D1319716

THE ARCHAEOLOGY
OF
EARLY CHRISTIANITY

THE ARCHAEOLOGY OF EARLY CHRISTIANITY

A History

William H. C. Frend

Fortress Press
Minneapolis

THE ARCHAEOLOGY OF EARLY CHRISTIANITY
A History

First published in North America by Fortress Press, 1996
First published in Great Britain by Geoffrey Chapman, a Cassell imprint, 1996

Design: John Leath, MSTD
Cover Photo: Kenneth Fraser
Author Photo: Visibility

ISBN 0–8006–2811–X

Printed and bound in Britain by Hartnolls, Bodmin, Cornwall

Manufactured in Great Britain   AF 1–2811

00   99   98   97   96   1   2   3   4   5   6   7   8   9   10

Contents

Illustrations

BLACK AND WHITE PHOTOGRAPHS

Giovanni Battista de Rossi

COLOUR PHOTOGRAPHS

To

MY WIFE

Glossary

aedicula	small shrine, usually set in a wall, having flanking pillars either side of the niche and a gabled roof
ambon	pulpit, not found in the West before the Byzantine reconquest
architrave	flat lintel resting on the column supports of a doorway
arcosolium	curved ceiling above a wealthy tomb in a *cubiculum* (q.v.) often decorated with biblical or naturalistic scenes
area	lit. 'courtyard', but term used by Christians for open-air cemetery in the pre-Constantinian period
arenaria	quarries and their approaches that sometimes formed the nucleus of a later catacomb
atrium	rectangular courtyard in front of a church
barrel vault	half-cylindrical vault
basilica	church based on a longitudinal plan with side aisles flanking a main nave and usually ending in a curved apse
basilica discoperta	a type of basilica supposedly set round an open courtyard instead of a roofed nave
cathedra	the throne or seat of a bishop in a church
choir	that part of a basilica-type church between the apse and nave, reserved for clergy and choir
chrism	(from the Greek *chrismon*) the sacred monogram ☧. Later (late fourth century) flanked by α/ω.
ciborium	canopy placed over a sacred object, such as a tomb or baptismal font in a church
confessio	small chamber dug below ground in or near the sanctuary of a church to house the body of someone held in special reverence, such as a martyr
crypt	subterranean gallery, below floor level of the choir of a church, often used for burials
cubiculum	richer and more elaborate family tomb-chamber in a catacomb, usually rectangular in shape
cupola	rounded dome forming the roof of a church in many Byzantine-period churches, generally square or octagonal in plan
diaconicon	small square chamber usually placed on the south side of the base of the apse of a church. Served as a vestry and place where books, liturgical vestments and sacred vessels were stored
domus ecclesiae	originally a meeting-house for worship. After the Peace of the Church, a general name for a complex of buildings set round a church serving as the bishop's residence and administrative offices

fenestella confessionis	a small window or squint allowing worshippers to view a *confessio* (q.v.)
graffito	writing or hand-cut inscription by an individual, often invoking prayers or aid at a martyr's tomb
hypogaeum	underground tomb-chamber, reserved for a family or funerary society
Liber Pontificalis	list and brief biographies of Popes from St Peter to Nicholas I (d. 867). When begun is not known, but repeatedly updated and contains many valuable original documents. Other major bishoprics, such as Ravenna, had their own similar *libri*.
loculus	simple, usually tiled, grave dug into the walls of a gallery in a catacomb
martyrium	building erected over the tomb of a martyr
mensa	lit. 'table'; either a wooden altar or rectangular stone slab used for eucharistic commemoration of martyr's death
narthex	entrance hall or vestibule at west end of church, occupied during the celebration of the Eucharist by catechumens and penitents. More usual in the East
opus sectile	covering of floor or (as at Knossos) a tomb with decorative marble cut into rectangular shapes.
orante	figure often found in the catacombs, shown standing and praying with arms outstretched and hands open turned towards the heavens
pallium	mantle thrown over the shoulder round the neck, as worn by the figure of Christ on the Hinton St Mary mosaic
pilaster	rectangular column, usually engaged in a wall and often supporting a chancel arch
prothesis	small chamber on the opposite side fo the apse to the *diaconicon*, where offerings were brought for use in the celebration of the Eucharist
pyx	small casket of silver or wood used to contain the consecrated bread for the Eucharist, or, in some cases, relics
reliquary	casket, or in Donatist North Africa often a cooking pot, used to house relics of a saint or martyr
sacristy	small room built on to the choir of the church, used for keeping sacred objects and serving as a vestry for the clergy. Similar function to the *diaconicon*
sanctuary	that part of the church reserved to the clergy, containing the altar, where the liturgy was performed
souterrain	in ecclesiastical sense, an underground chapel or martyr's shrine
synthronos	benches or seats reserved for clergy, set sometimes in a semicircle around the episcopal throne; sometimes placed either side of the throne, further down the sanctuary, and nearer the nave
transept	transverse part of basilican or cruciform church, situated between the nave and apse and normally separated from these by a colonnade
trefoil chapel	building whose interior is shaped like a three-leaf clover, usually erected to cover a martyr's shrine
twin churches (basilicas)	cathedral embodying two separate churches whose axes are usually placed parallel to each other. One would seem to be for congregational worship, the other probably a funerary church reserved for services commemorating martyrs or clergy buried within its precincts

Abbreviations

AA	*Archäologischer Anzeiger* (Berlin)
ABAW	*Abhandlungen der Academie der Wissenschaften in Berlin*
ABSA	*Annual of the British School at Athens* (London)
ACW	Ancient Christian Writers, ed. J. Quasten and J. C. Plumpe (Westminster, MD and London)
AG	*Analecta Gregoriana* (Rome)
AJ	*Antiquaries Journal* (London)
AJA	*American Journal of Archaeology* (Princeton)
AS	*Anatolian Studies* (London)
ASS	*Acta Sanctorum*, ed. Socii Bollandiani (Antwerp, 1643– ; Venice, 1734– ; Paris, 1863–)
Atti	*(Acta, Akten) Atti, Congressus Internationalis Archaeologiae Christianae* (1894–)
BAC	*Bollettino degli Amici delle Catacombe* (Rome)
BAR	British Archaeological Research
BCH	*Bulletin de correspondance hellénique*
BCTH	*Bulletin archéologique du Comité des Travaux historiques et scientifiques* (Paris)
BEFAR	*Bibliothèque des Écoles françaises d'Athènes et de Rome* (Paris)
BJRL	*Bulletin of John Rylands Library* (Manchester)
BullAC	*Bulletin d'archéologie et d'histoire du comité des travaux historiques et scientifiques* (Paris)
ByzZ	*Byzantinische Zeitschrift*
CArch	*Cahiers Archéologiques, Fin de l'Antiquité et Moyen Age* (Paris)
CCL	*Corpus Christianorum Latinorum*
CEFR	*Collection de l'École française de Rome* (Rome)
CIG	*Corpus Inscriptionum Graecarum*
CIL	*Corpus Inscriptionum Latinarum*
CRAI	*Comptes-rendus de l'Académie des Inscriptions et Belles-Lettres* (Paris)
CSEL	*Corpus Scriptorum Ecclesiasticorum Latinorum* (Vienna)
CT	Codex Theodosianus, ed. T. Mommsen and T. Meyer (Berlin).
DACL	*Dictionnaire d'archéologie chrétienne et de liturgie* (Paris, 1907–53)
DCB	*Dictionary of Christian Biography*

DHGE	*Dictionnaire d'histoire et de géographie ecclésiastique* (Paris, 1909–)
DNB	*Dictionary of National Biography*
DOP	*Dumbarton Oaks Papers* (Harvard University, 1950–)
EEC	*Encyclopedia of the Early Church* (Cambridge)
GCS	*Die griechischen christlichen Schriftsteller* (Berlin–Leipzig)
HE	*Historia Ecclesiae / Historia ecclesiastica*
HTR	*Harvard Theological Review* (Cambridge, MA)
ICUR	*Inscriptiones christianae Urbis Romae*
ILCV	*Inscriptiones latinae christianae veteres*, ed. E. Diehl (2nd edn, 1960)
JA	*Journal asiatique* (Paris)
JARCE	*Journal of the American Research Centre in Egypt*
JbAC	*Jahrbuch für Antike und Christentum* (Münster, 1958–)
JDAI	*Jahrbuch des deutschen archäologischen Instituts* (Berlin)
JEA	*Journal of Egyptian Archaeology* (London)
JEH	*Journal of Ecclesiastical History* (Cambridge)
JHS	*Journal of Hellenic Studies* (London)
JÖAI	*Jahreshefte des österreichischen archaeologischen Instituts*
JRS	*Journal of Roman Studies* (London)
JS	*Journal des Savants* (Paris)
JTS	*Journal of Theological Studies* (Oxford)
LAAA	*Liverpool Annals of Archaeology and Anthropology* (Liverpool)
LCC	Library of Christian Classics (Philadelphia–London 1953)
LCL	Loeb Classical Library
MAMA	*Monumenta Asiae Minoris antiqua* (London–Manchester, 1928–)
MEFR	*Mélanges d'archéologie et d'histoire de l'École française de Rome* (1881–)
MGH	*Monumenta Germaniae Historia* (Hanover–Berlin)
NBAC	*Nuovo bollettino di archeologia cristiana* (Rome)
OC	*Oriens christianus* (Wiesbaden)
OCA	*Orientalia christiana analecta* (Rome)
ODCC	*Oxford Dictionary of the Christian Church*
Pap. Oxy.	*The Oxyrhynchus Papyri* (London, 1896–)
PBA	*Proceedings of the British Academy*
PBSR	*Proceedings of the British School at Rome*

PG	*Patrologia Greco-Latina*, ed J.-P. Migne
PL	*Patrologia Latina*, ed. J.-P. Migne
PLRE	*The Prosopography of the Later Roman Empire*
PMR	Patristic, Medicval and Renaissance Conference (Villanova, PA)
PO	*Patrologia Orientalis*
QDAP	*Quarterly of the Department of Antiquites of Palestine*
RA	*Revue archéologique* (Paris)
RAC	*Rivista di archeologia cristiana* (Rome, Vatican City)
RACh	*Realexikon für Antike und Christentum* (Stuttgart, 1950–)
RAfr	*Revue africaine* (Algiers)
RB	*Revue biblique* (Paris)
RC	*Recueil des notices et des mémoires de la Société archéologique de Constantine*
RecAug	*Recherches augustiniennes* (Paris)
RHE	*Revue d'histoire ecclésiastique* (Louvain)
RHLR	*Revue d'histoire et de littérature religieuses* (Paris)
RHR	*Revue d'histoire des religions* (Paris)
RQ	*Römisches Quartalschrift* (Freiburg im Breisgau)
RSLR	*Rivista di storia e letteratura religiosa* (Florence)
SBAW	*Sitzungzberichte der Berliner (or Königlicher) preussischen Akademie der Wissenschaften* (Berlin)
SC	*Sources chrétiennes* (Paris)
SCH	*Studies in Church History* (Cambridge)
Syria	*Syria: Revue d'art oriental et d'archéologie* (Paris)
TDGNHAS	*Transactions of the Dumbarton and Galloway Natural History and Archaeology Society*
TRE	*Theologische Realenzyclopädie*
TU	*Texte und Untersuchungen zur Geschichte der altchristlichen Literatur* (Leipzig–Berlin)
VChr	*Vigiliae Christianae* (Amsterdam)
ZKG	*Zeitschrift für Kirchengeschichte* (Stuttgart)
ZNTW	*Zeitschrift für Neutestamentliche Wissenschaft und die Kunde der älteren Kirche* (Berlin)
ZPE	*Zeitschrift für Papyrologie und Epigraphik* (Bonn)

Introduction

In 1902 Adolf Harnack published his monumental *Die Mission und Ausbreitung des Christentums in den ersten drei Jahrhunderten*, translated into English in 1904 as *The Expansion of Christianity in the First Three Centuries*. Apart, however, from G. B. de Rossi's annual *Bollettino di archeologia cristiana*, very largely concerned with discoveries in the Roman catacombs, Harnack used little archaeological material with which to build up his picture of the gradual expansion of Christianity throughout the Roman world. With regard to North Africa in particular, he stated roundly that because of geographical conditions, namely the mountain ranges and steppes, Christianity was not able to strike roots almost anywhere among the Berbers.[1] Yet eight years before, the French archaeologists Henri Graillot and Stéphane Gsell had completed a survey of ruins which included numerous early Christian sites in Numidia, north of the Aurès and the heartland of the Donatist movement.[2]

Harnack's successor at Berlin University, who had the title of Professor of New Testament and Christian Archaeology, was Hans Leitzmann, and his scholarship embraced both fields with equal enthusiasm. Through Lietzmann's contact with Louis Poinssot, Inspector-General of Antiquities in Tunisia, I was able to travel to North Africa in 1938 and 1939 and see the vast extent of Christian remains there for myself. In 1939 I was entrusted with work on the rural site of Kherbet Bahrarous, north-west of Timgad, and excavated a church which appeared to form part of a larger agricultural complex, including an olive press and storage rooms.

These experiences, followed after the war by other opportunities of fieldwork in Asia Minor, Crete, Upper Egypt, Carthage and, latterly, Roman Britain, have prompted me to try to add to Harnack and Lietzmann's work by writing this history of Christian archaeology. I also had the chance of visiting the cemetery beneath the Vatican in August 1944 under the guidance of Professor Ernesto Iosi, Trier in 1965, Sardinia in 1968, and Salona in 1994. Hence, with the important exceptions of the Middle Eastern countries of Palestine, Syria and Jordan, I have been able to gain first-hand experience of most areas where early Christian churches have been found.

I have attempted to outline the growth of interest in Christian archaeology from the Renaissance onwards, describing briefly excavations in the

main areas of discovery, and placing these developments within the framework of cultural and religious movement of the day. Discoveries in the Roman
catacombs from the seventeenth century onwards have naturally had an enormous but not always helpful influence in the development of the subject, as
these were too often used for apologetic purposes, to prove that the Roman
Catholic Church was indeed 'The Church of the Martyrs', while paintings
decorating many of the richer tombs were held to prove the legitimacy of the
Church's teaching, for instance, concerning the Eucharist and the status of
the Virgin. It might have been thought that the progressive exploration of
other parts of the Mediterranean basin would have counterbalanced this tendency. One would reckon, however, without the influence of Napoleon.
Napoleon regarded his Egyptian campaign of 1798 as an expedition of exploration as well as conquest, and he was well served by the scholars that
accompanied his forces. The result was to integrate French archaeological
scholarship overseas with French cultural and political ambitions. This was
to be demonstrated during the conquest of Algeria (1830–44), and reinforced
during the episcopate of Cardinal Lavigerie as archbishop of Algiers (later of
Carthage) (1867–92). Nationalism allied to clericalism proved a formidable
combination, and I have not hesitated to describe as 'Catholic archaeology'
work in the catacombs, Syria and North Africa during the years 1867–94.

These tendencies were eventually outweighed, first by W. M. Ramsay's
exploration and discovery of early Christian sites in Asia Minor, and then by
the enormous extension of the range of discoveries in the twenty years leading up to the outbreak of the First World War. Egypt and Nubia, Palestine
and Syria and Central Asia were added to the areas where early Christian
remains were being encountered, while in North Africa, thanks to the great
influence of Stéphane Gsell, the clericalism of the Lavigerie era was replaced
by high and impartial standards of scholarship. In Rome too, the work of
G. B. de Rossi showed how the impartial study of archaeological remains
could live with loyalty to the Roman Church.

The period 1894–1914 was to my mind the decisive period in the story of
Christian archaeology. Not only were a great number of sites found, but these
opened up new and unexpected horizons for research. Among the discoveries
made by Ramsay in Asia Minor and Gsell in Algeria were inscriptions which
were clearly Montanist and Donatist respectively, while the journeys in Central Asia undertaken by Sir Aurel Stein and German and French explorers
brought back the first documents relating to the Manichaean religion.
For the first time, dissenting traditions persecuted by the Church and the

imperial government in the fourth, fifth and sixth centuries were being enabled to speak for themselves.

Unfortunately, discovery was not combined with excavational skills. Down to the end of the Second World War most of the excavators had had their training as architects. Their primary aim was to draw up accurate plans of the main building they were excavating, be it a temple or a Christian basilica. The upper levels which could provide clues to the building's subsequent history and destruction were often neglected; later buildings, sometimes Byzantine churches, were destroyed without record, and small finds, unless they were valuable, ignored. Pottery was not evaluated and dated. The result has been the loss of an immense amount of valuable historical evidence from important sites.

The inter-war years witnessed further discoveries accompanying growing popular interest in the past. Archaeological activity now extended to Greece and the Balkans, where the newly independent countries found in the discovery and excavation of churches a means of expressing a national, Christian identity. Outstanding finds also were not lacking. In 1931 the German papyrologist Carl Schmidt identified a collection of papyrus psalms and homilies belonging to a Coptic Manichaean community. Their importance was that they demonstrated the same dualistic beliefs and mythology as was contained in the manuscripts brought back from Central Asia. St Augustine had indeed been a member of a sect with world-wide ambitions during ten of the formative years of his life (373–383).

Next year, the Franco-American expedition to Dura Europos, the Roman fort on the Euphrates frontier, uncovered a Christian church and in 1934 a Jewish synagogue. On the walls of the synagogue and of the baptistery were magnificent biblical frescos, showing that in both communities prohibitions against representing biblical scenes in pictures were not being followed. In addition, the date of the building of the church (*c.* 232) reflected the growing influence of Christianity and revealed the Christians as holding their own corporate property. Near the end of this inter-war period the excavations of the town of Gerasa (Jerash) in Jordan demonstrated the gradual transformation of a pagan city into an entirely Christian one through the late fourth to the sixth century. The imprint of Justinian's determination to turn the Holy Land (in its widest interpretation) into an exclusively Christian territory was illustrated by the conversion of a synagogue into a church in his reign and the building of up to a dozen churches in the town.

The post-war period, again, has seen an immense number of new early Christian sites discovered and excavated, in most instances far more skilfully than earlier in the century. The period has been dominated by two major developments. First, the great discoveries: the Dead Sea Scrolls, the Nag Hammadi Gnostic library, and the cemetery and 'trophy' in honour of the apostles Peter and Paul beneath the Vatican; and secondly, the collaborative effort of international teams to save what could be saved of Christian and other remains threatened with destruction by major irrigation projects in Egypt and Iraq. As a result of the first, another non-orthodox tradition, the Gnostics, could at last represent its own views, and in the Vatican excavations considerable light was thrown on the Petrine tradition in the Church in Rome. The UNESCO 'Save Nubia' project revealed for the first time the splendours of the Nubian Monophysite civilization in the Nile valley which flourished between 500 and *c.* 1450. Finally, I have written two chapters to bring the story of discoveries and discussions surrounding them down to the present day, emphasizing the role of the International Congresses of Christian Archaeology.

In all this, Roman Britain has stood out as an exception. While Britain has produced a number of wealthy hoards, such as Mildenhall, Water Newton and Hoxne, intensive research has revealed few traces of early Christian churches (Silchester and Colchester are exceptions) such as have been found elsewhere in western Europe. Moreover, traces of outright opposition to Christianity have come to light in the form of the destruction of lead baptismal fonts and possibly, in some cases, their division into fragments as loot. Why this should have been so is as yet unknown, but it may provide a clue why, unlike on the Continent, the Church in Britain did not survive the barbarian invasions of the fifth century and continuity with Latin Christianity was lost.

The questions which interested this generation of architect–excavators have been largely those that concerned the shape and size of basilicas and baptisteries, and the significance of various architectural features connected with them. In the Roman catacombs, art historians and theologians have debated the precise meaning of the splendid murals that decorated many of the richer tombs. Historical questions relating to the spread of Christianity and evidence derived from pottery, coins and other small objects have tended to take second place.

I have discussed these problems to the best of my ability within the historical framework of my study. I have not intended an 'Einführung in die christlichen Archäologie',[3] nor an architectural or iconographic study. I would recommend students to the excellent works of F. W. Deichmann, Krautheimer, J. Kollwitz and Ernst Kitzinger among others, as the experts in these fields.

Finally, I would like to thank Mrs Deborah Taylor for all her unstinted help in typing a difficult manuscript, and Felicity Crowe, Ruth McCurry, Fiona McKenzie and their colleagues in Cassell for encouragement, help and patience on all occasions.

W. H. C. Frend

NOTES

1. A. Harnack, *Die Mission und Ausbreitung des Christentums in den ersten drei Jahrhunderten* (1902), p. 517n.
2. See below, Chapter 8, p. 118.
3. The title of Deichmann's study (Darmstadt, 1983)

I

In the wake of
Queen Helena

We start this survey more than a thousand years before the study of archaeology, as we understand it, begins. The discovery of the 'True Cross' by the
empress Helena, mother of the emperor Constantine, in 326, allegedly by digging at a spot revealed to her in a dream, began a tradition of excavating for
relics that lasted into the Middle Ages. It also indicated to future, more scien-
tifically oriented ages that historical information could be recovered from
under the ground as well as from literature.

The date is 325. The Council of Nicaea summoned by Constantine and
meeting for nearly two months, between early June and 25 July of that year,
marked the point at which the Greco-Roman world turned decisively towards
Christianity. Opinions differ on the role of the emperor in its proceedings. He
had assembled the bishops from both parts of his empire at Nicaea in preference to Ancyra, ostensibly on the grounds of better climate and convenience,
but also that Nicaea was nearer his temporary capital at Nicomedia at the
head of the Gulf of Iznik, and hence more susceptible to imperial pressure.
Whether he actually presided over any sessions, as opposed to intervening at
times, is uncertain,[1] and similarly the exact part he played in putting forward
the formula that declared Jesus Christ to be 'of one substance with the
Father' (*homo-ousios*), but his deep interest in the Council's decisions is sure,
and his letters to the Churches and separately to the Egyptians urging them
to obey the decrees of the Council and to observe peace and harmony[2] are the
genuine utterances of one to whom the unity of the servants of the Supreme
God was now a matter of first importance.

No sooner had the bishops been sent on their way than Constantine revealed far-reaching and ambitious plans to restore the Holy Places in Jerusalem and Palestine to the Christians.[3] Even for an autocrat such as Constantine was, this was a daunting task. Since the end of the Second Jewish War in 135 there had been no such place as Jerusalem, only Aelia Capitolina, symbolizing the victory of the emperor Hadrian and Jupiter Capitolinus over the Jews and their God, Jahwe. In almost two centuries after that event Aelia developed as a purely pagan city dominated by its forum, temples and other public buildings. Herod's Temple remained a blackened ruin, a warning to Jews, who were forbidden entry to Aelia, of what happened to those who rebelled against Rome. When in the Great Persecution (303–312) an Egyptian confessor told the governor of Palestine that 'Jerusalem was his city', the latter had no idea what he meant, and asked him 'in what part of the world it was situated', thinking even that it was some city 'at enmity and hostile to the Romans'.[4]

This was in 310. Even a decade later, the idea of Holy Places rang hollow to Eusebius, bishop of Caesarea (*c.* 269–339), the historian of the Church and future religious adviser to Constantine. In his view the actual places connected with the Lord's earthly life, Jerusalem included, were of little importance compared with a right understanding of Jesus as the divine Logos (Word) incarnate.[5] In any event, he was Metropolitan of the capital of the Roman province of Palestine (*Palestina Prima*) at Caesarea. He wanted no rival to that title in the person of the bishop of Jerusalem.

Constantine had other ideas. For him the Holy Places connected with the birth, crucifixion, and ascension of Christ were to be commemorated worthily for all time[6] and he aimed at Jerusalem being transformed into a Christian city. In quick succession in 325, he ordered the building of 'churches on the site of the Holy Sepulchre, the locality of our Saviour's Ascension' (the Mount of Olives), and above the grotto of the Nativity[7] at Bethlehem.

Contantine's determination had obliged Eusebius to fall into line. The historian describes step by step how Constantine's orders were carried out. He claims that a temple of Venus had been erected deliberately on the site of Christ's tomb, which he describes as a 'cave'.[8] Constantine had the temple destroyed and, not content with that, ordered that the 'polluted earth' be dug up and dumped a distance away. Then the excavators unexpectedly found themselves confronted with a knoll of natural rock, probably the remains of a quarry, and this was accepted eagerly as Golgotha itself,[9] the successful result of the first recorded excavation.

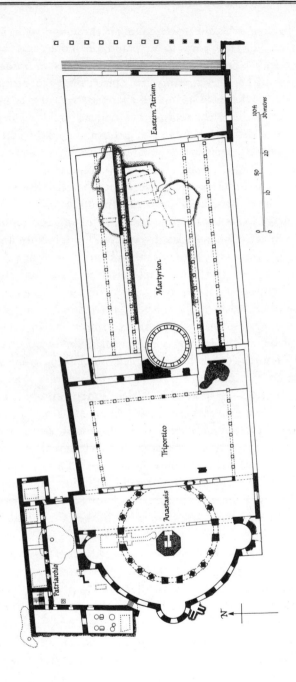

Church of the Holy Sepulchre, Constantinian phase

Constantine then ordered that a church of 'rich and royal greatness' be built on the site. No expense was to be spared; the money was to be raised by provincial governors. The emperor took an enthusiastic interest in the work, using Macarius, bishop of Jerusalem (314–333) as his agent and telling him just how the church designed 'to excel the fairest structures of any city of the empire' should be built.[10] The result was a 'huge Church' (*Praise of Constantine* ix), a great five-aisled basilican building, oriented east–west, approached through a rectangular courtyard (*atrium*) paved with polished marble. It was centred on the site of the 'cave' that had been hailed by Eusebius as the *Martyrion* ('witness to our Saviour's Resurrection': *Life* iii.28). Beyond this was a second court incorporating the rocky outrop into its south-east corner. At the west end of this court was a space enclosing the reputed tomb of Christ. The tomb itself was marked by a small building with a pointed roof, later covered by a rotunda. There was also a baptistery. 'A new Jerusalem was constructed on the very site that witnessed the Saviour's sufferings', claimed Eusebius.[11] Basilica and baptistery were already built when the Pilgrim of Bordeaux visited Jerusalem in 333.[12] Right or wrong regarding the site, credit goes to the Dominicans F. M. Abel and L. H. Vincent of the Ecole Biblique at Jerusalem just before the First World War for discovering what appears to have been the foundation of the Constantinian church,[13] and guiding later expert work.

Next year, in 326, Constantine's mother Helena and his mother-in-law Eutropia visited Jerusalem and sites round about. Bringing gifts and offerings, Helena dedicated two churches, one on the Mount of Olives associated with both Christ's teaching and Ascension (cf. Acts 1:11) and the other at Bethlehem.[14] Eutropia visited the site of the oak of Mamre, north of Hebron, where she found the area 'defiled by certain of the slaves of superstition in every possible way'.[15] In fact, the area was sacred to both Jews and pagans, and excavations between the World Wars established the existence of a structure built in the time of Herod (37–4 BC) and a sacred grove. She reported her discovery to Constantine. Macarius was ordered to have all traces of paganism removed and a church built on the site.[16]

Eusebius says much about Helena's 'pious conduct in the churches', and her 'mingling with the worshippers', but nothing about her excursion into archaeology that led to the discovery of the True Cross.[17] A vivid account of her discoveries, however, is preserved in a letter written by Paulinus of Nola to his friend the Gallic chronicler Sulpicius Severus *c.* 403,[18] to whom he was sending a 'sliver of the wood of the Holy Cross' as a gift. As Eusebius before him, Paulinus describes how Helena with Constantine's agreement set out for

Jerusalem to clear all the sites 'on which out Lord's feet had trod', to remove pagan temples and statues from them and build basilicas on them in their stead. He adds how, once arrived in Jerusalem, Helena included the site of the Passion and Crucifixion in her quest. No one seems to know where it was. After consulting local Christians, however, she assembled 'the most learned of the Jews to inform her of their native wickedness, in which, poor men, they even boast'. No doubt glad to satisfy her, they all agreed on a site. Their judgement was confirmed by a divine revelation to the empress, and digging started.[19]

The excavation was successful. 'Deep digging' by a corps of soldiers and civilians came upon three crosses. But which was the Saviour's? A Lazarus test was applied. A newly-dead man was brought to the spot. Two crosses were touched by the body without result, but at the third, 'death was shaken off' and like Lazarus the dead man stood up! So, the True Cross was discovered, and Paulinus had no doubt as to the living power of its fragments in his own day.

Paulinus was recounting an established tradition, for the episode was known to Ambrose, bishop of Milan, in 395,[20] and to the historian Rufinus a few years later.[21] The 'wood of the Cross' had become a symbol of the resurrection by 348, the date of Cyril of Jerusalem's lectures to catechumens, but it was not explicitly connected with Helena.[22] Cyril's account may have had a more parochial aim, that of increasing the importance of Jerusalem against its rival Caesarea, the Roman provincial capital, which had been Eusebius' see. The fame of the True Cross was spreading. Most interesting is a reference inscribed on a large commemorative stone (a *mensa martyrum* or altar?) from a North African church, dated precisely to AD 359 (see below, pp. 114–15).[23] Among the martyrs mentioned in the dedication on the stone slab was 'the wood of the Cross (and earth?) from the land of promise where Christ was born'.[24] This proves that an account of the discovery of the True Cross was circulating widely, and perhaps that the story of Helena's exploit had by now begun to gain currency.

In the next century, the tale was elaborated by the Constantinopolitan lawyer Sozomen in his *Ecclesiastical History*, written *c.* 440 or a little later. By now, 'signs and visions' had guided Helena and documents had been presented to her by a Jew who had inherited them through his forebears.[25] Not only were three crosses found, but nails and Pilate's superscription in white letters in Hebrew, Greek and Latin, 'Jesus of Nazareth, king of Jews'. A miracle of healing identified the Cross on which Jesus had hung.[26]

The accounts of Helena's excavation were to have far-reaching consequences. There had been a tradition in the Greek-speaking Church which respected the study of antiquity, especially when research upheld the Church's claim to be the true and natural religion of mankind that had existed since the beginning of time.[27] Josephus' *Antiquities of the Jews*, written *c*. AD 90, had attempted to prove the same on behalf of the Jewish people. Eusebius records in his account of the life of the Alexandrian theologian Origen (185–253), in Book vi of his *Ecclesiastical History*, how *c*. 217 Origen found a scroll of the Psalms hidden in a pot near Jericho.[28] This he was able to use as a further version of the Hebrew text in his compilation of what he hoped would become a final version of Scripture to which Christians could refer in controversies with the Jews.

Such early glimmerings of scientific scholarship relying partly on archaeological discovery were, however, to be snuffed out by the stories surrounding Helena's visit to Jerusalem and her alleged find of the True Cross. From now on and for many centuries to come, archaeology was harnessed almost exclusively to the discovery of wonder-working relics. Helena herself would look down, long-handled spade in hand, at the side of her husband from gilded mosaics on the congregations of many a rich mediaeval Byzantine church. Wherever possible, the burial places of apostles and martyrs were sought out, and bodies where found were dissected for their use as relics. Thus, by 424, St Augustine (354–430), bishop of Hippo in North Africa, had received relics of the martyr Stephen discovered in Palestine nine years before and had dedicated a chapel for them. In Book xxii of *De Civitate Dei* he lists an extraordinary sequence of miracles attributed to the relics of Stephen on their arrival in North Africa. The blind had their sight restored, the bishop of a neighbouring see to Augustine's was cured of a fistula; others who were seriously ill with a variety of ailments were cured and a staunch pagan converted by being restored to health.[29] Some of these cures served apologetic ends, for Augustine had previously upbraided his Donatist opponents in North Africa for their superstitious belief in the powers of earth brought from Palestine.[30] Now he himself accepted its miraculous powers. The miracles attributed to the relics of St Stephen were another nail in the coffin of the rival Church.

Augustine was neither the first nor the last to use archaeological discoveries to further the aims of his Church. Forty years before the incidents he describes in *De Civitate Dei*, Ambrose of Milan, whose teaching had been a powerful influence in persuading him to return to orthodox Catholicism in 386, had dug up the bones of Protasius and Gervasius, two supposed martyrs of the persecution of Diocletian (303–305). Augustine records how the site of their graves was revealed to Ambrose in a dream. Excavation was ordered, Ambrose himself participating, and the result was the discovery of two giant human skeletons whose bones 'still bore traces of blood' (i.e. red ochre; they may have been Palaeolithic burials). They were transported in triumph to Ambrose's church and on the way healed a blind man.[31] This time the target was the Arian minority in Milan and the empress Justina who favoured it. Ambrose was successful. Justina was discredited and Milan received its own pair of famous martyrs.

A final instance of this type of early Christian 'archaeology' may be quoted from the early years of the sixth century. The scene is Constantinople in the reign of Anastasius (491–518). The year 511 witnessed acute controversy between the patriarch of Constantinople, Macedonius, and the monk Severus, later to become patriarch of Antioch and inspirer of a Monophysite theology in regard to the Person of Christ. Severus believed that Christ as God's Word Incarnate was incapable of physical death and that the blood and water that issued from his side as the result of the soldier's lance thrust (John 19:34) should be interpreted symbolically as the 'stream of salvation' (for humanity) that welled forth from his side.[32] His opponent, Macedonius, believed that Christ existed in two natures, human and divine, and, quoting a version of Matthew 27:49 which included a Matthean record of the lance thrust, pointed out that the incident took place before Christ had died (Matt 27:50) and that in his physical nature he did in fact die. Severus was embarrassed. He could not deny the words of Scripture. But at the last stage of the debate archaeology came to his rescue. He found in the library in the imperial palace a copy of Matthew's Gospel that had been discovered in the reign of Zeno (474–491) at a site in Cyprus. It had been dug up with the body of the 'holy Barnabas', and it did not contain the offending passage. Severus triumphed. Macedonius was deposed and exiled (7 August 511).

Today one may smile at these examples of the misuse of archaeology. One is, however, dealing with people who had no idea of past civilizations beyond what might be gleaned from Scripture. Augustine, for instance, writes of his own discovery of large bones that had become exposed on the shores of the seaside town of Utica, north of Carthage. There was 'a human molar so enormous that if it were divided up into pieces to the dimension of our human teeth, it would, so it seemed to us, have made a hundred of them. But that molar I suppose it belonged to some giant.'[33] (Compare Gen 6:4.) Augustine was no worse informed than Ambrose had been, or the popular tradition recorded by Thucydides eight centuries earlier regarding the Cyclops, or the villagers who appear to have included fossils among votive offerings.[34]

There was, however, another powerful reason why the scientific study of the material remains of the past failed to prosper in the patristic era and through the European Middle Ages. The limits of human research and speculation concerning nature had been fixed by divine ordinance embodied in the tradition of the Church. Curiosity (*curiositas*), the attempt to push the bounds of knowledge further, was associated with an heretical spirit. At first the argument was directed specifically against the Gnostic sects who claimed that mystical knowledge (*gnōsis*) of the Beyond was essential for individual salvation. Thus, early in the third century, the North African theologian Tertullian (*c.* 160–*c.* 230), writing against the Gnostics, claimed that their favourite text was 'Seek and ye shall find' (Matt 7:7).[35] It was not an example to be encouraged. Nearly two centuries later, Ambrose of Milan, preaching at the funeral of his brother Satyrus, asserted 'Moses described the things that bear on our eternal welfare. He did not think it his duty to tell us how much of the air is occupied by the shadow of the earth when the sun leaves us at the close of day to illuminate the lower parts of the heavens, or how the moon is eclipsed when it passes into the regions of the earth's shadow. These things do not concern us.'[36] This attitude persisted. Thomas à Kempis warned how 'our own curiosity hindereth us in reading the Scriptures', and urges his readers 'Cease from an inordinate desire of knowing; for therein is much distraction and deceit. There are many things, to know which doth little profit the soul.'[37] Theology dominated the individual's perspective. Archaeology might be useful if the supposed remains of King Arthur, reputed descendant of Joseph of Arimathea, found by the monks of Glastonbury and translated to a marble tomb in their church, resulted in higher royal payments to the monastery.[38] But that was all. The twelfth century was 'the golden age of mediaeval forgery'.[39] Archaeology sometimes helped to create the requisite legends. It would need the Renaissance and Protestant Reformation to make it a handmaid of scientific inquiry.

NOTES

1. For this period see T. D. Barnes, *Constantine and Eusebius* (Cambridge, MA: Harvard University Press, 1981), pp. 212–19.
2. Eusebius of Caesarea, *Life of Constantine* (= *Life*) iii.17–21 and 23; Eng. trans., *The Greek Ecclesiastical Historians* (London: Samuel Bagster and Sons, 1845).
3. *Life* iii. 25.
4. Eusebius, *The Palestinian Martyrs* xi.10; ed. H. J. Lawlor and J. E. L. Oulton (SPCK, 1954), I, pp. 385–6.
5. See P. W. L. Walker, *Holy City, Holy Places* (OUP, 1990), p. 59. Eusebius was convinced that Palestine and its historic sites, including Jerusalem, were theologically redundant. In general, ch. iii.
6. *Life* iii. 25.
7. Ibid., 41 and 43.

8. Ibid., 26. Caves were also described by Eusebius as the scene of Jesus' birth and his Ascension on the Mount of Olives. See also Joan E. Taylor, *Christians and the Holy Place* (OUP, 1993), ch. 8, 'Caves and tombs', and ch. 7, 'Eleona'.

9. *Life* iii.27. Interesting that Constantine's first consideration seems to have been to get rid of the temple of Venus. Only when that had been done did the 'hallowed monument of our Saviour's resurrection' appear, 'contrary to all expectations' (iii.28), leaving the question open whether this traditional site of Golgotha is in fact correct. See Taylor, op. cit., pp. 138–42; Martin Biddle, 'The tomb of Christ: sources, methods and a new approach' in K. S. Painter (ed.), *Churches Built in Ancient Times* (London: Society of Antiquaries, 1994), pp. 73–147; esp. pp. 96–105, and full bibliography. The Jerusalem Church thought the site was somewhere around the Roman forum; Eusebius believed the spot was 'north of Mount Sion': *Onomastikon* 74.19–21.

10. This show of favour to Macarius could only have annoyed Eusebius, who studiously avoids the term 'Golgotha' in his account of events. See *Life* iii.30–32 (Constantine's instructions to Macarius) and 33–40 (Eusebius' description of the church).

11. Ibid., 33.

12. *The Pilgrim of Bordeaux* 594; Eng. trans, J. W. Wilkinson (1971), p. 158.

13. L. H. Vincent and F. M. Abel, *Jérusalem: recherches de topographie, d'archéologie et d'histoire*, II: *Jérusalem nouvelle* (Paris, 1914), pp. 40–300; J. W. Crowfoot, *Early Churches in Palestine* (The Schweich Lectures of the British Academy, 1937) (London, 1941), ch. 2. For the plan, see *EEC* II, fig. 164.

14. *Life* iii.43.

15. Ibid, iii.51–53.

16. Ibid.

17. Ibid., 42 and 45 (pious conduct) and 44 (gifts). For her journey, see E. D. Hunt, *Holy Land Pilgrimages in the Later Roman Empire* (OUP, 1982), ch. 2.

18. Paulinus of Nola, *Letter* 31, esp. 4–6: Eng. trans. P. G. Walsh, *Letters of St Paulinus of Nola*, II = *ACW* 36 (Westminister, MD, 1967), pp. 125–33.

19. Ibid., 5: p. 131.

20. Ambrose, *De obitu Theodosii* (on the death of Theodosius; preached on 25 February 395) 46; *CSEL* 73, 395.

21. Rufinus, *HE* ix.17: *PL* 21, 475; the patient was 'half dead' but had not expired! Interestingly, neither Eusebius of Caesarea nor the Bordeaux Pilgrim writing a pilgrim's gazetteer of the Holy Land *c.* 333 mentions the event. See S. P. Brock, review of J. W. Drijvers, *Helena Augusta, Waarheid en Legende* (Groningen, 1989), *JRS* 80 (1990), pp. 243–4 on the possible part played by Cyril's nephew Gelasius in propagating the legend.

22. See Walker, op. cit., pp. 126–30. Cyril referred to the 'recent discovery' five times during his series of catechetical lectures in 350: ed. A. Piédagnel, *SC* 126 (Paris, 1966).

23. *CIL* VIII, 20600. See below, pp. 114–15.

24. 'Memoria sancta. De terra promissionis ubi natus est Cristus'; later addition: 'Et Dabula et de ligno Crucis' (see below, p. 114).

25. Sozomen, *HE* ii.1.4; ed. Bidez and Hansen, *GCS* 50 (Berlin, 1960); Socrates, *HE* i.7; Theodoret, *HE* i.18.

26. Sozomen, i.6–7.

27. Eusebius, *HE* i.5.19.

28. Ibid, vi.16: an indication, perhaps, that not all the Dead Sea Scrolls were located in one area only.

29. Augustine, *De Civitate Dei* xxii.8. His previous scepticiom: *Letter* 88.3. Dedication of church: *Serm.* 318.

30. Augustine, *Letter* 52.2: 'unde [from the east] terra si adferatur, adorant'.

31. Augustine, *Confessions* ix.7.16 and *De Civitate Dei* xxii.8.2; Ambrose, *Letter* 22. See also *DACL* vi, 1232–1239.

32. See W. H. C. Frend, 'The fall of Macedonius in 511; a suggestion' in A. M. Ritter (ed.), *Kerygma und Logos (Festschrift für Carl Andresen zum 70. Geburtstag)* (Göttingen, 1979), pp. 183–95, at p. 193; for the recovery of the St Matthew's gospel 'buried with the holy Barnabas' at a site in Cyprus, see Severus of Antioch, *Letter* 108; ed. E. W. Brooks, *PO* 14, pp. 266–9.

33. Augustine, *De Civitate Dei* xv.9.

34. Robert Leighton, 'Antiquarianism and prehistory in western Mediterranean islands', *AJ* 69.2 (1989), pp. 183–204; E. D. Philips, 'The Greek vision of prehistory', *Antiquity* 34 (1964), pp. 171–8.

35. Tertullian, *De praescriptione haereticorum* 8.

36. Ambrose, *Hexaemeron*: *CSEL* 32, p. 209; and *De excessu Satyris* ii.86; and also compare Augustine, *De quantitate animae* 19.33: *CSEL* 89, p. 173. The pagans, at least, were asking recognizably scientific questions. In general see F. Homes Dudden, *Saint Ambrose: His Life and Times* (OUP, 1935), pp. 12, 504 and 558; and Ambrose's succinct 'We are bidden to believe, not to inquire': *De fide* i.78.
37. Thomas à Kempis, *The Christian's Pattern*, Eng. trans. J. Wesley (1854), 1.ii.2 and v.2.
38. Accounts of monastic 'archaeology' at Glastonbury near the end of the reign of Henry II in search of Arthur's tomb are given by Giraldus Cambrensis, and collated by Lewis Thorpe in his edition and translation *Gerald of Wales: The Journey through Wales: The Description of Wales* (Penguin Classics, 1978), pp. 281–8.
39. Cited from Karl F. Morrison, *Understanding Conversion* (University Press of Virginia, 1992), p. 40.

FURTHER READING

T. D. Barnes, *Constantine and Eusebius* (Harvard University Press, 1981).

Martin Biddle, 'The tomb of Christ: sources, methods and a new approach' in K. S. Painter (ed.), *Churches Built in Ancient Times* (London: Society of Antiquaries, 1994), pp. 73–147.

F. W. Deichmann and A. Tschira, 'Das Mausoleum der Kaiserin Helena und die Basilika der heiligen Marcellinus und Petrus an der Via Labicana von Rom', *JDAI* 72 (1957), pp. 44–110.

J. W. Drijvers, *Helena Augusta, Waarheid en Legende* (Groningen, 1990); reviewed by S. P. Brock, *JRS* 80 (1990), pp. 243–4.

E. D. Hunt, *Holy Land Pilgrimage in the Later Roman Empire* (OUP, 1982).

Robert Leighton, 'Antiquarianism and prehistory in western Mediterranean Islands', *AJ* 69.2 (1989), pp. 83–204.

Joan Taylor, *Christians and the Holy Places: The Myth of Jewish-Christian Origins* (OUP, 1993).

L. H. Vincent and E. M. Abel. 'Jérusalem: recherches de topographie, d'archéologie et d'histoire' in *Jérusalem nouvelle* (Paris, 1914), pp. 40–300.

P. W. L. Walker, *Holy City, Holy Places* (OUP, 1990).

2

Renaissance stirrings

Archaeology, including the archaeology of the early Church, is the child of the Renaissance. It is one aspect of the intellectual revolution in western Europe in the fifteenth century that ended the thousand-year dominance of Latin in moulding religious thought. It enabled scholars to study the Scriptures in their original languages of Greek and Hebrew and, in the Protestant countries, the ordinary folk to read them for themselves in their own speech. We may detect, perhaps, an anticipation of the new interest in the Classical past in the ruins of temples, basilicas and baths that found their way into the rural landscapes which Florentine artists designed as background to their religious masterpieces. Ancient Rome was beginning to come into its own.

The study of material remains of early Christianity, however, started in an environment that was not Classical and which for centuries had known only religious values. In *c.* 413 Jerome had recalled his Sunday visits with friends and fellow-students to the catacombs while a young man studying liberal arts in Rome nearly fifty years before. He carried a lifelong memory of the 'horror of the black darkness' of the passages that housed the bodies of countless Christians, including martyrs and Apostles.[1] Christians from Pope Damasus (366–384) downwards, intent on reliving the heroic times of the Persecutions, sharing vicariously in their sufferings and commemorating their feast-days, followed Jerome's example and visited the tombs. From the seventh century onwards, detailed guides or *Itineraries* were compiled, describing in accurate detail the route a pilgrim should follow if he wished to venerate a particular tomb.[2] Thus, the *Itinerary* of William of Malmesbury (1120–40), the latest, designed perhaps for the Crusaders, reads 'Between the Via Appia and the Via

11

Ostiense is the Via Ardeatina where are Marcus and Marcellianus, and where Damasus lies in his church, and not far away are St Petronilla, Nereus and Achilleus, and many others'. The *Topography of Einsiedeln* (after 750) stated that these sites were 'at (the cemetery) of St Soter'.[3] Put to the test by explorers from the seventeenth century onwards, and particularly by G. B. de Rossi (1822–94), the information was demonstrated to be exact. Read together with facts contained in the 'Book of the Popes' (*Liber Pontificalis*) the Itineraries were an essential guide to archaeological research. They eased the identification of individual catacombs and told explorers what they could expect to find, and where.

Though the compilers of the *Itineraries* were interested in antiquity, their prime aim, like that of their contemporaries, was religious, to provide accurate guidance for pilgrims starting out from major European religious centres. Exploration with a scientific motive had to await the last quarter of the fifteenth century. The previous hundred years, during the Papacy's move to Avignon (1309–77), had seen pilgrimages to the catacombs decline and the catacombs become neglected and even forgotten. In January 1475, however, the founder of the Roman Academy, Pomponius Laetus (Leto) (1428–97), entered what proved to be the San Callisto catacomb on the Appian Way. He and his companions brought with them a new, enquiring and somewhat irreverent spirit. They discovered walls covered with paintings of biblical scenes, but could not resist leaving their names as souvenirs and dedicating their investigations to 'Pope Pomponius', much to the displeasure of the official holder of the title, Pope Paul II. The 'academicians' were arrested and charged with conspiracy against the Pope and paganism, but were eventually freed, thanks, it was said, to the influence of powerful friends.[4]

These *perscrutatores antiquitatis* (investigators of antiquity) had recovered the sites of the Praetextatus and the Peter and Marcellinus catacombs as well as San Callisto. Their condemnation, however, served as a deterrent to other would-be explorers. For nearly a century the catacombs resumed their role as places for meditation and veneration of the saints. Philip Neri (1515–98) was one of those who entered their galleries for this purpose, meditating in the San Sebastiano catacomb how to promote the Catholic Reformation. A few important finds were, however, made in the area of the catacombs. Thus in 1551 a mutilated marble figure seated on a chair, without its arms or head, was found by Pirro Ligorio at a spot between the Via Nomentana and Via Tiburtina. On the sides were incised an Easter *computus* (calculation of dates) calculated in seven cycles of sixteen years between 222 and 333, and on the right-hand post of the chair a list of thirteen works corresponding largely to a list given by Eusebius of Caesarea of the works of (the presbyter) Hippolytus (*HE* vi.22), and the statue was restored as though it was Hippolytus. Today there are some doubts, though why anyone should inscribe the presbyter's works dating precisely to the reign of Alexander Severus on anyone else's statue also needs explanation.[5]

On 31 May 1578, however, the whole scene changed. The catacombs had been dug in the friable subsoil formed by volcanic tufa along the roads leading away from the city of Rome up to a distance of three miles from the walls of Aurelian (built *c.* AD 274). Much of this land was occupied by vineyards, and on that day workmen, planting vines in the Vigna Sanchez three miles along the Via Salaria Nuova north of the city, dug too deep and opened up a hole disclosing a vast underground cemetery. The adventurous who descended were well rewarded. Investigation revealed a classic combination of galleries lined with tiled graves and larger, more opulent tombs. These *cubicula* were more spacious. The grave was set into a shelf placed within a curved arch (*arcosolium*), the walls of which were often painted with vivid scenes taken from the Bible. The catacomb of the Jordani that had been discovered proved to be one of the finest, and even then was seen to contain paintings of Daniel in the lions' den, the Good Shepherd, and an Epiphany scene. It was, as Cesari Baronius (1538–1607) exclaimed, a 'city beneath the earth' – *Roma sotteranea*.[6]

For a short time excitement was intense, but then interest flagged, for the energies of the Papacy, in particular of Pope Sixtus V (1585–90), were directed towards a great clearance and salvage operation of ancient monuments that lay littering the site of the Roman Forum and the precincts of St Peter's itself. Egyptian monuments were rediscovered, raised and re-erected, including two large 'needles' which embellish the approaches to St Peter's. While dignity was being restored to the city there was little time for its honoured dead.

However, the discovery on the Via Salaria Nuova was not forgotten. It had inspired Baronius himself to compile his *Annales Ecclesiastici*, thus beginning that combination of literary and archaeologal material that has served the study of Church history so well. In the last decade of the century exploration was started again, Alphonso Chacon (Ciacconio) and Philip de Winghe (d. 1592) seeking out and copying (not always accurately) frescos that were now being discovered. De Winghe, however, had found a more able successor. Before he died he gave a young Maltese student copies of the frescos he had been discovering.

Antonio Bosio (1573–1629) was in Rome with his uncle, who was agent for the Knights of Malta.[7] He was studying philosophy and law, but de Winghe had turned his mind towards archaeology and the exploration of the

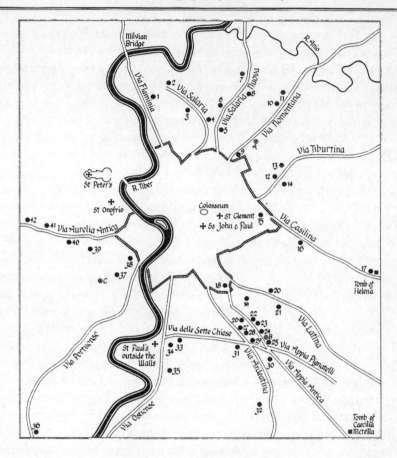

Rome and the catacombs in its vicinity

catacombs, which was to be his career. His first essay, however, was nearly his last, for descending with a friend into the as yet unidentified catacomb of Domitilla on the Via Ardeatina on 10 December 1593 he got lost in the maze of galleries and only just found an exit before becoming exhausted.[8] The experience only whetted his appetite, for it proved to him the vast extent of the underground cemeteries constructed by the early Christians. Before the year was out, he had visited the catacomb on the Via Salaria Nuova and another on the Via Tiburtina. In 1594 he explored the Via Nomentana in the north and the Via Appia south of the city. That on the Via Nomentana was a Jewish catacomb, the first to be discovered, and revealing that the Roman Jews as well as the Roman Christians were burying their dead in catacombs, also decorated by frescos representing biblical scenes. In 1595 Bosio turned his attention to the Via Ostiense, and the following year he and his followers found frescos in a catacomb on the Via Latina which they copied. Like their predecessors in the Roman Academy, they sometimes left their names and the date of their visit above the fresco they had copied. Thus we learn that on 10 June 1596 Bosio and his associate Toccafundo discovered the catacomb of Marcus and Marcellianus on the Via Ardeatina and painted their names and date above the magnificent picture of the Three Magi bearing gifts to the Virgin and Child.[9] Bosio continued his explorations. In August 1601 he descended into the catacomb on the Via Nomentana through one of the light-shafts (*lucernaria*) that provided enough light for the diggers to excavate new tombs in the darkened galleries. His final expedition was to the Monte Verde in 1615, beneath which he found the cemetery of Pontianus.[10]

Bosio relied on *Acta Martyrum* (Acts of the Martyrs) and local information provided by owners of vineyards for knowledge where to look for cemeteries, and he attempted to identify a catacomb with the name of a marytr. Of the *Itineraries*, only that of William of Malmesbury seems to have been used by him. From his careful notes it is evident that he found the entrances of thirty catacombs. Among his most important finds was the representation of the Heavenly Banquet in the catacomb of Peter and Marcellinus on the Via Labicana.[11] He was not primarily an excavator, but at the same time was far more than a cataloguer of discoveries. His method was to seek entrances and explore when the galleries were free from debris. In the intervals of exploration he searched patristic works for every reference to cemeteries and the liturgies associated with them. His great four-volume *Roma Sotteranea*, written between 1615 and 1629, was a magnificent work seeking to blend archaeological with literary evidence in a single theme of historical scholarship, an outlook far in advance of his time.

It was the period, however, of the Thirty Years War (1618–48) and the times were not friendly towards dispassionate scholarship even in the service of Catholic orthodoxy. Severanus, who edited Bosio's work in 1634 after his death, was intent on showing that the catacombs were uncontaminated by pagan, schismatic or heretical use. Apparently pagan scenes and symbols were, he claimed, taken over by the Christians and given a new significance – correct in some instances, but hardly in a polemical sense, to be used as ammunition against the opponents of Catholicism.

In St Peter's itself, work to reconstruct and enlarge the original Constantinian basilica had been going on since 1452, and did not end until 1667 with the completion of the porticos on each side of the piazza. Pope Clement VIII (1592–1605) planned to excavate beneath the newly constructed high altar where builders thought they had seen the cross which Constantine was believed to have placed on the tomb of the apostle Peter. He desisted, however, fearing that he might find nothing. However, substantial traces of the cemetery beneath St Peter's, which were finally brought to light in 1940, continued to be found, and Bosio was disappointed in not being able to explore in the wake of the architects.

The most famous of their discoveries was the sarcophagus of Junius Bassus, prefect of the city of Rome, who had died in 359 at the age of 42, while still in office, and whose tomb had been dug within the nave of Constantine's basilica. The discovery was made in 1595, and to this day the sarcophagus remains one of the finest exmples of early-Christian art. Bassus had been converted on his deathbed to Christianity. While at the end of the sarcophagus are scenes of harvesting putti, the two registers of the decorated side of the sarcophagus are divided into panels illustrating alternately scenes from the Old and New Testaments. The sacrifice of Isaac is followed by the arrest of Peter, Christ seated in majesty holds the scroll of the New Law; then the healing of the paralytic precedes Adam and Eve, and Daniel standing serenely between two quiescent lions contrasts with the execution of Paul. Not all follows logically, but the sculptor had attempted to include some of the most famous incidents in Scripture, perhaps of 'salvation history', to accompany the illustrious convert to his final home.[12]

Not all the discoveries during the reconstruction were so edifying. In 1626, while excavating an area in which to place the new high altar, workmen unearthed a third-century(?) pagan sarcophagus with an inscription in honour of Flavius Agricola, a native of Tibur (Tivoli). He was shown reclining at a funerary banquet and described himself 'taking care of himself and never going short of wine'; his wife for 30 years was a 'chaste worshipper of Isis'. His final injunction to his friends was 'Mix the wine, drink deep, wreathed with flowers, and do not refuse pretty girls the sweets of love. When death comes, earth and fire devour everything.' This cheerful epitaph of an Epicurean shocked those who expected to find something more suitable beneath so sacred a place. On the orders of Pope Urban VIII the irreverent object was removed and hidden away for the time being before being thrown into the Tiber, but not before the inscription had been copied.[13]

In view of such sensitiveness, emphasized by the condemnation of Galileo in 1633, it is not surprising that Bosio had no immediate scholarly successors, and that it was not until the mid-nineteenth century and de Rossi that his work was fully appreciated. Though the fighting between the Protestants and Catholics ended with the Peace of Westphalia in 1648, underlying hostility continued through the rest of the century. Pope Innocent X had condemned the Peace in unmeasured terms, regarding it as a betrayal of Catholicism. The second half of the seventeenth century was the age of Catholic, mainly Jesuit, missionary endeavour from Thailand to Lake Superior and of the attempt by Louis XIV to subjugate Europe to a Catholic monarchy. It was the age of Bossuet, Queen Christina, and James II, all ardent apostles of their faith. The catacombs were regarded as an inexhaustible mine of relics for export throughout the Catholic world. The frescos were regarded as an armoury for Catholic apologists, providing evidence for the primitive status of the cult of the Virgin, for prayers for the dead, for the Catholic eucharistic liturgy and the heroic continuity of the Roman Church itself. In 1678 Pope Clement X attempted to control the removal of material from the catacombs by establishing the office of Guardian of the Sacred Relics, but the Italian holders of the appointment were men of their time and hardly effective as researchers until the nineteenth century. Scholarly research was not helped, either, by non-Catholic scepticism. If the Benedictine scholar Jean Mabillon (1638–1707) had doubts about the authenticity of relics from the catacombs arriving in France,[14] Protestants were openly scoffing. In 1685–86, the historian Bishop Gilbert Burnet visited Italy, and rashly concluded that the catacombs were in reality old quarries, that the burials were pagan as well as Christian (true!), and the frescos were the work of mediaeval monks, 'Gothic style', Burnet claimed.[15] His study was closely followed by that of the still more radical F. W. Misson, who belived that the catacombs were common burial places and not fundamentally Christian. Some, even, were comparatively modern. These observations were hugely popular in Protestant circles: Burnet's continued to be published in London and Rotterdam until 1718, while Misson's final French edition was published only in 1739.

Elsewhere, in Catholic Europe, not least in the Habsburg dominions, confessional aims were combining with local patriotism to promote the Catholic cause. In *c*. 1693 the Jesuit seminary at Laibach (Ljubljana) had fake Latin and early-Christian inscriptions built into the walls of the seminary building to demonstrate its continuity from the Roman city of Emona. Like the 'discoverers' of the Piltdown Man, they believed that there *was* a link with the past, in this case, the Classical and early-Christian past, and if they could not find it then they would at least demonstrate its existence![16]

There were signs, however, of the slow emergence of a less partial spirit in some other European countries. France, despite its government by successive cardinals, Richelieu and Mazarin, and the anti-Protestant preaching of Bossuet, showed that pre-mediaeval discoveries could arouse scholarly as well as religious interest. In 1653 the tomb of the Frankish king Childeric (d. 481) was discovered in the St Brice district of Tournai during repairs to the presbytery of the Church.[17] There was great excitement. The tomb was identifed thanks to a gold signet ring on the finger of the skeleton inscribed with the name of its owner, Childeric. He was the father of Clovis, and had been buried with a great abundance of jewellery, arms, more than 200 silver coins and 100 gold coins, the latter minted in Constantinople. He was, of course, a pagan, but his relationship to Clovis, the founder of the Catholic Merovingian dynastry, gave the discovery an early-Christian as well as purely 'Merovingian' significance. Early-Christian archaeology in France may be said to date from the account of the tomb given by Jean-Jacques Chifflet, a learned physician of Antwerp, *Anastasis Childerici I*, published in Antwerp in 1655.[18]

Chifflet's account found an interested public, an interest kept alive by other valuable late-Roman and Merovingian finds in this period. Memories survived of the design of a cross said to have been offered to King Dagobert (629–639) and of the golden chalice of Chelles of the same period, which was copied in 1653.[19] But these, with much else, fell victim to the anticlericalism of the French Revolution (see below, p. 41). Around Arles, in the suburb of Trinquetaille, the first sarcophagi of what proved to be a major Christian cemetery were being unearthed, only, alas, to be broken up and looted.[20] A similar fate befell the massive silver hoard weighing 114 kg found near Trier in 1628. Two small platters survived, in the centre of one of which was a figure with a radiate crown, and round the rim the names 'Petrus Paulus Justus Hermes', enough to allow speculation about a hoard of Christian silver of Mildenhall proportions.[21]

Despite encouragement of untrammelled Classical studies symbolized by the foundation in 1663 of the Académie des Inscriptions et des Belles Lettres, scholars (mainly Benedictines and Jesuits) interested in the early-

Christian period played safe. They used their massive learning to initiate vast encyclopaedias that never risked the taint of unorthodoxy. Mabillon devoted his life with those of his fellow-Maurists (Benedictines of the Abbey of St Maur) to compiling chronologically an *Acta Sanctorum*, of the lives of monastic saints. The first volume, to AD 600, was published in 1668 and five others followed in the next dozen years. Meantime the Bollandists (Jesuits) had embarked on their huge *Acta Sanctorum*, designed to record the life and death 'of all Catholic saints' wheresoever venerated, and not least of martyrs for each day of the year. The first two volumes were completed in 1643, but the last, for December, only in 1940.[22] In the same vein, another scholar, Le Nain de Tillemont (1637–98), assembled the *Mémoires pour servir à l'histoire ecclésiastique des six premiers siècles*, in sixteen volumes of information drawn from the Fathers. There was little scope for interpretation, and in the age which witnessed the revocation of the Edict of Nantes (1685) little incentive to make any, especially for one who was inclined towards Jansenism. Tillemont, however, provided Edward Gibbon with the raw material from which he could fashion his interpretation of the role of Christianity in the fall of the Roman empire.[23] His volumes also provided a unique guide through the literary evidence for future investigators of the material remains of early Christianity.

Across the channel interest in early Christianity was moving in an opposite direction. Britain has produced splendid hoards of Christian silver. Mildenhall, Water Newton and Hoxne will always remain memorable but there has never been the steady flow of discoveries that indicate the irreversible progress of the faith as in other Roman provinces. In this period, the Rendelsham silver crown weighing 60 oz, dug up in 1687, and belonging perhaps to a member of the East Anglian royal house, was the only major discovery relating to early Christian times.[24] But scholarship, particularly that aimed at throwing light on antiquity and the coming of Christianity to Britain, was unhindered by fears of denunciation for unorthodoxy.

William Camden's *Britannia*, published in Latin in 1607 after twenty years of research and writing, was, like those of his French counterparts, an encyclopaedic work, but it was also an example of different attitudes prevailing in Britain and the Continent. Camden's aim was scientific, to 'restore Britain to antiquity and antiquity to Britain' and 'to recover a certainty in our affairs which either the carelessness of writers or the credulity of readers have bereaved us'.[25] The results were huge folio volumes, in which he told, first, the story of Roman Britain and Anglo-Saxon England, using every scrap of known literary evidence and, where possible, inscriptions, such as one from Boulogne referring to the rule of Magnus Maximus and Flavius Victor

(383–388).[26] This was followed by a county-by-county survey of known antiquities, so detailed as to provide the basis of all future county histories. True, Camden believed that the Britons were descended from the Trojans; that a 'monotheism taught by Druids prepared the way for acceptance of Christianity'[27] by the British, and that 'Hengist defeated the Britons at Stonehenge'.[28] But he also poured cold water on the claims of Glastonbury to be associated with Joseph of Arimathea, though he believed King Arthur was associated with Glastonbury. He was interested in archaeological discoveries as such, recording pagan funerary inscriptions 'fetched out of the earth' from Walcot Field near Bath, and he believed that the abbey at Bath stood on the remains of a temple of Minerva.[29] More even than Bosio he was a follower in spirit of the early 'investigators of antiquity' in Rome, and the first of a long line of British scholars of antiquity, whether secular or clerical, to whom the establishment of objective truth was the sole justification for their efforts.

Though confessional rancours were never far below the surface, as the attitude of so gifted an historian as Gilbert Burnet towards the Roman (and Neapolitan) catacombs showed, learning was now beginning to unite as well as divide. Exchanges of letters took place between the Bollandists and English scholars on and off throughout the seventeenth century, notably between Daniel Papebroch (d. 1714) and John Mill the New Testament scholar, and William Dugdale (d. 1685), the editor of *Monasticon Anglicanum*. These contacts showed that where scholarship and early-Christian history was concerned, dogmatic differences could sometimes be allowed to fade.[30]

With the eighteenth century we enter a period when confessional strife was less strident and an admiration for the Classics became the almost universal mark of an educated man, but so long as Christian archaeology was dominated by the catacombs, confessional interests would remain. Meanwhile, however, increasing trade links with the Ottoman empire enabled Europeans to travel through the one-time centres of Christianity in North Africa, Syria, Palestine and Asia Minor, and see there the majestic ruins of the Classical and Christian past. The dawn of the Enlightenment was preparing the way for the study of both as part of human history.

NOTES

1. Jerome, *Commentary on Ezekiel* 40.5–13: CCl. 75, 468. See J. N. D. Kelly, *Jerome* (New York: Harper and Row, 1975), p. 22.
2. See J. Stevenson's short but excellent description of the history and construction of the catacombs, as well as the purpose and routes followed by the *Itineraries: The Catacombs Rediscovered* (London: Batsford, 1978), chs 1–3.

3. William of Malmesbury, *De Gestis Regum Anglorum*; cited from O. Marucchi, *Eléments d'archéologie chrétienne* (Paris/Rome, 1903), II, p. 97 n.1. Examples of directions given in other *Itineraries* are given ibid., p. 52 n.1.

4. See Stevenson, op. cit., pp. 47–8, and J. B. de Rossi, *Roma Sotteranea* (Rome, 1867–76), I, pp. 3–9.

5. See *ICUR* VII (1933–35), p. 409; E. Prinzivalli, 'Hippolytus, statue of', in *EEC* I. Eusebius believed he was a 'Bishop' (*HE* vi.20.2). For the view that the statue may originally have been that of a pagan philosopher, Themista of Lampsacus, see M. Guarducci, *Epigraphia Graeca*, IV (Rome, 1978), pp. 535–46. For an exhaustive examination of the problem, see Allen Brent, *Hippolytus and the Roman Community* (Leiden: Brill, 1995).

6. See H. Leclercq, 'Catacombes', *DACL* II.2, 2436.

7. For Bosio's career, see H. Leclercq, 'Bosio', *DACL* II.1, 1083–1093, and for a short account, Stevenson, pp. 50–1.

8. For the chronology of Bosio's discoveries, see Leclercq, 'Bosio', 1085.

9. Ibid.; Stevenson, op. cit., p. 51. For his exploration of the catacomb and cemetery on the Via Latina, see E. Iosi, 'Cimitero cristiano sulla Via Latina', *Rivista* 16 (1939), pp. 19–48, 197–240.

10. Leclercq, 'Bosio'.

11. Bosio left his signature with that of Pomponius above the scene! See Stevenson, op. cit., p. 95, fig. 71.

12. Discussed by H. Grisar, 'Der Sarkophag des Junius Bassus', *RQ* 10 (1896), pp. 313–33; and E. S. Malbon, *The Iconography of the Sarcophagus of Junius Bassus* (Princeton University Press, 1990). Finely illustrated in Marcel Simon, *La Civilisation d'Antiquité et le Christianisme* (Paris: Arthaud, 1972), plates 107 and 147.

13. *CIL* VI.3, 17958a. See J. M. C. Toynbee and J. Ward Perkins, *The Shrine of St Peter and the Vatican Excavations* (London: Longmans, 1956) p. 58.

14. As Mabillon expressed to his friends on being presented with a catacomb skeleton, supposedly that of a martyr. See David Knowles, 'Jean Mabillon' in *The Historian and Character* (CUP, 1963), ch. 10, p. 230; and for the continued use of catacomb discoveries for apologetic purposes, see F. W. Deichmann, *Einführung in die christliche Archäologie* (Darmstadt, 1983), p. 17.

15. See Stevenson, op. cit., p. 52.

16. Recorded by A. von Premerstein, 'J. G. Thainitsches Antiquitates Labacensis', *JÖAI* 5 (1902), pp. 7–31.

17. P. A. Février, 'La naissance d'une archéologie chrétienne' in *Naissance des arts chrétiens: Atlas des monuments paléochrétiens de la France* (Paris, 1991) (= *Naissance*) pp. 336–47, at p. 338.

18. Antwerp and Tournai were in the Austrian Netherlands, but the treasure was eventually transmitted to Louis XIV, who as king of France claimed to be lawful successor of the Merovingians. Much of the treasure was stolen from the imperial art gallery in Paris in 1831 and not recovered.

19. *Naissance*, p. 314.

20. See L. A. Constans, *Arles antique* (*BEFAR* 119; Paris, 1921); reviewed in *JRS* 10 (1921), p. 284.

21. F. Baratte and C. Metzger, 'L'orfèvrerie christianisée' in *Naissance*, p. 306.

22. For the Bollandists, see H. Delehaye, *The Work of the Bollandists Through Three Centuries 1615–1915* (Eng. trans.; Princeton, NJ, 1922); D. Knowles, *Great Historical Enterprises* (Cambridge, 1963). The scale of the Bollandist project is indicated by the title of the first two volumes published in Antwerp: *Acta sanctorum quotquot tota orbe coluntur vel a Catholicis Scriptoribus celebrantur, quae ex Latinis et Graecis aliarumque gentium antiquis monumentis collegit, digressit, notis illustravit Johannes Bollandus.*

23. For Gibbon's praise mingled with some criticism see *Decline and Fall* (new edition 1802), VIII, ch. 47, p. 317 n. 72. and I, p. 306 n.70: 'The learned M. de Tillemont never dismisses a virtuous emperor without pronouncing his damnation.'

24. See H. Munro Chadwick, 'The Sutton Hoo burial: who was he?', *Antiquity* 14 (1940), p. 77. John Dee, the seventeenth-century antiquary, narrowly missed finding the Anglo-Saxon treasure at Sutton Hoo: C. W. Phillips, 'The Sutton Hoo ship burial', *Antiquity*, ibid., p. 11. See below, p. 255.

25. William Camden, *Britannia*, Eng. trans. by Edmund Gibson, bishop of London (1722; 4th edn 1772), Preface.

26. *Britannia*, I, p. 54.

27. Ibid., p. 57. A view widely accepted, not least by Stukeley in the next century. (See below, p. 29.)

28. Ibid., p. 207.

29. Ibid., pp. 322–3. Camden also made use of the newly-discovered Peutinger Table to try to fix the location of Romano-British towns.
30. See B. de Gaiffier, 'Religion, érudition et critique à la fin du XVIIe siècle et au début du XVIIIe' (Paris: Bibliothèque des Centres d'études supérieures specialisées, 1967), pp.4–5 of offprint.

FURTHER READING

R. Baratte and C. Metzger, 'L'orfèvrerie christianisée' in *Naissance des arts chrétiens: Atlas des monuments paléochrétiens de la France* (Paris, 1991), pp. 300–19.

Allen Brett, *Hippolytus and the Roman Community* (Leiden: Brill, 1995).

L. A. Constans, *Arles Antique* (*BEFAR*, fasc, 199;) Paris, 1921.

F. W. Deichmann, *Einführung in die christliche Archaelogie* (Darmstadt: Wissenschaftlihcche Buchgesellschaft, 1983), ch. 3, 'Geschichte'.

P. A. Février, 'Naissance d'une archéologie chrétienne' in *Naissance des arts chrétiens*, pp. 336–47.

H. Grisar, 'Der Sarkophag des Junius Bassus', *RQ* 10 (1896), pp. 313–33.

D. Knowles, *Great Historical Enterprises* (Cambridge, 1963).

E. S. Malbon, *The Iconography of the Sarcophagus of Junius Bassus* (Princeton University Press, 1990).

J. Stevenson, *The Catacombs: Rediscovered Monuments of Early Christianity* (London: Thames and Hudson, 1978): essential reading.

Articles in *DACL* by H. Leclercq: 'Bosio', 'Catacombes', 'Mabillon' and 'Ruinart'.

3

Antiquaries, travellers and enlighteners

The controversies at the end of the seventeenth century over the age and authenticity of the galleries and frescos in the Roman catacombs were symptoms of the continuing hostility between Catholics and Protestants in western and central Europe. The defeat of Louis XIV in the War of the Spanish Succession (1701–13) restored to a large extent the balance of power between the nations representing the two religions. From now on, though suspicion and acts of religious repression persisted, these tended to be overlaid by other more positive factors. Advances in scientific and historical knowledge led to a greater willingness to challenge the orthodoxies of the past. The age of the Encyclopaedists in France was also the age of the first critical histories of the early Church, of Isaac de Beausobre's two-volume work on the religion of the Manichees (*Histoire critique de Manichée et du Manichéisme*, 1734–39), of von Mosheim's *Ecclesiastical History* (1747, Eng. trans. 1767), and finally, to Gibbon's *Decline and Fall of the Roman Empire* (1776–87).

Alongside these great works of critical scholarship there was a slow but steady increase in the discovery of the material remains of the early Church. Improving diplomatic and trade relations with the Ottoman empire enabled individuals to travel under safe conduct and even escort in Syria and Palestine, and also in North Africa. Descriptions of the vast ruins, reminders of a Greco-Roman and Christian past, filtered back to the new learned societies being established in the European capitals. Such accounts found a ready hearing among those whose culture was dominated by Classical studies. In Italy the discovery of Herculaneum by a peasant in 1711 and of Pompeii in 1748 furthered interest in archaeology. At this stage, however, the collector gained most. King Charles III of Naples, tunnelling tirelessly to wrest as many sculptures from Herculaneum as possible, was the example followed.[1] The breakthrough that would enable archaeology to contribute towards understanding early Christianity did not occur. This had to await the French conquest of Algeria in the next century.

The Roman catacombs had shown what might be revealed, but throughout the eighteenth century progress was disappointing. Here, in particular, the spirit of the collector and pious fraud overcame that of the researcher. Bosio had no competent successors. Pope Clement XII's (1730–40) plan to have his works re-edited miscarried. Giovanni Bottari (1689–1762), appointed to that task, had little inclination to check Bosio's accounts of his explorations on the ground.[2] Though he published an important fresco depicting the Israelites crossing the Red Sea, he preferred to study Bosio's drawings from the comfort of his rooms. His three-volume *Roma Sotteranea* (1737–54) contained little new.[3]

Unfortunately Bottari typified the prevalent lethargy and indifference towards the catacombs. Marco Antonio Boldetti (1663–1749), a Hebrew scholar whom Pope Clement XI (Pope 1700–21) appointed as Custodian of the Sacred Cemeteries, began well enough.[4] In 1715 he entered a catacomb beneath the walls of the church of St Cyriacus seven miles along the Ostian Way, which Bosio had first identified.[5] Not long after he penetrated the great gallery of the catacomb of Commodilla and discovered the vault of the martyrs Digna and Emerita, victims of the persecution under Valerian (257–259), and a small chapel adjoining with frescos representing Christ and his saints. He considered, rightly as it happened, that the catacomb was in too dangerous a state to explore further,[6] and it was not entered again until the end of the next century. In 1720, he published his *Osservazione sopra i cimiteri di santi martyri ed antichi christiani di Roma*, a useful, if not always accurate, work but one which shows what material was then accessible, but is now lost. Unfortunately, Boldetti was a collector and a hoarder. The sub-title of his work, 'Riflessioni pratichi sopra il culto delle sagre Reliquie', showed where his inclinations lay. He removed inscriptions, including pagan inscriptions, and where he could, frescos,[7] tombs were opened in search for martyrs' relics, and these, with a multitude of small objects he found, were transported to his own and other churches in Rome. Perhaps the kindest estimate of his thirty years' regime was that of Henri Leclercq: 'Mgr Boldetti pilla les catacombes pour mieux servir religion.'[8] On his death in 1749 at the age of 86 his church and presbytery must have resembled a cross between a repository for antiques and a charnel house. His friend and successor Marangoni (1673–1753) was little better. The catacombs were neglected and often stonework was robbed by vineyard owners. It was the 'dark age' of research, as later scholars termed it.[9] Scientific study was resumed only in the 1830s by G. Settele (1770–1840) and the Jesuit Giuseppe Marchi (1795–1860), who inspired the young de Rossi with his life-long enthusiasm for the Roman catacombs.

Boldetti was not untypical of his age. The eigthteenth century was the period of the aristocratic traveller on whose whim whatever was spectacular or valuable found in excavations was removed without reference to its associations or historical context. Prominent among such connoisseurs and collectors were heirs to the great aristocratic houses in Britain finishing their education with the Grand Tour of Italy, and in 1764 the man who would become the greatest English historiographer, Edward Gibbon.

The one major exception in this era of genteel pillage was at Aquileia.[10] The antiquities of this Roman and early-Christian centre had aroused interest since 1544, when G. Candido had suggested that the church of St Martin on the road to Grado had been built on the site of a temple of the god Belenus. A town-plan of what was known of ancient Aquileia was drawn up in 1693, and working from this Canon Gaetano Bertoli (d. 1759) excavated the baptistery attached to the cathedral of the ancient city, part of a cemetery associated with the church of St Hilarius, allegedly the second bishop of Aquileia, martyred in 284 (long before the Great Persecution),[11] and also a three-nave church dedicated to Sts Felix and Fortunatus. His most notable find was an inscription showing a baptism in which the catechumens stood naked in a large basin while the priest poured water over them.[12] There was no descent into the font for threefold immersion, but a rite possibly similar to that practised in Roman Britain, where the catechumens seem to have stood in a lead font placed on the ground. (See below, p. 372.) Bertoli published his survey of Aquileia's Christian and secular antiquities in 1739 and a second shorter study in 1749. It was the last decade of the nineteenth century before his work was followed up.

In France also there was promise but little achievement. In the 1720s Canon L. A. Bocquillot (1649–1728) discovered a group of Merovingian sarcophagi at Quarré des Tombes in Burgundy and published them.[13] This and the discovery of the sarcophagi of Childeric II, his wife Bilihilde and son Dagobert beneath the choir of the church of St Germain des Prés[14] and four sarcophagi from within the church of St Martin at Artonne north of Clermont were among valuable archaeological funds that pointed the way to future progress.[15] More immediately important was the Maurist (Ruinart)[16] publication of the works of Gregory of Tours (d. 594), especially the *Historia Francorum*. Apart from recording the grim and gory events of early Frankish history Gregory often described in detail the construction of churches, not least in his own

Tours,[17] and the organization of Church life, which would guide research once the archaeologists began in earnest. In the eighteenth century, however, French interest in early Christianity and its remains was very largely confined to the learned Benedictines and clergy. The Revolution would be needed before it was shared with lay scholars drawn from the emergent middle classes.

In Britain, on the other hand, there were no such inhibitions. Since the Elizabethan settlement (1559–62), Church and scholarship had tended to work together. We have already noted William Camden's contribution to knowledge of early Britain. Among the clergy, Bishop Townsend of Chichester had been among the founders of the Royal Society in 1677. His colleagues Bishops Burnet, Wanley and Gibson had all contributed to historical studies. The Reverend William Stukeley was the first secretary to the society which became the Society of Antiquaries of London, formed in 1717. He was a physician and an FRS. A similar honour was accorded to the Reverend William Borlase, the Cornish antiquary who first put forward the idea, now proved to be true, that the Isles of Scilly were once one island, 'though not with towns and churches'.[18] For a scholar to be an MD as well as a DD was not altogether rare.

Antiquarian learning, which included delving into genuine and supposed remains of early Christianity in Britain, was often aided by aristocratic patronage. The period following the Treaty of Utrecht (1713) was among the most prosperous for the English landed gentry. As Basil Williams remarked, 'Apart from politics, the life of polite society in the reigns of the first two Georges must have been as agreeable as such life can ever be.'[19] The Palladian design of many of the great country mansions was completed by the building of Classical-style temples in the grounds, and by collections of Roman imperial busts and other acquisitions from the Grand Tour, or like those of the fourth Earl of Carlisle in Castle Howard, from a lengthy, leisured stay in Rome itself.

THE ANTIQUARIES

Such acquisitions were being supplemented by discoveries nearer home. It was not long before the 'Antiquarian Society of London' was fulfilling the expectations of its founders. In 1712 a Roman mosaic was excavated at Stonesfield near Woodstock, and duly recorded in the minutes of the Society on 7 December 1721. In 1727 the first evidences for the existence of the Roman baths and temple to Minerva were discovered at Bath.[20] In 1732 John Horsley published a three-volume *Britannia Romana*, an outstanding pioneer work, which included an inscription found at Chichester recording the building of a temple to Neptune and Minerva by Cogidumnus 'the legate' for the protection of the Divine House (i.e. the emperor Claudius). This was the opening chapter in the story of the British king of the Regni who sided with the invading Romans in 43 and was rewarded with the means of building the imperial-style villa at Fishbourne.[23] In 1736, another Roman villa, that at Cotterstock near Oundle, was located[22] and at the same time the first traces of the Roman mansion at Littlecote came to light with its Orpheus (possibly Christian) mosaic.[23]

Amidst all this activity, two discoveries (perhaps three, if one includes the recently (1994) identified lead tank found at Icklingham in 1725)[24] related directly to early Christianity. Both the Risley dish and Corbridge dish (or *lanx*) were found within a few years of each other, in 1729 and 1735 respectively. Both were recovered by accident and preserved by the instinctive curiosity of individuals who otherwise lacked formal education.

The Risley dish[25] was found on 9 June 1729 by a ploughman a few inches below the surface. It had been broken into some twenty pieces, probably from the impact of the plough. Stukeley heard of the find, visited the site, and probably saw the centre part of the dish which had been handed in by the ploughman to the lady of the manor, Lady Aston.

The dish seems to have been rectangular, measuring $7 \times 5\frac{1}{2}$ in (18×13 cm) and standing on a small foot of the same shape. It has been identified as a *lanx* whose central panel was filled by a hunting scene, huntsmen and dogs chasing a wild boar with 'a very antique type of temple with a statue in it of Pan' in the foreground(?). On the frieze round the edge were pastoral and hunting scenes. The dating would appear to be *c.* AD 350 or a little later, but this fine example of late-Classical silverware would have been regarded as pagan were it not for an inscription scratched on the back, 'Exsuperius episcopus ec(c)lesiae Bogiense dedit ☧'. Stukeley asked the right questions: who was this bishop, where was his see, and how did this splendid silver dish reach Risley Park? His answers, however, were antiquarian speculation typical of his time, believing that it was loot taken during an action near the town of Bouges in Touraine in 1421 and brought back to England.[26] Today the mystery of Exsuperius' see remains unsolved.[27] The Risley *lanx*, however, takes its place among the Christian silver treasures combining pagan and Christian motifs that were buried in Britain, with increasing likelihood, during the troubled period 360–370.

Stukeley reported the Risley find to the Antiquarian Society of London on 8 April 1736, with other pieces of Roman silverware that had been recovered in or near the banks of the Tyne near Corbridge in the previous five years.

Corbridge (Corstopitum) was the Roman supply base for the garrison on the Wall, and the five pieces recovered, though found separately, probably formed part of a collection belonging to a senior officer. The most imposing item was a silver dish, found in February 1735, of the same shape as the Risley *lanx*, but larger, measuring 19 × 15 cm and weighing 148 oz, supported like the Risley *lanx* on a rectangular foot. The central panel was also occupied by a pagan religious scene, a gathering of deities, as Roger Gale described in a letter to Stukeley in 1735. The exact nature of the gathering is still uncertain, but the five more important figures represented are all deities, the principal being Apollo standing at the entrance of a shrine.[28] He is confronted by Artemis, Athena and two other female deities, one of whom is perhaps Leto.[29] The scene is most likely placed at Apollo's shrine at Delos at a date that 'fits best the spirit of Julian's revival'[30] (i.e. 361–363).

Whatever the answer, the *lanx* would have no apparent connection with Christianity had not one of the other pieces in the group, found in 1736, been a bowl on whose rim were inscribed a series of six ☧ amid naturalistic decoration. This suggests that the Corbridge silver also had a Christian connection comparable to other similar treasures, such as that found at Mildenhall in 1943.[31] In this, the great silver dish featured Oceanus and Maenads, but five spoons with Christian inscriptions were also found as well as a strainer whose handle was shaped in the form of a dolphin, used possibly to filter wine dispensed at the Eucharist. In fourth-century Britain the wealthy Christians who owned these fine objects were evidently not opposed to combining their faith with a ready acceptance of the contemporary artistry of pagan mythology.

Stukeley's descriptions of the silver objects from Risley and Corbridge were not too wide of the mark, though his speculations concerning the arrival of the Risley dish from France during the Hundred Years War were nonsense. He himself demonstrates the mixture of theological and Classical learning, precise observation and curious theorizing that was the feature of much of British antiquarianism in the eighteenth as well as in the previous century. Born in 1687 at Holbeach (Lincs),[32] he graduated from Pembroke College, Cambridge, before his ten-year tenure of the secretaryship of the Antiquarian Society of London brought him into contact with increasing discoveries of the Roman period in Britain. A surgeon by profession, he was distinguished enough to be elected an FRS in 1717 and FRCP in 1722, but in 1729 he took Orders, believing as he said, 'the whole course of learning was requisite to the study of Divinity'.[33] For his time, he was a superb field archaeologist, locating the Avenue and Cursus at Stonehenge. He was tireless in searching for and describing visible antiquities of Britain from Avebury and Stonehenge to Car

Dyke, Richard of Cirencester and mediaeval castles, combining an enquiring mind with a firm Christian faith, demonstrated by a lecture to his medical colleagues on 'The miracles of healing'. In 1764, near the end of his life, as vicar of St George's, Queen Street, London, he postponed Morning Service for an hour so that his congregation should witness an eclipse of the sun. Stonehenge with its association of sun-worship and Druids fascinated him. He set out to prove that the Druids were connected with early Christianity. In 1763 he published *Palaeographica Sacra*, in which he suggested that the Druids were of the 'patriarchal religion of Abraham', that Abraham himself was 'the first Druid', and that Christianity was 'a republication of the patriarchal religion'.[34] This might have pleased Eusebius of Caesarea, who also argued that Christianity 'could claim the Hebrew patriarchs as its ancestor',[35] but as a piece of antiquarian lore it remains a curiosity of the age of the Enlightenment. Stukeley died in March 1765, his work on the coinage of Carausius the 'British emperor' (286–293) (though not his invention of a new 'empress' Oriuna, through misreading the reverse side 'Fortuna') taking its place alongside his research on the Risley and Corbridge Christian silver as a contribution to knowledge of late antiquity in Roman Britain. He may have been a 'fanciful man' as a contemporary (Thomas Hearne) described him, but not everything he wrote was 'built on fancy'.[36]

THE TRAVELLERS

Events meantime in the eastern Mediterranean were beginning to move scholarship to more solid ground. The eighteenth century witnessed more relaxed relations between western Europe and the Ottoman empire. Trade succeeded wars of conquest. The British and French both established 'factories' or trading-posts in the Levant and in North Africa. The British 'Levant Company', with its headquarters at Constantinople, was a notable example. Members used leisure periods for travel and adventure and left lengthy descriptions of their experiences. Apart from these off-duty traders, members of Catholic Orders sometimes found themselves embarking on journeys in their efforts to find and ransom Christian prisoners taken captive by corsairs operating from North African ports. There were also independent scholars, and members of scientific missions sponsored by European governments, notably the Prussian, who aimed at gathering geographic information in the hitherto closed territories of the Ottoman empire.

All were struck by the wealth of Classical and early-Christian remains that they encountered. Shaw[37] and Bruce[38] both record finding 'heaps of ruins', 'remains of large cities now completely deserted'. The Frenchman Jean Peyssonnel (1694–1759) described Sbeitla (Suffetula), which he claimed to have visited in 1724, as a city that 'had not been destroyed but simply fallen into ruins'.[39] He may have mistaken the site for another Roman city in south-central Tunisia, but his contemporary, Father Ximenes, described how he found Bedouin growing tobacco and onions among the majestic ruins of Sbeitla's temples and churches.[40]

What was the reason for this? The short answer is that the Ottoman empire in the Middle East and North Africa coincided almost exactly with the vast area overrun by nomadic tribes from the sixth century onwards, of which the Arab invasions of the seventh century were the most massive and decisive. Already, however, at the end of the Vandal occupation of Roman North Africa (c. 520) the plains of central Tunisia were being dominated by the Louata, Berber nomads originally from Cyrenaica. Their camels, flocks and herds were destroying the livelihood of the settled North African population before this was restored by the Byzantines, only to be destroyed again by the Arab invaders in the second half of the seventh century. In Syria the process was the same, once-prosperous villages being rendered uninhabitable by the arrival of the Arab armies in the 630s and their accompanying nomad tribesmen. In Asia Minor the culprits were the Seljuk Turks and their Turkoman allies, gradually seeping into areas occupied for centuries by a rural Christian population, destroying crops, driving the people off the land, and finally rendering the towns, the centres of Christian authority, uninhabitable. In Nubia, south of the Egyptian border, the enemy of the settled Christian population had been Sahara nomads coming in from the west, exerting pressure, not necessarily capturing the villages and strong points held by the Christian Nubians but driving them into poverty until abandonment remained the only course. The story was similar from Morocco to the Black Sea provinces of the Turkish empire and from Alexandria to Khartoum. Greco-Roman and Christian civilization, the way of life of a settled population, fell victim to nomadic or semi-nomadic invaders.[41]

Nomads, however, by their nature were not town or village dwellers. Occasionally once-prosperous Roman towns in North Africa, such as Dougga,[42] Macri[43] or Tiddis[44] limped along as inhabited areas for a century or so after the Arab conquest, but the great majority of sites were simply abandoned. The buildings constructed with the skill of Roman engineers and native craftsmen stood untenanted. Not many bothered even to rob them of their stonework. They stood surviving wind and weather, majestic symbols of 'the glory that was Rome' until rediscovered by scholarly travellers in the eighteenth century.

The Turkish provinces in Asia Minor and the Middle East provide the first accounts of European travel. Before the end of the seventeenth century members of the staff of the British 'factory' at Aleppo had visited Palmyra, the city of the third-century Queen Zenobia, and the Byzantine fort and city with its sixth-century shrines and churches at Resapha (Sergiopolis) in Mesopotamia. They had identified monasteries with cells and churches there.[45] From Smyrna (Izmir) British and French employees of their 'factories' had also visited the ruins of Prusa, the home town of Cynic and temporarily Christian Peregrinus,[46] described by Tournefort as 'the most magnificent in Asia, its walls still standing'.[47]

A journey which combined archaeological enterprise with contemporary relevance to the relations between the Anglican, Orthodox and Roman Christian traditions was that undertaken by Sir George Wheler. Wheler was interested in furthering Anglican–Orthodox relations as a counterweight to the continued pressure of Rome represented by Britain's potential enemies, France and Spain.[48] After visiting Roman and early-Christian ruins along the Dalmatian coast he decided to visit major sites in Syria and Palestine to check how far Eusebius of Caesarea's descriptions of the great church at Tyre (*HE* x.4) and the Holy Sepulchre at Jerusalem (*Life* iii.31–39) corresponded to what had survived. He also wanted to assess how far Orthodox rites, recognizable by reference to the plan of these and other churches in Syria, could be found to correspond with the liturgy of the Church of England.[49]

It was not a futile mission. During the seventeenth century relations between the Anglican and Orthodox Churches had been cordial. Letters had been exchanged between Archbishop Abbot (1572–1638) and Cyril Lukaris, archbishop of Alexandria in Charles I's reign. Cyril's gift to the king of the Codex Alexandrinus has remained in Britain ever since. At the Restoration, Anglican divines who were interested in liturgy knew a good deal about Orthodox rites.[50] Wheler was able to show in the account of his travels in 1689 that, in contrast to the Roman usage, the baptismal fonts in the Orthodox churches remained within the church and not placed in separate baptisteries, and in this respect the Anglican and Orthodox rites shared common ground. For the first time archaeological research had played a part in fostering relations between two Christian traditions.

Wheler's travels were not forgotten. Palestine and Jerusalem were visited by A. Reland in 1713 and results published with copious illustrations.[51] In the autumn of 1749 Robert Wood (1716–71) accompanied by John Bouverie and James Dawkins, Oxford graduates, set out from Rome on a long tour that would take them through Asia Minor to Damascus and, finally, eastwards to

Palmyra.[52] Wood's account mentions Wheler's journey. His and his companions' discoveries were similar to those of their contemporaries travelling in North Africa, though hardships and malaria caused the death of John Bouverie at Guzel Hissar in northern Turkey in September 1750. Ruins on the site of Ephesus were still standing, so also was the theatre at Laodicea and the church of St John at Pergamum. They copied inscriptions embedded in the city walls of Geyre (Aphrodisias), visited the vast ruins at Baalbek, and went on to the former cathedral of St John at Damascus, before spending five days early in April 1751 amid the ruins of Palmyra. Their sketches, added to those of Wheler and Thomas Shaw (1694–1751), who travelled in Palestine before his expeditions in Algeria, demonstrated the wealth of Classical and early-Christian remains awaiting exploration there.

Shaw's main contribution was to be in North Africa where in the 1720s and 1730s scholars were already discovering the wealth of the heritage of the past. In 1724, three years before Shaw began his travels in Tunisia and Algeria, Jean Peyssonnel and Father Ximenes, a priest of the Order of the Most Sacred Trinity already mentioned, had penetrated into central Tunisia.[53] Peyssonnel was a doctor from Marseilles whose interest in archaeology took second place to natural history. In May 1724 he set out on a mission authorized by Louis XV to collect rare plants and seeds in Tunisia and also to visit Roman ruins. An account of his journey from Tunis down the coast to Sousse, thence inland to El Djem (Thysdrus) and finally north-west to Le Kef (Sicca Veneria) is contained in seven letters to his friend Abbé Bignon, and also in what appears to be a copy of the report he submitted to Louis XV on his return to France the same autumn. Father Ximenes' primary purpose for being in Tunis from 1720 to 1735 was to work among, and if possible negotiate the ransom of, Christian captives, but he was able also to travel extensively throughout the kingdom. Whether he or Peyssonnel was the first European visitor to the ruins of Sbeitla is still a matter of debate, but Ximenes, who certainly was there, had no doubt that Sbeitla had been 'an episcopal city in the time of the Catholic emperors'[54] and that there were tombs of 'many martyrs' housed there. Beyond discussion, however, is that their joint endeavours opened the eyes of Europeans to another mine of early-Christian remains awaiting exploration in Tunisia.

Another European journey was that of Dr Karl Ludwig and J. E. Hellenstreit, who were instructed in 1732 by Duke Frederick Augustus of Saxony to 'undertake a journey to Barbary' mainly to observe the geography and flora of the country. Though Ludwig proved to be an accurate observer and recorded 52 Latin inscriptions, mainly from Constantine and Calama, his results remained unpublished until they were found by the Austrian scholar

Otto Fiebiger in 1902.[55] The real credit for awakening the courts and scholars of Europe to the vast extent of the remains of the Roman and Byzantine period surviving in North Africa belongs to Thomas Shaw and, a generation later, to the explorer James Bruce.

Shaw was twelve years chaplain to the English 'factory' at Algiers, appointed in 1720. But he was an inveterate traveller, and before he embarked on a journey to Tunis and the ruins of Carthage in 1727 he had already visited Egypt and Sinai in 1721, and Jerusalem and Mount Carmel in the following years.[56] Where he was out of touch with English and French 'factories' he had found welcome among Arab Khans in the countryside, taking their hospitality as it came and never showing the least signs of wealth. His journey through Algeria in 1731 is a travelogue. He was more interested in natural history than archaeology, while noting features such as the extent of the ruins of Cherchell, 'almost as extensive as those of Carthage',[57] and the 'Tomb of the Christian' ('Tombeau de la Chrétienne') south-east of Tipasa (probably the tomb of King Juba II), which he associated rightly with 'the royal family of the Numidian kings', in preference to that of 'a Christian woman'.[58] His *Travels and Observations relating to several parts of Barbary and the Levant*, published at Oxford in 1738, describes the countryside he passed through with its plants, animals and fossils, alongside archaeological remains. He was always on the look-out for resemblances between the Kabyle and Arab customs of his day and descriptions of the Numidians given by Sallust, reinforced by suggested similarities to be found in the Bible. He pointed to the burnous as a garment that had not altered in 3,000 years. Inscriptions he copied carefully. Lambaesis, the headquarters of the Third Legion, still had 'several' of the 'forty gates' Arab traditions attributed to it, and an amphitheatre surviving.[59] Zana could be identified with Diana Veteranorum through an inscription on the triumphal arch.[60] At Auzia he found an inscription commemorating the defeat of the Moorish rebel Faraxen in 260.[61] At Announa (Thibilis) he reported the existence of a 'chapel of the Christians', a small square building surviving nearly complete with the figure of the cross cut on the door lintel.[62] At a site west of Cirta (Constantine) he found a Byzantine church with the inscription 'Domine protege nomen/gloriosum' (O Lord, protect the glorious name), with crosses cut on each upright of the entrance.[63] Further east, where Dr Ludwig was to visit the next year, he found 'numerous inscriptions' built into the wall of the citadel (Byzantine fort).[64] There were the ruins of Roman towns everywhere he went.

Shaw returned to Algiers, married the widow of Edward Holden, the British consul, and returned to England in 1733. He settled in Oxford, became Principal of St Edmund Hall and left his collection of coins and Roman busts to the University. More than any previous traveller, he had raised the curtain on the wealth of Classical and Christian remains awaiting discovery in North Africa.

Thirty years later the British consul in Algiers was James Bruce (1730–94), who became one of the earliest of that community of explorers who sought between 1770 and 1870 to lighten the 'Dark Continent' of Africa. In his case it was to discover the source of the Nile.[65] Bruce himself was not always an accurate observer and his work was to be criticized sharply by Salt, who travelled in Abyssinia in 1809 (see below, p. 48). His journey, however, through Algeria, Tunisia and Libya in 1765–66 was minutely prepared. He was accompanied by a draughtsman with what he called a 'camera obscura'.[66] With these aids he was able to make a series of drawings of the Roman ruins he found on what was otherwise uninhabited steppe. Diana (Zana), Lambaesis, Cirta, Sbeitla, Djilma, Thysdrus and Tripoli were among the deserted Roman town sites he visited. At Lambaesis, he saw 'seven gates still standing' (*Travels*, p. xxix). Though these sketches were only published fully in 1876 they showed what had survived the end of Byzantine rule down to the eighteenth century. Together Shaw's and Bruce's accounts were to prove invaluable to archaeologically-minded French officers that accompanied the invading forces in Algeria in the 1830s and 1840s.

In 1765 Bruce gave up his consular post to concentrate on his ambition to explore ancient sites in Algeria and then to find the source of the Nile. In 1768 he sailed up the Nile as far as Aswan, acquiring probably at Akhmin in the following year a Coptic codex, which he brought back to England for the Bodleian Library to acquire ultimately in 1848. It took nearly another forty years before the Frenchman Emile Amélineau and the German scholar Carl Schmidt examined the Codex Brucianus and revealed one of the few then known original Gnostic documents, the *Books of Jeu*.[67]

Bruce was more interested in the Nile than in Coptic codices. He entered Abyssinia via the port of Massawa and reached Gondar, the capital, in February 1770. On the way he visited Axum on 18 January 1769, though he made little of the great obelisks in honour of King Ezana (*c.* 350) there.[68] For two years he enjoyed fame and fortune among the not inhospitable people, established the source of the Blue Nile, and returned to Europe in 1773. He brought back three MSS of the Ethiopian version of the *Book of Enoch*. This, too, had to wait until 1821 before it was transcribed, and 1838 until published at Oxford by Laurence.[69]

Apart from Shaw, Gibbon was to be critical of the work of the 'blind travellers'[70] that were promenading through the Roman provinces that lay under

Ottoman control. This was not always just, for the value of their work in alerting scholars to the possibilities of discoveries in areas previously closed to research is obvious today. There were now enough Christian inscriptions available for J. A. Morcelli, a scholarly Jesuit priest at the Vatican, to edit the first collection of these in 1781. Gibbon, for one, saw the value of the new dimension which archaeology could provide for his momentous study of the *Decline and Fall of the Roman Empire*.

THE ENLIGHTENERS

No one is ever likely to equal Le Nain de Tillemont's sixteen volumes of the *Mémoires pour servir à l'histoire ecclésiastique des six premiers siècles* (published 1693–1712), for sheer erudition. But the *Mémoires* are what they claim to be, *mémoires* or memoranda, described as patristic texts linked together with a minimum of narrative with questions of chronology and authorship relegated to learned footnotes at the end of each volume.[71] The change of outlook that took place in the next thirty years is shown by Johann von Mosheim's (1694–1755) four-volume *Ecclesiastical History*. This was written in the 1740s when the author was Chancellor of the University of Göttingen and translated into English by the Reverend Archibald Maclaine, chaplain to the English Church at The Hague in 1767. This is a straightforward history with no more bias towards patristic orthodoxy than to be found in more recent authors. 'Ecclesiastical history', wrote the author, 'is a clear and faithful narration of the transactions, revolutions and events that relate to that large community, which bears the name of Jesus Christ and is vulgarly known under the denomination of the Church.'[72] He divides his narrative into the internal and external history of the Church. In general he was favourable to orthodoxy. Irenaeus turned his pen against the Church's internal and domestic enemies by attacking 'the monstrous errors adopted by many primitive Christians'.[73] On the other hand, 'the venerable simplicity of earliest Christianity was not of long duration. Its beauty was gradually effaced by the laborious effort of human learning and the dark subtleties of imaginary science'[74] (e.g. the 'nice distinctions' of philosophical Christians). Regarding the persecutions suffered by Christians, he asks the historian's question why in view of 'the excellent nature of the Christian religion' it was persecuted by the Roman authorities.[75] Von Mosheim's was the first modern Church history, but it was written while many of the catacomb inscriptions were still suspect and those found elsewhere were too few for historians to use.

Von Mosheim established a tradition of the relatively impartial record of Church history which Gibbon (1737–94) was to follow. His also was to be 'a candid but rational inquiry into the progress and establishment of Christianity'[76] but assessed within the wider framework of the inquiry, being 'considered as a very essential part of the history of the Roman empire'. He contrasts the 'pleasing task' indulged in by the theologian of describing 'Religion as she descended from Heaven arrayed, in her native purity', and that of the historian whose 'melancholy duty' is to discover the inevitable mixture of error and corruption which she contrasted in a long residence on earth among a weak and degenerate race of beings.[77] On the persecutions, like von Mosheim, Gibbon asks why 'so benevolent a doctrine', 'with the sanctity of its moral precepts, and innocent and austere lives of those who in the first ages embraced the faith', should have been the object of persecution.[78]

Gibbon was able to draw on the beginnings of archaeological evidence to supplement texts. Thus in a footnote he quotes an inscription to confirm statements by Aelius Aristides that the duties of Asiarchs included that of holding the sacred games at their own expense. In discussing the Great Persecution, he draws on James Gruter's *Inscriptions of the city of Rome* to point out that Adauctus, the treasurer of the imperial domains, was the person 'of rank and distinction who appears to have suffered death'.[79] He also quotes Damasus' critical epitaph of Pope Marcellus from the catacomb of Priscilla to illustrate the disorders that broke out in the Church of Rome after the Great Persecution, and the tolerant attitude of (the usurper) Maxentius towards the Christians.[80] Gibbon was using available archaeological material as a critical historian.[81] Unfortunately, as we have seen, material from the catacombs suffered throughout the eighteenth century from poor stewardship. He and von Mosheim had, however, paved the way for Church history to become an historian's field of study using material as well as literary remains. Archaeological evidence was beginning to increase, and there was now an incentive to discover more. The first papyrus document was brought to Europe from Egypt in 1778, revealing a new and unsuspected source of information.[82] Bruce's codex was as yet undeciphered, but in 1785 the British Museum acquired manuscripts in Coptic from the heirs of another British traveller, Dr Askew, which proved to be the Gnostic tract *Pistis Sophia* (Faith-Wisdom).[83]

Two serious difficulties remained. First, over much of the Continent, study of the history of the early Church continued to be largely the preserve of clergy and monastic institutions. Secondly, the ancient languages of Egypt and the Near East, whose decipherment would give an enormous impetus to biblical and early-Christian studies, remained a mystery. In 1784, in the last decade of the *Ancien Régime*, Herder wrote 'In the Near East and neighbouring Egypt everything from the ancient times appears to us as ruins, or as a dream

36

that has disappeared.... The archives of Babylon, Phoenicia and Carthage are no more; Egypt had withered practically before the Greeks saw its interior. Thus, everything shrinks to a few faded leaves which contain stories about stories, fragments of history, a dream of the world before us.'[84]

It was a pessimistic view. Many of the writers and thinkers of the Enlightenment saw progress towards understanding the biblical and ancient worlds stalled. It needed a new generation of scholars, the heirs to the Enlightenment, drawn from the middle classes and less beholden to the Catholic Church and the aristocracy, to bring about change. It needed also the lucky find and flash of insight to exploit it. The French Revolution opened the way for a scientific spirit among the European middle classes to assert itself. The genius of Napoleon harnessed that spirit to his military vision of French domination of the known world. Luck, through the discovery of the Rosetta stone, unlocked the secrets of this hitherto submerged world of the Egyptian past and inspired the work of Layard and his associates to achieve the same in Mesopotamia. From that time on, Christian archaeology would be advancing. We turn now to the unwitting architect of this development, Napoleon Bonaparte.

NOTES

1. For a short account of work in the eighteenth century at Herculaneum and Pompeii, see J. Seznec, 'Herculaneum and Pompeii in French literature of the eighteenth century', *Archaeology* 2 (1949), pp. 150–6.
2. For his career, see H. Leclercq in *DACL* II, 1096–1098.
3. Bottari, *Roma Sotteranea*, plates XL and CXCIV.
4. For Boldetti's career, see H. Leclercq in *DACL* II, 974–975. Boldetti was priest-in-charge of the church of Santa Maria Trastevere, well placed for the catacomb exploration.
5. See F. Fornari, 'Le recenti explorazioni nel cimitero di S. Ciriaco', *MEFR* 36 (1916–17), pp. 52–72.
6. H. Marucchi, *Elements d'archéologie chrétienne* (Paris and Rome, 1903), II, p. 87.
7. Such as those from the earliest part of the Domitilla catacomb, known as the Vestibule of the Flavii: see Marucchi, op. cit., II, pp, 111–14.
8. H. Leclercq, 'Boldetti', 974. Also Marucchi, p, 114: 'pieux vandale'.
9. Erich Becker, 'Ein Katakomben-besuch in Jahre 1767', *RQ* (1911), pp 105–11; 'saeculum obscurum'.
10. F. Cabrol, 'Aquilée' in *DACL* I. 2, 2654–2694, using Bertoli's illustrations of his discoveries. See also Carola Jäggi, 'Aspekte der städtbäulichen Entwicklung Aquileias', *JbAC* 33 (1990), pp. 158–96, esp. pp. 173ff.
11. D. Bertoli, *Le antichità d'Aquileja profane e sacre per la maggior parte finora inedite* (Venice, 1739), p. 410 for the church of St Hilarius; and Jäggi, op. cit., p. 189 (built on top of the disused Cardo Maximus, south of the ruined civil basilica).
12. Illustrated in *DACL* I.2, 2672 after Bertoli.
13. Cited from *Naissance des arts chrétiens* (Paris, 1991), p. 357.
14. Ibid., p. 357.

15. Found in March 1702 during 'excavations' to discover the remains of St Vitalianus. See E. Leblant, *Les Inscriptions chrétiennes de la Gaule antérieures au VIIIe siècle*, II (Paris, 1865), pp. 312–22. Leblant also records the discovery of an important fourth-century Christian inscription commemorating the high official Flavius Memorius (d. 374) from Arles, preserved in the *Correspondance de Montfaucon* in 1722: ibid., pp. 243–5.
16. Ruinart (d. 1709) was interested mainly in the Acts of the Martyrs, compiling his *Acta sincera* partly to controvert W. Dodwell's assertion that before the Great Persecution martyrs had been few. An underlying anti-Anglican tendency among French ecclesiastical historians would continue throughout the first part of the eighteenth century, even the Orientalist Le Quien having a tilt against Anglican Orders.
17. Gregory of Tours, *Historia Francorum* ii.14 and 17; ed. *MGH, Scriptores historiarum merovingicarum* I.1 (Berlin, 1884), pp. 81–216.
18. See O. G. S. Crawford, 'Lyonesse', *Antiquity* (1927), pp. 5ff. Borlase's ideas were an initial inspiration.
19. Basil Williams, *The Whig Supremacy* (Oxford, 1939), p. 141 and in general, ch. 15, 'The arts'. See also Geoffrey Waywell's essay on the collection and display of Classical sculpture in the great houses of the day in R. Jenkyns (ed.), *The Legacy of Rome: A New Appraisal* (OUP, 1992).
20. Barry Cunliffe, *Roman Bath* (Research Reports of Society of Antiquaries of London 24; Oxford, 1969): the bronze statue of Minerva was found while digging for a sewer along the centre of Stall Street on 12 July 1727. Evidence for the temple of Minerva, spring and surrounding colonnades came to light during building work on the Pump Room in 1790.
21. John Horsley, *Britannia Romana* (1732), Book II, pp. 332–4 (2nd edn ed. Eric Birley, Newcastle upon Tyne, 1974); also W. Stukeley, *Itinerarium curiosum* (1724), p. 188.
22. Stephen Upex, 'The Roman villa at Cotterstock', *Durobrivae* 5 (1977), p. 24. Excavations were undertaken on the site in 1736 and 1798.
23. Charles Thomas, *Christianity in Roman Britain to AD 500* (London: Batsford, 1981), p. 181.
24. Frances Mawer, 'The lead tank from Icklingham, Suffolk', *Britannia* 25 (1994), pp. 232–6.
25. C. Johns, 'The Risley Park silver lanx: a lost antiquity from Roman Britain', *AJ* 61.1 (1981), pp. 53–72.
26. Ibid., pp. 57–60. Stukeley was very proud of his theory!
27. See K. S. Painter, *AJ* (forthcoming) on a possible Romano-British origin.
28. See F. Haverfield, 'Roman silver in Northumberland', *JRS* 4 (1914), pp. 1–12; O. Brendel, 'The Corbridge *lanx*', *JRS* 31 (1941), pp. 100–27. The *lanx* survived, and was in the possession of the Dukes of Northumberland at Alnwick Castle until it was acquired by the British Museum in 1993. The original finder was a nine-year-old daughter of a Corbridge blacksmith, Isobel Cutler.
29. Thus Brendel, op. cit., p. 100.
30. Ibid., p. 127.
31. K. S. Painter, *The Mildenhall Treasure* (British Museum Publications, 1977). See also below, pp. 349–50.
32. Details from *DNB*, and Stuart Piggott, 'Stukeley, Avebury and the Druids', *Antiquity* 9 (1935), pp. 22–32.
33. Stukeley, *Palaeographica Sacra* (London, 1763), Preface.
34. Ibid., For his absorption with the Druids, see T. D. Kendrick, *The Druids* (London: Methuen, 1927), pp. 9–12.
35. Eusebius, *HE* i.4.
36. Hearne's comment is cited from Stuart Piggott, op. cit., p. 23.
37. T. Shaw, *Travels or Observations relating to Several Parts of Barbary and the Levant* (Oxford, 1738), p. 85 (relating to the site of 'Herba').
38. James Bruce, *Travels to discover the Source of the Nile* (Edinburgh 1790): Dougga 'a large scene of ruins, the temple being Antonine'; 'Tipasa was easily the most extensive scene of ruins': p. xxvi.
39. See N. Duval, 'La solution d'une énigme: les voyageurs Peyssonnel et Gimenez à Sbeitla en 1724', *Bulletin de la Société Nationale des Antiquaires de France* (1965), pp. 94–135. at p. 101.
40. Ibid., p. 132.
41. I have summarized the evidence in 'Nomads and Christianity in the Middle Ages', *JEH* 26 (1975), pp. 209–21 and as ch. 23 in *Religion Popular and Unpopular* (London: Variorum Reprints, 1976). For more on Asia Minor, see below, p. 93.
42. In 1938 I observed two occupation levels in section in a part of the forum above the Byzantine level.
43. Glass Abbasid coins found on the surface of the site and on display in the museum at Macri.

44. A. Berthier, *L'Algérie et son passé* (Paris, 1951), p. 149. Berthier found Arab coins, pottery and jewellery during his excavations of Tiddis. (See below, p. 334.)
45. The Revd Wm. Halifax, 'A relation of a voyage from Aleppo to Palmyra in Syria', *Philosophical Transactions* 19 (1695), p. 109. He visited Resapha on a second journey. Resapha was also visited by Sellers in 1696, when he saw an inscription mentioning 'Bishop Sergius'.
46. Lucian, *On the Death of Peregrinus* 12–15.
47. Tournefort, *Relation d'une voyage du Levant;* cited in *BCH* 24 (1900), p. 364.
48. Sir G. Wheler, *Account of the churches described by Eusebius* (London, 1689).
49. Ibid., p. 35.
50. See C. J. Cuming, 'Eastern liturgies and Anglican Divines', *SCH* 13 (1976), pp. 231–8.
51. A. Reland, *Palestine Illustrated by Ancient Monuments* (London, 1714).
52. See E. A. Hutton, 'The travels of "Palmyra" Wood 1750–1751', *JHS* 46 (1927), pp. 102–28.
53. See N. Duval, 'La solution d'une énigme', op. cit. It is uncertain whether Peyssonnel actually reached Sbeitla or confused this site with another, such as Djilma (Cillium) or Vegesela, which are hill-sites, whereas Sbeitla was built on a plain.
54. Duval, op. cit., p. 130.
55. Recorded and published by O. Fiebiger, *JÖAI* (1902), when Hebenstreit's and Ludwig's report at last came to light.
56. Details of his career in 'Thomas Shaw' in *DNB; Travels and Observations*, pp. 38–41. See also ibid., p. 45.
57. P. A. Février, *Approches du Maghreb romain* (Edisud, 1989), p. 29.
58. On the monument, see Margaret and Robert Alexander, 'Kober Roumia', *Archaeology* 2.2 (Summer 1949), pp. 88–90; M. Christofle, *Le Tombeau de la chrétienne* (Paris, 1951).
59. Shaw, *Travels and Observations*, p. 118
60. Ibid., pp. 109–10.
61. Ibid., p. 83.
62. Ibid., p. 123.
63. Ibid., p. 125.
64. Ibid., p. 173, from Thignica (Ain Tounga).
65. Career 'James Bruce', in *DNB* VII, pp. 98–102; also Février, op. cit., p. 30.
66. James Bruce, *Travels to discover the Source of the Nile* (Edinburgh, 1790), I, pp. viii–xi; *DNB* VII, p. 99. His drawings were exhibited in 1937 at the Institute of British Architects, but Colonel Playfair included them in his own study in 1876. For an account of Bruce's journey in Libya, see D. Cumming, 'James Bruce in Libya, 1766', *Society for Libyan Studies. First Annual Report (1969–70)* (London, 1970), pp. 12–18.
67. See below, pp. 145–6; C. Schmidt and W. Till, 'Die beiden Bücher des Jeû', *GCS* (2nd edn 1959); also edited with Eng. trans. by Charlotte A. Baynes, *A Coptic Gnostic Treatise Contained in the Codex Brucianus* (CUP, 1933).
68. *DNB* VII, p. 99. See below, p. 48.
69. Thus R. H. Charles, *The Book of Enoch* (Oxford, 1912), Intro., pp. ix–x.
70. Edward Gibbon, *The Decline and Fall of the Roman Empire* (London, 1776–87), IV, ch. 24 (p. 164 n. 49 of 1802 edn which I have used). Gibbon began his work in 1771, publishing vol. I in 1776, but his initial inspiration came from his visit to Rome and its ruins in October 1764, as he says himself at the conclusion of *Decline and Fall*. Gibbon was in fact quite generous to travellers to whom he owed information. Bernier, for instance, he says, described 'with great accuracy' the 'immense moving city of Ctesiphon' (I, p. 333 n. 41). He is more severe on armchair 'explorers' like Voltaire who 'unsupported by either fact or probability has generous bestowed the Canary Islands on the Roman empire' (I, p. 42 n. 87).
71. See 'Tillemont', *ODCC*, p. 1358.
72. J. L. von Mosheim, *Ecclesiastical History*, Eng. trans. A. Maclaine (Dublin, 1767), Introduction, p. xxiii.
73. Ibid., I, p. 140.
74. Ibid., p. 142.
75. Ibid., p. 48.
76. Gibbon, op. cit., II, p. 265. For appreciations of Gibbon's career, character and work, see the essayists in 'Gibbon and the Decline and Fall of the Roman Empire', *Daedalus* (Summer 1976).
77. Gibbon, op. cit., p. 266.
78. Ibid., p. 381.

79. Ibid., p. 480; J. Gruter and T. Reinesius, *Syntagma, inscriptionum antiquarum cumprimis Romae veteris* (Leipzig and Frankfurt, 1682). Cf. Eusebius, *HE* viii.11; A. Ferrua, *Epigrammata*, 7.
80. Gibbon, op. cit., pp. 481–2.
81. Thus in 1764 Gibbon copied the Veleia tablet (*ILS* 6675) illustrating *inter alia* the accumulation of wealth and honours among a few in the reign of Trajan, but declined to use this 'dry and ungrateful work': cited from P. Brown, 'In Gibbon's shade', *New York Review of Books* 23 (1976), pp. 14–18.
82. By Cardinal Stefano Borgia and published in 1788 by N. Schow. It was the only survivor of a group of manuscripts found by peasants in the Fayum and brought to Cairo. Antique dealers kept one as a curiosity, destroying the remainder as worthless. The papyrus lists workmen employed in AD 191 as forced labour on the dykes controlling Nile flooding. See Sir Frederick Kenyon, *The Bible and Archaeology* (London, 1940), p, 205.
83. See C. Schmidt and W. Till, 'Die Pistis Sophia', *GCS* (2nd edn 1959) and bibliography to 1964 in Altaner–Stuiber, *Patrologie* (Freiburg, 1966) p. 132. The *Pistis Sophia* was a third-century work, later than the *Books of Jeu* which the Codex quotes. It also contained another separate Gnostic work, 'On Repentance'.
84. Cited from J. P. S. Moorey, *A Century of Biblical Archaeology* (Cambridge, 1991), p. 1.

FURTHER READING

Charlotte A. Baynes, *A Coptic-Gnostic Treatise Contained in the Codex Brucianus* (CUP, 1933).

O. Brendel, 'The Corbridge *lanx*', *JRS* 31 (1941), pp. 100–27.

P. Brown, *Society and the Holy in Late Antiquity* (Faber and Faber, 1982) (two essays on Gibbon).

M. Christofle, 'Le Tombeau de la Chrétienne' in *Fouilles et Consolidations.... de l'Algérie, 1933–1936* (Algiers, 1937), pp. 86–97.

O. G. S. Crawford, 'Lyonesse', *Antiquity* (1927), pp. 5ff.

C. J. Cuming, 'Eastern liturgies and Anglican Divines', *JHS* 46 (1927), pp. 102–28.

D. Cumming, 'James Bruce in Libya' embodied in *First Annual Report of the Society for Libyan Studies 1969–1970* (London, 1970).

N. Duval, 'La solution d'une énigme: les voyageurs Peyssonnel et Gimenez à Sbeitla en 1724', *Bulletin de la Société Nationale des Antiquaires de France* (1965), pp. 94–135.

W. H. C. Frend, 'Nomads and Christianity in the Middle Ages', *JEH* 26 (1975), pp. 209–21.

W. H. C. Frend, 'Edward Gibbon and early Christianity', *JEH* 45 (1994), pp. 661–72.

E. A. Hutton, 'The travels of "Palmyra" Wood 1750–1751', *JHS* 46 (1927), pp. 102–28.

C. Johns, 'The Risley Park silver lanx, a lost antiquity from Roman Britain', *AJ* 61 (1981), pp. 53–72.

Sir Frederick Kenyon, *The Bible and Archaeology* (London, 1940).

Basil Williams, *The Whig Supremacy* (OUP, 1939), especially ch. 15, 'The arts'.

Articles in *DACL*: F. Cabrol, 'Aquileia': I.2; H. Leclercq, 'Boldetti' and 'Bottari': ibid., II.

4

Napoleon

Gibbon had ended his great work two years before the French Revolution broke out in 1789. His superb understanding of the relations between the church and the Roman empire had been founded on an unrivalled knowledge of the literary evidence, though where possible he had used such inscriptions as had been found. However, without more material evidence study of early Christianity could not progress, not least because literary evidence favoured the orthodox viewpoint overwhelmingly. The rise of Christianity as a movement in history could never be told fully.

As its outset, however the French Revolution boded ill for early Christian archaeology. The Assembly decreed in October 1790 that Church treasures should become national property. Many of the finds made in the previous century were associated with monasteries and were scattered or destroyed as too tarred with the brush of 'clericalism'.[1] Such was the fate of the treasure of the Abbey at St Denis, and also Cluny, first vandalized in 1790 and then destroyed in 1793. The same treatment was meted out to some forty churches in Cologne and its neighbourhood during the French occupation.[2] At the same time, however, the energies of the middle classes, so long victims of an outdated caste system, were given a proper place in society through leadership of the professions. There was a new-found urge towards researches of every sort, from which science and the humanities benefited.

In England public opinion moved from the enthusiasm felt by Burke and Wordsworth towards the first events of the Revolution, through apprehension at its growing intolerance, to outright hostility as the revolutionary armies swept into the Austrian Netherlands (Belgium) to threaten Britain's maritime interests and the prosperity of the port of London.[3] The emotional tinder that turned these fears into war was provided by the execution of Louis XVI in January 1793. By the end of the month conflict had again broken out between England and France. This time all Europe became engulfed in a struggle that lasted 22 years, broken only by the brief Peace of Amiens in 1802. At the end, the world had changed almost beyond recognition in nearly every particular, from the conduct of war and international relations to industry, ideas of revenue-raising, everyday dress and, finally, the tools available to the scholar of biblical and early-Christian history.

England managed to survive the early onrush of the French armies, though its allies did not. Though the years 1795 to 1797 one after another of France's enemies had fallen. The revolution had found a general of genius in the youthful Napoleon Bonaparte. In April 1796 he conquered most of Piedmont, and in four days after his victory at Lodi on 7 May, almost the whole of Lombardy. Milan fell to him on 15 May. Further victories followed, until on 17 October 1797 at Campo Formio, not far from Udine in north-east Italy, he dictated peace with Austria. He returned to France to an ecstatic welcome. He remembered, however, that he had trained as a mathematician as well as artilleryman. He found men who shared his interests in the Institute of France (more properly Le Conservatoire des Arts et Métiers) organized by the National Convention amidst the horrors of the Terror in 1793. Now, four years later, it was beginning to find its feet as an academic institution. When he arrived in Paris, Napoleon had let it be known that he wished to become a member. He read some short papers before the Section of Mechanics in the Science Department (Classe des Sciences) and, more important, was greeted with enthusiasm by the new 'intellectuals' that controlled its workings.[4] He did not forget.

In 1798 largely on his own initiative, and to the relief of members of the Directory who wanted him as far away as possible, he was charged with an expedition to Egypt. It was aimed ultimately against England but the first phase was to control the Mediterranean through the occupation of Malta and conquest of Egypt. Thence France could threaten India. Napoleon himself believed that his country's destiny lay in this direction. He was a Corsican and a Latin; the *mare nostrum* of the Roman past struck a chord in his consciousness. It was, however, to be no ordinary military expedition however grandiose. This time civilization was to be combined with conquest. The expedition that set out on 19 May 1798 included not only Napoleon's best commanders, but a contingent of the same intellectuals whom he had charmed the year before. There were men of letters, scientists and artists to give the military campaign a secondary objective of mounting a scientific expedition. It was to be a campaign of conquest and exploration.

Napoleon landed at Alexandria on 30 June and amid the astounding successes of the following months against the Mameluke rulers of Egypt, the Institut d'Egypte carried out its work of survey, coping hieroglyph inscriptions and even making some summary excavations. The result of three years' work (1798–1801) was the monumental eighteen-volume *Description de l'Egypte* (1809–23), a magnificent work, its origins befitting the heyday of Napoleon's rule.

This work had, of course, no direct bearing on promoting interest in early-Christian remains, but it made the new generations of scholars in Europe aware of the possibilities of discovery of the past in Egypt, and further south in the once-Christian kingdoms of Nubia. It demonstrated also that henceforth scientific and cultural advance would form an essential part of French military expeditions, particularly in the Mediterranean basin. Officers in a French army might be expected to be alert to the antiquities in the area in which they were operating, especially if these related in some way to Rome's imperial past. (See below, p. 56.) From now on the spread of French culture became an objective of every incumbent of the Quai d'Orsay.

One find made by an officer in the artillery was to lay the foundation for the scientific study of Christian antiquities outside the bounds of Rome and the catacombs, namely the Rosetta stone. Like many sensational discoveries this was an accident.[5] In August 1798 an artillery officer was directing work for a fort near Rosetta in the Nile Delta and suddenly noticed an irregular slab of black granite covered with writing. Work stopped while the stone was extracted. Part of the writng he recognized as Greek, but there were two other scripts. One could be seen on Egyptian monuments, but the other was unknown. The three registers into which the writing was divided proved to be hieroglyphs, Demotic script, and Greek. It was a trilingual inscription dated 196–197 BC set up by priests, recording a decree of Ptolemy V conferring honours upon them and exempting them from paying taxes. The recipients had thought these considerable favours warranted formal record in the traditional cult-language of Egypt as well as in the ordinary script of the time and in the language of the government. The defeat of the French by the British, first in the battle of the Nile and subsequently near Alexandria in 1801, meant that the stone ended up in the British Museum, where it remains. Its discovery, however, opened the way to decipherment of Demotic and hieroglyphics, unlocked a vast range of information about the history of Egypt that forms the background to the story of the people of Israel, and threw additional light on the Greco-Roman period. The age of biblical scholarship seen in terms of material remains had begun.

Despite being marooned in Egypt after the battle of the Nile and their repulse at Acre, the French maintained themselves for over two years. Nominally Napoleon had claimed to have been acting on behalf of the Sultan at Constantinople, with whom the revolutionary government wished to cultivate good commercial relations. Hence, after his capture of Alexandria on 5 July 1798, he issued a proclamation 'to the people of Egypt' as he had two years before to 'the people of Italy'. 'We have come to restore your rights, punish usurpers (i.e. the Mamelukes) and uphold the Moslem religion.' 'Have we not destroyed the Pope who preached against the Moslem religion?'[6] The French came as the friend and ally of the Sultan (Selim III), and should be received as such. Strong words from a true son of the Revolution, but it did not last. Selim turned against the French and after varying fortunes the Armée de l'Orient capitulated to the forces of Lord Abercromby in the autumn of 1801, thus removing the final obstacle to the conclusion of the Peace of Amiens.

The French occupation, extending for a time as far as Aswan (captured 16 May 1799), had, however, given the Egyptians a glimpse of what orderly government could achieve. A hospital service had been established. The administration under Napoleon's lieutenant and successor in Egypt, General Kléber, was efficient and not corrupt. Law and order reigned as never before. The work of the *savants* copying and drawing the ancient monuments was pushed forward in the name of the Institut d'Egypte, and they included individuals such as Baron Vivant Denon who had a real interest in the people of Egypt. The lessons of benevolent despotism were not lost on a merchant from Kavalla (now in Greece) who had accompanied the British army on its expedition to Egypt in 1801. His name was Mehmet Ali (1769–1848).

The British eventually left Egypt in the autumn of 1803. There was a brief return of Ottoman rule with the Mamelukes retaining control of Upper Egypt. In 1805 Mehmet's army was strong enough to oust the Ottoman Pasha, three years later to beat off a further British attempted invasion in the name of the Sultan, and finally, in 1812–13, to destroy the Mameluke power in Upper Egypt. In 1812 Mehmet's son Ibrahim Ali stormed the fortress of Qasr Ibrim in Egyptian Nubia whither the remains of the Mameluke army and their dependants had fled. With that event the modern history of Nubia begins, and the progressive unfolding of the Christian civilization that had once dominated the territory

Apart from providing Mehmet Ali with an administative model for governing Egypt, Napoleon's legacy was to be fulfilled in two other directions. First came the enormous impetus to Pharaonic studies through the decipherment of the Rosetta stone by Dr Young of the British Museum and the genius

Giovanni Battista de Rossi
(1822–94)

Sir William M.
Ramsay
(1851–1939).
Portrait
by Sir George Reid

W. M. Calder FBA
(1881–1960)

Franz Joseph Dölger
(1879–1940)

Jean-François Champollion (1790–1832). Champollion had already in 1807 suggested that Coptic was in essentials the language of ancient Egypt and his patient work with Young gradually deciphered both the Demotic and hiero-glyphic sections of the Rosetta stone. His theory was vindicated. Successful research, however, led to the removal of Pharaonic monuments from Egypt to grace the British Museum and the Louvre and add distinction to London and Paris. Belzoni's removal with British consular support of the huge statue of the young Memnon from Thebes for shipment to England in 1812 was only the first of these combinations of exploration, scientific study and also pillage which the work of Napoleon's *savants* inspired.

The second result was less equivocally beneficial. It brought about the beginning of the exploration by Europeans of Nubia, the area of the cataracts, extending up the Nile from Aswan to Dongola. The Swiss explorer Jacob Burkhardt, the Frenchmen François Gau and Count Vidua, and, a generation later, Richard Lepsius are all heirs to the *savants* who accompanied Napoleon's army. Together, they ended the Dark Age of Nubia that had opened with the establishment of the Ottoman garrison (including Bosnians and Magyars) by Sultan Suleiman at Aswan, Ibrim *c.* 1560 and Sai in 1584 to guard the south-ern frontier of the Ottoman empire against the Funj state.[8]

Jacob (John Lewis) Burckhardt was a member of a Swiss family from Basel. His prospects of succeeding to a part of the family wealth were blasted by events of Napoleon's campaign against the Austrians, when he was accused, falsely, of betraying a French bridgehead at Huningen to the latter. He devel-oped a strong aversion to the French Republic and after much hesitation took service with the British. He became an Arabic specialist, and came into con-tact with members of the Africa Association associated with the Royal Society and aiming at the exploration of the interior of Africa. After travels in Syria he arrived in Cario in 1812, hoping to lead an expedition south-westwards through the Fezzan and towards the Niger. Finding this impossible for the current year he decided to take advantage of the defeat of the Mamelukes to travel south, up the Nile, 'making perhaps some lateral excursions into the Nubian desert'.[9] In the event he was to spend two-and-a-half years (1813–15) including two expeditions into Nubia as far as the Third Cataract, often trav-elling disguised as a poor Muslim trader.

Burckhardt's letters to the Africa Association and his diary give the first account of the Nubians, their way of life and economy, their customs and dis-tant reminiscences of a Christian past.[10] Two tribes even claimed Christian origins (Ouled el Nasara). The groups of houses round palm-trees and the large villages he encountered could not have differed much from the Nubian

Christian settlements of five centuries before. On 3 March 1813 he reached Ibrim, 'built on an insulated rocky hill just above the river', and saw for himself the destruction and resulting famine which the war against the Mamelukes had wrought. While the few remaining inhabitants described themselves as 'Turks, and not Noubas', Burckhardt also saw the 'remains of two public buildings, probably Greek churches, built in the same style as the ancient wall' (surrounding the fortress), and mentions 'the small grey granite column' in the church which had survived intact.[11] Further south, on one of the islands of the Batn el Hajar (between the Second and Third Cataract) he was not a little surprised to find himself in a 'Greek chapel'. 'Figures of saints were painted in gaudy colours up on the walls' and the names of many visitors and pilgrims inscribed.[12] Another church near the cataract of Wadi Halfa (Second Cataract) he found had been turned into a mosque.[13]

Burckhardt's interests were primarily those of a traveller, recording the language and customs, the diseases even, of the people, and the fauna and flora of the areas through which he passed. His account of early-Christian remains, however, is a primary source as well as his comments on their high state of preservation. His record of traditions how Islam and the Arabs had overthrown the Nubian kingdoms and transformed their people into Arab tribes is a priceless document of the times. It laid the foundations for future research into the story of the rise and fall of Christianity in Nubia.

Soon, others were taking advantage of the relative security imposed by Mehmet Ali to follow in Burckhardt's footsteps. Legh and Belzoni were at Ibrim in 1817. In 1818 the French architect François Gau took the same route as Burckhardt in search of Egyptian temples. On one, built by Rameses II on the banks of the Wadi Seboua, between Aswan and Ibrim, he saw and copied graffiti in a strange script. Beyond Ibrim he came on the fortified settlement of Djebel Adda, and found there an inscription written with the same type of letters. The writing was Old Nubian, used in the Christian Nubian kingdom.[14] He also was the first to discover the famous inscription in Greek, dated to *c.* 535, in honour of the Christian Nubian king Silko, on the walls of a temple at Talmis (Kalabsha). Silko claimed to be king of both the Nobades (northern Kingdom of Nubia) and the Ethiopians, and to have conquered a catalogue of heathen enemies, including the Blemmyes, with the aid of 'God' (*Theos*).[15]

The early 1820s witnessed a veritable procession of travellers, each adding a little to a store of knowledge of Nubian Christianity. In 1820 Count Vidua reached as far south as Colasua, south of Faras, where he beheld the abandoned remains of a Christian town and monastery. He returned with the record of two important inscriptions, one the epitaph of a bishop of Pachoras (Faras) and his daughter, dated AD 692, and the other of that of Bishop Tamer, dated 1193, a revelation at the time of the long survival of Christianity in Nubia.[16] Next year de Bellefonds explored as far as Meroë, sighting on the way Christian remains on the island of Meinarti, Kiniarti and Delmarti, surviving frescos at Gemai and the existence of an ancient Nubian castle at El Kab (see below, p. 299).[17] In 1824 Caillaud described a small Nubian church at Abusir near the Second Cataract on his way towards the beckoning south.[18] Despite all these discoveries it was over-ambitious and premature to publish in 1832, as did Jean Letronne, a survey of existing discoveries on which he believed the history of Christianity in Egypt, Nubia and Abyssinia (Ethiopia) between the fifth and eighth centuries could be based. It was not until the 1840s that some idea of the extent of surviving Christian remains in Nubia could so much as be guessed.

Richard Lepsius provided the first detailed descriptions and drawings of Nubian sites that have been the centre of more recent exploration. Lepsius was interested overwhelmingly in Pharaonic remains, and the Nubian section of his journey records in detail hieroglyphic inscriptions he copied at Kalabsha, Amada, Derr, Aniba and other temple sites. At Ibrim, however, he drew an accurate plan of the cathedral showing that the remains of the twelve columns that flanked the central nave could still be seen, as well as a decorated capital similar (if not the same) to one found by the Egypt Exploration Society expedition in 1964. His survey defined five major periods of occupation, namely, under the XIX Dynasty, Taharqa, Roman under Petronius, Nubian Christian and finally Arab. His short survey proved immensely valuable to the EES expedition.[19]

Lepsius travelled through Nubia during the years 1842–44 recording antiquities as he went south to a point beyond Khartoum. From the ruins of the mediaeval city he found there, probably Soba, the capital of the southern Nubian kingdom of Alwah, he brought back two fragments of a Christian marble tombstone datable to AD 897.[20] But the main value of his work lay in his superb descriptions and the accurate sketches he made at his discoveries and reproduced in his immense twelve-volume record of Egyptian and Nubian antiquities (1849–56). He visited Ibrim twice, emphasizing its strategic importance on a projecting cliff high above the Nile (see colour plate), leaving the impression in his line drawings of the cathedral, though turned into a mosque, as surviving as a majestic stone building whose arcades could pass for Gothic.[21]

In his journal Burckhardt had remarked on the prospect of early exploration of Abyssinia and the importance of Massawa and Suakim for trade.[22] While Napoleon regarded Egypt as a key objective in any conquest of the Middle East and India, the British were seeing their commercial objectives from the standpoint of their predominance in India. Possibilities of forging connections

with the Arabs who dominated the Horn of Africa and the Abyssinians inland
had been increased by the reannexation of Cape Colony in 1806. The Dutch
and Huguenot settlers had protested and grumbled but there had been no
uprising. A valuable staging-post on the road to India had been secured,
which also enabled contacts to be made with the various Arab rulers on the
east African littoral.

In July 1814, Henry Salt FRS (later British consul-general in Cairo) presented to the Prince Regent an ample account of his lengthy voyage
undertaken five years earlier via Madeira, where the British had a garrison
(1807–14), and the Cape to Massawa, and thence inland into the territories of
the emperor of Abyssinia.[23] He had carried a letter of greetings from George
III to the emperor. The expressed aim of the journey was to further British
commerce, 'enlarge the bounds of knowledge and ameliorate the general condition of mankind'. Salt was following in the footsteps of James Bruce and
Lord Valentia and was determined to see the strange obelisks both had
described at Axum.[24] Salt was a careful observer. His journal criticizes Bruce
frequently for his lax work and inaccurate detail, and on his arriving at Axum
recorded a detailed description and drawing of the most prominent visible
monument. 'This highly-wrought and very magnificent work of art', he
wrote, 'formed a single block of granite and measured a full 60ft high.'[25] It
produced a 'forcible impression' on his mind. The obelisk, which he copied,
carefully recorded the victory of King Aezanias, ruler over the Axumites, the
Homerites (in south-west Arabia) of Raeidan, and of the Aethiopians and
Sabaeans, over the rebellious Beja tribes, and catalogued the booty taken from
them. In this inscription King Aezanias (or Ezana) calls himself 'king of kings,
son of God the invincible Ares'. There is no sign of monotheism or
Christianity, to which other obelisks at Axum indicate that Ezana later progressed.[26] The influence of Frumentius, the Christian captive from Syria who
had become his chief adviser,[27] was not in evidence as yet. The language of the
inscription was Greek and the influence of the now-Christian Greco-Roman
world would soon be making itself felt. The inscription dated probably from
c. 345–350, a dozen years or so before the emperor Constantius would be writing to 'the Princes of Axum' exhorting them to reject Frumentius and accept
a non-Nicene form of Christianity.[28]

Salt showed the wealth of antiquities of the Christian period awaiting further discovery at Axum. It was less than twenty years since Napoleon had set
down a European army accompanied by French scholars on the shores of
Egypt. In these years new opportunities for archaeological discovery of
Christian sites in the Nile valley and beyond had been opened up. Something

was at last becoming known of the three Christian kingdoms of Nobatia, Makurrah and Alwah that had existed there for 1,000 years (500–1500) despite Islamic pressure. Archaeological scholarship was beginning to come into its own, even if on the Continent, thanks largely to Napoleon, it would be as the handmaid of foreign policy. Though Napoleon had failed to achieve his grand ambitions of ruling the continent of Europe and refounding New France from New Orleans, his legacy for scholarship was destined to be lasting. The *savants* who accompanied his army to Egypt would be succeeded by a generation of officers like Ravoisié and Delamare who shared that tradition[29] when in 1830 France decided to embark on the permanent occupation of Algeria. From the standpoint of archaeology, the Egyptian expedition had not been a failure. More than a century later, it provided an example which a French commander in the First World War was glad to quote,[30] and French *savants* in Algeria glad to remember.[31]

NOTES

1. Examples quoted by F. Barathes and C. Metzger, 'L'orfèvrerie christianisée' in *Naissance des Arts chrétiens* (Paris, 1992), p. 314. Some of the the the treasure belonging to St Denis turned up in the British Museum: see Seymour de Ricci, 'Un calice du trésor de Saint-Denis', *CRAI* (1923), pp. 335–9.
2. Information from K. Hellenkampfer, Hon. Fellow of the Society of Antiquaries, April 1993.
3. The transition can be followed in Wordsworth's memories of the period included in *The Prelude* (published 1805). In 1789 he was writing 'Bliss was it in that dawn to be alive. But to be young was very heaven' (*Prelude* xi). In 1790, still optimistic, ''Twas a time when Europe rejoiced, France standing on the top of golden hours. And human nature seeming born again' (*Prelude* vi). But in September 1792, 'Head after head and never heads enough. For those who bade them fall' (*Prelude* x).
4. For Napoleon's interest in science, see Louis Madelin, *The French Revolution*, Eng. trans. (London, 1930), p. 567. France's interest in Egypt and its antiquities may be traced back *inter alia* to the Jesuit Fr Claude Sicard's rediscovery of Thebes in 1719.
5. The discovery of the Rosetta stone is described in Sir Frederick Kenyon, *The Bible and Archaeology* (London, 1940), pp. 59–62 (photo, plate v); see also Carol Andrews, *The Rosetta Stone* (London, 1994).
6. Cited from Alan Palmer, *The Decline and Fall of the Ottoman Empire* (London, 1992), p. 58.
7. A second was the journal of William J. Bankes, who visited Abu Simbel and recorded two obelisks covered in bilingual Greek and hieroglyphic inscriptions at Philae in 1815. Eventually one of the obelisks was transported by Belzoni to England in 1820 and ended up on the lawn of Bankes's mansion at Kingston Lacey, Dorset: *The National Trust Magazine* 71 (1994), pp. 36–7.
8. For the presence of an Ottoman garrison at Qasr Ibrim from the sixteenth century, see J. L. Burckhardt, *Travels in Nubia* (London; John Murray, 1822), pp. 31 and 124 (republished by Darf Ltd., 1988). Research by V. L. Ménage indicates that Ibrim did not become a frontier fort until *c.* 1560: 'The Ottomans and Nubia in the 16th century', *Annales Islamologiques* 24 (1988), fn. 34.
9. See the Memoir giving Burckhardt's life and travels, forming the Introduction to Burckhardt's record. For Burckhardt's original intention to journey to the Fezzan, ibid., p. li.
10. W. Y. Adams, *Nubia, Corridor to Africa* (London: Allen Lane, 1977), pp, 563–8 and 584–90, quotes salient passages from Burckhardt.
11. Burckhardt, op. cit., pp 30–2. Burckhardt refers to the security he found existing at Ibrim and the honesty of the 'Turks' there.
12. Ibid., p. 72.
13. Ibid., p. 80.

14. Recorded by Seymour de Ricci, *CRAI* (1909), pp 144–65.
15. The date may be before the arrival of Theodora's mission at the Nobatian court in 543.
16. Presented to the Turin Museum. Cited from *JEA* 11 (1925), p. 262. For a full list of early travellers to Nubia, their aims and works, see W. Y. Adams, *Nubia*, pp. 594–5.
17. See *The Journal of Linant de Bellefonds*, ed. M. Shinnie (Sudan Antiquities Service Occasional Papers 4; Khartoum, 1958) pp. 3–4.
18. *Voyage à Méroë et au Fleuve Blanc* (Paris, 1826), Texte iii, 260.
19. See J. M. Plumley, *JEA* 50 (1964), pp. 1–3 and below, p. 307.
20. C. R. Lepsius, *Denkmäler aus Aegypten und Aethiopien* (Berlin, 1849–56), V, pp. 130–2 (Ibrim) and VI, 12a and b; re-edited by Naville (Leipzig, 1913).
21. Ibid., VI, 12a and b.
22. Burckhardt, op. cit., pp. 322 and 389ff. The East India Company had an agent at Mokha in south-west Arabia.
23. Henry Salt, *A voyage to Abyssinia and travels into the interior of that country* (Cass Library of African Studies: Travels and Narratives no. 16; London, 1967), Preface. For his career, see *DNB* L, pp. 212–13.
24. Bruce had arrived in Axum in January 1769. See his *Travels to discover the source of the Nile* (London, 1790), III, pp. 129–33.
25. Salt, op. cit., p. 405.
26. Ibid., pp. 411–12. See below, p. 155.
27. For the facts see Rufinus, *HE* x.9; Socrates, *HE* i.9; Sozomen, *HE* ii.24.
28. Athanasius, *Apologia ad Constantium* 31; Eng. trans. in *Creeds, Councils and Controversies*, ed. J. Stevenson and W. H. C. Frend (SPCK, 1989), p. 37.
29. Another example was Major (Aide-major) Lamare Picquot, a detachment commander in the French forces occupying Corfu in 1808–14. He initiated excavations to keep the garrison busy and was among the founders of the Académie Ionienne. See C. A. Rhomaios, 'Les premiers fouilles à Corfou', *BCH* 49 (1925), pp. 190–218, at pp. 203–11.
30. How real and lasting this tradition was is demonstrated by the action of General Sarrail, commanding the Allied forces in Salonica in 1916. On 21 February 1916 he ordered all units to preserve 'objets d'art et d'archéologie' and assemble these 'fidèle à la tradition française d'Egypte et Morée'. On 20 May he established an Antiquities Service, one of whose achievements was a topographical survey of ancient sites in the area occupied by the Allies. See L. Rey, 'Observations sur les premiers habitants de la Macédonie', *BCH* 41–43 (1917–20; published 1921), and especially the prefatory letter by Rey to the Ministre de Guerre.
31. Thus M. Georges Marçais, President of the Société historique Algérienne, in his address at the centenary celebrations of the society in 1956: 'La tradition créée par Bonaparte en Egypte revivait dans cette armée de l'Afrique': *RAfr* 100 (1956), p. 9.

FURTHER READING

A. Browne, *Bonaparte in Egypt and Egypt to-day* (London, 1907).

J. Bruce, *Travels to discover the sources of the Nile* (1768–73). ed. and abridged by C. F. Beckingham (Edinburgh, 1964).

J. L. Burckhardt, *Travels in Nubia* (London, 1822) (reprinted by Darf Publishers Ltd, 1988).

F. Caillaud, *Voyage à Méroë et au Fleuve Blanc* (4 vols; Paris, 1826–27).

Linant de Bellefonds, *Journal d'un voyage à Méroë dans l'année 1821 et 1822*; see M. Shinnie, *The Journal of Linant de Bellefonds* (Sudan Antiquities Service Occasional Papers 4; Khartoum, 1958).

Henry Salt, *A voyage in Abyssinia and travels into that country* (Cass Library of African Studies: Travels and Narratives no. 16, London, 1967).

S. J. Shaw, *Ottoman Egypt in the Age of the French Revolution* (Harvard Middle Eastern Monographs no. 11: Cambridge, MA, 1964).

5

Conquest and archaeology in Algeria, 1830–1870

The end of Napoleon's Hundred Days brought with it the permanent restoration of peace in Europe after 22 years of warfare. While new opportunities for research and exploration in the humanities would be opening up,[1] the chief beneficiary from the departure of Napoleon was the Roman Catholic Church. Free-thinking, and at first even the objective scholarship promoted in the Enlightenment, had become associated in the minds of many with the Revolution and its evil offspring, the Terror. The career and intellectual evolution of Robert de Lammenais (1782–1854) from a member of a liberal-minded Breton family that supported the early phases of the Revolution to an ardent propagator of the papal ultramontane cause, and then on the fall of Charles X in 1830 to a form of liberal though orthodox Catholicism, was typical of many in this period.[2] Napoleon's Concordat with Pius VII had been hailed with relief as liberation from the Goddess of Reason and her cult, while his subsequent quarrel with the papacy had eroded his popularity. In 1815 his defeat and exile to St Helena enabled the Papacy to emerge reinvigorated and enjoy renewed prestige and authority.

The changed conditions were not lost on the Jesuit scholar Stephano Antonio Morcelli (1737–1821), already before the Revolution the author of three volumes of *De Stilo inscriptionum Latinarum* (Rome, 1781). Now in old age he set about compiling a history of early-Christian North Africa, publishing a massive three-volume work in 1816–17.[3] Extracting every piece of information available from patristic works, and in particular the *Proceedings* (*Acta*) of the Donatist–Catholic confrontation at Carthage in 411, he provided a near-complete gazetteer of the North African Christian bishoprics with notes about the individual bishops and, where possible, their location. The second and third volumes traced the history of Christianity in North Africa from the execution of the Scillitan martyrs at Carthage in July 180 to the last known flickerings of the Church in the eleventh century. While his descriptions were confined of necessity very largely to literary evidence, he valued archaeology material when it was available and was able to reinforce his identifications of Numidian sites such as Thignica, Diana Veteranorum, Thubursicum Bure and others through existing collections of inscriptions.[4]

Morcelli's ideas extended beyond those of an antiquarian compiler of historical records. In his preface, addressed to the Pope Pius VII, he claimed that his work was a response to calls by scholars for him to write authoritatively about the Christian legacy in North Africa. He had done so to extol the civilizing work of the Romans and also in the hope of spreading Christianity. In particular he hoped for the emergence of a 'second Belisarius' who would defeat 'the Saracens' and restore the Catholic faith in North Africa,[5] and he records with obvious sorrow one of the last attempts in that direction, the attack on North Africa in 1087 by Genoese and Pisans inspired by Pope Victor, and its failure. There were now no traces of the Christian past, he comments.[6]

Morcelli provided both a framework of information and a goal for the representative of any Catholic European power that cared to listen. In 1817, however, European statesmen were still wrestling with the aftermath of Napoleon's wars. Spain and France, the principal powers that had a history of intervention in North Africa, were otherwise preoccupied. The subjects of the Dey of Algiers, the Bey of Constantine and various lesser rulers were Muslim. Though the ultimate suzerainty of the Ottoman empire sat lightly on them, they were ready enough to support the Muslim cause when threatened by Christians, as it was to be as a result of the Greek uprising of 1821.

The relative prosperity, however, of the Muslim principalities, and the laxness of the ultimate Ottoman control had resulted in the ports along the North African coast becoming homes of pirates and corsairs that preyed on commerce plying through the Mediterranean. The end of the Napoleonic wars enabled their victims among the maritime nations to take reprisals which led ultimately to the permanent French occupation of Algiers in 1830. In 1815 an American squadron had bombarded Tripoli, followed next year by an attack on Algiers by a British squadron under Lord Exmouth which imposed a temporary cessation of the slave trade there. In the 1820s relations between the European powers favouring the Greeks and the North Africans supporting the Turks worsened.[7] There was a general assent that piracy in the Mediterranean must be ended. A series of incidents involving the French brought a tense situation to a head and caused the government of Charles X to declare war on the Dey of Algiers in the spring of 1830.

It was almost inevitable that the French should have taken the lead in a conflict between the Europeans and the North Africans. For centuries, since the crusade of Louis IX (1270), France had been drawn spasmodically towards the twin objectives of restoring Christianity in North Africa and creating a sphere of influence for itself there. Partly to counter similar Spanish ambitions in the sixteenth century, Catherine de Medici had toyed with an idea of proclaiming her son Henry (later Henry III of France, 1574–89) 'king of Algiers'. In the reign of Louis XVI there had been correspondence between the King and Hassan Pasha of Algiers: and the French had remained alert when Count O'Reilly attempted unsuccessfully to seize Algiers in 1775 in the name of Charles III of Spain. Plans for the capture of that city and Tunis had been drawn up at Napoleon's order in 1808, as yet another means of threatening British naval supremacy in the Mediterranean,[8] but these came to nothing.

It was not until 1827 that an incident took place which led to France being able to satisfy its long-standing aims. The French consul had come to wield considerable influence in Algiers, and on 29 April 1827, Consul Deval visited its ruler, Husain Dey, with a complaint. There was an argument. The Dey lost his temper and struck the consul with his fan. The 'incident of the fan' increased bad blood between the two countries as France was a member of the coalition Christian powers, with England and Russia pressing for Greek independence while the Dey was assisting the Turks.[9] At first, however, France aimed at an alliance with another Muslim power to punish the Dey, Mehmet Ali, the Sultan's rebel viceroy of Egypt. This seemed a possibility when in September 1829 the Duc de Polignac, Charles X's chief minister, proposed to Mehmet Ali that he should abandon his planned attack on Syria and join with France in an attack on Algiers. A modified proposal would have left France free to attack Algiers while Mehmet mounted assaults on Tripoli and Tunis. France would retain control of Algerian ports.[10] It was a bold move, calculated to increase French influence in the Ottoman empire while avoiding the odium of a Christian aggression against Islam. At the same time it would counterbalance England's power in the Mediterranean and carry France's influence into the heart of Asia. Mehmet Ali hesitated and then declined. Much as he disliked the Sultan he feared the consequences of alliance with a Christian power against a Muslim one. He turned instead to England, which with Malta and Gibraltar in its hands had no further ambitions in the Mediterranean area.

There had been further incidents, including an attack on a French warship as she left Algiers harbour. Charles X decided that France must move on its own. On 14 June 1830 an army of 37,000 men under the command of General de Bourmont began to disembark at Sidi Ferruch on the western approaches to Algiers. On 5 July the Dey surrendered. The object at this stage was to gain a position for France at a conference aimed at settling the problem of the Barbary pirates once and for all. In fact, France had embarked on an adventure that was not to end until 1962.

It was the last effort by the Bourbons. The July revolution, and the substitution of Louis-Philippe for Charles X, and the capture of Algiers with the Dey's treasure did not, however, alter these plans. Algiers, the Algerian ports of Oran, Arzew, Mostaganem, Bougie and Bône were captured and their retention remained the limited objectives of the campaigns down to 1833. Why, then, did the French push into the interior? Partly, the decision was military. Since the time of the emperor Charles V, Christian armies had captured ports on the Algerian and Tunisian coasts. Soon these positions were cut off by hostile populations and had become untenable. The British had discovered this during their occupation of Tangier (1661–84). Control of viable surrounding areas was therefore a necessity and this objective was gained by 1833 through the convention signed with the Algerian Commander Abd-el-Kader. However in the decade following new circumstances were making advances into the interior possible. The railway age was beginning and communication between various headquarters could be maintained through the invention of the electric telegraph.[11] Soon the French had advanced inland to Blida and eastwards towards Constantine, which fell on 23 September 1837.

One must not neglect other, religious impulses behind the conquest. Strategy was combined with a certain crusading zeal. Whether or not Morcelli had been studied by anyone in authority there were French deputies who saw the insult to Consul Deval as a heaven-sent opportunity to restore the Catholic faith in a long-lost territory. Thus, Lainé de Villevêque, deputy for Loiret, wrote to Charles X in 1827: 'In regard to religion, what an honour it is for the eldest son of the Church to restore the sacred flame of Christianity, to raise the standard and altars of Christ in provinces made famous by the episcopates of Augustine and Cyprian, and finally to enable the Catholic religion to flourish anew there, where previously it had shone so brilliantly.'[12] Great hopes, which were echoed by Charles X's Minister of War, the Marquis du Clermont Tonnerre, in the spring of 1830 before the campaign had gone under way; 'God has willed that Your Majesty should have been brutally provoked in the person of his Consul by the most treacherous enemy of the Christian name. It is not without special objectives that Providence has called thus the son of St Louis to avenge at one and at the same time religion, humanity and the insults he himself has suffered ... Perhaps we shall in good time have the good fortune of civilizing the natives to make them Christian.'[13] Against this background of history and missionary purpose, the French pressed on. In 1834, their conquests were designated 'Possessions françaises dans le Nord de l'Afrique'. The French were there to stay. From simple reprisal, involving the occupation of some notorious pirate lairs, they had embarked on a policy of conquest and settlement with far-reaching results for the future history of Africa. Following the fall of Constantine, they advanced south and east. In May 1842 Tebessa (Theveste) was captured by General Négrier and the Tunisian frontier reached. Other forces moved south of the Aurès mountains to establish a southern frontier of the conquered province looking on to the desert, a challenge in the next generation for French missionaries and explorers.

We may leave the story of the French conquest and settlement of Algeria with the final surrender of Abd-el-Kader in December 1847, and turn to the immense harvest of Roman and Christian antiquities that confronted the troops of the expeditionary army and the first settlers. Why these ruins stood so complete 1,200 years after the end of the Byzantine occupation and the last of Christianity in North Africa has already been explained (above, p. 30). Now, as French garrisons were established, their officers found scope in off-duty time to study imposing remains of the past. The first early-Christian building found was in the ruins of Rusguniae (Cap Matifou). It was the remains of a basilica identified in 1832 by Captain Rozet, an engineer officer in the geographical service of the army.[14]

The archaeology of the early Church did not, however, benefit automatically from interest by soldiers and civilians in Classical monuments. The fall of Charles X had ended the explicitly Catholic rule of the Bourbons. With Louis-Philippe (1830–48) there was a return of a lay, anti-clerical spirit among many of the soldiers and settlers.[15] 'Civilization and Christianization' might be proclaimed as ultimate goals, but their more immediate aims were conquest and settlement. The Muslim population, while respecting French arms, were disillusioned by the apparent absence of any religious convictions among their conquerors. In the first years of the occupation there was scant religious presence among the nominally Catholic population. Not until the appointment of Mgr Dupuch as bishop of Julia Caesarea (later Algiers) in 1838 did this situation begin to change. Dupuch himself was not a fortunate choice. A priest from Bordeaux, he was energetic and sincere, but naïve and indiscreet.

He began the exploration of Christian sites such as the 'cathedral of Tipasa' that were still visible, collecting his results in *Essai sur l'Algérie Chrétienne*, but his zeal ran away with him. His attempts to convert his Muslim servants aroused derision. His stay ended in December 1846 amid a mass of debt, but he had done enough to establish a Catholic presence in Algeria and its interest in Christian antiquity. Among his legacies that bore fruit was a small museum of inscriptions preserved in his episcopal residence.[16]

The cause of methodical archaeological exploration was saved by the higher command and the initiative of individual officers. In Paris the Napoleonic tradition combining conquest with scholarship had survived in the person of Marshal Soult (1769–1851), Wellington's opponent in Spain, who had weathered every political storm since Napoleon's defeat and exile in 1814. Retaining his Napoleonic title of Duke of Dalmatia, he was now *Chef de Cabinet* to Louis-Philippe's government. In 1833 he wrote to the permanent Secretary of the Académie des Inscriptions et Belles-Lettres. After informing him of the archaeological treasures that were coming to light and emphasizing their importance to scholarship, he went on:

> The occupation of the Regency of Algiers by French Troops ... should not remain without results for science, and on its side science itself can contribute to that work of civilization which is beginning in Africa under the protection of our arms ... some individuals who have devoted an intelligent interest in the affairs of Algiers have pointed out to me, and I have felt myself, how the double interest of arms and civilization could offer a good understanding of the geography of Mauretania under ancient civilization and the history of Roman colonization in that country, the institutions that it founded and the relations it established with the natives. I have no need to stress the scientific interest of these researches and their interest for the administration is not less evident.[17]

As in Egypt thirty years before, the conquest of Algeria was to result in the minds of the officials and military responsible for its conduct in serving the wider purpose of scientific study, including Roman and Christian civilization.

The years of French advance from 1833 to 1847 were to show that many French officers shared the Duke of Dalmatia's ideas. Captain Rozet's discoveries at Cap Matifou were followed by others which were recorded in three articles in the *Journal des Savants* of 1837.[18] At Bougie the enterprising garrison commander Colonel de Larachette, converted his officers' mess into a *société des essais et recherches*, the first of the many natural history and archaeological societies that sprang into life in the first generation of the French occupation.[19] These activities were given official blessing on 13 October 1837 by General Damrémont within a few weeks of his capture of Constantine. The general issued a decree establishing a commission as part of the army expeditionary forces, which was especially charged with the 'collection of manuscripts, inscriptions, objects of art and antiquity that could be discovered in the double interest of science and the arts' in the territory occupied by the army.[20]

The French in Algeria were in the van of general movement furthering interest in archaeological and geological discovery taking place in western and northern Europe. The 1820s and 1830s were the years of Lyell's geological discoveries that effectively substituted geological for biblical time as the measure of creation. It was the period of the archaeological discoveries in Kent's Cavern at Torquay and Goat's Hole Cave at Paviland that established the existence of the 'Red Lady' and the Palaeolithic implements associated with her, thus contributing to remove the Flood from the centre of the world's historical stage.[21] There was a developing scholarly appreciation of archaeological remains, and 'the men of intellect' who were accompanying the French expeditionary force were sharing in the same movement. One of these was Adrien Berbrugger, who arrived in Algiers in 1834 as secretary to General Clauzel.

Adrien Berbrugger (1801–69) was the right man at the right time.[22] A graduate of the Ecole des Chartes, he was fully aware from the outset of the possibilities for discovery and research into the past that the conquest of Algeria offered. He was to spend the next 35 years in research that extended from the Neolithic to the 'Tomb of the Christian', which he was convinced was the tomb of the kings of Mauritania,[23] and Byzantine remains. He made journeys everywhere in the province and then southwards into the Sahara, foreshadowing the direction of future French imperial expansion from Algeria. In 1835 he became the first curator of the municipal library in Algiers and founded the first historical society in the province, though the Société historique de l'Algérie had to be refounded after the revolution of 1848. Berbrugger was determined that the archaeological riches of Algeria should stay where they were, that was in Algeria. As he wrote in 1845, 'Algeria having become French should not be despoiled as though it was still an Ottoman pashalik'.[24] In this cause he resisted successfully the project supported by Marshal Soult himself to create a Musée algérienne in Paris and transport thither an arch built in honour of the emperor Caracalla (211–217) at Cuicul (Djemila) that the Duc d'Orléans had fixed his eye on during a brief bivouac on the site, 19 to 21 October 1839. Ten years later he co-operated with Léon Renier (sub-librarian of the Bibliothèque Nationale) to mitigate so far as possible the destruction of Lambaesis, headquarters of the Third Legion, by contractors engaged in building a prison mainly to house those convicted of crimes committed during the revolution of 1848. Renier could not prevent the destruction of the magnificent amphitheatre, but his success may be measured by the 1,409 inscriptions he catalogued from Lambaesis out of a total of 4,417 from Algeria as a whole, which he published in 1855.[25]

Berbrugger was tireless in encouraging the recording and preservation of Algerian antiquities using contacts with the army and his official position to effect this. Unlike many of his fellow-countrymen, he saw the value of international co-operation in this task, opening the *Revue Africaine* to contributions from overseas scholars.[26] Though he recorded and catalogued the Christian inscriptions found at Caesarea, Berbrugger's interests were not primarily early-Christian. In the lay climate shared by settlers and the army alike the first decade of the occupation recorded few major discoveries relating to the Church. In 1843, however, Commandant Tripier of the *Génie* (Engineers) was clearing ground for the new French settlement of Orléansville (Castellum Tingitanum) in the valley of the river Chelif, south-west of Algiers. He came on a large Christian basilica with five aisles and floors entirely covered with mosaics. It was too important to be destroyed and the clergy hoped to reconstruct the church on the site and preserve the mosaics. The matter was referred to Paris, and instructions came back from the War Ministry to General Bugeaud that funds for preservation would only be forthcoming if the body of a bishop was found. To general astonishment the body of Reparatus, who died in July 475 after an episcopate of nine years and eleven months, was discovered. The Ministry, which had relied on asking the impossible, at first refused to contribute, but eventually the mosaics were saved and preserved in the local church. The first 'battle of the bulldozers' resulted in a draw.[27]

The French advance into the Constantine area and thence south-east to Tebessa also benefited early-Christian discoveries. One of the first acts of General Damrémont's commission was to despatch two experienced officers on a survey mission through eastern Algeria. Captains Amable Ravoisié and Adolphe Delamare were excellent choices. Ravoisié in particular was conscious of following the example of the previous generation of French scholars in Egypt. He was a superb draughtsman, while Delamare had the instincts of a classical scholar and antiquary. Ravoisié's line-drawings of major Roman buildings, done on the spot in 1840–42, demonstrate the enormous extent of surviving Roman ruins. The baths at Calama (Guelma) were shown rising to their original height with a native house nestling within the apse of the central hall.[28] (See plate.) The Christian basilica at Thibilis (Announa) was similarly recorded.[29] At Djemila (Cuicul) the two surveyors identified and carried out excavations on a large church, uncovering a pefectly preserved mosaic and recording in watercolours the first of the wealth of early-Christian mosaics that were awaiting discovery.[30] At Constantine itself they discovered the Rock of the Martyrs outside the city, bearing an inscription commemorating the martyrs Jacobus and Marianus executed at Constantine during the persecution under the emperor Valerian (257–259).[31]

In the south-east of the province, the commander of the Second Regiment of the Foreign Legion, Colonel Carbuccia, stationed at Batna, was also a scholar determined to preserve the antiquities in his area of command. In the summer of 1847 a cavalry detachment on a foraging expedition in the valley of the Chemorra came on extensive ancient ruins at Henchir Guessaria. Some prodding about resulted in the discovery of a church and a mosaic floor. Next year Carbuccia sent Lieutenant Viénot, a skilled draughtsman and graduate of the Ecole Polytechnique, to record the mosaic, and came himself with a detachment to excavate the site. The result was the uncovering of a large church (22.50 × 15 m) with transepts at either side of the apse. The latter and much of the nave had been covered with a richly ornamented mosaic with two main motifs: peacocks flanking a eucharistic chalice below which was an aquatic scene with fish of every size represented as swimming in calm waters. A text, whose full meaning is not completely clear even today, recorded the building of the church by three individuals in fulfilment of a vow, 'with the help of God', but the final phrase, 'Gadiniana flore', still defies an agreed explanation.[32] This, together with a small church 300 yards away, was the first 'Christian' excavation in Algeria, but showed that major Christian remains were not confined to towns. The Christian archaeology of Numidia had begun.

Carbuccia reported his find to Berbrugger in March 1849. Two years later the Académie des Inscriptions et des Belles Lettres awarded him its medal. But Carbuccia had a military career before him. Promoted *Général-de-Brigade*, he found himself commanding French forces supporting the British and Turks against Russia in the Crimean War. Tragically he died of cholera at Gallipoli on the way to the war zone in 1854, at the age of 46.

By this time the Second Republic had become the Second Empire and Algeria effectively an extension of France. During the eighteen years of the Empire's existence under Napoleon III (1852–70) archaeology flourished despite the continuous threat to sites by settlers and contractors in search of building stone. Apart from Lambaesis, the sites of Thagaste (Augustine's birthplace), Diana Veteranorum (Zana) and Caesarea were among those that suffered severe depredations. Individuals, however, could now count on the support of powerful Departmental societies enjoying official patronage and the support of local clergy. The year 1858 saw the foundation of a central museum at Algiers to which archaeological material found in Algeria was to be sent. In 1852 the Société archéologique et historique was founded at Constantine, publishing its proceedings yearly from 1853 (*Recueil des notices et des mémoires de la Société Archéologique de Constantine*), and four years later the Société historique algérienne published the first number of the *Revue Africaine* with Berbrugger as editor. On 31 December 1856 Berbrugger himself discovered a superb fourth-century sarcophagus at Dellys (Igilgili) on the coast. The sarcophagus had been decorated on one side with seven scenes set between pillars separating each panel. All figured a young man bearing a scroll, apparently healing individuals. At first any Christian significance appeared to be ruled out, since none of the scenes seemed to fit descriptions of Jesus' healing miracles. The figure of an old man with a cock at his feet suggested preparations for a sacrifice to Aesculapius.[33] Berbrugger put forward this intepretation and it was only later research that proved these were indeed scenes from Jesus' life, and that the elderly figure was Peter and the cock a reminder of his denial. Healing and liberating from sin were the aspects of Christian teaching that had drawn that aristocratic family to the new religion. Despite these accumulating discoveries some clergy were lamenting the evident lack of Christian remains. One, Abbé Godard, writing in the first number of the *Revue Africaine* (March 1856) concerning the ruins of Tifech (Tiddis) and Mdaurouch (Madauros), complained that 'the great Christian ruins were very few in number', and that one could hardly point out more than 'two or three basilicas almost wholly in ruins'.[34] How wrong he was!

In the 1850s and 1860s, in fact, the number and extent of discoveries relating to Christianity in Roman and Byzantine Algeria increased steadily. In 1851 Ravoisié found and recorded more mosaics and the large church first seen by him in 1840 in what was later identified as the bishop's quarters in the Christian centre outside the Roman town of Cuicul.[35] In 1856 Capitaine Moll of the Bureau arabe at Tebessa (Theveste) began to excavate among the vast surviving ruins of the basilica of Theveste as well as to record and map the Byzantine fortresses in the area.[36] There were now frequent *voyages d'exploration* by officers of the garrisons at Tebessa and Batna. In 1863 Laurent Féraud, *Interprète de l'Armée*, explored the Romano-Berber settlement at Henchir el Ateuch.[37] This was typical of the many abandoned settlements north of the

Aurès mountains. It covered some 30 hectares (about 75 acres); remains of a great church could easily be distinguished. Féraud was able to trace out on the ground the outlines of three naves and a sanctuary flanked by sacristies, while the upright stone slabs that had marked this off from the rest of the church were still in place. Abandonment seemed to have been rapid and complete. Back at Theveste Moll's successors, Commandants Clarinval and Sériziat, began a series of excavations on the complex of Christian buildings there which was to continue in one form or another until after the Second World War. In 1867 the excavators made their first major find, the tomb and mosaic commemorating Bishop Palladius, possibly of Idicra, who could have been the same Palladius who had been exiled by the Vandal king Huneric in 483 and died *probatus*, i.e. in exile. Sériziat also found a sarcophagus on which one of the figures appeared to be Christian Rome. In addition, they saw abundant evidence of burning, a clue which should have pointed their successors the way towards solving the riddle of the end of Christian civilization in that part of Algeria.[38]

Another clue relating to Christianity in south-eastern Algeria was not fully appreciated. Among the Christian inscriptions that were beginning to accumulate were some unusual texts. From Henchir Sef el Dalaa came a stone with the acclamation 'Deo Lau/des ...',[39]; another incorporated the rousing Pauline text (Rom 8:31) '[Have] faith in God and walk. If God is for us, who is against us?' ('Fide in Deo et ambula/Si Deus pro nobis quis adversus nos').[40] Another from Ksar el Kelb emphasized the 'Catholic' character of the Church.[41] (It was in fact a Donatist church dedicated to the honour of the Donatist martyr Bishop Marculus, who died in November 347.[42]) No one at this time suspected that these might be Donatist inscriptions, pointers to the allegiance of the vast majority of the inhabitants of this area during the fourth century.

Donatism[43] was never a popular cause among the French in Algeria. Sense of the Roman imperial past and of Catholic mission entailed hostility towards the Donatist rival to African Catholicism in the fourth and early fifth centuries. Berbrugger himself spoke for many of his contemporaries. In an article on Julia Caesarea in the first number of the *Revue Africaine*, he denounced the Donatists as 'pitiless foes' of Catholicism, 'more cruel than the pagans', and the Circumcellions (agrarian revolutionaries associated with the Donatist Church) as a destructive force against Christianity, a force that he associated in his mind with the spirit of 'Berber independence' centred on the Aurès mountains.[44] This attitude was to find support among later generations of French historians and archaeologists in Algeria (see below, p. 126). Not surprisingly, there was a reluctance to acknowledge traces of Donatist churches and monuments. Their full extent was not known until the expeditions of Henri Graillot and Stéphane Gsell in the country north of the Aurès, southern Numidia, in 1893–94. (See below, p. 117.)

On 21 July 1869 Berbrugger died during a short visit to France. He could no longer sustain the strenuous life he had led in the previous 35 years. Next year the empire of Napoleon III ended with the defeat of the emperor at Sedan by the Prussians, on whom France had unwisely declared war. The old order, however, was beginning to change. Much exploratory work would continue to be done by army officers and administrators, particularly in the Bureaux arabes, but the establishment of colleges of higher education at Algiers and Constantine, together with the continued flourishing state of the two Departmental learned societies, were encouraging new men to the fore who combined enthusiasm with expertise derived locally. Among these was Albert Cherbonneau (d. 1878), Professor of Arabic at the *lycée* at Constantine, and Emile Masqueray (d. 1894). A generation later there was Stéphane Gsell, who began his career in Algeria as a professor in the institute of higher learning (not yet a university) at Algiers. They were to be helped by civil administrators such as A. Poulle (1824–1902) and soldiers such as Capitaine Reboud, whose career in Algeria spanned 40 years, from 1849 to 1889. Meantime a new era for Christian archaeology opened with the arrival in May 1867 of the new bishop of Algiers, Charles Lavigerie. He was to inspire his clergy with the duty of preserving and recording the evidences of past Christian civilization while he himself saw archaeology as a powerful means of furthering his aim to restore Catholic Christianity to its lost homeland in North Africa.

NOTES

1. The first issue of the *Journal des Savants* is 1816.
2. See A. R. Vidler, *Prophecy and Papacy: A Study of Lamennais, the Church and the Revolution* (London, 1954).
3. S. A. Morcelli, *Africa Christiana* (Brixiae, 1816–17).
4. Ibid., I, pp. 150 (Diana Veteranorum), 324 (Thignica) and 324 (Thubursicum Bure). His reliance on epigraphic evidence where possible: I, p. 3.
5. Ibid., Praefatio, p. xi.
6. *Africa Christiana*, I, p. 129, note.
7. M. de Voulx, 'Co-opération de la Régence d'Alger à la guerre d'indépéndence grecque', *RAfr* 1 (1856–57), pp. 129, 207, 299, 464 (documentation); 2 (1857–58), pp. 131–8.
8. Cited from André Berthier, *L'Algérie et son passé* (Paris, 1951), p.183.
9. For an account of this incident see C. A. Julian, *Histoire de l'Algérie contemporaine* (Presses Universitaires de France, 1964), pp. 26–8.
10. See C. W. Crawley, 'The Mediterranean' in *The New Cambridge Modern History*, X (Cambridge, 1960), ch. 16, p. 427, quoting Polignac, *Etudes Historiques*, p. 227; Julian, op. cit., pp. 34–6.
11. Berbrugger's view as an eyewitness of the campaigns, *RAfr* 5 (1861), p. 13.

12. Cited from Berthier, op. cit., p. 185.
13. Ibid., p. 185.
14. See Paul-Albert Février, *Approches du Maghreb romain* (Aix-en-Provence: Edisud, 1989), I, p. 31. I acknowledge the debt owed to the author of this fine survey for much of the information in this chapter.
15. M. Emérit, 'La lutte entre les généraux et les prêtres au début de l'Algérie française', *RAfr* 97 (1953), pp. 67–97. For 'opening of Algeria' to European civilization as the French aim, see C. B. Hase, *Journal des Savants* (1837), p. 428.
16. Emérit, op. cit., p. 83.
17. Février, op. cit., p. 30.
18. Hase, op. cit., pp. 428, 648 and 706; Hase collated contributions by serving officers. Christian inscriptions: pp. 642 (Tlemçen), 704 (Bône) and 710 (Guelma).
19. Février, op. cit., p. 31.
20. Ibid., pp. 31–2.
21. See Glyn Daniel, *The Idea of Prehistory* (London: Watts, 1962), pp. 30–9.
22. For an appreciation of Berbrugger's contribution to archaeology in Algeria, see Georges Marçais' address at the celebration of the centenary of the first appearence of the society's journal in 1856: *RAfr* 100 (1956), p. 8.
23. See Margaret and Robert Alexander, 'Kober Roumia', *Archaeology* 2.2 (summer 1949), pp. 88–90.
24. Cited from Février, op. cit., p. 45.
25. L. Renier, *Inscriptions latines de l'Algérie* (Paris, 1858).
26. A. Berbrugger, *RAfr* I (1856–57), Introduction, p. 7.
27. The story is told by Février, op. cit., pp. 37–8. See also H. Leclercq, 'Orléansville', *DACL* XII.2, 2719–2730.
28. A. Ravoisié, *Exploration scientifique de l'Algérie pendent les années 1840–1842* (2 vols; Paris, 1846), II, plate 24.
29. Ibid., II, plate 15.
30. Ibid., I, p. 48 and plates LI–LIII.
31. Ibid., I, p. 15.
32. See N. Duval and M. Janon, 'Le dossier d'églises d'Henchir Guessaria', *MEFR* 97 (1985), pp. 1079–1112.
33. Described by Berbrugger, *RAfr* 2 (1857–58), pp. 309–17, but the Christian identification is proved conclusively by H. Leclercq, 'Catacombes (art des)', *DACL* II.2, 2462–2463, fig. 2182. Leclercq was scornful of Berbrugger's original interpretation, an indication of his distaste for lay and Protestant contributions to Christian archaeology. Berbrugger is not given an entry in *DACL*.
34. L. Godard, 'Observations générales sur les ruines chrétiennes en Afrique', *RAfr* I (1856–57), p. 163.
35. Février, op. cit., p. 37.
36. Ibid., p. 41. Moll mapped the forum of Theveste in 1857 before it was lost to new constructions.
37. L. Féraud, *Recueil de Constantine* 8 (1864), pp. 292–4 (under reports of 'Archéologie').
38. Commandant Clarinval, 'Rapport sur les fouilles faites à la basilique de Tébessa', *Recueil de Constantine* 14 (1870), pp. 605–11; also Sériziat, ibid., 12 (1868), pp. 473–7; and Chanoine Jaubert, ibid., 46 (1913), pp. 87–8.
39. *Recueil de Constantine* 11 (1867), p. 218 (recorded by Capitaine Dewulf).
40. Ibid., 15 (1871–72), p. 421 (recorded by Colonel Lucas, *Administrateur* of the district of Tébessa).
41. Ibid., 11 (1867), p. 219.
42. P. Cayrel, 'Une basilique donatiste de Numidie', *MEFR* 51 (1934), pp. 114–42. See below, p. 229.
43. For the Donatist Church, see the author's *The Donatist Church: A Movement of Protest in Roman North Africa* (3rd edn; Oxford, 1985), and for the Circumcellions, ibid., pp. 171–5.
44. A. Berbrugger, 'Julia Caesarea, inscriptions chrétiennes', *RAfr* I (1856–57), p. 119.

FURTHER READING

A. Berbrugger, 'Julia Caesarea, inscriptions chrétiennes', *RAfr* I (1856–57), pp. 115ff.

A. Berthier, *L'Algérie et son passé* (Paris: Editions J. Picard, 1951), ch. 8.

Commandant Clarinval, 'Rapport sur les fouilles faites à la basilique de Tébessa', *Recueil de Constantine* 14 (1870), pp. 605–11.

C. W. Crawley, 'The Mediterranean' in *The New Cambridge Modern History*, X (CUP, 1960), ch. 16.

N. Duval and M. Janon, 'Le dossier d'églises d'Henchir Guessaria', *MFER* 97 (1985), pp. 1079–1112.

M. Emérit, 'Les luttes entre les généraux et les prêtres au début de l'Algérie française', *RAfr* 97 (1953), pp. 67–97.

P. A. Février, *Approches du Maghreb romain*, I (Aix-en-Provence: Edisud, 1989).

S. Gsell, *Exploration scientifique de l'Algérie pendant les années 1840–1845: Archéologie* (Paris, 1912).

C. A. Julien, *Histoire de l'Algérie contemporaine* (Paris; Presses Universitaires de France, 1964).

N. Yacono, 'L'Algérie depuis 1830', *RAfr* 100 (1956); also contains appreciations of Berbrugger's work.

G. Yver, 'La conquête et la colonisation de l'Algérie' in *Histoire et Historiens de l'Algérie* (Paris; Alcan, 1931), pp. 267–306.

Articles by H. Leclercq in *DACL*: 'Cap Matifou (Rusguniae)' and 'Orléansville'.

6

Archaeology and Catholicism:
Lavigerie, de Vogüé and de Rossi,
1869–1894

LAVIGERIE

Adrien Berbrugger's sudden death in July 1869 did not leave North African archaeology leaderless. Not the least of his gifts was his ability to inspire colleagues and successors over the whole range of archaeological study that North Africa offered. After a tribute to his career in the service of French Algeria, M. Albert Cherbonneau, an Arabist as well as an archaeologist, took over the chairmanship of the Société historique Algérienne. The *Revue Africaine* and its sister publication the *Recueil de Constantine* continued as before recording new sites and excavations. In all these activities the officers of the Bureaux arabes and in the garrisons were prominent, and their efforts were being supported increasingly by members of the clergy. The alliance was necessary if antiquities, whether Classical or early-Christian, were to be salvaged. The arrival in 1871–72 of some 10,000 refugees from Alsace-Lorraine who refused to accept transfer to German rule renewed the demand for new settlements. Much of what remained of some Roman towns such as Iomnium (Tigzirt), Satafis (Ain el Kebira) and Novar... (Sillègue) was lost to the building contractors.[1] In advance of the latter, however, A. Poulle, now in the relatively powerful office of *Inspecteur* (later *Directeur*) *des domaines*, catalogued a further 80 inscriptions from threatened sites in north-central Algeria. At one, Ain Regada, he found an inscription commemorating a group of non-canonical martyrs (Nivalis, Matrona, Salvius and Fortunatus) commemorated on 5 November.[2] Another important inscription was recovered from the site of a native *castellum* (fortified community), Castellum Elephantum, submerged under the settlement of

Rouffach, which commemorated the deaths of the martyrs of Milevis under the governor (*praeses*) Florus, 'in the days of the incense-throwing' (*thurificationis*), i.e. during the Great Persecution. The inscription shows that there was indeed a 'day of sacrifice' as well as a day when sacred books had to be handed over to the authorities (*dies traditionis*), and also raised problems concerning the exact area which Florus governed.[3]

Most exploration, however, was taking place around Tebessa (Theveste), led characteristically by officers of the Bureau arabe there. Thus Capitaine de Bosredon recorded early-Christian sites at Ain Ghorab, Ain Segar and Henchir Magroun,[4] names familiar to archaeologists in the 1930s. Ain Ghorab was particularly interesting. It was a Donatist centre in the fourth century, where de Bosredon found a dedication to the martyr of Abitina, Emeritus, and Louis Leschi a 'Deo laudes' inscription in 1936. The Abitinian martyrs were claimed by the Donatists as their own. However, de Bosredon also found a fragment of a second inscription in honour of the apostles Peter and Paul, but probably dating from a century or so later, under the Vandals, when the church appears to have fallen under the control of the Catholic presbyter Probantius. From Rome, G. B. de Rossi, who was consulted, was able to show that it was likely the text had been modelled on one in the church of St Peter ad Vincula in Rome, built in the time of Pope Xystus III (432–440).[5] What exactly was happening in rural Numidia at this time and how this connection with a church in Rome came to be established remain to be researched. Not far away, at Henchir Goussa, the first acknowledged Donatist inscription was found: a defiant 'Deo laudes' cut 7 cm (2¾ in) high and deep into an upright pillar at the entrance of the church.[6]

Meantime, Emile Masqueray was working west of Theveste, finding a series of Romano-Berber village sites as he went.[7] Some of these were littered with architectural fragments, including many that showed Christianity as having been the religion of the inhabitants. Olive presses were prominent among the remains of buildings, indicating their staple crop in late Roman and Byzantine times. Finally, on the site of Timgad he came on a slab bearing the names of those who held office in the city. This fragment of the Album of Timgad was to be a valuable document, dating to AD 365, showing how far the new religion in this most Christianized of Numidian towns had penetrated the ruling class there.[8]

The study of early-Christian Algeria was not to remain a matter of chance. The Catholic Church was now well established. Algiers had been promoted to an archbishopric (3 January 1867) with suffragans at Oran and Constantine, a considerable staff, and a network of parishes covering the increasing number of

French settlements in what were now Departments of France. Moreover the archbishop who arrived to take up his post in May 1867 was a man of learning, zeal and vision, who regarded the archaeology of the early Church as a powerful means of restoring Christianity to North Africa under the aegis of France.

Charles-Martial Allemand Lavigerie (1825–92) was born in a village near Bayonne of middle-class parents.[9] At an early age he showed a strong interest in religion, and this persuaded his parents to commit him to a seminary education, first locally and then in Paris where his first experience of the capital was in the relatively liberal seminary directed by Mgr (later Bishop) Dupanloup. Thence he moved in October 1843 to the great seminary of St Sulpice. He progressed to doctoral research in the Faculty of Letters in the University of Paris where he discovered an interest in the history of the early Church. In July 1850, he submitted a doctoral thesis entitled 'L'Ecole chrétienne d'Edessa' adding 'Bardaisan, Lucien d'Antioche, Eusèbe d'Emèse, et Ephrem Syrus', but concentrating on the first and last named. Shortly afterwards he completed his Latin doctoral thesis on the life and writings of the second-century Jewish(?) Christian Hegesippus (*fl. c.* AD 170). These early researches might have led him to an interest in Syria, where French missions were established among the considerable Christian population.[10] In 1853, however, he met Mgr Dupuch, now returned from Algeria a sadder and wiser man, but still an enthusiast for the country. He had not lost his hope of opportunities as he saw them, for mission among the Muslims and even further south across the Sahara to the pagan tribes beyond. Lavigerie was impressed, but another thirteen years were to pass before he had the chance of following in the older man's footsteps.

He advanced steadily. In 1857 he became Professor of Church History in the newly-constituted Faculty of Theology in the Sorbonne. Two years later political events on the wider scene altered his prospects once more. Rivalry between Catholics (mainly French) and Orthodox (mainly Russian) over the guardianship of the Holy Places had contributed to the outbreak of the Crimean War. The Peace of Paris in 1856 that ended hostilities enhanced the French position in the Middle East. Turkey was obliged to grant religious toleration to all its subjects and the French missions in Syria were to benefit most from this. Catholic schools began to increase, resulting in a furious reaction on the part of the Druze population in southern Syria. Christians were subjected to a series of massacres and forced displacements during 1860. In this situation the Ecoles d'Orient, the parent body of the French mission schools in Syria, turned to Lavigerie and sent him out on a 'fact-finding tour', also to distribute some 3 million francs of alms among the Christians in the threatened areas. He returned in December of that year determined on a missionary career and determined also to persuade the government of Napoleon III and the Vatican to co-operate in a more active role in Syria. In his mind's eye he already saw a French protectorate over Syria and the Lebanon, if only to resist Protestant and above all 'jealous resistances especially of England'.[11]

He was never to return to Syria. Instead he became successively consultant to the Congregation of Oriental Rites in Rome (1861) and auditor of the Holy Rota, and bishop of Nancy in March 1863. In November 1866 Marshal MacMahon, the governor of Algeria, a firm Catholic, asked for Lavigerie to be appointed to fill the vacant archbishopric of Algiers following the death of Mgr Pavy that month. The request was granted on 16 May 1867. Lavigerie landed in Algiers as a leader of a well-organized Church. One of his first general instructions to his diocesan clergy in December 1867, was that they should register all archaeological and historical discoveries in their parishes relating to the early Church in North Africa.[12] This was carried out, and in the next two decades clergy, especially in the Department of Constantine, were among the most enthusiastic researchers into Christian antiquities. In parish clergy such as Abbés Delapart at Tebessa and Abbés Saint-Gérand and Grandidier at Tipasa the Service des Monuments historiques found devoted and well-informed allies.

Lavigerie had given a powerful impulse to Christian archaeological research. In 1877, he himself participated in excavations on the site of Caesarea (Cherchell) where an important Christian cemetery was found[13] and encouraged work by Mgr Toulotte from 1870 to 1880 at Tigava *castra* in the plain of Chelif, where he hoped to place Algerian Christian villages.[14] In the first years of his episcopate he also provided evidence for his strong views and far-reaching aims. In 1868 famine in Algeria was followed by cholera. Though critical of the administration and the government of Napoleon III for inadequate remedial action, he criticized the people of Oran for 'selling their faith for British Protestant gold' when they accepted supplies from a Protestant mission based in Gibraltar.[15] Despite showing a relatively liberal outlook when bishop of Nancy towards Pius IX's *Syllabus of Errors* (1864), he never lost his antipathy towards Protestantism and England as its chief representative. In May 1869 he wrote to the superiors of seminaries in Algeria that his aim was 'assurer à la France catholique une prépondérance marquée dans les destinées de l'Afrique du Nord'.[16] Such an intention involved missionary work affecting the Muslim population which ran contrary to French official policy since the conquest. This was based on a concept of the 'royaume arabe' existing with its own religion and customs within 'l'empire français'. Lavigerie considered, on the countrary, that to bring civilization to the Algerians involved missionary contact with Christianity.[17] He believed this could succeed and that 'en très peu d'années nous rendrons la Kabylie chrétienne'.[18] How wrong he was! His efforts were not confined to setting up orphanages and hospitals in Algeria. He was looking further afield: southwards across the Sahara whither the suppression of a revolt by the tribes of the Mzab in 1864 had extended French rule. If the Romans could push as far south as Ghadamès, ruminated Lavigerie, could not France send her missionaries even further?[19]

The story of Lavigerie's grandiose schemes that eventually placed the Missionaires d'Alger (the White Fathers) in Uganda is outside the scope of our narrative. The expansion south was, however, only part of the archbishop's vision. Nearer home was Carthage and the prospect of restoring the fame of St Louis, not least through exploiting its archaeology in the service of the Church. From 1872 Tunisia as a future French possession began to occupy his thoughts.[20]

In the 1870s the situation in Tunisia favoured such an initiative. Despite their spacious consular buildings at La Marsa, north of Carthage, the British were not interested in expanding their influence there, while Italy was too weak to take advantage of the large Italian population in Tunis. Lavigerie began to make yearly visits to the small French mission in Tunis, and in June 1875 purchased land on the Byrsa in order to build a chapel in honour of St Louis.[21] It was to be served by two missionaries whom he told 'the sanctuary that you will erect shall be for faith, fidelity and the ancient honour of France'. Eighteen months later, in January 1877, he expanded his purchase to 9 hectares, including in this practically the whole area of the Carthaginian acropolis. He appointed as his representative on the site the young Père A. L. Delattre (1850–1932), who proved himself an excellent organizer of mission and an energetic excavator who attempted (though not always successfully) a careful record of his two major discoveries before the First World War, the Basilica Majorum and Damous el Karita outside the north wall of Carthage. His first season's work at Damous marks the beginning of Christian archaeology in Tunisia.[22] During 1880 French intervention in Tunisia became a clear possibility. Before that took place in May 1881, Lavigerie sent a long letter on 11 February of that year to the Secrétaire perpétuel (Permanent Secretary) of the Académie des Inscriptions et des Belles-Lettres, outlining a series of suggestions for what may best be described as 'political archaeology' in the service of France.[23] Archaeology in Tunisia, he argued, was a matter of national honour. France must not be anticipated by other countries. 'We must take advantage of the ownership of the land that is ours on the Byrsa.' The Missionaires d'Alger were already on the scene with Delattre in charge and he had reported finding 3,822 architectural fragments including 1,530 Christian fragments of inscriptions during his excavations there. It was time to create a Musée National at Carthage, and further to establish at Carthage a Collège National de Saint Louis de Carthage with Delattre as archaeological director, so as to keep the finds on the site of discovery. At present no museum existed. There were also many other promising sites which well-wishers had pointed out. Finally, to support his argument, Lavigerie described what has been done in the previous few years. A cemetery north-east of Carthage (Mappalia area) had been located, where Cyprian had been buried. Another cemetery, reserved for imperial slaves, had also been found. Delattre had started work on a Christian site known as Damous el Karita (north of the city wall) and already recovered 600 fragments of Christian inscriptions.[24] For good measure Lavigerie had written a brochure describing discoveries on the Byrsa, which he forwarded.

Lavigerie's letter reveals something of his ambitions for France and Catholicism in North Africa. When the invasion of Tunisia took place a few months later, in May 1881, he welcomed it. The establishment of the protectorate under the treaty of the Bardo, 13 May 1881, was the triumph of Christian civilization in these barbarous parts,[25] and he looked forward to the regeneration of Carthage as a centre of religious life as well as government. He himself was appointed provisionally apostolic administrator in Tunisia on 28 June 1881, an indication of the confidence he enjoyed at the Vatican.[26] In April 1882 he was promoted cardinal. He had had to overcome unfriendly intrigues in Rome as well as the perpetual tensions between the lay and anti-clerical French government and the powerful French Catholic Church which was suspected of harbouring monarchist sympathies.[27] Lavigerie himself was a monarchist in sympathy, but his view of the monarchy was constitutional.[28] He would have retained the republican tricolour and much else, and could not be reconciled with the backward-looking outlook of the claimant to the throne the Comte de Chambord (d. 1883). Nor, must it be said, was this outlook realistic in the decade 1873–83 when the Republic, shorn of memories of the Revolution, became accepted as the legitimate government of France.

For all his activities in France and at the Vatican, Lavigerie's horizon remained Africa, and in particular, Carthage. In 1882 he established a shrine in memory of the martyrs Perpetua and Felicitas (d. 203) on the site of the amphitheatre,[29] which he was able to buy from the Great Mosque of Tunis. In November the same year he obtained a decree establishing a Museum of Archaeology (largely Christian) in the Bardo palace outside Tunis. In June 1884 he moved his archbishopric from Algiers to Carthage and a papal bull

Mater ecclesiae charitas (10 November 1884) confirmed Carthage as the primatial see of Africa itself, looking forward to the triumph of Christianity on that continent under its aegis. A vast (and monstrous) domed cathedral, aided by a legacy of 100,000 francs from the will of the Comte de Chambord, was now rising on the Byrsa.[30] It was completed in 1890 and consecrated by Lavigerie on Ascension Day that year in honour of St Louis. With this act he believed that the foundations of a French and Catholic Tunisia has been truly laid.

Archaeology continued to play its part in his ideas. In 1886 he persuaded Mgr Toulotte to undertake a revision of Morcelli and update it with the discoveries of the previous half century. Toulotte worked with energy and in 1888 the first edition of *La Géographie de l'Afrique chrétienne* was ready and dedicated to Lavigerie. 180 new churches were recorded. Careful cataloguing of the results of excavation was combined with Morcelli's vision of a restored Christian North Africa.[31]

On the ground Lavigerie was planning a 'reconstruction of Christian Carthage, beginning with the Harbour area'. His assistant, Delattre, meantime was excavating the Jewish (and early Christian) cemetery at Gamart two miles north of the walls of Carthage. In 1883 yet another vast basilica was discovered, the Basilica Majorum where the martyrs Perpetua and Felicitas were believed to have been buried. (See below, p. 124.) This excavation would have to await the next century before Delattre could give it his attention. His hands were full with the Damous. Year after year his reports published in the *Recueil de Constantine* tell of his progress. By 1886 he had found a huge basilica 45 m long and 65 m wide with a semicircular atrium on the east side. There were nine naves and over 100 columns.[32] In 1890 Delattre believed that there were 6,000 tombs associated with the church; many of these were the graves of clergy. In 1892 he claimed to have found thousands of fragments of inscriptions. Skeletons lay in a bed of lime to preserve them intact (for the Judgement) and their owners proclaimed their hopes in decorating their sarcophagi with biblical scenes, such as the Epiphany, the Good Shepherd, the multiplication of the loaves and the disobedience of Eve. Delattre had justified Lavigerie's trust in him.

Tunisia and Carthage did not exhaust Lavigerie's archaeological interests. As he got older he would spend the winter months at Biskra, south of the Aurès mountains, where he explored neighbouring Roman ruins with his friends. In 1887 he bought from M. Rousset, an official of the Service de Ponts et Chaussées (Bridges and Roads), for a sum between 1,000 and 2,000 francs, a fine oval silver casket that had been rescued three years before from the crypt of a church at Ain Zirara near Theveste that lay in the path of a highway. The casket was a reliquary, its lid showing the martyr standing, holding his crown of martyrdom with the hands at his breast. Another hand can be seen coming out of a cloud, placing a crown on his head. The casket itself is decorated with pastoral scenes. The combination of martyrdom and Donatist predominance in the Theveste region suggests that the reliquary may have belonged to a Donatist community.[33] But no one thought about that at the time and in 1889 Lavigerie presented the reliquary to Leo XIII to mark the fiftieth anniversary of his ordination. Coinciding with de Rossi's immense contribution to the study of the Roman catacombs, the gift symbolized the firm links that bound Christian archaeology to Catholicism in much of the Mediterranean.

No wonder that Lavigerie's previously robust health was beginning to fail. The consecration of the cathedral of St Louis at Carthage as his seat as cardinal marked the apogee of his influence in Africa. It coincided with Delattre's further excavation of the Jewish (and early-Christian) cemetery at Gamart and continuance of work on the vast Christian complex (even now never finished) of Damous el Karita. It also coincided with another important French Catholic venture, the foundation in November 1890 of the Ecole Biblique de Jérusalem, directed by the Dominican Père Albert Lagrange. In 1891 Lavigerie had the satisfaction of learning that Abbé Louis Duchesne and Stéphane Gsell had excavated what was believed to be the funerary church of the martyr Salsa at Tipasa.[34] That was his final bow. He died at the age of 67 on 26 November 1892.

Apart from the collapse of any lingering monarchical hopes his last years were clouded by a major disaster. This was the relative failure of the mission of the White Fathers in Uganda which had started in 1880 with outstanding success. Caught in a cross-fire of Muslim hostility and an Anglican predominance assured by the proclamation of the British protectorate in 1890, Catholicism was destined for the role of an influential minority in an area where Lavigerie hoped to create yet another French sphere of influence.[35]

At this distance of time, in a different religious and political environment, it is not easy to do full justice to the cardinal. In some ways he was a sort of ecclesiastical Cecil Rhodes, aiming always at the extension of French power southwards from Algeria, eventually to dominate all sub-Saharan and central Africa. Algeria, Tunisia, the Sahara and Uganda all formed part of a single vision of French rule and Catholic authority. Archaeology and, in particular, anything that related to previous Christian civilization had a major role. He had a genuine love of the subject derived from his seminary studies in early-Christian history, but he was a politician, xenophobic and intolerant towards all opinion that did not conform to his ultramontane view of the world. His zealous hunt for Christian inscriptions led to a deplorable lack of method in archaeological research, particularly at Damous el Karita, where the stages of development of this vast Christian complex as well as its possibly Jewish origins have been lost.

Lavigerie had his problems but these were not helped by his disdain for his secular fellow-countrymen, exemplified by his refusal of academic honours which would have rendered him less isolated from his peers and from the lay, non-clerically inclined portion of the French population in Algeria. But as a man of his age one would recall the view of Paul Cambon, Resident-General of Tunisia, on 22 November 1884: 'C'est un homme sage, droit et juste qui comprend merveilleusement la situation',[36] above all, he was a servant of France. This last sentiment Lavigerie echoed himself when he wrote to Mgr Dauphin, Director of the Ecoles d'Orient, in December 1882 'Nous suivons le drapeau de France sans même nous préoccuper des mains qui le tiennent'.[37]

DE VOGÜÉ

North Africa was not the only area where the French sought to develop their influence with the aid of archaeological research. Five years before Lavigerie landed in Algiers, Comte Charles de Vogüé had made an epic journey of archaeological discovery in Syria. De Vogüé shared with Lavigerie membership of a group of clergy and laymen formed in 1855 to promote the interests of France and Catholicism in the eastern Mediterranean by establishing schools and orphanages. The prospects were far more promising than in North Africa. Lebanon had retained a Christian majority since the Crusades, while in Syria and Palestine there were native Christian communities that had held firm through centuries of Muslim predominance. The visible remains of early-Christian civilization in the form of churches and monasteries were more impressive than those in North Africa. Some major buildings had survived almost intact. At Bostra, for instance, where the cathedral was dated precisely to 512, the square walls survived to full height, as also the clerestory above. Barrel vaults were in place over five sections of the east end, and the chancel arch still stood.[38] De Vogüé's fine lithograph drawings of this and other sixth-century churches showed how these had survived all the hazards of Muslim rule. The church at Turmanin and the vast monastic complex that had grown up around Simeon Stylites' (d. 459) pillar at Qalaat Semân were among many buildings that had weathered more than a thousand years of abandonment, sun, and rain. In the 1860s their walls were still standing nearly as they had been left.

Their discoverer was a member of an aristocratic family that had served France with distinction in war and peace for centuries.[39] The first part of Charles de Vogüé's long life (1829–1912) was divided between career-diplomacy and archaeological travel in Palestine and Syria. At first he had considered a life as a scientist but in the confused situation that prevailed in France in 1848–49 he failed to win a place at the Ecole polytechnique. Instead, he became an attaché at the embassy at St Petersburg (1849 to 1851), but the failure of his first choice of career provided a blessing in disguise. De Vogüé's preparation for the Ecole had included a course of draughtsmanship which enabled him to record the ruins he visited in the precise detail that Ravoisié had shown in Algeria. His successful tenure of a junior embassy post opened a diplomatic career to him, and in pursuing this he also found time to write up his archaeological discoveries.

St Petersburg awakened an interest in the Orthodox and other Eastern Churches. In 1852–53 he was able to travel in the East, to Jerusalem and Palmyra, and see Roman, Byzantine and Crusader ruins at first hand. The results of his study were published in 1860 (republished 1862, 1869 and 1911) as *Les Eglises de la Terre Sainte*. Official duties recalled him to Paris in 1854, but eight years later he was able to join the two experienced Asia Minor travellers Waddington (future French ambassador in London) and Perrot on another visit to Palmyra, and through an area between Aleppo and Damascus strewn with Byzantine ruins, and thence south to Bostra and beyond. In the autumn of 1862 Waddington returned to France, and de Vogüé, after a brief stay in Jerusalem, set out for the Hauran (ancient Batanea) to record the majestic Greco-Roman ruins to the area. In the introduction to his monumental *Syrie centrale: architecture civile et religieuse de Ier au VIIe siècle*, which was finished in 1876 during his time at the French embassy in Vienna, he describes the scale of late-Roman settlement in the area.[40] With some exaggeration perhaps, he recounts visits to deserted towns with paved streets and colonnades still flanking them practically intact. In some places houses still served as the abode of Druze squatters. One was occupied by the local sheik and his family. There were remains of stables, cisterns, porticos, gardens even. Today it would be an archaeologist's paradise. For de Vogüé it was the chance to record a vanished Christian civilization.

The high state of presevation of the ruins such as the magnificent apsed church at Qalb Louzeh[41] provided de Vogüé with evidence not only about the architecture of churches and monasteries but of the faith of the inhabitants and the economy that supported them. In the fifth and sixth centuries the Hauran had been wholly Christian, with a prosperity based, as in North

Africa, on its vineyards and olive plantations. The Monophysite-inclined belief of their inhabitants was shown by inscriptions cut on doorways proclaiming trust in 'the one God' and their fervour in calling on the aid of Christ.[42] In this period important secular buildings, such as the *praetorium* of a fort at Mousmili, had been converted into a church[43] and the civil basilica at Chaqqa had undergone a similar change simply by adding an apse to the existing building.[44] De Vogüé believed that this example proved the origin of the basilican form of church to which the great majority of Syrian churches conformed, while the cupola-roofed churches were Byzantine.[45]

During most of the fourth century, however, the new religion had spread comparatively slowly. A funerary inscription dated to 369 recorded that the owner of the tomb was 'Eusebius the Christian', as though his identity was unusual.[46] Another inscription, however, from Deir el Ali (Lebaba) south of Damascus was dated to 318–319.[47] It recorded the building of 'a synagogue of the Marcionites' by the presbyter Paulus. At the time this was the earliest known dated inscription relating to a Christian church, but it was a Marcionite building, and it was called a 'synagogue' and not a church. In addition, the date in the reign of Licinius showed that the emperor had extended toleration to all Christian traditions, unlike Constantine, whose benevolence was restricted to 'members of the Catholic belief'.

De Vogüé's main discoveries were the churches and monasteries of the fifth and sixth centuries. His superb drawings and descriptions preserved a record of these at a time when the Arab population inland was relatively small and transhumant. The stone buildings stood as they were when the Byzantine population finally abandoned them. From the eighteen churches he examined, he was able to show something of the nature of Syrian Christianity at the height of its prosperity in the fifth and sixth centuries and the economic basis on which that prosperity rested. He laid the foundation for the more technically expert work of Caquot and Tchalenko, while asserting his country's interest in a part of the world where France had aspired to predominance since the Crusades.

De Vogüé's work in Syria, though pioneering, should not be seen as an isolated episode. Though the archaeology of the Old Testament falls outside our scope the period of his exploration and the publication of his masterly *Syrie centrale* comes in the middle of the first period of biblical archaeology in neighbouring Palestine and Jordan. Ernest Renan (1823–92) compiled his *Mission de Phénicie*, recording every type of surviving ancient monument in Phoenicia in 1864, as a result of research when he was archaeological adviser to Napoleon III's expedition to the Lebanon following the anti-Christian outbreaks there in 1860. His controversial *Vie de Jesus* (1863) was the first 'Life' that was familiar with, and used, archaeological evidence. In 1865 the Palestine Exploration Fund was founded and an archaeological survey begun, mainly with an eye to discovering Old Testament sites.[48] There was an almost immediate success, for in 1868 the black basalt 'Moabite Stone' (an inscription of King Mesha of Moab; compare 2 Kings 1:1 and 3:4–27) was found by chance at Dibon in Jordan.[49] In 1873 Charles Clermont-Ganneau, a friend of Renan and French consul in Jerusalem, claimed that a collection of ossuaries found on the Mount of Olives might show evidence for the earliest Jewish-Christian community in Jerusalem. He believed that the rough crosses cut on some of them indicated Christian discipleship. He was probably mistaken, for some of the ossuaries may be considerably later than the first century. Nonetheless Jerusalem was now becoming recognized as a field for early-Christian research.[50]

People, not necessarily well-educated, were beginning to report discoveries of unusual objects. In 1884 a chance discovery in a Byzantine Christian church at Madaba near Amman (Philadelphia) on the road to Mount Nebo gave to the world the mosaic map of the Holy Land which, apart from the Peutinger Table, is its only visual representation in antiquity.[51] Originally the map probably covered the entire width of the church and may have been as large as 22–24 m by 6 m. Today only 10.5 m by 5 m survive, but this is enough to show what some learned cleric living early in the reign of Justinian (527–565) thought were the most important features of the Holy Land. Jerusalem with the rotunda at Christ's tomb and the great *martyrium* occupies the centre. But among the churches and monasteries of Palestine are Jewish sites such as Modim, the birthplace of the Maccabees, and some of the tribal territories of ancient Israel. The map may have been designed as a pilgrim's map, and as such provides in mosaic what Eusebius of Caesarea's *Onomasticon* or Egeria's travelogue described in narrative.[52] Though the emphasis of the European and American societies in the Bible lands in these years lay on biblical discoveries, early Christianity was not being neglected.

THE CATACOMBS

Cardinal Lavigerie's gift of the Ain Zirara reliquary to Pope Leo XIII was apt, despite the doubtful orthodoxy of the original owners. The papacy was now actively encouraging archaeological research into Christian origins, particularly in the Roman catacombs. As we have seen, guardianship had been lax and research practically non-existent throughout the eighteenth century.

Sarcophagus of Junius Bassus, AD 359

The Roman baths at Calama. Drawing by A. Ravoisié, 1842

Two fragments of the
Avircius inscription

Mosaics in the church of
Theodore, Aquileia
(314–320)

The catacombs discovered by Bosio had become a prey to looters and relic-hunters as well as ill-considered efforts at preservation by removal to city churches. (See Chapter 3 above.) Not until 1840, when Pope Gregory XV appointed the Jesuit Giuseppe Marchi (1795–1860) as Superintendent of the Sacred Relics and the Cemeteries, was there a real improvement.[53] Marchi was a good scholar and one of the first Roman researchers who understood that archaeological material must be studied in relation to its associated finds and should not be transported elsewhere. His *Monumenti delle Arti cristiane* (1844) may have been overambitious but it was the first scholarly attempt to establish a chronology for the known catacomb paintings. Next year he was rewarded on 21 March by discovering the catacomb of St Hermes and the crypt of the martyr Hyacinthos. He insisted that the inscription identifying the martyr should stay in place and not be transported to a church. Between 1838 and 1851, 300 inscriptions had been found and recorded in the catacombs.[54] His method and resolve made an impression on a young friend who had already begun to be known as an archaeologist of pagan and Christian Rome.

Giovanni Battista de Rossi (1822–94) was the greatest of the nineteenth-century Roman archaeologists.[55] Like the cockney, who is 'born within the sound of Bow bells', de Rossi was a Roman of Rome, born near the Campus Martius, completely loyal to the papacy, and seldom out of the city. Pius IX instructed that his publications should bear the Vatican imprint. De Rossi, however, was a researcher who accepted the evidence as it stood regarding the date and purpose of each catacomb he investigated. So, as early as 1856, he was subjected to the wrong-headed charge from jealous critics that he was 'the ally of the Protestants', singularly misplaced for a man who throughout his life was profoundly 'white' (i.e. papalist) regardless of the possible non-Catholic implications of his discoveries. He believed in 'the good sense that should always guide archaeological judgements'.[56] A brilliant student who had copied Greek MSS in the Vatican at the age of fourteen, he was already planning at university the major project of assembling and publishing all Christian inscriptions found in Rome and surroundings. The project started in 1842 took fifteen years to complete. The 1,126 inscriptions, from AD 71–589, contained in *Inscriptiones christianae Urbis Romae* were published by the Vatican press in 1857. Later editions in the nineteenth century increased the total to 1,374 after weeding out the first four as not being geniune. This left as the earliest Roman Christian inscription the memorial of Caracalla's chamberlain and treasurer Prosenes (d. 217), and so, to date, it has remained.[57] Another notable find, however, was the graffito scratched on a building on the Palatine, a crude representation of a donkey being 'crucified', with the comment 'Alexamenos you worship this god', a mockery of Christianity dated to about the same period.[58]

Meanwhile de Rossi had been following up Marchi's exploration of the catacombs. Building on Bosio's research, but making more use of the *Itineraries* than he, he began in 1848 with the catacomb of Praetextatus on the Appian Way. This catacomb contained the famous frescos representing Susanna and the Elders and, teaching the same moral lesson, the shepherd defending his flock against a wild ass and a wild boar, the personifications of the devil and impurity.[59] Next year he made his first and perhaps his most important discovery while working in the area between the Ardeatine and Appian Ways. The actual location of 'the cemetery of the Popes' was not known, though it was belived to be very near the *coemeterium Callisti* on the Appian Way. This would have been the original catacomb whose administration Pope Zephyrinus entrusted to his deacon Callistus *c.* 200. Investigating in this area, de Rossi came upon an inscribed fragment of white marble used in a stairway belonging to a vineyard store. It read ...]NELIUS MARTYR. There was only one name that could fill in the beginning of the text, namely 'Cornelius', Pope between 251 and 253, whom the emperor Gallus had exiled to Civitavecchia where he died; hence his claim to the title of martyr.[60] Cornelius' was the only papal epitaph in the third century to have been written in Latin. He was a member of the great Roman house of the Cornelii and had been buried in a chamber belonging to the family.[61] The *hypogaeum* (burial vault) became part of the crypt of Lucina and included in the vast network of galleries that composed the cemetery of Callistus. From 1852 onwards, hard work and good fortune were to enable de Rossi to establish this. In one of the galleries he found a series of white marble slabs bearing the names of third-century Popes from Anteros (235–236) to Eutychian (275–283) simply inscribed in large Greek capitals.[61] This proved to be the crypt of the Popes, containing fourteen epitaphs of Popes from Anteros (235–236) to Miltiades (311–314); those from 235–314 except Gaius (283–296), Marcellinus (296–304) and Marcellus (304–308).[62] The frescos that decorated the walls and remains of sarcophagi included the Good Shepherd, the sacrifice of Abraham, the feeding of the five thousand, and Ulysses (a not unusual representation of Christ in the third century) bound to the mast of a ship.[63] De Rossi believed with justice that the catacomb had been prepared during the relative peace of the Church in the reign of Alexander Severus (222–235), and therefore the first Pope to be buried there was the short-lived Anteros.[64]

On the other side of the city, on the Via Salaria Nuova, de Rossi excavated the catacomb of Thrason (1872) and of (the martyr?) Priscilla, where he was working throughout the 1880s. The most discussed finds such as the '*fractio panis*' fresco were made by his pupil Josef Wilpert in the next decade (see below, Chapter 8).[65] Nonetheless, he was also able to identify in the Priscilla catacomb the crypt of the Acilii Glabriones, a member of which family had been executed by Domitian (81–96) in AD 95. He was associated with Flavius Clemens, and his wife Domitilla, relatives of the emperor but accused of 'falling into Jewish customs', perhaps Christianity, as well as, in Clemens' case, 'sluggishness in religious observances'.[66] Rather to the disappointment of traditionalists, de Rossi dated the crypt as not earlier than the end of the second century.[67] (In fact, Stevenson points out that the inscriptions, with one exception dating to the third century, are religiously-speaking neutral.[68]) De Rossi found in the catacomb of Nicomedes near the Via Nomentana the earliest then known dated tomb, AD 287.[69] Catacombs of the third century, however, marked the beginnings of the conversion of some members of senatorial families such as the family of Pomponia Graecina and Pomponius Bassus. From now on, Christian and pagan cultures in Rome were becoming increasingly intermingled.[70]

To publish his discoveries de Rossi had initiated the *Bollettino di archeologia cristiana*, the first number appearing in January 1863, and recording his earlier researches. Next year, however, the first volume of his massive three-volume study of 'underground Rome' (*Roma Sotteranea*) in 1864, 1867 and 1877, appeared, which he dedicated to Pope Pius IX. A good deal of the work, particularly in the first volume, is historical. There is lavish praise for Bosio, condemnation of the seventeenth-century critics who claimed that the catacombs were at least in origin non-Christian,[71] and scarcely less mercy for his incompetent eighteenth-century predecessors. These, he pointed out, despite some zeal for their service had destroyed frescos and removed sarcophagi, inscriptions and bones to swell the numbers of 'martyrs' relics'.[72]

Much of the remainder of these huge volumes was taken up with detailed descriptions of the Lucina and Callisto galleries. These studies, however (for some technical aspects he was indebted to his brother, Michele de Rossi), enabled him to draw a series of conclusions most of which remain valid. He pointed out that far from the Christians opposing the representation of biblical and liturgical scenes in pictures, the earliest frescos in the catacombs were usually of a higher artistic standard than the later.[73] Hence also, the first generations of Christians buried in the catacombs were by no means poor and needy, but well-organized members of Christian burial societies.[74] He was able to show that the catacombs themselves were not used to celebrate the liturgy or as refuges for Christians in time of persecution until the persecution under

Valerian (257–259). He suggested, however, that they could have become meeting-places for the celebration of funeral and other liturgies in the years between the abdication of Diocletian and Maximian (305) and the restoration of church property in Rome by Maxentius in 311.[75] He was too optimistic in believing that the 'chronology of the catacombs was now abundantly assured',[76] and, no more than his contemporaries, attempted to assess adequately pottery, lamps, and even the coins sometimes embedded in the mortar used in making the tile-graves that lined the galleries. At the same time the limits of Christian ownership and use of the catacombs – from the second half of the second century (not the apostolic period!) to the fifth century – has been proved correct.

He established a reputation, finally, for attention to detail. In 1872 workmen struck a Christian burial vault and unearthed a complete glass vase about two-thirds full of a red liquid. 'The blood of martyrs', everyone presumed. Not so, thought de Rossi. The liquid was subjected to exhaustive tests by the standards of the time, and the verdict, 'animal's blood' (what, he could not say: 'positivamente ed essentialmente animale') – a discovery of great interest, but not a surviving witness of a martyr's death.[77] As he wrote years later to M. Lecour-Gayet in correspondence reproduced in the *Mélanges de l'Ecole française de Rome* of 1891, 'Rien n'est à négliger en archéologie'. He was discussing the presence of ostensibly pagan medallions of Antonine date found in a catacomb. How did they get there? If pagan, what was their significance for the history of the catacombs?[78] Thus he restored the greatest single source of information about early-Christian liturgy, art, and hope in the hereafter to the level of scientific study. His foundation on 12 December 1875 of a Società dei Cultori di Archeologia Cristiana was to prove immensely worthwhile, enabling scholars to meet regularly in Rome from 1877 onwards, and report and discuss the latest discoveries relating to Christian archaeology.

He also was among the first scholars to realize the importance of spreading his knowledge to the people. He conducted what might be termed 'adult education classes' on site, especially on saints' days. Numbers had to be restricted, as on 6 August, the anniversary of the martyrdom of Pope Xystus II and his four deacons in 258. 'On this very place', he would tell his audience in the San Callisto catacomb, 'where we are standing, on 6 August 258 Pope Xystus II was presiding with his deacons over a meeting of Christians ... Then the police arrived. The old pastor refused to flee. They seized him and took him away. A few paces from where we stand they beheaded him, his deacons with him. That same evening he was buried in a crypt beneath your feet.'[79] It was dramatic, like his contemporary Charles Dickens reciting publicly from his writings. But like another contemporary, Cardinal Lavigerie, de Rossi refused all honours offered by the Italian governement, 'the Piedmontese', as he called them. Divisions between clericals and nationalists ran deep in the Italy of 1870s and 1880s. Scholarship itself could not escape its effects.

De Rossi's *Bollettino* was translated into French as each issue appeared and *Roma Sotteranea* found readers in Britain as well as France. Visits to newly-found Christian remains, such as the catacombs associated with St Januarius at Naples, coupled with sound advice, personal contacts and friendships with European scholars raised the standing of Christian archaeology throughout Europe.

His example inspired other Italian scholars to discover and excavate catacombs and Christian cemeteries in their own cities where there was evidence for early Christianity. Syracuse, whose bishop, Chrestus, was invited to the Council of Arles in 314, was one of these. De Rossi called it 'Rome's little sister' (*sorella minore*) on account of the extent of its burial-places. There between 1891 and 1894 Paolo Orsi excavated the San Giovanni catacomb north-east of the site of the ancient city and later, the smaller catacombs of Vigna Cassia and Santa Lucia.[80] San Giovanni was immense; galleries containing 164 sepulchres in all, leading off a broad central 'street' like an urban *decumanus maximus*.[81] This city of the dead had remained in use probably from as early as the mid-third to the mid-fifth century. Unlike most burials in the Roman catacombs the graves were usually dated exactly by consular dates while the age of the deceased was also often given in years, months and days. Nearly all the inscriptions were in Greek, showing the language of the Christian community who buried their dead there. There were also informative snatches, such as the fact that one aureus or solidus bought a *topos*, or simple grave space.[82] Others, more elaborate, cost more. Occasionally, as in Asia Minor, the deceased felt the need of some reassurance from pagan custom, one body being buried with a donkey's bridle laid beneath him.[83] Why, is uncertain, for he had been buried amid orthodox paintings of Daniel, the Good Shepherd, Lazarus and the entry into Jerusalem, but age-old belief was never far below the surface, even in fifth-century Sicily.[84]

Orsi was aided by the work of a Bavarian scholar, G. Führer, who looked for early-Christian sites throughout the island, and in 1897 published a monograph, *Forschungen zur Sicilia Sotteranea*. These two scholars were examples of the successful spread of scholarly interest in the catacombs of Italy and Sicily at this time. De Rossi's final article (published in 1894) concerned finds at Terni.[85] His lifelong enthusiasm was infectious, and no one benefited from it more than a young French civil servant whom he met as he was visiting Rome in 1847 to see the collections of Christian antiquities already assembled, notably in the Jesuit Collegium Romanum.

Edmond Leblant (1818–97) was a double-career man. The archaeological side flourished thanks largely to the generosity of his employers, the Customs Service department of the Ministère des Finances.[86] It would appear that in tacit exchange for a middling grade throughout his official career (1843–72) it allowed him time to maintain his abiding interest in Christian antiquity. His meeting with de Rossi came at a crucial moment, when the latter was just embarking on his first discoveries, and transmitted his enthusiasm to his friend. Leblant returned to France intent on taking up the same studies himelf. In November 1848 he obtained from the Republican Ministère d'Instruction publique permission to travel throughout France and collate inscriptions referring to early Christianity that had found their way into museums and private collections. He went about his work with a will, discovering Christian inscriptions embedded in the walls of houses, and even in that of the museum of Arles.[87] A year later he reported the discovery of 228 texts from the south of France of which 47 were previously unedited. In 1852 he undertook another journey including Sens and Dijon on his route as well as the promising areas of Lyons, Nîmes and Marseilles. The result of these travels was the publication of two volumes of *Inscriptions chrétiennes de la Gaule antérieur au viiie siècle, remises et annotées* (Paris, 1856 and 1865). The author insisted that ecclesiastical history must be based on material remains as well as texts. Archaeology, he believed, reflected the ideas of the great mass of Christian believers who influenced the leaders, while the literary works of the latter influenced a few only.[88] This view could be accepted today though in former times conscious propagandists, such as Augustine and Athanasius, took pains to ensure that their views in pamphlet form reached as wide an audience as possible. Leblant stressed the importance of inscriptions and attempted always to connect information gleaned from them with relevant texts and the ever-increasing material being found by de Rossi in Rome.

As early as 1849 his attention had been drawn to sarcophagi found in cemeteries in the neighbourhood of Arles, already known in the seventeenth century. He had to wait ten years before his was able to study them seriously, and at last in 1878 published his results in detail.[89] Most belonged to Gallo-Roman aristocrats converted to Christianity during the fourth century.[90] Leblant saw how, as in the catacombs, a large proportion of the scenes represented on the sides referred to Old Testament incidents which were given a new Christian significance, but there were also events in Christ's ministry such as the healing of the paralytic, the judgement before Pilate and the Resurrection, but never apparently the Crucifixion.[91] The continuity of the message of salvation, and hope rather than suffering and despair at death, were the lights that lightened the memories of these educated Gallic, and also the Roman, Christians.

Retirement from the Customs Service enabled Leblant to concentrate his energies on archaeology. He was rewarded by appointment as Director of the Ecole française de Rome in 1883, a post which he held for five years. His interest never flagged. In 1886 he published *Recueil des Sarcophages chrétiens de la Gaule*, using the most up-to-date methods of illustration and having extended his research from Arles to cover all France; 295 sarcophagi and texts were recorded and commented on.[92] In the last years of his life he was still contributing important articles on the relations between Christianity and paganism[93] and not least, evidence for the concealment of pagan statues and other cult objects in marshes to prevent their desecration by Christians.[94]

De Rossi and Leblant were pioneers of early-Christian archaeology in western Europe. Both there, however, and in now established areas of research in French North Africa the 1880s are a period of great activity. The creation of the Ecole française de Rome in November 1875, housed in the spacious Palazzo Farnese, was to enable some of France's brightest Classical and early mediaeval scholars to have the chance of working on North African sites, including those connected with early Christianity. In North Africa itself there was a continuous day-to-day activity undertaken by the Service des Monuments historiques and by keen members of the archaeological societies based in Algiers and Constantine. Thus, Lieutenant-en-retraite Dufour, retired officer turned settler, excavated a church at Thibilis (Announa).[95] There was also unceremonious looting as when an inscription bearing the name 'Argentius' (in reality Arcentius) led excavators and settlers to join in digging a great hole in the apse of a church near Lamiggiga (Seriana), north-west of Batna, in the hope of finding buried treasure.[96] More officially work was begun on the site of Timgad in 1882, partly to anticipate the depredations of contractors who saw the ruins as a prize quarry,[97] and in 1888 on what proved to be a major basilica at Tigzirt on the coast.[98] In Tunisia, the protectorate opened the way to research and excavations at Dougga and Bulla Regia in the west,[99] Ammaedara in the south-east, Djilma (Cillium) in the centre, and Gigthis in the south, as well as Delattre's continuing work in Carthage.

It was all go. Archaeological discoveries were being supplemented also by new literary finds such as the MS of the *Didache* found in 1875 by Bryennios in the library of the Orthodox Patriarch of Jerusalem at Constantinople. More would follow. The climax, however, of this period was the First International Congress of Christian Archaeology held under the patronage of Pope Leo XIII and the emperor Franz-Josef at Spalato (Split), the site of Diocletian's palace and only a few miles from the newly-discovered Christian remains at Salona.[100] As long ago as 1864, de Rossi had guessed the importance of Salona as an early-Christian centre. He was justified, for by 1890 two of the principal Christian sites of Marusinac and Manastirine had been discovered and exploratory excavations had produced inscriptions and sarcophagi. A new journal, *Ephemeris Salonitana*, had been launched. For the last three years of his life de Rossi had worked tirelessly for the success of this project, but he was to die soon after it met on 20 August 1894. While its interconfessional aims and universal scope were stressed by its organizers, it was largely a gathering of clerical scholars working on the catacombs and on the Dalmatian sites in the Austro-Hungarian empire. Neither the work of Ramsay nor that of Stéphane Gsell was included in the programme. Christian archaeology on the higher levels was progressing unevenly, and perhaps precociously. The congress resolutions call for the creation of university courses in Christian archaeology, for the publication of *corpora* of Christian monuments, of sculpture and funerary frescos, especially those in the Austro-Hungarian empire. Looking ahead (perhaps further than anticipated), the Academy of Arts and Sciences of the South Slavs based on Spalato (Split) was encouraged to publish a *corpus* of mediaeval inscriptions 'from Dalmatia and other South Slav territories' (Resolution of the Fifth Section). Another conference was to be held in 1898 at Ravenna – it met eventually in Rome in April 1900.[101]

The First Congress was over-ambitious. Publishers turned down requests to publish the hugely expensive *corpora*, and of the great men of the previous decade de Rossi had passed from the scene, Leblant was ageing and Duchesne had other commitments. The basis, also, of the work was too narrow and exclusive, too much the sphere of the art historian and liturgiologist and too little that of the archaeologist. Method also was still in its infancy. Developments in France at the time were giving sharp reminders of this. There, this was the epoch of unskilful and wasteful excavations in search of early-Christian and Merovingian cemeteries.[102] On the one hand, there were Leblant's outstanding scholarly studies of Christian inscriptions and sarcophagi of late-Roman and Merovingian Gaul, to which should be added Abbé J. A. Martigny's attempt (albeit premature) to assemble known Christian archaeological material into a great *Dictionnaire des antiquités chrétiennes* (1865). On the other hand, the 1870s and 1880s were the classic epoch for unskilful and unproductive quarrels between 'Gallo-Romans' and 'Germanists', each claiming that fifth- and sixth-century cemeteries and artifacts proved their case for the origins of the French nation. Resources at the disposal of the Commission des Monuments historiques had to be spent on the upkeep and restoration of the cathedrals of France, leaving little for archaeology.

SILCHESTER: THE CHURCH, ACTUAL STATE

The Silchester church

In North Africa offical excavations were entrusted to young architects whose horizons were often concentrated too heavily on single buildings, such as the triumphal arch at the west entrance of Timgad or the market of Sertius, to the neglect of associated features and above all, stratigraphy. At Timgad the excavator's comments on five churches that were found in the first year's excavation was that these were of 'no architectural merit',[103] and also that 'a considerable amount of earth' was removed from the ruins of the theatre.

In some contrast, in England the Society of Antiquaries' excavation at Silchester in 1892 of what is almost certainly a small church has some claim to have been a model of care and scholarly research for the day. The curious features of the building, constructed *c.* 335 but out of use as a church only 35 years later, still raise questions. How did it come to occupy a space near the forum, when most churches of that period were built in Christian cemeteries outside the city? Why the small square water-tank in a courtyard at the west end – baptism or ablutions? – and why did the building apparently become a haunt of squatters within a generation of construction? No complete answers have yet been found.[104]

Roman Britain consistently stands on its own. Elsewhere, while new areas of discovery were being opened up in the Roman catacombs, in Syria, and in Tunisia, overall there brooded the shadow of confessional intolerance, To Lavigerie and the Roman clergy, Protestants were opponents to be outwitted and defeated, not fellow-Christians and allies in the same field of research. Even lay critics of ill-founded theories were sometimes deplored as 'subscribers to a *loi odieuse* of criticism'.[105] The era of Vatican I was not friendly to independence of mind and scholarly research. Only a few like Louis Duchesne were able to hold in tension loyalty to the Roman Catholic Church and scientific integrity. This outlook boded ill for the peace of Europe, with Prussia (and, for Lavigerie, England) representing 'Protestantism' and France, with its unrequited claim to Alsace-Lorraine, 'Catholicism'. In the midst of these continental storms we turn with some relief to a more harmonious field of New Testament and early Christian studies opened up by the work of W. M. Ramsay and his British and American colleagues in Asia Minor.

NOTES

1. For examples of salvage work in advance of road-building and construction work at this period, see A. Poulle, 'Inscriptions de la Numidie et de la Mauretanie Sétifienne', *RC* 17 (1875), pp. 351–440, and 'Inscriptions diverses de la Numidie', *RC* 24 (1888), pp. 189–98.
2. A. Poulle, *RC* 17, pp. 379–84.

3. Poulle, *RC* 18 (1876–77), p. 505; *CIL* VIII, 6700 = 19353. For discussion of its significance, see G. E. M. de Ste Croix, 'Aspects of the Great Persecution', *HTR* 47 (1954), p. 90.

4. Capitaine L. de Bosredon, 'Inscriptions receuillies à Tébessa et aux environs', *RC* 18, pp. 379–80.

5. De Bosredon, ibid., pp. 378–80. The link with the Roman inscription was established by de Rossi, *Bollettino* (1878), pp. 17–20; and for the community's Donatism, see L. Leschi, 'Basilique et cimitière donatistes de Numidie' (Ain Ghorab), *RAfr* 78 (1936), pp. 27–43.

6. *RC* 17, p. 390 (Henchir Goussa). The village consisted of a Donatist church, an olive grove and remains of dwellings.

7. E. Masqueray, 'Deuxième rapport sur la Mission dans le Sud', *RAfr* 21 (1877), pp. 33–45.

8. Masqueray, 'Sur quelques inscriptions trouvées à Thamgad', *RC* 17, pp. 441–7.

9. Most of the information has been taken from Louis Baunard, *Le Cardinal Lavigerie* (2 vols; Paris, 1922), supplemented for Lavigerie's involvement in French and Vatican politics, by J. Tournier, *Le Cardinal Lavigerie et son action politique (1863–1892)* (Paris, 1913).

10. Baunard, op. cit., I, ch. 2.

11. Ibid., p. 62.

12. Ibid., pp. 185–6. Compare also Lavigerie's recall of the past glories of the Church in North Africa in his opening address to his clergy: ibid., p. 164.

13. P.A. Février, *Approches du Maghreb romain* (Edisud, 1989), p. 48. Lavigerie believed that the absence of inscriptions was due to Christians hiding their identities for fear of 'violent persecutions' extending even to the dead!

14. Février, op. cit., p. 47; Baunard, p. 274 (Catholic agricultural settlements).

15. Ibid., p. 274.

16. Ibid., p. 297.

17. Ibid., p. 189. His conflict with pro-Islamic officials, I, p. 169. In a letter to Marshal MacMahon in May 1868, Lavigerie said roundly that France must either give the Muslim people the Gospel or expel them into the desert: p. 241.

18. Ibid., p. 251. In fact after three-quarters of a century of endeavour the White Fathers abandoned Kabylie. The Protestant Mission Rolland based at Tizi-Ouzou persisted with some success (as I witnessed in May 1939), and had come round to the idea that only a small native Kabylie Church could take root.

19. Ibid., p. 269 (letter to Abbé Bourret, 10 August 1868).

20. Ibid., p. 375.

21. Ibid., ch. 15, pp. 488–98 and II, p. 124.

22. Some rather desultory excavations had been carried on in Carthage in the 1850s and 1860s; Sir Thomas Read, the British Consul, and Nathan Reed had worked there, as had Charles-Ernest Beulé, Professor of Archaeology at the Ecole Impériale, but to Delattre belongs the credit for the first systematic excavations.

23. 'De l'utilité d'une mission archéologique permanente à Carthage'.

24. Ibid.

25. Baunard, op. cit., II, p. 154.

26. Tournier, op. cit., p. 144.

27. Ibid., p. 177.

28. Lavigerie considered that the monarchy had in reality 'committed suicide' through the attitude of the Comte de Chambord. He tried in vain during a visit in 1874 to secure from him an undertaking to accept the role of a constitutional monarch. See Tournier, pp. 36–41.

29. Baunard, II, pp. 225–6 – another example of the astonishing state of the preservation of many of the Roman ruins.

30. Ibid., pp. 246–7.

31. Ibid., pp. 421–3. The Numidian section, published in 1894, was criticized for inaccuracies by S. Gsell, *MEFR* 15 (1895), p. 319.

32. A. L. Delattre, 'Inscriptions chrétiennes trouvées 1884–1886 dans les fouilles d'une ancienne basilique à Carthage', *RC* 24 (1886–87), pp. 37–68; 25 (1889), pp. 279–396; 26 (1892), p. 189. Discovery to date of 6,000 inscribed fragments.

33. See A. Poulle, *RC* 25, pp. 410–12; previously described by de Rossi, *Bollettino* (1887), pp. 118–29; illustrated in *RC* 46 (1912), plate viii. Now in the Vatican Museum.

34. Recorded by S. Gsell, 'Tipasa', *MEFR* 14 (1894), pp. 291–450.

35. Not completely extinct today. Note the *Times* report that the object of French military intervention in Rwanda was to check the 'advance of Anglo-Saxon influence' in the area: *The Times*, 22 August 1994.
36. Baunard, I, p. 405.
37. Ibid., I, p. 236.
38. See Margaret Golding, 'The cathedral at Bosra', *Archaeology* 1 (1948), pp. 151–7 (plan).
39. See H. Leclercq, 'de Vogüé', *DACL* XV.2 (ed. H. I. Marrou; Paris, 1953), 3149–3186.
40. C. M. de Vogüé, *Syrie centrale: architecture civile et religieuse du Ier au VIIe siècles* (Paris: Baudry, 1865–67).
41. Ibid., plate 126.
42. Ibid., I, p. 7.
43. Ibid., p. 40.
44. Ibid., pp. 56–7.
45. C. de Vogüé, *Les Eglises de la Terre Sainte* (Paris, 1860), p. 39.
46. De Vogüé, *Syrie centrale*, p. 119.
47. H. von Harnack, 'Die älteste Kirchensinschrift', *SBAW* (20 October 1915).
48. P. R. S. Moorey, *A Century of Biblical Archaeology* (Cambridge, 1992), pp. 17–19.
49. Ibid., p. 20.
50. C. Clermont-Ganneau, 'Epigraphes hébraïques et grecques sur des ossuaires juifs inédités', *RA* (3rd series) 1 (1883), pp. 257–68; and see J.B. Frey, *Corpus Inscr. Jud.* (1952), I, pp. 265–320.
51. R. L. Wilken, *The Land Called Holy* (Yale University Press, 1992), pp. 172–3 and fig. vi b. For a full description and discussion of the Madaba mosaic, see H. Leclercq in *DACL* X.1, 806–885.
52. Wilken, op. cit., p. 177.
53. For Marchi's career, see H. Leclercq in *DACL*: for his contribution to catacomb research, A. de Waal, 'Funde in der Katakomben in den Jahren 1838–1851', *RQ* 12 (1898), pp. 335–60; 13 (1899), pp. 1–16.
54. Ibid.
55. See H. Leclercq, 'de Rossi', *DACL* XV.1, 18–99; too fulsome and lengthy but, with a bibliography of his work, a useful starting point for an assessment of de Rossi's life and work.
56. Unpublished essay by G. B. de Rossi, 'Sulla questione del vaso di sangue' in P.A. Ferrua (ed.), *Studi di Antichità cristiana* 18 (Vatican City, 1944), p. 49.
57. *ILCV* 3332 a and b, quoting de Rossi, *ICUR* I.5, Suppl. 1378, and other literature.
58. *ILCV* 1352c, and see 'Ane', *DACL* I. The date could be earlier, some time in the second half of the second century.
59. See Stevenson, *The Catacombs* (London, 1978), p. 100. De Rossi records his researches in the first number of *Bollettino di archeologia cristiana* (January 1863). The owner of part of the land under which the catacomb extended prevented full examination for many years. Not until 1920 was the final phase of examination begun.
60. De Rossi described his find in *Bollettino* (1864, July issue) and *Roma Sotterranea*, I, pp. 250, 287ff. and 305.
61. Ibid., I, p. 255; H. Marucchi, *Eléments d'archéologie chrétienne* (Paris, 1903), II, pp. 140–6. Pope Eusebius, who died in exile in 310, was also buried separately: *Roma Sotterranea*, I, p. 252.
62. Ibid., pp. 254–5; Stevenson, op. cit., p. 28.
63. Illustrated in *Roma Sotterranea*, I and described pp. 346–51; see also Marucchi, op. cit., II, pp. 138ff.
64. *Roma Sotterranea*, I, pp. 198–9.
65. The catacomb of Priscilla was published by de Rossi, *Bollettino* (1880), pp. 5–60; (1887), pp. 5–35; see also H. Leclercq, 'Priscille', *DACL* XIV.2, 1799–1874; illustrated in Stevenson, op. cit., p. 95. The fresco seems to portray a banquet in Paradise with the food, bread and fish displayed prominently. It is a family group and there appears to be no priestly figure dispensing bread and wine. Josef Wilpert's view published in 1885 as *Fractio Panis* (Herder, 1885), and followed by Marucchi, who claimed that this was 'la plus ancienne représentation du Sacrifice eucharistique' (p. 293), seems mistaken. (See below, p. 161 and 171 n. 242.)
66. Suetonius, *Domitian* 15: 'Flavium Clementem patruelem suum contemptissimae inertiae ...', and Dio Cassius, *History* 67.14.
67. *Bollettino* (1888), pp. 42ff.; further discussion by Leclercq in *DACL* XIV.2, 1807–1809.
68. Stevenson, op. cit., p. 28.
69. De Rossi, *Bollettino* 3 (1865), p. 51.
70. *Roma Sotterranea*, II, p. 363.

71. Ibid., I, ch. 5, praising Bosio; and referring to his 'marvellous researches'; also III, p. 593. His contempt for Burnet and other critics', 'indegna derisione de sotteranei nostri cemeteri': I, pp. 50–1.
72. Ibid., pp. 58–63, 'Damnosa e vituperevole negligenza delle cristiane antichità' in the eighteenth century, 'Barbara devastazione'.
73. Ibid., I, pp. 195–7.
74. Ibid., I, p. 209.
75. Ibid., III, pp. 225 and 481–2.
76. Ibid., III, p. 625.
77. Ibid., III, pp. 714–15. De Rossi had been involved in a similar controversy in 1862, and then had argued that while some vessels buried with the dead had contained blood the great majority of such instances were either post-Constantine or had been buried with children too young to be martyrs. Only relatively few were authentic martyrs' burials. The red liquid also could be either balsam or wine used in Eucharist. See de Rossi, 'Sulla questione del vaso di Sangue', pp. 49–54.
78. Letter published in *MEFR* I (1880), pp. 139–40.
79. Cited from Leclercq, art. cit., col. 25; see also L. Duchesne's tribute, *Revue de Paris* 5 (1894), p. 720.
80. Described by L. Lefort, 'Chronologie des peintures des catacombes de Naples', *MEFR* 3 (1883), pp. 67–9 and 183–201.
81. P. Orsi, 'Gli scavi à San Giovanni di Siracusa', *RQ* 10 (1896), pp. 1–59; see also Stevenson, op. cit., pp. 131–8.
82. Orsi, op. cit., p. 46. Two solidi seems to have been the price of a family grave.
83. Ibid., p. 6 and n. 1 for further examples of surviving pagan burial superstitions.
84. See the descriptive catalogue of the biblical and other scenes represented in the Sicilian catacombs: G. Agnello, *La pittura paleocristiana della Sicilia* (Collezione Amici delle Catacombe 17; Vatican City, 1952).
85. J. B. de Rossi, 'Due vergini martiri storiche effigiate in forma di orante in epitaphio di Terni', *RQ* 7 (1894), pp. 131–4.
86. Leblant's career is outlined by Heron de Villefosse in his valedictory address: 'Discours', *MEFR* 17 (1897), pp. 492–502; see also H. Leclercq in *DACL* VIII.2 (1929), 2143–2218.
87. Leblant, *Inscriptions*, II.
88. P. A. Février, 'Naissance d'une archéologie chrétienne' in *Naissance des arts chrétiens* (Paris, 1992), pp. 336–47 (p. 341).
89. *Etude sur les Sarcophages de la ville d'Arles* (Paris, 1878). Discussed by Leclercq, 2192–96.
90. Février, 'Les sarcophages decorées du Midi' in *Naissance*, pp. 270–87, especially p. 273.
91. Février, ibid.
92. Ibid., Heron de Villefosse, 'Discours', pp. 497–8.
93. Thus 'Les premiers chrétiens et les dieux', *MEFR* 12 (1892), pp. 1–16.
94. E. Leblant, 'De quelques statues cachées par les Anciens', *MEFR* 10 (1890), pp. 389–96, and published, *Les Persécuteurs et les Martyrs aux premiers siècles de notre ère* (1893).
95. *RC* 22 (1882), pp. 298–301.
96. Recorded by A. Domergue, *RC* 27 (1892), p. 154; published as *ILCV* 2032 (Arcentius). The inscription on the mosaic was eventually deciphered: 'Dignis dig/na patri Arc/entio coronam / Benenatus teselavit.' See also *Bulletin de la Société nationale des Antiquaires de France* 63 (1902), p. 196. Possibly Donatist.
97. A. Poulle, 'Nouvelles inscriptions de Thimgad, de Lambèse et de Announa', *RC* 22 (1882), pp. 331–406. Poulle asks the question how it had come about that these great sites occupied land now semi-desert: pp. 331–2.
98. See P. Gavault, *Ruines de Tigzirt* (1894), pp. 103–5. Tigzirt = Iomnium, a Donatist see in 411.
99. At Bulla Regia, the baths, temples and theatres could still be recognized before excavation: *RC* 23 (1884), p. 1.
100. See A. de Waal, 'Die Resolutionen des ersten Congresses der christlichen Archaeologen zu Spalato 1894', *RQ* 10 (1896), pp. 223–4. The *Acta* of the Conference were reprinted in preparation for the Centenary Conference of 1994 as *Studi di Antichità cristiana* 50 (Vatican City, 1993).
101. De Waal, op. cit., pp. 232–4.
102. See Xavier Barral i Altet, 'Les étapes de la recherche au XIXe siècle et les personnalités' in *Naissance*, pp. 348–67; B. K. Young, 'Les nécropoles (IIIe-VIIIe siècle)', ibid., p. 97.

103. *RC* 22 (1883), pp. 343 and 345. The market of Sertius was excavated by M. Sarazin, architect, in 1888: *RC* 25 (1888). pp. 406–9. For the ever-present danger of looting from the site see ibid., p. 347.
104. W. H. St J. Hope, *Archaeologia* (1893), pp. 563–8; S. S. Frere, 'The Silchester church: the excavation by Sir Ian Richmond', *Archaeologia* 105 (1976), pp. 277–302.
105. Février, op. cit., p. 344, and for other examples of clerical suspicion of archaeology, see Barral i Altet, op. cit., p. 352.

FURTHER READING

X. Barral i Altet, 'Les étapes de la recherche au XIXe siècle et les personnalités' in *Naissance des arts chrétiens* (Paris, 1992), pp. 348–67.

Louis Baunard, *Le Cardinal Lavigerie* (2 vols; Paris, 1922).

C. Clermont-Ganneau, 'Epigraphes hébraïques et grecques sur des ossuaires juifs inédités', *RA* (3rd series) I (1883), pp. 257–68.

A. Delattre, 'Inscriptions chrétiennes trouvées 1884–1886 dans les fouilles d'une ancienne basilique à Carthage', *RC* 24 (1886–87), pp. 37–68; 25 (1889), pp. 279–396; 26 (1892), pp. 189ff.

P. A. Février, 'Naissance d'une archéologie chrétienne' in *Naissance*, pp. 336–47.

P. A. Février, 'Les sarcophages décorées du Midi', ibid., pp. 270–87.

S. S. Frere, 'The Silchester church: the excavations by Sir Ian Richmond', *Archaeologia* 105 (1976), pp. 277–302.

Margaret Golding, 'The cathedral at Bosra', *Archaeology* I (1948), pp. 151–7.

E. Leblant, 'De quelques statues cachées par les Anciens', *MEFR* 10 (1890), pp. 389–96.

Louis Reekmans, *La tombe du pape Corneille et sa région cémétériale* (Vatician City, 1964).

J. Tournier, *Le Cardinal Lavigerie et son action politique (1863–1892)* (Paris, 1913).

A. de Waal, 'Die Resolutionen des ersten Congresses der christlichen Archaeologen zu Spalato 1894', *RQ* 10 (1896), pp. 223–34.

A, de Waal, 'Funde in der Katakomben in den Jahren 1838–1851', *RQ* 12 (1898), pp. 335–60.

H. Leclercq, articles in *DACL* on Leblant: VIII.2, 2143–2218, de Rossi: XV.1, 18–99, and Charles Melchior de Vogüé: XV.2, 3149–3186, and the Catacombs of Priscilla: XIV.2, 1799–1874 with bibliography to 1908, at 1872–74; and Thrason: XV.2. 2276–2283.

7

In the steps of St Paul: Exploration of Christian remains in Asia Minor, 1875–1895

If the story of archaeological research on early-Christian sites in North Africa is exclusively a story of France and French scholarship and ambitions, the study of similar remains in Asia Minor was shared by the British, Austrians and Germans as well as the French.

For over a thousand years Asia Minor had been at the heart of Christianity. Its Greek cities had been the scene of Paul's missions, and his three-year stay in Ephesus suggests that after Jerusalem Paul considered that city as the leading centre of the Christian mission. 'The Seven Churches that are in Asia' were all situated in western Asia Minor and may have been the centres of the Christian mission at the end of the first century. In the second century Christianity had continued to be strongest in the Roman provinces in Asia Minor. After the conversion of Constantine its bishops supplied the most numerous contingents to the ecumenical councils of Nicaea, Ephesus and Chalcedon held on its soil. Even rural paganism seemed to have been destroyed in Justinian's reign, and throughout the early centuries of the Byzantine empire its people were the main source of the armies that kept the Arabs at bay.

It was the disastrous effort of Romanus IV to extend the empire eastwards into Armenia that led to his decisive defeat at the hands of the Ottoman Turks at Manzikert in 1071. A complete change in the religious and political life of Asia Minor resulted. As already mentioned (Chapter 3, p. 30), gradually through the twelfth and thirteenth centuries the Ottomans and their semi-nomadic Turkoman allies took over previously Christian areas, seeping in like a human tide, isolating and finally destroying once-prosperous Christian towns and villages. By the time Constantinople fell in 1453, much of Asia Minor had already passed from Christianity to Islam.

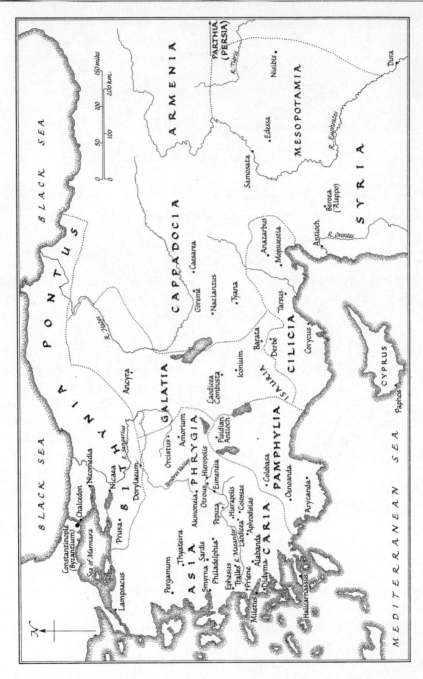

Asia Minor, c. AD 300

As in North Africa and Syria, however, a large proportion of the Islamic invaders were nomads, and where these newcomers were ready to settle they often chose areas adjacent to but separate from the remaining Christian population. The result was that many Anatolian town and even village sites were left abandoned and, like their North African and Syrian counterparts, degenerated into vast areas of ruin. In the nineteenth century skeletons of temples, churches, theatres, market-places and other public buildings thrust broken columns and walls skywards, mute witnesses to past civilizations awaiting discovery by travellers and archaeologists. Roman milestones still marked the route taken by once-great highways crossing the country from west to east. Even older Hittite and Phrygian monuments had been left standing where they had been set up 3,000 or so years before. A harvest of enormous wealth awaited those who had the wit and resource to gather it.

This had to wait until the 1830s and 1840s. Then valuable groundwork had been carried out by the British explorer James Hamilton (1835–36) and by Le Bas and Waddington, two intrepid French explorers who had journeyed through parts of Asia Minor and noted nearly 2,000 Greco-Roman inscriptions on their way.[1] In 1877, the fourth volume of the *Corpus Inscriptionum Graecarum* (1828–77) contained only 179 epitaphs from Asia Minor, gleaned from previous collections.[2] When W. M. Ramsay began his exploration of remains in the interior of the country in 1881, some of the sites of major Greek cities, such as Colossae, Dorylaeum, Laodicea, Amorium and Caesarea were known, but very little about them. While Le Quien had catalogued the bishoprics of Asia Minor and Syria,[3] as Morcelli had those of North Africa, archaeologically Asia Minor beyond the coastal fringe was almost a blank.

The 1870s, however, saw increased interest in the archaeology of the eastern Mediterranean as in North Africa. Western European schools of archaeology were being established in Athens and there were Schliemann's sensational finds on the site of Troy in 1871 to whet appetites for adventure and discovery. The beginnings of serious archaeological research in Palestine, largely in the hope of vindicating the truth of the Old Testament, was bound to encourage parallel research in Asia Minor on the Pauline missions. It was with the similar motive of being able to demonstrate that Luke was a 'great historian'[4] that W. M. Ramsay started out on his astonishing career of exploration and record of Greco-Roman and early-Christian sites in the Roman provinces of Phrygia and Galatia.

Ramsay himself (1851–1939) had already shown his qualities as a scholar when he first set foot in Asia Minor in May 1880.[5] He was born in Aberdeen, with a strong Presbyterian family background. After taking First Class Honours in Humanity (Classics) at Aberdeen University he came south to

Oxford, where he gained Firsts in Classical Moderations (1874) and Greats in 1876. He was able to spend the Long Vacation of 1874 at Göttingen, where tuition in Sanskrit inspired him with a wish to explore the borderlands of European and Asiatic civilization. The chance to fulfil this ambition did not come at once, but in January 1880 he was elected to a studentship at Oxford for travel and research in Greek lands. At Smyrna he was lucky enough to meet Her Majesty's 'military consul in Anatolia', Colonel Sir Charles Wilson, who persuaded him to travel in the interior rather than stick to the better-known coastal sites. 'That was the place for explorers', he urged. The result was two long journeys into Classical Phrygia in 1881 and 1883, accompanied by Sir Charles and by R. C. S. Sterrett of Amherst and, later, Yale University. In 1882 Exeter College awarded Ramsay a Fellowship and three years later he was appointed to the new Chair of Classical Archaeology by Lincoln and Merton Colleges. Return journeys to Asia Minor were subsidized by the Asia Minor Exploration Fund. In 1886, after further successful travels in Asia Minor, he was elected Professor of Humanities at Aberdeen, which Chair he held until retirement in 1911. Meantime, after a break between 1891 and 1899 (due in part to having contracted cholera), he resumed his travels in Asia Minor, continuing until the outbreak of war in 1914. His retirement was exceptionally active and fruitful, his last work being a consideration of the 'Social basis of Roman power in Asia Minor' which his pupil J. G. C. Anderson published posthumously. He died in March 1939.

Ramsay dominated exploration and recording of ancient sites in Asia Minor from 1881 down to the publication of *Cities and Bishoprics in Phrygia* (2 vols; Oxford, 1895 and 1897), and he contributed further when he resumed his work there in 1899. This chapter will centre on his activities and those of his collaborators Sterrett and Hogarth. His most successful research turned out to be on early Christianity, but his approach was that of an historian of the Roman empire and an archaeologist. In Asia Minor, however, he saw that the two could not be separated. De Rossi had come to similar conclusions concerning Rome in the third century, and would probably have agreed with Ramsay's view that 'Christianity was not merely a religion but a system of life and action', to understand which one must explore and understand its remains on the ground.[6] His researches contributed greatly to New Testament studies and to the impact of Greek civilization on the people of Asia Minor. Greek was the vehicle also of Christian mission, and the native languages such as Lycaonian and Phrygian gave way before it. In his *Historical Geography of Asia Minor* (1890) he threw light also on the advance and decline of the empire's institutions on the conflict between Byzantine and the Arabs in south-east Anatolia, and finally, on the character of the long drawn-out Ottoman conquest in the twelfth and thirteenth centuries and the gradual Islamization of Asia Minor.

One of his contemporaries, writing on the flyleaf of *St Paul the Traveller and the Roman Citizen* (1895), described Ramsay as 'arbitrary and headstrong, who makes everyone yield to his views'.[7] He certainly pressed his opinions, and his prolix and orotund lecturing style, recorded almost verbatim in his numerous books, suggests pomposity, but he was more often right than wrong. As no one before him, he opened western Asia Minor to scholars and scholarship, and he made the reading public in Britain aware of the importance of detailed work on the ground for understanding Paul and the mission of the Church. He stood aside from the bickerings of Catholics and Protestants in Europe over the theological significance of his finds. For all his faults he remains one of the great pioneers in the study of the material remains of the early Church.

The early 1880s favoured renewed archaeological research in Asia Minor. The Treaty of Berlin (1878) had consolidated good relations between Britain and Turkey. While communications were improving, expeditions through Asia Minor by foreigners were still hazardous (see below, p. 103). Ramsay was lucky in having Sir Charles as his companion and the resources of the consulate at Smyrna to draw upon during his first two journeys in the interior.

What turned out to be his most significant single discovery came early. In May 1881, he and his companions came on a series of ruins of Greco-Roman towns in the valley of the Glaukos river, a tributary of the Maeander. These included Eumeneia (Ishekli) to the west, Pepuza (the Montanist centre), Otrous and Hieropolis further east, the last two known through the activities of their bishops against Montanism (180–200).[8] At Kelendres, the probable site of Otrous, Ramsay discovered a funerary inscription commemorating a certain Alexander son of Antonius and dated precisely to AD 216. The first lines of the inscription, however, read 'I, a citizen of a distinguished (*eklektēs*) city made this [tomb] while I was still alive that my body may have a resting-place before the eyes of men (*phaneros*)'. Further on it claimed that Alexander had been 'a disciple (*mathētes*) of the holy shepherd'.[9] The phrasing at once suggested a Christian owner, the more so since it reproduced a line from the *Acts of St Avircius (Acta Abercii)*, a document written *c*. 375–400 in honour of Avircius Marcellus, the anti-Montanist bishop of Hieropolis who had died *c*. 190–195. Ramsay's researches proved that *c*. 216, the date of the Otrous inscription, sentences that were to be found later in the *Acta Abercii* were well enough known to be used on the tombstone of a Christian of a neighbouring town.[10] This was a sensational discovery, and it was to be followed by one of even greater importance.

In 1883 Ramsay and Sterrett returned to the same area. They were again in luck. Exploring the ruins of a bath-house at the hot springs three miles south of the now identified Hieropolis, they came on three fragments of what appeared to be an ordinary pagan altar of the late second century. Closer examination, however, revealed words such as 'ichthun' (fish), 'golden-' and 'Euphraten' (the river Euphrates). Then it became clear that the owner of the epitaph had been described, like Alexander the son of Antonius, as 'the citizen of a distinguished (or elect) city' and a 'servant of the shepherd'. At the age of 72 he had set up a memorial for himself recording his journeys that extended from Nisibis and the Euphrates to Rome. On these he 'had been accompanied by Paul with Faith leading the way', and he had found 'all gathered together', and provided 'by a pure virgin with bread and wine for him and his friends, to partake'. It was clear that Ramsay and Sterrett had now found the original memorial set up on Avircius' instruction from which the text of the *Vita Abercii* was taken. 'Abercius' was indeed none other than Avircius Marcellus, the bishop of Hieropolis during the last quarter of the second century, who had inspired the anonymous historian quoted at length by Eusebius to write against the sectaries.[11] He had stood for the unity of the 'people bearing the seal' whose liturgy he had found to be identical throughout the cities he had visited from Rome to the eastern frontier of the empire. This contrasted with Montanist division.

Ramsay's find supported the evidence preserved by Eusebius from Hegesippus and others[12] of the unity of the Greek-speaking Church in the period 170–200 under episcopal control.

In 1888 Ramsay returned once more to Hieropolis and organized the transfer of the inscription to the Lateran Museum.[13] Gradually controversy built up along confessional lines, until by 1894 there was a first-class row between the Catholic supporters of a Christian-universalist interpretation of the inscription accepted by Ramsay himself, and a scepticism represented largely by the German Protestant scholars in Berlin. Doubts, in particular, surrounded the French and Catholic interpretation of 'Rome' and 'royal and golden-sandalled' as referring to the Church in Rome.

On 11 January 1894, Adolf von Harnack read a paper to the Prussian Academy of Sciences which had been written by Dr Gerhard Ficker, an ingenious young scholar who had studied Ramsay's discoveries. Ficker pointed out a number of pagan aspects in the form and wording of the inscription which led him to deny its Christian character and suggested instead that it might be the memorial of a priest of Cybele.[14] The 'chaste shepherd' could be a Phrygian god and the fish symbol was not necessarily Christian at this period. The remainder of the symbolism could also be interpreted in a non-Christian sense. Ficker's paper, if detailed, was pedantic and hypercritical and could probably have been forgotten had it not been read by Adolf von Harnack, which implied that eminent scholar's approval. A storm broke out immediately. In the *Römische Quartalschrift* of the autumn of 1894 de Waal poured scorn on Ficker's analysis, and his example was followed by other Catholic scholars.[15] Early in 1895, Harnack himself wrote to defend his protégé and put forward his own interpretation of the inscription. With great learning, and assisted by a new inscription found at Salona[16] where a dedicant recorded that she had built a temple to Magna Mater and included a fish and a dolphin among the creatures representing the goddess, he went to work to demonstrate that the inscription was not orthodox Christian.[17] He was able to show that heathen–Christian syncretism was rife in Asia Minor during the early centuries AD.[18] The use of a pagan-type altar did not indicate Christianity and much of the symbolism was unusual, at least in orthodoxy. The mention of 'Pistis' along with 'Paul' as the dedicant's companions suggested Gnosticism,[19] and while a Christian element was not ruled out, a coalescence with the worship of Magna Mater or Cybele would appear to be the right interpretation.[20]

In an article in the *Mélanges de l'Ecole française de Rome* in the same year, Louis Duchesne, now an established early-Church historian, who had travelled in Asia Minor nearly twenty years before, discussed these suggestions. He reinstated the orthodox-Christian interpretation of the inscription,[21] to which Ramsay gave wholehearted support in his account of the discovery in *Cities and Bishoprics*. However, questions of detail raised by Harnack remained and still remain, Who was 'the holy maiden' who gave the 'big fish from the spring to friends' together with bread and wine? Above all, the 'golden-sandalled queen' whom Avircius saw in Rome: who was she?[22] In rejecting the interpretation that the virgin was the Virgin Mary or the Church, Harnack had pointed to the use of 'spring' in the Jewish-Christian *Gospel according to the Hebrews*, and to that writer's use of 'virgin' as well as 'mother' as an attribute of the Holy Spirit.[23] That a Jewish-Christian as well as an anti-Montanist element had some credibility can be argued from the parallels which Ramsay himself noticed in the Jewish-Christian *Sibylline Verses*. These refer to Babylon and the vast extent of her empire, which was destined for destruction by 'the blessed man from the heavenly spheres' (ll. 415–416). In this description one also finds 'mountains' associated with the river 'Euphrates' (l. 437), but in the poem 'the golden-sandalled queen' is 'Babylon mistress of the world' (ll. 435–436).[24] The *Sibylline Verses* can hardly be later than mid-second century and the compiler of Avircius Marcellus' tombstone could have had them in mind as he cut the text. The 'queen' was neither the Roman Church nor the Roman emperor but Rome herself, mistress of the world.[25] In the 1890s the ramifications of Jewish-Christianity and its continued influence on Christian ideas were not fully appreciated. One can see, perhaps, the memorial to the anti-Montanist bishop as itself strongly influenced by a pervading Jewish-Christianity among the Churches in Asia Minor in the second century that was also present to a high degree among the Montanists.[26] It was not altogether favourable to the Roman empire even while enjoying relative peace and toleration.[27]

Harnack mentions Ramsay only in connection with the Salona inscription he quoted, and it is unfortunate that the controversy aroused by this single find obscured temporarily the significance of Ramsay's many other discoveries. In 1883 he reported the discovery of no fewer than 450 inscriptions in Phrygia, and progress also towards establishing a map of ancient Phrygia.[28] Visits to the ruins of nearby Ishekli (Eumeneia) in 1883 and 1887 showed him that in this relatively wealthy town the Christians themselves may have contributed to their toleration by discretion towards their pagan contemporaries. Tombstones in Asia Minor, and in particular in Phrygia, normally included a threat against anyone who attempted to insert a body into the grave without the owner's permission. The usual formula was a curse on the offender and a demand that he should pay a stated, considerable sum of money to the public treasury.[29] A number of inscriptions found by Ramsay contained the additional threat 'he shall have to account to God', or sometimes 'to the living God' or even 'God the judge'. These formulae, implying a divine judgement, could originally have been pagan, and sometimes may have been Jewish, but they were found on undeniably Christian inscriptions such as one from Philomelium and another from Iconium, where the words 'who will judge in the future the living and the dead' have been added.[30] In view of the fact that they seem to have been introduced in the third century, with dated inscriptions ranging from *c.* 224 to 270 and extending only rarely into the fourth century, Ramsay believed that the great majority of the 26 inscriptions he found (or otherwise was made aware of) on the site were Christian. The formula could be read by contemporaries as a pious aspiration on the part of any conscientious citizen, but in fact concealed the identity of Christians.[31] There was, he claimed 'no violent break between Greek and Christian culture in Eumeneia'.[32]

The idea was reasonable. Eumeneia had possessed a bishop since *c.* 160, when Eusebius preserves the tradition of the martydom of Bishop Thraseas there.[33] The formulae were sometimes associated with Christian names, such as Philip and Paulina, words such as a *koimētērion* instead of *herōon* denoting a burial area, and the emerging pre-Constantinian Christian monogram ☧.[34] The case for their Christianity was strong. Ramsay's arguments were accepted by Duchesne and still hold good.[35]

Possible but less certain was Ramsay's further claim that Eumeneia was the Phrygian town recorded by both Lactantius[36] and Eusebius[37] of Caesarea as having been burnt down and its inhabitants exterminated at Diocletian's order during the Great Persecution.[38] From being an overwhelmingly Christian town, where conversion to the new religion had been led by its leading citizens, Eumeneia degenerated through the fourth century into an intellectual backwater, whose bishops were ill-educated and undistinguished.[39]

The inscriptions indicate also that during the last half of the third century the urban Christians did not regard themselves as aliens from their city or hostile to the empire. Fines for tomb-violations were to be paid to the public treasury, copies of wills would be deposited in the public archives; there was pride in one's city.[40] Was there a sudden change in relations at the outset of the persecution? We do not know. The circumstantial evidence is strong, however, as Eumeneia was a Christian centre whose inhabitants might be expected to resist the emperor's command to cease from Christian worship and surrender their Scriptures. Refusal would have involved severe penalties. But until excavations on the site have been undertaken, and have revealed a tell-tale destruction layer and a church destroyed by fire, Ramsay's identification remains unproven.

Ramsay was, however, also fortunate enough to find what may well have been an echo of the final phase of the Great Persecution in 312–313. There were the few years (311–313) when the Asiatic provinces were being governed by Maximin, who had occupied them on Galerius' death on 5 May 311. Maximin paid lipservice to Galerius' decree of toleration issued on 30 April 311, just a week before he died. In fact, Maximin connived at the continuation of the repression of the Christians and, as both Eusebius and Lactantius state,[41] encouraged individual provincial and town councils – the most conservative institutions in provincial life – to petition him to remove 'atheists' (Christians) from their territories. At the same time he inspired so far as possible a revival of pagan morale through reorganizing the temples and priesthood on the basis of a hierarchy opposing the Christian hierarchy. In addition, he instigated a propaganda war against them by circulating in schools a bogus *Acts of Pilate*, purporting to be Pilate's report on the trial of Jesus, in which he describes him as a charlatan.[42]

At this point archaeological evidence supported Eusebius' indictment. In 1892 an Austrian expedition under Benndorf and Bormann exploring Greco-Roman sites in southern Turkey arrived at Aruf (ancient Arycanda). There they had the luck to find an inscription recording a petition by 'the peoples of Lycia and Pamphylia' – in fact the provincial councils – 'to the three emperors Maximin, Constantine and Licinius' (in that order). These they hailed as 'the saviours of the human race', requesting them precisely to expel 'the atheists' from their territories.[43] They almost certainly obtained the same grandiloquent reply that Eusebius records the citizens of Tyre receiving for their similar request.

The long inscription found by Ramsay at Akmonia in Phrygia was cut on four sides of an altar and may also relate to these times. The inscription mentions four high priests, who appear to have been active supporters of Maximin's policy. They were well-to-do citizens and city councillors (*nomothetes*) serving 'the immortal gods' (i.e. of Rome). One of them, the priestess Ispatale, was recorded as having 'ransomed many from evil torments' (Christianity?). Little wonder that the Christians of a later date defaced the inscription by incising a cross in place of one of the figures.[44]

The Avircius inscription had shown the reality of the controversy aroused by Montanus at the end of the second century. While orthodoxy gradually gained the upper hand during the next century in the towns, the countryside told a different story. Already in the 1840s Lebas and Waddington had penetrated into the Tembris river valley in northern Phrygia. It was an area, probably an imperial estate, in which the inhabitants lived in farms and villages. In this remote part they had found three inscriptions in which the dedicants had confessed openly their Christianity, proclaiming themselves 'Christians for Christians'.[45] Ramsay himself found three more and published them together with the Le Bas–Waddington discoveries in 1888.[46] The unconcealed assertion of faith contrasted with the discretion of the Eumeneia memorials, and since the dating appeared to fall between 249 and *c.* 310, preceding the peace of the Church, they were obviously exceptional.[47] Ramsay at first seems to have inclined to the view that they were the result of the arrival in northern Phrygia of more rigidly inclined missionaries from Bithynia. There was also a comparatively lax administration by the authorities of this remote part of the province of Asia which included Phrygia at that time, far away from the cities and centres of government. There was, he argued, 'community of life, little social organization and great individual liberty' among the people of the Tembris valley.[48] The simpler explanation that they were Montanists and confessed their faith openly as a matter of principle he does not seem to have accepted until later.[49] Then, first J. G. C. Anderson and later W. M. Calder provided evidence that seems today all but conclusive.[50] Ramsay himself pointed to the similarity of the formula to that put into the mouths of confessors of this period.[51]

Apart from these historical texts supporting literary evidence, archaeological journeys undertaken by Ramsay and his companions threw light on the popular religion and organization of the Church in western Asia Minor. Clergy were married and, like Aquilas, presbyter from Akmonia, were commemorated as 'leaders of the people'.[52] The latter were often known as 'brethren',[53] forming identifiable brotherhoods. Resources were used to found orphanages, and other charitable works (though these may also have been undertaken by Jewish communities);[54] thus corroborating the complaint of the emperor Julian in his letter to Arsacius, high priest of Galatia, in 362, that the 'atheists' looked after their own poor, and even those of the pagans.[55] On matters of doctrine one inscription invokes Christ as 'the power of God' and 'Wisdom of God', subordinationist phrases that could also hark back to Judaism, and as they stood, could have been accepted by Arius.[56] Angels, particularly the Archangel Michael, figure on church dedications.[57] Christians left land, such as a burial area, for the benefit of the church; curiously, one such bequest recorded on an inscription from Akmonia requires also that rose petals (*rosalia*) should be scattered on a particular, but unnamed, anniversary.[58] If by the mid-third century the Christians of Phrygia were numerous and self-reliant, they also retained memories of a pagan past, especially when sudden and unexplained deaths occurred. Thus, a presbyter of Dokimaion records that he had prepared a tomb for his two daughters who had died young, blaming the powers of Fate for their deaths, 'the winds that had hurried the maidens from earth before their prime'. Ramsay dates the inscriptions to the period after the peace of the Church.[59] Sudden disaster would sometimes then as now bring back to the sufferer the comforts of age-old beliefs which Christianity could not dispel.

The Jewish communities also figured in Ramsay's discoveries. The six fragments of a large inscription he found near Akmonia record the existence of three families of royal Phrygian and Galatian descent intermarrying *c.* AD 60–80, but one of their members, Julia Severa, was a Jewess,[60] who ranked as leader of the synagogue. This suggests that the other notables mentioned on the inscription were also Jews. Be that as it may, Julia Severa confirmed the description in Acts 13:50 of the 'devout and honourable women' among Jewish sympathizers who opposed Paul and Barnabas at Pisidian Antioch. Relations between Christians and Jews appear to have remained close through the second century, and mention of the Jewish feasts of Unleavened Bread (Azymon) and Pentecost on an inscription which appears otherwise to be Christian reinforces this conclusion.[61] The tendency among Jews to regard their city as 'their country'[62] and assimilate into the Greek majority also confirmed what Acts 16:3 has to say about the result of the marriage of the Jewess Eunice to a Greek in Lystra, that Timothy, their son, should not be circumcised according to the Mosaic law.

Ramsay was thus able to confirm the general accuracy of the description given by Luke of the Jewish communities in the Greek cities of Asia Minor, and strengthened the claims of the 'south Galatian' direction of Paul's missionary journeys.[63] Archaeology, however, had helped him less than he may have hoped. The Jews of southern and western Asia Minor he could claim justly were 'an active, intelligent and prosperous minority', which 'must have exercised strong influence on their neighbours'.[64] He and Sterrett were able to establish that Pisidian Antioch was the centre of the *regio*, a massive imperial estate (or group of estates) through the discovery of a tombstone of a 'regionary centurion'.[65] But major discoveries which would have enabled him to press the claim of Luke to be 'a great historian' eluded him. It was not until 1905 that the inscription previously found at Delphi established the date of Gallio's proconsulship of Achaea as 52–53 (cf. Acts 18:12ff.). (See below, p. 135.) Disappointingly much of the discussion on Ramsay's *St Paul, the Traveller and the Roman Citizen* (1896) had to rely largely on literary evidence.

Ramsay's successes inspired imitators on an international scale. Since 1883 he had invited the co-operation of the Ecole française d'Athènes. Now the Austrians, as already mentioned, and the American School at Athens organized expeditions, the precursors of greater effort from the end of the century onwards. For once, however, the Germans were slow off the mark. Ramsay's stay at Göttingen in 1874 had made him aware of the strengths and weaknesses of German scholarship in the humanities. He was unstinting in his praise for the textual and literary work of their scholars. Karl Holl's reconstruction of Church and politics in the late fourth century, *Amphilochius von Ikonium* (1904), he described as 'one of the great modern studies in its department'.[66] But equally, the pedantic, unconstructive criticism of Ficker and his colleagues, pontificating about sites they had never visited, filled him with scorn. For much of the time during the 1880s that Ramsay was making his journeys of discovery, the Germans had sat on the sidelines. New factors were hastening change. Turkey in its effort to modernize itself both militarily and politically was turning increasingly to France and Germany for help. The countryside was becoming safer. Foreigners were better regarded and protected. The result was that from 1890 onwards scholarly research was taking the form of archaeological journeys (*Reisen*) through specific areas by young scholars, on the lines Ramsay had pioneered. Germans, Austrians and French were active. The German embassy at Istanbul had sponsored archaeological journeys by Freiherr von Goltz and Colonel von Diest, both members of the staff, through the ancient province of Bithynia in 1881, 1890 and 1895. These aimed at locating the Byzantine forts guarding the crossing of the river Sangarius which formed the last effective barrier between the Bosporus and the Turkish advance in mediaeval times.[67] Apart from these partially military excursions, German scholars were beginning to mount archaeological journeys similar to those undertaken by Ramsay and his colleagues. In 1889–90 Carl Humann and Otto Puchstein trekked through south-eastern Turkey into northern Syria and visited the site of Constantia in Mesopotamia. Some fifth-century Christian inscriptions were found, including one commemorating a Bishop Abraham who died in 456.[68] This expedition was successful and both researchers became leaders of German archaeological work in Greece and Turkey, the one in Athens and the other in the Hieropolis area of Phrygia. Less fortunate was Karl Buresch (1862–96). He was a fine Classical scholar who was interested also in the topography of south-western Asia Minor, especially the province of Lydia. Except for the discovery of a fifth-century(?) chapel built in honour of St George at Basch-Bojük, his three expeditions in 1891, 1894 and 1895 added little to early Christian studies.[69] He died of malaria in March 1896, and the memoir written by his friend Otto Ribbeck which published his results shows the hazards Europeans still encountered. Near Thyateira in the Lycos valley Buresch was threatened by hostile villagers who refused him help when his horse was disabled crossing a river. He found himself at the mercy of 'men dressed like bandits'; malaria, to which he eventually succumbed, was endemic.[70] Once out of the main towns the rudiments of civilized life in the form of roads, inns, or medical resources hardly existed. Buresch's fate, dying at the age of 34, showed that even officially sponsored archaeological travel could be dangerous.

French scholars from the Ecole française d'Athènes began equally unpromisingly. Most of the effort of the Ecole concentrated on Delos but in 1876 the future early-Church historian Abbé Louis Duchesne and Henri Collignon, both students there, travelled through southern Asia Minor with an eye to discovering and recording new sites and inscriptions. It was a journey dogged by misfortune. News of the assassination of the French and German consuls in Salonica, followed by the abdication of Sultan Abd-el-Aziz, made the Turks suspicious of Westerners. The report by the young scholars on their return to Athens contained little beyond generalities.[71] Duchesne, however, had better luck next year, discovering a long and detailed inscription on the site of Chalcedon, recording the dedication of a *martyrion* in honour of St Christopher on 22 September 452 – a year after the great council – the first known dedication to that saint.[72] In 1879 he travelled south to Isauria to visit and re-edit where necessary inscriptions at Seleucia and Claudiopolis (in Isauria) first seen by Waddington.[73] From then on in the 1880s, while Ramsay was working in Phrygia, students of the Ecole d'Athènes were making yearly expeditions exploring the Roman and Byzantine provinces. Among the areas visited were Sebaste far to the east of Ramsay's explorations,[74] Aphrodisias in Caria, and Thyateira.[75] At Aphrodisias Pierre Paris found an inscription pronouncing anathema, invoking the authority of the '318 Fathers' (of Nicaea) against any who damaged the walls of a church.[76] It needed luck, however, as well as persistence to make great discoveries. Finding the fragments of the large and enormously important Epicurean inscription set up by Diogenes *c.* AD 200 at Oenoanda by Holleaux in 1884 and its publication by Cousin in 1892 was not paralleled by any sensational new early-Christian material.[77] This, in fact, occupied a relatively minor role in the reports of these early expeditions. Doublet's interesting find from the site of Euchaita in Paphlagonia of a dedication of a church to St Stephen by Eudocia, wife of Theodosius II, in gratitude for relief of pain in her left knee and foot due to an accident, was almost an exception.[78]

The tally of discoveries, however, continued to mount. In 1895 enough Christian inscriptions from Asia Minor had been gathered to allow a young Belgian scholar, Franz Cumont, to publish a catalogue amounting to 445 inscriptions, including 70 from Phrygia.[79] Their dates ranged from 'before 216' for the Avircius inscription to a stone from Lydia dating to 1460, or seven years after the fall of Constantinople. A feature was the considerable number of inscriptions dated to the eighth century and later. As the editor commented, all the great events in the life of the Church, such as the persecutions, its defeat of paganism, 'the struggle against the heresies', as well as evidence for the organization and the wealth of some churches and monasteries were represented in the catalogue.[80] He complained quite rightly of the neglect of early-Christian and Byzantine remains by previous scholars.[81] What was missing, however, perhaps by carelessness and inexperience rather than design, was a fitting tribute to Ramsay. 'M. Ramsay', though he had been Professor of Humanities at Aberdeen since 1886, received some mentions in the long introduction that preceded Cumont's catalogue. There was little to indicate that without his exertions through ten years of exploration in the Phrygian countryside the editor's work would not have been possible, nor, indeed, that the Avircius inscription would not have been discovered. In the approaching climax of the 'age of imperialism', scholarship would not escape the rivalries and antipathies of the European powers.

NOTES

1. P. Le Bas and W. H. Waddington, *Voyage archéologique en Grèce et Asie Mineure fait pendant les années 1843 et 1844* (8 vols; Paris, 1847–73); vol. V deals with Asia Minor: *Inscriptions grecques et latines recueillies en Asie Mineure* (Paris, 1870). Ramsay had high praise for their work. Waddington, as we have seen, also travelled in Syria in 1861–62, and became French ambassador in London in the 1880s. Ramsay met him in 1881 and he showed Ramsay how coin evidence and inscriptions could each contribute towards identifying sites: Grégoire (below, n. 5). p. x.

2. A. Boeckh, *Corpus Inscriptionum Graecarum* (4 vols; Berlin, 1828–77), nos 9155–9287; 152 were published in vol. IV, 27 in vols I–III.

3. M. Le Quien, *Oriens christianus in quattuor patriarchas digestus* (Paris, 1740).

4. W. M. Ramsay, *St Paul, the Traveller and the Roman Citizen* (London, 1906), p. 14.

5. See J. G. C. Anderson's article in *DNB 1931–1940* on Ramsay, and Henri Grégoire's memoir, *Byzantion* 6 (1931), pp. v–xii.

6. *St Paul*, p. 1; and compare *The Church of the Roman Empire*, p. xi.

7. Arthur Wright, Fellow of King's College, Cambridge. Note also Ramsay's admission that 'egotistic self-assertion' was a criticism made by 'many English critics' of his work: *Cities and Bishoprics of Phrygia*, II (Oxford, 1897), Preface, p. viii.

8. Eusebius, *HE* v.16.3 and 5; and line 22 of MS of *Acta Abercii*.

9. For Ramsay's account of the discovery of the Alexander inscription see *BCH* (1882), pp. 518–19, and *Cities and Bishoprics*, II, pp. 720–2. In 'The tale of Saint Abercius', *JHS* 3 (1882), pp. 339–52, he demonstrates the link between this inscription and the *Acta Abercii*.

10. See Ramsay's account of this find in *Cities and Bishoprics*, II, pp. 722–9, inscription 657.

11. Eusebius, *HE* v.16.3. Ramsay dates the inscription as 'probably' 192: *Cities and Bishoprics*, II, p. 713. An English translation of the *Acta Abercii* is given in J. Stevenson rev. W. H. C. Frend, *A New Eusebius* (1987), pp. 111–12, document 92.

12. Eusebius, *HE* iv.22.1. Hegesippus explained in his *Memorials* how when travelling as far as Rome he mingled with many bishops and he found the same teaching among them all.

13. Part of the inscription was donated by the Sultan to Pope Leo XIII, part in Ramsay's keeping, sent direct to the Lateran.

14. *SBAW* (1 February 1894), pp. 87ff.

15. H de Waal, 'Die Inschrift des Abercius', *RQ* 8 (1894) pp. 329–31.

16. A. Harnack, 'Zur Abercius-Inschrift', *TU* 12.4b (1895).

17. Ibid., Appendix.

18. Ibid., pp. 17–20.

19. Ibid., p. 13. 1894 was the time when the Gnostic tract *Pistis Sophia* was receiving the attention of scholars.

20. Ibid., pp. 25–6.

21. Louis Duchesne, 'L'épitaphe d'Abercius', *MEFR* 15 (1895), pp. 155–82. Some Roman Catholic scholars pressed the evidence too far. Thus, H. Marucchi considered the inscription 'most important of all from the point of view of dogma'. It alluded to the doctrine of the Eucharist, to the cult of the Virgin, the communion of saints, prayers for the dead and the supremacy of the Roman Church: *Eléments d'archéologie chrétienne*, I (Paris/Rome, 1905), p. 307, and compare T. M. Wehofer, 'Philologische Bemerkungen zur Aberkiosinschrift', *RQ* 10 (1896), pp. 61–84.

22. For a more recent attempt to solve this problem, see W. M. Calder, 'The epitaph of Avircius Marcellus', *JRS* 28 (1939), pp. 1–5. Calder, however, does not take into account the possible Jewish-Christian overtones of the inscription with 'Babylon' = 'Rome'.

23. Harnack, op. cit., p. 15 n.i. This was by far the author's most useful suggestion, and it could have been even more relevant if he had quoted the similarities of the inscription with the *Sibylline Verses*. 'Friends' (*philoi*) was not a usual Christian identification in place of 'brethren' (*adelphoi*). Useful also would have been a comparison with the language of the Pectorius Greek inscription found in 1839 near Autun (*DACL* I, 3196). Line 16 starts '[member] of the heavenly race of the divine Ichthys, preserve a saintly heart, thou who receivest among mortals the eternal fount of divine water'.

   The reference to people 'of the fish' and baptism is common to both inscriptions, suggesting that this was the usage by Christians in the period 180–230. For Pectorius, see H. Leclercq, 'Pectorius', *DACL* XIII.1, 2884–2898: a detailed study with bibliography to 1935.

24. *Sibylline Verses*, ed. and Eng. trans. H. N. Bate, *The Sibylline Oracles, Books III–V* (SPCK, 1918), lines 434–437. I accept Bate's dating as 'the last quarter of the first century' (p. 27) as a possibility, but the period 115–135, when the Jews felt violent hostility towards the empire, seems more likely. The use of this hostile tract by the otherwise loyal Avircius Marcellus is a puzzle.
25. Ramsay, *Cities and Bishoprics*, p. 727.
26. Thus J. Massingberd Ford, 'Was Montanism a Jewish-Christian heresy?', *JEH* 17 (1956), pp. 145–58.
27. As shown by the last line of the text of the Abercius manuscript.
28. Recorded in Ramsay, 'The cities and bishoprics of Phrygia', *JHS* 4 (1883), pp. 370–436.
29. Examples quoted by Ramsay, *Cities and Bishoprics*, pp. 496–9, together with appeals to God (or the gods) for the punishment of the offender.
30. See W. M. Calder, 'Philadelphia and Montanism', *BJRL* 7 (1923), p. 316.
31. Ramsay, *Cities and Bishoprics*, pp. 499–502. One Eumeneian inscription using the formula 'let him answer before the living God' was set up for a bishop: Ramsay, *JHS* 4 (1883), p. 400.
32. Ramsay, *Cities and Bishoprics*, p. 503.
33. Eusebius, *HE* v.24.4.
34. Christian names: *Cities and Bishoprics*, p. 532; general discussion of evidence, and for the 'monogram', *JTS* 4 (1883), pp. 433 and 514–33. See also S. Mitchell, *Anatolia* (OUP, 1993), II, pp. 40–1.
35. L. Duchesne, op. cit (above, n. 21), pp. 168–9, and in *Revue des Questions historiques* (1883), p. 25.
36. Lactantius, *Div. Inst.* v.11.
37. Eusebius, *HE* viii.11. Both near-contemporary accounts.
38. Ramsay, *Cities and Bishoprics*, pp. 505–9.
39. Ibid, pp. 508–9.
40. The evidence is marshalled by F. Cumont, 'Les inscriptions chrétiennes d'Asie Mineure', *MEFR* 15.1 (1895), pp. 266–7.
41. Eusebius, *HE* ix. 7.3–14 (Tyre) and Lactantius, *De Mort. Persec.* 36.3.
42. Eusebius, *HE* ix.5.1; compare i.9.3–4.
43. *CIL* III, 1.2132 = *ILCV* I; and see *DACL* I.2 (Arycanda) and *Arch. epigraph. Mitteilung* 16 (1893), pp. 93ff. A similar inscription was found by S. Mitchell in July 1986 on the site of Colobasa (Kusbaba). The inscription, however, records Maximin's reply, given at Sardes on 6 April 312, to the people of Colobasa in Pisidia, agreeing to their petition (to be rid of Christians) and informing them that they could ask for 'whatsoever they wanted' because of their 'zeal for the sacred rites of the immortal gods'. Maximin's rhetoric recalls that used in his letter to the people of Tyre: *HE* vii.9.10. See Stephen Mitchell, 'Maximinus and the Christians in AD 312; a new Latin inscription', *JRS* 68 (1988), pp. 105–24.
44. Ramsay, *Cities and Bishoprics*, pp. 743–4, inscription 684.
45. Le Bas and Waddington, *Voyage archéologique: Inscriptions*, III, nos 727, 785 and 1783.
46. Ramsay, 'The early Christian monuments in Phrygia, a study in the early history of the Church', *The Expositor* (3rd Series) (1888), pp. 241 and 400; (1889), pp. 141, 253, and 392; esp. (1888), pp. 251–55.
47. Ramsay, 'Early Christian monuments', *Expositor* (1888), pp. 404–5.
48. Ibid., p. 405.
49. Inscription 393: op. cit., pp. 536–7, which Ramsay dates to the last quarter of the third century AD: 'The bold uncompromising proclamation of the religion of the persons who have made the grave recalls Montanist principles.' Compare inscription 444 from Trajanopolis in north-west Phrygia.
50. See below, p. 195. Calder's principal article is 'Philadelphia and Montanism', *BJRL* 7 (1923), pp. 309–55. For recent discussion, see Mitchell, *Anatolia*, II, p. 40.
51. Ramsay, *Cities and Bishoprics*, p. 537.
52. Ramsay, *Expositor* (1888), p. 260 and *JHS* 4 (1883), p. 260, inscription 12: Aquila remembered 'as leader of the people', with his wife Cyrilla.
53. Ramsay, *Expositor* (1888), p. 409.
54. Ramsay, *Cities and Bishoprics*, inscription 412, from Akmonia, dating from 190–200 though Judaism should not be ruled out.
55. Julian, *Letter* 49, to Arsacius, high priest of Galatia; ed. W. C. Wright, 429D.
56. Ramsay, *Cities and Bishoprics*, p. 558, inscriptions 441 and 442 from Ushak (Trajanopolis).
57. Inscriptions 404, 427 and 678.
58. Inscriptions 455, Ramsay, pp. 562–64.
59. Inscriptions 441–442, Ramsay, p. 558.

60. Ramsay, pp. 449–51 and 673. Note also the appearance of Noah's ark on the local coinage of Apamea in the reigns of Septimius Severus (193–211), Macrinus (217–218) and Philip (244–249).
61. Inscription 411 (Akmonia)
62. Inscription 561 (near Akmonia)
63. That is, that Paul did not journey into the northern parts of the province of Galatia. (The 'south Galatian' theory was more favourable to the general accuracy of Acts.) See Ramsay, *St Paul*, ch. 6 and Preface, p. xiii.
64. Ramsay, *St Paul*, p. 144. Compare *Cities and Bishoprics*, p. 675: Jews of Akmonia described as 'accepting the Roman empire as their country, even to the extent of engaging in the loyal worship of the emperors'.
65. Discovered by Sterrett: see Ramsay, *St Paul*, pp. 102–4: probably not merely a provincial sub-division but the centre of a network of imperial estates administered by an imperial official.
66. K. Holl, *Amphilochius von Ikonium in seiner Verhältnis zu den grossen Kappadoziern* (Tübingen and Leipzig, 1904). Ramsay's praise: *Luke the Physician* (London: Hodder and Stoughton, 1908), Preface, p. vi.
67. W. von Diest, 'Von Pergamon über den Dindymos zum Pontos', *Petermanns Mitteilungen* (Ergänzungs-heft 1889), pp. 92ff.; Freiherr von der Goltz, *Anatolische Ausflüge* (Berlin, 1896).
68. C. Humann and O. Puchstein, *Reisen in Kleinasien und Nordsyrien* (Berlin, 1890), pp. 405–6.
69. K. Buresch and O. Ribbeck, *Aus Lydien, epigraphische und geographische Reisefrüchte* (Leipzig, 1898), p. 108.
70. Ibid., Introduction, pp. vi–xii.
71. *BCH* 1 (1877), pp. 371–6.
72. *BCH* 2 (1878), pp. 289–98.
73. *BCH* 4 (1880), pp. 195–205.
74. P. Paris, 'Inscriptions de Sebaste', *BCH* 7 (1883), pp. 448–57.
75. M. Clerc, 'Inscriptions de Thyatire et ses environs', *BCH* 10 (1886), pp. 398–423.
76. P. Paris and M. Holleaux, *BCH* 9 (1885), p. 83. Another useful journey was that of C. Radet and P. Paris into southern Turkey (Pisidia, Lycaonia and Isauria), published in *BCH* 10 (1886), pp. 500–14.
77. G. Cousin, 'Inscriptions d'Oenoanda' (recording the discoveries by successive French expeditions since the origianal find by Paris and Holleaux in 1884), *BCH* 16 (1892), pp. 1–70.
78. G. Doublet, 'Inscriptions de Paphlagonie', *BCH* 13 (1889), pp. 293–319.
79. F. Cumont, 'Les inscriptions chrétiennes de l'Asie Mineure', *MEFR* 15 (1895), pp. 245–99.
80. Ibid., p. 247.
81. Ibid., p. 246.

FURTHER READING

M. Clerc, 'Inscriptions de Thyatire et ses environs', *BCH* 10 (1886), pp. 398–423.

Louis Duchesne, 'L'épitaphe d'Abercius', *MEFR* 15 (1895), pp. 155–82.

Gerhard Ficker, 'Die heidnische Character des Abercius Inschrift', *SBAW* (February 1894), pp. 87ff.

A. Harnack, 'Zur Abercius-Inschrift', *TU* 12.4b (1895).

J. Massingberd Ford, 'Was Montanism a Jewish-Christian heresy?', *JEH* 17 (1956), pp. 145–58.

S. Mitchell, 'Maximinus and the Christians in AD 312: a new Latin inscription', *JRS* 68 (1988), pp. 105–24.

S. Mitchell, *Anatolia: Land, Men and Gods in Asia Minor*, II: *The Rise of the Church* (OUP, 1993).

W. M. Ramsay, *The Church of the Roman Empire to AD 170* (London, 1893),

W. M. Ramsay, *St Paul, the traveller and the Roman Citizen* (London, 1896),

W. M. Ramsay, *Cities and Bishoprics of Phrygia* (2 vols; Oxford, 1895–97),

H. de Waal, 'Die Inschrift des Abercius', *RQ* 8 (1894), pp. 329–31.

For the controversy following Ficker's article, see H. Leclerq in *DACL* I, 86–87.

8

Following the flag, 1894–1914

The twenty years leading up to the outbreak of the First World War were the classic period of European scholarship, as they were of European imperialism. There seemed to be no reason why the dominance of the European empires over the rest of the planet should not last for ever, and similarly, the dominance of Europe in industry and the arts as well. The industrial power that enabled, for instance, the British to extend their empire in a great arc in the Indian Ocean from the Cape of Good Hope to Australia, or the French to control North Africa and much of sub-Saharan Africa, resulted in a steady advance in the living standards of most Europeans. This in turn created an increased public interest in the arts including scientific and archaeological discoveries. In Britain major civic universities at Birmingham and Manchester and the University of Wales received their charters. Liverpool (chartered in 1883) was to become a prime sponsor of fieldwork in Egypt and Nubia, which led to greatly increased knowledge of the once prosperous Christian civilizations there. Museums in towns, 'reading rooms' in villages, testified to the public's will to self-improvement. Elsewhere in Europe there were similar developments. In France, Germany and Austria-Hungary the great museums in the capitals were acquiring the lion's share of the portable discoveries made by their nationals in officially-sponsored excavations overseas. Europe led the world of scholarship in a way never again to be achieved.

Archaeology, and not least Christian archaeology, would play its part in enhancing the cultural life of western Europe. There was optimism regarding its potential and results. Thus, M. Noël Valois, ending his annual report to the Académie des Inscriptions et des Belles Lettres on 14 November 1913,[1] praised the work of young French archaeologists from Algeria to Cambodia, and declared his belief that in the coming year yet more of the veils that continued to 'hide a great portion of the secrets of the history of humanity' would be lifted. Such hopes were, alas, doomed to be sacrificed within that time to the rivalries of the Great Powers which underlay the successive crises before the war.

Major archaeological projects were themselves becoming matters of national pride. In Asia Minor while Ramsay and his colleagues subsisted (effectively) on grants from Aberdeen and Oxford universities, their colleagues from France, Germany and Austria-Hungary were carrying out grandiose programmes of excavation on prestigious sites on the coast, planned and subsidized by their respective Ministries of Culture. Ephesus, Pergamum, Priene and Miletus were among the prime mainland sites where the representatives of the Powers sought influence and concessions from the Ottoman authorities, with the same zeal that they drove strategic railways through Anatolia or established rival post offices in the major cities.

Religious antipathies also continued to simmer. The period witnessed the continuance of the siege mentality engendered by Vatican I expressed in suspicions of biblical and historical criticism. These were reflected by the encyclicals *Pascendi Gregis* (8 September 1907) and *Lamentabili* (July 1907), which placed intolerable burdens on the scholarship of men such as Alfred Loisy and even on the ever-loyal Louis Duchesne. In Jerusalem, Albert Lagrange was harassed by whisperings that his works of biblical criticism were tainted with 'rationalism' and 'modernism'. He felt obliged to write a profound submission 'on his knees' to the papal consistory imploring its blessing.[2] Such 'reform Catholics' were unwelcome. Conservative attitudes in Rome were hardened also by the radicalism of some New Testament critics, such as Karl Kautsky, whose *Foundations of Christianity* (1908) suggested that Christ himself never lived,[3] and Albert Schweitzer, whose *Quest of the Historical Jesus* emphasized the apocalyptic elements in Jesus' recorded teaching. There was, too, just enough new archaeological material from Asia Minor regarding the beliefs and religious practices of peoples in the ancient Near East for scholars to draw parallels between these and Christian doctrine and liturgy, and imply that Christianity was no more credible than a mystery religion. Thus the idea of the suffering god could be parallelled in the cult of Attis, the resurrection in that of Osiris, judgement in the beliefs of the Zoroastrians and the Eucharist in Mithraic rites. The School of the History of Religions associated with Loisy[4] and Richard Reitzenstein[5] carried considerable conviction in the first decade of the century. Scholars of equal weight, however, such as Karl Holl would be asking why, if this were all true, did

Christianity prevail and become a world religion?[6] Similarities between Christianity and some major contemporary pagan cults existed but were not to be accounted for by mere borrowing by Paul and his successors. Some adaptation may have taken place during the early centuries, but the originality of the Christian message of salvation and liberation remained. No mystery religion preached the moral values emphasized by Christian leaders such as Origen (185–253) that attracted thousands to the faith. The Light of the World (*Lux Mundi*), Charles Gore had argued in 1889, could accept the insights provided by archaeological scholarship (he was thinking mainly of the Old Testament) without qualm.[7]

Unfortunately the hopes and ambitions of the archaeologists and architects who conducted major excavations in North Africa and Asia Minor were seldom matched by their skills.

The French would still be carrying out a great deal of the work. Since Napoleon's time archaeology overseas had been regarded as the handmaid of colonial and foreign policy. Metropolitan France, however, lacked an effective network of local archaeological societies such as existed in Britain, able to provide a background to successful work abroad and produce skilled excavators to support the efforts of the officials and architects in charge of overseas sites. Above all there was no French or European equivalent of General Pitt-Rivers, someone to teach from experience on the equivalent of Cranborne Chase the importance of accurate observation of levels and association of finds with these, without which archaeology ceases to be a science.

In this period the main objective on most sites was *déblayage*, the horizontal clearing and planning of large public buildings, with little concern either for stratigraphy or consideration how these buildings integrated into the life of the communities which had erected them. There was tendency, too, particularly in Asia Minor and in the Greek islands, to 'get rid of' the upper layers of sites, which would be those most likely to contain early Christian remains, so as to find treasures of earlier civilizations beneath and send back these to state museums as proof of success. At Delos, for instance, excavations in this period destroyed four churches and a monastic building in the diggers' zeal to find Classical buildings beneath them.[8] Only occasionally did more far-sighted scholars, such as Albert Ballu, chief architect of the Inspection des Monuments historiques in Algeria from 1889 to 1928 and the excavator of Timgad, remark on the significance of 'ruins that had been systematically destroyed' and of the 'finest paved roads encumbered by walls resting on the paving-stones themselves'. He noted how the columns once belonging to the theatre had been removed to build houses. Unfortunately he had destroyed the evidence that would have enabled him to suggest when and why, and to reconstruct the various phases in the life of the town.[9] As Stéphane Gsell pointed out, 500,000 francs had been spent on Timgad down to 1902. Everyone knew by now that the streets had been paved and the town laid out on a set plan. Money should have gone on smaller sites, including rural and early Christian localities.[10] Something, one might add, should have been left for his successors to work on.

Conscientious though he was, Ballu's identification of Christian monuments in Timgad did not go beyond the preconceptions of he day. Neither he nor his colleagues René Cagnat and Paul Monceaux, for instance, realized that the impressive buildings that occupied a five-acre eminence south-west of the city were not those of a Catholic monastery but the cathedral of Bishop Optatus (388–398) and a centre of Donatist pilgrimage and power.[11]

In every area open to Europeans, great efforts were being made by individuals working as field archaeologists and, in central Asia and Nubia, as explorers. The pace, however, was too hot even in an era when many believed in the permanent upward progress of mankind. Much was uncovered but much also was destroyed.

(1) French North Africa

'Faced with the difficulties that archaeological excavations are encountering at this moment in Italy, Greece and Turkey we sincerely hope that the Director of the Ecole française de Rome will continue to turn the scientific activities of young scholars whose research he directs towards the exploration of French Africa.' The difficulties proved to be temporary, but it was thus that the President of the Académie des Inscriptions et des Belles Lettres, M. Barbier de Meynard, pinned his hopes on North Africa in an address to his colleagues in November 1889.[12] In so doing he initiated a policy that was to continue uninterrupted until the Second World War.

The emphasis on 'French Africa' responded to the mood of the time. In 1891 the writer and historian Gaston Boissier, author of *L'Afrique Romaine*, addressed members of the annual congress of the Sociétiés savantes de France. 'The natives', he said, 'call us *roumis*. They look on us as the heirs and descendants of those who had long governed them and concerning whom they still retain a confused memory. Gentlemen, let us accept our heritage. We shall

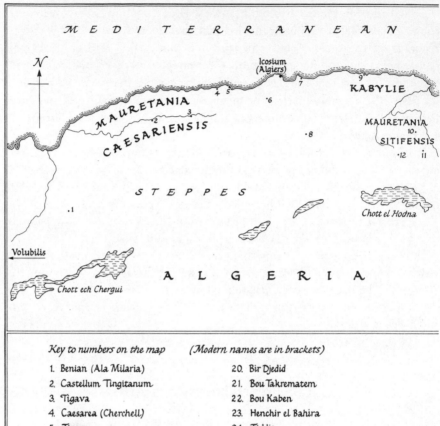

Key to numbers on the map   (Modern names are in brackets)

1. Benian (Ala Milaria)
2. Castellum Tingitanum
3. Tigava
4. Caesarea (Cherchell)
5. Tipasa
6. Tanaramusa Castra (Mouzaïaville)
7. Rusguniae (Matifou)
8. Gouea
9. Iomnium (Tigzirt)
10. Sertei
11. Thamalla (Tocqueville)
12. Equizetum
13. Satafis
14. Cuicul (Djemila)
15. Kherbet Bahrarous
16. Kherbet Bou Addoufen
17. Bir Younkene
18. Mechta Azrou
19. Azrou Zaouia
20. Bir Djedid
21. Bou Takrematem
22. Bou Kaben
23. Henchir el Bahira
24. Tiddis
25. Henchir Guessaria
26. Henchir el Ateuch
27. Henchir Akhrib
28. Zarai
29. Nif en Nisr
30. Ain Beida
31. Telergma (Ferme Laurent)
32. Bou Lhilet
33. Foum el Amba
34. Oued Rhezel
35. Seriana
36. Lambiridi
37. Foum Seffane
38. Ain Fakroun

Algeria and Tunisia

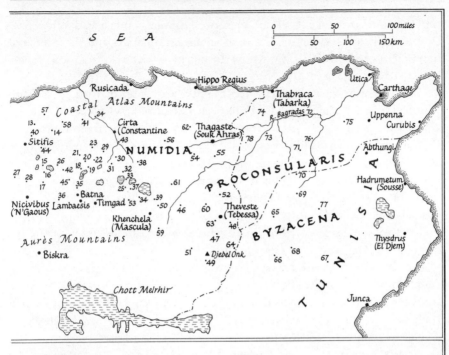

39. Bagai
40. Sillègue
41. Milevis
42. Nova Petra
43. Tigisis
44. Tixter (Oum el Adham)
45. Diana Veteranorum (Zana)
46. Ksar el Kelb
47. Rouis
48. Henchir Brisgane
49. Ain Telidjen (Manichaean documents)
50. Henchir Guesses
51. Ain Ghorab
52. Morsott
53. Henchir Ghorai
54. Thubursicum Numidarum (Khamissa)
55. Madaura
56. Thibilis (Announa)
57. Ain Regada
58. Rouffach

59. Zoui
60. Sef el Dalaa
61. Calama (Guelma)
62. Ain Zirara
63. Tebessa Khalia
64. Fundus Tuletanus
65. Ammaedara (Haidra)
66. Thelepte
67. Suffetula (Sbeitla)
68. Cillium (Kasserine)
69. Althiburos
70. Mactar
71. Thignica (Ain Tounga)
72. Abitina
73. Dougga
74. Bulla Regia
75. Furni
76. Thuburbo Maius
77. Hadjeb el Aioun
78. Sicca Veneria (Le Kef)

find it to our advantage ... We are merely continuing a great work of civilization. We take possession once more of an ancient domain, and these ancient monuments before which the Arabs do not pass without awe and respect. These are our title deeds.'[13]

These were brave words, repeated twenty years later in 1912 by another Classical historian, Jules Toutain.[14] They echoed also the views of the Church whose leaders continued in the tradition of Lavigerie, regarding Roman and Byzantine Christian buildings as part of its inheritance. Thus on 21 October 1894 the bishop of Constantine, Mgr Laférrière, celebrated Mass in the newly-excavated 'Catholic cathedral' (north church) of Timgad. His predecessor but one, Mgr Robert, an enthusiast, had himself excavated the apse of the main basilica at Thibilis (Announa) during his short episcopate in the mid-1870s. As already noted he found wholehearted support from among his clergy in the Department of Constantine.

Not everyone in Algeria accepted the practical consequences of the Christian heritage. The arrival of the first *scolaires* from Rome in 1890, Auguste Audollent and J. Letaille, helped stem the prevalent vandalism against Roman remains, the 'fureur de destruction qui possède certains habitants', as Audollent reported.[15] Such attitudes must seem extraordinary but it was only luck and the sharp eye of an engineer that preserved for posterity one of the most important individual Christian inscriptions from North Africa which Audollent discusses in detail. Curious writing and decoration on a large stone probably from a basilica unearthed during road construction near Tixter (Oum el Adham) aroused his interest and he informed Audollent.[16] The inscription recorded the commemoration by two Christians, Pequaria and Benenatus, in 359 on a *mensa martyrum* (a flat stone on which an altar would be erected and dedicated to martyrs) 'the wood of the Cross from the land of promise where Christ was born', followed by 'the apostles Peter and Paul' and 'the names of the martyrs (*nomina martyrum*), Datian, Donatian, Cyprian, Nemesian, Citin and Victoria', with the Mauretanian provincial date of 320 = 359, to which had been added later, above the main inscription, 'Victorinus, Miggin, seven Ides September' (= 7 September). The sacred monogram within a crown cut in relief and the words 'memoria sa(n)cta' had been inscribed in the centre of the stone.[17]

Audollent was able to solve much of the puzzle presented by what still appears to be an extraordinary mixture of names of persons and relics – wood of the cross, apostles, bishops and local martyrs. Cyprian was the martyr-bishop of Carthage (d. 14 September 258). Nemesian was in all probability bishop of Tubunae (Tobna), a correspondent of Cyprian, who in 257 had been condemned to the mines.[18] Datianus and Victoria figured among the martyrs of Abitina, victims of the Great Persecution in 304.[19] Miggin and Cittin were native martyrs, the former despised by pagans as typical of the rejection of civilization identified with the cult of martyrs.[20] The veneration of the True Cross, Audollent was able to parallel from an inscription from Rusguniae (27 km east of Algiers) from a church built by Flavius Nuvel (Nubel?) in 373. He was probably the Kabyle chief and father of Firmus who led a revolt against Roman authority 372–375.[21] The apostles Peter and Paul featured on the inscription from Ain Ghorab mentioned previously (p. 66).

The pattern of orthodoxy seemed evident, but there were some features not easily explicable. Victorinus and Miggin appear on Jerome's *Martyrology*, but not on 7 September. Peter and Paul were associated also with native martyrs such as Mettun and Baric not mentioned on any martyrology and with the Abitinian confessor, Emeritus.[22] The Abitinians, apart from being steadfast upholders of the faith, were also reckoned opponents of the archdeacon Caecilian, whose election as bishop of Carthage in 311/312 set off the Donatist schism.[23] Cyprian was also regarded by the Donatists as one who had upheld the exclusive nature of the Church and consecrated his views by his martyrdom. Finally, the True Cross; this had been allegedly discovered by the empress Helena in 326 but not before 415 did it become popular with other relics from the Holy Land as a relic among Catholic North Africans.[24] Instead Augustine, writing to his Donatist cousin Severinus *c.* 400, complained that 'if anyone brought them [the Donatists] a bit of earth from the east they would worship it'.[25] It looks as though this was what may have happened, and Audollent had recovered a priceless fragment of information concerning Donatist liturgy in the mid-fourth century.

Audollent's pleas for the establishment of more local museums was partially successful and collections were formed at Tebessa, Khenchela, Annouina and Constantine itself, all containing early Christian material. His and Letaille's journey through the country north of the Aurès mountains, however, confirmed Masqueray's view that here was 'a vast field for the study of Christian archaeology'. His words were heeded by a young lecturer at the Ecole des Lettres (soon to be a university) at Algiers, who had already made his mark as a Classicist and archaeologist, Stéphane Gsell (1864–1932).

Gsell is one of the 'greats' in North African archaeology, his importance there the equal to Ramsay's in Asia Minor. His interests, like Berbrugger's before him, spanned the entire range of antiquity from Berber-Neolithic to early-Arab, in which the discovery and record of early-Christian antiquities claimed a major place. His family were Swiss Protestants from St Gall originally but also had links with Protestants in Alsace.[26] His father was a painter and had moved the family to Paris, where Stéphane was born on 7 February 1864. He had a brilliant scholastic career, obtaining the top *agrégation* in history at the Ecole Normale (entered in 1883) in 1886. His next four years were spent as a student at the Ecole française at Rome where he carried out the excavation of an Etruscan cemetery at Vulci which was praised highly for its detailed observation and precise work,[27] and, at the same time, prepared a thesis on the emperor Domitian. Friendship with Louis Duchesne drew him to Christian archaeology in North Africa. In November 1890 he was appointed *Chargé de Cours* at the Ecole des Lettres at Algiers. Next year he embarked on what turned out to be three years of intensive work at Tipasa, first with Duchesne and then with Abbé J. B. de Saint-Gérand, *curé* of Tipasa. This resulted in a series of major discoveries, including that of the 'great basilica' there.[28]

The site had attracted attention for the previous fifty years. Duchesne pointed out an area on a promontory west of the city walls where the owner of most of the area, M. Trémaux, was prepared to allow excavations.[29] In 1892, working with de Saint-Gérand, Gsell uncovered a late fourth-century basilica built by Bishop Alexander who had recorded on a mosaic inscription that the basilica contained the graves of the 'iusti priores', in all probability his predecessors. Nine stone coffins were found in a crypt below the altar and, given a reasonable length of time for each episcopate,[30] Tipasa would have had its bishop since the mid-third century. The fervent Christian belief prevailing among the inhabitants in the fourth century was demonstrated by Gsell's excavation of the vast basilica measuring 52 m by 45 m, excluding the apse, with seven aisles and floors paved with mosaic, just within the north-west wall of the city (plan in Gsell, *Tipasa*, p. 359). Previously, outside the east boundary of Tipasa amidst many hundreds of tombs extending in date to Punic times, he and de Saint-Gérand had found what they could claim reasonably as the church covering the tomb of the martyr St Salsa, allegedly a maiden aged fourteen and the victim of the Great Persecution. The church was smaller than that at the opposite side of the town, having three aisles separated by arcades. It had been built in the mid-fourth century, enlarged in the middle of the fifth century by Bishop Potentius and again during Byzantine times. While the tomb itself was a third-century cylindrical stone memorial to 'Fabia Salsa', a *matrona* who died at the age of 64, pious imagination and plaster over the precise details of the deceased converted it into the tomb of the fourteen-year-old martyr, and it was placed at a point of honour in the middle of the nave of the church.[31] At least from 362, however, Tipasa had opted for the Catholic side in the Donatist–Catholic controversy. Bishop

Alexander proclaimed his allegiance. The citizens had resisted Donatist
attack in 362–363[32] and twelve years later provided Count Theodosius with a
safe headquarters in his war against the pro-Donatist rebel Firmus.[33] For
three centuries, until sometime in the seventh century, the church of St Salsa
remained a centre of pilgrimage, including pilgrims from overseas. Even when
the basilica itself was destroyed by fire an effort had been made to preserve
the tomb but this, too, succumbed finally to flame and destruction: the date
of this event even Gsell's careful excavation failed to reveal satisfactorily.

Success at Tipasa was followed by an important journey of record and
exploration in the country north of the Aurès mountains. In company with
Henri Graillot of the Ecole française Gsell planned to follow up the work of
Masqueray and Audollent but concentrating on non-Classical antiquities.
Their report, together with a survey of sites north and west of Ain Beida, was
published in consecutive numbers of the *Mélanges de l'Ecole française de Rome*
and was a model of its kind. It threw light not only on the extent of the Christian antiquities in the area, but on their nature and probable Donatist
allegiance. They told something also of the economic life of the inhabitants
and, perhaps most interesting of all, of the non-Classical, Berber, artistic tradition that found its outlet on the stonework cut by masons for the chancels
and entrances of the church.[34]

The archaeologists' route lay along the line of the Roman military road
that had once linked the fortress towns of Timgad and Zarai. These fortress
settlements had been designed to block the valleys leading out of the Aurès
mountains to the more open country beyond. This, and the high plains to the
north of Ain Beida which they also explored, was Numidia, Berber country,
and so remained to a great extent as late as 1939. In the first century AD the
Musulamii, a nomadic tribe who fought against Roman occupation, had been
dominant. Nomadism had, however, given way to settled agriculture made
possible by planting olives as a crop that could flourish in dry conditions.
These geographical conditions resulted in there being few towns and only a
scattering of large villa establishments in southern and central Numidia. The
overwhelming majority of the people lived in villages, *coloni* on the imperial or
private domains that seem to have occupied much of the area.[35] Berbers
though they were, they had accepted the Punic religion of Baal-Hammon, disguised in Roman form as Saturn, supreme over the crops and herds and over
life and death, whose command, sometimes communicated to the worshipper
in a dream, required blood sacrifice. By the third century a lamb could be
substituted for the original human victim.[36] Down to the middle of that century shrines in honour of this all-powerful but ill-humoured and feared deity

dominated the religious life of the whole region. Sacred sites or temples dedicated to Saturn were to be found in city and village alike. Then, quite suddenly, probably in no more than a generation (*c.* 260–290), the religion of the great majority of the Numidians swung irreversibly towards a biblically-inspired form of Christianity in which the blood-sacrifice of martyrdom replaced the blood-sacrifice to Saturn. This was southern and central Numidia, the heartland of the Donatist movement.[37]

Gsell and Graillot were convinced of the overwhelmingly Christian character of the whole area from the fourth century until the Arab conquest. 'After the peace of the Church', they wrote, 'Christianity north of the Aurès experienced an extraordinarily intense life. Everywhere churches and chapels were built, whose architecture or their symbols allow us to date from the end of the fourth century to the beginning of the fifth century.'[38] This dating may have been correct in some cases, but future researches were inclined to accept it literally, with the result that too little attention was paid to church building earlier in the fourth century, and to occupation and reconstruction in the Vandal and Byzantine periods. But in the state of then existing knowledge the assessment was fair.

Rural life revolved round churches, olive presses and granaries. There were few if any public buildings such as would be associated with Roman towns. One inscription showed how a large church was built by the co-operation of three tribes or extended kin.[39] Others were built by clergy or individual worshippers, often in memory of a martyr. The most important discovery, however, came from a local museum preserving inscriptions salvaged from the sites around the Roman town of Mascula (Khenchela) which had been ransacked for stone. A group of rectangular flat stone panels had been decorated with a finely executed chequer-board pattern in low relief; the centre was occupied by a Christian monogram, and in one case by the Donatist watchword 'Deo laudes'; the lower register was occupied by the stylized carving of a doorway. The art owed nothing to Classical models, and the doorway was reminiscent of the decoration sometimes found on the false doorways of megalithic tombs.[40]

The expedition had fulfilled all expectations and prepared the ground for intensive working the same area by the Ecole française and by André Berthier of the Musée Gustave Mercier at Constantine in the 1930s. (See below, p. 231.) It was only expected, also, that Audollent's and Gsell's researches would arouse interest among scholars in Europe. In 1893 Walter Thümmel, a young Lutheran pastor at the University of Halle in central Germany, submitted a thesis for his licenciate entitled *Zur Beurtheilung des Donatismus* ('Towards an assessment of Donatism'). Thümmel was able to combine

Duchesne's researches published in the *Mélanges de l'Ecole de Rome* of 1890 which established the authenticity of all or nearly all the documents on the outbreak of the Donatist controversy preserved by Optatus of Milevis (*c.* 365), with the latest archaeological evidence. He considered that while there was a theological dimension in the Donatist controversy the strife could not have lasted for so long – over a century – unless it had been sustained by other factors. These Thümmel defined as 'Berber nationalism'.[41] He pointed to the Numidian origins of many of the Donatist leaders and Donatism's support among rural communities, and to an apparent coincidence of Donatism with areas in which a native language, which he believed was Punic, survived. This brought him to conclude that Donatism was an essentially native revolt against the Catholic church in North Africa which drew its support from the non-romanized classes.

Thümmel had opened up a new and promising line of research in North African Church history, not least because in the same year Gsell and Graillot themselves had pointed to the identity of the intensely Christian region north of the Aurès as 'the centre of Donatism', and also the rural character of the late-Roman occupation.[42] Far from welcoming Thümmel's research, however, Gsell poured cold water on it. In a short, carping review in the *Mélanges* of 1895, he pointed out that the Donatists were not anti-Roman. Only the Circumcellions participated in social revolt, and that in many details, especially geographical, Thümmel was inaccurate.[43] It was an ungenerous assessment showing that Gsell, too, could be as possessive towards French pre-eminence in Algeria as Boissier or Lavigerie. Outsiders, especially Germans, were to be discouraged.

In the same year 1895 Gsell, now titular professor of *Antiquités d'Afrique* at the Ecole des Lettres, took over a feature in the Mélanges that had been started by Jules Toutain.[44] The 'Chronique archéologique africaine' brought to a wider public immediate knowledge of the results of archaeological research in Algeria and Tunisia, with a considerable emphasis on early-Christian discoveries. In the ten years of its life under Gsell Christian sites of great importance were recorded. Among these was the church at Morsott, north of Theveste, a building 45 m long from which a large quantity of fragments of Communion vases was recovered, suggesting intense congregational participation in the liturgy.[45] Another equally imposing building was excavated at Cap Matifou (Rusguniae) by Commandant Chardon in 1899–1900, belonging to a wealthy congregation.[46] Before this Gsell had recorded further work by himself on the churches at Satafis and Thamalla in Mauretania Sitifensis.[47] In 1897 he published a report prepared by Pierre Gavault, *Inspecteur des édifices départementaux d'Alger* on the great basilica at Tigzirt (Iomnium), who had died in 1895 before his work had been completed. The church, one of five now known to have existed in this Donatist see on the coast east of Algiers, had been preserved from destruction when the French village was built in 1867. The floors were covered entirely with mosaic, geometric patterns predominating, but some were inscribed, probably with the names of donors. As important were the architectural fragments, the capitals of columns which were decorated in the same type of low-relief wood-carving technique and patterns that had been found on sites north of the Aurès, another example of native tradition finding a new vigour through Donatist Christianity.[48]

Two years later, in 1899, Gsell made a further discovery relating to the Donatists, this time in the military zone in the far west of Algeria, at Ala Miliara (Benian). The church he discovered on the east side of the Roman fort had been built on earlier military and religious foundations. In the crypt were a number of burials dating between 422 and 446 of Donatist clergy including successive bishops of Ala Miliara and Robba, and a *sanctimonialis* (woman in vows) who was murdered by the *traditores* (Catholics) at the age of 50 on 22 March 434, more than twenty years after Donatism had been formally proscribed by imperial decree (30 January 412). The Vandal invasion five years before had not ended sectarian strife.[49]

In 1901 Gsell, now Inspector of Antiquities in Algeria, published his two-volume *Monuments antiques de l'Algérie*, the second volume of which was devoted almost entirely to Christian remains. Here were listed 169 churches already discovered, from large basilicas in Roman towns to insignificant chapels in the Numidian countryside, many of which he had found himself. The publication coincided with Charles Diehl's *L'Afrique byzantine,* itself the product of careful survey-work on the ground. Some of Diehl's ideas may be challenged today, relating to the strategic planning behind the location of Byzantine fortresses, but the plans and photographs are a unique record of the buildings as they stood in the 1890s before stone-robbers got seriously to work on them.

In 1902 Gsell excavated a small but important church in south-western Numidia at Henchir Akhrib where for the first time he found in the form of a reliquary evidence of an assimilation of Byzantine saints (Pastor and Julian) into the native Christian martyrology (the martyrs Felix and Cassian) during the Byzantine occupation (534–c. 660).[50]

In 1904 and 1905 Gsell worked with C. A. Joly, continuing the excavations carried out earlier in the main church at Thibilis (Announa). From 1912 onwards, however, he was mainly in Paris,[51] having been appointed Professor of North African history at the Collège de France. Meantime he had been preparing what must be regarded as his most important study of Algerian archaeology, the *Atlas archéologique de l'Algérie* published in 1911. It was founded on military maps (which also had noted antiquities) based on a 1/200,000 scale, but combined accurate geography with the marking and short description of every known prehistoric, Roman, early-Christian and Byzantine site, together with references to existing reports. In the four sheets covering central Numidia, Gsell recorded 1,200 sites.[52] In the later Roman period, there was a village with its church or chapel every 2½ miles. Some of these villages were very large, like Kherbet Bahrarous where the writer was working in 1938 and 1939 which covered 50–60 acres (20–30 hectares).[53] Herodian's comment, made *c.* 240, that Libya (North Africa) was heavily populated and, hence, well farmed[54] was confirmed, and in the fourth century this large rural population was overwhelmingly Donatist-Christian.

In the years 1900–14 work was continuing in Algeria unabated. This has still remained the most intensive period of archaeological research there. Nearly all the splendid ruins of Roman cities that greet the tourist were uncovered in the years before the First World War. Timgad first. Despite Gsell's criticism of the waste of money on what he regarded as repetitive effort, work continued through the decade 1900–11. By then ten of the eleven known churches had been brought to light, the plan of the 'monastery' and its imposing baptistery excavated,[55] and work started on what proved to be a huge Christian cemetery on a hill south of the city containing some 15,000 graves, mainly poor tile covered burials, the bodies laid out in plaster so that their features would be preserved in the Last Day.

While Ballu was working at Timgad, C. Joly was completing excavation of 'the great church' at Thibilis (1906), as well as finding what was possibly the Byzantine cathedral church.[56] In 1912 Joly turned his attention to Madaura which had remained a pagan stronghold as late as the 380s,[57] but where he found and excavated a basilica.[58] In the same year. Ballu moved to Djemila, where he began the long process of uncovering the cathedral, baptistery, ecclesiastical offices and dedications to martyrs – the complete Christian quarter that had grown up on high ground to the south-west of the town.[59] In the countryside an energetic administrator of the *Commune mixte* of Ain el Ksar renewed work on the large church at Henchir Guessaria.[60] The equally keen *Chef de Bataillon, Commandant Supérieur du Cercle de Tébessa*, E. Guénin, excavated a Byzantine fort, and in 1907 drew up an inventory of inscriptions, many of them Christian, in his area.[61] Among the few potentially important sites that witnessed only the beginnings of major excavations was Hippo Regius, Augustine's see. These would have to await the period immediately succeeding the Second World War.[62]

Meantime a great deal was happening in Tunisia. The establishment of the French Protectorate had provided scope for the same grouping of architects and archaeologists in government service, army officers, interested settlers and enthusiastic amateurs to research and restore the magnificent Roman, Christian and Byzantine remains that confronted them almost everywhere. The Medjerda valley alone, leading south-west from the Gulf of Tunis, contained no fewer than 200 sizeable Roman settlements, and throughout the fertile areas in the north extending across the central steppes to the Chott el Djerid there were a vast number of occupation sites ranging from farm settlements to once populous cities such as Thysdrus, Thelepte, Sbeitla and Ammaedara some of which had been visited by travellers a century before. In addition, the Protectorate government saw the immediate advantage of research connected with the numerous water cisterns that had survived centuries of nomadic occupation as a means of bringing land apparently desert back into cultivation.[63] The successive reports by Paul Gauckler assisted by a team of army officers of the *Brigade Topographique* and by *contrôleurs civils*, on the various types of water installations discovered throughout Tunisia between 1895 and 1900, opened the way to the exploration of more major sites and further evidence for the spread and development of Christianity.

Leadership by the Direction des Antiquités et Arts, actively seconded by army officers and settlers, was responsible for major excavations at Dougga (Dr Carton and Abbé Chabot), Uchi Majus (Henchir Douemis) (Merlin and Poinssot), Bulla Regia and Althiburus (Merlin), Thuburbo Maius (Poinssot) and Ammaedara (Sadoux and Gsell) between 1897 and 1913. Though large public buildings of the first three centuries were the main preoccupation, numerous discoveries relating to early Christianity were also made. At Ammaedara, Sadoux discovered and wrote a preliminary report on what proved to be the 'church of Bishop Melleus', who lived in the reign of Justin II (565–578). His name is preserved as the bishop presiding over the deposition of relics of Cyprian in the church in 568/569.[64] At Uchi Majus, the cemetery produced inscriptions, including a dedication to the virgin Eulalia which recalls the Spanish martyr during the Great Persecution. Was there a cult in her honour in North Africa?[65] In 1909 Merlin reported the discovery near Hadjeb el Aioun of a number of square panels made of tiles, probably hung on the walls of a fifth- to sixth-century church. The scenes depicted included the temptation of Adam and Eve, Daniel in the lions' den, and also a mounted military figure destroying a serpent, named as St Theodore, a Byzantine military saint (suggesting, in this church also, a blend of traditional North African and Byzantine martyr-theology).[66] At Sbeitla (Suffetula) work on the site known to eighteenth-century travellers was begun in 1907 and continued to 1922, during which time Alfred Merlin published churches and temples he found as he excavated the forum in the Roman and Byzantine town.[67]

Most spectacular were the series of magnificent mosaics found at Tabarka on the coast. A Christian cemetery there had already been known since 1884, which produced a dedication to Anastasia and her companions, but it was left to another military archaeologist to make the discoveries for which Tabarka has become famous. Capitaine Benet, the officer commanding a detachment based at this strategically important coastal town, began to excavate a large church built round what appeared to be a martyr's tomb. To his amazement as his work advanced he found the choir filled with burials many of which had been richly ornamented with mosaics. Altogether 33 complete mosaics were found. These remain a classic series, unmatched examples of North African Christian art in the second half of the fourth century and important witnesses to the triumphant beliefs of Christians at this time. There is a scribe standing, pen poised behind his table, as though recording the *Acta* of a martyr. Another mosaic depicts a church with the details of its construction from atrium to apse and with burning candles on the altar. This was the *ecclesia mater* of the faithful. Another tomb commemorated Crescentianus 'companion of the martyrs'. The names of the deceased are recorded, encircled by crowns of martyrdom. One, that of Privata and Victoria, bore the acclamation 'Gaude triumfa consecratae virginitatis et confessionis victricia portentes tropaea veste'. With yet another acclamation 'Digna dignis, vincentibus corona', it is difficult not to see Donatist influence in these inscriptions. Paul Gauckler, *Directeur des Antiquités et des Beaux-Arts* in Tunisia, described and analysed Benet's discoveries.[68] The basilica was a vast funerary chapel, its nave filled with burials; many were those of martyrs transported thither from elsewhere. There were nine layers of tombs followed by a destruction layer on top of which were found Byzantine graves. But here also, faulty excavation allowed too many questions to remain unanswered. When was the original basilica built? What was its relation to the two monasteries referred to by Victor Vitensis *c.* 490?[69] What was the persecution that claimed so many victims – Diocletian's, Catholic measures against the Donatists, or Vandal against the Catholics? When was the church destroyed, and by whom? The excavators did not say and the means of discovery have now in all probability been lost. Brilliant artistic remains had been preserved but a record of events that caused their assemblage has almost certainly perished.

Work at Carthage under the energetic guidance of Delattre continued to reward. In 1895 after work on a first- to second-century AD cemetery apparently reserved for the use of officials and their families, he had turned to the amphitheatre which had witnessed the deaths of Perpetua and her companions. It was unfortunately a typical *déblayage* resulting in the reconstruction of the plan, at the expense of the removal of stratigraphical evidence. Further excavations of a finely decorated fifth-century(?) *hypogaeum* (funerary vault) on the Byrsa and cemeteries both pagan and Christian followed, until in 1906 his attention was drawn to a patch of rising ground at Mcidfa north-west of the city, covered with olive trees.[70] Some fragments of inscriptions had been found, and Delattre began excavations in March 1906. Already his first season revealed a very large church (61 m long and 45 m wide, with the central nave 16 m across and seven aisles in all) and surrounding cemetery which yielded more than 3,300 inscribed fragments. On 20 March 1907 Delattre came on fragments of a greyish marble tablet, probably of Byzantine date, recording the names of Felicitas, Saturus and Revocatus, the martyr Perpetua's companions. In the next days further pieces filled in the names of Saturninus and Perpetua herself. The possibility that he had discovered not only the Basilica Majorum traditionally associated with Perpetua,[71] but the site of the martyr's tomb itself was strengthened when he found what appeared to be a *c.* third-century inscription reading simply 'Perpetue filie dulcissimae' in letters 3 cm high while another bore the family name of Vibia.[72] One of a group of three large decorated sarcophagi contained a body wrapped in gold cloth while another nearby contained that of a child. Final honours to an obstinate but dearly loved daughter and her young child, or coincidences, we do not know; but whatever the answer, the church was centred on an elaborate *confessio*, a small chapel (3.60 × 3.70 m) placed in the middle of the main nave, covered with mosaic and set in the midst of a vast cemetery, burials being found wherever there was room. By the end of 1907 6,500 fragments of inscriptions had been recorded, and this number rose to more than 7,000. A few feet away from the *confessio* a pit was found filled with human bones down to a depth of 30 m – hundreds of bodies. The possibility struck Delattre that these could be the remains of Donatist supporters massacred in 317 whose fate was recorded in the Donatist saga, the *Passio Donati et Avocati*.[73] Again, except for the fact that nearly all inscribed fragments found were 'early', there can be no certainty. The inscriptions recovered show that the worshippers came from a wide span of occupations, including a *bestiarius* and a *medicus*. One group had died in a plague (*eripuit pesta*). The *area* (cemetery) and *confessio* could be as early as the third century. By the fourth century the site had developed into a huge cemetery basilica, and possibly one of the centres of Donatist Carthage.

At Sousse (Hadrumetum, down the coast) another soldier, Colonel Vincent of the 4me Tirailleurs, had come upon a Christian catacomb west of the town. From 1903 to 1905 he loaned soldiers 'on charge' (*disciplinaires*) as labour to work through the stifling galleries under the supervision of the *curé* of Sousse, Abbé (later Mgr) A. F. Leynaud, and Dr Carton. By the end of 1905, 260 *loculi* had been found and 100 metres of gallery cleared. (Eventually 10,000 burials were identified.) Marble plaques decorated with Christian symbols such as the Good Shepherd covered some of the tombs. Others showed the pathos of the times alongside the Christian hope. Victoria had died at the age of 28. Her infant son Lucilus was buried at her feet. A mosaic covered their tomb inscribed with the Christian monogram.[74]

The variety and amount of new discoveries were now beginning to have their effect on the approach of historians (but not yet theologians) to the history of early Christianity. In 1902 Harnack had regretted that there was not much help to be gained from material finds for his great *Mission and Expansion of Christianity in the First Three Centuries*.[75] Five years later Henri Leclercq gave a decisive answer to this pessimism. It remains a mystery how this Belgian Benedictine monk, whose first inclinations were towards a military career and who had shown little early scholastic promise, became the greatest self-taught scholar of all time. He combined the ability to compile articles with an unerring sense of the important amid the detail of a mass of archaeological reports, and to write rapidly and convincingly on a very wide variety of topics relating to the early Church.[76] Leclercq himself was a French nationalist. He had little liking for German or Anglo-Saxon Protestant and lay scholarship. This applied also to the country, Britain, that gave him forty years of hospitality, the means of working in the British Museum, and of earning a livelihood as a chaplain after he had been secularized in 1924. Even so, the *Dictionnaire d'archéologie chrétienne et de liturgie*, the first volume of which was published by Fernard Cabrol, his superior at Farnborough Abbey, in 1907, with Leclercq as his assistant, was a massive work of fundamental importance. The whole series was not completed until 1943 (and the last volume published by H. I. Marrou in 1951). As one reads the articles written by Leclercq in North Africa before 1914, accompanying his two-volume *L'Afrique chrétienne* published in 1904, one can only be thankful that this superb compiler was on the scene at the right time.

If the skeleton of the Christian period of North African Church history had been provided by Leclercq, the flesh was added by Paul Monceaux. Monceaux had already written the first volume of his *Histoire littéraire de l'Afrique chrétienne* (Paris, 1901–23) in 1901 with a account of the possible Jewish origins of the North African Church[77] and a study of Tertullian. The second and third volumes were devoted to the Cyprian and the Catholic tradition in fourth-century North Africa respectively, but the fourth, fifth, sixth and seventh volumes concerned different aspects of the Donatist movement, stopping short however at St Augustine's career except for his relations with the Donatists.

Monceaux had worked on Numidian sites and was fascinated by the Donatists. His preliminary articles, however, in the *Journal des Savants*[78] never allowed their leaders to be anything better than just below par. Obstinacy, stupidity and arrogance were qualities often attributed to them. He was, however, the first scholar who sought to determine the influence of Donatism rather than its wrong-headedness. He set out to identify Donatist inscriptions and hence learn the organization and the liturgy as well as the viewpoint of the Donatist Church.[79] Continuation of the exclusive view of the Church of Cyprian's day was all-important, indicated by inscriptions confining entry to a church to 'the righteous' or 'the saints',[80] expressing the virtues of martyrdom and praise to God and devotion to the word of Scripture. 'In God I will praise the word. My conversation will rest in God with praise. I place my hope in God. I do not fear what man shall do to me' (cf. Psalm 55(56):11).[81] Exaltation of martyrdom and triumphant songs of praise, often inspired by the Psalms, filled their worship.[82] The ideal of the gathered community embattled against the world is expressed in inscriptions directly quoting Paul's letter to the Romans, 'If God is for us who is against us' (Rom 8:31),[83] and the all-important rite of baptism marking the believer's complete renunciation of the world. 'Praise to God over the waters of baptism by the people of Novar...',[84] and one can only regret that the rest of the inscription, together with so much else from this site, was lost.

Monceaux's work was supplemented in 1912, the same year as he published his chapter on Donatist inscriptions in vol. IV of the *Histoire littéraire*, by Père J. Mesnage's *L'Afrique chrétienne: évêchés et ruines antiques*. This was a scholarly gazetteer of North African archaeology revising and updating the work of Toulotte, twenty years before. Painstaking research enabled Mesnage to catalogue 1,800 sites with Christian remains and map the bishoprics recorded at the conference of Carthage in 411 when Donatist and Catholic bishops faced each other in a decisive trial of strength. The result confirmed literary evidence regarding the predominance of Donatism in Numidia and of Catholicism in the more Romanized proconsular Africa.[85] For Numidia, Mesnage's results were elaborated by Canon H. Jaubert in 1912–13 in his catalogue of Christian remains in Numidia and Mauretania Sitifensis. Together these were a permanent landmark in early-Christian research in North Africa.[86]

The outbreak of the war in 1914 interrupted Roman and Christian archaeology in its full vigour. Never again was the achievement of these years to be repeated. While there had been a tragic, avoidable loss of historical data, a great amount had been recovered in advance of the population explosion among the North African peoples that has since threatened to destroy archaeological remains for ever. There were always enough interested army officers, clergy and settlers to second the efforts of the Service des Monuments historiques in Algeria and Tunisia in its work of discovery, salvage and reconstruction. Mme Dufour digging up remains of buildings of Hippo Regius in her garden, or M. Chevillot hunting for objects in his, provided a background against which more expert work could succeed.[87] As a result much of the archaeological map of North Africa and Christianity's place in it had been established. Magnificent churches had been cleared and planned while the haul of inscriptions provided evidence for the beliefs and hopes of the Christian people, their organization and liturgy and, above all, of the division between Catholic and Donatist among them. Evidence for the transition between worship of Saturn and acceptance of Christianity in the late third century was emerging, as well as the social and economic changes in the countryside which seems to have accompanied that change of belief. The evidence provided by Optatus of Milevis (*c.* 365), and by Augustine a generation later, of a non-theological dimension to the Donatist movement were being discovered from research into the impact of Christianity in rural areas of Numidia. The long history of tension between the concepts of a universal Church as against those of a gathered community could be traced back into the patristic era. There was optimism that even more would be found out in future, thanks to archaeology. As Henri Leclercq himself wrote in 1904, 'Discoveries mainly archaeological were reducing imperceptibly but continuously the measure of our ignorance'.[88]

The gains and losses of this period may be summed up from work carried out on one major site. At Tebessa (Theveste) in the south-east corner of Algeria the ruins of the great church and its associated buildings had survived through the ages. As we have seen (above, p. 60), these ruins had challenged a succession of *curés* at Tebessa and officers of the Bureau arabe located there, and some excavation had taken place. It was, however, largely the needs of salvage, to stop the continuous robbing of the fine-cut stonework of the ruins by the *colons* in Tebessa, that spurred the Service des Monuments into five years of continuous excavations from 1888. The result was the restoration of the plan of the main complex and a chronology which seemed entirely convincing at the time, but which further excavations in the 1960s revealed as seriously flawed. Ballu believed that there were four periods of construction.[89] The first was a Constantinian phase resulting in an imposing three-naved basilica 46 m long and 22 m wide built on a raised podium, and preceded by an atrium (rectangular court in front of the entrance) adjoining a small trefoil-shaped chapel built on to the right or south side. The chapel was linked to the basilica itself by a flight of steps. It had been the resting-place for the large marble sarcophagus found by Commandant Sériziat in 1868, which had featured Christian Rome flanked by two other still unidentified figures. The floor of the basilica had been paved throughout with mosaic of brilliant naturalistic and geometric designs. A second phase concerned the approaches to the basilica. A wide paved square measuring 55 m × 42 m entered from a monumental gateway was built on the west side of the basilica. Later in a third phase a large building which had occupied one side of the square was divided into a series of chambers (monastic cells),[90] and a portico was added on either side of the entrance of the basilica. The whole complex was surrounded by a wall enclosing an area of 190 m × 90 m. This period, *c*. AD 400, marked the grandiose climax of the basilica's prosperity.

Apart from this last fact Ballu's reconstruction was proved to be seriously misleading. The whole complex with the exception of the trefoil chapel had been built, probably at one time, in the reign of Theodosius I (379–395), and oriented on the existing martyr's chapel.[91] The idea of a monastery attached to the basilica was speculative. However, Ballu was justified in believing that the basilica continued in use through much of the Vandal period, for tombs of that date were found, the latest being a child's tomb dating to AD 508.[92] Then came a massive destruction and fire to such an extent that the Byzantines did not restore the church but converted much of the space into a barracks. A small chapel was built for the use of the soldiers, or workmen employed in rebuilding Theveste at General Solomon's orders in 540. The barracks may also have been as speculative as the 'monastery', for the line of stables on one side of the courtyard seem to have been contemporary with the basilica complex and could have served pilgrims as well as the military 150 years later.

Where all were agreed, from the time of Abbé Delapart's suggestion in the 1860s to the twentieth century, was that the great basilica and trefoil chapel were both connected with honouring the martyr Crispina (martyred 5 December 304). It was also evident that the destruction of the complex had occurred *c*. 520, at the hands of either Aurès Berbers or the even more deadly Louata nomads. The writer may claim that when he visited the site in 1939 he preferred the idea of a pilgrimage centre to the prevailing theory of a 'monastery'. He also wondered how the association of Theveste with the Donatist council *c.* 363, recorded by Optatus of Milevis (*De Schismate Donatistarum* ii.18), fitted into Ballu's picture. The verse epitaph in mosaic covering the tomb of the virgin Urbica found in the atrium of the great basilica included a triumphant 'laudes in excelsis' instead of the usual 'gloria in excelsis', 'Deo laudes' being the Donatist war-cry.[93] These problems remain. They were not addressed by Ballu and his colleagues, nor was stratigraphy used, while the numerous coins and pottery sherds from the site were neglected. Even the mosaics were not safeguarded from deterioration and vandalism.[94] Visitors were provided with a splendid Christian site to admire but much of its history was lost; the story of North African archaeology to 1914.

FURTHER READING

A. Audollent, *Carthage romaine* (Paris, 1901).

A. Audollent (with J. Letaille), 'Voyage épigraphique en Algérie', *MEFR* 10 (1890), pp. 397–588.

A. Ballu, *Les ruines de Timgad: sept années de découvertes* (Paris, 1911).

G. Boissier, *L'Afrique romaine*, Eng. trans. (New York, 1899) *Roman Africa*.

G. Boissier, *La fin du paganisme* (Paris, 1903).

J. Christern, *Das frühchristliche Pilgerheiligtum von Tebessa* (Wiesbaden, 1976).

Louis Duchesne, 'Le dossier du Donatisme', *MEFR* 10 (1890), pp. 590–643.

P. Gauckler, 'Mosaïques tombales d'une chapelle de martyrs à Thabraca', *Monuments Piot* 13 (1907), pp. 173–207.

R. Gavault, *Etude sur les ruines romaines de Tigzirt*, fasc. II (Paris: Ministere d'Instruction publique, 1897).

S. Gsell, 'Tipasa', *MEFR* 14 (1894), pp. 291–450.

S. Gsell, *Monuments antiques de l'Algérie* (2 vols, Paris, 1901).

S. Gsell and Henri Graillot, 'Exploration archéologique dans le départment de Constantine', *MEFR* 13 (1893), pp. 461–541; 14 (1894), pp. 17–86.

H. Leclercq, *L'Afrique chrétienne* (2 vols; Paris, 1904).

J. Mesnage, *L'Afrique chrétienne, évêchés et ruines antiques* (Paris: Leroux, 1912).

P. Monceaux, *Histoire littéraire de l'Afrique chrétienne* (7 vols; Paris: Leroux, 1901–23), especially IV.

P. Monceaux, *Timgad chrétien* (Paris: Imprimerie nationale, 1911).

K. von Nathusius, *Zur Charakteristik der Circumcellionen* (Greifswald, 1900).

W. Thümmel, *Zur Beurtheilung des Donatismus* (Halle, 1893).

J. Toutain, *Les cités romaines de la Tunisie* (Paris, 1896).

J. Toutain, *Les cultes païens dans l'Empire romain* (3 vols; Paris: Leroux, 1920).

(2) Asia Minor and further south

The story of Christian archaeology in Asia Minor between 1895 and 1914 differs from that in North Africa. In both areas there was great activity and effort, in Asia Minor fuelled by increased scholarly interest in Acts and the Pauline epistles as history. Whereas, however, in North Africa work was monopolized by the French, in Asia Minor it mirrored the rivalries of the European powers France, Austria-Hungary, and Germany to win influence over the weak but strategically placed Ottoman empire.[95] In archaeological terms they struggled to secure *firmans* (authorizations) to excavate prestigious sites to enhance their standing in Constantinople and enrich their national museums. In this fierce competition the goal was the treasures of Classical archaeology. Upper levels of sites, even of New Testament fame and containing early-Christian antiquities, were often ignored and swept away.

We can start, however, with *Britain* and Ramsay and his pupils working mainly in the interior of Anatolia. In contrast to the Continental countries, their research was funded by universities and private sources rather than by national Ministries of Culture carrying out government policy. At this period, however, the British system had advantages. Instead of concentrating on the discovery of *trésors scientifiques* with the emphasis on *trésors*, and undertaking expensive and not always productive *Reisen* (archaeological travels) through Asia Minor, the British were obliged to concentrate on individual inland sites already visited which promised the best scholarly results acceptable to their university paymasters.

Ramsay had returned to Aberdeen in 1891 to spend the next eight years lecturing and writing up the results of ten years' incessant fieldwork told in *The Church in the Roman Empire to AD 170* (1893) and his masterpiece, *Cities and Bishoprics in Phrygia* (2 vols: Oxford, 1895 and 1897). He did not come back to Asia Minor until 1899. Meantime, his student J. G. C. Anderson had explored the Lake Tatta region of Phrygia, and in 1895 revisiting the Tembris valley found an important inscription recording a petition by the *coloni* of Araguë to the emperor Philip (244–249) protesting against exactions by soldiers and officials.[96] The inscription shows an articulate and independent community whose representatives could express themselves in good Greek. Though there is no hint of Christianity on the inscription, which starts with the normal invocation to Agathē Tychē (Favourable Fate), one may place this alongside the equally determined 'Christians for Christians' inscriptions from the same area as an indication of the spirit of these farmers on a imperial estate at a period when the transition from paganism to Montanist Christianity was beginning.

Apart from confidence in their faith, the qualities which were praised on these latter inscriptions, of which Anderson found another nine, included 'showing kindly hospitality towards strangers'.[97] This was a virtue attributed wryly by the emperor Julian to the Christians in Asia Minor a century later.[98]

Ramsay returned to the scene at the end of the century and in the next years (1904–05) explored the borderlands of Lycaonia and Isauria, finding further evidence for crypto-Christianity among the inhabitants during the third century.[99] In 1905 and 1907 a hard trek brought him to the Kara Dagh (Black Mountain) and to the site of Bin Bir Kilisse (Thousand and One Churches) 160 km (100 miles) east of Konya (Iconium), which he had visited earlier in his career in 1882.[100] This was and remains one of the most spectacular early-Christian sites in Asia Minor. It occupies a plateau surrounded on three sides by mountains, the Kara Dagh to the south rising to 2,000 m (7,000 ft). In the fifth century AD it was, he believed, the town of Barata (Maden Shehir) centred on a spectacular group of churches and monasteries. While some scholars had tended to place these as no later than the seventh century, Ramsay remained convinced that they spanned almost the entire history of Byzantine church architecture from the fifth to the eleventh century, and he was almost certainly right. The site had survived the first Muslim raids of the latter part of the seventh century, but in the early ninth century pressure from the Arabs increased and it seems that the inhabitants retreated to the protection of the mountains to the north, founding another ecclesiastical settlement there. They returned to the original site at the time when the victories of John Tzimisces and Basil I had thrown back the Arabs from Asia Minor and much of Syria (960–1025). Abandonment was due to the attacks of the more successful Ottoman invasions *c.* 1100, and the site was never re-occupied. Hence there survived an astonishing assemblage of churches, monasteries and houses, built from stone quarried from the Kara Dagh, preserved for posterity. There were some 28 churches and monasteries on the plateau and almost the same number in the refuge site to the north. Many of the visible remains appear to date from the latest phase of occupation, 850–1100.

The site was first visited by James Hamilton in 1836 and thereafter had become a magnet to attract the adventurous. In 1900, Anderson, Smirnov, and J. W. Crowfoot, at the outset of a distinguished career in Middle Eastern and Egyptian archaeology, and finally, in 1903, the German engineer Carl Holtzmann were among the more notable arrivals. Anderson and Smirnov photographed, and Holtzmann planned many of the ruins, publishing his account in 1904.[101] His work was of enormous value to Ramsay on his visit to the site the next year. This time he was accompanied by younger colleagues and met Gertrude Bell. The latter represented in every way the intrepid late-Victorian women ready to demonstrate their independence by scientific journeys in out-of-the-way parts of the world or, when the situation demanded, by serving as nurses with the Serbian army in the Balkan wars of 1912–13. These were raising the status of women by achievement rather than by agitation.

Gertrude Lowthian Bell (1869–1926)[102] had taken full advantage of financial independence and diplomatic connections to pursue a career of scholarship and travel in the Middle East. She was the daughter of a successful Yorkshire businessman, had won a place at Lady Margaret Hall, Oxford, and was the first woman to be awarded First Class Honours in Modern History. A connection with the British ambassador in Bucharest kindled in her an interest in the Ottoman world and the Near East. This was increased by a visit to Teheran in 1892 and a stay in the embassy, where she took the opportunity to learn Persian and Arabic. There the tragic death of her fiancé seems to have reconciled her to being unmarried. Today she would have already embarked on a diplomatic career but in the 1890s this was impossible. She decided, therefore, to direct her energies into study of the archaeology and customs of the people of the Middle East. She was courageous and resourceful, spoke fluent Arabic and commanded respect wherever she went. Not surprisingly she became an invaluable aide first to Ramsay and after the war to Leonard Woolley at Ur of the Chaldees and in the British High Commission at Baghdad. She was one of the few individuals in that period who understood the Druzes of Hauran and spoke their language.

In January 1905 she set out on a six months' journey through Hauran to Damascus, Aleppo, the site of Antioch, and thence to Konya, where she met Ramsay. She wrote up the account of her journey in a series of articles for the *Revue Archéologique* in 1905–06.[103] Her main interest at this time was early-Christian architecture. She was not disappointed. The ruins of churches and monasteries were often as substantial as in de Vogüé's day. Early Christian and Byzantine churches at Budrun, on the site of Anazarbus, Sheher, and Corcyrus (Korghaz) in Cilicia, were planned and photographed. At this time Stéphane Gsell's work on the churches in Numidia was becoming known outside Algeria, and Gertrude Bell was struck by similarities in the plans of the churches in northern Syria and Cilicia with those in Algeria. She pointed out how in both, apart from the basilican plan and sacristies, the altar stood in an enclosure surrounded by a low wall at the east end of the nave, and as at Morsott and Benian, the Cilician church also had oblong chambers behind the apse. The North African cult of martyrs had, however, no real parallel in Syria, and whether the similarities were more than functional remains unclear.

Bell, however, was already well versed in the technicalities of early-Christian architecture when she arrived at Bin Bir Kilisse. After a month drawing and planning the most prominent Christian remains, she moved on to Konya. There she met Ramsay, who had been continuing his exploration of the Lycaonian border in search of Byzantine sites. She asked him for help in deciphering an inscription she had found in one of the churches, which she believed contained the clue to dating the building. Ramsay revisited the site himself, confirmed Bell's impression, sent her a copy of transcription and arranged a joint expedition to the site, which took place in 1907.

Their efforts were to be fruitful as well as timely. In their account of their work they showed that churches representing the entire evolution of early-Byzantine church architecture could be seen.[104] There were the early, fifth-century basilicas, the cruciform churches modelled on those built by Justinian in Constantinople; there were examples of the later tenth-century cruciform churches and octagonal churches surmounted by a cupola. There were also a number of smaller polygonal and trifoliate chapels. It was a paradise for the historian of Byzantine architecture. In addition some of the monasteries were so well preserved that one could trace out the lines of the long dormitories that Justinian had instructed that monks should sleep in, as well as refectories, assembly halls, and the great rectangular court around which the buildings, including the church, were set.[105]

Ramsay and Bell had arrived at the right moment, for already the abundant water supply and fertile soil were attracting population on the plateau.[106] Even after an interval of only two years (1907–09) some stone-robbing had taken place. When the writer visited the site in 1954 the remains of the larger churches were still moderately preserved, and in the great church (no. 1 in Ramsay–Bell) near the entrance to the largest village, dating to *c.* AD 550, one could still pick out a painting of the Virgin in the apse and a yellow fresco, but the design was largely obscured by whitewash.[107]

Ramsay was to make another important discovery in the same area in 1911. With Anderson he discovered the mountain sanctuary of Men Askeinos in the territory of Pisidian Antioch.[108] It lay, however, on a site approachable only by crossing the river Anthinos and climbing the 5,500 ft range of the Sultan Dagh. The efforts of the party in surveying the site were more than worthwhile. The Hieron (shrine) and adjacent theatre produced a number of inscriptions honouring the pagan emperors Galerius (293–311) and Maximin (308–313) and others relating to a strange pagan brotherhood called the 'Tekmoreians' or Guest-friends. Inscriptions relating to them dated from 220 to 315, but more interesting even than the date, which spanned the period of pagan–Christian tension and the Great Persecution, was that the ritual of the brotherhood included a common meal at which unleavened bread was used.[109] As Ramsay claimed, this seems to have been a deliberate challenge to the Christians, an imitation of the Eucharist.[110] Also, it might be added, it was a possible indication how individual Christian congregations were regarded as brotherhoods, whose central activity was a common meal in which the eating of unleavened bread and drinking wine played an essential part.

Another inscription found on the site of Laodicea Combusta (Ladik) (though not published until 1920) illustrated a different side of the tensions between Christian and pagan during Maximin's brief but eventful rule. Marcus Julius Eugenius served as an officer in the *officium* (staff) of the Governor of Pisidia. He married another aristocrat, Flavia Julia Flaviana, described as of 'senatorial rank'. But Eugenius was a Christian. He was harassed and forbidden to quit the imperial service by Maximin (probably in 311 when Maximin took over Galerius' provinces in Asia Minor). He survived and became *c.* 315 bishop of Laodicea, which post he held for 25 years.[111] These inscriptions show how deeply divided were parts of southern Asia Minor in the period of the Great Persecution. The inscriptions from Arycanda and Colobasa complete the picture painted by Eusebius of Caesarea, who was observing at first hand one of the great turning-points in the cultural and religious history of the Mediterranean peoples.

Ramsay retired from his Chair at Aberdeen in 1911. His students and successors in the field, Anderson and W. M. Calder (1881–1960), first turned their attention to a problem opened up by Karl Holl in a notable article in *Hermes* in 1908, which sought to correlate the survival of native languages in Asia Minor, such as Phrygian and Lycaonian, with the popularity of non-orthodox Christian sects such as the Montanists and Novatianists.[112] In 1908 and 1910 Calder, who was to contribute greatly to the study of these in the years after the First World War, was working in Phrygia. He and Anderson found a number of bilingual Greek–Phrygian inscriptions, showing that Phrygian was spoken as far south as Iconium (Konya) as late as the third century AD, thus confirming one part of Holl's theory.[113] Its correlation with Montanism, however, though possible, still needs further research.

In retrospect it was a pity that Ramsay's work was followed up so sporadically, and also that Calder had so strong a preference for survey as against excavation. As Gertrude Bell remarked, British scholars had been the pioneers in archaeological work in the interior of Anatolia,[114] and if a rural site in the Tembris valley and an urban community such as Laodicea or Colossae could have been selected then for long-term research, the results would have been worthwhile. Colossae in particular, it was pointed out in 1939, was of 'historical renown, accessible and completely unoccupied'.[115] As it was, lack of funds, the down side of reliance on non-governmental support, prevailed. Even to employ an architect to check the plans of the churches discovered at Bin Bir Kilisse would cost, it was calculated, £300; to mount a full-scale excavation, at least £5,000.[116] The money was not there; Crete and Arthur Evans' excavations at Knossos and work on Mycenaean sites in mainland Greece were absorbing available funds from the British School of Athens and from Oxford. There were calls for help for the new discoveries in Egyptian Nubia and the Sudan. Bin Bir Kilisse could not compete. The British were slow to see the value of good scholarly relations with foreign governments and investment in archaeology as aids towards trade and diplomatic influence. The Continentals saw matters more clearly in the two decades that preceded the First World War. *French* archaeological research was focused on North Africa. In the eastern Mediterranean the work of the Ecole française d'Athènes concentrated on two main sites: Delphi and Delos, and on the mainland of Asia Minor at Pergamum in the 1890s and Aphrodisias in Caria from 1902. Also, that monument of self-importance set up by the Epicurean Diogenes at Oenoanda in Lycia *c.* AD 200, in which he set out in flowery language his credo for all to see, was the subject of exhaustive study.[117] Early Christianity took second place in these researches. Evidence, however, for the conversion of the temple of Apollo at Delphi into a large Christian church, richly adorned with marble plaques and the most ornate Corinthian and Ionic style capitals, was found during the excavations.[118] At Rheneia (Delos) excavators came on a grisly reminder that all was not peaceful trading among the Jewish community there. An inscription recorded the murder of two young women and demanded divine vengeance on the murderers.[119]

Back at Paris, however, the most important discovery was made by a doctoral student, Emile Bourget, in 1905. Working through the mass of epigraphic fragments from Delphi he found four that came from the same inscription but had been overlooked on the site. It was a rescript from the emperor Claudius to the proconsul of Achaea, Gallio. This fixed precisely the date of his proconsulship to between April 52 and April 53. This in turn fixed Paul's stay in Corinth to between the autumn of 51 and the end of 52. A pivotal date in Paul's missionary career had been established.[120]

In Asia Minor scholars of the Ecole française continued their *voyages archéologiques* through the imperial provinces, but the emphasis always lay on Greco-Roman inscriptions. Two exceptions may, however, be mentioned. In 1908 Gustave Mendel, later to become *Conservateur* (Curator) of the Imperial Ottoman Museum at Constantinople, was working among recent finds exhibited at the museum at Brusa. A stone casket had been brought in the previous year by a local farmer who had been looking for building-stone on his land and noticed the writing on it. It was a reliquary honouring 'the martyr Trophimus', and threatened any who 'cast out his bones shall be answerable before God' i.e., the third-century 'Eumeneian formula'. The martyr's *Acta* stated that he had been martyred at Synnada in Phrygia in the reign of Probus (276–282). There was no Christian symbol on the casket. To an outsider the text could be Jewish, but as it was it seems likely that the *Acta* were preserving a true record of an event that demonstrated the precarious character of the status acquired by Christians even in the 'long peace' of 43 years (260–303) that preceded the Great Persecution.[121]

The results of the second *voyage archéologique* were to be even more far-reaching. The remote petrified landscape between the town of Göreme and Ürgüb in Cappadocia, 85 km west of Kayseri (Caesarea), had not escaped the eye of Byzantine monks. They had hewn their monasteries and churches out of volcanic rock, and these strange sites had attracted European travellers since the eighteenth century. Louis XV had regarded Paul Lucas as deranged when he described the plateau covered with 'pyramids, rounded domes of rock, pillars and great isolated boulders in terms more applicable to a moonscape than anywhere on this planet'.[122] Monks, however, had found the rock soft enough to excavate cells, and chapels. From the end of the iconoclastic controversy in 843 until the thirteenth century generations of monks succeeded one another in this desolate region. Chapels were enlarged into churches, their walls covered with brilliant frescos rivalling in decorative power those of Faras in Nubia. The representation of the Last Supper, the Betrayal and the Pantocrator on the ceiling of the church of Karandih Kilisse is one of the finest examples of mediaeval Byzantine art, and most of the churches and monasteries were adorned by frescos representing the Birth narrative, martyrs, and angels and archangels. Such was the scene that greeted, first, the German scholar Hans Rott in 1906[123] and then more effectively the Jesuit Père Guillaume de Jerphanion in two journeys in 1907 and 1912.[124] At this period when tolerable relations existed between Christians and Muslims in Asia Minor Jerphanion was able to record and photograph at will. His account, beautifully illustrated, had to await publication in a series of monographs after the war, but it preserved just in time a record of the religious and superb artistic achievement of mediaeval Byzantium in Anatolia.

Two months after Jerphanion had left the scene in 1907 his place was taken by Henri Grégoire, a young Belgian scholar, destined to leave a permanent mark on Byzantine studies. His report brought an entirely fresh approach to the annual *voyages* undertaken by his colleagues at the Ecole. Not only did he write with verve but he had an eye for Christian remains, which he described thoroughly and related them to their surroundings. He corrected Rott's somewhat inaccurate transcription of an inscription on a pillar in the Sari Kilisse (Yellow Church) at Kücük Burungum, and identified it as a church subordinate to a monastery at which a bishop resided. He found new monasteries in the Ürgüb area, inscriptions that Jerphanion had missed, and corrected the readings of others that scholars had misunderstood.[125] He himself had taken the first step towards sharing with Norman Baynes and George Ostrogorsky the title of the foremost Byzantinist of his time.

The year 1908 saw another French enterprise, this time in Constantinople itself. From Paris the Ministry of Public Instruction initiated a record and survey of Byzantine churches extending from the fifth to the fourteenth centuries, converted into mosques.[126] By coincidence, fierce fires in the years 1908, 1911 and 1912 which destroyed a large number of wooden buildings clustered round the Sultan Ahmed mosque revealed the vaulted ruin of the Byzantine imperial palace and traces of earlier buildings. In 1912 a range of Byzantine buildings lying between the palace and hippodrome were exposed[127] and in October to December of the following year work started on the 'House of Justinian', an imposing façade bordering the Sea of Marmara.[128] The way was prepared for research that would reveal the splendour of the palace in early Byzantine times.

Syria and Anatolia both formed part of the Ottoman empire, and Gertrude Bell had found little difficulty in making her journey unaccompanied from Aleppo to meet Ramsay at Konya. It was to be expected that French archaeologists would be extending their activities southwards from Asia Minor into Syria. The hinterlands of cities such as Antioch and Beirut (Berytus) had hardly been explored. Following up the work of Baron de Vogüé, in 1901 Victor Chapot explored the extensive ruins of Bishop Theodoret's (d. 458) see at Cyrrhus in northern Syria, and also Samosata in 1902. Two years later he had better luck so far as concerned early-Christian remains further east, at Resapha. This was Justinian's strongpoint against the Saracens, whose walls still stood 5 metres high, and its churches were equally well preserved. An inscription recording Bishop Sergius, son of Maronius, the *chorepiscopus*, showed that even in the sixth century episcopal celibacy was by no means a universal rule.[129]

Most of these sites, as well as those discovered in Transjordan by members of the Dominican Ecole Biblique in Jerusalem, would await the end of the First World War before investigation assisted by air photography was possible.[130]

Throughout the pre-war decade, however, work was going on under the direction of Père A. Lagrange, L. H. Vincent and F. M. Abel on the sites of alleged Constantinian basilicas in and around Jerusalem. In 1910, for example, the Ecole followed up the keen observation of one of its seminarists. He had identified the site of the church of Eleona (i.e. on the Mount of Olives) on land belonging to the Benedictine convent. Building material was strewn around over an area of 1,500 metres, but no one had associated this previously with Constantine's church. Seven months of excavation revealed a basilica, smallish by Jerusalem standards (30 × 18.60 m), preceded by a broad atrium with a colonnade on all four sides. The basilica itself had been built over a cavern that had been enlarged so as to form a crypt chapel beneath the apse and altar area. The church had been evidently built at a single time, but had been repaired under Justinian. It commemorated where Christ was said to have taught and also the site of his Ascension.[131] Its position above the cave seems to confirm once more the accuracy of Eusebius' account of the site (*Life* iii.41) and of Constantine's aim of building finely-appointed basilicas on the site of Christian holy places so as to restore these without compromise to Christianity (*Life* iii.31ff.).

Altogether, France was served well by its religious orders, whether at Carthage or Jerusalem. The Ecole Biblique would be in the forefront of research on biblical sites in the 1920s and 1930s. When the Dead Sea Scrolls were found in 1945, it produced in Père Roland de Vaux a scholar whose archaeological ability was matched by a real sense of brotherhood among scholars of all Christian (and indeed, non-Christian) traditions.

In the pre-war years, whether in North Africa, Asia Minor or Palestine, the French showed how teamwork involving home government, commercial enterprises on the spot[132] and sponsored scholars could provide continuity to scientific research, and at the same time enhance the prestige and influence of France.

The *Austro-Hungarian empire* had had its consulate at Smyrna, and its post offices in the Ottoman empire since 1867 and, sharing a common frontier with the Ottomans in the Balkans, had political and commercial interests as well. In the 1890s these were being supported by prestigious and successful archaeological projects. Josef Keil and Anton von Premerstein became the classic explorers of the Roman provinces of Asia Minor in the fifteen years before the war. Even so the main Austrian contribution to early-Christian scholarship was at Ephesus. In 1893, funded by the Ministry for Religious Affairs (*Cultus*) and Education, planning was begun for a major excavation. Ephesus had been a major port and capital of the Roman province of Asia, where St Paul had spent three years of hard and eventful missionary work and left behind a flourishing Church. Thanks, however, to a slight fall in the sea level and the silting up of the Maeander river, the Greco-Roman city was stranded on a marshy plain some three miles (five km) from the coast, and the site was practically uninhabited. Between 1863 and 1874 preliminary work had been carried out by J. T. Wood, mainly on the temple of Artemis, but had not been followed up until the Austrians arrived on the scene.

In 1895 they were ready to begin. Work was entrusted to Rudolf Heberdey, who had already undertaken journeys in Cilicia in 1891 and 1892, and in western Asia Minor in 1893 and 1894. In the next sixteen years he carried out a systematic clearing as well as planning excavation of major buildings which made Ephesus famous in the past and a prime tourist attraction today. In the first season Wood's theory that the temple of Artemis (Diana) had been destroyed by the Goths in AD 263 and never rebuilt was established as in all probability correct,[133] thus providing a further instance of the growing weakness of Greco-Roman paganism in Asia Minor in the second half of the third century. The celebrated temple had been destroyed by fire and the site re-occupied only by wretched buildings of no religious purpose and indeterminate date. Its stonework provided an almost inexhaustible mine for street repairs and new building during the fourth century.

Thereafter clearance operations went on year after year. Successively, the theatre where the populace had rioted against Paul (Acts 19:29; see colour plate) and the stadium where Paul claimed he had fought 'the beasts of Ephesus' (1 Cor 15:32), the library of Celsus, and across the finely-paved street, the temple of Hadrian with its splendid series of second-century friezes were uncovered. By 1912 Classical Ephesus had been opened up to tourists as a Turkish counterpart of Dougga and Timgad in North Africa.

It was not until 1902 that Heberdey turned his attention specifically to Christian Ephesus. His report from that year recorded the discovery and excavation of a Byzantine church.[134] Two years later, however, work started on the ruin of a huge church, north of the agora on the site of the Museon and not far from the east end of the ancient harbour.[135] Already, the 1904 season had identified a great basilica-type church 144 m long and 31.5 m wide, with narrow side aisles. It had been dedicated to the 'Ever-virgin Mary' and hence could reasonably be accepted as the scene of the three Councils held at Ephesus (431, 449 and 475).[136] The wide central nave provided a splendid setting for the Council of 431 which witnessed the triumph of Cyril of Alexandria, with the aid of Bishop Memnon of Ephesus, over Nestorius; and equally in 449 for Dioscorus' bid for supreme ecclesiastical power. Even that of 475, sponsored by the usurper Basiliscus (475–476), was impressive. All three Councils supported the Alexandrian

Christology that tended towards recognizing the Incarnate Christ in One Nature, and that divine, in contast to the orthodox perception of Christ 'in two Natures' (human and divine) as defined at the Council of Chalcedon in 451.[137] Great though this church was, ensuing excavations in 1910 and 1911 revealed a huge complex, extending 265 m along the west side of the Museon, a 'double basilica', as the excavators termed it. It consisted of the main three-naved basilica, paved with mosaic of floral and geometric designs, ending in a rectangular atrium at the west end, on to which had been built a second smaller church with its apse at the west end. (See map on p. 192.) A baptistery had been constructed on its north side. This may have been a separate baptismal church originally, like some of those in the West. Later, probably in Justinian's reign, the basilican church had been converted into a smaller cupola-roofed building, apparently no longer connected with the smaller baptismal church.[138]

The original 144 m long church had been built during the first half of the fourth century. Its position, alongside the centre of learning and culture in the Classical city, symbolized the triumph of Christianity as surely as the blackened ruins of the temple of Artemis symbolized the downfall of paganism in Ephesus.[139] An inscription found near the Library of Celsus expressed this truth, celebrating the destruction of the 'demon Artemis' and attendant idols through the 'divine cross', the 'victorious, deathless symbol of Christ',[140] though another showed that, while they might be Christians, some citizens of Ephesus still thought in terms of Minos, Lycurgus and Solon when they wanted to praise the equity of a just official.[141]

The Austrian approach to archaeology in Asia Minor was a model for its day. The exhaustive *Reise* undertaken by Keil and von Premerstein were supplemented by a major piece of research at Ephesus. There was continuity of control through Heberdey and financial support from the imperial government at Vienna. Major sites relating to the New Testament and early Christianity had been preserved, and further work planned on sites surveyed by Keil southwards from Ephesus towards Priene. It was a tragedy that the fortunes of war, first in Europe and then in Anatolia, prevented the Austrians from building on their work. However, in 1926 they were back in Ephesus itself, benefiting from the increased American interest in and sponsorship of archaeology in Turkey and the Middle East.

The Austrians had begun to provide a balanced and informative picture of Ephesus in Classical, Greco-Roman times, and as a Christian and Byzantine city. The *Germans* used their far greater resources primarily on Classical archaeology, and in the interior on the excavation of the great Hittite centre of Boghaz Koy.

During the 1890s Germany gradually became the most influential European power in the Ottoman dominions. The Germany of Bismarck had shown limited interest in Turkey but after his fall in March 1890 perspectives changed. Sultan Abdulhamid (1876–1908) had cause to distrust each of the other powers. Russia was regarded as permanently hostile, France had seized Tunisia, Italy had ambitions to do the same in Libya, and Britain, he believed, had deceived him in taking over a predominant role in Egypt. Germany on the other hand was a formidable military power whose advisers had enabled the Turks to win a rare military campaign in 1897 in Thessaly, and was prepared to invest in a grandiose scheme for a railway linking Berlin with Baghdad and Basra[142] across the heart of the Ottoman empire. *Firmans* permitting spectacular excavations at Pergamum, Priene and Miletus were an acknowledgement of services received.

The excavations on all three sites were on a massive scale, organized and funded centrally from Berlin. At Pergamum, Wilhelm Dörpfeld was employing between 100 and 125 workmen (half Greek and half Turks) on a ten-year programme (1900–10) that concentrated on the gymnasium, temple of Athena and the road leading thence to the great altar, an area where the French had been working a decade previously. In 1906 he moved to the palace of the consul Attalus and the Greek theatre. His interest was, however, almost exclusively concentrated on these monuments of Classical architecture, large parts of which were destined to form the heart of the Pergamon Museum in Berlin. His colleague Wilhelm Kolbe, cataloguing 405 inscriptions found in 1904 and 1905, did not include a single Christian stone.[143]

At Miletus and Didyma ten miles (16 km) away, Theodor Wiegand showed greater awareness of the potential of the site for discoveries relating to the New Testament and early Church. In excavating the theatre at Miletus in 1906 he found a number of inscriptions identifying the owners of seats. In the fifth row of the second block from the west he came on one reserved as 'Place of the Jews and also the God-fearers', indication that the Jews attended shows but sat separate from the rest of the audience, and that God-fearers were included among the Jews but also regarded as separate from them as they were from the pagans. Christians down to *c.* AD 100 might have found an identity among the God-fearers.[144] Wiegand excavated and planned a church at Miletus but he could also be equally as careless of post-Classical remains as Dörpfeld. At Didyma excavation of the temple of Apollo involved the demolition of a Greek village and the 'removal' of an early-Byzantine church before work could begin. The temple doors, however, were found, panelled with ivory.[145] Amid discoveries such as this Christianity came well down the excavators' priorities.

A major exception to this scale of values were the extensive journeys undertaken by Hans Lucas and Max von Oppenheim in northern Syria and Mesopotamia in 1899 and by Hans Georg, Duke of Saxony, in 1909. As in Vogüé's day the travellers found the region littered with Roman and Byzantine remains. A few of the churches, notably Harab es Schems between Aleppo and Kalaat were almost intact. Between Hamah and Aleppo Lucas and Oppenheim noted nearly 200 sites, with 'numberless churches'.[146] Inscriptions there, as further south in Hauran, proclaimed the Christians' Monophysite belief in 'One God'. Biblical quotations were almost 'Donatist' in their assertions of righteousness; 'This the tower the just may enter' read an inscription from Kasr Ibn Wardan. Pressing on further east they reached the site of the Byzantine–Persian frontier city of Nisibis and saw frescos surviving in a church there. The journey opened the eyes of scholars to the possibilities of the Roman fortress sites in the Euphrates valley, and hence prepared the way for the epoch-making excavations at Dura Europos in the 1920s and 1930s.

The *Americans* would be taking up this challenge. While they had concentrated their efforts on the Classical sites of Sardes and Halicarnassus,[147] and on the mainland at Corinth, their scholars were also showing interest in Christian remains in Syria. Princeton University and H. C. Butler organized expeditions in 1899–1900, 1904–05 and 1909 in northern Syria, east of Antioch. It was the land of the pillar saints of the fifth and sixth centuries, and some basilicas associated with them, such as Kal'aat Sem'an associated with Simeon Stylites, stood hardly disturbed by time. In southern Syria, archaeologically practically unknown at the time, the expedition of 1904–05 carried out thorough surveys of ruins also described as 'untouched by man'. Eleven temples, 87 churches, twelve convents and groups of ecclesiastical buildings, 52 houses, eight villas and two palaces were among the harvest of remains examined.[148] Some of the ruins were dated by the provincial era. The dated inscriptions confirmed the impression gained from literary sources of the victory of Christianity throughout the area in the fifth century. The earliest inscription (AD 344/345, on a lintel in a church at Umm el Jemal, east of Amman[149]) was later shown (see below, Chapter 13) to refer not to the building of a church but to a cemetery belonging to the Christians of the town at that date. The community there was probably still a minority.

Finally, the *Ottoman government* itself was taking an interest in the civilization its ancestors had supplanted in Asia Minor. Work was undertaken at Sardes, and also on the site of the great fifth-century monastery at Alabanda (Alahan).[150] This latter site the Goughs would be excavating fully in the 1950s. (See below, p. 341.) Turkey, however, was determined to prove itself a modern European power involved, as were other Europeans, in preserving its archaeological heritage.

In 1914 archaeology in Asia Minor, and even more further south in Syria and Palestine, was still a patchwork. In Asia Minor the emphasis was overwhelmingly on the recovery of Classical civilization and the prestige to be gained by excavation of major Classical sites. Few besides Ramsay, Gertrude Bell, their British colleagues, and Henri Grégoire put early-Christian remains in the forefront of their research. Yet, as in North Africa, important results were achieved. In particular, inscriptions were filling out details of the period of the Great Persecution and so confirming the accounts of Lactantius (*Institutes*, Book 5) and Eusebius (*HE*, Books 8 and 9). In addition something of the great importance of Ephesus as a Christian centre in the fifth century had been revealed by the Austrian excavations. At Constantinople itself research combined with accident was providing glimpses of the splendours that lay beneath the banal structures of the Ottoman period. Finally, scholars, not least the Viennese scholar Josef Strzygowski and Gertrude Bell, had become aware of the vitality and originality of early-Christian art and architecture in Asia Minor.[151] In moments of enthusiasm Strzygowski saw nearly every distinctive feature of Christian art and architecture, including even the basilica, as belonging to the heritage of the East. Ephesus, and Nazianzus, together with the great centres of Antioch, Tyre and Alexandria, not Rome, were the sources of Christian architectural and artistic achievement.[152] These ideas proved to be exaggerated,[153] but what seems to have been true is that, as in North Africa and among the Copts in Egypt, Christianity appeared to have liberated a native genius in Asia Minor which eventually would lead to Anthemius of Tralles' masterpiece of Sancta Sophia. Despite the predominance which the Classics retained in the priorities of international scholarship new fields of research were opening out for studying early Christianity at the very moment when the rivalries of the Powers spilled over into war.

FURTHER READING

J. G. C. Anderson, 'Paganism and Christianity in northern Phrygia' in W. M. Ramsay (ed.), *Studies in the East Roman Provinces* (Aberdeen, 1906), pp. 183–227.

G. W. Bell, 'Notes of a journey through Cilicia and Lycaonia', *RA* 7 (January–June 1906), pp. 1–29 and 385–414; 8 (July–December 1906), pp. 2–36 and 225–52.

G. W. Bell with W. M. Ramsay, *The Thousand and One Churches* (London, 1909).

W. M. Calder, 'Studies in early Christian epigraphy', *JHS* 40 (1920), pp. 42–54.

V. Chapot, 'Antiquités de la Syrie du Nord', *BCH* 26 (1902), pp. 161–208.

Adolf Deissmann, *Light from the Ancient East,* Eng. trans. L. R. C. Strachan (London, 1911).

Henri Grégoire, 'Voyage dans le Pont et en Cappadocie', *BCH* 33 (1909), pp. 3–170.

M. Hardie, 'The shrine of Mēn Askeinos at Pisidian Antioch', *JHS* 32 (1911), pp. 111–33.

Karl Holl, 'Das Fortleben der Volksprachen in Klein-Asien in der nachchristlicher Zeit', *Hermes* 43 (1908), pp. 240–54.

G. de Jerphanion, *Les Eglises rupestres de Cappadoce,* I (Paris, 1925) and II (Paris, 1936).

J. Kamm, *Daughter of the Desert* (London, 1956)

Max von Oppenheim and Hans Lucas, 'Griechische und lateinische Inschriften aus Syrien, Mesopotamien und Kleinasien', *BZ* 14 (1905), pp. 1–72.

Alan Palmer, *The Decline and Fall of the Ottoman Empire* (London, 1992).

A. M. Ramsay, 'Isaurian and Phrygian art of the third century' in *Studies in the East Roman Provinces* (Aberdeen, 1906), pp. 30–58.

J. Strzygowski, *Orient oder Rom: Beiträge zur Geschichte der spätantiken und frühchristlichen Kunst* (Leipzig, 1901).

J. Strzygowski, *Kleinasien ein Neuland der Kunstgeschichte* (Leipzig, 1903), and for a critical assessment of Strzygowski's views, E. Weigand, 'Die Orient-oder-Rom Frage in der frühchristliche Kunst', *ZNTW* 22 (1923), pp. 233ff.

For the Austrian excavations at Ephesus, see the successive articles by Rudolf Heberdey, 'Vorläufige Berichte über die Ausgrabungen in Ephesus', *JÖAI* (1895 Beiblatt–1912).

Work on Constantine's churches in *Jerusalem* during this period is described by F. M. Abel and L. Vincent in *Jérusalem nouvelle* (Paris, 1914 and 1926).

(3) The Nile valley, 1885–1914

EGYPT

Christian archaeology under the British suzerainty of late nineteenth-century Egypt means mainly papyri, and then only hesitatingly so. The sheer abundance and impressive majesty of the Pharaonic monuments ensured that these would remain the centre of interest for scholars and the incipient tourist pioneers alike. The prestige of the work of Champollion and Mariette (d.1881) also contributed to the natural inclination of the Egyptian Antiquities Service towards a study of Pharaonic history that could now been seen to have extended back over 5,000 years. In addition, the legacy of the Rosetta stone had concentrated research on hieroglyphic records, towards finding possible links between the history of Egypt and that of ancient Israel, links it was hoped would confirm the historical narrative contained in the Old Testament.

In contrast, Roman, Byzantine, Coptic Christian remains attracted less attention. The Copts, in particular, were regarded by the Egyptian administration and the French archaeologists who dominated the Antiquities Service as nuisances. 'Méchants Coptes' was the verdict.[154] These were the people who had thrown down great monuments of Egypt's past, and had defaced the walls of temples with graffiti. Why should trouble and expense be wasted on their remains?

Even amidst this onslaught some dissenting voices were being raised. In 1884, A. J. Butler had published his *Coptic Churches of Egypt*, and in 1893 Jacques de Morgan had brought the great monastery known as St Simeon's, two miles from Aswan, to scholars' attention by publishing a survey of the ruins.[155] Before the end of the century the Coptic cemetery at Bagawat in the oasis of Khargeh (Kufra), which included some 200 funerary chapels, small round or square buildings with domed roofs, was beginning to yield frescos rivalling those of the Roman catacombs. In a large chapel at the north end of the cemetery of this 'Christian Pompeii' were murals representing biblical scenes, including the crossing of the Red Sea by the Israelites, the Old Testament type of Christian liberation from idolatry. The style was Greek-Alexandrian and the scenes recalled those, such as the Creation or Noah's Ark, found in the catacombs.[156] The new trend was aptly expressed by Josef Strzygowski, already an authority on sub-Classical Christian art in Asia Minor, in an article in the *Römische Quartalschrift* in 1898: 'Egypt is a cultural volcano that today is dormant', but 'one day it would burst into life'. From a study of the small number of Coptic sarcophagi he was able to see he concluded that Coptic Christian art had developed within the framework of late Greco-Roman art, and that it also formed the basis on which Arab art would develop in Egypt.[157] The East had as much claim to be the source of Christian art as Rome itself.

The written records of Coptic Christianity represented by papyri and parchment were also finding a champion in the wayward genius of Emile Amélineau. In 1881 he had begun to study the fragments of a papyrus codex acquired by James Bruce in 1769 during his journey of exploration to find the source of the Nile. Eventually the codex with other Coptic manuscript fragments had found its way to the safe-keeping of the Bodleian Library, Oxford, where Amélineau recognized the contents as two Gnostic tracts identified as the *Books of Jeu*.[158] Until then the only Gnostic work known had been the *Pistis Sophia* (Faith-Wisdom), the contents of the Codex Askewanus which had been brought to England by an English traveller and physician, Dr Askew, and acquired by the British Museum (see above, p. 36). In 1851 a Latin translation had been made by Dr M. G. Schwartz in Berlin, and Amélineau now recognized that what he had in the Codex Bruce was related to the *Pistis Sophia*.

Amélineau published his results in 1891, but at that very moment a young German scholar, Carl Schmidt, handed in his Berlin thesis on the same text which was duly published later the same year.[159] Amélineau was the pioneer – he published a new edition of *Pistis-Sophia* in 1895 – but Schmidt was the more thorough and complete scholar. He pointed to mistakes in Amélineau's rendering, and his own compendious 690-page edition has not unnaturally remained the *editio princeps*. The 'two books of Jeu' as they are now called, are a revelation of the 'great unseen God' by a revelation of the risen Jesus to his disciples, to whom he reveals the secrets of the world beyond. The second book includes a revelation of the secrets that lie behind individual letters of the Greek alphabet, which the believer must know so as to pass through spheres controlled by planetary deities to the heavenly realm beyond.[160] With this beginning it is not surprising that Carl Schmidt dominated German papyrological research for the next 40 years, until his death in 1938.

Between 1892 and 1896 more Gnostic texts and apocryphal gospels used by the Gnostics were published. In 1892 U. Bouriant published a codex found in a mediaeval Coptic grave at Akhmin (Latopolis) which proved to be large parts of the *Apocalypse of Peter* and the *Gospel of Peter*.[161] Four years later Akhmin yielded another codex, of 71 pages (five or six were missing) containing hitherto unknown Gnostic works. The *Gospel of Mary*, the *Secret Teaching (Apocryphon) of John*, and the *Wisdom (Sophia) of Jesus Christ* as well as a fragment of the *Acts of Peter* were all works included among the Gnostic codices found at Nag Hammadi in 1945.[162] Unfortunately, Schmidt, to whom the collection was entrusted, did not follow up his preliminary survey with a full publication. An accident destroyed proofs of his study, and he did not resume it before he died in 1938. Eventually, the texts were published in 1955 by the Austrian scholar Walter Till (see below, p. 280). These discoveries allowed Harnack to compare Irenaeus' denunciations of Gnostic beliefs with actual Gnostic documents. There was little doubt that Irenaeus had some of these to hand when he wrote *Adversus Haereses c.* 185. Hence the documents in question must date back earlier in the second century. New light had been shed on an important aspect of Egyptian-Greek Christianity at that early period.[163]

These additions to knowledge of Christian Egypt were being obtained by scholars working in European libraries. Interest, however, in the written records of the Roman and later periods of Egyptian history had gradually been increasing since a moment in 1877 when peasants working on the site of the Greco-Roman city of Arsinoë in the Fayum came upon a large collection of papyri of Roman date. It became clear that here was another valuable source of information for the social and economic conditions in that period. In 1883 the Egypt Exploration Fund was founded with papyrological research as a main objective and results to be published annually. Next year Flinders Petrie working for the Fund came on baskets containing 228 Demotic papyri on the site of Tanis in the Nile delta. These, with 38 Greek texts, he sent to the *savant* Ernest Reveillout in Paris for study. Alas, after 40 years the texts were still unpublished! 'A complete year's work wasted', commented Petrie in his memoirs.[164]

The setback was temporary. The Fayum was now firmly in the sights of archaeologists. In 1893 Dr Fritz Krebs published in Berlin (through Harnack) what proved to be the first of a series of documents throwing a vivid light on the way in which the authorities carried out the emperor Decius' order in 250 for a general sacrifice to the Roman gods to assure the preservation of the empire. The document was a *libellus* (certificate) recording how Diogenes, an old man of 72, identified by 'a scar over his right eyebrow', had 'always sacrificed to the gods' and now did so 'in accordance with the edict', by pouring a libation and partaking of the sacred victims. He asks that his action should be certified 'by the commission chosen to superintend the sacrifices' at the village of Alexander's Isle.[165] This information confirmed that from other sources, notably the letters of Cyprian, bishop of Carthage (*c.* 248–258), that commissions of prominent citizens (*primores*) supervised the sacrifices on this occasion.[166] Texts and archaeological evidence were working together. At length 42 similar texts have been found.

It was also from a rubbish tip near Oxyrhynchus that in 1895 two Oxford scholars, B. P. Grenfell and A. S. Hunt, came upon fragments of a codex containing remains of a gospel that seemed to preserve hitherto unknown sayings of Jesus. One ran: 'Jesus saith, Except ye fast to the world, ye shall in no wise find the kingdom of God; and except ye keep the Sabbath as a sabbath, ye shall not see the Father'. And another: 'Jesus saith, A prophet is not acceptable in his own country, neither doth a physician work cures on those that know him'.[167]

The handwriting indicated the third century AD. A second season's work at Oxyrhynchus in 1903 produced another fragment but not of the same manuscript.[168] This had been copied on the back of a lengthy land-survey and consisted of 42 incomplete lines of sayings. The date appeared to be late second century AD. The beginning could be reconstructed. 'These are the [......] words which Jesus the living [Lord] spake to [......] and Thomas, and he said unto them, Whosoever [shall hearken] unto these words shall not taste [of death].' The volume included a saying quoted by Clement of Alexandria *c.* 200 as from *The Gospel According to the Hebrews*. It reads: 'Jesus saith, Let not him that seeks [the kingdom?] cease until he find it and when he finds it [he will be astonished]. Astonished he shall attain the kingdom and [having attained] he shall have rest.'[169] The same papyrus contained another group of sayings which seemed to suggest that no thought should be taken for the morrow, for God would provide all necessary clothing. Nakedness (like that of Adam?) was not to be ashamed of.[170]

While some critics, notably Charles Guignebert, were unimpressed by the discoveries,[171] the finders had no doubt about their importance.[172] At least, the sayings appeared to have links with Jewish-Christian works circulating in Egypt in the late second century. Were the sources of such works different from those of the Gospel writers, but nonetheless authentic? Other texts, New Testament in character but not canonical, have suggested that this might be so.[173] The discovery of the complete *Gospel of Thomas* among the Nag Hammadi documents has as yet not entirely answered the question.

In the first decade of the new century the pace of discovery quickened. Jean Clédat excavated the monastic complex of Apa Apollo at Bawit, discovering in the remains of two churches associated with it carvings and frescos, including a full-length painting of St George. But the little cemetery chapel where generations of monks had been buried yielded some of the most spectacular. Christ throned in glory with the apostles and Virgin standing as petitioners for the soul of the deceased was most often found, but one chapel portrayed David as a musician, and another, the military saint Sisinnios. The centre, built in Justinian's reign and destroyed sometime in the second half of the twelfth century, justified completely Strzygowski's prediction concerning the future importance and individuality of Coptic Christian art, and also provided an early insight into the religion centred on the Virgin and the military saints that the Nubian Christians were making their own.[174]

In addition, a multitude of papyri was being found at Oxyrhynchus, their information supplemented by texts which for a long time had remained unnoticed in big private collections, such as that belonging to the Amherst family. This collection now produced a large fragment of the *Shepherd of Hermas*, an early second-century work written in Rome in Jewish-Christian circles with a strong emphasis on prophetic teaching.[175] Its presence in Egypt showed the continued existence of the same tendency among Christians there alongside Gnosticism. Another papyrus from the same collection published by Grenfell and Hunt showed how in the episcopate of Maximus of Alexandria (265–282) Christian corn merchants in Arsinoë were using the bishop and his steward

Theonas (later bishop of Alexandria 282–300) as their intermediaries in trade with merchants in Rome. Maximus was in Rome receiving money owed from the transaction. In this period Christians had little to fear from the authorities and their leaders were engaged openly in profitable secular activities.[176] A few years later, the situation had changed. A letter from a presbyter, Psenosiris, to a colleague, Apollo, written at the outset of the Great Persecution in 303–304, concerning, apparently, the return of a woman from exile in the Great Oasis and his worry for her well-being. Exile, therefore, was being used as a punishment, as it had been in the persecution under Valerian in 257–259.[177] Persecution failed, and 40 years on Egypt was overwhelmingly Christian. Deissmann published one example out of a deposit of 60 letters representing the correspondence of a Christian officer, Flavius Abinnaeus, serving at Dionysias in the Fayum *c.* 343–351. The letter from the priest (*Papas*) Caor, of Hermupolis, asks Abinnaeus to pardon a deserter who now wished to rejoin his unit.[178] *Plus ça change!*

Ostraka were also proving their worth to the Church historian. These were potsherds which could be used to write receipts on, but sometimes for short letters. One of the most interesting recorded in the 1900s was a plea by three candidates for the diaconate to their bishop, Abraham of Hermouthis (*fl. c.* AD 600). They ask to be accepted, stating their readiness to keep the canons, to observe the commands of their superiors, and not to take usury. Moreover they would learn St John's Gospel by heart – a glimpse of theological training in late sixth-century Egypt.[179]

Accompanying these discoveries went a lessening of prejudice against Coptic remains. In 1903 Clédat excavated the church belonging to St Simeon's monastery. In the next few years Somers Clarke, to whom Nubian Christian research would be vastly indebted, devoted the second part of his *Christian Antiquities in the Nile Valley* (Oxford, 1912) to recording major surviving Coptic churches and monasteries north of Aswan. Monasteries showed how self-sufficiency on the Pachomian model had continued as long as these were inhabited by monks. Just a few still had residents. The monastery buildings would be protected by high walls and a watch-tower and equipped with ovens, mills and oil presses, to which were sometimes added vegetable gardens and date palms. The wells were often still usable.[180] Monasteries were the obvious target for future study but in 1913–14 R. Campbell Thompson, working for the Committee of the Byzantine Research and Publication Fund, excavated an abandoned Coptic village site on the Wadi Sarga, 15 miles south of Assiut. A cave had been turned into a church and paintings included the Three Holy Children in the fiery furnace. Thompson brought back to the

British Museum an array of humble artefacts, such as baskets, tapestry and *ostraka*. It was a poor man's site, and its abandonment in the first half of the eighth century may reveal one aspect of the transition from Christianity to Islam in this corner of Egypt.[181]

NUBIA

Somers Clarke had begun restoring some dignity to the story of the Coptic past. It was, however, the building of the dam at Aswan in 1899 (raised in 1907) that drew attention to the need of exploring and salvaging the monuments of Nubian Christianity. Nubia, comprising southern Egypt and Sudan, traditionally a much despised neighbour of Egypt, would soon be repaying handsomely those who ventured down the Nile between Aswan and Khartoum in the wake of Burkhardt and Lepsius. In 1899, following the battle of Omdurman (1 September 1898), an Anglo-Egyptian condominium was established over the Sudan. Half a century had elapsed since the publication of Karl Lepsius' graphic and scholarly but vast account of his travels down the Nile valley and the vestiges of a vanished early-Christian civilization he encountered on his way as far south as Khartoum.[182] Now, awakening interest in the Copts and their Christian heritage, together with the need of salvaging as much as possible as the waters of the Nile began to flood the low-lying areas along its course behind the Aswan dam, prompted immediate survey-work on the numerous endangered sites. In January and February 1899, Somers Clarke, an honorary member of the Comité de Conservation des Monuments et de l'Art arabe at Cairo, made a rapid survey of sites on the way as far south as Ibrim, concentrating on visible remains of forts, such as Kor.[183] On his report an archaeological survey was set up with the American scholar George A. Reisner as Director and C. M. Firth and F. Ll. Griffith, an Oxford scholar, as members.[184]

Their brief included excavation as well as survey, and both Reisner and Firth were 'diggers', while Griffith was a philologist, mainly interested in the Nubian language. Digging concentrated on the numerous cemeteries between Shellal to the north and Wadi es Sebua, where no fewer than 150 were excavated, containing some 8,000 graves. The main Christian cemetery was at Shellal, where Reisner's workmen excavated 1,625 individual burials. They found no grave-goods, as the Christians did not bury any with their dead, but this was a frustrating experience at a time when the recovery of portable objects for museums was a prime aim of any excavations. Reisner never again opened any appreciable number of Christian graves, and his frustration was

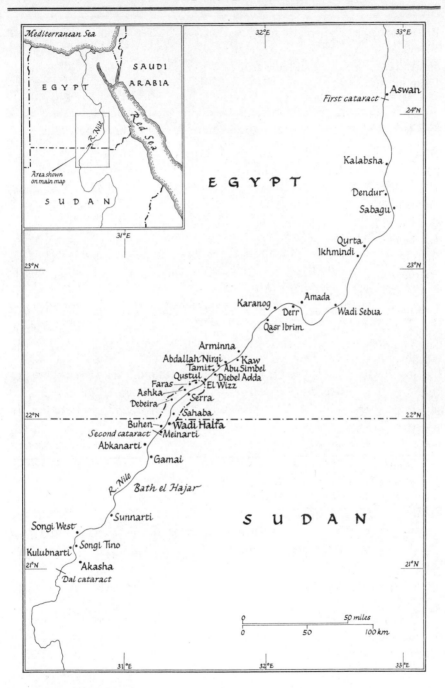

Principal archaeological sites in northern Nubia

reflected in the rather cursory recording in their last season's work.[185] This was a misfortune, for Reisner and Firth had appreciated the importance of salvage archaeology. Unfortunately they believed that the most informative as well as productive sites would be cemeteries, rather than the remains of churches, monasteries and forts. Survey and small-scale excavations on a selected number of such sites in immediate danger of flooding would have been of great value at this time.

As it was, their contribution to Nubian Christian archaeology was overshadowed by the work of Somers Clarke and G. S. Mileham, and by expeditions sponsored by Oxford, Philadelphia and Liverpool universities. Clarke's expeditions in 1899, 1907, 1909 and 1910 between Aswan and Dongola, accompanied by F. W. Green and Professor Sayce, recorded the existence of many of the sites that would be excavated by the international teams in the 1960s.[186] These included Serra, Kulb, Kulubnarti, el Ghazali and Sunnarti among others, household names to Nubiologists.

Clarke opposed large-scale excavation, rightly considering that with the resources available these would do more harm than good.[187] The only digging he records was an abortive attempt to find the base of the one surviving upright column in the cathedral at Ibrim.[188] He did not, however, realize that the floor of the latter lay nearly five feet below ground level! (See Chapter 12 below, p. 307.) Instead of excavations Clarke concentrated on drawing up accurate on-the-spot plans of the remains he visited. These were mainly churches. He found that despite decay and being obscured by vegetation, some of the churches were still in a fair state of preservation, even with parts of their roofs and walls standing. He was able to begin to build up a typology of Nubian church architecture, extending from the early basilican plan of churches such as Ibrim to later cruciform models with barrel vaults and, finally, small square buildings topped by a cupola, developments in many ways similar to those in the Byzantine empire itself.[189] This work provided a foundation for the studies of Shinnie and Adams half a century later (see below, p. 313) as his descriptions and plans of major sites – he was particularly interested in Ibrim[190] – helped the international teams preparing for large-scale salvage operations in the 1960s.

Clarke was interested in Christian Nubia as a whole. He identified numerous Christian villages, and drew attention to the relatively large Nubian population dwelling each side of the Nile between the ninth and thirteenth centuries AD. At one of these smaller sites he made a discovery on 7 December 1909 which showed what might be expected of future Nubian archaeology. The church at Abd-el-Kader near the Second Cataract was 'a diminutive ruin of crude brick', of total dimension 9.20 × 5.50 m, with the eastern chamber barely 4.50 m square and aisles only 0.80–1 m wide, but much of the roof had survived and the walls rose to a height of more than 2.50 m. The roof consisted of 'diminutive barrel vaults' over a central area entered from the hall or narthex which 'rested in part on the cross arches'. At a point on the wall of the central barrel vault is painted a 'Christ in majesty' filling up the whole available space, and in all other parts fragments of painting are to be seen, fairly well preserved.[191] An inconspicuous exterior plus accumulation of debris had aided in preserving the vaulting and paintings, anticipating what could be expected in larger and more distinguished buildings. The author remarked, finally, that this church unfortunately lay not far from the tourist track. 'The tourist is a greater enemy to an ancient building than an ignorant native. He takes away relics and momentos, crowds into the little chambers and blunders about with sticks, sunshades and nailed boots, doing more damage, innocently no doubt, than dozens of horned beasts.'[192] In 1909 the tourist in the Nile valley was not much different from his successor eighty years later.

Somers Clarke's work was complemented by Arthur Weigall and G. S. Mileham. Arthur Weigall succeeded Maspéro as Chief Inspector of Antiquities in Egypt in 1905, and at once under took a journey between Aswan and Abu Simbel with the main object of estimating the likely damage to monuments resulting from the Aswan dam. Most of his work, however, concerned temples and cemeteries. He found Derr 'very dirty' and Abu Simbel still 'partly covered with sand'. He noted the existence of 'Greco-Roman ruins' 4 km north of Abu Simbel, but apart from a brief description of the cathedral at Ibrim he had little to say about the Christian period when he published his report in 1907.[193]

Mileham's contribution was in the tradition of Clarke. His expeditions in 1908 and 1909 were sponsored by the Echley R. Coxe Jr Fund at Pennsylvania university and covered the area between Aswan and the Sudanese frontier, or Lower Nubia. Mileham, like Somers Clarke, was determined to end the neglect that had beset Coptic and early-Christian archaeology. The first task he set himself was to locate, clean and plan some major early-Christian churches. His report provides detailed accounts of Nubian methods of church-building, the construction of the brick vaults which almost always surmounted either the nave or the apse, and the methods used by the Nubians to counteract their chronic shortage of wood.[194] Thus, the churches at Debereh,[195] Faras,[196] Addendan,[197] and Serreh[198] were all surveyed, cleared of accumulated debris and described. At Debereh, Mileham found the first Christian inscription from that site, an elaborate funerary text in Coptic and

Greek commemorating the deacon Peter who died in the 45th year of the era of the martyrs, i.e. 1029.[199] He also identified a big building near the church at Serreh as a fort, anticipating thus the equation of fortified settlements with the later periods of Christian Nubian history.[200] His large surface collection of pottery sherds from the various sites he visited enabled him to begin a classification of the finely-decorated pottery of the Classic Nubian period (ninth and tenth centuries).

Faras, however, was the site that attracted Mileham's attention. No area in Nubia, he pointed out, 'contained so many ruined churches', and he deduced from this that Faras must have been the capital of the 'Lord of the Mountain' and kingdom of Nobatia.[201] He had been anticipated there in 1895 by Professor Sayce of Cambridge and Dr Maheffy, but his descriptions of the churches north and south of the main settlement were pioneering guides for future work. While he found no frescos, he recorded the Coptic inscriptions he found on the walls of the North Church and in tombs he located outside the main site.[202]

Some of the inscriptions he saw may have been in Old Nubian, and these years witnessed a major advance towards deciphering inscriptions in that language. Some Nubian inscriptions had already been identified as such and Christian inscriptions catalogued.[203] Now there was to be a major advance. In November 1906 Heinrich Schäfer deciphered a parchment document in Nubian, which Carl Schmidt had purchased for the Royal Library at Berlin.[204] Schäfer had been able to identify biblical passages through recognizing the words 'Herod the King' and use a knowledge of spoken (Maknass dialect) Nubian to achieve a promising result. He then generously handed over his work to F. Ll. Griffith, who had already worked on two texts, and by 1913 had become a corresponding member of the Prussian Academy of Sciences. Griffith's communication to the latter in July 1913 proved to be the foundation of Old Nubian studies.[205]

At the time he had only five documents and a number of graffiti to record. Two documents, however, were substantial, consisting of a text relating to the legend of St Menas the Egyptian (seventeen pages) and a Nubian copy of an Arabic version of the canons of Nicaea. There also existed a Nubian Christmastide lectionary,[206] an apocryphal address by Christ to his disciples before his ascension,[207] and a leather scroll recording a legal transaction (sale of land) in the reign of the Nubian king of Dotawi, Eilte (*c.* tenth century).[208] Griffith was able to publish adequate translations and show also the type of liturgical and legal documents likely to turn up (as they did at Ibrim: see below, Chapter 12, pp. 309–310) on sites during excavations.

As over the whole of the Greco-Roman world that had lain for centuries submerged under Islam, represented since the sixteenth century by Ottoman rule, the decade before the war was a time of discovery and increasing excitement. In Egypt and Sudan new fields were opening up and with new opportunities for research. In 1913, there were expeditions by Firth and Reisner (Firth this time being the leader) and by Oxford University. The latter, working at Faras from 1909 to 1913, proved to be one of the most important undertaken in Nubia. It confirmed that the site contained remains from every period of Nubian history from the New Kingdom to the Turkish domination, and with the discovery of the Rivergate Church and the North and South Churches, demonstrated what awaited the next generation of archaeologists.[209] These studies were interrupted by the war, but already archaeologists in the Nile valley were piecing together previously lost sections of the Christian history of its peoples. Particularly in Nubia, the outlines of the once-prosperous Christian civilization were emerging and even more clearly understood through the discovery of its works of art and decipherment of its language. Above all, what in 1884 Flinders Petrie described as the bane of archaeologists, their 'greed for small valuables',[210] was giving way to an interest in the objects found on sites primarily as data for research. Foundations had been laid for which scholars would be grateful when the construction of the High Dam endangered practically every Nubian site between Aswan and Wadi Halfa.

ETHIOPIA

After Salt's expedition in 1809 Ethiopian archaeology failed to arouse interest in Europe until near the end of the century. (See below, p. 385.) Then, the German explorer and antiquary Theodore Bent visited Axum and began to record the great quantity of antiquities that confronted him. His account of his discoveries together with an incipient German political interest in the Abyssinian empire, resulted in a well-equipped expedition being fitted out in 1906 under Daniel Krenker and Enno Littmann. Littmann and his companions spent three months on the site of Axum (Aksum). Their discoveries were such as to fill five large volumes. No fewer than 78 stelae of the pillar type recorded by Salt were found and mapped.[211] These included eleven which Littmann identified as having been erected by King Ezana, 'king of Aksum and of Himyar' (south-west Arabia), acknowledging the aid of divine powers in his victories over 'the peoples of Noba (Nubia)' and other enemies. On four of these stelae Ezana proclaimed himself 'son of the inconquerable god

Ares',[212] but on one, Inscription 11, there is a change. Instead of Ares, Ezana attributes his victories to 'the might of the Lord of the Heavens' and 'the Lord of All, who has created me'.[213] Littmann believed this inscription proved that Ezana was converted to Christianity and that he and his brother Sazana were the princes of Axum addressed by the emperor Constantius II in 357,[214] and that by then they were Christians. A gold coin of Ezana with a cross on it seemed to confirm this belief.[215]

Another Ezana inscription, this time acknowledging the 'power of the Father and the Son and the Holy Spirit', discovered in 1969, appears to vindicate Littmann's general thesis. However, the inscription dedicated to 'the Lord of Heavens' indicates a monotheist phase in the king's religious development which was not necessarily Christian, while the Greek cross on the coin could be later than the mid-fourth century. The possibility also of two rulers named Ezana, one pagan and the other, later, Christian, cannot be ruled out. Littmann's results, published in 1913, showed however what was to be found at Axum and prepared the ground for the research of the French archaeologists Anfray and Caquot in 1969,[216] the British excavations under Neville Chittick in 1974,[217] on behalf of the British Institute in Eastern Africa, and in 1993 and 1994 by David Phillipson.

FURTHER READING

W. V. Adams, *Nubia, Corridor to Africa* (London: Allen Lane, 1977): a fundamental study for all aspects of Nubian civilization and religion known to 1976.

F. Anfray, A. Caquot and P. Nautin, 'Une nouvelle inscription grecque d'Ezana, roi d'Axoum', *JS* (1970), pp. 260–73.

Wallis Budge, *Texts Relating to Saint Mena of Egypt and the Canons of Nicaea in Nubian Dialect* (London, 1909).

Somers Clarke, *Christian Antiquities in the Nile Valley* (London, 1912).

J. Clédat, 'Baouit', *DACL* II, 203–251.

F. Ll. Griffith, 'The Nubian texts of the Christian period', *ABAW* (July 1913).

F. Ll. Griffith, 'Oxford excavations in Nubia', *LAAA* 11 (1924), pp. 115–180; 12 (1925), pp. 57–172; 13 (1926), pp. 17–37; 14 (1927), pp. 57–116.

Sir Frederick Kenyon, *The Bible and Archaeology* (London, 1940).

G. S. Mileham, *Churches in Lower Nubia* (University of Philadelphia Press, 1910).

S. C. Munro, *Excavations at Aksum* (Chittick's excavations 1972–74; London: British Institute in East Africa, 1989), memoir 10.

H. Leclercq, articles in *DACL*: 'Bagouat (el)', II, 31–62 and 'Papyrus', XIII, 1370–1520.

Fish and anchor
fresco from
the Roman
catacombs

The theatre at
Ephesus

Tombs in the
church of
St Domnio,
Manastirine,
Salona

Wall painting in the synagogue, Dura Europos

Last church on the point below Qasr Ibrim

(4) Central Asia

The archaeological expeditions during the first decade of the century following the ancient Silk Route that once linked the Roman empire to China were yet another example of the thrust and rivalry of the European powers into potentially strategic areas of the world. Central Asia and, in particular, the oasis of Turfan in Chinese Turkestan proved to be a magnet for successive expeditions by German, British and French explorers and archaeologists. They were rewarded richly by hauls of documents that threw new and completely unexpected light on the mingling of peoples, languages and cultures that had taken place along the Route in the first ten centuries of the Christian era.[218]

Turfan had been the capital of the semi-nomadic Turkish tribe of Uigurs in the eighth and ninth centuries. It was a meeting-place for Buddhists, Nestorians and Manichees, and for speakers of Syriac, Soghdian (a sort of Middle Persian), Proto-Turkish, Chinese, Brahmini and Gupta. Texts were found in all these languages. Though the predominant culture was Buddhist, the *Khagan* (ruler) of the tribe had been converted to the dualist sect of Manichaeism in 762, and the most important result of the various expeditions that visited the area was evidence for the impact of Manichaeism on the different cultures its missionaries had encountered. An assertion by the Muslim Arab writer Al-Biruni *c.* AD 1000 that 'most of the eastern Turks, of the peoples of China and Tibet and some of the Hindus adhere to Mani's law and doctrine',[219] may well have had some truth in it.

The first arrivals were the two Germans, Grünwedel and Huth, in 1902–03.[220] They were in luck, discovering part of a copy of a long document written by Mani to King Bahram (276–293) (not King Sapor (242–276), as originally thought),[221] explaining and defending his message, as well as fragments of homilies and hymns. They were published by the Prussian Academy of Sciences by F. W. K. Müller in 1904. This success inspired further officially sponsored expeditions. Grünwedel and Albrecht von Le Coq were again at Turfan in 1904 and 1907. The latter visit was extraordinarily productive. New documents in Uiguric (Old Turkish) referred to 'the mighty Apostle', and to conflict between Zarathustra and the demons in the holy city of Babylon.[222] 'The mighty Apostle' could be St Paul, whom the Manichees regarded as *the* interpreter of Jesus' message, but could even be Mani as 'the Apostle of Jesus Christ'. The explicit dualism of the eternal conflict between Good and Evil was the hall-mark of Mani's teaching. No further proof was needed for the influence of Manichaeism among the Uigur people. The texts from the haul of documents, probably from a Manichaean library, were written in a special script on paper, parchment, and palm-leaf in a variety of languages. One document proved to be the first pages of the Khuastanift or 'Confessional for the Hearers'. It defined fifteen types of sin for which a Hearer must seek forgiveness and set out the duties of Hearers in regard to the Elect (fully initiated Manichees).[223] Another document recorded the end of the primeval conflict between Light and the Demons that resulted in the creation of the world.[224] Particularly revealing from the point of view of Manichaean missionary tactics were those that showed how the legends concerning the Buddha as well as Buddhist phraseology had been adapted by the Manichee missionaries. These, true to the teaching of Mani, had evidently attempted to combine existing religious traditions of Christianity, Zoroastrianism and Buddhism into a synthesis based, however, on a strict dualism of eternal conflict between Light and Darkness.[225] For the inhabitants of Turfan, Mani was the 'Buddha of Light', and the terminology of the texts was 'of unmistakably Buddhist[226] origin'. Mani himself was represented on the murals on the walls of his sect's monasteries as a Buddha-figure.

These German expeditions were quickly followed by the French, though the main thrust of the latter, represented by Edouard Chavannes and Paul Pelliot, was 300 miles further east along the Silk Route. The site was the cave-temples of Tun-Huang where the Frenchmen followed in the footsteps of Sir Aurel Stein, who visited the area at the end of a survey of the Han *limes* (fortified frontier) in Central Asia in 1908. Stein[227] had been at Turfan in November 1907 and found manuscripts, but his short visit to Tun-Huang proved to be even more fruitful. The temple library there contained many thousands of scrolls. It had been preserved because the cave which had served as a depository had been sealed in 1035 to prevent its desecration by marauders.[228] A Taoist priest had made the original find but Stein was luckily on the spot and able to take a small selection of the rolls of manuscripts back with him to India, and thence they came eventually into the care of the British museum. Most were Buddhist, but one proved to be the entire text of the Khuastanift already known from the Turfan manuscript in Old Turkish, which showed that the Manichaeans of Turfan had pushed east into China itself.[229]

Chavannes and Pelliot were at the caves in 1909 and 1911, acquiring documents for the Bibliothèque Nationale. Their discoveries, combined with a hymn scroll and a document known as *The Compendium* containing an account of Mani's life and tenets found among the British Museum documents, enabled them to piece together something of the beliefs and culture of the Chinese Manichees. They were also able to edit an even larger document, known as the

Treatise, which Chinese scholars had found at the caves and taken to Peking.[230] This document showed that the Manichees insisted that he who wished 'to enter the religion' must discern the existence of the (eternal) principles of 'Light and Darkness', and also the Three Moments of the Past, the Present and the Future.[231] Its authenticity became clear when one compared its demand with the opening words of Mani's 'Fundamental Epistle', preserved by Augustine: 'Accordingly, hear first if you please, what happened before the settlement of the world, and how the battle was carried on, so that you may be able to distinguish the nature of light from that of darkness.'[232] The Manichees, too, formed a distinct sect, calling themselves 'The Association of the Religion of Light'.[233] That the story of Light and Darkness and the invasion of Light by the kingdom of Darkness was not regarded simply as esoteric legend is shown by another document explaining how the eternal conflict was mirrored exactly in the experience of each individual, his good but isolated soul being invaded by alien uncontrollable forces of evil.[234]

In China, however, the religion never lost its foreign, imported and exclusive character. It had arrived largely through the tributary Uigur people and ultimately expressed the language and ideas of the far west in Persia.[235] The Hymn Scroll, for instance, containing praises of Mani, consisted of translations of hymns from the Parthian. They included elaborate instructions how the refrains were to be sung, as though they had been transcribed phonetically.[236] Not surprisingly, the documents also showed how the Manichees were often treated with suspicion by the Chinese authorities and their religion proscribed, though it is now known that groups managed to survive into the fifteenth century.[237]

The Manichees did not, however, have the field to themselves in China. Christian Nestorian missionaries, also from Persia, were active at this same time. There was a Metropolitan in China not later than *c.* AD 630 and Nestorian monks in 638, when an imperial decree accorded them protection on the grounds that their preaching 'fixed the essentials of life and perfection'. It was not a popular post, for a Persian monarch wishing to intimidate a Christian bishop would threaten to banish him to China, putting him on board a merchant ship plying between the Persian Gulf and China.[238] The great Nestorian monument erected in 779 (or 781) at Si-ngan-fu, though originally dug up in 1625, was not fully published in English until 1916.[239] It mentions a Patriarch Huanisho in whose name it was set up, also other clergy such as Yohannis, deacon and monk, and a priest who was *chorepiscopos* ('country' or auxiliary bishop) of Kundan. It claims that the original Nestorian missionary Alo-pen was received by the emperor T'ai Tsung, 'the cultured emperor', in

635 and that 'The Scriptures were translated in the Royal Library and their doctrine examined in the Private Apartments'.[240] These were signs of favour. The Nestorians, moreover, were not regarded by the Muslims with such antipathy as the Manichees, and they remained an influence throughout central Asia until the rise of the Tartar empire and their rulers' acceptance of Islam in the mid-thirteenth century.

Manichees and Nestorians can be seen as intrepid missionaries, each anticipating the Jesuits in their ability to adapt their teaching to the culture and customs of their prospective converts. Whatever the rivalry of the Powers that contributed to the expeditions to Turfan and further east in the first decade of the twentieth century, these threw new light on the success of the Manichaean missionaries and the beliefs of the sect. As late as 1897,[241] scholars had discounted the possibility of discovering the writings of this least popular and most secretive of Christian dissenting traditions. Thanks to the Turfan and Tun-Huang documents, a new era for Manichaean studies had dawned.

FURTHER READING

Peter Brown, 'The diffusion of Manichaeism in the Roman Empire', *JRS* 59 (1969), pp. 92–103 (= *Religion and Society in the Age of Saint Augustine* (London: Faber and Faber, 1972), pp. 74–93) and *Augustine of Hippo* (Faber and Faber, 1967), chs 4–9.

F. C. Burkitt, *The Religion of the Manichees* (Cambridge, 1924): discussion of discoveries in Central Asia.

W. B. Hemming, 'The date of the Sogdian Ancient Letters', *BSOAS* 12 (1948), pp 601–15.

A. V. W. Jackson, *Researches into Manichaeism with Special Reference to the Turfan Fragments* (New York, 1932).

Samuel N. C. Lieu, *Manichaeism in the Later Roman Empire and Mediaeval China: A Historical Survey* (Manchester University Press, 1984): a fundamental work, with full bibliography relating to Manichaeism in China.

Samuel N. C. Lieu, 'Polemics against Manichaeism as a subversive cult in China', *BJRL* 62 (1979), pp. 151–67.

H. C. Puech, *Le Manichéisme, son fondateur, sa doctrine* (Paris 1949).

P. Y. Saeku, *The Nestorian Monument in China* (SPCK, 1916).

M. Aurel Stein, *Ruins of Desert Cathay* (2 vols; London: Macmillan, 1912).

Other works relating to Manichaeism in Egypt and North Africa, and the career of Mani are included in *Further Reading* under Chapter 9.

(5) The catacombs

De Rossi had worked and published to the last year of his life and his legacy continued after him. Exploration, research and organization went on apace. Though of his three outstanding disciples, Enrico Stevenson, Orazio Marucchi and Josef Wilpert (1857–1944) Stevenson died in 1897, Marucchi and Wilpert maintained de Rossi's ideals for another thirty years, surviving the First World War to give catacomb research a generation-long leading role in Christian archaeology. They made an excellent team. Marucchi was the explorer historian and organizer, Wilpert the artist and dogmatist. Wilpert's enormous *Pitture della Catacombe* (*Malerei der römischen Katacomben*) (2 vols; Rome, 1903) put on permanent, if sometimes idealized, record a great number of catacomb frescos which otherwise would have faded into decay through exposure. Marucchi's *Elements d'archéologie chrétienne* (Paris/Rome, 1903) brought together the history and results to date from North Africa and the catacombs to reinforce the claim for the study of Christian archaeology to be essential for the study of the later Roman empire. Both men, however, were strongly conservative, as one would expect in Rome in the latter years of the pontificate of Leo XIII (d. 1903) and that of Pius X (d. 1914). This sometimes led them to attempt to find the origins of Roman Catholic beliefs and liturgy in catacomb art where other explanations were more convincing. Was the banquet scene in the *Capella graeca*, the little subterranean chapel in the Priscilla catacomb, forming part of 'the earliest representation of the eucharistic sacrifice'?[242] Was one justified in believing that the painting itself could be related to the memory of the Apostle Peter?[243] Or should it be asserted that a young woman aged 25 kneeling before Christ and the apostles Peter and Paul, her arms outstretched in supplication to a welcoming Christ, represented 'the Mother of God praying to the Child Jesus', instead of the deceased's fervent entry into Paradise?[244] Sometimes, however, they were justified, such as on a judgement scene in the catacomb of Hermes where a soul appears to be conducted by a saintly patron before a seated Christ, while an accuser (?) stands on his left. This could be an early representation of an individual's patron saint necessary to guarantee him or her the hoped-for *refrigerium* (refreshment) in Paradise.[245] What catacomb art demonstrates is that in addition to the aspirations of the deceased, some of the almost universal liturgical practices and sacraments of the Churches were being illustrated as early as the third century AD.[246]

The vast increase in the amount of material available for study was resulting in the debate widening, especially in Germany. Already scholars were beginning to ask whether the art of the catacombs was simply a projection of Classical art into a Christian medium, or whether Christian art was essentially a new art form corresponding to the originality of the new Christ-oriented religion. Did it owe more to the East than to the classical world?[247] In this debate Wilpert and Strzygowski became the champions of radically opposed views, Wilpert asserting the predominance of Rome, Strzygowski, of the

East.[248] Both scholars exaggerated their position. Wilpert became increasingly dogmatic. Strzygowski pushed his search for origins ever eastward, to Armenia and even to the Turkish peoples. The discovery of Dura Europos would have prevented his wilder surmises. Both had some right on their side, and take credit for opening a debate that lasted throughout much of the century.

Meantime, the Second International Congress of Christian Archaeology eventually assembled in Rome on 21 April 1900. Duchesne presided, and the scope was wider than its predecessor at Spalato (see above, pp. 83–4). Delattre reported on his latest discoveries at Carthage and Gsell on the churches he had excavated at Ammaedara and Thelepte in south-east Tunisia. The Austrians gave an account of their *Reisen* in Turkey. Bulić spoke of the great Christian cemetery of Manastirine he had discovered at Salona. Carthage was chosen as the site of the next meeting.[249]

The geographical extension was to the good, but once again resources available were unequal to the task of organizing and publishing the work of these assemblies. In the next decade the best results were achieved by Duchesne's and Marucchi's smaller monthly meetings of de Rossi's Società in Rome. Once such was the rapid reporting in 1911 of the existence of the important fifth- to sixth-century Christian cemetery at Ain Zara in Italy's recent conquest of Tripolitania.[250]

In Rome itself discoveries were following thick and fast. A new source was being exploited. Study of the foundations of some of the city's churches revealed more catacombs, one below the church of San Pancrazio on the Via Aurelia, another beneath a building belonging to the convent of the Dorotheans. Even more productive was Enrico Stevenson's discovery on property just north of the Via Casilina where the Sisters of the Holy Family planned to build either a refectory or chapel. They could hardly have succeeded, for already de Rossi had perceived that the whole area was honeycombed with subterranean passages and put Stevenson on the trail. Two seasons' work (1895 and 1896) enabled him to locate a crypt in the centre of which were two *loculi* placed one above another.[251] Their position fitted the description given by Einhard in the ninth century of the burial-place of the martyrs Peter and Marcellinus,[252] executed during the Great Persecution. Pilgrims' graffiti helped to confirm the identification. Marucchi published the discovery from Stevenson's notes, opening the way to the exploration of a vast catacomb and cemetery *Ad Duos Lauros* established in the second half of the third century.[253] This would contain memorable paintings, such as Christ touching the water jars with a magic wand at the feast of

Cana, the Heavenly Banquet, one among several at which two serving maids are named 'Agape' and 'Irene', whether real names or symbols for 'Love' and 'Peace' is not yet known.[254] There was also the multiplication of loaves and Moses striking the rock, as well as a cemetery containing thousands of third- and fourth-century graves, and dominated by the Constantinian basilica and mausoleum built for the empress Helena.[255]

Marucchi and Wilpert meantime were concentrating on the catacomb of Domitilla on the Ardeatine Way. Part of this had been left since Boldetti's time as too dangerous to enter, but in 1897 the two scholars were able to resume exploration and another great gallery of *loculi* and *arcosolia* discovered. On the side of one of the latter there was a representation of Christ crowning a group of martyrs.[256] and in the same area Wilpert came on a chapel used by Christian members of a corporation of bakers that depicted granaries and barges transporting grain.[257] There was also a representation of Orpheus originally discovered by Bosio, whose central figure had, however, been vandalized and removed in the eighteenth century. The animals, tamed by Orpheus' music, could still be recognized and the third-century date showed how Orpheus, representing Christ, was attracting educated people in Rome to Christianity.[258] The way to the faith was leading along roads other than biblical.

Though accurate dating was still in its infancy, neither scholar was willing to accept that pagans and Christians had been laid to rest in the same catacombs. It needed a representation of the labours of Hercules and Medusa alongside biblical schemes from the catacomb on the Via Latina (published in 1960) to resolve most doubts.[259] (See Chapter 13 below.)

Marucchi and Wilpert were more willing to accept a heretical, Gnostic interpretation for one fine series of paintings from the vault of Trebius Justus, also on the Via Latina, excavated in March 1911.[260] Trebius is shown as a wealthy young man seated with writing materials, or as generous landowner and as a supervisor of the building of a villa (or town house). The centre of the vault was occupied by a representation of the Good Shepherd. To the present writer there seems nothing mysterious about this choice of artistic motifs. They could depict simply the many activities in which Trebius was engaged when he died sometime in the second half of the third century. Others, however, saw hidden symbolic meanings behind what appeared to be straightforward illustrations of the life of a 'noble master'. Eight years later, the vault of the Aurelii on the Via Manzoni would provide clearer evidence for the existence of a Gnostic community in third-century Rome.

FURTHER READING

H. Leclercq, *Manuel d'archéologie chrétienne* (2 vols; Paris, 1907).

O. Marucchi, 'La cripta storica dei SS Pietro e Marcellino recentemente scoperta sulla Via Labicana', *NBAC* 4 (1898), pp. 137–94.

O. Marucchi, *Elements d'archéologie chrétienne* (2 vols; Paris/Rome, 1903).

O. Marucchi, 'L'Ipogeo sepocrale di Trebio Giusto', *NBAC* 17 (1911), pp. 209–35; 18 (1912), pp. 83–9.

J. Wilpert, *Fractio Panis: Die älteste Darstellung des eucharistischen Opfers* (Freiburg im Breisgau, 1895).

J. Wilpert, *Le pitture delle catacombe romane* (Rome, 1903) (German trans. *Die Malerei der römischen Katakomben*).

For a critical assessment of Wilpert's scholarship, see E. Dassmann, 'J. Wilpert und die Erforschung der römischen Katakomben', *RQ* Suppl. 35 (1977), pp. 160ff.

See also Stevenson, *The Catacombs*, and *DACL* art. 'Domitilla'.

For catacombs outside Rome explored in this period see:

E. Becker, *Malta sotteranea* (Strasbourg, 1913).

J. Führer and V. Schultze, *Altchristlichen Grabstätten Siziliens* (Berlin, 1907).

(6) The Balkans and western Europe

The subjects of the Austro-Hungarian empire played a prominent part in the Congress of Christian Archaeology in August 1894. Salona–Spalato was chosen as its twin location and among the moving spirits were two Croat clergy, Fr. L. Jelić of Zara who carried out excavations there, and Mgr Francesce Bulić. The latter was to spend fifty years of a long life (1846–1934) working on the Christian monuments of Salona.

Bulić had started to work there in 1885, but it was not until 1899 that he discovered the Christian cemeteries of Marusinac and Manastirine outside the city.[261] The Marusinac complex had developed round the tomb of Anastasius the fuller who had actually sought maryrdom in Salona in 304 as his native Aquileia was not dangerous enough! The church and cemetry at Manastirine had probably grown up round that of Domnio, the first bishop and also a martyr during the Great Persecution.[262] Domnio was a member of what appears to have been an immigrant Syrian Christian family that had settled in the town, and created a Christian community *c.* 300, for which he paid with his life.[263] He was succeeded by his nephew Primus.[264] The story, reconstructed from inscriptions mostly found and reported by Bulić, confirms that Christianity was a late arrival in the West, often brought by merchants from the eastern provinces. More surprisingly, these show also that the custom of keeping the bishopric in the family died hard, instanced by Polycrates of Ephesus *c.* 190 who had succeeded eight successive kinsmen.[265] Both Marusinac and Manastirine became centres of pilgrimage, as had Tipasa in North Africa. An inscription from Manastirine asserted that this was 'the cemetery of the holy Christian law' — Christianity still immigrant and sectarian in outlook in the fourth century.

Though most of the excavation was to be carried out between the wars by the Danish architect/archaeologist Einar Dyggve and his Austrian colleague Rudolf Egger, Bulić was able to establish the three main Christian centres in Salona. In the cemetery area north of the city walls were Marusinac and Manistirine, but within the walls east of the amphitheatre from 1903 to 1909 he and an Austrian colleague, Dr Gerber, excavated an imposing episcopal cathedral complex. This was centred on parallel-standing churches (double churches), one probably for congregational worship and the other yet another memorial church reserved for the cult of martyrs' relics. The area included a large baptistery, rooms (domestic), a self-contained water-tower, and space for an oil reservoir and for storing wine. Oil and wine were manufactured on the spot and would have increased episcopal revenues accordingly.[266]

Salona was eventually destroyed by the Avars *c.* 614: the inhabitants moved to Spalato three miles to the south, and the site was not re-occupied. The undisturbed remains of three centuries of Christian history have deservedly made it the show-piece as well as a major centre for the study of Christianity in the Balkans.

Its status however as the archaeological magnet was being challenged in the first decade of the twentieth century by Aquileia. The Roman city, which lay within the Austrian frontier with Italy, was providing equally important material. Despite Bertoli's discoveries in the 1730s little work had been carried out in this enormouly promising site. In 1894 Wilpert had published Christian epigraphy found to date there, including the important inscription showing baptism by affusion (i.e. the convert standing in a large font while baptismal water was poured on him).[267] In 1908, however, a series of excavations began beneath the eleventh-century cathedral. The work was handsomely rewarded. A church was discovered whose floor was wholly paved with mosaic and on one side was a suite of rooms which included a baptistery and the bishop's residence.[268] The mosaics were extraordinary by any standard. A large area was taken up with an elaborate scene depicting fishermen in their boats catching a variety of fish in calm waters: right and left were frames showing animals grazing or standing around peacefully. A centre panel portrayed the busts of individuals, reasonably identified as the donors of the mosaic, and at the bottom were three panels, two with geometric patterns and one portraying further human busts (see photograph). The only specifically Christian symbol was accompanying the inscription 'Theodore felix / hic crevisti / hic felix' (Blessed Theodorus, here you have increased, here you are blessed).[269] Theodorus of Aquileia was mentioned among the bishops attending the Council of Arles in 314. The church can therefore hardly be later than *c.* 320. It was supported by wealthy citizens, and Theodorus himself had probably converted his family home (there was an earlier mosaic below the church) into an episcopal residence. Aquileia thus provided a further example of the progress of Christianity in another major western centre in the first decade of the fourth century.

Pola (Pula) and Salonica both produced substantial evidence for Christianity in the fourth century. At Pola[270] a large church was found in an area where Constantine had a villa. This had witnessed grisly episodes. His son Crispus and wife Fausta met their ends there, and the unfortunate Caesar Gallus was executed in 354 at the order of his cousin Constantius II.[271] At Salonica, still very much part of the Turkish empire, an early example of salvage archaeology, carried out by R. Perdrizet and his colleagues, enabled the study of much of a large Christian cemetery soon to be submerged in the foundations of a hospital.[272] Their work suggested, however, that this Pauline missionary centre, like others, only became Christian in the Constantinian period.[273]

In the western provinces comprising the Gallic prefecture (Spain, Gaul, Germany and Britain) there was less activity. *Britain* would have to await the discovery of the Traprain Law treasure in 1919 before early Christianity was represented again among its Roman antiquities. In France and Germany the main efforts of archaeologists had, as we have seen, been overseas.

In *France*, Edmond Leblant had no outstanding successor. As in Britain there were a multitude of local natural history and antiquarian societies but in many discovery of valuable objects from cemeteries, took pride of place. There was an 'enthousiame pour l'archéologie funéraire' often leading to the looting and spoliation of Gallo-Roman and Merovingian cemeteries,[274] as scholars attempted to judge the degree of fusion between Gallo-Roman provincial and Germanic populations to form the French nation. One archaeologist was reputed to have opened 10,000 Merovingian graves in the valley of the Aisne without making plans of any of them.[276] Another pillaged a rich site at Marcheleport (Somme) and allegedly sold his finds to dealers.[277] It was fortunate when occasionally a cleric such as Père Camille de la Croix (1831–1911) spent a long period of his life in one parish and became interested in the local antiquities. In the neighbourhood of Poitiers, de la Croix excavated a cemetery with 300 graves, among which was the magnificent stone-built vault of the presbyter Mellobaudes. Later he excavated one of the best preserved Gallo-Roman baptisteries, that of St John.[278] Like Mgr Bulić's at Salona, his was an individual effort, but in his case not well supported by his colleagues.

In Paris the situation was better. Watchfulness and appreciation of the importance of the city's past allowed Théodore Vacquet (1822–99) to record some 2,000 early-Christian (Gallo-Roman) and Merovingian sarcophagi of the sixth to eighth centuries, in forty years of observation (1858–98).[279] One major success was the discovery of Christian buildings below St Germain des Prés (1873–77); another the Cimitière Saint-Marcel (1868–74).[280] His persistence was rewarded in the last year of his life by the creation of a Commission du Vieux Paris. The example of Paris was followed in other municipalities. It was uphill work. The first early Christian church was excavated in 1913 at St Bertrand de Comminges,[281] but only in the south, where Roman remains were often visible, and Christian cemeteries, such as those around Arles, had been long known, was real interest being shown. In this period French archaeology was part of French culture to be disseminated in their empire and spheres of influence.

The *Germans* had been well represented at Spalato, and in 1908 and 1913 a corpus of Christian inscriptions with an appendix for Jewish inscriptions was published in Bonn.[282] But fieldwork was still in its opening stages. Trier, however, was beginning to yield, in the cemetery of St Eucharius surrounding the church of St Matthias, a rich harvest to be gathered in the inter-war years. The late-Roman cemetery had been cut through by the railway and sarcophagi protruded along one side of the cutting, inviting investigation by local archaeologists.[283] Another Christian cemetery was found at Cologne, but the meagre results in their homelands demonstrated the importance laid by the European Powers on archaeological work in strategic areas overseas. In these years archaeology was indeed following the flag.

FURTHER READING

E. Dyggve, *History of Salonitan Christianity* (Oslo, 1951)

P. A. Février, 'Naissance de l'archéologie chrétienne' in *Naissance des arts chrétiens* (Atlas archéologiques de France; Paris, 1991), pp. 336–47.

A. Gnirs, *Pola, ein Führer durch die antiken Baudenkmäler und Sammlungen* (Vienna, 1915).

B. K. Young and P. Perin. 'Les nécropoles (IIIe–VIIIe siècle)' in *Naissance des Arts chrétiens*, pp. 94–121.

J. Zeiller, *Origines chrétiennes de la Dalmatie* (Paris, 1906).

H. Leclercq, major articles 'Bulić' and 'Salona' in *DACL*.

Conclusion

This long chapter needs no excuse. In the twenty years before the First World War scholarship was moving forward in every field. The study of early Christianity was no exception. New literary texts were coming to light, such as the Armenian version of Irenaeus' *Exhortation of Apostolic Preaching*, found in December 1904,[284] and the potentially vast discoveries awaiting their finder among the papyri from the rubbish-tips of the Fayum. All round the Mediterranean there were new discoveries to be made. It was an archaeologist's paradise. Ancient sites still stood undisturbed, and if today one reproaches the archaeologists for their lack of skill and loss of valuable historical evidence, one must concede that but for their efforts the sites would soon have been lost to the bulldozer. Already, as population was growing, there were increasing numbers of those like the village headman in northern Syria who told Gertrude Bell 'When I want some cut stones, I only have to dig in this ground'.[285]

Temples, amphitheatres, fora and private dwellings were salvaged, along with churches and baptisteries, to inspire the tourist with a sense of wonder at the 'glory that was Rome' and of the vanished Christian civilization. Apart from the plans of the individual churches and greatly increased knowledge of Christian liturgy and aspirations, the chief gain had been in the new knowledge of the Christian dissenting movements whose works and leaders the Great Church did its utmost to suppress. Donatists, Montanists, Manichaeans and Coptic and Nubian Monophysites at last could begin to speak for themselves through inscriptions, papyri and the steady accumulation of material evidence. The uncovering of a Christian past both accompanied and fuelled growing popular interest. De Rossi's lectures at spots he believed actual maryrdoms had taken place in the Roman catacombs during the persecutions drew crowds of hearers. Ramsay aimed at bringing his studies of the Roman empire and Christianity in Asia Minor to the widest public. In turn, *The Church in the Roman Empire to 170*, *St Paul, Traveller and Roman Citizen*, *The Seven Churches That Are in Asia*, and *Luke the Physician* went through edition after edition. Fame and fortune were won by their author, and a growing public was made aware of the story told from archaeology of the progress of Christianity from Jewish sect to world religion.

The two congresses of Christian archaeologists in 1894 and 1900 may have been over-ambitious and were not repeated until the 1930s, but they inspired Continental universities to include archaeology in their courses of Church history. One of those who took advantage of this was Franz Joseph Dölger

(1879–1940), who published in 1910 his first essay on 'The fish symbol in early Christian times', a study that combined epigraphic with literary evidence, not least to show how in the fifth century the symbol had been used to protect houses.[286] He opened up, as one (Protestant) theologian stated, 'a new world in early Christian research'.[287] Dölger, however, suffered for his openness. After Professor (later Cardinal) Faulhaber had written 'So long as I have influence, Dölger will never be a Professor',[288] Dölger never attempted to fuse his studies in the detail of relationship between Christianity and the pagan provincial world into a general history. It was too risky. Protestant theologians suffered no such impediment. New Testament scholars, such as Hans Lietzmann, successively professor at Jena and Berlin, included graffiti and papyri in their courses. A visit to the newly-discovered sites in Greece and Tunisia in 1913 filled Lietzmann with enthusiasm for archaeology. 'I understand', wrote his friend Karl Holl in May 1914, 'you are completely taken up with archaeology.'[289] Three months later the achievements of the previous half century were threatened with total loss and oblivion by the outbreak of war. The optimism of two decades of imperial self-confidence would never be revived. Archaeology would survive, but as it became more professional and dour something of the *Light from the Ancient East*, Adolf Deissmann's vision, was extinguished.

NOTES

1. Noël Valois, *CRAI* (1913), pp. 548–9.
2. See L. H. Vincent, 'Le Père Lagrange', *RB* 47 (1938), pp. 321–54, at pp. 346–9.
3. E.g. K. Kautsky, *Foundations of Christianity*, Eng. trans. of 13th edn by J. W. Hartmann (Berlin, 1980): 'We are not even certain that he [Jesus] ever lived'. Christianity was a 'social product': ibid., p. 42.
4. Alfred Loisy's *Les mystères païens et les mystères chrétiens* (1st edn; Paris, 1912) is a well-documented survey. He points in ch. i and pp. 104–20 to some similarities beween the worship of Attis in Asia Minor and the Christian liturgy and to similarities in the way pagan and Christian hopes in the afterlife were being expressed in the fourth century: p. 118 n. 2.
5. Particularly in his *Hellenistische Wundererzählungen* (Leipzig, 1906). Reitzenstein suggested that many of the miracle stories recorded in orthodox and Gnostic Christian Acts of the Martyrs and lives of saints, were adapted from existing pagan, particularly Cynic, models.
6. Karl Holl, 'Urchristentum und Religionsgeschichte', *Antike* (1925), pp. 161–74.
7. Charles Gore (ed.), *Lux Mundi* (1889), p. vii, The Church, because 'the truth makes her free', 'is able to assimilate all new material, to welcome and to give its place to all knowledge ... shewing again and again her power of witnessing under changed conditions to the catholic capacity of her faith and life'. Similar ideas are expressd on p. 262.
8. Reported by Anastase Orlandos, 'Délos chrétienne', *BCH* 60 (1936), pp. 68–100, esp. pp. 69 and 87ff.
9. Citing the report from P. A. Février, *Approches du Maghreb* (Edisud, 1987–89) p. 73. For burnt and destroyed area in Timgad, see A. Ballu, *Les ruines de Timgad: sept années de découvertes* (Paris, 1911), p. 46.

10. S. Gsell, 'Chronique d'archéologie africaine', *MEFR* 22 (1902), pp. 33–45. Gsell also somewhat perversely criticized time spent on excavation of 'méchantes bâtisses byzantines et berbères', for these would have been included in the smaller sites in Numidia which he urged should be tackled, and would have provided useful information on the last phases of major sites.

11. P. Monceaux, *Timgad chrétien* (Paris, 1911). Proof that this huge Christian complex was indeed the Donatist cathedral was established by E. Albertini, *CRAI* (1939), pp. 100–1, briefly reporting the discovery of a mosaic within the main church, laid on the instructions of Bishop Optatus (Donatist bishop 388–398): 'Hic iubente sacerdote Dei Optato peregi'. In 1913 R. Cagnat found a fine mosaic in a fourth-century chapel on the site dedicated to 'the martyrs' with the salutation usually regarded as Donatist, 'Dignis digna': *CRAI* (1913), pp. 381–4.

12. *CRAI* (1889), 'Séance de 22 novembre 1889', p. 457; also *MEFR* 10 (1890), p. 397.

13. Gaston Boissier, cited from Février, op. cit., p. 89.

14. J. Toutain, 'Les progrès de la vie urbaine dans l'Afrique du Nord sous la domination romaine' in *Mélanges René Cagnat* (Paris, 1912), pp. 319–347 at p. 347.

15. A. Audollent and J. Letaille, 'Mission épigraphique en Algérie', *MEFR* 10 (1890), pp. 397–588, at p. 400.

16. Ibid., pp. 440–70; illustrated on p. 441.

17. Ibid.

18. Cyprian, *Ep.* 76; ed. W. Hartel, *CSEL* 3.2, 827.

19. *Acta Saturnini* 18: *PL* 8, 701. For the particular veneration of these martyrs by the Donatists, see P. Monceaux, *Histoire littéraire* IV (Paris, 1912), p. 467.

20. Augustine, *Epp.* 16 and 17.

21. Audollent and Letaille, op. cit., p. 457 = *CIL* VIII, 9255 and *DACL* X.2, 2670–2677. For Firmus' 'pro-Donatist tendency', see W. H. C. Frend, *The Donatist Church*, pp. 197–9. Donatists dubbed 'Firmiani' by Augustine, *C. Ep. Parm.* 10.16.

22. See Frend, 'The Memoriae Apostolorum in Roman North Africa', *JRS* 30 (1940), pp. 37–49.

23. *Acta Saturnini* 17: *PL* 8, 700.

24. Augustine made great play of these relics against the Donatists in the period 417–426. See *De Civ. Dei* xxii.8 for the miracles attributed to St Stephen's relics in aid of the Catholic cause and above, p. 6.

25. Augustine, *Ep.* 52.2.

26. I have taken the facts from E. Hubert's article in the *Dictionnaire de Biographie française*, XVI, 1395 and E. Albertini's memoir 'Stéphane Gsell', *RAfr* 73 (1932), pp. 20–53.

27. By G. Perrot, *CRAI* (1890), pp. 67–70.

28. See S. Gsell, 'Tipasa, ville de Maurétanie césarienne', *MEFR* 14 (1894), pp. 291–450; the chronology of the work done is given on pp. 291–3. See also H. Leclercq, 'Tipasa', *DACL* XV.2, 2338–2405.

29. A short account is given by Duchesne, *CRAI* (1890), p. 116.

30. Gsell, op. cit., pp. 314 and 390–1, giving the text of two inscriptions forming part of mosaics, and Saint-Gérand, 'Une basilique funéraire de Tipasa', *BAC* (1892), p. 466. For further mosaics found in 1939, see *BAC* (27 May 1940), pp. xii–xx.

31. Gsell, op. cit., pp. 386–7, and *Recherches archéologiques de l'Algérie* (1893). For discussion of this curious inscription, see H. Grégoire, 'Sainte Salse', *Byzantion* 12 (1937), pp. 213–24.

32. Optatus of Milevis, *De Schismate* ii.18; ed. Ziwsa, p. 53.

33. Ammianus Marcellinus, *Res Gestae* xxix.5.17 and 31. Tipasa is portrayed as a friendly city to the Romans where Count Theodosius was able to establish his base in 374–375; and Salsa was credited with the discomfiture of Firmus (*Passio Salsae* 13).

34. See S. Gsell and H. Graillot, 'Ruines romaines au nord de l'Aurès', *MEFR* 13 (1893), pp. 461–541; 14 (1894), pp. 17–86; and 'Ruines romaines au nord des Monts de Batna', *MEFR* 14, pp. 501–609.

35. Gsell and Graillot observed that many of the inscriptions they found outside the fortress towns were written in grotesque 'Latin' indicating a lack of assimilation between Roman settlers and natives: *MEFR* 13 (1893), p. 473. On the economy of a Romano-Berber village see Frend, 'A note on religion and life in a Numidian village in the Later Roman Empire', *BCTH* n.s. (1981/82; published 1984), pp. 261–71.

36. J. Carcopino, 'Survivances par substitution des sacrifices d'enfants', *RHR* 106 (1932), pp. 592–9.

37. See Frend, *The Donatist Church*, pp. 82–4.

38. *MEFR* 13, pp. 472–3: Donatism was 'une sorte de réveil d'independance indigène'.

39. *MEFR* 14, pp. 24–5, Inscription no. 78.

40. *MEFR* 13, pp, 497–500, plate vii; and P. Salama, 'Recherches sur la sculpture géometrique tradition-nelle', *El Djezair* 16 (1977), p. 17.
41. W. Thümmel, *Zur Beurtheilung des Donatismus* (Halle, 1893), esp. pp. 63ff.
42. *MEFR* 13, pp. 473.
43. Gsell, *MEFR* 15 (1895), p. 526: 'Le mémoire de M. Thümmel est assez malordonné et contient nom-breuses inexactitudes de détail'. On the other hand, Leclercq, whom no one could accuse of pro-Donatism, accepted that Donatism was a social as well as a religious movement: *L'Afrique chrétienne*, II (Paris, 1907), p. 345. Thümmel was weak in that he thought the Circumcellions originally *pagans* and separate from the main Donatist Church (Thümmel, p. 93). The Circumcellions were identified as a revolutionary and Donatist group by French and German scholars alike. Thus K. von Nathusius, *Zur Charakteristik der Circumcellionen* (Greifswald, 1900); F. Martroye, 'Une tentative de révolution sociale en Afrique', *Revue des questions historiques* 76 (1904), pp. 353–416; 77 (1905), pp. 1–53.
44. He had since 1892 been editing a similar survey for the *Revue Africaine*.
45. *MEFR* 18 (1898), pp. 118–19; S. Gsell, *Monuments antiques*, II, pp. 231–4.
46. *BCTH* (1900), pp. 129–49 (full account); also 'Matifou', *DACL* X, 2670–2677. The whole floor was covered with what amounted to 700 square metres of mosaic, much of which would have been donated by members of the church.
47. S. Gsell, 'Satafis (Périgotville) et Thamalla (Tocqueville)', *MEFR* 15 (1895), pp. 33–70: references to previous work at Satafis, p. 33 n. 2.
48. P. Gavault, *Etude sur les ruines romaines de Tigzirt* (Paris, 1897). More recently, S. Lancel, 'Architecture et décoration de la grand basilique de Tigzirt', *MEFR* 76 (1956), pp. 30–7 (see below, pp. 345–5); compare S. Gsell, 'Grand mausolée de Bled Guitoun', *CRAI* (1898), pp. 481–99 on the native-type art exemplified at Tigzirt.
49. S. Gsell, *Les fouilles de Bénian* (1899), and briefly, *CRAI* (1899), p. 277; Monceaux, op. cit., IV, pp. 480–3.
50. S. Gsell, 'Chapelle chrétienne à Henchir Akhrib', *MEFR* 24 (1903), pp. 1–25; H. Jaubert, *RC* 46 (1912), pp. 141–4, plate vi.
51. Personal tragedy in the form of the death of his wife in 1910 prompted Gsell's return to France.
52. Recorded by A. Berthier and colleagues, *Les vestiges du christianisme antique dans la Numidie centrale* (Algiers, 1942), pp. 22–5, referring to *Atlas*, feuilles 335 and 340: Constantine (516 sites) and Ain Beida (280 sites); 26: Batna (388 sites) and 27: Bou Taleb (193 sites). Berthier's explorations revealed 250 Roman sites and 72 churches and chapels. (See Chapter 10 below.)
53. For Kherbet Bahrarous, see Berthier, op. cit., p. 156. Another example is Kherbet Bou Hadef (*Atlas*, Bou Taleb 64), extending over 800 m in one direction, p. 24 and 158: described by Gsell, *Atlas*, text, Bou Taleb, p. 4 as 'vastes ruines romaines'. Further evidence for Numidian population in the fourth century: see below, p. 231.
54. Herodian, *Ab Excessu divi Marci* (ed. K. Stavenhagen) vii.4.14, commenting on the situation in North Africa *c.* 238.
55. A. Ballu, *Les Ruines de Timgad* (Paris, 1911), giving an account of his work in 1898–1910. See for full bibliography I. Gui, N. Duval and J. P. Caillet, *Basiliques chrétiennes de l'Afrique du Nord* (Paris, 1992), pp. 263–84.
56. S. Gsell and C. A. Joly, *Announa* III (Paris, 1905), pp. 92–5. Basic description and bibliography repro-duced in Gui–Duval–Caillet, op. cit., pp. 337–41. Also excavated Basilica II in the north-west part of the ruins: Gsell and Joly, op. cit., pp. 95–9. The entire campaign was published by both scholars between 1914 and 1922 as *Khamissa, Mdaourouch, Announa* (Service des Monuments historiques, Algiers).
57. See Augustine, *Ep.* 16 and 17 (correspondence with his old pagan tutor Maximus of Madaura).
58. Reported by S. Gsell, *BCTH* (1915), pp. 222–34 (Madaura). Also Duval, op. cit., pp. 327–31.
59. A. Ballu, *BCTH* (1914), pp. 304–8 (Djemila) and *CRAI* (1913), pp. 219 and 404.
60. Recorded by A. Ballu, *BCTH* (1909), pp. 82–3 (Henchir Guessaria). Inscriptions: *CIL* VIII, 8344–8348; *Bulletins des Antiquaires de France* (1913), p. 279. Final report by N. Duval and M. Janon, *MEFR* 97 (1985), pp. 1079–1109.
61. E. Guénin, 'Inventaire archéologique du cercle de Tébessa', *Nouvelles archives des Missions scientifiques* 17 (1908), pp. 138ff.
62. Thus P. Monceaux during his lecture on 'Un couvent de femmes à Hippone' to members of the Insti-tut: *CRAI* (1913), p. 572.
63. Thus P. Gauckler's report to René Millet, Resident-General in 1897, *Enquête sur les Installations hydrauliques romaines* (Tunis, 1897), followed by others similar.

64. Sadoux' findings were incorporated in a paper given by Gsell at the Second Congress of Christian Archaeologists in Rome, 1900 (*Atti*, pp. 225–8) and reprinted in *Revue Tunisienne* n.s. 3 (1932), pp. 277–82, through Charles Saumagne after Gsell's death. For Duval's excavations in the 1960s see Chapter 13, p. 356 n. 79.

65. A. Merlin and L. Poinssot, *Les Inscriptions d'Uchi Maius d'aprés les recherches du Capitaine Gondonin* (Notes et Documents publiés par la direction des antiquitié et d'arts (Tunis) 2; Paris, 1908), inscription 159, pp. 99–102.

66. A. Merlin, *BCTH* (1909), pp. 1–7.

67. A. Merlin, 'Forum et églises de Sufetula', *Bulletin des Antiquaires de France* (1912).

68. A full account is given by P. Gauckler, 'Mosaïques tombales d'une chapelle de martyrs à Thabraca', *Monuments Piot* 13 (1907), pp. 173–227. Also his *Eglises chrétiennes de la Tunisie 1894–1904* (Paris, 1907); R. Massigli, 'Notes sur quelques monuments chrétiens de Tunisie', *MEFR* 31 (1912), pp. 13–26. At Upenna a mosaic was discovered recording the names of martyrs, including Bishop Honoratus, a victim of Vandal persecution: *CRAI* (1903), p. 5.

69. Victor Vitensis, *Historia Persecutionis africae provinciae* i.10: ed. M. Petschenig, *CSEL* 7.

70. Delattre's work on the sites described vividly by H. Leclercq in the course of his long article 'Carthage', *DACL* II.2 (Paris, 1910), 2190–2330 at col. 2237. Also Delattre's interim reports, *CRAI* (1906, 1907, 1908 and 1917).

71. Victor Vitensis, *Historia* i.3: 'Ubi corpora sanctarum martyrum Perpetuae et Felicitatis sepulta sunt'.

72. Leclercq, art. cit., 2246–2248 (photo).

73. *Passio Donati et Avocati*: PL 8, 752–758; defilement of the basilica and murder of its congregation and refugees there: ibid., iv and vi. See Leclercq, art. cit., 2249–2250.

74. Abbé Leynaud, 'Les fouilles des catacombes de Sousse', *CRAI* (1905), pp. 504–17. For the tragedy of Lucilus, *CRAI* (1913), pp. 432–3.

75. A. Harnack, *Mission und Ausbreitung des Christentums* (Leipzig, 1902 edn), Preface, p. vi. (See Introduction above, p. xv.)

76. See T. Klauser, *Henri Leclercq 1869–1945: von Autodidakten zum Kompilator grossen Stils* (*JbAC* Ergänzungsband 5; Münster, 1977), reviewed by the writer, *JTS* n.s. 30 (1979), pp. 320–34. Klauser points to the streak of anti-Germanism in Leclercq's work, which outlook he shared, as we have seen, with other French ecclesiastics of the day: op. cit., pp. 76–7, and 87.

77. P. Monceaux, *Histoire littéraire de l'Afrique chrétienne* (Paris, 1901).

78. For instance, *JS* (January and April 1909), pp. 19 and 157 and *Histoire littéraire*, on the career and outlook of Parmenian.

79. *Histoire littéraire*, IV (Paris, 1912)

80. Ibid., p. 453, Inscription from Henchir el Olga (south-west of Tebessa): 'Sanctorum sedes, Domu(s) Domini, qui pure petit (ac)cipit'.

81. Ibid., pp. 447–8: Thamalla.

82. Ibid., p. 457: from the same church, excavated in 1907.

83. Ibid., p. 448: numerous sites.

84. Ibid., p. 458.

85. Reported by Noël Valois in his anniversity address to members of the Institut des Inscriptions et des Belles Lettres, *CRAI* (1913), p. 542.

86. H. Jaubert, 'Anciens évêchés et ruines chrétiennes de la Numidie et de la Sitifienne', *RC* 46 (1912) published 1913), pp. 1–218. The general picture of Donatist predominance in Numidia has been confirmed by S. Lancel's studies in *Actes du Concile de Carthage en 411*, I = *SC* 195, pp. 273–90. For a detailed study of the religious situation within Augustine's diocese of Hippo (early fifth century) see Lancel, 'Etude sur la Numidie d'Hippone au temps de Saint Augustin', *MEFR* (Antiquité) 96.2 (1984), pp. 1085–1113.

87. See F. G. de Pachtère, 'Nouvelles fouilles d'Hippone', *MEFR* 30 (1911), pp. 321–47.

88. H. Leclercq, *L'Afrique chrétienne* (1907 edn), I, p. 20.

89. H. Leclercq. 'Tébessa', *DACL* XV.2, 1998–2028 (with biblio. to 1946); A. Truillot, 'Autour de la basilique de Tébessa', *RC* 62 (1939), pp. 115–200, reviewing the evidence as it then stood; photographic record by E. Fercot, 'Visions du Passé', *Société de préhistoire et d'archéologie de Tébessa* I (1936–37), pp. 259–65. For a series of plans and photographs representing various phases of research, see N. Duval, *Basiliques chrétiennes de l'Afrique du Nord* (Paris: Institut d'Etudes augustiniennes, 1992): Inventaire de l'Algérie i.2, illus. 150–158.

90. For the monastery theory, see A. Ballu, *Le monastère byzantin de Tébessa* (Paris, 1897).
91. Thus Jürgen Christern; see below, Chapter 14, pp. 363–4.
92. Truillot, op. cit., pp. 53–4 of offprint; Duval, op. cit., p. clviii, fig. 3.
93. Recorded by Monceaux among the Donatist inscriptions: *Histoire littéraire*, IV, pp. 477–8.
94. Truillot, p. 50 of offprint, for the destruction of the mosaics; for the destruction of the basilica and town of Theveste (Tebessa), ibid., p. 79.
95. For the relations between the European powers and Turkey during the 1890s, see Alan Palmer, *The Decline and Fall of the Ottoman Empire* (London, 1992), ch. 12.
96. See J. G. C. Anderson, *JHS* 17 (1897), pp. 417ff. and M. Rostovtzeff, *Social and Economic History of the Roman Empire* (2nd edn rev. P. M. Fraser; Oxford, 1951), p. 741.
97. J. G. C. Anderson, 'Paganism and Christianity in northern Phrygia' in W. M. Ramsay (ed.), *Studies in the East Roman Provinces* (Aberdeen, 1906), pp. 183–227, at pp. 223–4: tombstone of Trophimus from Ain Kuruk.
98. Julian, *Letter* 49.
99. A. M. Ramsay, 'Isaurian and Phrygian art of the third century' in *Studies in the East Roman Provinces*, pp. 30–58: fish symbol in fig. 51; doves, fig. 53.
100. Ramsay visited the site with Sir Charles Wilson in 1882, and considered its ruins as 'perhaps the most interesting in Asia Minor for church antiquities': W. M. Ramsay and G. Bell, *The Thousand and One Churches* (London, 1909), Preface. For the history of the site see ibid., ch. 1.
101. C. Holtzmann, *Bin-Bir-Kilisse* (Hamburg: Boysen and Maasch, 1904). His work has been anticipated in part by that of J. Strzygowski, *Kleinasien ein Neuland der Kunstgeschichte* (Leipzig, 1903), drawing on Anderson and Smirnov's study.
102. I have used the sketch of Bell's life by Josephine Kamm, *Daughter of the Desert* (London, 1956). See also the memoir by A. D. Hogarth in *DNB 1922–1930*, pp. 74–6.
103. 'Notes on a journey though Cilicia and Lycaonia', *RA* n.s. 7 (January–June 1906), pp. 1–29, 385–414; 8 (June–December 1906), pp. 2–36 and 225–52: describing her work at Bin Bir Kilisse in 1905.
104. Ramsay and Bell, op. cit., p. viii and *passim*. At the same time the authors pointed out the 'non-Hellenic character of this rustic city': p. 23.
105. Ramsay and Bell, op. cit., p. 460.
106. Ibid., Preface, p. viii.
107. As part of a journey undertaken under the auspices of Gonville and Caius College, S. A. Cook Bye-Fellowship, in 1954. On the way to the site I found a rock-carving in honour of the goddess Gaia (Earth) not apperantly noticed by previous travellers: 'Two finds in central Anatolia', *Anatolian Studies* 6 (1956), pp. 97 and plate vi a. No. 1 church is described in Ramsay and Bell, op. cit., pp. 41–50.
108. M. Hardie, 'The shrine of Men Askaenos at Pisidian Antioch', *JHS* 32 (1912), pp. 111–33.
109. W. M. Ramsay, 'The Tekmoreian guest-friends', *JHS* 32 (1912), pp. 134ff; 'Studies in the Province of Galatia', *JRS* 8 (1918), pp. 107–45, at pp. 137–44. Half the Tekmor sanctuary inscriptions were later than AD 250.
110. *JHS* 32, p. 154: 'The analogy with the Christian Eucharist is striking'. At this period the copying, if such it could be, was likely to be by the pagans.
111. W. M. Calder, 'Studies in early Christian epigraphy', *JHS* 40 (1920), pp. 42–54, at pp. 42–7. Also, *MAMA* I (ed. Calder, 1928), nos 170 and 171.
112. K. Holl, 'Das Fortleben der Volksprachen in Klein-Asien in der nachchristlicher Zeit', *Hermes* 43 (1908), pp. 240–54.
113. Anderson, 'Corpus Inscriptionum neo-Phrygarum', *JHS* 31 (1911), pp. 161–215; art. *JHS* 33 (1913), pp. 97–105.
114. Ramsay and Bell, op. cit., p. 299. Gertrude Bell also pointed to opportunities for work on sites in eastern Syria and Mesopotamia, such as Amida, Edessa and Nisibis.
115. Thus the view of Buckler and Calder, *MAMA* VI (1939), p. xi.
116. Ramsay and Bell, Preface and p. 9.
117. Thus G. Cousin, M. Holleaux and P. Paris, 'Inscriptions d'Oenoanda', *BCH* 16 (1892), pp. 1–70. Garth Fowden points out that the inscription was carved on part of the city walls next to a doorway leading from the city into a tower and could be read by passers-by: *JRS* 78 (1988), p. 178. See also C. W. Chilton, *Diogenes of Oenoanda: The Fragments* (OUP, 1971).
118. J. Laurent, 'Delphes chrétien', *BCH* 23 (1899), pp. 206–79.
119. *Corpus Inscr. Jud.* 1,725; Adolf Deissmann, *Light from the Ancient East*, pp. 423–5.

120. E. Bourguet, *De Rebus Delphicis imperatoriae aetatis capita duo* (Paris thesis; Montepessulano, 1905), pp. 63ff. Bourguet's discovery was assessed first by A. J. Reinach, *Etudes grecques* 20 (1907), p. 49 and then by A. Deissmann, *St Paul: A Study in Social and Religious History*, Eng. trans. C. R. M. Strachan (London, 1912). Appendix I. See also A. Brasssc, 'Une inscription de Delphes et la chronologie de Saint Paul', *RB* n.s. 10 (1913), pp. 36–53.

121. G. Mendel, 'Catalogue des monuments grecs, romains et byzantins du Musée impérial ottoman de Brousse', *BCH* 33 (1909), pp. 245–442, at p. 342.

122. In 1839 Charles Texier described his journey to the area: *Description de l'Asie Mineure* (Paris, 1839).

123. H. Rott, *Klenasiastische Denkmäler aus Pisidien, Pamphylien, Kappadocien und Lycien* (Leipzig, 1908).

124. G. de Jerphanion, *Les Eglises rupestres de Cappadoce* (Paris, 1925). Frescos reproduced in *Les Merveilles de Cappadoce, Monastères et églises* (Ankara: Direction générale de la Presse, de la Radiodiffusion et du Tourism, 1951), plates.

125. H. Grégoire, 'Voyage dans le Pont et en Cappadocie', *BCH* 33 (1909), pp. 3–170: his identification of a great monastery at Eski Gumusch, pp. 132–5.

126. M. Ebersolt and A. Thiers, 'Les églises byzantines de Constantinople', *CRAI* (1909), pp. 214–17.

127. Same authors, 'Les ruines du palais des empereurs byzantins', *CRAI* (1913), pp. 31–8.

128. Same authors, *CRAI* (1914), pp. 444–51.

129. V. Chapot, 'Resapha-Sergiopolis', *BCH* 27 (1904), pp. 280–91.

130. Thus Abel and Vincent did not publish a full account of their work on the Constantinian churches until 1926: *Jérusalem nouvelle 1914–1926*.

131. H. Vincent, *RB* n.s. (1911), pp. 219–65; J. E. Taylor, *Christians and the Holy Places* (OUP. 1993).

132. Thus Gustave Mendel was assisted during his journey through Bithynia in 1899 by officials and engineers of the French-managed Société des chemins de fer ottomans d'Anatolie: *BCH* 24 (1900), p. 362.

133. R. Heberdey, 'Vorlaüfige Berichte über die Ausgrabungen in Ephesus', *JÖAI* (1895), Beiblatt, pp. 59–60.

134. Heberdey, ibid, 5 (1902), Beiblatt, pp. 53–66 at p. 60.

135. Ibid., 8 (1904), Beiblatt, pp. 73–8.

136. Ibid., 10 (1907), Beiblatt, p. 74.

137. For these events, see Frend, *Rise of the Monophysite Movement* (CUP, 1979), chs 1 and 4.

138. *JÖAI* 15 (1912), Beiblatt; J. Keil, *Führer durch Ephesos* (Vienna, 1915), pp. 17 and 41–3.

139. Recorded by J. P. Droop, 'Archaeology of Greece 1912–1913', *JHS* 33 (1913), p. 364.

140. Grégoire, *Recueil des Inscriptions grecques d'Asie Mineure*, p. 104.

141. See *JÖAI* 25 (1930), Beiblatt, p. 61, 1.

142. Palmer, *Ottoman Empire*, ch. 12. The British, on the other hand, had been outraged by the Armenian massacres of 1895, and said so.

143. W. Kolbe, 'Die Arbeiten zu Pergamon 1904–05', *Deutsche arch. Inst. in Athen* 32 (1907), pp. 241–469.

144. See A. Deissmann, citing information from T. Wiegand, in appendix IV of *Light from the Ancient East*.

145. T. Wiegand, fifth interim report on excavations at Didyma, *SBAW* (1906), pp. 249–65. His excavation of the Miletus church is recorded in his sixth interim report, *ABAW* (1908), Anhang VI, pp. 29–32.

146. Max von Oppenheim and Hans Lucas, 'Griechische und lateinische Inschriften aus Syrien, Mesopotamien und Kleinasien', *ByzZ* 14 (1905), pp. 1–72. For further Christian inscriptions from this expedition, see Deissmann, op. cit., app. VI. For Hans Georg's contribution, see *RQ* (1911), pp. 72–9.

147. W. B. Dinsmoor, 'The Mausoleum at Halicarnassus', *AJA* 13 (1908), pp. 3–29 and 141–7; for Sardes, H. C. Butler, 'First preliminary report on the American excavations at Sardes in Asia Minor', *AJA* 14 (1910), pp. 401–16.

148. H. C. Butler, 'American expeditions 1899–1900, 1904–1905 and 1909', *Publications of Princeton University Archaeological Expedition to Syria in 1904–05* (Leiden, 1907–09 and 1913), Introduction, pp. iv and vii. For dated churches, see R. Krautheimer, *Early Christian and Byzantine Architecture*, pp. 150–70.

149. Butler, op. cit., 'Southern Syria, division II, part II: Umm el Djemal' (Leiden, 1913), p. 173. Butler did not think the inscription was *in situ*. See also G. M. Wheeler, 'Inscriptions from the Hauran', *AJA* 10 (1906), pp. 289–94; W. K. Prentice, 'Magical formulae on Syrian lintels', ibid., pp. 137–50.

150. Reported in *CRAI* (1905) pp. 443–55, and (1906), pp. 407–22.

151. See A. M. Ramsay, *Studies in the East Roman Provinces of the Roman Empire* (Aberdeen, 1906), pp. 3–92, on non-Classical influences on early-Christian art in Isauria. For Gertrude Bell's support of Strzygowski's ideas, espcially regarding the trefoil-shaped church as an example of Christian originality in the field of architecture, see *Thousand and One Churches*, pp. 348ff.; and for detailed discussion, L. H. Vincent, 'Le Plan trèfle dans l'Architecture byzantine', *RA* ser.5, 11 (1920), pp. 82–111.

152. J. Strzygowski, *Kleinasien, ein Neuland der Kunstgeschichte*, esp. p. 128, 'die Bauform der christlichen Basilika als Ganzes ... erschient es heute schon möglich, dass sie im Orient geboren ist' (i.e. the East was a more important source than Rome for the plan of the Christian basilica); two years before, in *Orient oder Rom* (Leipzig, 1901), he emphazises the debt owed by Christian architecture to late-Hellenistic models.

153. E. Weigand, 'Die Orient-oder-Rom Frage in der frühchristlicher Kunst', *ZNTW* 22 (1923), pp. 233–56.

154. Somers Clarke, *Christian Antiquities in the Nile Valley* (Oxford, 1912), pp. 1 and 189–90: 'Les méchants Coptes' was the view of Maspéro, the Director-General of Antiquities to 1894.

155. J. de Morgan, *Catalogue des Monuments et Inscriptions de l'Egypte antique* (Cairo, 1894), p.130.

156. C. M. Kaufmann, *Ein altchristliche Pompey in der libyschen Wüste: die Necropolis der 'Grossen Oase'* (Mainz, 1902); H. Leclercq, 'Bagouat (el)', *DACL* (1910) 31 62 at 47. Excavations in 1898.

157. J. Strzygowski, 'Die christliche Denkmäler Aegyptens', *RQ* 13 (1898), pp. 1–41.

158. E. Amélineau, *RHR* 21 (1891), pp. 176–215 and 'Notice sur le papyrus gnostic Bruce', *Notices et Extraits des Manuscripts dans la Bibliothèque nationale et aux autres bibliothèques* 29 (1891), Part 1. For Bruce's purchase, see above, Chapter 3, p. 34. For the controversy between Amélineau and Schmidt, see G. R. S. Mead, *Pistis Sophia: A Gnostic Miscellany* (London, 1963), pp. lvii–lx.

159. C. Schmidt, 'Gnostische Schriften in koptischer Sprache aus dem Codex Brucianus', *TU* 8.2 (1892), Part 1.

160. Summarized in Kurt Rudolf, *Gnosis*, Eng. trans. R. McL. Wilson (Edingburgh, 1983), p. 27.

161. U. Bouriant, *Mémoires publiés par les membres de la Mission archéol. française au Caire* 9 (1892), pp. 137ff.; commented on by A. von Harnack, 'Bruchstücke des Evangeliums und der Apokalypse des Petrus', *SBAW* (1893), pp. 895–903 and 949–65.

162. C. Schmidt, 'Ein vorirenaeisches gnostisches Original-werk in Koptischer Sprache', *SBAW* (1896), pp. 839–47.

163. See A. Harnack, *Chronologie der altchristlicher Literatur bis Eusebius* (Leipzig, 1897) 1.713, in which Harnack points out that the *Acta Petri* were also used by the Manichees.

164. Flinders Petrie, *Seventy Years in Archaeology* (London, 1933), p. 51.

165. K. Krebs, 'Ein *Libellus* eines Libellaticus von Jahre 250n. Chr. aus dem Faijum', *SBAW* (1893), pp. 1007–14.

166. Cyprian, *Ep.* 55.14. Other examples are given in J. R. Knipfing, *HTR* 16 (1923), pp. 363ff.

167. *Pap. Oxy.* 1; translation cited from Sir Frederick Kenyon, *The Bible and Archaeology* (London, 1940), p. 214, illustrated on plate xxv. In 1920 H. G. Evelyn White suggested 'not later than 140' as the date of the papyri: *The Sayings of Jesus from Oxyrhynchus* (Cambridge, 1920), p. lxvii.

168. *Pap. Oxy.* 654, and compare 655. Deissmann, *Light*, translates *Pap. Oxy.* 654, pp. 436–40, and gives relevant literature to 1908, ibid., p. 3 n.3.

169. Cited from Kenyon, op. cit., p. 215 and Deissmann, op. cit., p. 436.

170. Kenyon, op. cit., p. 216.

171. C. Guignebert, *Le Christ* (1939), p. 14.

172. Thus Grenfell and Hunt, *Oxyrhynchus Papyri* IV (1904) p. 21, commenting on *Pap. Oxy.* 654.

173. The known Christian non-canonical texts from papyri were published by C. Wessely, 'Les plus anciens monuments du Christianisme, écrits sur papyrus; textes grecs, édités, traduits et commentés', *PO* 4.2 (Paris, 1907). Also, H. Leclercq, 'Papyrus', *DACL* XIII.1 (1937), 1370–1520.

174. See J. Clédat, 'Baouit', *DACL* II, 203–251; frescos from the funerary chapel: 226ff. Clédat published his final survey as 'Le monastère et la nécrople de Baouit', *MIFAO* 60 (Cairo, 1943); see also his early report, *CRAI* (1904), pp. 517–26.

175. See Deissmann, op. cit., p. 4.

176. P. Amherst, Part i, no. 3a; see Deissmann, op. cit., pp. 192–201, which gives references and discussion to 1908. Also E. Hardy, *Christian Egypt: Church and People* (OUP, 1952), pp. 33–4.

177. Deissmann, op. cit., pp. 201–3 = Grenfell and Hunt, *Greek Papyri*, Series II (Oxford, 1897), no. 73.

178. Deissmann, op. cit., pp. 205–10.

179. Ibid., pp. 210–14.

180. Somers Clarke, *Christian Antiquities*, pp. 95–110, devoted largely to St Simeon's. He goes on to describe churches at Edfu, Esna, Medinet Habu and 'the White Monastery' at Sohag among those he visited.

181. Described briefly in the *British Museum Guide to Early Christian and Byzantine Antiquities* (1921), p. 177.

182. K. R. Lepsius, *Denkmäler* (Berlin, 1849–53), V and VI. Lepsius' main interest was in Pharaonic remains, but he did not neglect Christian remains when he saw them.
183. See Somers Clarke, 'Ancient Egyptian Frontier fortresses', *JEA* 3 (1916), p. 163.
184. W. Y. Adams, *Nubia, Corridor to Africa* (London: Allen Lane, 1977), p. 1.
185. See ibid., p. 72.
186. See Somers Clarke, *Christian Antiquities*, under chapter headings.
187. Ibid., pp. 54 and 196: objections to 'mere aimless digging', and 'well-intentioned excavations', as at Sobha, near Khartoum, a probable allusion to those of the Governor-General of Sudan, Sir Reginald Wingate, and a party of volunteer officials and their wives on the site of the great church in 1903(?): see P. C. Shinnie, *Excavation at Soba* (Khartoum, 1955), p. 8.
188. Somers Clarke, op. cit., p. 77.
189. Ibid., pp. 90–4 and plates XXV and XXVI, 'Type Plans'.
190. Ibid., pp. 75–81. His plan of the main church proved not to be accurate so far as concerned its east end. This had been built over a previous palatial structure which influenced its alignment to the remainder of the church.
191. Ibid., p. 54. Paintings 'well preserved'. Also Monneret de Villard, *Nubie medioévale*, I, pp. 214–17; and see below, pp. 227–8.
192. Somers Clarke, op. cit., p. 54.
193. A. Weigall, *Report on the Antiquities of Lower Nubia* (Oxford, 1907). Weigall was interested in the rock carvings he found (plate 67), but he also visited Ibrim: pp. 119–20.
194. G. S. Mileham, *Churches in Lower Nubia* (University of Philadelphia Press, 1910), ch. 2: 'Nubian church construction'. For the 1960s excavations at Serra, see James Knudstad, 'Serra East and Dorginati', *Kush* 14 (1966), pp. 165–86.
195. Mileham, op. cit., ch. 3 (Debereh).
196. Ibid., ch. 4 (Faras)
197. Ibid., ch. 7 (Addendan).
198. Ibid., ch. 8 (Serreh).
199. Ibid., pp. 19, 21 and plate 7. A second long funerary text on an inscription was acquired by S. de Ricci at Luxor, and published in *CRAI* (1909), pp. 144–65, but its original provenance is not known.
200. Mileham, op. cit., ch. 8.
201. Ibid., p. 26.
202. Ibid., ch. 5.
203. Listed by H. Leclercq, 'Ethiopie', *DACL* VII, 618–622.
204. H. Schäfer and Karl Schmidt, 'Die ersten Bruchstücke christlicher Literatur in altnubischer Sprache', *SBAW* (8 November 1906), pp. 774ff. The nearest surviving dialect, the authors believed, was that spoken in the Barabra country (Batu el Hajar) between the Second and Third Cataracts, i.e. the southern part of the region occupied by the kingdom of Dotawo as late as the end of the fifteenth century.
205. Recorded by Griffith in his paper, 'The Nubian texts of the Christian period', *ABAW* (Phil. Hist. Klasse) (July 1913).
206. Wallis Budge, *Texts Relating to Saint Mena of Egypt and the Canons of Nicaea in Nubian Dialect* (London: British Museum 1909), folio 1b and 10b. Budget did not apparently know of Schäfer's researches and believed the Nubian language was still 'unknown'. See also Griffith, *JTS* 10 (1909), pp. 545–53.
207. Schmidt and Schäfer, *SBAW* (20 June 1907), pp. 602ff. See also researches by S. de Ricci: *CRAI* (1909), pp. 144–65.
208. Griffith, *ABAW* (1913), pp. 53–5.
209. The Oxford University expedition's results were published by Griffith after the war: 'Oxford excavations in Nubia' (esp. IV–VII), *LAAA* 11 (1924), pp. 115–80; 12 (1925), pp. 57–172; 13 (1926), pp. 49–93 (Faras, Rivergate Church); 14 (1927), pp. 57–116 (Church in the Mastaba field and Anchorite's Grotto); 15 (1928), pp. 63–88 (Abd el Kader church).
210. Flinders Petrie, *Seventy Years in Archaeology*, p. 51.
211. Cited from Neville Chittick, 'Excavations at Aksum 1973–74: a preliminary report', *Azania* 9 (1974), pp. 159–205.
212. See Erich Dinkler, 'König Ezana von Aksum und das Christentum', *Aegypten und Kusch* 13 (Festschrift F. Hintze; Berlin, 1977), pp. 121–32.

213. Ibid., p. 125.
214. See Athanasius, *Apol. ad Constantium* (written in 357) 31: *PG* 25, 636–637.
215. Dinkler, op. cit., p. 129.
216. F. Anfray, A. Caquot and P. Nautin, 'Une nouvelle inscription grecque d'Ezana, roi d'Axoum', *JS* (1970), pp. 260–73.
217. See S. C. Munro, *Excavations at Aksum* (Chittick's excavations 1972–74; London: British Institute in East Africa, 1989), memoir 10.
218. The best recent study is that of S. Lieu, *Manichaeism in the Later Roman Empire and Mediaeval China* (Manchester University Press, 1985); also F. C. Burkitt, *The Religion of the Manichees* (Cambridge, 1925).
219. Cited from Burkitt, op. cit., p. 6.
220. F. W. K. Müller, 'Handschriften Reste in Estrangelo Schrift aus Turfan', *SBAW* (1904), pp. 348ff, and 'Handschriften Reste II', *ABAW* ix (1904), pp. 10ff, especially 80–84. Grünwedel was Director of the Imperial Ethnographic Museum of Berlin.
221. See H. C. Puech, *Le Manichéisme, son fondateur, sa Doctrine* (Paris, 1949), p. 27.
222. A. von Le Coq, 'Ein christliches und ein manichäisches Manuschriftfragment aus der Turfan', *SBAW* (1909), pp. 1202–18; see also his 'Köktürkisches aus Turfan', ibid., pp. 1047–61, (describing his discovery of the manuscripts); 'Ein manichäische Fragment aus Idiqut Schahri', ibid. (1908), pp. 398–414.
223. Described by Burkitt, op. cit., pp. 48–9, 51–9.
224. Von Le Coq, *ABAW* (1912).
225. Grünwedel and von Le Coq, *SBAW* (1909), art. cit., and for the Mani teaching concerning 'the Tree of Life and the Tree of Death' in a Chinese context, see Le Coq, 'Türkische Manichaica aus Chotscho I', *ABAW* (1912), Anhang, pp. 8–9. Chotscho (Khotscho) is near Turfan. For a Coptic Manichee version, see below, Chapter 10, p. 225.
226. Lieu, op. cit., ch. 8, p. 204, and see Le Coq, art. cit. (1909), p. 204.
227. See M. A. Stein, *Ruins of Desert Cathay* (2 vols; London, 1912), I, pp. 159–219 and II, ch. 82.
228. Ibid., II, chs 65 and 66; the scrolls are illustrated on plate 192 facing p. 180.
229. Translated by Le Coq. See A. von Le Coq, 'Dr. Stein's Turkish Khuastanift from Tun-Huang', *Journal of the Royal Asiatic Society* (1911), pp. 277–314; analysed in Burkitt, op. cit., pp. 48–63.
230. Lieu, p. 202.
231. Chavannes and Pelliot, 'Un traité manichéen retrouvé en Chine: deuxième partie', *JA* ser. 11, I (1913), pp. 99–199 and 261–383, at p. 114: 'Rules for entry into religion'.
232. Augustine, *Contra Epistolam Manichaei quam vocant Fundamenti* xii.15: *PL* 42, 182.
233. Chavannes and Pelliot, p. 333. Mani was regarded as the 'white (robed) Buddha': p. 334.
234. Chavannes and Pelliot, 'Traité' (première partie), *JA* ser.10, 18 (1911), p. 547. See also P. Brown, *Augustine of Hippo: A Biography* (1967), p. 52 n.2.
235. There had been Persian Manichaean missionaries at the Chinese court since 694 (Chavannes and Pelliot, p. 376) but the religion was associated primarily with the Uigurs, who were unpopular tributaries.
236. Lieu, pp. 203–4.
237. Ibid., p. 262.
238. A. Mingana, 'The early spread of Christianity in Central Asia and the Far East; a new document', *BJRL* 9.2 (1925), p. 33 of offprint.
239. P. Y. Saeki, *The Nestorian Monument in China* (SPCK, 1916). On the date, Mingana, op. cit., pp. 36–9.
240. Extract from W.G. Young, *Handbook of Sources Materials for Students of Church History* (Indian Theological Library; Madras, 1969), p. 32.
241. Chavannes' view, cited from Lieu, p. 203.
242. Illustrated in Stevenson, *Catacombs*, p. 95. The fresco seems to portray a banquet in Paradise with the food, consisting of bread and fish, displayed prominently. This is consistent with a family group. There appears to be no priestly figure dispensing bread and wine. Josef Wilpert's view (*Fractio Panis: die älteste Darstellung des eucharistischen Opfers*, Herder, 1895) was that this was 'the oldest representation of the Eucharistic sacrifice'. This seems mistaken, for the catacomb artists were concerned more with destinies in the after-life, and much less with current liturgical practice. See also Chapter 6 above, p. 88 note 65.
243. Marucchi. *Elements*, II, pp. 393–4; but Wilpert, *Pitture*, pp. 264–5, while insisting in the liturgical character of the painting, does not mention St Peter in that connection.

244. J. Wilpert, 'Maria als Fürsprecherin mit dem Jesusknabe', *RQ* 4 (1900), pp. 309–15. This seems far-fetched. A fresco in a Syracuse catacomb shows the deceased, Marcia, being welcomed to Paradise in a similar fashion; see Stevenson, op. cit., pp. 137–8.
245. Marucchi, op. cit., p. 479 (illustration). Or the two figures might be local martyrs friendly towards the deceased's soul.
246. Notably the painting of the consecration of bread (and another indistinct offering) on a table by a priest, while a woman (the deceased?) stands in prayer (*orante*), from the San Callisto catacomb (Marucchi, op. cit., p. 154), and also the many representations of baptism.
247. Thus the claim by Ludwig von Sybel, *Christliche Antike* (1906), p. 10: 'In der christlichen Kunst vollendet die Antike ihren Lauf, vollzieht sich ihr letztes Schicksal.'
248. See F. W. Deichmann, *Entstehung der christlichen Archäologie*, pp. 28–30.
249. The *Acta* (II; Rome, 1902) are difficult to come by. Gsell's article on the churches at Ammaedara and Thelepte was reprinted in *Revue Tunisienne* (1932), pp. 5ff.
250. S. Aurigemma, *NBAC* (1911), pp. 242–6; *RQ* 55 (1912), p. 85; see also below, p. 189.
251. O. Marucchi, 'La cripta storica dei SS Pietro e Marcellino recentemente scoperta sulla Via Labicana', *NBAC* 4 (1898), pp. 137–94. Examples of graffiti invoking the saints are reproduced in *Elements*, p. 244.
252. Eginhard (Einhard), 'Historia translationis beatorum Christi martyrum Petri et Marcellini', *Acta Sanctorum* (2 June), pp. 177–201.
253. See J. Guyon's exhaustive discussion of this vast site in *La Cimitière aux Deux Lauriers, recherches sur les Catacombes romains* (Bibliothèque des Ecoles françaises d'Athènes et de Rome 264; Rome, 1987); and Marucchi, op. cit., pp. 239ff.
254. There has been recent discussion about the 'serving maids' Agape and Eirene who occur eight times on separate frescos in the catacomb: P. Düchers, *JbAC* 35 (1992), pp. 147–67.
255. Recorded by Marucchi, pp. 253–7. The continuance of the *agapē* as the prefiguration of the Heavenly Banquet as late as the fourth century is interesting.
256. Ibid., pp. 123–4. See 'Domitilla', *DACL* IV.2, 1404-1442 for discoveries to 1920.
257. Wilpert, *NBAS* (1897), p. 138; Marucchi, p. 122.
258. Marucchi, p. 124. For Orpheus in catacomb art, see 'Orphée', *DACL* XII.2 (1933), 2735.
259. See J. Stevenson, *Catacombs*, pp. 124–5; and below, Chapter 13, pp. 344–5.
260. Marucchi, 'L'Ipogeo sepocrale di Trebio Giusto', *NBAC* 17 (1911), pp. 209–35; 18 (1912), pp. 83–9; P. Franchi di Cavalieri, 'Iscrizioni graffite nel vestibolo dell' Ipogeo di Trebio Giusto', *RQ* 26 (1912), p. 53.
261. Bulić worked at Salona from 1885 until his death in 1934. He was responsible for the discovery and excavation of most of the early-Christian buildings found on the site of Salona before 1914. The first early-Christian discoveries were made by Lanza in 1826. See J. Zeiller, *Origines chrétiennes de la Dalmatie* (Paris, 1906); H. Leclercq, 'Salona', *DACL* XV.1, 609ff., and IV.1, 21–110. For a memoir on Bulić himself see H. Leclercq, *DACL* XV.1, 618–621.
262. See J. Zeiller, 'Les dernières fouilles de Salone', *MEFR* 22 (1902), pp. 429–37; Leclercq, 'Dalmatie', *DACL* IV. IV.1, 21–110.
263. *DACL*, ibid., 23–27.
264. Ibid., 26; XV.1 (Salona), 604ff, for illustrations of the basilicas. Plan of episcopal centre ibid., 607.
265. Eusebius, *HE* v.24.6. In a letter to Pope Victor, Bishop Polycrates of Ephesus claimed that he was the eighth in a succession of kinsfolk to the bishopric. The bishops of Salona as known are listed by E. Dyggve. *History of Salonitan Christianity* (Oslo, 1951), p. 22.
266. Dyggve, op. cit., ch. 2.
267. First reported by de Rossi, *Bollettino* (1876), pp. 7–10, and see J. Wilpert, *Ephemeris Salonitana* (1894), pp. 1–21 (reprinted, with ATTI I, 1994), and *DACL* I.2, 2672.
268. Anton Gnirs, *Die christliche Kultanlage aus Konstantinischer Zeit am Platze des Domes in Aquileja* (Vienna, 1915); Hans Lietzmann, 'Die Doppelkirche von Aquileja', ZNTW 20 (1921), pp. 249–52; more recently, L. Jaeggi, 'Aspekte der stadtbaulichen Entwicklung Aquileias', *JbAC* 33 (1990), pp. 173–6.
269. Lietzmann, loc. cit.
270. For Pola, see Gnirs, *Pola, Ein Führer durch die antilen Baudenkmäler und Sammlungen*; *DACL* XIV, 1340–1346. The Austrians were accused by Leclercq of 'vandalism': 1341.
271. Ammianus Marcellinus xiv.11, 20–22.
272. P. Perdrizet, *MEFR* 19 (1899), pp. 541–48 and 'Inscriptions de Salonique', ibid., 25 (1905), pp. 85–95.

273. Alexander was the first recorded bishop of Salonica. He was present at the Councils of Nicaea (325) and Tyre (335): *DACL* XV.1, 634. An inscription (no. 16; *DACL*, 710) shows that an individual paid three solidi for the priviledge of being buried near the tomb of the martyr John.
274. Thus B. K. Young and P. Perin, 'Les nécropoles (III–VIIIe siècle)' in *Naissance des arts chrétiens* (Paris, 1991), pp. 94–121, at p. 94.
275. Ibid., p. 97.
276. Recorded ibid., p. 97.
277. Ibid.
278. P. A. Février, 'Naissance de l'archéologie chrétienne' in *Naissance*, pp. 336–47, at p. 334; X. Barral i Altet, 'Etapes de la recherche au XIXe siècle', ibid., pp. 348–67 at pp. 364–5 (illustration).
279. Barral i Altet, ibid., pp. 361–2.
280. Ibid., p. 362.
281. Noel Duval, ibid., p. 209.
282. *Lateinische (alt)christliche Inschriften mit einem Anhang jüdischen Inschriften* (2 vols; Bonn, 1908–13). See also S. Loeschke, *Frühchristliche Denkmäler aus Trier* (Trier, 1936), p. 97, illus. 9. The first Christian sarcophagus with a representation of Noah's Ark (early fourth century) was found in 1780 on the line of the road of the road cutting the St Eucharius cemetery.
283. *BJ* 120 (1910), p. 325 for Trier; J. Popplereuter, 'Die römische Gräber Kölns', *BJ* 114 (1906), pp. 372–3.
284. Found in the church of the Blessed Virgin at Erevan in Armenia; editied in *TU* 30.1 (1907); Eng. trans. J. Armitage Robinson, *St Irenaeus: The Apostolic Preaching* (SPCK, 1920).
285. Gertrude Bell, *RA* (1906), p. 10.
286. F. J. Dölger, *Das Fischsymbol in frühchristlicher Zeit* (1910), pp. 239–58.
287. Cited from Karl Baus, 'Franz Joseph Dölger', *RQ* 47.1 (1942), p. 3.
288. Cited from Georg Schöllgen, 'Franz Joseph Dölger und die Entstehung seines Forschungsprogramm "Antike und Christentum"', *JbAC* 26 (1993), pp. 7–23, at p. 9.
289. K. Aland, *Glanz und Niedergang der deutschen Universität, 50 Jahre deutsche Wissenschaftsgeschichte in Briefe an und von Hans von Lietzmann (1892–1942)* (Berlin/New York, 1979), p. 299.

9

Picking up the pieces, 1919–1931

The optimism of the first decade of the twentieth century perished in the fateful week 28 July to 5 August 1914. Grave-faced gentlemen in frock-coats and top hats called at the Foreign Ministries in the European capitals to present declarations of war and request their passports. The situation was not without its paradoxes. In Vienna it is related how on 12 August Sir Maurice de Bunsen, the British ambassador and Count Mensdorff at the Austro-Hungarian Foreign Ministry, whose countries had been dragged into the general war without either enmity or conflicting interests, performed the necessities of declaring mutual hostility and then sat down for an hour to discuss what a peace settlement might be.[1] Among the peoples affected, however, the outbreak of war was greeted with enthusiasm. Sir John Reith's diaries, 29 July 1914, record 'WAR. Tremendous excitement. Austria v. Serbia. Russia, Germany and France will probably join in, England also.'[2] It was as though some evil genius had been suddenly freed from the bottle imprisoning him. 'Nach Paris', 'À Berlin' proclaimed the troop-trains conveying reservists to the front. 'It will all be over by Christmas' reflected the mood in Britain. It was not to be. Four and a quarter years of carnage and destruction came to involve nearly every nation in the world. The Europeans came out worst. The best of their manhood had been swallowed up, their finances and industries ruined, their hegemony as world leaders gone for ever. The Americans, the sole victors, would now be taking centre stage, including a central role in archaeological research in Turkey and the Middle East. Dura, Ephesus and Antioch would all bear witness to their enthusiasm and expertise as well as their sponsorship.

Cultural life was not to escape damage from the catastrophe of the war, but as an exception archaeology benefited from the new popular culture that emerged in its aftermath, and from the new methods of discovery evolved through the struggle for the mastery of the air by the combatants. The dozen years following the end of hostilities on 11 November 1918 were to be a period of recovery, hope, and, above all, achievement by the digger. This was particularly true in Britain. The popularity of the works of Ramsay and Deissmann had already revealed the attraction of early-Christian archaeological discoveries among the wider public. Now, events far removed from Church history were to accelerate this movement. In November 1922 Howard Carter discovered the almost undisturbed tomb of the Pharaoh Tutankhamen in the Valley of the Kings. The filming of the removal of successive finds of treasures, each more fantastic than the last, stirred public imagination as no other archaeological discovery before or since. Next year Leonard Woolley began to publish his even more important discoveries of the Babylonian temples and royal tombs at Ur of the Chaldees, extending, as he said, 'from unknown date in prehistoric times to the seventh century BC'.[3] Abraham's journey towards the Negev (Gen 12:9) was given a visible starting point.

Moreover the war had involved the combat of mass armies, and one aspect of its revolutionary aftermath was popular interest in the history of humanity, its varied cultures and religions. In 1918–19, H. G. Wells wrote his *Outline of History* in the hope of satisfying 'multitudes of people, all the intelligent people in the world', who were 'seeking more or less consciously to get the hang of world affairs as a whole'.[4] From another angle popular curiosity was being satisfied by the successive publication of the seven volumes of *Peoples of All Nations* (1920–22), providing brief, well-illustrated descriptions of the history, geography and anthropology of every known distinct people.[5] In this environment O. G. S. Crawford launched *Antiquity* in 1927 with the claim that there was a 'universal interest in the past', and hence his aim of surveying world archaeology over a time span of a million years.[6] The enormous early volumes packed with information justified the claim.

Antiquity quickly found scope for discussions relating to early-Christian sites.[7] Their study had already been furthered by Henri Grégoire's *Recueil des Inscriptions grecques chrétiennes d'Asie Mineure* (1922; reprinted 1980) and above all, by his launch of *Byzantion* in 1924. For Rome and the West, Ernst Diehl's publication in 1925 of a complete and elaborately indexed compendium of Latin Christian inscriptions found to date (*Inscriptiones Latinae Christianae Veteres*) served a similar cause.

Pope Pius XI had put the Vatican printing press at Diehl's disposal when publication in Germany became impossible because of the economic crisis.[8] Rome, and the Vatican as a neutral, had escaped the effects of the war and work in the catacombs had continued under Marucchi and Wilpert, and their younger colleagues Franco Fornari and Ernesto Iosi. Duchesne died on 21 April 1922 and Marucchi now became the Nestor of Christian antiquities. Iosi, whose work was to include the Vatican excavations of 1939–50, quickly made his mark by publishing yet another harvest of frescos and inscriptions from the catacomb of Peter and Marcellinus, including a fine scene of Christ healing the woman with the issue of blood (Mark 5:21–34), the result of excavations in 1914.[9]

These continuous new discoveries were requiring fuller publication than possible even in the *Nuovo Bollettino*. In 1924 this was succeeded by the *Rivista di archeologia cristiana* as the *Acta* of the Pontifical Commission of Sacred Archaeology. Soon this widened its range beyond the study of catacombs to all types of Christian archaeology. In the Vatican itself, meanwhile, de Rossi's stress on the need for objective assessment of the material from the catacombs was bearing fruit. On 11 December 1925 Pius XI issued a decree (*motu proprio*) setting out new ordinances of the Pontifical Commission of Sacred Archaeology which had been in existence as the Pontificia Accademia Romana di Archeologia since 1852, and creating a Pontifical Institute of Christian Archaeology designed as a centre for teaching and research for students.[10] J. P. Kirsch (1861–1941) in his inaugural address in June 1926, emphasized that Christian archaeology was 'an historical science', a 'critical study based on authentic sources and observing absolute objectivity'[11] – a milestone on the long road to inter-confessional co-operation.

Improvements in excavation technique were also making these aims realistic. Though most of the excavations in the Mediterranean and Middle East continued to involve large numbers of unskilled and often inadequately supervised workmen, directors now had one major technical advantage over their predecessors. Woolley's account of his excavations at Ur in the *Antiquaries Journal* was prefaced with a photograph: 'Aeroplane view of Ur. (Photograph taken by the R.A.F. published by permission of G.H.Q.)'.[12] Progressive improvements to aircraft design and the extension of the fighting to the outlying but archaeologically-rich territories of the Ottoman empire had revealed the possibilities of air-photography for archaeology where there had been little or no previous work. No longer would archaeologists be digging 'by guess and by God'. Whether in rural sites in North Africa or on the Roman *limes* in Syria, air-photographic survey was henceforth an essential preliminary to research on the ground.

The presence of Allied (in reality, British and French) armies of occupation in the Ottoman territories, however, was a mixed blessing. Vast new fields of research were opened up and the French in particular were willing to use troops as diggers whether in Constantinople, Byblos or Dura Europos. Unfortunately Napoleonic appetites were whetted and the French sought monopoly positions for archaeological research in Persia and Afghanistan (as well as in their Mandate of Syria), as a means of furthering political aims.[13] In neither area were they completely successful: a protest from the Foreign Office obliged French agreement to British participation in work in Afghanistan, while by 1927 a German expedition was uncovering sixth-century Christian churches at Ctesiphon, thus confirming the strength of Christian influence in pre-Islamic Persia.[14]

Apart from the Roman catacombs, *North Africa* was the one major area that had escaped operations during the war. Throughout the decade North African archaeology continued to produce a lion's share of early-Christian discoveries. At the fifth International Congress of Archaeology at Algiers in April 1930, North African themes dominated. Djemila, Timgad and Christian churches of the late-Byzantine era in western Mauretania were all represented.[15] All the time 'Fouilles et consolidations' had been going on as before. The men of the pre-war generation, Albert Ballu, Dr Lucien Carton and Louis Poinssot, were able to continue work, passing on experience and tradition to their successors. New names, such as Eugène Albertini, future *Directeur des Antiquités de l'Algérie*, Prosper Alquier, *Conservateur en Chef* at the Musée Ernest Mercier at Algiers, and his wife Jeanne, and Louis Leschi, also a future *Directeur*, begin to appear. In the background, ready to help with his immense knowledge of North African archaeology, stood Stéphane Gsell, though occupied with what he hoped would be a completed life's work, the *Histoire de l'Afrique du Nord*. Alas, the eighth volume ended only with the fall of Juba's kingdom in AD 39 and the definitive establishment of Roman rule. The volumes on the empire in North Africa were never written before Gsell's death on 1 January 1932.[16]

In Carthage, though the needs of the war had reduced their numbers drastically, the Perès Blancs under Delattre continued to discover and excavate early-Christian sites. The excavation of the Basilique de Sainte-Monique on a plateau overlooking the sea just to the north of the Theodosian walls of Carthage was the last which Delattre supervised personally, and also that which gives him his best claim as a field archaeologist. In 1915 he had noticed a change in the colour of the earth, from the natural brown-red of the face of the Hamilcar ravine to grey-black. There were no other surface indications. A single fragment of a Christian inscription, however, alerted him to the possibility of a basilica, and as the land belonged to the archbishopric, permission to explore was granted readily.[17] Delattre's excavation followed the methods he had used on the Damous and Basilica Majorum sites. A scrupulous count was kept of all fragments of inscriptions, and when he reported the end of his campaign in 1920 he claimed that the total had reached 9,400.[18] He also drew up convincing-looking but in fact not accurate plans showing the great atrium on the east side, 35 m long and 55 m wide, that led into the church 60 m long with its seven naves, and a comparatively small central apse flanked by sacristies. Unfortunately, this was *déblayage* on a grand scale. Trenches were taken down to the foundations of the church, involving the total loss of intervening floor-levels. At the same time, he made little attempt to explore earlier buildings, represented by a large cistern on the north side of the atrium and walls over which the entrance to the church was built, and which could be seen by a visitor as late as 1978. No stratigraphic sections were drawn. It was the old story. Delattre's enthusiasm and collector's instinct got the better of the needs of scientific historical research. He was not interested in the pagan or Jewish origins of the sites he excavated and whose remains lay below the basilicas. He was determined to prepare the site for the Eucharistic Congress to be held in Carthage in 1930, and other considerations had to give way. While his work on salvaging and exposing major Christian sites in Carthage is beyond praise it also deserves Noel Duval's criticism. He had 'good will, energy and persistence, but lacked any truly scientific concern and professional rigour'. He had no training, his archaeological methods were 'destructive', and he failed to provide adequate descriptions of his finds. He made faulty restorations and listed his inscriptions without proper order and in a way in which these were not easily usable by researchers.[19] Harsh words, but intelligible to those who had to review his results in the 'Save Carthage' campaign more than 50 years later.

In 1920 Delattre was 70, and thereafter shared his work with Père Chales. Unfortunately, the latter lacked Delattre's skills and energy. American researchers working for 'Save Carthage' found much excavation remained to be carried out on the Bir Kinissia[20] cemetery-basilica erected within an extensive Christian *area*, situated west of the harbour area, where Chales worked in 1923. The writer had a similar experience with an apparently Byzantine church situated on the ridge above the Résidence, very near the local railway. This had been left partly excavated. In particular, the baptistery on the south side contained a large two-period font. Part of the earlier, hexagonal basin (probably fourth century) had been filled in to form a smaller, round basin of Byzantine date, perhaps indicating a different emphasis regarding the rite between late-Roman and Byzantine times. The basilica sited within the walls, and overlooking much of the city, may have had a particular status in the late fourth century. Was it a cathedral?[21]

Elsewhere, in *Tunisia* no less than 31 separate sites were investigated during the 1920s. The small oratory found at Dougga may typify events in some Roman towns in the latter part of the fourth century. The construction was very largely from materials robbed from the theatre, a temple of Saturn and other monumental buildings along with fragments of pagan sarcophagi.[22] The North African towns still had a level of prosperity, but it would seem that the concerns of their inhabitants had altered considerably from their heyday at the end of the second century. The transition from Vandal to Byzantine rule was also documented. Citizens were prepared to knock down or use the remains of former pagan buildings to build churches, such as a basilica built by Bishop Simeon at Furnos Maius (Henchir Ain Fourna) in 528, during the period of active toleration for the Catholics under the pro-Byzantine Vandal king Hilderic (523–530).[23] The Byzantine occupation itself was illustrated by the magnificant mosaics that covered almost every inch of the floor-space of the church at El-Mouasset (11 km north-west of Mahres) – wonderful designs, perhaps, as the excavators believed, from models from Constantinople, but hampered by the poverty of material used.[24]

In *Algeria* much of the work could be described as 'fouilles et consolidations', concentrating on sites examined before the war. These included more work at Timgad, Djemila, Lambaesis, Lambiridi, Tebessa and Tipasa. There were also useful surveys of sites in the countryside. That by Louis Leschi in 1928 confirmed that the rural areas surrounding Tebessa had begun to prosper from the mid-third century onwards.[25] The predominant Donatism in the area had evidently accompanied relative prosperity and not depopulation and despair.

This same area produced the most surprising discovery of the decade in North Africa: 13 fragments of a Manichaean work written on parchment, found by chance in June 1917 in a cave 25 km south of Telidjen and 75 km from Tebessa. The finder, M. Reygasse the *administrateur* of the *Commune Mixte* of Tébessa, was a prehistorian and was exploring the cave in search of Stone Age artifacts. At first a Manichee identity was not suspected, and at a meeting of the Académie des Inscriptions et Belles Lettres in 1918 Henri Omont reported the find as a possible lost work of Niceta of Remesiana.[26] The mistake was soon corrected by Prosper Alfaric, who had been researching the Manichaean phase of Augustine's career. In 1920 he published an article showing conclusively that the fragments formed part of a treatise which appeared to define the respective roles of the Elect and the Hearers, the two grades (*gradus*) in the Manichaean sect.[27] The writer (clearly not Mani himself[28]) describes the Elect as the few chosen among the many who are called (Matt 10:22) The catechumens, on the other hand, are regarded as living 'in the world' (*saeculo*) and must serve the Elect.[29] Relying largely on Pauline quotations, the writer asserts the spiritual perfection of the Elect on the basis of Colossians 3:15–16, the necessary distinction between the responsibilities of Elect and Hearers, representing the spiritual and carnal followers of the Prophet (Mani), from 2 Thessalonians 3:12–13.

Other features of Manichaeism in North Africa were revealed in the text. The Christian ideal of the wandering missionary (the Elect) was justified from 1 Thessalonians 5:12 and Philippians 2:16 and 25 and that the Elect were filled with grace from Philippians 1:15. That they had no need to work (in obedience to 2 Thess 3:10) could be shown from Paul's injunction to Titus (Titus 3:8). They relied on the Hearers for their food and upkeep.[30] It was clear that in the fifth century the Manichees regarded themselves as 'Christians'. They accepted Paul as the interpreter of Christ's teaching while Mani himself was his prophet. This manual throws some light on the reliance which Augustine's Manichee contemporaries, such as Fortunatus, placed on Pauline texts. In addition a Christian sect that had ostensibly the same episcopal hierarchy as the Catholics but which combined freedom of enquiry and acceptance of the Classics as a stepping-stone towards the truth, and rejected the morality of much of the Old Testament, was calculated to appeal to Augustine during the formative years of his life.[31] Why the manuscript was deposited in a cave is anyone's guess. Recurrent insecurity in Vandal Africa might be sufficient reason.

That insecurity was illustrated by other discoveries. At Madaura an inscription on a *mensa* records the deaths of two brothers, Theodorus, a deacon, and Faustinus, 'killed by the Moors',[32] the fate also suffered by a bishop of Tanaramusa (Mouzaïaville) between Blida and Tipasa in May 495.[33] Balancing this picture of the breakdown of civilized life, were, however, two other discoveries. The first was an inscription from Berrouaghia in Mauretania Sitifensis dating from 474. It recorded how a Berber chieftain Iugmena, styling himself 'prefect', 'began a church which God completed'. 'God', however, in this case included the 'Zabenses' (i.e. tribesmen round the town of Zabi) who stated that they 'had finished' (the work). This shows that beyond the Vandal frontier to the west the Berbers had established principalities, kept the Roman provincial dating, and, unlike during the collapse of the Byzantine administration in the mid-seventh century, retained an organized Christian Church.[34]

Relative peace and prosperity for much of the Vandal period[35] was also indicated from the Theveste area, where in April 1928 Alexis Truillot, Secretary to the *Administrateur* of Morsott, but resident in Tebessa, reported to Albertini the discovery of 34 inscribed tablets of cedar wood among the inscribed pottery sherds found by a French farmer in ruins in a remote area between the Djebel Onk and Tamerza. Eventually 56 documents or fragments were recovered. These proved to be acts of sale and transactions relating to a dowry, and came probably from the archives of a landowner. They were of the greatest interest in themselves, but the date, 'the tenth year of King Gunthamund' (i.e. 494), and the Christian cross at the beginning of one of the tablets, together with the reference to the Lex Mancia, demonstrated how in this part of the North African countryside the Vandal occupation had brought few changes to the daily lives and status of the inhabitants. The Roman legal system, (non-Arian?) Christianity and the Latin language continued to prevail.[36]

One important excavation carried out through the war years and in the first decade after showed probably as well as any other the character of the transition from Roman to Vandal Africa, and thence to the Byzantine re-occupation and the final phase of decline and disappearance of community life. Djemila (Cuicul) in Mauretania Sitifensis had attracted the attention of archaeologists since Ravoisié's time. The campaign of excavation begun in 1909 by Albert Ballu continued uninterrupted to 1925. To a substantial Christian basilica in the north of the town Ballu and his colleagues added the discovery of a complete Christian quarter on high ground to the south-west.[37] Two basilicas, one larger than the other, with a complete baptistery and baths attached, and rooms which must have included an episcopal residence and various 'offices' were found.

The smaller of the two churches indicated the steady advance of Christianity in the town through the third and fourth centuries. There had been a bishop in 256 at the time of Cyprian's council (the seventh council) at Carthage on the (re-)baptism issue on 1 September 256.[38] In the Great Persecution Cuicul had suffered its martyrdoms, the names of nine victims being preserved in two churches found in other parts of the town.[39] When, however, the new church and complex were built on the hill outside the city, its floor was paved with mosaics donated by high officials (*honestissimi*) and an individual holding the title of *sacerdotalis* i.e. the title once of a priest of the imperial cult but now purely a civic office. (Re)used in the foundations, too, was a dedication of the Temple of Tellus, evidence that that cult had no longer many adherents in the town.[40] The great baptistery immediately outside this church symbolized perhaps the triumph of Christianity in the town. There, as a text of a mosaic proclaimed, Illumination would be won.

In the fourth century Cuicul was divided between Donatists and Catholics, but at the time of the conference of Carthage in 411 the Donatist bishop had just died,[41] and his Catholic rival Cresconius was able to unite the Christian community under his banner. A very much larger church was built on the south side of the original building. This time a richly adorned mosaic celebrated in verse the ending of the schism and 'the crowd of Christians assembled in a single body' under Cresconius the bishop. It may also have had a cult relating to martyrs and his predeccessors, the 'justi priores' referred to also on the mosaic.[42] Whatever the relations between the two churches, Cresconius had only a few years to enjoy his triumph before the Vandal invasion in 429. Cuicul, however, seems to have been less affected than areas further east. A priest Turasius died in 454[43] and an inscription on his tomb dated this event with the Roman consular dates. Later on, however, the Vandals took over and during their occupation a hoard of 180 gold coins dating a little after the accession of the emperor Anastasius in 491 was hidden in the crypt of the great church.[44] This may have the resulted from a raid by Kabylie tribes, and this period also may have witnessed the destruction of the smaller church,[44] and insecurity similar to that prevailing elsewhere in North-Africa. Byzantine reconquest brought a partial restoration. There was a Bishop Crescens of Cuicul summoned by Justinian to the fifth general council at Constantinople in 553. That is the final mention of Cuicul in history.[45] The last episode in the life of the splendid Christian quarter was marked by the establishment of olive presses amidst the ruin of episcopal rooms and the decay of the churches.[46] Gradual decline of Christianity rather than sudden catastrophe has been the verdict of archaeology in a number of urban sites, including Carthage itself. (See below, pp. 316–17.)

How the decline was taking place in the first half of the seventh century was demonstrated by another chance find. In July 1924 work on the Ferme Laurent near Telergma in eastern Algeria led to the discovery of a small sheet of lead, perhaps from a reliquary casket. This bore an inscription recording the deposit of martyrs' relics by three bishops at a date which could be calculated as 8 February 637. The interest of the reliquary lay not only in the late date, in the reign of Heraclius (610–641), but the names of the martyrs, Stephen, Focius, Theodore and Victor, illustrated once more how in the Byzantine period Byzantine saints were being accepted into the traditional Numidian cult of martyrs and their relics.[47] Such adaptation should have proved a source of strength to the Christians even when threatened by the

Marianos (d. 1036),
bishop of Pachoras
(Faras) 1005–36

Martyr's(?) tomb in
sixth-century church
at Knossos, Crete

The Great Dish from
the Mildenhall Treasure

Mosaic from
Hinton St Mary

The silver chalice
from Water Newton

Arabs and Berber nomads in the remainder of the century. However, the dedication showed that another of the main supports of Christianity was failing, namely the Latin language, which had survived during the Vandal rule. Though the general meaning of the text was clear from the outset, it took several attempts and forty years of scholarly effort before all its secrets were unlocked, so obscure had the language become.

Curiously, the opposite tendency was coming to light in the far west of Roman Africa. Excavations at Volubilis, and at some other centres in western parts of *Mauretania Caesariensis*, were revealing dated inscriptions of the late sixth and seventh centuries written in good Latin. One, an epitaph of Julia Rogativa, was dated by the provincial calculation to 655, and commemorated her 'domum eternale' erected by her parents. Julia is called 'vicepraepositus', an official Roman title. It could be that, as in sixth-century Britain, Christianity and Latinity were identified with each other, and as the inscription had been found re-used in the 'House of Columns' in Volubilis, this situation could have lasted until the end of the seventh century.[48]

At the other extreme of Latin-speaking North Africa, the Italian occupation of *Libya* was being accompanied by the excavation of secular and early-Christian monuments in the chief Roman towns. At Sabratha, Bartoccini's excavation revealed splendid Byzantine churches showing how that community had been revived through Justinian's reconquest of the province.[49] The Ain Zara cemetery south of Tripoli, reported to the Società in 1911, had proved sensational (see above, p. 162). It was a rural *area* containing 121 tombs apparently in use during the Vandal occupation. This was interesting enough, another instance of how little rural life changed during that century-long period. Unique, however, in North Africa were the liturgical inscriptions painted on the plaster covering the graves. On 26 were the words 'Requiem aeternam det tibi Dominus et lux perpetua luceat tibi. Amen' (May the Lord give you eternal rest and may light perpetual shine upon you. Amen) or 'Sanctus Deus, sanctus fortis, sanctus immortalis miserere mei' (Holy God, holy and strong, holy and immortal, have mercy on me) or 'Deus Sabaoth'. Fish either side of a mixing bowl were a favourite decoration in plaster in the tomb itself. These inscriptions surely reproduced phrases of the funerary liturgy that have survived in the Western Churches to our own day. One commentator pointed out how the burial and inscriptions resembled in many ways those from the cemetery of En-Gila, also in Tripolitania but four centuries later.[50] As Henri Leclercq had stated before the war, every year was producing new material relating to Christianity in North Africa,[51] and this process would only be checked by the Second World War and its tragic aftermath throughout the Maghreb.

Asia Minor and *Constantinople* suffered more from warfare. Archaeology was disrupted successively by the Great War and in its aftermath by the Greco-Turkish war of 1921–22. In December 1916 the French School at Athens was closed by order of the pro-German administration there and did not reopen until 1919. In Asia Minor the Turks vented their feelings on the Christian Greeks by destroying antiquities, such as the church of the Assumption of the Virgin at Nicaea,[52] while many valuable smaller finds were lost in the great fire that swept through Smyrna on 13–14 September 1922.[53] In the brief interval between these crises, however, some discoveries were made. In Constantinople members of the French army of occupation excavated two churches, one of which produced a Latin inscription referring to the emperor Theodosius (uncertain whether I or II), thus adding to knowledge of the Christian topography of the city in early Byzantine times.[54] At Philippi not far from the Turkish frontier, Charles Picard took up where the French had begun in 1914, to initiate twenty years of extremely successful work. In his first season he found inscribed on the uprights of the Neapolis gate leading out of the city a version of the Letter of King Abgar to Jesus, recorded by Eusebius (*HE* i.13).[55] That this document with its powerful sacred implications was used to protect cities and even private homes is shown by Jesus' recorded reply found inscribed on the underside of a lintel at the entrance of a private house at Ephesus.[56] Fragments of the whole 'correspondence' were found at Faras,[57] a further indication how despite the existence of Muslim Egypt the kingdom of Nobatia retained its cultural and religious links with the rest of the Byzantine world.

Peace was restored to Asia Minor by the treaty of Lausanne in 1923. The exchange of populations agreed involved a massive exodus of Greeks from Asia Minor. Kemal Atatürk's nationalist government encouraged research into his people's 'Hittite heritage', rather than into Christian antiquities associated with his enemies. In addition, as the European Schools of Archaeology gradually resumed work, they tended once more to concentrate on prehistoric, Mycenaean and Classical sites where they had left off in 1914. The British were engaged at Mycenae and Knossos, the French at last concluded fifty years' work at Delos and Delphi, the Germans went back to Pergamum in 1927, a shadow of the great clearance operations undertaken there and at Miletus and Priene before the war,[58] while the Americans restarted excavations at Corinth.

There were, however, two notable exceptions, namely the Austrian-led excavations at Ephesus from 1926 onwards, and continued British exploration of Greco-Roman and Christian sites in Anatolia. Austria had suffered most from the peace treaties of 1919–22. The Austro-Hungarian empire was finished. Its various components had been divided up among the successor states of Czechoslovakia, Yugoslavia and Hungary itself. Vienna remained an imperial capital of a small German-speaking country. With commendable effort Austria, however, continued to send its scholars to Asia Minor to take up work that had to be abandoned in 1914. Returning to Cilicia, Samuel Guyer investigated and excavated partially the church of St Thecla at Meriamlik. He found that the grotto which was said to have served as Thecla's abode after her conversion to Christianity by St Paul had retained its sacred character. It had been a centre of pilgrimage before a large basilican church had been built on the site in the fourth century. This had been succeeded in the reign of Zeno (474–491) by a domed church preceded by an extensive atrium, the latter reminiscent of a similar feature that had extended in front of the Carthaginian church of Damous el Karita. In the sixth century cisterns were built, perhaps to tap springs in the area whose healing properties were an additional attraction to pilgrims.[59]

Not far away, at Corcyrus, Guyer, accompanied by Josef Keil and Adolf Wilhelm, visited sites that had first been seen by Gertrude Bell a generation before. Fifth-century monastic buildings were identified but none of this research would have been possible without the sponsorship of the American Society for Archaeological Research in Asia Minor.[60]

In 1926 funds from the J. D. Rockefeller Foundation enabled Keil to return to Ephesus, where work on a new site, the church of St John, had been started by Soteriou in 1919 but abandoned with the collapse of Greek power in western Asia Minor in September 1922. The site was north of the temple of Artemis/Diana on high ground known as Ayasolouk. Keil was again director and his chief colleagues were the veteran scholar Adolf Deissmann and a young professor from the Vienna Technische Hochschule, Franz Miltner, working under the auspices now of the Turkish State Museum of Izmir (formerly Smyrna). Before work was resumed on the church site the excavators had turned their attention to a large Christian cemetery about a mile away containing hundreds of graves. These were found to centre on a cavern incorporated into the crypt of a domed church built on the site in the fifth century. It commemorated the Seven Sleepers. The legend had been immensely popular. It told how seven Christians of Ephesus, victims of the Decian persecution in 250, had been entombed in a cave but had been miraculously delivered unharmed in the reign of the pious emperor Theodosius II (402–450). They left their tomb, walked into the city's market place, and attempted to make purchases from their astonished and disbelieving fellow-citizens with coins 160 years out of date! The site attracted pilgrims for centuries, and these included Frankish crusaders and, as late as 1444, Armenian Christians, i.e. within a decade of the fall of Constantinople.[61]

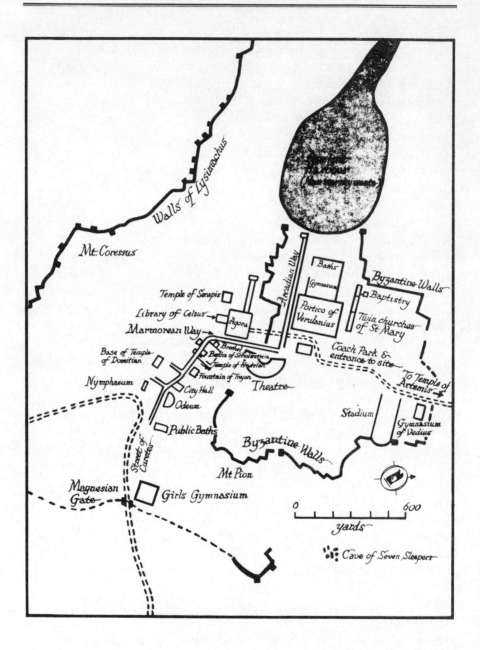

Plan of Ephesus

Keil now returned to St John's, built presumably over the remains of the Apostle's tomb. The excavation was difficult. The collapse of the domes of Justinian's church with their supporting vaulting and beams had created heaps of rubble up to 20 feet high.[62] It took two complete seasons' work (1927 and 1928) with some hundreds of workmen to finish the task. But the result was worthwhile. In the early fourth century a small square chapel had been erected on the site of the tomb. This had been massively enlarged until it formed a fine cruciform building. In Justinian's reign this had in its turn been transformed into a huge structure, 110 m long, with transepts, entered from a narthex (entrance hall). The main roof consisted of six cupolas, whose collapse had resulted in the building being concealed under a huge mound of ruin. An interesting find was a capital bearing the monograms of both Justinian and his Monophysite wife Theodora.[63] This strengthened evidence for their keen rivalry which literary works indicated regarding Ephesus, where dissent was active enough to enable the arrival of John (of Amida) as Monophysite bishop in 558. By this time Ephesus, like other great cities of the East Roman Empire, had finally become Christian, though only then were some of the one-time temples converted into churches.[64]

One of Ephesus' other troubles, this time with its neighbour Smyrna, was illustrated by a long inscription found by Keil in the church of the Virgin, dated 441. In this, the Smyrnaeans were denounced as 'godless' (*anhosioi*) for pursuing a claim to ecclesiastical precedence over Ephesus.[65] Eventually this was settled by Smyrna's elevation to an archbishopric while Ephesus retained the status of Metropolitan.[66]

The Christian heritage of Asia Minor was also being preserved effectively through Henri Grégoire's *Byzantion*. The early volumes provided scope for Byzantine historical studies and a continuing record of archaeological discoveries in the Byzantine world. A climax in this period was a *Festschrift* in honour of Ramsay's eightienth birthday in 1931.

This was richly deserved even though his work had been recognized in the volume of *Anatolian Studies* presented to him in 1923. The survey work of the British in inland sites in Asia Minor had continued despite difficulties caused by the Greco-Turkish war. In 1923, W. M. Calder, Ramsay's younger colleague, now Professor of Greek and Lecturer in Christian Epigraphy at Manchester University, published an article in which he drew together the results to date of research into early Christianity in western Anatolia.[67] Following Ramsay, he pointed out obvious differences of outlook demonstrated by the 'crypto-Christian' epitaphs from central Phrygia and the Hermus valley, but principally from the town of Eumeneia (that any who sought to intrude a new

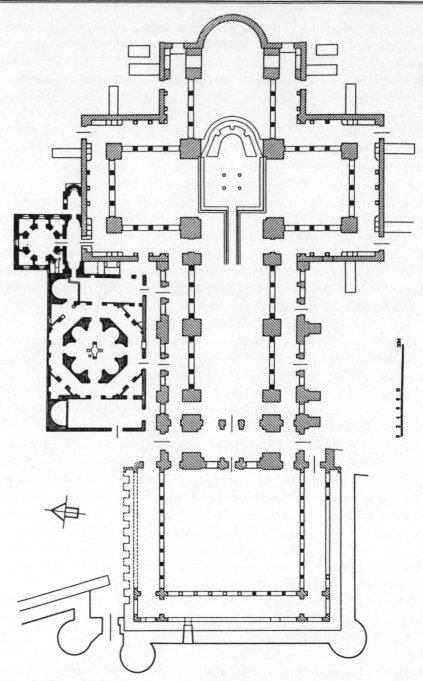

Church of St John the Evangelist, Ephesus: Justinianic phase

corpse into the deceased's grave 'will answer before the living God'), and the uncompromisingly Christian 'Christians for Christians' inscriptions found 30 miles north in the Tembris valley. Calder believed that the 'concealed' epitaphs resulted from an orthodox-episcopal Christianity spread inland from Ephesus and Laodicea (Pamukkale) contrasted with a prophetic form of Christianity represented by Philadelphia. Regardless of the correctness of this it would seem clear that an inscription (from Ai Kuruk) on which the dedicator describes himself as 'a great soldier', must be Montanist.[68] 'Miles Christi' was 'almost a technical term in Montanist phraseology',[69] and an inscription from a Donatist church at Henchir bou Said, in the Theveste area of Algeria, portrays a *miles Christi* standing in chains – a permanent reminder to the congregation of what were the demands of martyrdom.[70] Nothing similar on a Catholic epitaph has been found. Moreover, the Tembris valley was the home of other dissenting traditions in the fourth century. There was a Novatianist bishop of Kotaion (Cotiaeum), the metropolis of the Tembris valley. In the same period an epitaph records how Ammia the daughter of Telesphorus died 'a virgin', 'having my faith unsullied having light eternal and (continuing?) among the holy Novatians'.[71] The pattern seems clear; in the late third century there was an ardently Christian Montanist population on the imperial estates covering the Tembris valley, surrounding a still largely pagan city of Cotiaeum. The argument urged by Elsa Gibson that the same stonemasons made 'Christians for Christians' epitaphs and as well as others and hence there was no proof of Montanism does not outweigh considerations supporting Calder's theory accepted during this period.[72]

Calder published more 'Christians for Christians' inscriptions in his contribution to Ramsay's first *Festschrift* in 1923[73] and others in an article in the *Bulletin of the John Rylands Library* in 1929.[74] In 1930, further field research jointly with the American Society for Archaeological Research in Asia Minor convinced him that the Montanists' 'holy cities' of Tymion and Pepuza were at Uc Kayu and Bekilli near the north bank of the river Maeander.[75] An inscription from a marble episcopal chair from a church in the Bekilli area was dedicated to a man and woman who made open profession of Christianity, either as priests or prophetesses, while another, fifth-century, stone recorded '... of Montanus the protodeacon'.[76] The assertion of faith, the name 'Montanus' and unconventional status of 'protodeacon' point towards Montanism, and to Bekilli, at least, being for three centuries an important Montanist centre.

Material remains of another group of dissenters, the Encratites, centred apparently on Laodicea Combusta (Ladik), were found in the expeditions of Calder, Cox and Buckler in southern Asia Minor in 1924 and 1926. Laodicea, situated south of Iconium (Konya) and in an area where Phrygian was still spoken at the end of the third century AD, produced a number of Christian inscriptions, three of which were in honour of members of the sect.[77] The Encratites were teetotallers, rejecting even the use of wine at Communion, and one epitaph found by a villager in 1928 castigated the orthodox as 'winebibbers'.[78] A more constructive tone was preserved on the grave of the deacon Pancratius, recorded as a 'wise and faithful judge' who had been an 'assessor to governors' and who 'taught the heavenly doctrine to the youth'. His wife, 'sprung from the priests', 'loved the brethren' and was 'a faithful stewardess of continence',[79] all qualities that gained the Christian clergy in Asia Minor respect during the fourth century.

In 1928 when Calder published volume I of *Monumenta Asiae Minoris Anti-qua*[80] it could be claimed that Phrygia rivalled the Roman catacombs for information about expansion of the Church in the pre-Constantinian period.[81] This claim, however, was soon to be challenged by the sensational discovery of a Christian church dated to *c*. AD 232 in the Roman frontier fortress of *Dura Europos* on the Euphrates. The discovery was typical of the times. The end of the war had witnessed the end of the Ottoman empire. Of the Arab lands, Hejaz became independent. France reasserted its influence in Lebanon and Syria under the guise of a League of Nations mandate, and Britain gained the same status in Mesopotamia, Jordan and Palestine. The Arabs were not happy, and early in 1920 there was a rising in Mesopotamia. Captain Murphy and an infantry detachment were ordered to occupy Saliliyeh, a strategic point commanding a stretch of the Euphrates valley from the west. The ruins there provided cover and a good field of fire. On 31 March trenches were being dug. There was a startled shout: one of the men had struck the inner wall of a building. The soil peeled away, revealing a dark, vicious-looking face with deep-set slit eyes, crowned by what appeared to be a dunce's cap. The painted mural seemed to descend indefinitely. It was like a scene from Aladdin, but the djinn remained dumb. Soon three another similar figures were revealed. Captain Murphy made a rapid coloured sketch. The hole was filled in, and a report despatched to GHQ at Baghdad. The staff was interested, the more so because Gertrude Bell was on hand to point out the importance of the discovery. As luck would have it, an archaeological expedition from the University of Chicago led by Professor J. H. Breasted had just arrived at Baghdad. He was contacted, and on 23 April shown Murphy's sketch. He was urged to go to Saliliyeh as quickly as possible and given the information in confidence that because of the unrest it was proposed to move the Mesopotamian frontier upstream, leaving the site as part of Syria.[82]

Breasted was told that he could not be given more than 24 hours on the site, but was provided with a platoon of British troops to do any digging. He arrived at Saliliyeh on 4 May and worked with a will. The results were astonishing. Murphy had stumbled on one room of a chapel dedicated to the Palmyrene gods, and the fresco represented the family of a certain Conon performing sacrifice before a group of assembled priests. In an adjacent room, there was another scene of sacrifice, this time by an officer of the Roman garrison, Julius Terentius. At his side was the regimental standard and the *imagines* (statues) of the deified emperors. The imperial cult was being celebrated in the third century in a way reminiscent of Pliny's description in his letter to Trajan concerning the Christians of Amastris in Bithynia 100 years before (*Letters* x.96).

With incredible speed Breasted dug, drew and photographed, his last photographs being taken as dusk was falling. At the end of the day, however, these and his sketches demonstrated both the strength of this most advanced of Roman fortresses on the Euphrates frontier, as well as something of the character of the religion of its garrison and well-to-do citizens. Above all, as he pointed out, the murals provided a clue to the transition between Hellenistic art and the semi-Orientalized art of the Byzantines.[83]

The Mesopotamian frontier was duly withdrawn, and Saliliyeh fell within the borders of Syria and the French Mandate. In 1922 excavations were entrusted to Franz Cumont and Commandant Renard of the French Army of the Levant, assisted by troops from the Foreign Legion. Cumont had written a perceptive tailpiece to Breasted's article in *Syria*, and identified the fort with Dura Europos.[84] Dura had been originally a Seleucid stronghold, then a Palmyrene caravan city, before it became a fortress guarding the road between Palmyra and Antioch after the advance of the Roman frontier eastwards under Lucius Verus (161–169). Its capture by the Persians under Sapor I in 256 was a disaster that led ultimately to the defeat and capture of the emperor Valerian in 260 as he strove in vain to drive the Persians from the eastern provinces of the empire. The temple found by Breasted was indeed that dedicated to the Palmyrene gods and among the finds was an inscripti on in honour of the emperor Alexander Severus in 229–230.[85]

Nothing as yet indicated either the destruction of the city or any Christian presence. In 1927, however, after a break of four years arrangements with the Syrian government were made for work to resume on a large scale through co-operation between Yale University and the Académie des Incriptions et Belles Lettres with Franz Cumont and Michael Rostovtzev as Directors. Actual excavations were delayed until April 1929, but these were followed up by successive campaigns to 1937 and the site gradually yielded up its secrets. Two hoards of antoniniani, none of the coins minted later than 256, were found near the citadel, suggesting one end-date for the occupation.[86] Another clue was a coin of the Persian king Sapor I found among the burnt ruins of the temple of Atargatis.[87] Then the excavators turned to the outside wall on the south, or more approachable side of the town, facing the desert. They found that instead of standing vertical, this had been approached from inside the town by a series of mud-brick walls and embankments, the effect of which was to form a glacis, the slope of which had destroyed buildings standing in its way. The defenders had been given a broad defensive platform from which to fight off enemy attacks. The manoeuvre had delayed the town's capture, since the besiegers had been forced to tunnel below both the wall and the defensive embankment before they could penetrate the city.[88] Excavations in 1932–33 were to show evidence for hand-to-hand fighting in the murky darkness of tunnels as each side attempted to ambush the other. Skeletons marked where combatants had fallen.[89]

The 1931–32 season produced a completely unexpected discovery. Working down through part of the glacis, the excavators came upon the remains of a large house evidently built towards the end of the second century AD. It proved to be no ordinary dwelling. A room capable of holding about 70 people had been turned into a chapel. At one end was a raised platform, probably for an altar table. Adjoining was a baptistery. Paintings covered the walls of the baptistery, representing biblical scenes[90] with the theme of Fall and Deliverance. Christ himself was portrayed both as Great Physician healing the sick as exemplified by the paralytic, and as the beardless figure of the Good Shepherd, saving his followers from the power of demons and fate that reduced humans to the condition of slaves.[91] It was not an accident that a painting of Adam and Eve representing the Fall of man was placed immediately below that of the Good Shepherd. Old Testament scenes also portrayed liberation, such as David's overthrow of Goliath, prefiguring Christ's destruction of Satan, or deliverance from temptation, such as the Jonah sequence, The universal appeal of Christianity through baptism was exemplified by the Samaritan woman whom Jesus met at the well.[92] The Old Testament was used alongside the New to teach moral lessons to the Greek and Syrian congregation[93] that Christ was a healer and liberator to be invoked at the Eucharist in favour of faithful departed.[94] He was a greater Moses and baptism through him provided the means of illumination and salvation.

The Dura church ranks with major finds in the catacombs, Asia Minor and North Africa, among the most important discoveries in Christian archaeology. Alone its date, approximately AD 232, makes it the earliest Christian building yet found. Its existence demonstrates that toleration was real during the reign of Alexander Severus (222–235). It provides a glimpse of the possible strength and limitations of this Christian community living in the environment of a garrison town where traditional Roman and Semitic ceremonies were being sedulously observed. The building, too, must have belonged to the local church (perhaps the bishop's residence), thus proving its status as a property-holding association. The vivid murals show that at Dura as in the catacombs there was no prohibition against pictorial representation of biblical scenes. It adds greatly to our knowledge of Christian art in the first half of the third century, symbolic and allegorical in character as was the interpretation of Scripture. The faithful learned the Christian message through pictures, as did the Jews in their synagogue to be discovered not far away (below, p. 236), but with the Christians the importance of the Old Testament was that it prefigured the New. The Scriptures were integrated into a system of doctrine, teaching the same lessons of salvation and hope that were being expressed in the language of picture alike in Rome and in the empire's far-flung outpost on the Euphrates.[95]

A second major site was *Gerasa* (*Jerash*), the city of the Decapolis in Transjordan. Here also Yale University was prominent, this time, however, co-operating with J. W. Crowfoot (now retired from the Egyptian Civil Service and Director of the British School at Jerusalem) and a mainly British team working for the British School of Archaeology at Jerusalem. Like Dura, Gerasa was originally a Macedonian city which developed into a Roman *colonia* with a mixed Greek and Arab population, Greek being the predominant language. But here the resemblances ended. Gerasa never became a garrison town and never, it would seem, was threatened by the Persians before Chosroes II's great invasion of Palestine and Syria in 614. (What happened during the confusion following the capture of Valerian by the Persians in 260 is not known.) In the second and third centuries the city was dominated by the temple of Artemis standing among temples, public buildings and an amphitheatre. Then, probably during the reign of Constantius II (337–361), Christianity began to progress. A bishop of Gerasa took part in the Council of Seleucia in 359–360, and by that time the cathedral, a great building 45–50 m in length, may already have been built.[96]

199

Excavations began in 1928 and continued for three seasons. No fewer than eleven churches were found within the city walls and one outside. A complete transformation of the city took place between the fourth and sixth centuries. The temple of Artemis was used as a quarry to furnish dressed stone for the cathedral, itself built on the probable site of the temple of Bacchus, and just to the east of a spring sacred to the infant Dionysus. In the fifth century the conversion of the population progressed rapidly. Another church was built in honour of the prophets, apostles and martyrs in 464–465 in the north-east of the town. This was a cruciform church with a small apse at the east end. It was an early example of a domed church; Jean Lassus was to find an outstanding example of this outside Antioch (see below, p. 238) and Heisenberg had identified a third in the church of the Apostles at Constantinople before the war. The cruciform plan marked the beginning of a new style of Byzantine architecture, its earliest examples being at this stage from Syria and Jordan in the second half of the fifth century.[97]

Thirty years later, in 494–496, another church was built, this time in honour of the soldier-martyr St Theodore. It contained an inscription on a mosaic that indicated one reason why Christianity had been preferred to paganism. The builder was the 'chief priest' Aeneas, who proclaimed that St Theodore rejoiced that an area 'once polluted by the stench of four-footed animals that toiling died and were cast forth here' and travellers had to hold their noses as they passed, was now a 'scented plain' of 'lovely beauty' where passers-by would sign themselves with the cross.[98] The wholehearted rejection of animal sacrifice is recorded by Arnobius[99] and Lactantius[100] in the era of the Great Persecution. The waste and futility of hecatombs of sacrifices was not lost on a population already becoming disillusioned with the traditional pagan deities.

The sixth century saw the completion of Gerasa's transformation. Between 526 and 533 five new churches were built, four by Bishop Paul between 529 and 533. A synagogue which occupied a high point in the south-west part of the town was converted into a church involving its sacred area being switched from west (facing Jerusalem) to east. Its third- and fourth-century mosaics, one featuring Noah's ark with the animals and the 'creeping things' processing into it, were covered over by still finer Christian-inspired patterns.[101] Justinian was determined that the Holy Land should be exclusively Christian: not a 'sorry parody of the past',[102] but a new concept of city life centred on the Church. The Church's triumph was emphasized by two further churches built in his reign, one occupying part of the great Propylaea leading to the temple of Artemis.[103] In the seventh century a final church was built by Bishop Genesius in 613, just three years before the Persian invasion.[104]

Gerasa survived as a Christian city for another century. Only in the caliphates of Omar II and (more likely) Yezid II were the mosaics within the churches damaged through smashing any human or animal form represented on them. The end came suddenly, not, however, through persecution, but a massive earthquake that struck the city on 18 January 746. Workmen left tasks half completed as they fled and never returned. Crowfoot's excavations had revealed a complete Christian history of a large and prosperous town. Thanks to dated inscriptions he enabled the stages of Christianization to be followed step by step, including an example of the persecution of the Jews in Justinian's reign, a persecution for which the Christians would pay dearly when the Persians gave the Jews and Samaritans their chance of vengeance.

In *Syria*, meantime, the French had been quick to re-examine sites located by Renan and de Vogüé in the previous century. Military labour was used to excavate a church east of Byblos, discovered by Renan in 1864, and in so doing to bring to light splendid wall-paintings showing the Virgin with John the Baptist and the four Evangelists.[105] In *Palestine*, the Ecole Biblique made a possible identification of the site of Jesus' trial before Pilate. At least, it would seem that the massive flag-stones of the pavement covering the courtyard of the Antonia fort in the north-west corner of the Temple-area must be the *Lithostroton* (Pavement) where Pilate sat to deliver judgement (John 19:13). The impressive discovery made by Père Vincent beneath the school and convent of the Sisters of our Lady of Sion would be hard to dispute.[106]

Less open to doubt were the results of A. E. Mader's excavations in 1926–28 on another Constantinian site, that of Mamre near Hebron where Abraham was recorded to have entertained the angels (Gen 28:13).[107] Eusebius mentions the site as being holy to pagans, Jews and Christians. As we have already seen (Chapter 1), Constantine, urged, it is said, by his mother-in-law Eutropia, who visited the spot in 326, was determined to enforce a Christian monopoly of the site, and he succeeded.[108] Mader's excavations showed that it had long been sacred. Since Herod's time (37–4 BC) there had been an enclosure surrounding a tree, a well, and an altar supposedly built by Abraham. The Constantinian church had been built within the enclosure against the end wall of the Herodian shrine. Its existence confirmed the truth of Eusebius' account of Constantine's determination after the Council of Nicaea to further the Christian cause wherever possible, and especially in the reputed holy places in Jerusalem and Palestine.[109]

In *Egypt*, archaeological research on the ground concentrated on the Coptic monasteries. Evelyn White and members of the New York Metropolitan Museum Expedition explored monastic sites in the Wadi Natrun, recovering fragments of apocryphal gospels, showing that the monks did not restrict their study to canonical and orthodox work.[110] This was to become even more evident after a close examination of the bindings of the codices from the fourth-century Gnostic library found in 1945 at Nag Hammadi. (See below, p. 282.)

Papyri acquired by the British Museum in 1922 and 1923 among 'a quite miscellaneous collection' proved to be particularly important for unravelling the history of the relations between Athanasius and his Meletian opponents in the years 333–335.[111] The Meletians were dissidents whose quarrel with the Alexandrian bishops arose out of the treatment of those who had lapsed during the Great Persecution. Meletius, bishop of Lycopolis in Upper Egypt, demanded a more rigorous policy towards penitents who wanted to be re-admitted to Communion than Bishop Peter of Alexandria would accept. The martyrdom of the latter on 25 November 311 seemed to give divine sanction to the more clement policy, but Meletius persisted. A schism developed, with the Meletians receiving substantial support from Coptic-speaking Christians and from the incipient monastic movement. The schism, however, never reached the proportions of the Donatist Church in north Africa.[112] In 325 the council of Nicaea worked out a compromise. Meletius himself was to retain his title of bishop but exercise no functions. Those ordained by him would be re-ordained and then retain their rank and functions with the understanding that if their orthodox rival died first the Meletian should succeed him. There were however ambiguities, and when on 17 April 328 Bishop Alexander of Alexandria died, the Meletian leader John Arcaph, who had succeeded Meletius on the latter's death *c.* 327, believed he had the right of succession. The Egyptian bishops, however, after six weeks of haggling elected Alexander's archdeacon Athanasius on 8 June, 'an upright man and a virtuous, a good Christian, one of the ascetics'.[113]

Friend of the monks, especially Anthony[114] and Pachomius, Athanasius certainly was, but not of the Meletians, and his antipathy was worsened by their making common cause with the Arians and eastern (Eusebian) opposition to him. The papyri (with one certain and one doubtful exception) were all letters either written by or addressed to a certain Apa Paieous. The most important can be dated to either 334 or 335. Paieous was a Meletian presbyter and possibly also a 'confessor' (i.e. he had suffered in the Great Persecution).[115]

The letters leave no doubt as to Meletian support among Coptic-speaking monks.[116] The earliest (Pap. Lond. 1913) dated 19 March 334, deals with the appointment of a deputy to the priest Pageus to oversee the affairs of the monastery of Hathor. Pageus had been summoned by Constantine to attend a council at Caesarea where the charge against Athanasius was that he had Arsenius, Meletian bishop of Hypsele, murdered. The charge proved to be groundless, for Arsenius was found safe and well, and later made his peace with Athanasius. The latter, however, seems to have been determined to wreak his displeasure on the Meletians. A second important letter (Pap. Lond. 1914) from Callistus, a Meletian monk or cleric, to Paieous dates probably to June–July 335, shortly before the larger and more impressive Council of Tyre was due to meet. At this, Athanasius would be convicted of various acts of indiscipline, such as causing the breaking of a chalice in the church of the Meletian presbyter Ischyras, and violence against the Meletians.[117] The papyrus shows the sort of violence Athanasius was allowing to happen. Callistus reports how on 20 May (335) Athanasius' supporters raided the camp outside the city of Alexandria where Meletian clergy, including the bishop of Letopolis, were dining with Heraiscus, Meletian bishop of Alexandria. Though the raiders were frustrated through the soldiers hiding the clergy in their quarters, Athanasius' supporters found and severely beat four monks, while Bishop Heraiscus was apparently detained in the camp for his own safety. It would seem that Athanasius was determined at all costs to prevent his opponents confronting him at the impending council meeting. No wonder then, that he was 'very despondent' when he realized that these misdeeds were unlikely to remain concealed; and after loading his baggage on to a ship bound for Tyre, unloaded it, only deciding at the last moment to attend the council.[118]

Other documents in the collection demonstrate the weight of taxation falling on individuals at this time, forcing some to sell even the clothes they were wearing, and to pledge their children as sureties for debts incurred in paying the taxes. The Meletian monasteries were not idle but were carrying on small-scale industrial enterprises, such as making cloaks. We see them as organized communities sharing neither Anthony's ideal of the solitary anchorite nor the large-scale self-sufficient institutions established by Pachomius.[119] In general, the documents show how Egyptian monasticism had roots in Meletianism as well as orthodoxy. They show, too, that 'Athanasius contra mundum' was a reality in these years, perhaps understandably so.

Knowledge of early-Christian civilization in *Nubia* was also reaping the rewards of earlier survey and excavation combined with the discovery of important written records. Success of the former had now established Faras as the provincial capital of the area, and that by the ninth century there was a flourishing Coptic monastic settlement to the west of the main Nubian town.[120] The foundations on which the Poles were to build with outstanding success in the 'Save Nubia' campaign (1961–65) had been laid by the Oxford University expeditions in the pre- and inter-war years. (See below, p. 302.)

A similar expedition in 1927 working near the Second Cataract south of Faras described the tiny church their members had seen at Abd-el-Kader and 'probably the most complete ecclesiastical building that survives in Nubia', 'so perfect that it can hardly be described as a ruin'.[121] It produced a remarkable series of wall-paintings including a figure of the ruler of Nobatia now identified with the Byzantine title of eparch clothed in embroidered garments and wearing a horned crown decorated with the star of David.[122] The figure of Christ behind his right shoulder was raising the right hand to give a blessing, with the fingers held according to Byzantine ritual. Graffiti incised on the walls in Greek honoured the military martyr/saints George and Mercurius. Provisionally, the excavators dated the church to *c*. AD 1000.[123] Its condition suggested a simple abandonment of Christianity rather than its violent destruction.

Another indication of the continued use of Greek by the Nubian Christians and their adherence to Byzantine-type liturgies (even if they claimed a Coptic Monophysite identity) was provided by inscriptions found by Crowfoot in the long stretch of river valley between Wadi Halfa and Old Dongola, occupied by Makurrah, the middle of the three Nubian kingdoms. One of these inscriptions, dated to AD 982, included prayers from the Byzantine *Euchologion Mega*, commendatory intercessions for the dead, though Nubia had been cut off from the rest of the Byzantine world for three and a half centuries.[124]

F. Ll. Griffith, following up his pre-war researches, was showing that not only the Church but the Nubian royal administration had retained a Byzantine heritage. In 1928 he published a series of Christian documents from Nubia.[125] These included legal documents in the Nubian language written in black ink on leather scrolls of the type which J. M. Plumley and the writer were to find at Qasr Ibrim. (See below, p. 309.) The scrolls mentioned individuals holding titles such as *meizoteros* (mayor of the palace?), *protomeizoteros* (premier super-mayor!), *domesticus*, *primacerius* (secretary) and *eparchos*. Whether in Coptic or Nubian documents, the original Greek title was preserved – all high-sounding titles modelled on those of the Byzantine court.[126] Communications, however, were also being maintained with Coptic Egypt. Evelyn White's exploration of the monastery church of Deir es Suriyan in the Wadi Natrun in 1921 had recovered a large white marble tray (perhaps for offerings) found leaning against a wall of the sanctuary, where it had been left behind by the monks after their final service. The bilingual inscription in Greek and Nubian consisted of a funerary prayer beseeching refreshment and rest for the soul of King George, and forgiveness of all his sins. The Nubian text revealed that George was born in 1106, ascended the throne in 1130 and died in 1158.[127] He was probably king of Makurrah.

Another link in the story of Nubian Christianity was the decipherment of a long graffito in debased Greek uncovered at St Simeon's monastery. It could be dated to 7 April 1322.[128] The moment was dramatic, for the Nubian king Kudanbes (d. 1323), styled 'president of the Caesars', was about to leave Egypt on what proved to be a final, fatal, struggle with a Muslim rival for the throne of the Nubian kingdom whose capital was Dongola. He lost, and at the time the graffito was discovered he was thought to have been the last Christian ruler of a Nubian kingdom. Though discoveries at Qasr Ibrim in 1964 proved that this was not so, another blank in Nubian history had been filled in.

For *Europe* completely different circumstances prevailed. It was not a question of expeditions searching for long-vanished Christian civilizations in a Muslim world, and of excavations employing hundreds of labourers.[129] Research was fuelled by heightened popular curiosity and awareness of the heritage of the past. In the *Balkans* renewal national self-consciousness and in *Greece* determination to rise above the disaster of 1922 were allied to a strong Christian sense of identity which favoured research into the early spread of the faith in their countries. The mid-1920s witnessed some of the first excavations of *églises paléochrétiennes*, i.e. churches built in the late fourth and early fifth centuries, that were to show eventually how the western provinces of the empire (except Britain) yielded to the advance of Christianity in the last decades of the fourth century AD.

Work continued on the pre-war sites of Salona,[130] Salonica[131] and Diocletian's palace at Split (Spalato),[132] as well as Philippi, recorded above. The legacy of Mgr Bulić's work at Salona was taken up by a Danish expedition in 1920–21 and 1922–23 under Einar Dyggve and then by Rudolf Egger, resulting in the discovery of the Basilica of the Five Martyrs, and sixth-century oratories built amoung the ruins of the amphitheatre, which in turn had been incorporated in the defences of the town before it fell to the Avars *c.* 615. But equally important for the future of Christian archaeology were the smaller sites often found by accident but now taken up by scholars working for their national museums. Such was Anastasi Orlandos' excavation at Lochrida, north-east of Arkitsa in eastern Greece. The site had been found by peasants searching for an ikon of St Catherine which one of them said he had seen in a dream.[133] A hole had been dug in the apse before the Ministry of Education stepped in. The church was indeed worthy of St Catherine. It was an imposing building, the chancel flanked by sacristies and the floors paved with a patterned mosaic. It had been built, probably early in the fifth century, by Eugenius, a personage of consular rank, and his wife Dionysia. As such it represented the conversion of educated Greek provincials from Hellenism to Christianity. Its end by fire in the late sixth century told of the closing of the Byzantine Christian era, in face of the most pervasive and destructive of all the mass migrations of peoples in Europe, that of the Slavs. Orlandos also excavated the church of St John at Gortyna in Crete,[134] the see attributed to Titus (Titus 1:5), and we learn from Eusebius (*HE* iv.23.5) there was a church there whose bishop, Philip, seems to have been the leading bishop in Crete about AD 170.[135] However, no material remains of Christianity earlier than the fourth century were found.

New churches were discovered on other islands, on Chios, Lesbos (three churches) and Samos.[136] Most promising for the future, however, was G. A. Soteriou's excavation of two churches at Nea Anchialos (Thebes) in Thessaly begun in 1925.[137] The catalogue of new discoveries showed that by the end of the fourth century Christianity was well on the way towards replacing paganism as the religion of the people. Mainland Greece also was developing its own architectural style, apparently more akin to that of Syria and the West than Constantinople, reflecting its dependence on Thessalonica, and thence on Rome. Soteriou believed that Greece had a claim to be regarded as an independent cultural province in early-Christian architecture as well as organization. He pointed to the absence in Greece of the polygonal apse normal in churches in the capital. At the same time, churches that he and Orlandos had discovered were of a Syrian or Western basilican type with a *prothesis* and *diaconicon* either side of a semicircular apse.[138]

Macedonia, though politically part of *Yugoslavia*, obviously fell within the same cultural province. Soteriou claimed with justice the fourth- to fifth-century episcopal church at Stobi excavated by an Anglo-Yugoslav team as a typical Greek basilican-style church.[139] Dispute between Greece, Yugoslavia and Bulgaria, each claiming the cultural heritage of Macedonia, was never to be far below the surface.

In *Bulgaria* there was a similar groundswell of interest in the nation's early-Christian past. The discovery of a large Christian cemetery surrounding the church of St Sophia at Sofia (Serdica) reminded scholars that Serdica had been in 342–343 the scene of the first important meeting between Eastern and Western bishops, which resulted also in the first major dispute between the Latin and Greek Churches. The relative wealth of the local Christian community was illustrated by the frescos found in some of the larger tombs in which, as elsewhere in the fourth century, Classical themes were richly intermingled with biblical scenes as, for instance, in a bucolic representation of Paradise as a garden.[140]

The Balkans were now attracting the systematic exploration of early-Christian sites hitherto the prerogative of territories further east. In *western*

Europe, however, Christian archaeology was continuing to be largely a matter of work on accidental discoveries.. Thus, in *France*, the fourth-century baptistery at Fréjus came to light during the restoration of its tenth-century successor.[141] At Narbonne, where Christian sarcophagi had been found since 1658, chance revealed an ornate inscription dated to 455 commemorating the building of a church outside the walls by Bishop Rusticus dedicated to St Felix, at which members of the Gallo-Roman nobility, and possibly Visigothic nobility as well, were present (the mention of 'Glismoda comitissa' suggests this). The church was succeeded by another referred to by Gregory of Tours, the find thus confirming his account.[142] In *Spain*, however, where up to this time Christian archaeology had hardly existed, accident changed the situation permanently. In 1923 a large state-owned tobacco factory was to be built on the outskirts of Tarragona. In levelling the ground, however, builders came on the remains of a vast Christian cemetery and a basilica. The contractors were not amused, and exploration was confined to salvage without the possibility of systematic excavation. Nonetheless, much was accomplished. It could be established that during the fourth century the cemetery had been used by members of all classes, from humble tile graves and 'coffins' composed of amphorae cut in half (both found in North Africa) to marble sarcophagi, lead coffins and tombs covered with mosaics. A figure depicted on one of these wore a toga, an indication of Christianity among the highest classes in Tarragona, and their hopes after death were expressed by the inscription 'Sancta Christi in sede requiescis' ('May you rest in the holy seat of Christ')[143] The cemetery and basilica, combined with an adjoining baptistery of exactly the same plan and dimensions as one found belonging to a basilica at Hippo,[144] suggest the possibility of the emergence of a 'western Mediterranean province' of Christian building and liturgy during the fourth century which would continue until the onset of Islam.

In the *Rhineland* a new field for archaeological work was opening up through repairs and renovation in or around the mediaeval cathedrals at Bonn, Mainz and Cologne, and at Trier at the ancient churches of St Eucharius/Matthias south of the city and St Paulinus on the northern edge. These provided evidence for the arrival of Christianity in the late third century and its progress through the fourth century. Christian worship on these sites was shown to have been continuous from *c.* 370 (the reign of Valentinian I) to the present day.[145] At Bonn repairs to the choir of the cathedral church of St Cassius in 1928 produced unforeseen results. The church lay about a kilometre from the *vicus* attached to the legionary encampment of Bonna. Repairs to a crypt beneath the choir revealed a memorial chapel (*cella memoriae*) which had been built in a cemetery among pagan graves of the second and third centuries, the latest dating to *c.* 260.[146] The chapel measured no more than 3.35 m × 2.55 m. It contained, however, two stone table blocks, while two recesses had been cut into the back wall. In one of these was a late Samian bowl of a mid-third-century type. One can imagine the small Christian community gathering in the chapel for eucharistic services and funerary meals amid the tombs of pagan provincials. In the late fourth century (reign of Valens or later) a rectangular hall was built above the chapel which served as a repository for sarcophagi, and the mediaeval cathedral was built on the site in the eleventh century.[147] At Cologne, also, the great mediaeval cathedral had been preceded by a Christian chapel.

Trier produced material of a different type in the form of Christian sarcophagi and marble memorial epitaphs.[148] As at Bonn the Christian cemeteries seem to have developed on the same sites as earlier, pagan cemeteries. Discoveries accumulating for over a century showed that the community if at first small had been able to attract wealthy members. The richly decorated sarcophagus of 'Eleuthera the sinner' from the crypt of the St Paulinus church[149] was the most opulent of many substantial stone and lead sarcophagi and marble plaques found in the St Eucharius/Matthias cemetery. Some of the sarcophagi were shaped similarly to Syrian sarcophagi.[150] This, together with the presence of Greek epitaphs and Greek names among clergy and laity, would suggest that as in parts of the Balkans Christianity could have arrived in Trier through merchants from the East Roman provinces.[151]

In the Rhineland, therefore, archaeological evidence was showing the presence of flourishing Christian communities by the mid-fourth century. In *Britain*, on the other hand, a major chance find illustrated some of the dangers which could befall a rich and triumphant Christianity during the invasions and barbarian raids in the early fifth century. In the summer of 1919 men working at the north end of the hill-fort at Traprain Law, some four miles from Edinburgh, came on a treasure hastily buried in a hole 2 ft in diameter and 2 ft deep.[152] Brought to the surface and cleaned, it was seen to consist of 170 separate silver objects, weighing 770 ounces (about 22 kg). The objects had belonged to wealthy owners. They included ten small flagons decorated with pagan and Christian motifs, pyxes, remains of chalices, spoons, and a strainer with a ☧ monogram formed by the perforations in its bowl. All had been broken up and thrown together in a heap. There were also four silver coins, one of Valens, one of Valentinian II (375–92) and two of Honorius (395–423), thus dating the hoard to the early years of the fifth century. It was loot, many of the objects having been cut up (some into rough squares) or bent out of shape ready for distribution to members of the band.[153] Romans and Christians and their churches had been singled out by the raiders, but not exclusively so. One of the least expected objects was a Visigothic-type brooch while other artefacts were stamped with Teutonic names.[154] Most of the treasure seems to be Gallic in origin but the identity of the raiders remains uncertain. Saxons allied to Picts is one possibility. Another, more specific, was William Ridgeway's theory that the hoard was booty captured by Niall of the Nine Hostages who was killed in 405.[155] But Niall raided from Ireland and nothing suggests an alliance between him and the Picts.

Whether or not the hoard was part of booty brought back by one of Niall's followers from his last fateful expedition to Gaul,[156] the rich assemblage of Christian vessels tells something about the wealth and also the liturgy of some of the Gallic-Christian communities in this period just before the onset of the Germanic invasions. There was also the same acceptance of pagan ornamentation (for example Pan and a Hermaphrodite),[157] even in eucharistic vessels, that was to characterize objects found as far apart as Water Newton and northern Syria. (See below, p. 377.) Some of the decoration, however, was wholly biblical and Christian, such as the silver flask that portrayed the Epiphany, the Virgin seated with the Child on her knee being approached by the three kings bearing their gifts. Above had been portrayed a small rectangular building with a steep tiled roof, perhaps a church.[158] The Traprain treasure invited comparison with another famous silver hoard in the west, namely the Esquiline treasure discovered on the Esquiline Hill, Rome, in 1793.[159] This included tall silver flasks, circular dishes, a silver saucepan and the domed silver bridal toilet casket belonging to a Roman lady named Projecta, the wife of L. Turcius Secundus. Projecta was a Christian and her epitaph was written by Pope Damasus (366–384),[160] but the treasure was not liturgical and whether it had continued in her family as an heirloom to be buried at the approach of Alaric on Rome in 410 or whether it was in some way connected with Projecta's early death and funeral *c.* 380 is uncertain. The two treasures taken together provide a glimpse of the wealth accumulating in the hands of the aristocratic patrons of the Church in Rome, and perhaps also of some Churches in the West in the last quarter of the fourth century.

Finally *Rome* itself continued to produce its wonders. In November 1919 a burial vault measuring some 7 m square was discovered accidentally as the result of demolitions near the Viale Manzoni. A mosaic showed that Aurelius Felicissimus had prepared the tomb for 'his brothers and fellow-freedmen'.[161] Two things were noticeable at once about the inscription. One of the 'brethren', Aurelia Primitiva, was named as 'a virgin', while the concluding formula 'bene merentibus' (deserving well), though religiously neutral and sometimes used by Jews, was also being used in the third century by Christians. During the exploration of the site an inscription painted on a wall of one of the lower chambers recorded a certain Remmeus Celerinus 'making a *refrigerium* in honour of Aurelius Epaphroditus'.[162] The Christian identity was therefore assured. Tiles employed in the construction could be dated to the reign of Caracalla (211–217), and the vault attributed to a Christian group not much later than AD 220.

But what group? The vault consisted of two floors each divided into two separate rooms with traces of passages leading from them. The rooms contained vaulted cubicles (*arcosolia*) and further tombs had been dug later in the floors and walls. The walls and ceilings of the original vault were covered with paintings beautifully executed. In one of the upper chambers there was a scene of the garden of Eden with Adam, Eve and the serpent, with another male figure in the background. It was a Creation scene with a difference. The male figure was youthful, reminiscent of the Demiurge or Archon rather than Jahwe, while the serpent was coiled round a tree, its jaws open, not offering the forbidden fruit but apparently speaking, teaching perhaps.[163] In a lower chamber was a banquet scene, perhaps the Last Supper or the meal at Emmaus, but here too there are other features that can hardly be reconciled with orthodoxy. Who was the woman standing behind the third and fourth seated disciple?[164] Was it perhaps Sophia of Gnostic teaching? Why are there some only of the apostles? What was the significance of the splendid painting of New Jerusalem and the four figures standing conversing with one another in Paradise outside the city?[165] Even more mysterious are the scenes depicting the return of Ulysses,[166] and the triumphant horseman approaching a city gate to be greeted by a group of welcomers.[167] Finally there is a painting of a shepherd (in addition to the Good Shepherd featured on a ceiling) seated on a mountain top, reading intently from a scroll while sheep and goats graze on the slopes below him.[168]

Orthodox explanations are possible. The shepherd could be Christ promulgating the New Law, but if so, why is he bent so intently over the scroll? Christ could be entering Jerusalem, but if so, he should be seated humbly on an ass (Zech 9:4) (as shown on numerous sarcophagi) rather than riding in triumph. It could be Antichrist, as Cecchelli suggests, or simply a freedman's vision of an imperial *Adventus*; but the subject is not the emperor, but perhaps himself, his illumined and emancipated spirit. The two detailed and explicit Homeric scenes suggest a community that held Homer in high regard as a guide for the soul. The evidence points not to a Montanist[169] or even a Monarchian[170] group but to a Gnostic one, more specifically, Naassene,[171] with the wise serpent instructing Gnosis and the inclusion of scenes from the Homeric narrative of Ulysses. The Naassenes of the early third century were said to magnify Homer as 'their prophet' and the Serpent as their object of worship.[172] If so, these extraordinarily fine funerary paintings belonged to a sect flourishing in Rome at the time the presbyter Hippolytus was writing against them.[173] The discovery revealed an artistic and religious genius among the Roman Gnostics.

Less convincing has been the claim that the cult centre beneath the church of St Sebastiano three miles along the Via Appia could also have belonged to a non-orthodox sect. Excavations began in 1915 and continued after the war. By 1933 it had become clear that down to the middle of the third century the centre had belonged to a pagan-mystical group of 'Innocentii'.[174] How and why these ceased to own the site so that it came into the possession of the Christians is not known. It would appear, even, that the same centre was used by both communities for some years. By the mid-250s Christians must have been sole owners, for, probably on 22 February 258, in the middle of the Valerianic persecution, the remains of the apostles Peter and Paul were moved from their burial places to the centre, and that on 29 June of the same year, the event proudly dated by the consular year of Tuscus and Bassus, their 'birthday' (*natalis*) was celebrated. Thereafter, as the 640 separate graffiti now show, the centre became the focus of an intense cult in which the prayers of the apostles were requested by pilgrims. In the first half of the fourth century a basilica named after the martyr Sebastian was erected on the site after the remains of St Peter (if not St Paul) had apparently been restored to what was believed to be their original resting-place in the Vatican cemetery. By the 380s, Pope Damasus wrote a stanza recorded by a seventh-century pilgrim, in honour of the apostles, how this site was where they had dwelt (*habitasse*), but implying they did so no longer.[175] Nothing suggests that the cult-centre was in other than orthodox Christian use, active for about 50 years from 258 until Constantine began to build the first St Peter's in honour of the apostle *c.* 322.

In the same month as the vault of the Aurelii came to light there was a almost equally important discovery in the garden of the Villa Torlonia.[176] It was a Jewish catacomb, one of six known (in 1975) in Rome and belonging probably to the community of 'Suburenses'. So far as dating is possible most tombs appear to be third-century. The very few *arcosolia* belonging to richer members were painted with pictures of the Ark, dolphins, lions and peacocks, the scrolls of the Law and the *menorah* (seven-branch candlestick), but no scenes from the Old Testament. Forty-nine out of the 53 inscriptions were in Greek, but a few graffiti in Hebrew could be deciphered on the tile graves that lined the galleries. The great majority of the graves were of poor people, with a striking proportion of children and adolescents. Unlike the catacomb on the Via Latina this belonged to a poor community and does not seem to be earlier than the Christian catacombs. This might indicate that Christian and Jewish catacombs begin at roughly the same date, namely end-second to beginning-third century,[177] and that their artistic development runs parallel. While Jewish and Christian formulae such as 'bene merenti' and the concluding 'in pace' are the same, Christian catacomb art in Rome would not seem to be derived from earlier existing Jewish models. (See below, p. 370.)

There were two more important discoveries in this period. In 1920 Ernesto Iosi excavated yet another vast catacomb, that of St Pamphilus on the Via Salaria Vetus which had flourished in the second half of the third century. Coins of Maxentius (306–312) and other pre-Constantinian emperors had been impressed into the mortar binding the tiles used in the burial galleries, while this was still wet.[178] The catacomb of Novatian belongs to the same period. Novatian, a leading presbyter in the Roman Church, had represented a rigorous attitude towards those who had lapsed during the Decian persecution (250–251). He failed, however, to secure consecration as the martyred Bishop Fabian's successor, but became opposition bishop with a following in North Africa, Syria and Asia Minor as well as in Rome itself. In 1926 a catacomb was found near the junction of the Via Tiburtina and Viale Regina Margherita. Significantly it was not mentioned in the Pilgrim's *Itineraries* or by any subsequent explorer of the catacombs. In 1932, however, at the end of seven seasons' work an inscription was found: 'For the most blessed martyr, Novatianus, Gaudentius the deacon made (this tomb)'.[179] The tomb was only large enough to house relics, and Novatian himself may have died in exile. As the tomb appears to date from 270–300 its association with the schismatic bishop seems likely, though the claim has been disputed in favour of a martyr named Novatian commemorated in the Hieronomyian Martyrology on 27 and 29 June.[180]

Time, however, now had to be spent on consolidation and salvage. Mussolini's seizure of power in 1922 benefited excavation in the Forum, but did not help Christian sites. Some of these were being threatened by new buildings. The *Rivista* of 1924 reports 'grave damage' to the famous catacombs of Felicitas, Hermes and Bassilla, and Jordanes through building work in the region of the Via Salaria.[181] Urban sprawl, the blight of Classical and Christian sites all round the Mediterranean in the year after the Second World War, was beginning to cast its shadow on Christian Rome.

This European 'era of good feelings' that witnessed signature of the Locarno treaty in 1925, marking the reintegration of Germany into the international community devised by the victors, was a period of archaeological achievement. Some areas, notably central Asia, had become practically closed to further discovery, but elsewhere pieces had indeed been picked up. The defeat of Turkey in the war had enabled new areas in Syria and Jordan to be open for archaeological research, while in Greece and the Balkans the new nations and governments arising out of the peace settlements were keen to establish their Christian heritage and their claims to scholarship. Furthermore, the long Indian summer of the European colonial empires enabled archaeological research to continue in North Africa and move forward strongly in Egypt and Sudan. Research in western Europe remained dominated by the Roman catacombs, though other catacombs, notably in Malta, were beginning to be explored. Paradoxically, the main threat to archaeological research in these years came from rising prosperity among all classes. Urban renewal in Rome that threatened some of the catacombs was repeated in a different form in Egypt. There in 1926 the American Professor F. W. Kelsey, excavating at Kum Ousin in the Fayum, wrote of 'the systematic destruction of ancient sites', and, in particular, of 'the total loss of Arsinoë', due to farmers using the papyrus-bearing earth from the ancient rubbish tip as fertilizer for their expanding farms.[182]

But all was not gloom. In the 1920s archaeology had widened further the horizons of Church history. Discovery of mid-seventh-century Latin epitaphs in western Mauretania (Oran and Morocco) was of major importance, as was the finding of Gnostic as well as Jewish catacombs in third-century Rome. Greece, Austria and Yugoslavia were now providing evidence for the progress of Christianity in the fourth century far beyond its established centres. The conversion of the Roman provinces in that period was shown to be a reality. The momentum of research was being sustained by the establishment of 'Christian archaeology' as part of the faculties of theology in Continental universities, such as Breslau, Münster and Freiburg. At Bonn, Franz Joseph Dölger, having moved from Münster, was inspiring the study of late antiquity and Christianity which would bear fruit in the *Reallexikon für Antike und Christentum* and later in the formation of the F. J. Dölger Institut for these studies at the University of Bonn. Dölger was to have the support of Hans Lietzmann at Berlin, who had assisted Hans Beyer in excavating the Jewish catacomb in the grounds of the Villa Torlonia, and in 1928 had surveyed part of the Byzantine walls at Constantinople.[183] In this age of renewed confidence and increasing discoveries of the material remains of early Christianity Benjamin Kidd's three-volume study of the *History of the Church to AD 461* (Clarendon Press, 1922) remains the last (if not also the greatest) history of the early Church that relied almost exclusively on patristic texts. Dölger's continued researches into the ramifications of the fish symbol in early-Christian epigraphy and Wilhelm Schepelern's *Der Montanismus und die phrygische Kult* (1929) were each showing how archaeological and literary evidence were needed to provide a convincing picture of early-Christian life and the cross-currents of its thought. For Phrygia, Schepelern gave full weight to the importance of traditional pagan rites as forming a background to the Montanist movement. He maintained, however, that the real inspiration for Montanism came from the Fourth Gospel and, in particular, the Johannine letters and the eschatology of the book of Revelation; and he pointed to the Montanist observance of the Johannine (Quartodeciman) calculation of the Easter Feast as evidence for this.

Henceforth, no study of early Christianity could afford to neglect the wealth of evidence from archaeology. The renewed hopes of the 1920s provided fresh opportunity for research not least in the fields of Christian art and architecture. The crises, at first economic but then political, that resulted in the Second World War would check but not destroy entirely these widening horizons.

NOTES

1. As related to the author by Lady Cecily Douglas, daughter of Sir Maurice de Bunsen (Aberfoyle, 1982).
2. Sir John Reith, *Diary* (29 July 1914); published in art. by Ian McIntyre, *Sunday Times* (22 August 1993).
3. C. Leonard Woolley, 'Excavations at Ur of the Chaldees', *AJ* 3.4 (1923), p. 319, relating to the temple of the moon-god and his consort.
4. H. G. Wells, *The Outline of History* (London: Cassell, 1920), p. 2.
5. Ed. J. A. Hammerton (London, 1920–22).
6. O. G. S. Crawford, *Antiquity* 1 (March 1927), pp. 1–4. Another example of the popularity of archaeology in Britain during this period was T. D. Kendrick and C. F. C. Hawkes, *Archaeology in England and Wales 1914–1931* (London: Methuen, 1932).
7. Thus, D. Talbot Rice, 'Monasteries of Mount Athos', *Antiquity* 2 (1928), pp. 443–51.
8. E. Diehl, *ILCV*, Introduction, p. viii. At this time (1925) Latin and Greek Christian inscriptions numbered at least 25,000: see. S. de Ricci, 'Recueil des inscriptions chrétiennes de Rome', *RA* 5th ser. 20 (1924), p. 162.
9. Enrico Iosi, 'Scavi nelle catacombe romane', *NBAC* 24–25 (1918–19), pp. 73–87, at p. 82, fig. i. Christ places his hand on the woman's head.
10. 'Motu Proprio del S. Padre Pio xi', *Rivista* 3 (1926), pp. 7–19. For the history of the Institute 1925–75, see Robert Jacquard (ed.) *L'Institut Pontifical d'archéologie chrétienne: Journal de cinquante années (1925–1975)* (Rome, 1975).
11. J. P. Kirsch, 'Prolusione per l'inaugurazione del Pont. Istituto di Arch. cristiana', *Rivista* 4 (1927), pp. 49–57.
12. Woolley, *AJ* 3 (4 October 1923), plate XXIV. On site, balloon photography was undertaken with success in Palestinian excavations: *Antiquity* 6 (1932), p. 148.
13. Thus Sir Hercules Read in his Presidential Address to the Society of Antiquaries of London (23 April 1923) said that the French themselves 'exercise a jealous control over what France considers her legitimate spheres of influences, and to an extent that has no parallel in England': *AJ* 3.3 (July 1923), p. 205. On Afghanistan, ibid., pp. 206–7: regarding Persia, p. 209. For disputes with M. Lacau, Direc-

tor of the Egyptian Antiquities Service (a position also monopolized by France), relating to the distribution of finds from Tutankhamen's and other tombs in the Valley of the Kings, ibid., pp. 212–13. France, after pressure, agreed to collaborate with the British on archaeological work in Afghanistan: *The Times* (25 May 1923).

14. Oscar Reuther, 'German excavations at Ctesiphon', *Antiquity* 3 (1929), pp. 439–51. The excavations describe (pp. 449–51) the single-aisled nave, supported on pillared walls without an apse, of a building which may have marked the tolerant policy of Chosroes II (591–628) towards the Christians in Persia.

15. Proceedings of the Algiers Congress, reviewed *RA* 6th ser. 3 (1934), pp. 145–6. Contributers estimated the population of Djemila at 5,000, and that of Timgad at 8,000, useful yardsticks in considering religious life in the North African towns in the Later Empire.

16. That these volumes were planned is shown by Gsell's slips with notes, e.g. to Tertullian, *De Praescriptione* 7, which were given to the present writer by Robert Esquer, librarian at the public library of Tunis, during his stay there in 1938.

17. A. L Delattre, 'Une grande basilique près de Sante-Monique à Carthage', *CRAI* (1915), p. 495. Also *CRAI* (1916), pp. 150–64 and 432ff.; (1917), pp. 507ff.; (1920), pp. 191–9. Delattre's reports were consolidated by F. Vaultrin, 'Basiliques chrétiens de Carthage', *RAfr* 73 (1932), pp. 182–318, at pp. 279–91.

18. Delattre, *CRAI* (1920), p. 195.

19. N. Duval, in his introduction to Liliane Ennabli, *Les Inscriptions funéraires chrétiennes de la Basilique dite de Sainte-Monique* (Collection de l'Ecole française de Rome 25; Rome, 1975). Mme Ennabli was able to recover only 403 inscriptions of those recorded by Delattre; some of these latter had been cemented into the wall outside the Pères Blancs' museum and may have been robbed by members of the German or Allied occupation forces in 1943–46.

20. Vaultrin, op. cit., pp. 309–18. See also Delattre and P. Chales, *CRAI* (1922), p. 302; (1923), p. 449 on their discovery of more than 200 fragments of inscriptions.

21. W. H. C. Frend, 'A two-period baptistery in Carthage', *CEDAC* (Carthage) (1985–86), pp. 42–3.

22. L. Poinssot and R. Lantier, 'L'église de Thugga', *RA* 5th ser. 22 (1925), pp. 228–47.

23. Poinssot and Lantier, 'L'archéologie en Tunisie, 1920–1932', *Atti* III (publ. Rome, 1934), pp. 383–410, esp. p. 393.

24. Ibid., pp. 393–8.

25. L. Leschi, 'Recherches épigraphiques dans le pays de Nemencha', *RAfr* 72 (1931), pp. 262–93: 'C'est dans la deuxième moitié du IIIe siècle et pendant le cours du IVe siècle que cette partie de la Numidie a été la plus peuplée': p. 293.

26. Described and reported by H. Omont, *CRAI* (1918). pp. 241–3.

27. P. Alfaric, 'Un manuscrit manichéen', *RHLR* n.s. 6 (1920), pp. 62–98. The MS was in a very poor state; only fragments were possible to decipher with any confidence.

28. Thus Alfaric, op. cit., p. 93. Against: F. Decret, 'Aspects de l'Eglise manichéenne' in *Signum Pietatis* (*Festgabe für C. P. Mayer*) (Würzburg, 1989), pp. 123–51, at pp. 125ff.

29. The Latin text of the first eight out of the 26 columns of writing is given by A. Adam, *Texte zum Manichäismus* (Kleine Texte 175; Berlin 1954, 2nd edn 1969), pp. 34–5: see lines 41–47 on the duties of catechumens.

30. Fragments reproduced by Alfari, op. cit.: see also W. H. C. Frend, 'The Gnostic-Manichaean traditions in Roman North Africa', *JEH* 4.1 (1953), pp. 13–26, at p. 21.

31. See P. Brown, *Augustine of Hippo: A Biography* (1967), ch. 5.

32. P. Monceaux. 'Deux victimes des Maures à Madauros', *CRAI* (1920), pp. 329–33. For attacks by the Moors especially from c. 490 onwards, see *Vita Fulgentii* (ed. P. G. Lepeyre) 28 and 65.

33. *CIL* VIII, 9286; H. Leclercq, 'Mouzaiaville', *DACL* XII.1, 377–378.

34. *CRAI* (1925), pp. 261–6; *Année épigraphique* (1926), inscr. 60.

35. Though increasing insecurity seems to have led to the abandonment or destruction of major towns; Theveste and Bagai had to be rebuilt by the Byzantines *a fundamentis*.

36. The original find was described by Alexis Truillot, *RC* 58 (1928–29), pp. 406–13, under 'Chronique archéologique'. Albertini gave his opinion in September 1928 that the Tablettes Albertini dated to the reign of King Gunthamund (484–496), were deposited probably in 494, and that they were deeds of sale, pehaps forming part of a local landowner's archive. For a definitive, detailed study, see C. Courtois, L. Leschi, C. Perrat and C. Saumagne, *Tablettes Albertini: Actes privés de l'époque vandale* (Algiers, 1952), dating the *Actes* to 493–496: p. 21.

37. A. Ballu, 'Ruines de Djemila', *RAfr* 62 (1921), pp. 201-76. For an excellent survey, see E. Albertini, 'L'Archéologie chrétienne de l'Algérie', *Atti* III, pp. 411–27.

38. *Sententiae Episcoporum* no. 71 (Pudentianus): *CSEL* III.1, ed. W. Hartel (Vienna, 1868), p. 457.

39. P. Monceaux, 'Les martyrs de Djemila', *CRAI* (1920), pp. 290–7. Also 'Découverte d'édifices chrétiens à Djemila', *CRAI* (1922), pp. 380–407; 'Cuicul chrétien', *Atti della Pontificia Accademia romana di archeologia* (1923).

40. See Y. Allais, *Djemila* (Paris, 1938), pp. 27–30.

41. *Gesta Coll. Carth.* (ed. S. Lancel) 1.121; A. Berthier, *DHGE* 13 (1956), pp. 1095–7. The relations between the two churches remains obscure. They could be contemporary and have formed a 'double church' on the lines of similar churches at Salona and Trier, and have constituted a centre of pilgrimage. See P. A. Février, *Djemila* (Algiers, 1971), p. 81 and plan.

42. The text is published in *CRAI* (1922), pp. 380–407, at p. 397.

43. Allais, op., cit. p. 30 and *Année épigraphique* (1924), no. 58. The inscription is dated by consular years, and hence Cuicul must still have been under Roman rule.

44. Allais, p. 31.

45. Ibid., pp. 31–2.

46. Own observations (1939).

47. The discovery was made by J. Bosco and P. Alquier and reported in *RC* 58 (1927), pp. 209–16, and also in *CRAI* (1927), pp. 98–103. Though the general meaning of the inscription was clear it was not until 1969 that a detailed study was published by N. Duval and P. A. Février, 'Procès-verbal de la déposition de reliques de la région de Telergma (viie siècle)', *MEFR* 68 (1969), pp. 257–320. For full bibliography, see Y. Duval, *Loca Sanctorum Africae* (Rome, 1982), pp. 231–6.

48. See J. Carcopino, 'Note sur une inscription chrétienne de Volubilis', *Hesperis* (1928), pp. 135–46; *Le Maroc antique* (Paris, 1943), pp. 293–4 and 298. The precise Latinity of the inscription contrasts with the decline of Latin in Numidia at this time. Julia may herself have been a noble member of the Baquates tribe who controlled Volubilis in the sixth and seventh centuries. For Christianity further east in the département of Oran, see S. Gsell, 'Le Christianisme en Oranie', *Bulletin de la cinquantenaire de la Société de géographie et d'archéologie d'Oran* (1928), pp. 19–32.

49. R. Bartocini, *Relazione sugli scavi* (1926).

50. The site was excavated and recorded by S. Aurigemma, *Studi di Antichità cristiana* 5 (Rome, 1932) and the comment is by J. B. Frey, 'Une ancienne nécropole chrétienne en Tripolitaine', *Rivista* 10 (1933), pp. 119–33.

51. H. Leclercq, *L'Afrique chrétienne*, p. 20. Inscriptions he regarded as the most important source of new information.

52. As recorded in *BCH* 45 (1921), p. 555; and Talbot Rice, 'Nicaea', *Antiquity* 3 (1929), pp. 60–4: see also art. 'Nicée' in *DACL*.

53. Recorded in *BCH* 46 (1922), pp. 547–8, five days after the abandonment of the city by the Greek administration.

54. Recorded in 'Les fouilles du Corps d'Occupation française à Constantinople', *CRAI* (1922), pp. 198–207; (1923), pp. 241–8.

55. Charles Picard, 'Texte nouveau de la Correspondance entre Abgar d'Osroène et Jésus-Christ gravé sur une porte de la ville à Philippes (Macédoine)', *BCH* 44 (1920), pp. 41–9.

56. Ibid., p. 50.

57. Ibid., p. 50. See F. Ll. Griffith, 'Oxford excavations in Nubia: the Anchorite's Grotto', *LAAA* 14 (1927), p. 83.

58. M. Schede, *Gnomon* 2 (1926), p. 746. No more excavations 'grössten Stils' as before the war . For a useful summary of German work in Asia Minor from 1924 to 1931 see 'Notes and news', *Antiquity* 26 (1932), pp. 218–21.

59. Recorded in S. Guyer (ed.), *MAMA* II (Manchester University Press, 1930).

60. See J. Keil and A. Wilhelm (eds), *MAMA* III (1931) in which are recorded results of the journeys by Austrian archaeologists in the area in 1892, 1914 and 1925.

61. J. Keil, 'XIII. Vorläufiger Bericht über Ausgrabungen in Ephesos', *JÖAI* 24 (1929), Beiblatt, pp. 10–20 and 51ff.

62. J. Keil, 'XIV. Vorläufiger Bericht', *JÖAI* 25 (1929), pp. 6–27.

63. Ibid., pp. 12–13.

64. See J. Keil, 'Antike und Christentum in Ephesos' in *Von Antike zum Christentum (Festgabe Viktor Schultze)* (Stettin, 1931), pp. 97–102, at p. 102; and *Ephesos: Ein Führer durch die Ruinenstätte und ihre Geschichte* (Vienna, 1930), pp. 25–7. Keil regarded the cruciform church of St John as the first purpose-built Christian building in Ephesus, which up to then, despite the huge church dedicated to the Virgin alongside the Museon, was still dominated by pagan buildings. Pagan attitudes continued to prevail among many of the townsfolk in the fifth century ('Antike und Christentum', pp. 98–9), though the earliest Christian shrine over the area sacred to the Apostle's memory could have dated from the third century.

65. Recorded by H. Grégoire, 'Chronique', *Byzantion* 1 (1924), pp. 712–15. Ephesus had a reasonable claim to seniority. An inscription of the reign of Gordian III (238–244) re-used in the church of St John gives it the title of 'the first and greatest metropolis in Asia': *JÖAI* 24 (1929), p. 18.

66. Recorded by Henri Grégoire, 'Chronique', *Byzantion* 1 (1924), pp. 712–15, and in his 'Recueil des inscriptions grecques chrétiennes d'Asie Mineure' in A. M. Ramsay (ed.), *Anatolian Studies Presented to Sir William Ramsay* (Manchester University Press, 1923), no. 100, pp. 154ff.

67. W. M. Calder, 'Philadelphia and Montanism', *BJRL* 7 (1923), pp. 309–55. In 1928 he was appointed to the Chair of Greek Epigraphy at Manchester University. For his career, see J. M. C. Cormack, *PBA* (1962), pp. 345–60.

68. Calder, ibid., pp. 343–6, fig. 4.

69. Ibid., p. 322.

70. P. Monceaux, *Histoire littéraire*, IV, pp. 475–6. The Donatists claimed to be 'milites Christi, Agonistici appellantur. Utinam ergo milites Christi essent': Augustine, *Enarr. in Ps.* 132.6.

71. W. H. Buckler, W. M. Calder and C. W. M. Cox, 'Asia Minor 1924, IV: a monument from the upper Tembris valley', *JRS* 16 (1927), pp. 54–7. For Novatians in Asia Minor, see S. Mitchell, *Anatolia* (OUP, 1993), II. pp. 96–103.

72. E. Gibson, *The 'Christians for Christians' Inscriptions in Phrygia* (Missoula, 1978), p. 43. Contrast Henri Grégoire's view supporting Calder: *Byzantion* 1 (1924), p. 708. In Dorset, mosaics bearing Christian and pagan motifs were being designed in the same workshop *c.* 340, but this does not invalidate the Christianity of those marked with a Christian symbol.

73. W. M. Calder, 'The epigraphy of the Anatolian heresies' in *Anatolian Studies Presented to Sir W. M. Ramsay*, pp. 58–91, at pp. 59ff.

74. 'Leaves from an Anatolian Notebook', *BJRL* 13 (1929), pp. 254–71.

75. W. M. Calder, 'The New Jerusalem of the Montanists', *Byzantion* 6 (1931), pp. 421–5.

76. Ibid., p. 424. See also Mitchell, op. cit., pp. 103–7.

77. W. M. Calder, 'Two Encratite tombstones', *ByzZ* 30 (1929–30; Festschrift A. Heisenberg), pp. 645–6. There was also a priest of the Catharists at Laodicea. See Henri Grégoire, *Byzantion* 1 (1924), pp. 699–700 for another Cathar priest. 'A rich cocktail of heretical texts': Mitchell, op. cit., p. 103.

78. W. M. Calder, 'Two Encratite tombstones', p, 646. The epitaph ends 'And if any one of the wine-bibbers intrudes (a corpse) he has to deal with God and Christ'. Dated c. AD 375.

79. W. H. Buckler, W. M. Calder and C. W. M. Cox, 'Asia Minor 1924, I: monuments from Iconium, Lycaonia and Isauria', *JRS* 14 (1924), pp. 24–84, at pp. 54–8. His father Nestor was recorded as a 'helper of virtuous widows'.

80. Reviewed fully by Grégoire, *Byzantion* 4 (1927–28), pp. 692–701. There were 130 Christian inscription out of a total of 440.

81. Grégoire's view expressed in *Byzantion* 4 (1927–28), p. 693.

82. *CRAI* (1922, session of 7 July), pp. 240–1: James H. Breasted's preliminary report. Also F. Cumont, ibid., pp. 425–8; J. H. Breasted's detailed record: 'Peintures de l'époque romaine dans le désert de Syrie', *Syria* 2 (1922), pp. 177ff.; *Monuments Piot* 25 (1923), pp. 1ff.

83. Breasted, op. cit., esp. p. 206.

84. F. Cumont, 'Rapport sur une mission à Saliliyeh sur l'Euphrate', *CRAI* (1923), pp. 12–41. For air photographs of the site see *Archaeology* 3 (1950), 158–62.

85. F. Cumont, 'Rapport sur une nouvelle mission à Saliliyeh', *CRAI* (1924), pp. 17–31. For an outline story of the excavations, see J. W. Crowfoot, 'Dura-Europos', *Antiquity* 19 (1945), pp. 113–21.

86. P. V. C. Baur and M. I. Rostovtzeff, *Preliminary Report of Second Season's Work at Dura Europos* (1931), pp. 10, 76 and 78; *Third Season* (1932), pp. 141–5.

87. *Third Season*, p. 164.

88. *Fifth Season, October 1931–March 1932* (London: Yale, 1934), pp. 9–13.

89. *Sixth Season 1932–33* (publ. 1936), pp. 188–205, and figs 16, 17 and 18.

90. *Fifth Season*: C. Hopkins, 'The Christian church', ch. 7, and P. Baur, ch. 8, 'The paintings in the Christian chapel'.

91. Ibid., pp. 259–62 and plates XLIV and XLV.
92. Ibid., pp. 275–9. A Roman analogy of the Samaritan women drawing water comes from the Catacomb of Domitilla: Wilpert, *Pitture*, p. 270. The themes at Dura seen to have been general in the third century.
93. *Excavations at Dura: Final Report* (New Haven, 1958), VIII.2: 'The Christian Church' (no certain Jewish names: p. 108).
94. An inscription read 'Remind Christ of Proclus among yourselves': *Fifth Season*, p. 284.
95. Photographs of the baptistery, assembly hall and some of the frescos in F. Van der Meer and C. Mohrmann, *Atlas of the Early Christian World*. Eng. trans. M. F. Hedlund and H. H. Rowley (2nd edn, London and The Netherlands, 1959), p. 46, as well as chs 40–51 of *Fifth Season Report*. The four examples of the ROTAS square found at Dura could be either Christian or Jewish (either an anagram of *Pater Noster* or a symbol of God's judgement on Rome, interpreting Ezek 10:2 as the angel sowing coals of fire between the wheels of Jahwe's chariot).
96. J. W. Crowfoot, *Churches at Jerash: A Preliminary Report of the Joint Yale-British School Expedition to Jerash 1928–30* (British School of Archaeology in Jerusalem Suppl. Paper 3: London, 1931), pp. 7–11.
97. Crowfoot, op. cit., pp. 32–3.
98. Ibid., p. 12.
99. Arnobius, *Contra Gentes* vii. 9.
100. Lactantius, *Div. Inst.* vi.1.
101. Crowfoot, op. cit., pp. 16–20; F. M. Abel, 'Les églises de Palestine récemment découvertes', *Atti* III, pp. 493–506.
102. A Classicist's view: see J. B. Ward Perkins, *Archaeology* 3 (1950), p. 27.
103. Crowfoot, op. cit., pp. 13–16.
104. Ibid., pp. 27–8.
105. C. Diehl, 'Peintures de Bhadidat en Syrie', *CRAI* (1927), pp. 328–30. Renan's publication was in *Mission de Phénicie* (Paris, 1864–74), pp. 186–236.
106. G. E. Wright, *Biblical Archaeology* (Philadelphia, 1957), p. 223, fig. 166. Also L. N. Vincent, 'Chronique: La cour dallée de l'Antonia et son entrée', *RB* 42 (1933), pp. 102–13.
107. Eusebius, *Vita* iii.52.
108. *Vita* iii.53. See above, p. 2.
109. A. E. Mader, 'La Basilica Constantiniana di Mamre presso Hebron', *Rivista* 6 (1929), pp. 256–312; *RB* 40 (1930), pp. 84ff. Also Crowfoot, *Churches in Palestine*, pp. 35 and 36.
110. H. G. Evelyn White, 'The monasteries in Wadi Natrun, the Egyptian Expedition', *Bulletin of the Metropolitan Museum of Art* (New York) (1920), pp. 34–9; (1921), pp. 54–60: recorded briefly by De Lacy O'Leary, 'Bibliography: Christian Egypt', *JEA* 8 (1922), p. 185.
111. H. I. Bell, *Jews and Christians in Egypt* (British Museum and OUP, 1924), pp. 38ff. for the story of the Meletian schism; for documents see J. Stevenson, *A New Eusebius: Documents Illustrating the History of the Church to AD 337*, 2nd edn rev. W. H. C. Frend (London: SPCK, 1987), documents 242–244.
112. A document submitted by Meletius to a council in 327, and quoted by Athanasius (*Apol. contra Arianos* 71) shows that in the Delta the Meletians had one bishop out of every six or seven towns, but this total rose to one in every two or three in Middle and Upper Egypt. Though a powerful movement among the Copts, it was never a majority as Donatism was in Numidia and Mauretania.
113. *Apol. contra Arianos* 6.
114. For the suspicion that Athanasius suspected Antony of Meletian sympathies, see L. W. Barnard, 'Did Athanasius know Antony?', *AS* 24 (1993), pp. 139–49.
115. Pap. Lond. 1913–1922. See Bell, op. cit., pp. 43ff.
116. Pap. Lond. 1913 and 1914. See also T. D. Barnes, *Athanasius and Constantius* (Harvard University Press, 1993), pp. 22–3 and 32.
117. For a pro-Athanasian account, see Sozomen, *HE* ii.23 and 25.
118. Bell, op. cit., pp. 61–2 (Pap. Lond. 1914).
119. Pap. Lond, 1915, 1916 (exactions), 1920.
120. F. Ll. Griffith, 'Pachoras–Bahkharas–Faras in geography and history', *JEA* 11 (1925), pp. 259–68; *LAAA* 11 (1924); 13 (1926), pp. 7–37 and 46–93; continued in *LAAA* 14 (1927), pp. 57–116.
121. F. Ll. Griffith, 'Oxford excavations in Nubia', *LAAA* 15 (1928) at pp. 63 and 64.
122. Ibid., plate XXXII.
123. Ibid., p. 79.
124. J. W. Crowfoot, 'Five Greek inscriptions from Nubia', *JEA* 13 (1927), pp. 226–33. See also H. Junker, 'Die christliche Grabsteine Nubiens', *Zeitschrift für ägyptische Spraches* 60, p. 131.

125. F. Ll. Griffith, 'Christian documents from Nubia', *PBA* 14 (1928).
126. Griffith, op. cit., pp. 15–17 (of offprint).
127. Ibid., plate I and pp. 2–12 (of offprint).
128. Ibid., pp. 18–29 (of offprint).
129. For an example, see the photograph of the Metropolitan Museum of Art's excavations at Mentu-Hotep temple in 1921–22: *Archaeology* 1 (1948), p. 143.
130. H. Leclercq, 'Salone', *DACL* XV.1, 602–624, expecially 607, where Dyggve's work on two previously undiscovered churches, found in 1923, is recorded.
131. L. Bréhier, 'Les monuments chrétiens de Salonique', *RA* 5th ser. 9 (1919), pp. 1–36 (review of early Christian and Byzantine archaeology and art). Also, further work on Byzantine churches recorded in 'Chronique', *BCH*, (1929), p. 509, and H. Leclercq's long article 'Salonique', *DACL* XV.1, 629–713.
132. J. Zeiller, 'Sur la place du Palais de Dioclétien à Spalato dans l'histoire de l'art', *Byzantion* 7 (1931), pp. 565–9.
133. A. Orlandos, 'Une basilique paléochrétienne en Lochride', *Byzantion* 5 (1929–30), pp. 207–28.
134. Recorded in *Byzantion* 4 (1927–28), p. 513 ('Chronique').
135. Eusebius, *HE* iv.23.5, Bishop Pinytus was the recipient of a letter from Bishop Dionysius of Corinth urging 'care against heretical error'.
136. Recorded by Orlandos, *BCH* 52 (1928), p. 506 (Lesbos): (1929), p. 531 (Chios); and *Byzantion* 4 (1927–28), p. 515. For Lesbos , see also H. Grégoire, *Byzantion* 4 711–15.
137. G. A. Soteriou, recorded in 'Chronique des fouilles', *BCH* 51 (1927), p. 485: church at Nea Anchialos with 'dependent structures', and a baptismal font found 'vers le milieu du diamètre d'apside'. What appeared to be a Slav grave was found in the upper levels of the site.
138. G. A. Soteriou, 'Hai palaiokhristianikai basilikai tēs Hellados', *Archaiologikē Ephēmeris* (1929), pp. 161–256; reviewed by E. Weigand, *BZ* (1993), pp. 150–2. In general see R. Krautheimer, *Early Christian and Byzantine Architecture* (Harmondsworth, 1965), pp. 124ff, in particular his discussion of the church at Epidauros built *c.* 400.
139. Recorded in *BCH* 54 (1930), p. 501. See also *Byzantion* 5 (1929–30), p. 514 and Krautheimer, op. cit., p. 138.
140. K. Miateff, 'Les peintures décoratives de la nécropole de Serdica-Sofiae, *Byzantion* (1924), p. 511.
141. V. Formigé, 'Le Baptistère de Fréjus', *Bulletin de la Société des Antiquaires de France* (1925), pp. 143–6 and 263; P. Pfister, 'Il Battistero di Fréjus', *Rivista* 5 (1927–28), pp. 345–64.
142. Gregory, *De Gloria Martyrum* i.92; H. Leclercq, 'Narbonne', *DACL* XII.1, 851–852; R. Cognat and M. Bessner, *RA* (1928) II, p. 376, inscr. no. 85.
143. E. Junyent, 'I monumenti cristiani di Spagna studiati in questi ultimi anni', *Atti* III, pp. 255–85.
144. Ibid.
145. J. Sauer, 'Frühchristliche Funde in Deutschland aus den letzten 25 Jahren', *Atti* III, pp. 169–81.
146. Sauer, pp. 162–5; C. P. Thiede, *The Heritage of the First Christians*, Eng. trans. K. Hein (Oxford; Lion Book, 1992), pp. 60–2. For discoveries in the cathedral area of Mainz: Sauer, pp. 170–1.
147. Thiede, op. cit.
148. S. Loeschke, 'Frühchristliche Denkmäler aus Trier', *Rheinische Verein für Denkmalpflege und Heimatschutz* 29 (1936), pp. 91–145.
149. Ibid., pp. 104–8.
150. Ibid., pp. 99, plate 11.
151. Ibid., pp. 132, 141 and 144.
152. A. O. Curle, 'The recent discovery of silver at Traprain Law', *AJ* (1921), pp. 42–8; *The Treasure of Traprain* (Glasgow, 1923), p. 3. Also H. Leclercq, 'Orfévrerie', *DACL* XII.2, 2484–2495.
153. Curle, Traprain, plate XXXIV.
154. Curle, Traprain, pp. 86–9 and plate XXXIII; S. Reinach, 'Le Trésor d'argenterie de Traprain Law', *CRAI* (1921), pp. 409–29, at p. 423.
155. W. Ridgway, 'Niall of the Nine Hostages', *JRS* 14 (1924), pp. 123–36; other opinions are listed by Leclercq, 'Traprain Law', *DACL* XV.2, 2699–2700. Curle himself was clear about the Gallic origin of the booty. 'There is little room for doubt that the booty was obtained in Gaul': *Traprain*, p. 108. Reinach, art. cit., pp. 424–8, was inclined to agree: 'Primiacum, a church in Poitou' (Pictavensis) being one of the victims of the raid.
156. Ridgway, p. 143.
157. Curle, *Traprain*, plate XI, p. 26, and 'The identification of Ulysses', plate XII.

158. Curle, *Traprain*, pp. 14–19. Adam and Eve, and Peter and the Betrayal of Christ are also represented.
159. M. T. Tozzi, 'Il Tesoro di Projecta', *Rivista* 9 (1932), pp. 279–314; and see J. P. C. Kent and K. S. Painter, *Wealth of the Roman World* (British Museum, 1977), pp. 44–9.
160. See A. Ferrua, *Epigrammata Damasiana*, no. 51.
161. The best summaries of the discovery are those of C. Cecchelli, *Monumenti cristiano-eretici di Roma* (Rome: Palombi, 1944) with reproductions of Wilpert's paintings of the main scenes in the *hypogeum* and J. Carcopino, *De Pythagore aux Apôtres* (Paris: Flammarion, 1956), Part II. Also Wilpert's view in *Atti della Pontificia Accademia Romana di Archeologia*, Memorie 1.2.
162. Carcopino, op. cit., pp. 96–8, and plate IIIb and Tavola IIIa.
163. See Cecchelli, op. cit., p. 81 and Tavola IIIa: Carcopino, op. cit., pp. 110–12 and plate Va. Irenaeus records how in the Valentinian system of Gnosis, the serpent represents Nous, whence the human spirit and soul were derived, while his 'father' Ialdabaoth (the Demiurge) imparted knowledge (of evil!) to Adam (*Adv. Haer.* 1.30.5). The Naassenes attributed even greater power to the Serpent: see notes 172 and 173 below.
164. Cecchelli, plate facing p. 80; Carcopino, plate XIIIb.
165. Cecchelli, p. 46 and figs on pp. 51 and 52; Carcopino, Plate XIIIa.
166. Cecchelli, p. 73 and plate facing p. 100; Carcopino, pp. 190ff. and Plate XIVb.
167. Cecchelli, pp. 26ff. (Antichrist?); Carcopino, plate XIVa.
168. Cecchelli, plates facing pp. 8 and 16; Carcopino, plates XI and XII.
169. As suggested by Cecchelli, pp. 100–1.
170. Stevenson's suggestion: *Catacombs*, pp. 116–17.
171. The view of Carcopino, p. 220, particularly in view of the Ulysses sequence.
172. On the Ophite/Naassenes and their veneration of snakes see H. Lerclecq, 'Ophites', *DACL* XII.2, 2157–2160.
173. Hippolytus, *Refutatio* v.3.1 and 4.
174. The situation up to 1926 is described by A. von Gerkan in Hans Lietzmann, *Petrus und Paulus in Rom* (1927), pp. 248–301. For later work, see J. Carcopino, op. cit., Part III; J. Toynbee and J. Ward Perkins, *The Shrine of St Peter and the Vatican Excavations* (London: Longmans, 1956), pp. 167–82 and 187 n. 45 (Bibliography); also F. Fornari, *Atti* III, pp. 315–24 and E. Iosi, ibid., pp. 325–73.
175. 'Hic habitasse prius sanctos cognoscere debes. Nomina quisque Petri pariter Paulique requiris' ('Here you should know that the saints once dwelt, you are seeking the names of both Peter and Paul'): cited from Toynbee and Ward Perkins, p. 168; see also Ferrua, op. cit., p. 142.
176. Paribeni, *Notizie degli Scavi di Antichità* 17 (1920), pp. 143–55. For the inscriptions, J. B. Frey, 'Inscriptions inédites des catacombes juives de Rome', *Rivista* 5 (1928), pp. 279–305, and for a full report H. W. Beyer and H. Lietzmann, *Jüdischer Denkmäler: Die jüdische Katakombe der Villa Torlonia in Rom* (Berlin/Leipzig, 1930). Also for the dating of the paintings in this and other Jewish catacombs, see L. V. Rutgers, 'Überlegungen zu den jüdischen Katakomben Roms', *JAC* 33 (1990), pp. 140–57.
177. Rutgers, art. cit., p. 154.
178. E. Iosi, 'Descrizione del Cimitero di Pamfilo', *Rivista* 1 (1924), pp. 54–119: 2 (1925), pp. 51–211; illustrated in *Atti* III, p. 102.
179. Iosi, 'Le più notevole scoperte avennute in questi ultimi anni nelle catacombe Romane', *Atti* III, pp. 311–12; Cecchelli, op. cit., pp. 157ff. and drawing of inscription, p. 158.
180. Iosi, *Atti* III, p. 312
181. C. Respinghe, 'Relazione di lavori ed excavazioni nei cimeteri delle Salare', *Rivista* 1 (1924), pp. 9–14.
182. F. W. Kelsey, 'Fouilles américaines à Kom Ousin (Fayoum)', *CRAI* (1927), pp. 81–90. Karanis was suffering similarly.
183. H. Lietzmann, 'Die Landmauer von Konstantinopel', *ABAW* (1929) and *AA* (1929), p. 339. See also A. M. Schneider, 'The city walls of Istanbul', *Antiquity* 11 (1937), pp. 461–8.

FURTHER READING

Prosper Alfaric, *L'Evolution intellectuelle de Saint Augustin* (Paris, Nourry, 1918; 1 vol. only).

Prosper Alfaric, 'Un manuscript manichéen', *RHLR* n.s. 6 (1920), pp. 62–98.

Yvonne Allais, *Djemila* (Paris, 1938)

A. Ballu, 'Ruines de Djemila', *RAfr* 62 (1921), pp. 201–76.

H. I. Bell, *Jews and Christians in Egypt* (British Museum, 1924).

H. W. Beyer and H. Lietzmann, *Die jüdische Katakomben der Villa Torlonia in Rom* (Berlin/Leipzig, 1930).

J. H. Breasted, 'Peintures de l'époque romaine dans le désert de Syrie', *Syria* 2 (1922), pp. 177ff.

L. Bréhier, 'Les monuments chrétiens de Salonique', *RA* 5th ser. 9 (1919), pp. 1–36.

W. M. Calder, 'Philadelphia and Montanism', *BJRL* 7 (1923), pp. 309–55.

J. Carcopino, *Le Maroc antique* (Paris, 1943).

J. Carcopino, *De Pythagore aux Apôtres* (Paris: Flammarion, 1956).

C. Cecchelli, *Mounmenti cristiano-eretici di Roma* (Rome: Palombi, 1944).

C. Courtois, L. Leschi, C. Perrat and C. Saumagne, *Tablettes Albertini: Actes privées de l'époque vandale* (Algiers: Gouvernement-Général de l'Algérie, 1952)

J. W. Crowfoot, *Churches at Jerash: A Preliminary Report of the Joint Yale–British School Expedition to Jerash* (*BSAJ* Suppl. Paper 3: London, 1931)

A. O. Curle, *The Treasure of Traprain* (Glasgow, 1923).

N. Duval and P. A. Février, 'Procès-verbal de la déposition de reliques de la région de Telergma (VIIe siécle)', *MEFR* 68 (1969), pp. 257–320: final report on discovery made by J. Bosco and P. Alquier in 1924, and full bibliography of subsequent research.

E. Gibson, *The 'Christians for Christians' Inscriptions in Phrygia* (Missoula: The Scholars' Press, 1978).

F. Ll. Griffith, 'Oxford excavations in Naubia', *LAAA* 15 (1928).

F. Ll. Griffith, 'Christian documents from Nubia', *PBA* 14 (1928).

S. Gsell, ed. Claude Lepelley, *Etudes sur l'Afrique antique: Scripta Varia* (important article on Christianity in Oran publ. in 1928: Lille, 1981).

E. Iosi, 'Descrizione del Cimitero di Pamphilo', *Rivista* 1 (1924), pp. 54–119; 2 (1925), pp. 52–211.

R. Jacquard (ed.), *L'Institut Pontifical d'archéologie chrétienne (Journal de cinquante années)* (Rome, 1975).

H. Leclercq, 'Salone', *DACL* XV.1, 602–624 (mosaics illustrated).

H. Lietzmann, *Petrus und Paulus in Rom* (Berlin, 1927).

E. Mader, 'La Basilica Constantiniana di Mamre presso Hebron', *Rivista* 6 (1929), pp. 256–312.

S. Mitchell, *Anatolia*, II (OUP, 1993).

A. M. Ramsay (ed.), *Anatolian Studies Presented to Sir William Ramsay* (Manchester University Press 1923).

M. Rostovtzev, *The Art of Dura Europos* (OUP, 1938).

M. Simon, *La Civilisation antique et le Christianisme* (Paris: Arthaud, 1970) (Dura frescos).

F. Vaultrin, 'Basiliques chrétiens de Carthage', *RAfr* 72 (1932), pp. 182–318.

H. G. Evelyn White, 'The monasteries in Wadi Natrun', *Bulletin of the Metropolitan Museum of New York* (1920).

IO

Sunset over imperial archaeology, 1931–1940

The end-date, 1931, of Kendrick and Hawkes' *Archaeology of England and Wales 1914–1931* may have been fortuitous. The year 1931, however, marks the transition from the gradual rise of optimism of the first decade of the inter-war years, to its collapse under the succession of crises that led to the advent of Hitler, to Mussolini's attack on Abyssinia, and inexorably to the Second World War. Yet most people, as the writer experienced, learned to live with insecurity. The nine years from the onset of the European financial crisis in the summer of 1931 to the end of the 'phoney war' on 10 May 1940 were by no means barren of archaeological achievement. They saw Dölger's launch of the periodical *Antike und Christentum* of which five numbers had appeared by the time of his death in 1940. Two considerable conferences of Christian archaeology were held; the first in Ravenna in September 1932 (preferred to the original choice in 1900 of Carthage), and the second in October 1938 in Rome. In both, Pope Pius XI's keen interest in archaeology ensured that the Vatican would remain the predominant partner, a situation which the excavations beneath the Vatican 1940–49 and 1952 onwards would consolidate.

Though there were mutterings about the number of papers offered to the Fourth Congress of Christian Archaeology, scholarship was not yet overwhelmed by the avalanche of material that poured in after the Second World War. At Ravenna the main task had been to record what had been going on in the previous 25 years, a task which the organizers were able to keep within limits. There was also still plenty of scope for local archaeological societies, and in Britain, directors of excavations would often be amateurs working for these societies on sites they may have discovered themselves. Even major digs such as Mortimer Wheeler's excavation of the Maiden Castle defences and important late Romano-Celtic temple there (1934–36) were social as well as scientific events, enlivened by the women students, some soon to be members of a newly-established (in 1937) Institute of Archaeology at London University, who acted as trench supervisors, successors to the pioneers of pre-war days.[1]

Kendrick and Hawkes scarcely mention Christianity in their survey of British archaeology, and Roman Britain's contribution was to be significantly negative. Elsewhere, however, the established fields of research of North Africa, the catacombs, Egypt and Nubia, Palestine and Syria, Constantinople and to a lesser degree Asia Minor continued to provide ever new material. In Yugoslavia, Salona was on the way to being systematically cleared, as was Philippi in eastern Greece, and new areas of discovery were appearing on Cyprus, Malta and in Italy outside Rome. Ecclesiastical sites in central and western Europe were providing further evidence for the continuity of Christianity through late-Roman and barbarian into mediaeval times.

Even so, the archaeology of the early Church, except in North Africa, contributed only a fraction of the total archaeological research in the decade 1931–40. The *Revue Archéologique* did not record a single early-Christian excavation in 1932, and next year only Emery and Kirwan's work at Ballana was 'Christian', and that only because of loot found in the barbaric royal tomb! This was an understatement of the position, but an indication that even when prospects seemed set fair, resources, as Ramsay himself found, would not always be forthcoming for work on early-Christian sites.

We start with another of those lucky finds that have altered permanently our understanding of a dissenting movement on the margins of orthodox Christianity. The hoard of Coptic Manichaean documents from Medinet Madi in the Fayum, identified by Carl Schmidt in 1931, was a watershed in the study of that religion.[2] Schmidt's account given in the pages of the *Sitzungs-berichte* (Proceedings) of the Berlin Academy in January 1933 reads, as he himself says, like a tale from the *Arabian Nights*.[3] In 1930 Schmidt had obtained a grant from the Notgemeinschaft der deutschen Wissenschaft (Emergency Aid Fund of German Scholarship) to visit Palestine and Egypt. His main objective, however, was Egypt. A papyrologist of great experience, he knew what his contacts among the antique dealers of Cairo might have to offer. He also wanted to put every moment of his trip to good scholarly use and had brought with him the proofs of Karl Holl's new edition of Epiphanius' *Panarion* in preparation for its publication as three volumes of *Die griechischen christlichen Schriftsteller*. He had reached the long section – chapter 66 – on the

Manichees at the point where Epiphanius describes the heresiarch's *Principles* (*Kephalaia*).[4] On arrival at Cairo he put aside his work for a visit to a lifelong acquaintance in the antiquities trade. After the usual black coffee the dealer brought out two thick wads of papyrus and laid them on the counter. They looked hopeless. Then Schmidt looked more closely. Discoloured through damp though they were, the leaves still showed a remarkably clear handwriting. On the right-hand corner he saw the word *Kephalaia*. He knew that the 'Principles' were cast in the form of a question-and-answer session between Mani and his disciples. He looked further. He could make out the words 'And now the Illuminator (*Phōster*) said ...'.[5] It was unbelievable. Here was a text purporting to be the words of Mani himself, the first ever found in the West. Schmidt, himself, was in no position to buy it, and his report, sent at once to his colleagues in Berlin, was greeted with scepticism even by Harnack, now in the last year of his life, and by Lietzmann, Harnack's successor as Professor of Church History in the university. However, on his way back at Jerusalem, Schmidt heard that Chester Beatty had been shown a similar papyrus, had taken the plunge and bought it. It was a collection of Manichaean psalms. The location of the find was now becoming certain. It had been discovered by a peasant in the cellar of a house at Medinet Madi in the Fayum. This had been a small military settlement and someone, either soldier or civilian, had placed these texts in a box which in course of time had become waterlogged, preserving the contents but in a shocking condition.[6]

Armed with the knowledge of Chester Beatty's purchase Schmidt persuaded the Prussian Ministry of Cults to subsidize a further visit to Cairo. This time he made sure of his identification of the documents, paid for them out of his own money and returned with them to Berlin. Quickly, co-ordination was arranged with Chester Beatty, and in the next seven years Schmidt, with the younger papyrologists H. J. Polotsky and H. Ibscher, published much of their share of seven volumes of Manichaean letters, homilies, treatises, including a life of Mani, while C. R. C. Alberry published the psalms for Chester Beatty.[7] Rapidly though Ibscher and Polotsky worked, they had not finished when war broke out. It is thought that some of the documents, including letters and a life of Mani, may have perished as the result of the bombing of Berlin, or even been taken by Soviet occupation forces in 1945.

The results even of incomplete publication were remarkable.[8] The only surviving Manichaean texts had been, as we have seen (above, p. 158), those discovered at Turfan and Tun-Huang in the first decade of the century. They were regarded widely as being either 'late' (i.e. mediaeval) or peculiar to an eastern extension of Manichaeism, with little relation to the religion to which

St Augustine had adhered for ten or eleven of the most formative years of his life (373–384).[9] Now these critics were shown to be wrong. Mani was a missionary who had preached from India to the frontier of the Roman Empire. He had indeed intended his religion to be worldwide and to incorporate 'the wisdom' of other previous 'apostles' such as Paul, Buddha and Zoroaster into a single wisdom of which he was the inspired interpreter.[10] It was still not known, of course, that Mani's upbringing had been among a Christian baptist sect in marshland south of Basra but that successive conversions had brought him in 240 at the age of 24 to regard himself as the bearer of a gospel akin to an extreme form of Gnostic dualism, but still regarding itself as a revelation of Christ and within a Christian framework (see below, p. 362).[11]

The copy of the *Kephalaia* identified by Schmidt made Mani's ambitions clear. In reply to a question put by his disciples why they should regard his religion as superior to the messages preached by his predecessors, Mani replied 'He who has his church in the West (i.e. in the Roman empire), he and his church have not reached the East; the choice of him who has chosen his church in the East has not come to the West ... But my hope, mine will go towards the West, and she will go also towards the East; and they shall hear her voice in all languages, and proclaim her in all cities. My church is superior in this first point to previous churches.'[12] These were confined to particular countries, whereas Mani's was universal. His 'wisdom' was also superior. His disciples were given their master's answer to the meaning of the two trees, one producing good fruit (Light) and the other evil fruit (Darkness), and explanations of particular parts of the Manichee myth of creation.[13] The attraction of the message could be seen also in the psalms in which, sung probably to a mournful lilting tune, the convert would proclaim his desire to be 'cleansed from all matter (*hylē*) that surrounds me', and 'to be cleansed from my sins. Glory and victory to the Father, the God of Truth, and his beloved Son, and the Holy Spirit, the Paraclete, Victory and renown to the soul of Mary.'[14] With their monasteries, ascetic ideal, dualistic outlook, and devoted veneration of the Virgin the Egyptian Manichees would prove a formidable rival to the orthodoxy of Antony and Pachomius. Their Docetic Christology did not allow Athanasius to make any concessions to his Eusebian, anti-Nicene opponents. If he had, the religion of Mani might have swept through Egypt.

This was a great find, and in the 1930s Egypt producd two others almost as significant. In 1934 the British Museum, in the person of its Keeper of MSS, Dr H. Idris Bell, purchased a miscellaneous collection of papyri of unknown provenance from a Cairo dealer, among which was a portion of three leaves of a codex datable from its script to the middle of the second century (P. Egerton

2). It turned out to be fragments of an unknown gospel, not Gnostic, but containing accounts of incidents in Jesus' ministry similar to those recorded in the Synoptic Gospels.[15] Its tone is sober, concise and matter-of-fact, just as the Gospel narratives. There were, however, some apparent connections with John, as for instance, when Jesus addresses lawyers; after telling them to punish wrongdoers and not him, he says 'Think not that I am come to accuse you to my Father; there is one that accuseth you, even Moses, on whom you have set your hope'. This is an evident reminiscence of John 5:45. Another passage, a version of the tribute penny, seems to relate to Matthew 22:16 = Mark 12:14 and Luke 20:21, as does the cleansing of a leper (Mark 1:40–42). On the other hand, a miracle describing Jesus sprinkling seed on the water's edge of the Jordan and its immediate growth occurs nowhere in the Gospels. It's a bizarre story, but no more so than those of the blasted figtree or the coin in the fish's mouth.[16] Apart from *agrapha* it would seem that by AD 150 numerous accounts of Jesus' ministry were circulating, not least in Egypt, having the Fourth Gospel as their main inspiration.[17]

That this was already in use by *c.* 120 was demontrated the same year by Colin Roberts. Working on the Rylands collection of papyri at Manchester University, he spotted a fragment (P. Ryl. 457) containing parts of John 18:31–33 and 37–38. The script could hardly be later than AD 140, if not earlier, and written presumably in Egypt.[18] Allowing time for the Gospel to reach Egypt from Ephesus where it seems likely it was first published, and its circulation, the Gospel could hardly be a 'late' compilation as some critics of the time claimed. Egyptian Christians must have had a continuous Gospel tradition from the early second century onwards, forming a background to the early Gnostic commentaries, such as Basilides' 24 Books of *Exegetica c.* 130, the first known commentary on Christian scriptures (Eusebius, *HE* iv.7.7).[19]

South of the Egyptian frontier in *Nubia* the main discovery belonged to the period immediately before the coming of Christianity, but in its savage splendour showed something of the constant threat that overhung Christian Egypt in the fourth century. The mounds at Qustul and Ballana south of Abu Simbel were so large that they were thought to be natural. Walter Emery and his young assistant Lawrence (later Sir Lawrence) Kirwan supected otherwise. Their suspicions were justified.[20] Three years of work (1931–34) revealed something of the barbarous society and its rulers that prevailed in northern Nubia in the fourth and fifth centuries AD. The Blemmye (?) rulers were buried amidst barbaric magnificence reminiscent of the Royal Tombs of Ur. The king was laid, with his silver crown on his head, in a vaulted funerary chamber. An iron sword in a silver-coated scabbard lay at his side. His dog accompanied him.

His horse also died with him, richly decked out in silver headgear and bejewelled harness. There was loot from forays against Christian Egypt, and the dead
monarch had companions, shown by the skeletons of slaves, and those of four
youths strangled with ropes. That the early-Christian mission took root in
Nobatia during the fifth century is a matter for amazement.

Apart from these grisly finds there were Oxford University expeditions to
Firha and Sai island, 100 miles south of Wadi Halfa, and to Kawa. Not a great
deal resulted from the early-Christian point of view. Sai revealed the remains
of numerous churches as well as a Christian building that seemed to be a
former cathedral. There and at Firha a pattern of fortified settlements was
emerging that would be the feature of the last period of Christian Nubia. The
enemy would be desert tribesmen rather than Mameluke invaders from the
north.[21] By 1934, however, just enough material had been assembled from literary and archaeological sources for an historian to contemplate writing a
history of Nubia in the European Middle Ages.[22] The task was taken up by
Ugo Monneret de Villard. The Milanese scholar set about his work with a
will. Italy had hardly been involved in the exploration of Christian Nubia, and
Villard was able to bring an outsider's perpective to the study of the evidence.
Between 1929 and 1934 he made yearly journeys to areas covered by previous
expeditions, working methodically from north to south, until he had covered
the whole area between Aswan and Dongola. He was spurred on by a belief
that the Egyptian government intended to modify the flow of the Nile so that
the drop between the Second Cataract to the sea would amount to 122
metres. He foresaw massive disruption of the Nubian Christian sites along
the river's banks as a consequence. This was happily not realized until the
building of the High Dam in 1965. The result, however, of his almost demonic
energies was an enormous two-volume compendium of known sites from near
Aswan to Dongola, including plans of churches and photographs of ruins and
surviving frescos.[22] In 1938 he followed this by a connected history of Nubia
from the time of Gallus' intervention in its affairs on behalf of the emperor
Augustus in 27 BC until AD 1330, the date of the last then known archaeological record of Christianity, found at Edfu.[24] In 1957 he produced two further
volumes discussing the art and architecture of the Nubian churches.

It is not easy to overpraise this work or overestimate its importance. As de
Villard pointed out, work had been going on in Nubia for a long time but the
result was a mass of unrelated, miscellaneous information. Scholars had failed
to agree on a reasonable division of Nubian history into periods. Reisner had,
he alleged, included both X-Group (pre-Christian) and early-Christian graves
in a single 'Byzantine period' extending from AD 200 to 400. Somers Clarke's

plans were faulty and his lack of sense of history was demonstrated by suggesting that Moses was the subect of an important fresco instead of a Nubian eparch.[25] Some of this was fair, but when de Villard attempted to compile his own consecutive history he found that he too had to rely mainly on literary evidence supplemented by Griffith's invaluable (acknowledged by him) decipherment of Nubian documents. With all said and done, however, his studies provided the essential, comprehensive framework for the survey undertaken from 1960 onwards in preparation for the great international 'Save Nubia' excavations, before the High Dam obliterated all low-lying sites betwen Aswan and Wadi Halfa. His historical writing, too, guided research along the right paths in assessing and adding to the picture of the Nubian Monophysite kingdoms that never lost their links with Byzantine civilization during their thousand-year existence from 500 to 1500. De Villard wrote his masterpiece with the outlines only of the clear chronological framework needed for a comprehensive study of Nubia, such as William Adams was able to achieve in 1977 with the benefit of the results of the 'Save Nubia' campaign.[26]

In the other great archaeological province on the south side of the Mediterranean, *North Africa*, the problem was also one of interpreting a mass of evidence, too often collected from sites where study of stratigraphy and association of objects with levels was largely lacking. Archaeologists and their attendant architects were spoiled by inscriptions and fascinated, justifiably enough, by the splendid mosaics that were recovered year by year from Roman and Byzantine urban sites. Changes in technique associated with Mortimer Wheeler at Verulamium and Maiden Castle and followed by his successors, however, had not spread to North Africa in this last decade before the war, when archaeological work could be carried out in security throughout the whole area once dominated by Rome or Byzantium.

Enough material was being recovered throughout North Africa to justify annual conferences from 1935 to 1939, of the Fédération des Sociétés savantes de l'Afrique du Nord at Algiers at which the latest discoveries were reported. For the years 1933–36 inclusive, edited descriptions of excavations in Algeria alone take up nearly 500 pages. If full reports had been published volumes more than double the size would have been needed.[27] At the Fourth International Congress of Christian Archaeology at Rome in October 1938, Louis Leschi's[28] and Père P. G. Lapeyre's[29] almost telegraphic reports of work in North Africa in the previous decade took up 100 pages.

In addition, a new province for archaeological field-work and reconstructions had opened in Libya and Cyrenaica under the energetic authoritarian regime of Mussolini's Italy. Here the most notable contribution to early

Christian history was the discovery of very large Byzantine churches in Leptis Magna, Sabratha, and Apollonia in Cyrenaica.[30] These were further examples of the triumphalist building of Christian churches and monasteries as part of Justinian's *reconquista* of former imperial territories and his aim of making the Mediterranean an orthodox Christian lake.

The main activity was taking place in Algeria. By now the number of early churches found there could be described as *innombrables*, and every year – almost every month – added to their total. There were two main reasons for this explosion of activity. First, the *bourses de voyage* (travelling scholarships) instituted by the Government-General of Algeria in 1919 mainly for the bene-fit of scholars researching at the Ecole française de Rome became used, apart from continuous work at Tipasa,[31] increasingly by individuals interested in the early-Christian sites found by Gsell and others on the Algerian high plains. Secondly, the Museé Gustave Mercier at Constantine was now headed by an exceptionally gifted and far-sighted archaeologist, André Berthier. He was able to form a team consisting of himself, M. Maurice Martin, owner of a farm at M'Chira on the northern edge of the once thickly populated high plains of Numidia, and Fernand Logeart, the Administrator of the *commune mixte* of Ain M'lila. Together between 1934 and 1940 they surveyed and in many cases partly excavated sites containing traces of some 73 churches and chapels as well as hundreds of oil presses and granaries.[32] They built up an extraordinarily complete picture of rural life in central and southern Numidia during the fourth and later centuries, including the impact of the Donatist Church throughout the whole region.[33]

The most important discovery in this period was Pierre Cayrel's identifi-cation of the basilica of the Donatist martyr bishop Marculus at Ksar el Kelb (Vegesela) in 1933.[34] His work was followed by a second campaign by the future eminent patristic scholar Pierre Courcelle in 1935.[35] Marculus was the Donatist bishop who in 347 defied the emissaries of the emperor Constans (340–350) when the latter attempted to force the Donatists into unity with their Catholic opponents.[36] According to the writer of the *Passio Marculi*, Marculus and other Donatist bishops met the imperial commissioners Paul and Macarius at Vegesela in Numidia and protested vigorously against their activities. Marculus was arrested and conveyed round the Numidian country-side with the object of making him an example and exciting ridicule against him. When this had the opposite effect he was imprisoned and, allegedly on 29 November 347, murdered by being thrown over a cliff to his death.[37]

That his supporters believed the truth of this account was now shown by the excavation of a large church on the site of Vegesela. This proved to be an imposing *memoria* to Marculus, whose actual see remains unknown.[38] It was more than twenty years after the events that the church was built, a milestone in the names of Valentinian I and II and Gratian (i.e. post-367) being recovered from the foundations of the apse.[39] Contrasting with the fine construction of the outer walls the floor was beaten earth laid on a brick foundation, with no traces of mosaic. At first it seemed that Cayrel was working on just another large (26 m × 12 m) Numidian basilica which had at one time been burnt down, but gradually its special features came to light. First, in front of the apse a rectangular ditch had been dug with great care, which contained a skeleton of a man.[40] Two superbly cut stones lay at the entrance of the choir bearing the inscription 'Domus Dei' and 'Aula pacis'. 'Peace' was very much a Catholic term and used as early as 393 by Augustine as such.[41] The natural conclusion was that this church had belonged to the African Catholics. But not for long; on the keystone of the chancel arch were inscribed the words 'Deo laudes h[ic] omnes dicamus' (Here let us all say 'Praise to God'). As Cayrel pointed out, the accent was on the unanimity of the faithful and their collective enthusiasm in maintaining everlasting combat chanting the Donatist watchwords.[42] In addition, the decoration on the surviving pillars was purely geometric, the masons employing the same wood-carving technique as used on similar pillars found near Khenchela (Mascula) some ten miles away.[43] Also, remains of elaborate plasterwork decorations were recovered, possibly symbolizing the Eucharist. Then finally, the basilica was identified beyond doubt by an incription 'Memoria Domini Marchuli' accompanied by a Constantinian monogram.[44]

The site was obviously important enough to warrant a second season of work. This was richly repaid. Pierre Courcelle concentrated on the area of the choir and sacristies. The apse had been raised 1.46 m, unusually high above the level of the rest of the church. The reason was soon evident. It had been built over eight tombs placed in two ranges, but the upper range of four tombs was arranged so that these did not fall into those below. These may have been the tombs of Marculus' companions, the untimely deaths of two of whom were indicated perhaps by large nails found near the skull of two of the skeletons. While no coffins were found within the basilica many had been placed around the walls. A defiant inscription read '[D]e dono [Dei] inimicis / [conf]usionem /[fe]cit', i.e. the martyr by the grace or 'gift' of God heaped confusion on his enemies.[45]

These discoveries recorded the spirit of Donatist Numidia and reflected accurately the provocative language of the Donatist tract, the *Passio Marculi*. The same accuracy was also being demonstrated at that moment by the researches of Berthier and his colleagues. They had chosen a rectangular area 70 miles by 25 miles (110 km by 40 km) covering the Numidian high plains between the then railway linking Algiers and Tunis and the salt lakes north of the Aurès mountains. In the fourth century there had been a large rural population, remains of villages being found on the average of one every 2½ miles, and some of these were very extensive.[46] In every village investigated there were traces of churches or chapels, some such as Oued Rzel on the plain of Bou Lhilet containing as many as seven, and seldom fewer than two.[47] The churches were all built on the same basilican plan with a raised apse, in front of which was an altar enclosure which housed martyrs' relics deposited in various receptacles protected by a stone covering. Some had transepts. The cult of martyrs was universal, and in some instances the martyrs' relics had been dedicated and rededicated several times, marked by layers of hard white plaster covering the reliquary.[48] Names of those commemorated were often those of the confessors of Abitina who had defied the authorities and whom the Archdeacon Caecilian was alleged to have prevented from receiving food at their prison during the Great Persecution.[49] Others were natives with names such as Miggin, Baric, Dacunis or Badin, martyrs not recorded on any orthodox martyrology and who aroused the contempt of educated pagans.[50] To be buried within the church near to the tomb of a martyr was a point of honour.[51] Inscriptions carried recognizably Donatist formulae.[52] While the *memoria* or *mensa martyrum* (altar of the martyrs) had a dominant role in the religion of these villagers, their eucharistic liturgy was illustrated by an ornate plaster panel from a vast agglomeration at Bou Takrematem showing peacocks flanking a chalice below which were fish representing the food and drink of Paradise.[53] The remains of many glass eucharistic chalices were also found there. Petitionary prayers were addressed to the martyrs, as well as psalms of praise, sometimes with a defiant edge and forming part of the worship. Over all, the sculptures often found on the pilasters supporting an arch above the apse emphazied the exclusive nature of the church. One example portrayed the martyr's crown associated with Noah's Ark – the saved securely within, sinners, supporters of Caecilian and the Catholic *traditores* (betrayers of the Scriptures) left to their fate without (see photograph). The mason had also left a permanent record of his tools and trade in stone.[54] The churches themselves sometimes formed part of larger complexes of what appear to be agricultural buildings. A silo for grain storage was found in the sacristy of the church at Mechta Azrou, providing a clue, perhaps, why the Circumcellions were said to dwell round *cellae* (chapels) 'for the sake of food'.[55] At Kherbet Bahrarous, the writer found that the church he was excavating formed the east side of a large rectangular building set round a courtyard, whose small rooms had been used for storing grain or olives. Ten metres to the south was an oil press. Indeed Berthier's excavations consolidated what had already been generally recognized about the rural communities in central Numidia. There were no monumental public buildings such as existed in quite modest towns; the whole area was occupied by granaries, olive presses and chapels. Each family seems to have possessed its silo for storing grain, and an olive press alongside. The remains of 87 olive presses found by the writer at Kherbet Bahrarous may represent the holdings of 87 family groups.[56]

A final discovery concerned the Circumcellions. In a number of his anti-Donatist treatises and in particular his latest, addressed to Gaudentius, Donatist bishop of Timgad in 420, Augustine refers to Circumcellions committing suicide in order to earn the merit of martyrdom, by leaping to their deaths from cliff tops.[57] The central Algerian high plains do not consist simply of plateau and salt lake, but are broken up by some steep and rocky mountains, such as the Djebel Guerion which rises to a height of 1,729 m. Around the base of one of these outcrops, the Djebel Nif en Nisr, Fernand Logeart found no fewer than 34 loose rocks on which had been roughly inscribed a name, a date, and the letters *r* or *red.* (*reditum*). The most plausible suggestion remains that these stones marked the date when some Christian returned his soul to the Creator; and those Christians could hardly be other than Circumcellions.[58]

The picture of Donatist rural Numidia in the fourth century had by now been largely filled in by the combined work of Louis Leschi, Director of Antiquities,[59] André Berthier and his colleagues, and the young researchers of the Ecole française de Rome. Donatism could be seen as a mass movement expressing the religious ideas of the overwhelming majority of the Numidians.[60] Its repression by Augustine and the imperial authorities after the conference of Carthage in 411 was a disaster for these communities. It could not avoid resulting in the most serious long-term consequences for North African Christianity as a whole.

There were also important discoveries relating to both the pre-Christian background and the last phase of Christianity in Maghreb. In 1932 Jerome Carcopino published a series of early third-century inscriptions found by Jeanne Alquier near N'gaous (Nicivibus) in south-western Numidia. These were dedications to Saturn dated to the beginning of the third century. They showed how the old nocturnal Punic ceremony of Moloch (Mochomor) had persisted. The dedicants, a husband and wife, had made a vow, and on its favourable outcome had obeyed the god's command to sacrifice, conveyed to them by dreams.

The sacrifice demanded was a blood sacrifice; a lamb, however, being accepted in substitution for a human being. On the other hand, Saturn had become Romanized, represented as a severe-looking figure, bearded and dressed in a priestly robe, holding a sickle; below which a lamb, the victim stood.[61] One is left to ponder why this worship that held its worshippers in such awe should have given way relatively rapidly and completely at the end of the century to a biblical martyr-inspired Christianity. Had the god become too much identified with official worship? Had his powers seemed less than those of Christ? The questions can only be asked, not answered satisfactorily.

Carcopino also invited an answer to a problem relating to the end of Christianity in North Africa. He had already published the inscriptions from Volubilis in Morocco indicating the continuance of Christianity there combined with good Latinity as late as 655 (see above, p. 189). He came to the conclusion that the Baquates, who were the dominant tribe in the region, had gained independence from the empire as the result of a strategic withdrawal of the western Mauretanian *limes* by Diocletian, but had accepted Christianity.[62] Freed from the shackles of imperial rule, the Christian faith and Latin civilization had prospered, unaffected by changes and upheaval in other parts of North Africa.[63] Tangier and a considerable area round the city had been retained by the empire, and joined to Spain as to form part of the Gallic prefecture.[64] A seventh-century Christian inscription similar to those from Volubilis had been found as far east as Albulae (Ain Temounchet),[65] and hence the Baquates' kingdom must have formed a powerful Christian entity in north-west Africa in the sixth and seventh centuries.

Despite the conservatism of the continued use of the Constantinian monogram and the retention of the traditional formula on grave memorials of D.M.S. (*Dis Manibus sacrum*) retained from paganism, the idea of an isolated Christian kingdom continuing to use the Roman provincial dating, where time had stood still for three centuries, was hard to accept. Christian Courtois said as much in his study of Vandal Africa in the 1950s,[66] and the discovery of a dedication to Constans and Constantius west of Columnata on the Mauretanian *limes* calls Carcopino's entire thesis into question.[67]

Archaeological research between the wars, however, produced some other clues how the Christian civilization in North Africa might have declined in the seventh century to the point where extinction was likely.[68] In Tunisia, one of the sites that attracted attention was Thuburbo Maius (Pont du Fahs), southwest of Carthage. The amphitheatre and capitol were cleared and restored, and work moved to the forum. The archaeologists were surprised to find that in Byzantine times part of the space had been occupied by a number of small, well-built basins used for storing olive oil. Conveniently, 150 gold solidi associated with them ranged from Phocas (602–610) to Heraclius (608–641), indicating occupation through the first half of the seventh century and probable cessation after the great Arab raid and defeat of the patrician Gregorius in 647. But by this time the occupation was purely agricultural. The olive farmers were wealthy, but the town as such had ceased to exist.[69] This pattern seems to have been repeated elsewhere. Sbeitla and Thignica have both provided evidence for olive presses replacing public buildings late in the Byzantine period.

In Numidia the Byzantine reconquest seems to have had as little effect on the lives of the inhabitants as the Vandal occupation had before it. In the south-west the Papacy had established estates large enough to warrant the appointment of Columbus, bishop of Nicivibus (N'gaous), as its special agent, administering a *regio* with doubtless a staff of clerical bailiffs under his control.[70] There were few signs of urban revival. By the end of the sixth century one former town site covering an area of two kilometres by one (Bou Takrematem) had reverted completely to a rural status, broken pillars and marble that may once have faced its public buildings being incorporated into the ruins of churches and olive presses.[71] One change, however, in religious life had taken place. Relics housed beneath the altars in chapels would now include those of Byzantine saints, including the military martyrs such as Theodore, popular throughout the Byzantine world, as well as local martyrs.[72] The old and new had blended so as to form an Afro-Byzantine cult that few could have foreseen.

This, as we have said, should have been a source of strength to Christianity, and have formed a sure base for its successful resistance to Islam. That it failed to do so is probably connected with, first growing insecurity and, secondly, the decline in the use of the Latin language, the Church's language of mission in the West. The Byzantine reconquest had required a massive programme of fortress building to defend towns throughout North Africa. In Numidia many of the larger villages also acquired a fort. They were not there for prestige or decoration. Near the fort of Foum Seffane was a large mound, 28 m in diameter and 6 m high. With André Berthier the writer found late Roman red ware, fragments of amphorae and Christian lamps on the surface. A trench dug through the mound revealed the remains of nearly 100 skeletons, partially burnt, heaped unceremoniously without any effort at proper burial.[73] At Oued Rzel not far away, where seven chapels had been found, houses nearby had been burnt and the skeletons of their last occupants lay as they had fallen.[74] Despite the victories of the Byzantine generals the threat from the independent Aurès tribes and the Berber nomads moving in from the south-east was never far away. At the end of the seventh century the Berber queen, the Kahena, was recorded as being no less a destroyer of the olive-based wealth of rural Numidia than the Arab invaders.[75]

Growing insecurity was accompanied by declining acquaintance with Latin and visible fall in standards of living and building. The dedication of the Byzantine and African martyrs in the church at Telergma was conducted by five bishops with a parade of loyalty to the Byzantine rulers. Yet, as we have seen (above, p. 188) the 'Latin' text took nearly 40 years before it was fully deciphered and published. At Hippo Regius, where one would have expected Latinity to have survived in the tradition of Augustine, a funerary inscription in atrocious script, probably seventh century, would be deciphered by H. I. Marrou and found to include half-remembered quotes from Virgil's *Aeneid* (vii.44–45 and 53, and xi.68).[76] Christian buildings, whether represented by the church erected by the patrician Gregorius at Timgad in 645 or the 'late chapels' in parts of central Numidia, display a decline in size and standard of workmanhip. They were simply native huts (*gourbis*) with an apse and burials within their precincts. The latest secular buildings in the villages were also the poorest.[77] One fragment of information came from the eastern extremity of Latin North Africa. The Christian cemetery at En Gila in Tripolitania yielded graves dated by the Byzantine era to 950–1003.[78] They showed, what would be evident from letter of Pope Gregory VII, that isolated groups of 'Afri' survived several centuries after the Arab conquest, when the vast majority of North Africans opted for Islam as their religion and Arabic as their language. How and why, archaeology does not yet tell us.

By 1939 though much remained to be done, it could now be better understood why the religious history of North Africa was to differ radically from that, for instance, of Coptic Egypt and Nubia. Hostile nomads, coupled perhaps with memories of persecution by the Catholics in the form of papal landowners as well as imperial authorities, may have contributed to an abandonment of Christianity in the early eighth century as irreversible as the abandonment of Saturn-worship at the end of the third century.[79] Much, however, was outstanding when war and call to the colours disrupted further archaeological work in Numidia. Some work was carried out on a chapel at Oued Rzel in the winter of 1940–41, and a curious reliquary containing bird bones found.[80] This seems to have marked the last serious work in the central Algerian *bled* (countryside). The arrival of the Anglo-American armies in Morocco and Algeria in November 1942, coupled with fighting throughout much of Tunisia in the spring of 1943, prevented a revival. No sooner had the war ended than the long Algerian revolution began (8 May 1945). Unlike Asia

Minor and Nubia, there was no British interest in following up work in North Africa when conditions allowed. The work of the writer was not wholly forgotten, but as the North African population expanded and the demands of agriculture increased, the square stone from churches and other buildings half exposed in the 1930s became a prey to robbing. There would be some revival of activity in the 1950s; largely on urban sites, such as Hippo Regius, Theveste and Tiddis. However, in 1994 it looked as though after 160 years of archaeological endeavour the bulldozer had finally triumphed, leaving major questions concerning the transition of Mediterranean civilization from Christianity to Islam without an answer.

In the *Middle East*, until 1937, *Dura* remained the major centre of operations. No new Christian building was discovered, but in 1933 a small fragment of Tatian's *Diatessaron* (Harmony of the Four Gospels) was found. This seems to have been a Greek translation of the original Syriac,[81] but whether the Christians of Dura were also Encratites as Tatian had been and the *Diatessaron* their only Scripture remains unknown.

Not far from the house-church, along the same stretch of the south wall, the 1932–33 excavations revealed the remains of a Jewish synagogue, the later and more opulent of two successive religious buildings. Due to the steep slope of the embankment against the city wall, part of the synagogue had survived to a height of nearly 20 ft (6 m).[82] Like the Christian church, it had been at one time a private house, whose final reconstruction had taken place only in 245. The main room used for worship was also comparable in size (8 m × 13 m) to the Christian, and as in the church the walls were covered with brilliant paintings. These were dominated by scenes from the life of Moses, starting with a vivid representation of Pharaoh seated on his throne, with Moses' mother nearby in the act of placing her son in a basket on the banks of the Nile. Moses grown-up was painted twice the size of the Israelite soldiers in the act of leading them to liberty across the Red Sea. Future generations were to behold the Lawgiver and Servant of God.[83] Other paintings reminded worshippers of great moments in Israel's history: the recapture of the ark of the covenant from the Philistines, and the destruction of Dagon's temple, demonstrations of God's will as shown in the sacrifice of Isaac and the story of Job, and the hope proclaimed by Ezekiel for the restoration of the people in this world and the next.[84] Inscriptions in Pahlavi-Sassanian perhaps provide a clue where Jewish sympathies may have lain.[85] Hebrew and Aramaic were used on the foundation inscription. Certainly the community was not popular, for the eyes of some of the painted figures had been gouged out, in all probability by soldiers and townsfolk building the glacis.[86]

The successive seasons' excavations enabled the church and synagogue to be placed in their proper perspective in the religious life of the town. Dura's importance was now revealed as the headquarters of the *dux ripensis* (military commander of the river (Euphrates) frontier) and hence a prime objective of the Persian invaders in 256. Though a Roman *colonia*, the deities that commanded most respect were Oriental, such as Atargatis, Aphlad, the Palmyrene gods, or Zeus Theos, the Greek assimilation of the Syrian supreme god, who was guardian of the city.[87] Christianity was the most recent of three imported religions, the Jewish being the oldest, as the first synagogue can be dated probably to the first half of the second century. There was also a Mithraic chapel, built *c.* 168 and repaired twice, *c.* 210 and 240, whose walls, like those of the church and synagogue, were decorated with scenes relating to the cult.[88] It must have been curious to behold seated in the cult niche two bearded figures in Perso-Palmyrene dress holding a scroll. They were probably Zoroaster and Ostranes, Persians and hence representatives of the Persian enemy across the river.[89] At the time of the siege Christianity was the religion of a small minority of Greeks and Syrians with no foreseeable prospects of triumph.

Dura was guarding the main route to *Antioch*, the real obective of Sapor's campaign in 256. It was by any standards a city, covering an area larger than Rome within Aurelian's walls. It was also a Christian centre, the metropolitan see whose authority in the fourth century extended from the borders of Egypt to Anatolia. In the reign of Constantius II (337–361) it had been the scene of an important Council in 341 presided over by the emperor on the occasion of the consecration of a magnificent church, the church of the Golden Dome.[90] There were high hopes for spectacular early-Christian discoveries when in March 1932 excavations began under the direction of Richard Stillwell, organized jointly by Princeton University and the Louvre. Among the latter's representatives was Jean Lassus, a young but experienced archaeologist who had worked at Tipasa in 1929[91] as a student of the Ecole française de Rome, and would be one of the last representatives of French archaeology in Algeria.

From the point of view of early-Christian archaeology the successive seasons' work to 1938 did not live up to expectations. The octagonal church of the Golden Dome begun by Constantine in 327 and finished under Constantius II was not found. Work concentrated on establishing the street-plan of the city and its walls and excavating the theatre. At every turn, however, there was evidence for the opulence of the city, as portrayed by the emperor Julian,[92] Ammianus Marcellinus,[93] Libanius,[94] and John Chrysostom.[95] Magnificent mosaics were found, often salvaged from the attentions of farmers, as they lay close to the surface, unequalled even in Roman Africa. But of the 239 recovered,[96] dating mainly to the fourth and later centuries, designs based on pagan mythology predominated and there was nothing to show from them how Julian had found Antioch, if pleasure-loving, an almost wholly Christian city.

It was in the suburb of Kouassie that Lassus made the most valuable early-Christian discovery. He found two churches; the more important had been constructed in the form of an equal-armed cross 25 m long and 11 m wide, the arms concentrating on a central square area 16 m across. It had been a large and important building. An inscription provided its date of completion as March 387, the year of the great riot and subsequent public dread at its possible results for them and their city. But the purpose of this church would seem to be as a memorial chapel, perhaps in honour of Bishop Babylas, martyred in 250 during the Decian persecution, a reasonable supposition since the successive bishops of Antioch, Meletius (d. 381) and Flavian (d. 397), were among those who initiated the cult of martyrs in the East.[97]

Christian buildings were still awaiting discovery when excavations were suspended after the 1938 season. The reality of Christian Antioch's wealth, however, was shown by the treasures of Christian silver found in and around the neighbourhood of the city. One such was the Antioch chalice, a magnificent silver vessel decorated with figures of Christ and the apostles.[98] Another was the finding of two hoards of Communion silver from Hama, east of Antioch, and believed to have been the product of silversmiths in Antioch.[99] Archaeology was confirming visibly and brilliantly the view that the wealth of the see of Antioch may have been on a par with that of its rival, Alexandria.

In *Transjordan*, Jerash had demonstrated the thrust of Christianity during the fourth and fifth centuries, and of Justinian's aim at an exclusively Christian Holy Land conceived in its widest context.[100] The discovery and excavation of a small church at Ma'in in 1937 provided further evidence. This church contained a mosaic of the Madaba type representing 24 cities and churches throughout Palestine and Transjordan, including Gaza, Ascalon, Gadara and Amwas (Emmaus).[101] The excavator was Père Roland de Vaux on his first major assignment. He would soon be better known for his research on the Dead Sea Scrolls.

In *Palestine* the same story was being unfolded, that of Christianization from the time of Constantine which reached its climax under Justinian. The church of the Nativity at Bethlehem had been worked on by Vincent and Abel just before the war, with the help of the Palestine Exploration Fund.[102] The establishment of the British mandate enabled a full-scale excavation to take place in 1933–34 with E. T. Richmond as Field Director and William Harvey as architect. This resulted in a successful blend of British skill and technique with the experience of the scholars of the Ecole Biblique. The original Constantinian building was identified, as also additions, possibly dating from the time of the empress Eudocia's stay in Jerusalem (457–460). Before Justinian's extensive reconstruction there was evidence for a destructive fire; possibly a trace of the Jewish and Samaritan uprising in the early years of the sixth century.[103] As the Holy Sepulchre, it was a pilgrim centre.

The work had had to contend with the presence of their latter-day successors and road-building designed to assist them. There were also the Armenian and Franciscan convents covering part of the site, and Crusader-period renovations. Nonetheless the excavation provided another glimpse of the extent of Constantine's enthusiasm for the Holy Places and the scale of the architectural innovations that resulted from this.[104] The Bethlehem church had been in existence since the time when the Bordeaux Pilgrim visited Palestine in 333.[105] It was larger than that over the Holy Sepulchre – 46.4 m long as against just 38 m and 28.5 m wide. It was a great basilican building with five aisles and four doorways, preceded, as was the church over the Holy Sepulchre, by a wide courtyard in the midst of which was a fountain. As in the Constantinian churches in Jerusalem and Rome, however, the church itself was simply the approach to the principal object of worship, in this case the grotto where the birth of Jesus was believed to have taken place. This was covered by an octagonal structure, with a domed roof. In the middle was a dais pierced by an aperture through which pilgrims could view the grotto. As Crowfoot describes,[106] it would be easy to picture pilgrims thronging up the steps from the nave of the basilica to kneel on the octagonal stairway to peer into the grotto below. The Constantinian churches in Palestine were not only following a uniform plan of construction but by being pilgrim-oriented were opening to worshippers access to the divinity which in the recesses of a pagan temple would have been shrouded from their gaze.[107] Architectural and religious revolutions were going hand in hand.

Evidence for the steady advance of Christianity in Palestine during the fourth century was provided by the creation of monasteries, such as that excavated by Bellarmino Bagatti on Mount Nebo.[108] The process was not accepted easily by the indigenous Jewish population. In 351 there was a revolt against the Caesar, Gallus,[109] and rumblings of discontent throughout the fifth century. Excavations carried out by Jewish scholars, notably Avi Yonah and E.L. Sukenik at Beth Alpha,[110] Capernaum, Chorazim and elsewhere, indicated the resilience and loyalty of the Jewish people to their religion through the three centuries of Christian predominance in Palestine.[111] *Asia Minor* saw less activity in this decade. Calder led British expeditions 1932–34 in further exploration of Pisidia (1932) and in central and northern Phrygia using Afyon Karahissar as a base in 1933–34. Not many new Christian texts were found, but at Akmonia a chance discovery of a bilingual (?) Greek–Hebrew inscription demonstrated that there as well as in Ephesus there had been a Hebrew-speaking Jewish community, reflecting the varied character as well as the strength and tenacity of Phrygian Judaism in the first two centuries AD.[112] It was a pity that at this point a site was not selected in Phrygia for long-term excavation. Surface inscriptions were dwindling, and the need was to build up associations of what had been found with the lives of the inhabitants of sites. With the keen and energetic young archaeologist C. E. Stevens of Magdalen College, Oxford, and the Classical scholar W. K. C. Guthrie (later Master of Downing College, Cambridge), Calder had the chance of training the next generation of field archaeologists to work in the hinterland of Asia Minor. As it was, he saw other priorities. His main effort and that of his colleagues lay with the publication of four successive volumes of the *Mounmenta Asiae Minoris Antiqua* (1933–39) with the co-operation of the American Society for Archaeological Research in Asia Minor, and Manchester University. These volumes consolidated work he had done in Phrygia from Eski Sheher in the north to Apamea (Dinar) in the south. Sir William Ramsay, now 80, lived to see the fruits of his genius securely on record before he died in March 1939.

The mantle for work in the field fell on the French scholar Louis Robert. Already in the early 1930s Robert was achieving a dominating role in Greek epigraphic studies. In 1938 M. N. Tod praised his mastery of Greek and Jewish epigraphy as well as his ability as an editor. But Robert was a loner and no easy colleague. In 1935 he was accused by A. Laumonier in an article in the *Bulletin de Correspondence Hellenique* of 'exercising tyrannical control' over inscriptions discovered in Caria, and of his *ton aussi désobligeant* towards his colleagues.[113] Years later the writer found that the inscription he had come upon in the museum at Afyon detailing a lawsuit between two villages in 237 regarding their respective duties relating to the *angareia* (in this case, the upkeep of roads and furnishing of beasts for transport along them) gave Robert no pleasure.[114] Nonetheless his publication in 1939 of *Etudes anatoliennes* was in its way a masterpiece. Robert, however, at this time concentrated purely on recording and discussing inscriptions of the Attalid and Greco-Roman periods. No Christian and only three Jewish inscriptions were included. One however, from Tralles, recorded that a close relative of a proconsul from one of the foremost families of the province of Asia was a

'God-fearer'.[115] The great days of Ramsay and Calder for Christian archaeology in Asia Minor had gone and were not destined to return.

In contrast to relative quiescence in Asia Minor, *Constantinople* (Istanbul) had now become a magnet for archaeologists and art historians. The government of Kemal Atatürk, though Islamic in background, was secular in practice. The great fire of 1912 had destroyed that part of Istanbul lying south-east of the mosque of Sultan Ahmed. The area thus cleared had become identified through literary sources with the probable site of the Great Palace of the Byzantine emperors.[116] The authorities had little objection to this hypothesis being tested. In 1932 the concession was granted to the British who had been working on the hippodrome, not far away. After some delay a team led by Professor J. H. Baxter of St Andrews University, and including Gunter Martiny from Berlin and two young British scholars, B. K. Stevenson and Gerard Brett, started work in 1935 and continued through four seasons to the summer of 1938.

The excavation was hugely successful.[117] Baxter uncovered a large open rectangular courtyard surrounded by a roofed colonnade, around which the main apartments of the palace had been built. These had included the church of the Theotokos, and the 'golden banqueting and audience hall' (*Chryso-triklinios*). There were also private suites belonging to the emperor which overlooked the sea of Marmara to the south, and those belonging to the empress on the south side of the colonnade. Modern buildings prevented further exploration. In their four years of work the team identified the site of the great palace securely, and in contrast to the excavation of many other early-Christian sites, recorded stratigraphy strictly. The result was that through the observation of sealed layers, Byzantine pottery, particularly of the ninth and later centuries, could be placed within a fairly tight chronology and the principal discovery dated.[118]

This was the great mosaic that had covered the whole area enclosed by the colonnade. Within a border ornamented with a continuous twisted ribbon design the central panel displayed a succession of scenes relating to various aspects of daily life and mythology. There were four hunting scenes, one depicting huntsmen on foot attacking a tiger, another using greyhounds; there were combats between animals, a snake struggling after being borne aloft in the mouth of an eagle, but there were also pastoral scenes, such as children driving geese or a woman with a jug on her shoulder, and scenes taken from pagan mythology such as Pan carrying the infant Bacchus on his shoulder.[119] There was no Christian symbolism, remarkable, as the mosaic could be dated securely to *c*. 410 (the reign of Theodosius II) and was repaired under Justinian *c*. 550.[120]

The whole composition shows how uneven was the impact of Christianity on taste even in the imperial court at the beginning of the fifth century. The mosaic itself would appear to be still in the tradition of the artistry of the mosaic of the Villa Armerina, the Sicilian residence of the emperor Maximian (286–305). Attempts to find parallels with the Tabarka or Zliten villa mosaics are not entirely convincing;[121] the figures at Tabarka are already more stylized than those in the Great Palace, and the gory amphitheatre scene on the mosaic at Zliten is at least a century and a half too early. The mosaic would seem to represent a last splendid representation of naturalistic Classical art, before it was superseded by the hieratic conventions of Byzantium.

Not far away work was beginning that in the course of time would throw light on the religion of the era of Justinian and his ninth-century successors. Since the fall of Constantinople, Sancta Sophia had been converted into a mosque and as such had been a standing provocation to Christians, especially the Orthodox. In 1934 Kemal issued a decree 'desacralizing' the building so that it could become a Byzantine museum of art bereft of sacred association for either religion. The chance was now taken to examine the Byzantine mosaics that had been hidden under plaster inscribed with Koranic texts. Already work had been undertaken in the forecourt of the building by the German Archaeological School at Istanbul that had succeeded in identifying remains of the second of the three great churches dedicated to the Holy Wisdom. This had been built *c.* 415 but destroyed by fire during the Nika riots of 532, when it was itself replaced by the existing Sancta Sophia.

Work on the mosaics, however, was entrusted to an experienced medieval archaeologist trusted by Kemal, Thomas Whittemore, then an independent American scholar but soon to become founder and first Director of the Byzantine Institute. He was to spend eighteen years at work on Sancta Sophia and when he died in 1950 this was still unfinished.[122] Preliminary surveys were followed by successive seasons' work from 1934 to 1939.[123] During this time Whittemore uncovered mosaics extending over 800 years, from the sixth to the fourteenth century. In the first phase of work, the mosaics above the narthex and southern vestibule had been restored to their former glory and copied and three main periods of work were identified. These were the original Justinianic (532–537); the mosaic in the central lunette in the narthex which could be dated in all probability to the reign of Leo VI (886–912); and in the southern vestibule the heroic period of Byzantine history, the reign of John Tzimisces (969–976). To this last period belongs the representation of Constantine and Justinian standing either side of a seated Virgin and Child against a golden background and presenting gifts in the form of the city of

Constantinople and Sancta Sophia respectively. These gifts expressed the devotion of the emperors to the Virgin as protector of the city, at a moment of triumph in the long history of Byzantium. Whittemore was also invited to restore other churches in the city, and after the outbreak of war, in which Turkey maintained its neutrality, was given special facilities to move between that country and the United States. Thanks largely to him, Constantinople (Istanbul) would continue to be a major centre of Christian archaeological achievement and research in which European countries and the United States co-operated.

Greece and the Balkans also witnessed a spate of activity during the 1930s, though the emphasis here was on national effort. At Philippi, however, the French continued their long-term commitment to the site until 1937. Once again excavations showed how Christianity gradually came to dominate a Greco-Roman city. One of the most interesting examples of the start of this process in the latter part of the third century (there was no material evidence for the Pauline community or its immediate continuation) was an inscription dating to 261–262 set up by Aurelius Capito to his wife Baebia Paula and son Elpidius, who describes himself as *presbyteros neos tēs katholikēs ekklēsias* (new (or junior) presbyter of the universal Church).[125] The term is not unique for the period, as it was used by the confessor Pionius in 250 in reply to a question by the proconsul of Asia, 'What is the cult or sect to which you belong?',[126] but one would like to know who were the opponents at this time, just after the restoration of Christian places of worship by Gallienus in 260. It is interesting too, that Aurelius Capito and his wife Baebia Paula appear to have been upper-class citizens, descendants of Roman veterans, who were the citizen class of the Roman *colonia*, but they give their son the Greek Christian name of Elpidius.

The Capitos' example was gradually followed. Temples, public buildings fell into disrepair and their stone was seized upon by the builders of a great Christian complex that rose above the north end of the forum. The church had a baptistery and an atrium that was approached by a monumental stairway leading up from the forum, a demonstration to the inhabitants of the triumph of the new religion.[127] Though this church and the large Byzantine churches that came to dominate the site in the sixth century relied heavily on re-used material from Classical-period buildings,[128] many of the latter remained. Philippi's Turkish name, Derekler or 'Pillars', indicated their survival. As at Ephesus, Philippi retained much of its Classical heritage long after Christianity had come to prevail.

Westwards along the Via Egnatia was Thessalonica (Salonica). Apparent hesitation by the Christians to turn major pagan buildings originating with the Tetrarchy (293–311) into churches was shown by Dyggye's excavation around the rotunda of St George. This had evidently been prepared by Galerius as a family mausoleum, and he had intended apparently to retire, as Diocletian had, to a palatial residence where he could contemplate the arch of triumph set up in 298 after his victory over the Persians. The onset of his fatal illness in the spring of 311 thwarted this plan. Licinius' hostility to his family prevented the rotunda being used as intended, but evidently it was not until early in the fifth century that it was transformed by the Christians into the church of St George.[129]

In the remainder of Greece more and more early-Christian sites character-ized by large basilica-type churches were being discovered and excavated by Soteriou and Orlandos in widely separated areas.[130] The most important site continued to be Nea Anchialos (Thebes) in Thessaly. Four large basilicas and what appears to have been a complete early-Christian settlement associated with them were found, occupied from the late fourth to seventh century. These churches were awe-inspiring buildings, paved with marble or mosaic with finely worked capitals on their columns, served by clergy clad in gor-geous vestments representing in their deportment and daily liturgy a reflection of the heavenly harmonies.[131] In the largest (Basilica D) there was a square raised platform (*bema*) in front of the apse which contained a decorated covering or *ciborium* protecting an altar. To the right were the seats for the presbyters arranged in a semicircle approached by a short flight of steps. Behind this *synthronos* the bishop's ceremonial chair was placed at the centre of the apse, also raised and approached by steps.[132] The liturgy in which the bishop took the principal part had become more elaborate in the fifth century. The new arrangement that emphasized the role of the bishop and presbyters, while still retaining the basilican plan of the church, corresponded to their ever more-exalted claims. That this was not peculiar to Nea Anchialos is evi-dent from similar plans of churches excavated at this time at Nicopolis (Preveza) on the Adriatic coast.[133] At the Fourth Congress of Christian Archaeology at Rome in October 1938 Soteriou presented his hearers with an impressive list of churches which he and his colleague had discovered in the previous decade. These included Sykion (Sicyon), Spetsai, Lokris, Delos (where a church had been built amid the ruins of an abandoned Greco-Roman house), Chios, Lesbos (three churches), Samos (three churches) and Cos.[134] When one adds the church at Ayios Philon in Cyprus, excavated by Miss Du Plat Taylor,[135] the Classical monuments such as the Parthenon which were converted into churches and the wealthy Christian cemetery outside Corinth excavated by the American School at Athens (where a burial plot cost $1\frac{1}{2}$ gold solidi[136]), one gets the impression of a strong, wealthy church in mainland Greece and the Greek islands from the end of the fourth century until after the death of Justinian. Some of these churches were majestic buildings; that at Nicopolis with its *synthronos* being over 60 m long and its five aisles paved with mosaic.[137] Justinian's reign marked the climax of prosperity. Decline set in thereafter. Few of these great Christian buildings, Soteriou indicated, were destined to remain intact and in use. Most had been destroyed, generally by fire.[138] In the Balkans and Greece the flourishing Christian civilization of the early Byzantine period had been almost completely wiped out by the Slav invaders by the first decades of the seventh century.

In the *West and in Italy outside Rome* discoveries continued to confirm the impression of Christianity victorious, at least in the towns by the end of the fourth century. As in the previous decade the results were produced by a mixture of luck and planned excavations. Luck played its part in the initial find of the complex of basilicas and baptisteries below the cathedral of St Pierre at Geneva. The need for improving heating installations led to the discovery of early-Christian structures beneath an aisle of the cathedral. The earliest of these proved to date from the latter part of the fourth century and indicated the existence of far more extensive remains[139] In Ostia, also, road repairs uncovered sarcophagi and the site of a Christian cemetery, strengthening the claim of a curious building to be either Christian baths or a baptistery with an associated suite of rooms of uncertain purpose.[140]

Following on work in the previous decade, cathedrals and abbeys of Italy and western Germany provided further evidence for the continuity of Christianity from late-Roman into the mediaeval period. At Milan there were large scale excavations round the church of San Lorenzo.[141] This showed that the existing church with its four towers had followed the exact plan of earlier buildings originating in the first half of the fourth century but could also have been connected with Milan as the seat of imperial government in the West under Constantius II from 353 onwards. At Cimitile, outside the walls of Nola in south Italy, Professor Chierici's excavations from 1933 to 1936 disentangled some of the problems relating to the tomb of St Felix (martyred in the Decian persecution in 250), the chapel of the martyrs, and Paulinus of Nola's commemorative basilica in honour of St Felix.[142] It would seem that the earliest structure on the site had been the chapel of the martyrs, built at the end of third century or, at the latest, early fourth century. Meantime St Felix's tomb itself had been protected by a simple wooden structure. In the fourth century,

a three-naved basilica had been built on the site followed, after 394, by Paulinus' elaborate building in honour of the saint whom he and his wife Therasia
revered. The excavations confirmed the long account which Paulinus wrote
about his building plans to his friend Sulpicius Severus *c.* 403. His was in fact
the fourth period of additions to an already substantial building.[143]

One other piece of research in this period deserves mention. In *Trier*,
Siegfried Loeschke had discovered a very extensive pagan cult-centre in the
Altbachtal outside the city. During the 1920s he had located over 70 Romano-
Celtic temples, a Mithraeum and a theatre in a vast area three times the size
of the sacred enclosure of Delphi. The temples, however, had been systematically destroyed, and Loeschke believed that Bishop Maximin, the powerful
leader of the Christians in Trier *c.* 330–340, had been responsible. Later
research has shown, however, that while there was a period of destruction
c. 337–340, which included the Mithraeum, some of the temples were repaired
and restored to use. Final destruction did not take place until the reign of
Valentinian I–Valens–Gratian (367–383) and a church was erected on the site
of one of the temples.[144] That this period confirmed a significant advance of
Christianity among the upper classes in Trier was evident from coins found
associated with nineteen Christian sarcophagi Loeschke opened dating
360–380.[145]

Rome. In the 1930s most roads still led archaeologically to Rome. Rome had
been chosen to be the meeting-place (venue!) of the Fourth International
Congress of Archaeology to open on 9 October 1938. A momentary panic
caused by the Munich crisis was overcome, and the Congress opened only a
week late, on 16 October, with 300 members from 23 countries. Pope Pius XI
was patron, Mgr Kirsch president, and a galaxy of high Vatican officials,
including Cardinal Pacelli (later Pope Pius XII), were among the members of
the honorary committee. The sessions took place in the Lateran palace, where
excavations had established that the Constantinian basilica overlay earlier
buildings. These were perhaps part of the barracks of the corps of cavalry
guards established by Septimius Severus but disbanded by Constantine after
they had sided with his defeated rival Maxentius in 312.[146]

In the previous decade much had been happening to necessitate a congress
largely devoted to bringing some system into the ever-increasing volume of
varied information. The same situation that Monneret de Villard had decried
regarding Nubia had been arising elsewhere, and not least in Rome. Work was
going on without a break but an overview, setting out the historical development of the catacombs, was urgently needed. Ernesto Iosi's excavation of the
catacomb at Viale Regina Margherita (on the right-hand side of the Via

Tiburtina) between 1932 and 1935 had added important new evidence for the progress of Christianity in Rome from the mid-third century. In 1932 he found the earliest dated burial yet discovered in the catacombs. It was that of Calpurnia Dionysia whose short life lasted from 13 May 263 to 13 August 266.[147] She had died of some unnamed malady in the heat of a Roman summer. Another inscription written in Greek recorded a burial in 270.[148] Altogether Iosi published 192 inscriptions from the catacomb, a large proportion being those of children. A second major excavation, that in the catacomb of Praetextatus, however, showed up some of the problems that had resulted from over-rapid and one-sided explorations.

The excavation had begun as a rescue dig, part of the surface above the catacomb having collapsed. The new harvest of inscriptions, dating from 273 to 475, included those of many clergy, *fossores* (diggers), members of the Roman aristocracy, and a freedman Quintus Lactearius who described himself as 'qui fuit de domium (*sic*) Laterani' (i.e. connected with the family after whom the Lateran palace was originally named).[149] But among the fragments of sarcophagus discovered were some which were clearly pagan. Examples such as a representation of the Argonauts on a second-century sarcophagus were already on display in the museum of Praetextatus.[150] An explanation for the intermingling of pagan and Christian memorials was overdue and was now attempted.

Paul Styger was a Swiss scholar who had been engaged in catacomb archaeology since 1915. Then he had worked on the cult-centre of Peter and Paul on the Appian Way. His work on *The Roman Catacombs*[151] concentrated on the *capella Graeca* in the Priscilla catacomb, and the catacombs of San Callisto and of Domitilla, as well as the new discoveries from Praetextatus. It was an immensely painstaking study, as though Styger had taken a tape-measure to each gallery, but his main results so far as dating was concerned were convincing. The catacombs were most used, he claimed, in the fourth century, after the Peace of the Church.[152] Some of the earliest Christian burials, for instance, in the Domitilla catacomb could date from the mid-second century,[153] but they were not necessarily the oldest burials on the plot. There and in the Praetextatus catacomb digging had gone on ever deeper as new galleries were required, followed by infilling. Fragments of sarcophagi from original pagan burials were used in this process and hence contaminated much later (and deeper) levels, some as late as fifth century. Hence earlier investigators had been deceived into believing that fragments, for instance, of sarcophagi belonging to the Acilii family found in galleries must be Christian. This was not so. There were no Christian catacombs of Apostolic or even sub-Apostolic date.[154]

Styger went further. He had little time for what he considered Wilpert's fanciful reconstructions of frescos and carved figures on sarcophagi.[155] Thus, the broken lid of a child's sarcophagus on which could be seen a Siren holding a scroll was not a symbol of heresy which the child represented by Ulysses was rejecting, but the mythological scene on a pagan burial.[156] Similarly he dismissed Wilpert's theory that the large open space within the *capella Graeca* had been designed to hold eucharistic and baptismal services as early as 150. The *capella* could hold ten people at most. Was it really where presbyters gathered to hold private services? There was no altar, only the remains of a child's grave, hardly a substitute.[157] Sometimes, however, he went too far and even was simply wrong.[158] He believed perversely that spelling ΙΧΤΘΥC instead of ΙΧΘΥC rendered an inscription non-Christian.[159] He wrote before the Dura frescos had been published, and these showed beyond doubt the symbolic character of paintings selected from Scripture and designed to represent the liberation of the soul and its progress towards the *refrigerium* of Paradise. This, as the early third-century *Passio Perpetuae* shows, was regarded as a place of happiness and relaxation. 'Go and play' were the imagined words of the Lord as the martyrs encountered him after their sacrifice.[160] The catacomb paintings were more than just literal representations of selected biblical scenes.[161]

Styger, however, had accomplished much. He had set out new guidelines for dating the different periods of catacomb construction less beholden to typology than usual at that time. He had swept away some of the mythology that surrounded the interpretation of the paintings – funeral meals rather than Masses for the dead were represented – and he had shown how the catacombs had developed from being the burial-plots belonging to individual families to the elaborate and organized galleries owned by the Church in the late third and fourth centuries. This could be demonstrated in numerous ways. The choice, he pointed out, of biblical scenes accompanying this change progressed from seven Old Testament scenes and six New Testament scenes before 312 to more than 60 in the rest of the fourth century.[162]

In face of these criticisms of method and result, clarity and systematization were a necessity for the Congress. It was, however, a pity that the choice of themes fell so completely to historians of architecture rather than to those concerned with the mission and expansion of the Church and the relations between orthodoxy and dissent which new discoveries had been illustrating. Instead, the Congress was asked to consider 'the true origins of the Christian basilica', its relation to the life and culture of the Christian community, and the development of the domed church from the end of the fifth century. How far was this a product of imperial Byzantine inspiration, and why did it spread to north Italy?[163] To these major themes were added, however, valuable accounts of regional excavations in the previous decade. Unfortunately, because of the war these latter were not published until 1948.

The general view of the origins of the basilica was expressed by Louis Leschi on the basis of a vast number of North African churches. 'It seems difficult to deny that the Christian buildings, are not, in their general construction, inspired by models provided by civil buildings spread throughout the empire. This was true particularly in that the basilican plan was favoured by Constantine's architects in Palestine.'[164] There were examples, also, such as at Madaura for civil basilicas being transformed into churches. The first dated Christian basilica was built at Castellum Tingitanum (Orléansville) in 324 and henceforth this pattern was followed in North Africa.[165] The churches in Europe, Syria and Palestine were of the same design with varieties of flanking chambers either side of the apse, some in-built but in other cases forming an external feature. The function of these chambers was debated. Were they 'mere store-rooms, like modern diaconica' as Crowfoot suggested,[166] or did they have a more pronounced liturgical role? The chamber on the left side would be the *prothesis* where the gifts needed in the celebration of the Eucharist would be kept, while the *diaconicon* on the opposite side of the apse would be used largely as a store for articles to be distributed for charitable purposes. It would also serve as the deacon's office where records of such disbursements were kept.

The cupola-roofed church, Samuel Guyer insisted, was, on the other hand, a Christian innovation.[167] No pagan builder used a cupola to roof a colonnaded structure divided into several naves. Instead he connected the cupola with the rise of cruciform and trifoliate churches related to martyrs' and saints' shrines. The earliest cruciform churches were built in Cappadocia, and this province could claim probably the earliest octagon church, that at Nazianzus, *c.* 370.[168] The most spectacular development of the cupola, however, was to be seen, of course, in the great Justinianic churches in Constantinople of Sergius and Bacchus and Sancta Sophia itself. It was the hall-mark of imperial Byzantine church architecture.

Guyer, like other members of the congress, was strong on description but less so on analysis. It was only after the war that André Grabar and John Ward Perkins between them provided some answers to the problem. Ward Perkins concentrated on the actual origins of the basilica. The term had royal connections extending back to its Hellenistic origins. It had always been a hall-shaped building used for official purposes.[169] At Trier, Constantine's basilica was a long aisle-less apsed hall. This form came naturally to the emperor's mind when he was planning his great Christian memorial monuments starting with St Peter's in Rome *c.* 322. These memorials, whether in Rome or in Jerusalem, all showed the same features, namely an approach through a broad ceremonial atrium, a basilican colonnaded hall leading to a small octagonal structure sheltering either a tomb or, as in the church of the Nativity, a 'cave'. The basilican form, or as the Pilgrim of Bordeaux called it, 'royal', soon became standard, particularly in the West.[170]

Ward Perkins realized the problem of the transition from the house-church normal before 312 to the basilica thereafter. He believed that the Lateran basilica was probably built on a basilican plan in time for Pope Miltiades to hold a council in October 313 and might provide the key. Whatever the final results of the excavations there, however, there could be also an explanation more firmly connected with the development of the Church's organization and liturgy. The second half of the third century had seen changes to both. It may have been coincidence but the basilican form of church with its apse, side chapels and sanctuary in front of the apse corresponded exactly to the requirements of a more clergy-dominated Church, and the celebration of the Eucharist in an area exclusively reserved to the clergy in the fourth century. Previously, as Tertullian (*c.* 200) said, the Church was 'an association or society (*corpus*) with a common religious feeling, unity of discipline and a common bond of hope', meeting 'to read the books' of God.[171] While the congregation was led by presbyters and the Eucharist celebrated, anyone could be called upon to prophesy at a service which was concluded with a meal (*agapē*). In such circumstances a house-church with a table or raised platform for the gifts of the people, such as at Dura, and an adjacent baptistery would serve the needs of the community.

From the time of Cyprian (248–258) a radical change took place. The position of the clergy was enhanced, that of the laity diminished. The raised semi-circular apse approached by steps would now accommodate the presiding presbyter (or bishop). The eucharistic liturgy was performed with the assistance of deacons within the sanctuary. This was closed off from the body of the church (*quadratum populi*) which was the domain of the laity, sometimes men and women separated by a broad central nave.[172] As Grabar pointed out, the relics of the martyrs were placed beneath the altar (cf. Rev 6:9), and this also fitted into the design of the basilican church.

The cupola or central dome that became familiar in the East also seems to have developed from two separate origins. It would be, first, a form of roof adapted for a small cruciform building, such as a baptistery or a *martyrium*,[173] but it would also have a doctrinal significance. It might represent an attempt to express the doctrines set out in the Nicene and Constantinopolitan creeds in terms of architecture. The dome was the dome of Heaven from which Christ in glory looked down on his people. Below him on the pillars supporting the central dome would be archangels and angels followed by apostles, evangelists, martyrs and, finally, the emperor and his court. In a sense this did correspond to the concept of the emperor as Christ's vice-gerent on earth[174] but the hierarchy extended downwards. Heaven looked down from its Creator through his representatives on earth to all Christians who shared the true faith and were bound together by the liturgy. To some extent church architecture, especially in the East, reflected the outlook of the emperors and their advisers, lay as well as clerical.

Would a similar claim be made in respect of the images of Christ that in the fourth and fifth centuries so decisively displaced those of Jupiter and the pagan pantheon in Christian art? An influential group of younger scholars, including Andreas Alföldi (1895–1981), Grabar himself, and Ernst Kitzinger, were all attempting to apply the formula of 'emperor mystique' to early-Christian imagery. They believed that the images of Christ used on fresco or sarcophagus were now derived from the images of the emperor. The relatively restricted art of the early catacombs and cemeteries was transformed into compositions that identified Christian with imperial iconography. Christ mystique became emperor mystique.[175]

As a critic has pointed out, all these scholars were refugees who had felt nostalgia for the imperial states they had served in the First World War and whose collapse they had witnessed. Then they had been forced to flee from Hitlerite Europe. At Princeton or Dumbarton Oaks they could research into the origins of Christian art and architecture from the material as presented to them by the archaeologists. From this they could establish, as they believed, the close connection between Christian and imperial majesty, and see in those connections the source of the imperial outlook so familiar to them in younger and happier days.[176]

Their theories, however, were not entirely untrue for, as we have seen, imperial models and religious outlook were among the inspirations of Christian imagery and architecture. But equally attempts at systematizing the existing results of Christian archaeology were only partially successful. Information was still unco-ordinated as well as incomplete. Even Hans Lietzmann, archaeologist at heart though he was, kept closely to his literary texts in the first two volumes of his masterly *Geschichte der Alten Kirche*, published in 1930 and 1936. There was something of a paradox that while methods of archaeology were being greatly improved by Mortimer Wheeler and his colleagues in Britain, Roman *Britain* itself could contribute little directly to the study of the material remains of the early Church.

The British Isles had only featured once in the proceedings of the Fourth Congress. On the final full day Ralegh Radford, Director of the British School at Rome, had read a paper on the Christian inscriptions of the fourth to seventh centuries from Celtic Britain.[177] These inscriptions have been found as far east as Wareham in Dorset, and show how Christianity and reminiscences of Roman rule through the titles of some officials had survived in the west, while eastern and most of central Britain was being conquered by the Anglo-Saxons. In 1939 Nash Williams published some of the 400 surviving Celtic crosses found in Wales, pointing out that some of the formulae used on the epitaphs were identical with those found on late Romano-Gallic tombs, suggesting that a tenuous contact was being maintained through the fifth and sixth centuries between the Churches in Britain and Gaul.[178]

Archaeological research in Roman Britain, however, was beginning to lead to the conclusion that Christianity had failed to maintain its momentum after progress during the first half of the fourth century. Its history in Britain, therefore, was indicative of a development different from that on the Continent, indeed from any of the other provinces in the Greco-Roman world.

Literary sources tell us little about Christianity in Britain in Roman times. To add to vague references in Tertullian (*c.* 200)[179] and Origen (*c.* 240)[180] to the faith having reached the Britons, there is the record of the martyrdom of Aaron and Julius at Caerleon and the more certain martyrdom of Alban, possibly during the Decian persecution (250), at Verulamium.[181] What is clear, however, from the records of the Council of Arles on 1 August 314, is that the Church in Britain was organized in the same way as that elsewhere on the Continent. There were town-based communities with a hierarchy led by bishops. London, York and either Colchester (Camulodunum) or Lincoln were episcopal sees.[182] After the Council of Nicaea in 325 Britain followed the lead of the Western provinces in supporting Athanasius and adhering to the creed of that council. It was, however, a notably poor Church, three of its bishops at the Council of Ariminum in 359 accepting the (non-Nicene) emperor Constantius' offer of travelling expenses, a step that needed explanation.[183] Two other snippets of information come from near the end of the century. In the 390s Victricius, bishop of Rouen, attended a council of British bishops assembled to discuss a matter of discipline which evidently affected the Church on both sides of the Channel.[184] At the same period we learn from St Patrick's *Confession c.* 440 that his father and grandfather had been Christian clergy; the family had been Christian, therefore, in a settlement worth raiding, since at least *c.* 350. Finally there are tantalizing references to Pelagianism in Britain. Pelagius himself may have been British, perhaps the son of an imperial official working in Britain. We learn from the south Gallic chronicler Prosper Tiro that Pope Celestine (422–432) tried to free Britain from 'this plague', and that a certain Agricola, son of Bishop Severianus, had corrupted the Churches in Britain 'by the secret inculcation of heresy'.[186] In these circumstances the visits of Germanus, bishop of Auxerre, to Britain in 429 and 447, the former explicitly to combat the heresy, become intelligible.[187]

From these sources it seems that the Church in Britain had firm links with its neighbours on the Continent and followed the same patterns of organization and doctrine as they. But unlike the Church in Gaul, Spain and Italy, it produced no great leaders, no one like Martin of Tours to convert, albeit by force, the rural populations, or to sustain it in face of the Anglo-Saxon invaders. So complete was its collapse during the fifth century in areas occupied by the latter that not even the alliance between the Jutish kingdom of Kent and the Catholic Merovingians in Gaul in the latter half of the sixth century could restore it. Vague reminiscences of martyrs and ruined churches were all that greeted Augustine's mission on it arrival at Canterbury in 597. Only the shrine of St Alban, on the ridge rising to the east of Roman Verulamium, the alleged place of his execution, linked Romano-British Christianity with that preached by St Augustine at the court of King Ethelbert.[188] Archaeology, however, had already been providing evidence for the scattered and even random nature of Christianity in Roman Britain. The small church at Silchester indicated a following in some towns, while the Risley Park and Corbridge silver dishes suggested some wealthy adherents; but there was no pattern. Discoveries connected with villas in the south, such as the pewter dinner-set buried below the floor of the villa at Appleshaw near Andover (Hants), a ☧ featured on a mosaic at Frampton (Dorset), and Christian symbols found on stone objects from Chedworth (Gloucestershire), added to the picture of support among a relatively wealthy landowning class.[189] Small objects, such as silver spoons from Dorchester and rings from the villa at Fifehead Neville (Dorset),[190] supported this view, and indicated that the impression gained from the poverty of the British bishops at the Council of Ariminum would need modifying.

Mortimer Wheeler's excavations at Lydney Park and Maiden Castle, however, would show that Christianity in Roman Britain was meeting with strong resistance from traditional Roman-Celtic religion. In 1928 when he began work on a hill-fort site near Lydney, the property of Lord Bledisloe, Wheeler was already a distinguished archaeologist, with the successful excavation of Segontium (north Wales) and the inspiration and plans for an Institute of Archaeology at London University to his credit.[191] Some systematic digging had been carried out in 1805 on part of the interior of the fort called the Dwarf's Chapel, and walls together with pottery and nearly 5,000 coins, mainly late-Roman, were found. Nothing, however, had prepared the excavators for the extent of their discoveries. A large and prosperous temple settlement had been founded not earlier than the reign of Valentinian and Valens (364–378), whose coinage was found in the make-up of the cement floor of the temple.[192] Along with the temple there had been a guest-house, sumptuous baths, and a long building of unknown purpose, the whole surrounded by a well-built precinct wall. The temple had been dedicated to the Celtic god, Nodens. Later, there had been some reconstructions. The settlement had been popular, attracting numerous worshippers over a considerable period. Apart from the coins found within the area enclosed by the precinct walls, 300 bronze bracelets, 320 or more pins and 40 bronze spoons, and bronze letters used in putting up votive inscriptions on the temple walls, attested to the devotion of a peasantry and pilgrims making their offerings to a god on whose healing powers they relied. The temple had a long life, for the floors of the buildings were patched, one such repair in the bath building concealing a hoard of 1,646 coins, fragments and tiny bronze minims.[193] Wheeler pointed out in his and his wife's report, published in 1932), the 'foundation of this sanctuary within the last generation of Roman Britain was clearly something more than a mere flash in the pan'.[194]

This was confirmed two years later by his excavation of the great hill-fort of Maiden Castle, three miles south of Dorchester. Here, too, the site had been occupied late in the fourth century. A Romano-Celtic temple with a two-roomed 'priest's house' approached by a metalled road, built not before AD 367, was uncovered. As at Lydney the construction had been of a high standard. Just to the south had been built a curious oval hut erected at the same period. This building (perhaps a throwback to pre-Roman, Celtic worship), unlike the temple, had been wrecked,[195] but both buildings had been in use in the reign of Honorius (395-423), a small hoard of gold coins of this period being found in the temple.[196] The temple itself was repaired not earlier than 379.

The message of these discoveries could only be that Romano-Celtic religion had continued to flourish, even after 380 when the emperor Theodosius decreed that Catholic Christianity was to be the sole religion of the empire.[198] The temples at Lydney and Maiden Castle had also been built within Iron Age hill-forts. Yet another apparent reversion to pre-Roman ways of life which

aroused considerable discusion at this period were the hanging bowls, embell-
ished with roundels of rich and elaborate La Tène-type Celtic ornament.[199]
These were found often in pagan Anglo-Saxon burials, almost exclusively in
eastern England. Nothing suggested that they had a Christian significance.[200]
On the other hand, a series of excavations on churches at Reculver, Wing, Brix-
worth and Brancaster confirmed their seventh-century Saxon date and the
advance of Christianity at this time but not before. Clearly, Britain had tended
to drift away from the remainder of the Christian West with the final withdrawal of the legions in 410, but for reasons which as yet remained obscure.

The final event in this decade of discovery in Britain was the most important of all, namely the Saxon boat-burial at Sutton Hoo. As O. G. S. Crawford
wrote in the special number of *Antiquity* (March 1940) devoted to its discovery and excavation, 'It is not the first time in the history of British
archaeology that knowledge had been signally advanced by the enterprise of
an enlightened land-owner – far from it'.[201] The work was a triumph of co-
operation between the perceptive amateur knowing the limits of his skills and
the professionalism of the archaeologists of the Office of Works and British
Museum, directed by C. W. Phillips.[202]

It was in the summer of 1938 that Mrs E. M. Pretty decided to investigate
some of the conspicuous group of eleven mounds that lay on heathland at the
head of the estuary of the river Deben not far from Woodbridge in east Suffolk. The mounds had been disturbed in the sixteenth century; in some, holes
had been dug, and even the remains of picnics buried, but the damage was less
extensive than feared. In 1938 one barrow yielded the remains of a boat some
18 ft long with an iron-bound stern (recovered by Basil Brown), while others,
where they had not been rifled, contained cremations and objects datable to
the sixth and seventh centuries. The site was therefore in use in pagan Anglo-
Saxon times.[203] In May 1939 a team including Basil Brown and supervised by
Guy Maynard of the Ipswich Museum began work on the largest of the group
of barrows. Working with great care Brown excavated what proved to be the
forepart of a large ship, and realizing the importance of the discovery called in
the British Museum.

As the political horizons steadily darkened through the summer the excavation became a race against time. Soon the outlines of a ship 85 ft long overall
and 14 ft at its greatest beam emerged, preserved in outline in the hardened
sand of the barrow. It had been clinker-built and propelled by 38 rowers.

At this stage a Viking origin was still suspected, but very soon objects
began to appear that dated the barrow and its contents securely to the Anglo-
Saxon period and to a royal personage. First, a whetstone 1 ft 9 in in length,

each end decorated by four human heads carved in low relief, suggested a
sceptre, a formal symbol of authority,[204] an impression reinforced by the discovery nearby of a shield boss of great size and weight belonging to a shield to
be carried into battle by a warrior king. The sword with gold-decorated hilt
and helmet told the same story. Other discoveries confirmed the sense of
wealth and power, and the farflung contacts that once had symbolized the
prestige of the dead man. The great silver bowl stamped with the monogram
of the emperor Anastasius I (491–518) had been buried with other silver
bowls of East Roman origin. Equally magnificent, but made probably in eastern England itself, was a hanging bowl whose ornamented enamel roundels
indic-ated the continuance of a native Romano-Celtic tradition of metal-work
into the seventh century.[205] Of the great haul of treasure that was coming to
light only two spoons were clearly of Christian origin, marked respectively on
their bowls ☦ Paulos and ☦ Saulos.[206]

Who was the ruler who had been laid to rest in so much barbaric splendour?
A purse of 40 gold coins (Merovingian tremisses) was among the jewellery
recovered. Three coins appeared to be Merovingian copies of the gold of Maurice Tiberius (582–602) but others could not be associated with certainity
with any Merovingian king.[207] The excavators were left with a date later than
600 and even as late as 640–650.[208] This late date seems less likely, as by that
time the Anglo-Saxon kingdoms, except Mercia, were opting finally for Christianity and kings and nobility would have been buried near the newly-erected
churches. In the previous generation, however, the pendulum had swung violently between paganism and Christianity. In Kent where King Ethelbert had
been converted to Christianity by St Augustine in 597 and died in 617, his son
and successor reverted to heathenism. Among the East Angles King Redwald
is said to have also been converted to Christianity on a visit to Kent, but to
have reverted to traditional paganism on his return.[209] He compromised by
setting up one altar to Christ and another to the Germanic gods in the same
sanctuary. Pagan sympathies, at least in funerary practice, seem indicated by
the number of drinking horns found.[210] Redwald was high king of the Anglo-
Saxons when he died in 625. His son Eorpwald was persuaded by the Christian
Northumbrian King Edwin to embrace Christianity *c.* 627 and his kingdom
thereafter became Christian. From this rather tangled tale, it seems that the
only ruler who possessed the status to warrant the Sutton Hoo burial was
Redwald. The pagan ritual of the ship burial, combined with Christian possessions such as the silver dishes and spoons, suggest those elements of religious
compromise coupled with massive wealth and influence that one could expect
of a high king. If so, the Sutton Hoo burial may mark the point of transition

from pagan to Christian Anglo-Saxon England, in which also the crafts of the conquered Romano-Celtic people also had a place.[211]

The removal of the most sensational finds began on 25 July and lasted a week. They reached the comparative safety of the vaults of the British Museum just in time.[212] August saw the balance between peace and war shift decisively towards the latter. Only on 26 August was the excavation concluded and the finest archaeological discovery ever made in Britain, perhaps in Europe, safeguarded. Three days before, on 23 August, after minimum negotiation, Ribbentrop and Molotov signed a non-agression pact between Germany and the Soviet Union (with a secret protocol partitioning Poland between them). Poland was doomed. On 26 August Hitler gave his General Staff the go-ahead for attack. On 1 September his armies crossed the Polish frontier. On 3 September after 36 hours of frantic hesitation, first Britain and then France declared war on Germany. The Second World War had begun.

Unheeded went the warning uttered by State-Secretary von Weizsäcker to Ribbentrop the previous year, on 30 June 1938, that if Germany went to war she would eventually be defeated and all Europe would suffer with her. Victory would go chiefly to the 'non-European and the anti-Social powers'.[213] In 1939 the sun was setting finally on Europe and her empires. For apart from the six years of fratricidal struggle in Europe that ensued, the colonial peoples, better educated and led, had become impatient with European control. In Tunis in 1930 a young man had watched with growing anger the Eucharistic Congress unrolling before his eyes. Was this to signal the end of Islam in North Africa? Not if he could help it. The Neo-Destour movement under Habib Bourguiba was born. In Egypt and the Middle East there were similar stirrings. The end of the war would see a vastly changed world. The era of 'archaeological imperialism' was nearly over.

NOTES

1. For the Maiden Castle 'dig' as an example of the 'social value' of archaeology in terms of 'a happy and human' public relations 'policy', see C. F. C. Hawkes, review of Wheeler's *Maiden Castle, JRS* 34 (1944), p. 155.
2. C. Schmidt, 'Ein Mani Fund in Aegypten', *SBAW* (1933), pp. 4–81.
3. Ibid., p. 4.
4. *Panarion*, ed. Holl, III, p. 18.
5. Schmidt, op. cit., p. 6.
6. Ibid., p. 9.
7. H. J. Polotsky, 'Abriss des manichäischen Systems' in Pauly-Wissowa, *Real-Encyklopädie der classischen Wissenschaft*, Suppl. 6, 241–272, and *Manichäische Homilien* (Stuttgart, 1934); C. Schmidt and H. J. Polotsky, *Kephalaia* (Stuttgart, 1935); C. R. C. Alberry, *A Manichaean Psalm-book*, Part II (Stuttgart, 1938).

8. Brilliantly exploited by H. C. Puech, *Le Manichéisme: son fondateur, sa doctrine* (Musée Guimet, Bibliothéque de Diffusion, 56; Paris, 1949).

9. For Augustine's Manichaeism, see P. R. L. Brown, *Augustine: A Biography* (London: Faber, 1967), ch. 5.

10. 'All apostles that have come into the world are sent by one and the same force but differ according to country': at the beginning of a book called *Shabuhragan* written by Mani for King Sapor I, perhaps *c.* 270. Also *Keph.* 143: see Schmidt, op. cit., pp. 59–62. For Mani's dependence on his predecessors' teaching, see W. Henning, 'Ein manichäische Henochbuch', *SBAW* (1934), pp. 27–35.

11. For Schmidt's reconstruction of his life, see op. cit., pp. 48–57.

12. *Keph.* 54, cited from J. Stevenson rev. W. H. C. Frend, *A New Eusebius* (1987), document 234, p. 266: Puech, op. cit., p. 63.

13. *Keph.* 2 (parable of the trees) and *Keph.* 7 on the relations of celestial beings such as the Father of Light to the 12 Aeons: Schmidt, op. cit., p. 22.

14. Cited from Psalm 242 = Alberry, op. cit., p. 49. Mariolatry was a feature of Coptic Manichaeism as it was of Coptic and Nubian Monophysitism (see below, p. 309).

15. H. I. Bell and T. C. Skeat, *Fragments of an Unknown Gospel and Other Early Christian Papyri* (British Museum, 1935).

16. Ibid., p. 30.

17. Ibid., p. 38, suggesting the possibility of the author's use of a source used by the writer of the Fourth Gospel. See also C. H. Dodd, 'A new gospel', *BJRL* 22, 2 (October 1928), pp. 3–39, at pp. 21–2. Fragments of another unknown gospel relatng to 'tribute' were published in *The Times* by Bell (25 January 1935).

18. C. H. Roberts, *P. Ryl.* iii.457; published in *BJRL*.

19. For another, early third-century, probably Gnostic commentary (P. Egerton 3) see Bell and Skeat, 'Fragments of a Gospel commentary', *Fragments of an Unknown Gospel*, op. cit., part II, pp. 42ff.

20. W. B. Emery and L. P. Kirwan, *The Royal Tombs of Ballana and Q'ustul* (2 vols; Egyptian Arch. Survey); review by R. Paribeni, *Aegyptus* 19 (1939), pp. 113ff, and briefly reported in *RA* (1932) under 'Nouvelles archéologiques et correspondences', p. 152.

21. L. P. Kirwan, 'The Oxford University Excavations in Nubia 1934–1935', *JEA* 21 (1935), pp. 191–8.

22. A useful brief outline was being constructed by Kirwan in his article 'Notes on the topography of the Christian Nubian Kingdom', *JEA* 21 (1935), pp. 57–62 (which de Villard may not have known).

23. U. Monneret de Villard, *La Nubie medioévale*, I and II (Cairo, 1935), III and IV (Cairo, 1957).

24. De Villard, 'Storia della Nubia cristiana', *Orientalia christiana analecta* 118 (Rome, 1938).

25. De Villard, *La Nubie*, I, pp. viii–xii. One suggestion made by de Villard, that a small Christian kingdom of Dotawo did survive to the fourteenth century, has been upheld.

26. W. Y. Adams, *Nubia the Corridor of Africa* (London, 1977) and also O. G. S. Crawford; review of De Villard, 'Storia': *Antiquity* 21 (1947), pp. 10–15.

27. Marcel Christofle, *Rapport sur les travaux de fouilles et consolidations effectuées par le Service des Monuments historiques de l'Algérie 1933–1936* (Algiers, 1937).

28. L. Leschi, 'La basilique chrétienne en Algérie', *Atti* IV.1 (Rome, 1940), pp. 145–67.

29. P. G. Lapeyre, 'La basilique chrétienne de Tunisie', ibid., pp. 169–244: a thorough survey of early-Christian church architecture in Tunisia.

30. P. Romanelli, 'La Basilica cristiana nell Africa settentrionale Italiana', ibid., pp. 245–89.

31. Work at Tipasa continued without interuption from 1925: *Rapport* 74, and also J. Lassus, 'Autour de la basilique de Tipasa', *MEFR* 47 (1929).

32. A. Berthier *et al.*, *Les vestiges du christianisme antique dans le Numidie centrale* (Algiers, 1942), pp. 9ff. (= *Vestiges*).

33. *Vestiges*, pp. 205ff.

34. P. Cayrel, 'Une basilique donatiste de Numidie', *MEFR* 51 (1934), pp. 114–42.

35. P. Courcelle, 'Une seconde campagne des fouilles à Ksar el Kelb', *MEFR* 53 (1936), pp. 166–97.

36. W. H. C. Frend, *The Donatist Church*, p. 179.

37. *Passio Marculi*: PL VIII, 761. Compare also Optatus, *De Schismate* iii.6 (Marculus and Donatus 'occisi').

38. Cayrel, op. cit., p. 133.

39. Ibid., p. 124.

40. Ibid., pp. 119–20.

41. Thus Augustine, *Psalmus contra Partem Donati* (composed *c.* 393): *PL* 43, 26: 'Omnes qui gaudetis de pace, modum verum judicate', and see P. Monceaux, *Histoire littéraire*, IV, pp. 473 and 478 (examples).
42. Cayrel, op. cit., p. 132.
43. Ibid., p. 126. See above, p. 118.
44. Ibid., p. 134.
45. Courcelle, op. cit., pp. 179–81.
46. Thus, Kherbet bou Addoufen extended over an area 800 m long and Kherbet Bahrarous 40 hectares: Berthier, *Vestiges*, pp. 158 and 156.
47. See map of sites in Berthier, *Vestiges*, facing p. 38.
48. Berthier, op. cit., Part III: 'Le culte'.
49. *Acta Saturnini*: *PL* 8, 700–701, See Frend, *Donatist Church*, pp. 9–10.
50. Berthier, op. cit., p. 129 (Bir Djedid) and 211. Compare Augustine, *Ep.* 16 (from Maximus of Madaura).
51. For instance, Ferme Gourdon, Church ii, contained 35 burials within its walls. For a similar cemetery-church at Ain Ghorab (see above, p. 66), see L. Leschi, 'Basilique et cimitière donatistes de Numidie (Ain Ghorab)', *RAfr* 78 (1936), pp. 27–42.
52. For example, from Foum el Amba, where inscriptions bearing the Donatist watch-word 'Deo laudes' and the emphatic 'Vitam eternam qu[i] iusti et q[ui] fecerunt', as the reward to those who built the church: Berthier, pp. 77 and 206–7.
53. Ibid., p. 133 and plate xxix, p. 58.
54. Ibid., plate xxiv, p. 46, from Oued Rzel.
55. Augustine, *Contra Gaudentium* i.28.32.
56. Berthier, op. cit., pp. 26 (Kherbet bou Hadef) and 25 (Kherbet Bahrarous). Also W. H. C. Frend, 'A note on the religion and life in a Numidian village in the later Roman empire' in *Archaeology and History* (Variorum Press, 1988), ch. xii.
57. Thus *Contra Gaudentium* i.22.25, 27.30 and 28.32.
58. F. Logeart, 'Les épitaphes funéraires chrétiennes du Djebel Nif en Nisr', *RAFr* 83 (1940) pp. 5–29; L. Leschi, 'A propos des épitaphes chrétiennes du Djebel Nif en Nisr', ibid., pp. 31–6.
59. Particlarly his conribution, 'Basilique et cimitière donatistes de Numidie (Ain Ghorab)'; op. cit.
60. Bethier, op. cit., Conclusion, pp. 220–4.
61. J. Carcopino, 'Survivances par substitution des sacrifices d'enfants', *RHR* 106 (1932), pp. 592–9.
62. J. Carcopino, 'La fin du Maroc romain', *MEFR* 57 (1940), pp. 349–448, at pp. 350ff., 367. Carcopino pointed to a comparative lack of Constantinian coins from Volubilis, also a lack of imperial dedications there after Carinus (283–284), contrasting with the flow of coins and official activity at Tingis (Tangier).
63. Ibid., p. 434.
64. Mauretania Tingitana was part of the *Dioecesis Hispaniarum* according to the Verona list (of Roman provinces) drawn up *c.* 297. Cited from Carcopino, op. cit., p. 349.
65. Listed with other similar late-Christian inscriptions, ibid., pp. 435ff. Up to 1925, 64 Christian inscriptions, dated between 450 and 651, had been found in the one-time military centres along line of the Mauretanian *limes* from Tiaret to the Moroccan frontier: Diehl, *ILCV* III, 271–272. Carcopino (pp. 436–7) lists three more from Volubilis dating from 599 to 655.
66. C. Courtois, *Les Vandales et l'Afrique* (Paris: Arts et Métiers, 1955), pp. 88–9; and see W. H. C. Frend, *JRS* 56 (1956), pp. 161–6, at p. 164.
67. P. Salama, *Libyca* II (1954), pp. 205–29.
68. For the general history of the Church in North Africa in Byzantine times see R. Devréese, 'L'Eglise d'Afrique durant l'occupation byzantine', *MEFR* 57 (1940), pp. 141–66.
69. L. Poinssot and R. Lantier, *BAC* (1925), pp. lxxv–lxxxiv.
70. Gregory, *Epp.* ii. 46, iii.47 and 48, vii.2, viii.14 and 15, xii.8 and 28.
71. Bou Takrematen was a large site covering 80 hectares, compared, for instance, with 61 hectares covered by Tipasa. It may have been the site of Nova Sparsa. See A. Berthier and M. Martin, 'Edifices chrétiens de Bou Takrematen' in *Ier Congrès de la Fédération des Sociétés Savantes de l'Afrique du Nord* (Algiers, 1935), pp. 137–52.
72. A good example is the deposition of the relics of St Julian of Antioch and St Lawrence and others by Bishop Columbus of Nicivibis on 3 October 581 or 582, the inscription being written in illiterate Latin: S. Gsell, *MEFR* 23 (1903), pp. 1–25. Another example came from Henchir Rouis, where the

Afican martyrs (d. 304) Maxima, Donatilla and Secunda are associated with the archangels Michael and Gabriel and St Vincentius: H. Jaubert, 'Ruines chrétiennes du Diocèse de Constantine', *RC* 57 (1912: publ. 1913), p. 196, plate vii.

73. A. Berthier, *Vestiges*, p. 90.

74. Own observation on site in 1939.

75. See E. F. Gautier, *Le Passé de l'Afrique du Nord: Les siècles obscurs* (Paris: Paycot, 1937), p. 276, citing the Arab author Al Bayano' l-moghreb.

76. H. I. Marrou, 'Epitaphe chrétienne d'Hippone à réminiscences virgiliennes' in *Tempora Christiana* (Collection de L'Ecole française de Rome 35; Rome, 1978), pp. 222–30. Optimistically, perhaps, 'Elle attesterait dans une Hippone en voie de barbarisation une étonnante persistance de l'ambition littéraire': p. 230.

77. Examples quoted by the writer, 'The end of Byzantine North Africa. Some evidence of transitions' in *Archaeology and History in the Study of Early Christianity* (Variorum Press, 1988), ch.13.

78. W. Seston, 'Sur les dernier temps du Christianisme en Afrique', *MEFR* 56 (1936), pp. 101–24, at p. 103 citing Paribeni's discoveries; 'Papal interventions in North Africa 146–1085' are quoted ibid., pp. 120–1.

79. Al Bayano, cited by Gautier, op. cit., p. 277, cites an example of the immediate conversion to Islam of Kahena's defeated army and their willingmess to serve under Hassan in 703.

80. Berthier, *Vestiges*, pp. 50–1.

81. *Sixth Preliminary Report*, pp. 416–17. For Tatian's authorship, see Eusebius, *HE* iv.29.6 ('still extant in some places', when Eusebius wrote).

82. *Sixth Preliminary Report*, pp. 309–96. Also Comte du Mesnil du Buisson's account in *RB* 45 (1936), pp. 86–90.

83. du Buisson, *Les Peintures de la Synagogue de Doura Europos, 245–256 après J. C.* (Rome 1939), plates XV–XXI.

84. du Buisson, op. cit., plate XXXIX (the Messianic restoration of Israel proclaimed by Ezekiel 37).

85. Ibid., plate LIX.

86. *Sixth Preliminary Report*, p. 309.

87. *Eighth Preliminary Report* (1939), chs iii–vii on the temples of Dura.

88. *Eighth Preliminary Report*, ch. ii on the history of the building. Also du Buisson, report of work during the 1934–35 season, *CRAI* (1935), pp. 275–304, at p. 280. The Mithraeum was in bad need of repair in 256. Lizards had apparently been nesting behind the plaster of part of the walls in the chamber where the cult was celebrated.

89. Illustrated in M. Simon, *La Civilisation antique et le Christianisme* (Paris, 1972), opposite p. 164 (fig. 62); and *Eighth Preliminary Report*, plate XVIII.

90. For the non-Nicene creeds agreed at this council, see J. Stevenson rev. W. H. C. Frend, *Creeds, Councils and Controversies* (SPCK, 1989), pp. 8–11. For the ecclesiastical background see B. J. Kidd, *A History of the Church to AD 461* (OUP, 1922), II, pp. 77–82.

91. For Lassus' contribution at Tipasa, see his article 'Autour des basiliques chrétiennes de Tipasa', *MEFR* 47 (1930), pp. 222–7 (plan: fig. 1, p. 225).

92. Julian, *Misopogon* 342B, ed. W. C. Wright: 'gay and prosperous city'.

93. Ammianus Marcellinus, *Res Gestae* xiv.8.8: 'Antioch a city known to all the world, and without rival so rich is it in imported and domestic goods'.

94. Libanius, *Ep.* 1119 put the population at about 150,000: the well-to-do tended to live in the city: *Orat.* i.4–5, and retire to wealthy houses in the suburb of Daphne in the summer: *Ep.* 419.

95. John Chrysostom, *Homil. in Matth.* 95.4 (*PG* 58, 762) states that the city contained 100,000 Christians.

96. J. Lassus, 'Les mosaiques d'Antioche', *CRAI* (1936), pp. 33–42; also R. Stillwell (ed.), *Antioch on the Orontes*, II (Princeton, 1938).

97. J. Lassus, 'L'Eglise cruciforme d'Antioche–Kouassie' in *Antioch on the Oronates* II, pp. 5–44 (inscriptions pp. 38–44); H. Delehaye, *L'Origine du Culte des Martyrs* (Brussels, 1912), p. 70.

98. Found in 1910 by Arab workmen digging a well near Antioch on a site traditionally associated with the cathedral; probably dated to the sixth century. See J. P. C. Kent and K. S. Painter (eds), *Wealth of the Roman World* (British Museum, 1987), p. 86, illustration no. 147.

99. See Frend, 'Syrian parallels to the Water Newton treasure', *JbAC* 27/28 (1984/85), pp. 146–50; for its possible connection with the Antioch Chalice, see Kent and Painter, op. cit., pp. 86–7; and for a brief summary on both Byzantine silver treasures from Hama, see Marvin C. Ross, 'A second Byzantine silver treasure from Hamah', *Archaeology* 3 (1950), pp. 162–3.

100. Crowfoot sums up the results of his work in *Gerasa, the City of the Decapolis* (New Haven, 1938).
101. R. de Vaux, 'Une mosaique byzantine à Ma'in', *RB* 47 (1938), pp. 226–58; Crowfoot, *Churches in Palestine*, pp. 141–6. Ma'in was five miles south-west of Madaba, and one might suspect that the same artist had constructed both mosaics. The church at Ma'in underwent repairs as late as 719–720.
102. The early excavations are recorded by L. H. Vincent and F. M. Abel, *Bethléem, le sanctuaire de la Nativité* (Paris: Gabalda, 1914) and by W. Harvey and colleagues, *The Church of the Nativity at Bethlehem* (London, 1910).
103. Vincent, 'Bethléem, la sanctuaire de la Nativité d'après les fouilles récentes', *RB* 45 (136), pp. 544–74; 46 (1937), pp. 93–121. Also *Atti* iv.2, pp. 65–78; Crowfoot, op. cit., pp. 22–30; E. T. Richmond, 'The Church of the Nativity: the Plan of the Constantinian Church', *QDAP* 6, pp. 63–6.
104. Richmond, 'Alterations carried out by Justinian', *QDAP* 6, pp. 67–72.
105. *Itinerarium*: *PL* 8, 792c: Ibi [Bethlehem] basilica facta est iussu Constantini.
106. Crowfoot, op. cit., p. 27.
107. The point made by Vincent, *RB* (1936), pp. 572–3.
108. P. Bellarmino Bagatti, 'Il monastero del Nebo e gli antichi monasteri della Palestina', *Atti* IV.2, pp. 89–110.
109. Aurelius Victor, *De Caesaribus*, ed. Pichlmayr, 42.9–13.
110. E. L. Sukenik, *The Ancient Synagogue of Beth-Alpha* (OUP, 1932). Built in the fifth century on a basilican plan. In the sixth century mosaics were added illustrating the Ark of the Covenant and the zodiac.
111. See, in general, Avi Yonah, *The Jews in Palestine* (Oxford: Blackwell, 1976), pp. 176–81.
112. *MAMA* VI (1939), p. 334, reading 'May there be peace upon Israel and upon Jerusalem and upon this place to the end of time'. The Greek is too fragmentary to claim bilingual status. For a prosperous synagogue in Greco-Roman Akmonia, ibid., p. 264.
113. *BCH* (1935), pp. 232 and 235. Robert was criticized for his 'ton aussi désobligeant' towards his colleagues. On the other hand, he was warmly praised by M. N. Tod for his 'mastery of the evidence, acuteness of observation and felicity of restoration'. He was a 'tireless worker': *JHS* 55 (1935), p. 210.
114. W. H. C. Frend, 'A third century inscription relating to *angareia* in Phrygia', *JRS* 46 (1956), pp. 46–56. The writer was characterized as 'le dilettante Frend' and A. M. Woodhead, with whom he worked on the inscription, as 'Monsieur Tête de Bois'! (Information from the late Dr Woodhead.)
115. *Etudes anatoliennes: Recherches sur les inscriptions grecques de l'Asie Mineure* (Etudes orientales 5: Paris, 1939), pp. 409–12. Other inscriptions referring to Jews were on p. 433 (Mastaura) and 568 (Mylasa).
116. See Constantine Porphyrogenitus, *Le Livre des Cérémonies*, ed. A. Vogt, I: *Commentaire* (2 vols; Paris, Budé, 1935–40).
117. Published by G. Brett, W. J. Macaulay and B. K. Stevenson, *The Great Palace of the Byzantine Emperors (First Report)* (OUP, 1947); briefly by H. Megaw, 'Archaeology in Greece 1935–36', *JHS* 56 (1936), p. 155.
118. *Great Palace Excavations*, ch. 2, B. K. Stevenson's section on 'The pottery', esp. p. 38 (coins and pottery dating).
119. *Great Palace Excavations*, ch. 3, Gerard Brett's section on 'The mosaics'. Late Roman pottery was found below the level of the mosaics.
120. For dating see ibid., pp. 16ff. and 31–2.
121. As suggested by Brett, loc. cit., pp. 94–7.
122. See the memoir on his life: by Edward W. Forbes, 'Thomas Whittemore 1871–1950', *Archaeology* 3 (1950), pp. 180–2.
123. Full results: T. Whittemore, *The Mosaics of the St Sophia at Istanbul* (4 vols; Paris/Oxford, 1933–53); preliminary results: Whittemore, *The Mosaics of St Sophia at Istanbul* (OUP for the Byzantine Institute at Princeton, 1936); and *AJA* 2nd ser. 43 (1938) pp 219–26. Also A. M. Schneider, *Die Hagia Sophia zu Konstantinopel* (Berlin, 1939).
124. See P. Collart, 'Inscriptions de Philippes', *BCH* 56 (1932), pp. 192–231; and successive reports by P. Lemerle in *BCH* 58 (1934), pp. 259–61; 59 (1935), pp. 160–3; 60 (1936), pp. 478–80; 61 (1937), pp. 465–8. Excavations continued to 1937.
125. J. Comfry and M. Fayel, 'Inscriptions de Philippes', *BCH* 60 (1936), pp. 37–58, at pp. 47–52. Also M. N. Tod, 'The progress of Greek epigraphy, 1937–38', *JHS* 59 (1939), p. 264.
126. *Acta Pionii*, ed. H. Musurillo (OUP, 1972), 19.5.
127. Lemerle and Comfry, *CRAI* (1937), p. 182. In 1937 another magnificent pre-Byzantine basilica was excavated. Its walls had been faced with marble, the baptistery adorned with mosaic and the *atrium* in front of the church flanked by ceremonial porticos: *CRAI* (1938), pp. 174–6.

128. P. Lemerle, *CRAI* (1935), pp. 180–1. A vast building, with three naves preceded by a courtyard and two chapels used as baptisteries.
129. Recorded in 'Chronique', *BCH* 63 (1939), pp. 313–14 and in *Byzantion* 14 (1939).
130. For a list of the sites explored and discussion, see G. A. Soteriou, 'Die altchristlichen Basiliken Griechenlands', *Atti* IV.i, pp. 355–80.
131. See below, p. 305 (the frescos at Faras illustrating Byzantine vestments).
132. Soteriou, op. cit., pp. 375, Abbildung 21, and 361. Soteriou gives a fifth-century date to this church.
133. Ibid., p. 367.
134. Ibid., p. 355.
135. Ibid., p. 378 and Abbildung 24 on p. 379. Also G. M. Young, 'Archaeology in Greece 1938', *JHS* 58 (1939), p. 227.
136. F. J. de Waele, 'The fountain of Lerna and the early Christian cemetery at Corinth', *AJA* (1935), pp. 352–9. There were 315 burials in the cemetery.
137. Soteriou, loc. cit., p. 371.
138. Ibid., p. 351.
139. Louis Blondel, 'Les premiers édifices chrétiens à Genève', *Geneva* 2 (1933), pp. 77–101. For Charles Bonnet's excavations, see below, p. 372.
140. Armin von Gerkan, 'Die christliche Anlage in Ostia', *RQ* 47 (1939), pp. 15–30.
141. Recorded by Gino Chierici, 'Di alcuni risultati sui recenti lavori intorno alla Basilica di San Lorenzo a Milano e alle Basiliche Paoliniane di Cimitile', *Atti* IV, pp. 29–47, at pp. 29–35.
142. Ibid., pp. 36–47. Phases of construction outlined: pp. 44–7.
143. Paulinus of Nola, *Ep.* 320.10–16 to Sulpicius Severus in 404: ed. W. Hartel, *CSEL* 29 (1894), pp. 285–91.
144. See S. Loeschke, *Die Erforschung des Tempelbezirkes in Altbachtale zu Trier* (Berlin, 1928), pp. 5 and 17, 'all destroyed in 337', blaming the powerful Bishop Maximin of Trier for this act. Later: *Der Tempelbezirk in Altbachtale zu Trier* (Berlin, 1938), p. vii. But, for some later pagan use, at least until the period of Valentinan I–Valens–Gratian (367–383), see E. Gose, *Der gallo-römische Tempelbezirk in Altbachtale zu Trier* (Trierer Forschungen und Grabungen VII: Mainz 1972), p. 140, relating to temple no. 38 in the sacred area.
145. Loeschke, *Frühchristliche Denkmäler*, pp. 123–4.
146. *Atti* IV.1, p. 53.
147. E. Iosi, 'Cimitero nella sinistra della via Tiburtina al Viale Regina Margherita', *Rivista archeologica* 10 (1933), pp. 187–233 at p. 209.
148. Ibid., p. 203.
149. Recorded in *RQ* 44 (1936), p. 295.
150. See M. Gütschow, 'Das Museum des Praetextatus', *Pont. Acad. Rom. Memorie* 4 (1938), pp. 46ff.; for third-century pagan saracophagi in the catacombs, 'Die Katakomben als Fundstätte heidnischen Sarcophagi', ibid., pp. 35–43.
151. P. Styger, *Die römische Katakomben* (Berlin, 1933).
152. 'Das 4 Jh. ist die Blütezeit der Katakomben': ibid., p. 3.
153. Ibid., p. 99. Styger dated the fresco depicting the raising of Lazarus to mid-second century: p. 142.
154. Ibid., p. 110.
155. Wilpert had published his catalogue *Sarcophagi cristiani antichi* (Rome, 1929–36).
156. Styger, op. cit., p. 140; he also disputed Wilpert's interpretation of a banquet scene on a fresco in the catacomb as a celebration of Mass (*Fractio Panis*, p. 31) – it was a funeral meal: p. 140.
157. Ibid., pp. 139–40.
158. As when he claimed that the Viale Manzoni frescos were pagan: ibid., p. 16.
159. Ibid., p. 339.
160. *Passio Perpetuae*, ed. H. Musurillo, 12.6: 'et dixerunt nobis seniores, Ite et ludite'.
161. Styger, op. cit., p. 362: 'Der ganze Bilderschatz der Katakomben ist eine volkstumliche, erzählrischer Widergabe der Hl. Schrift' (final opinion).
162. Ibid., p. 355.
163. J. P. Kirsch, *Atti* IV.1, 'Seduta inaugurale', esp. pp. 35–7.
164. L. Leschi, 'La basilique chrétienne en Algérie', *Atti* IV.1, p. 148. A fine example of a then extant apse flanked by small chambers was that of Le Kef: Leschi, ibid., fig. 20, p. 216.
165. Ibid., pp. 148–9.

166. J. W. Crowfoot, 'The Christian basilica in Palestine', *Atti* IV.1, p. 326.
167. S. Guyer, 'Les édifices à coupole de l'Orient', *Atti* IV.2, p. 3.
168. Ibid., pp. 4–5 and Krautheimer, *Architecture*, 242. That at Nazianzus is described by Gregory in *Or.* 18.39: a church with vaulted dome, built by his father (d. 374).
169. Krautheimer, *Architecture*, pp. 41–2,
170. *Itinerarium*: PL 8, 593. In general, see H. Brandenburg, 'Kirchenbau', *TRE* 18 (1989), p. 422. Plans of third-century churches generally still unknown.
171. Tertullian, *Apol.* 39. 1.
172. As described by Augustine, *Ep.* 55.15 and *De Civ. Dei* ii.28 (separation of sexes): see also H. Leclercq, 'Afrique (liturgie, post-nicéene de)', *DACL* I.1, 620–638.
173. As argued by André Grabar, *Le Martyrium* (Paris, 1946) and in 'Christian architecture, East and West', *Archaeology* 2 (Summer 1949), pp. 95–164. He points, in particular, to the importance of the rotundas covering the site of the Holy Places as furthering the use of the cupola roof: p. 99. He believed that 'in the East as well as the West, the same cult of martyrs tended in a decisive manner to determine the average style of mediaeval church'. But in the East, church architecture developed from the mausoleum dedicated to a martyr or holy place, while in the West any changes in architectural form affected only the choir, considered as the *martyrium*, and leaving the basilica nave changed: p. 103.
174. Eusebius, *In Praise of Constantine* i (end): '. . . the emperor receiving as it were a copy of the Divine sovereignty directs in imitation of God Himself, the administration of this world's affairs'.
175. Thomas F. Matthews, *The Clash of Gods: A Reinterpretation of Early Christian Art* (Princeton University Press, 1993), ch. 1.
176. Ibid., pp. 16–19.
177. Ralegh Radford, 'L'Epigraphia dal iv and vii secolo nella Britannia Celtica', *Atti* IV.2, pp. 335–46.
178. V. E. Nash Williams, 'Some Welsh early Christian monuments', *AJ* 19 (1939), pp. 147–56 (with plates and figures).
179. Tertullian, *Adv. Iudaeos* 7.
180. Origen, *Homil. iv in Ezekiel*, Hieron. interp.: ed. Baehrens, *GCS*, *Origens* 8 (Leipzig, 1925), p. 362.
181. Bede, *HE* i.7 (end) for Aaron and Julius, i.7 for Alban; Gildas, *De Excidio* 10 (Aaron and Julius and Alban); discussion of the evidence: W. Levison, 'St Alban and St Albans', *Antiquity* 15 (1941), pp. 337–59. Levison's verdict, '*Ignoramus* and *ignorabimus*' (p. 350), still stands.
182. On the council of Arles, see Jean Gaudemet, *Conciles gaulois du IVe siècle* (SC 241: Paris, 1977), pp. 35–67; J. G. Mann, 'The administration of Roman Britain', *Antiquity* 35 (1961), pp. 316–20.
183. Sulpicius Severus, *Chronicon*, ed. Halm (*CSEL*), ii.41.
184. Victricius, *De Laude Sanctorium* i: PL 20, 443–444.
185. Patrick, *Confessio*, ed. R. P. C. Hanson and C. Blanc (*SC* 249: Paris, 1978).
186. Bede, *HE* i.17: *Prosper Tiro Chronicon* ad ann. 429 and 431: PL 58, 594.
187. See Charles Thomas, *Christianity in Roman Britain* (Batsford, 1981), pp. 55–60: Germanus had been a military leader, *Dux*, before consecration as bishop. He died in 448.
188. Bede, *HE* i.7.18. For the existence of a shrine in Alban's honour *c.* 470, see Constantius, *Life of Germanus* 16 and 18; C. E. Stevens, 'Gildas Sapiens', *EHR* (1941), p. 373. The site of the shrine still eludes investigation (*The Times*, 24 August 1994).
189. For these see Thomas, op. cit., pp. 110–13.
190. Ibid., pp. 104–5.
191. Wheeler's account is given in *Still Digging* (London, 1955), ch. 5.
192. R. E. M. and T. V. Wheeler, *Report on the Excavation of the Prehistoric, Roman and Post-Roman Site in Lydney Park, Gloucestershire* (Society of Antiquaries Reports of the Research Committee 9; Oxford, 1932), pp. 60–3.
193. For the hoards of minims, see pp. 112ff., and plates XXXV–XLIX.
194. Ibid., p. 61.
195. R. E. M. Wheeler, *Maiden Castle, Dorset* (Society of Antiquaries Reports of the Research Committee 12: OUP, 1943), pp. 72–8.
196. Ibid., p. 74.
197. Ibid., p. 75.
198. *Cod. Theod.* xvi. 1. 2 (*Cunctos Populos*, 27 February 380). See N. Q. King, *The Emperor Theodosius and the Establishment of Christianity* (London: SCM Press, 1961), ch. 2.Theodosius ordered all forms of pagan religious observance to cease in an order addresssed to the praetorian prefect, Albinus, on 24 February 391: *Cod. Theod.* xci.10.10.

199. See T. D. Kendrick , 'British hanging bowls', *Antiquity* 6 (1932), pp. 161–84: E. T. Leeds, *Celtic Ornament* (OUP, 1933), ch. 6, 'The revival', referring to a 'Dark Age of Celtic art in Britain' (p. 137). Also Leeds, 'An enamelled bowl from Baginston', *AJ* 15 (1935), pp. 109–12.

200. Leeds, *Celtic Ornament*, op. cit., p. 154: 'Practically all [the enamelled escutcheons] have come to light within an area bounded on the west by the line of the Fosse Way' (i. e. pagan Anglo-Saxon England). Also T. D. Kendrick, 'The Sutton Hoo ship-burial: the large hanging bowl', *Antiquity* 14 (1940), pp. 30–9.

201. O. G. S. Crawford, 'Editorial notes', *Antiquity* 14 (1940), p. 1.

202. Phillips' account is published as 'The excavation of the Sutton Hoo ship-burial', *AJ* 20 (1940), pp. 149–202 (excellent photographs).

203. For the story of the excavation, see C. W. Phillips, 'The Sutton Hoo ship-burial: the excavation', *Antiquity* 14 (1940), pp. 6–27, at p. 8. and Phillips, *AJ*, pp. 152–203: for the 1938 excavations ibid., pp. 52–4 and 191.

204. *Antiquity* 14 (1940), p. 15.

205. See above, note 200.

206. Ernst Kitzinger, 'The Sutton Hoo ship burial V: the silver', *Antiquity* 14, pp. 40–63, at pp. 58–60 (the spoons).

207. O. G. S. Crawford, 'The coins', ibid., pp. 64–7.

208. Ibid., p. 67.

209. Bede, *HE* ii.15; H. Munro Chadwick, 'The Sutton Hoo ship burial VIII: who was he?', *Antiquity* 14 (1940), p. 76–87.

210. Phillips, op. cit., plate XXVIIb. and pp. 168–9. As many as nine horns and nine bowls found together.

211. Chadwick's conclusion: p. 87. For arguments for a later date on the evidence of the coins, see C. F. C. Hawkes, 'Sutton Hoo, twenty-five years after', *Antiquity* 39 (1964), pp. 252–6.

212. W. F. Grimes, 'Salvaging the finds', *Antiquity* 14 (1940), pp. 67–75.

213. *Documents on German Foreign Policy Series D*, II: *Germany and Czechoslovakia 1937–1938* (HMSO, 1950), p. 420.

FURTHER READING

C. R. C. Alberry, *A Manichaean Psalm-Book*, Part II (Stuttgart, 1938).

M. Avi Yonah, *The Jews in Palestine* (Oxford: Blackwell, 1976).

A. Berthier *et al.*, *Les vestiges du christianisime antique dans la Numidie centrale* (Algiers, 1942).

J. Carcopino, 'La fin du Maroc romain', *MEFR* 57 (1940), pp. 349–448.

P. Cayrel, 'Une basilique donatiste de Numidie', *MEFR* 51 (1934), pp. 114–42.

J. W. Crowfoot, *Gerasa, the City of the Decapolis* (New Haven, 1938).

J. W. Crowfoot, 'The Christian basilica in Palestine', *Atti* IV. 1, p. 328.

S. Guyer, 'Les édifices à coupole de l'Orient', *Atti* IV. 2, pp. 3ff.

T. D. Kendrick, 'The British hanging bowls', *Antiquity* 6 (1932), pp. 161–84.

T. M. Matthews, *The Clash of Gods: A Reinterpretation of Early Christian Art* (Princeton University Press, 1993).

V. E. Nash Williams, 'Some early Welsh Christian monuments', *AJ* 19 (1939), pp. 147–56.

H. J. Polotsky, 'Abriss des manichäischen Systems' in Pauly–Wissowa, *Realencyclopädie der classischen Wissenschaft*, Suppl. 6, pp. 241–72.

P. Romanelli, 'La basilica cristiana nella Africa settentrionale italiana', *Atti* IV.1, pp. 245–89.

C. Schmidt, 'Ein Mani Fund in Aegypten', *SBAW* (1933), pp. 4–81.

P. Styger, *Die römische Katakomben* (Berlin, 1933).

E. L. Sukenik, *The Ancient Synagogue of Beth-Alpha* (OUP, 1932).

R. E. M. Wheeler, *Maiden Castle, Dorset* (Society of Antiquaries Reports of the Research Committee 12; OUP, 1943).

R. E. M. and T. V. Wheeler, *Report on the Excavation of the Prehistoric, Roman and Post-Roman Site in Lydney Park, Gloucestershire* (Society of Antiquaries Reports of the Research Committee 9; OUP, 1932).

L. Michael White, *Building God's House in the Roman World* (Baltimore/London: Johns Hopkins University Press, 1990).

Various authors, *Africa Romana* (Istituto di Studi romani; Milan: Hoepli, 1935).

Dura Europos, Preliminary Reports (1929–38) and *Final Reports* (1953–58), ed. P. V. C. Baur, M. I. Rostovtzev and A. R. Bellinger (Yale University Press).

'Sutton Hoo, preliminary report', *Antiquity* 14 (1940), March issue.

Excavations on the Great Palace in Constantinople: G. Brett, W. J. Macaulay and B. K. Stevenson, *The Great Palace of the Byzantine Emperors (First Report)* (OUP, 1947).

II

The great discoveries,
1940–1960

Some of Carl Schmidt's treasures were to fall victim to the pitiless character of the war in the east, sharing the fate of much of Berlin itself. In North Africa and Italy, however, the opposing forces were able to maintain an element of civilized conduct, and neither wished to incur the reproach of needless destruction of antiquities. On the German side the Afrika Corps resisted temptation to destroy these on its final retreat from Cyrenaica and Tripolitania after El Alamein.[1] In Italy, Rome was evacuated as an open city (4 and 5 June I944), Florence similarly (though not the open spaces immediately surrounding the city, which were heavily mined) on II August, and Siena declared a 'hospital city', a large Red Cross being painted at the entrance of the piazza. At Ravenna the mosaics in San Vitale and San Apollinare Nuovo had been protected so far as possible from the effects of blast by layers of silver tinfoil.[2] As one German officer remarked to the writer, warfare in Italy 'was like trying to fight in an antique shop'.

In Cyrenaica and Tripolitania the Italian archaeologists had done their best to safeguard the Roman and Byzantine ruins excavated between the wars. Forty-six specialists together with women assistants under Dr Gennaro Pesce, Chief Inspector of Antiquities, put themselves at Brigadier Mortimer Wheeler's disposal after the fall of Tripoli on 16 January 1943. Archaeology, not least the safeguarding of the magnificent early Christian remains in Cyrene, Leptis Magna, Sabratha and Tripoli (Oea), were lucky to have Wheeler in the Eighth Army. One divisional commander was reported to have said 'What would it matter if the whole of these blank ruins were pushed into the sea?'[3] On 2 February, Wheeler published a series of detailed regulations safeguarding the antiquities in Leptis, Sabratha and Tripoli.[4] He was also able to appoint Major John Ward Perkins, long-time friend and later, in 1946, Director of the British School at Rome, as his executive officer to see that the regulations were carried out. With two other officers, C. G. C. Hyslop and Denis Haynes, he began to lay the foundations for successful British work, particularly on the Byzantine remains in Tripolitania (Libya) and Cyrenaica in the decade after the war.

The details of this work as well as the immense progress of archaeological research as it affected Christian antiquities will be reserved to another chapter. Here we discuss four major finds made in the 1940s and 1950s that have increased in contrasting ways our understanding of the history of the early Church and the outlook of its members. The excavations beneath the Vatican from 1940 to 1949 and from 1952 onwards, spurred on in the hope of finding the bones of St Peter, were uniquely significant in themselves, but also the incentive they gave to discussion of the history of Christianity in Rome that has lasted for decades. In addition to this 'set-piece' excavation, continuously rising standard of education and awareness of the value (not least monetary) of antiquities resulted in the preservation of material that would otherwise have been destroyed or lost. Workmen clearing a cave at Toura outside Cairo, needed for storing ammunition, finding a cache of papyri that included lost works of Origen and Didymus the Blind; a shepherd boy following a goat into a hole in rocky cliffs overlooking the Dead Sea at Qumran and finding instead the Isaiah Scroll; peasants coming upon and breaking a large storage pot in an ancient cemetery near Nag Hammadi in Upper Egypt and deciding (after some hesitation) to preserve its Gnostic manuscript contents: these discoveries have changed many perspectives relating to the history of heresy and orthodoxy in the first Christian centuries.

A. We start chronologically with the *excavations under St. Peter's*. Pope Pius XI died on 22 February 1939. Before he became Pope and during his pontificate he had shown more than usual interest in the scholarly study of Christian antiquities, particularly in Rome. Not surprisingly, therefore, his request to be buried in the *sacre grotte* or crypt of St Peter's was respected.[5] Preparations for his tomb were to provide an opportunity to turn this crypt into a spacious lower church; but work had hardly begun when workmen hit obstructions. Barely 20 cm below the existing floor they encountered, first, traces of the pavement of Constantine's church, and immediately below this, sarcophagi that had been sunk through its floor. More exciting even, they hit the top of a large tiled structure that proved to be the upper part of the façade of a pagan

Roman mausoleum, apparently complete except that part of the pediment and crown of the vault had been sliced off by Constantine's builders. These had then filled the interior with earth to make a level floor on which the pavement of the basilica could be laid. Pope Pius XII ordered as complete an excavation of the area as compatible with the safety of the church. There was to be scientific investigation of what lay below the papal altar and *confessio* down to virgin soil, to test among other things the truth of the tradition of the apostle's burial-place.[6] It was a courageous move.

The excavation itself proved to be extremely hazardous. The Constantinian basilica begun *c*. 322 and finished *c*. 349 had been built into the slope of the *Mons Vaticanus* and had required thorough scarping and levelling, and the destruction of any buildings, including the cemetery, that stood in the way. About one million cubic feet of earth had been displaced before a level platform had been created capable of sustaining the thrust of the foundations on which Constantine's massive church was built. The reverse process involved clearing about one quarter of the dumped earth, working 30ft under the floor of St Peter's, and taking steps to shore up and make safe the remaining foundations and floor level of the Constantinian church. Professor Iosi and his three companion directors, Apollonj-Ghetti, Kirschbaum and Ferrua, with their team of *Sampietrini* (hereditary workmen of the Vatican) handled these conditions with great ability and success. Though some of their work may be criticized in detail they preserved the splendidly built mausolea of the pagan cemetery[7] and also the shrine, constructed at a spot which Christians from the latter part of the second century onwards believed had a special connection with the apostle.

The writer was privileged to see part of the excavations for himself, accompanied by Professor Iosi, on 12 August 1944. By then the mausolea aligned north of the Via Cornelia beneath the nave of the Constantinian church had been cleared. One entered the excavation, as Toynbee and Ward Perkins have described, through a narrow opening built into one of the great foundations of Constantine's basilica.[8] In a moment one came face to face with the magnificent façade of Tomb D. This looked roughly south across a gallery running east to west some 3 m wide, lined on each side by house-tombs, most erected between *c*. 120 and the end of the second century; but used until *c*. 320. Tomb D was particularly impressive. The evenly laid courses of deep red bricks of the exterior were so finely jointed that they looked as though they had been set only yesterday. A rectangular travertine doorway with a lintel had been placed in the middle of the façade, above which was a white marble plaque with a space unfilled, for the name of the owner. Over this, part of the gable coping that formed the top of the tomb had survived.[9] It had been a family mausoleum, in many respects reminiscent of modern equivalents in cemeteries of Mediterranean countries.

The majority of the families whose memories and sometimes whose bodies were preserved were wealthy freedmen or their immediate descendants, and sometimes their patrons. Most of the names included a tell-tale Greek *cognomen* (third name) such as Quintus Marcius Hermes, buried with his wife in Tomb Φ directly opposite Tomb D. Some of the owners were very rich, such as Ostorius Euhodianus who embalmed his daughter Ostoria Chelidon in her coffin, and wrapped her in purple, covered with a fine veil of gold and adorned with a golden bracelet weighing 75 grammes.[10] Employment in accounting and secretarial work in the public services would seem to have been their principal, very profitable, occupations.

The interiors of the tombs were often as decorated as the exteriors were severe. Red and white roses were painted on the ceiling of an entrance arch; there were cupids bearing garlands, and a red panther chasing a red deer, perhaps symbolic of pursuing death; there were vine tendrils and ivy, often associated on mosaics in Roman Africa with the destruction of the power of the evil eye. Even in their sorrow many of the owners saw death in terms of hope. There was Flavius Agricola's cheerful Epicurean acceptance of fate that had so angered the Pope (see above, pp. 16–17); the painting of Silenus on the tomb of the Marcii[11] suggesting a joyful expectancy of the Beyond; and the judgement of Paris, an allegory of the soul choosing beauty and therefore immortality. Lucifer and Hesperus were painted on the walls of another tomb, symbolized as the morning and evening star, the dawn and eve of human life, or rebirth after death.[12] Most of the idealized portraits that adorned the marble sarcophagi would have hoped that just dealing, represented by a painting of a steward doing his accounts, would be rewarded hereafter.[13]

But as we have seen elsewhere, by the mid-third century Christianity was beginning to replace or absorb the previously well-tried guides of the soul in its progress to eternity. To the Christian burial in the Tomb of the Egyptians, guarded by a somewhat sombre wall-painting of the hawk-headed god[14] Horus, was added the striking testimony in a small tomb belonging to the family of the Julii.[15] There in a mosaic covering the ceiling, amid a veritable forest of apotropaic vine-scrolls on an orange background was a beardless male figure standing in a chariot, one arm raised, the other supporting a globe. It was Helios, or the sun god but with a difference, for behind his head the rays of the sun formed a cross, while the figure itself faced front, his hand raised as though to bless. Pagan symbolism was being adapted to give new, Christian meanings, as elsewhere in Roman cemeteries at this time.[16]

Christian or not, the tomb was not spared by Constantine's workmen. The basilica in honour of St Peter was being built on the same general plan as the emperor's great churches in Palestine. It was basilican in form, with five naves, preceded by a wide square open courtyard with a fountain in the middle. As in Palestinian churches the difficulty of the site was compensated by the aim of placing the focal point of the church over one particular spot. This, many Roman Christians had believed, was uniquely connected with the apostle.

How far were their ideas to be proved right? Hans Lietzmann's study of the literary and available archaeological evidence had convinced him that the tradition of Peter's stay and martyrdom in Rome was in all probability well founded.[17] The excavation of the cult-centre on the Via Appia in honour of the two apostles had strengthened this probability; for who, it could be asked, would inscribe such fervent invocations of the apostles on the walls of the centre if no firm tradition of their presence in Rome had existed? Yet doubts remained.[18] The last historical mention of St Peter is in 54 when Paul refers to his ministry in his first letter to the Corinthians (1 Cor 9:5). Paul does not mention him again, neither in his letter to the Romans, nor is Peter mentioned among his associates who send greetings from Rome to Colossae *c.* AD 60, while 1 Peter, supposedly written by the apostle in Rome, is not included in the Muratorian canon listing the Scriptures acknowledged by the Church in Rome *c.* AD 190. There are, however, numerous quotations from it by Polycarp of Smyrna in his letter to the Church at Philippi written *c.* 107, which suggests an origin in the province of Asia.[19] Nonetheless, the Church tradition for Peter's and Paul's presence and death in Rome is consistent, extending back to the Roman writer of *1 Clement* to the Church at Corinth *c.* 95–100,[20] and it remained so.[21] How far would the excavation solve the problem?

The writer did not see this part of the excavation. Indeed, the secret of what was found in the eastward continuation of the cemetery extending beneath the high altar of St Peter's was closely guarded until December 1951. Then on 19 December Apollonj Ghetti, Ferrua, Iosi and Kirschbaum delivered their joint two-volume official report of the excavations 1940–49 to Pius XII. Toynbee and Ward Perkins based their study on this.

Working conditions had been even more difficult than under the nave, not least because of the many alterations that had taken place in that area over the centuries. Nonetheless, the report, achievement though it was, suffered from two major omissions. First, there were no stratigraphical sections that would have allowed readers to understand the sequence of levels and character of the disturbances of earth surrounding any tombs that were found, and secondly, no firm bases existed for the accurate dating of pottery and small objects that Roman *fossores* could have dropped during their work.[22]

Nonetheless the excavators were able to establish that the object which Constantine aimed at preserving for veneration was a small niched structure, known as the Aedicula. This had been built into the 'Red Wall', a relatively narrow wall 45 m thick that formed the eastern boundary of a family tomb and an alley-way ending in steps (the Clivus) that gave access to this tomb and its neighbour. The Aedicula was contemporary with the Red Wall, which in its turn had been built *c.* 160.[23] It consisted of three niches built one on top of the other, two being above ground level, the third in some sense an after-thought dug into the Red Wall below ground. The gash in the wall was roughly triangular in shape, suggesting the attempted insertion or extraction of a tiled penthouse grave at this spot. Anyone approaching the Aedicula across a small open yard in front of it would have seen a structure like a memorial shrine, whose bottom part (1.40 m high and 0.72 m wide) was slightly larger than the top, and was separated from it by a single projecting slab of travertine. The shallow central recesses in each part were flanked by small columns. A slab of travertine also projected at ground level about one metre in front of the lower niche.[24] At some period a hole had been made in this, allowing access to the grave below.

This was without doubt the *tropaion* mentioned by the Roman presbyter Gaius *c.* 190, in honour of the apostles (i.e. both Peter and Paul) who were 'both martyred at the same time and who founded this (Roman) Church'.[25] Any visitor could see for himself a small shrine similar to others erected later at Salona.[26]

Gaius appears to have believed that this *tropaion* had been erected at the spot where Peter had been martyred. Though the shrine dated from the period of Marcus Aurelius as Caesar (147–161) the part of the cemetery in which the Red Wall stood had been used for a long time for burials of a much poorer type. These consisted of a stone or tile-lined cist with a penthouse tiled roof. There were five such burials in the immediate vicinity of the Aedicula. The only one for which an approximate date could be given was not older than the reign of Vespasian (69–79), and could be later.[27] This would be a decade too late for St Peter's burial. However, at one point the foundations of the Red Wall were much shallower, leaving an 'island' of earth on either side of which the foundations had been dug more deeply. As Toynbee and Ward Perkins point out, the hypothesis of a pre-existing grave would offer a reasonable explanation. Neither the Christians nor the owner of the family tomb behind the Aedicula would want to disturb it.[28] The Christians could have accepted this unnamed grave as that of the apostle and erected their shrine over the spot. Some bones were indeed found, but of what sex, or even if they were human, was not disclosed at the time.[29]

The question of Peter's tomb could not be settled one way or another. All that could be said was that by *c.* 160, nearly a century after his supposed death, Christians in Rome associated this small area with his martyrdom. However, in the autumn of 1950 another factor, in no way connected with archaeology, was emerging. On 1 November, Pius XII defined the doctrine of the Assumption of the Virgin in the decree *Munificentissmus Deus*, stopping short at declaring the Virgin 'Co-Redemptress', but asserting that 'having completed her earthly life she was in body and soul assumed into heavenly glory'. Next month, on 24 December, the Pope answered the question whether Peter's tomb had really been found, 'to this question the answer is beyond all doubt, Yes. The tomb of the Prince of the Apostles has been found.'[30] It is difficult to dissociate these two events entirely. A miracle, in the likely view of Pope Pius, had confirmed the new definition, just as the miracle of the appearance of the Virgin to Bernadette Soubirous at Lourdes in 1858 had underpinned the credibility of Pius IX's pronouncement of the doctrine of the Immaculate Conception three and a half years before. Pius XII's pronouncement made it difficult for any Italian scholar working on the site to disagree.

This must be borne in mind when assessing the second campaign of excavations which began in 1952, and will always be associated with Professor Margherita Guarducci. Guarducci never doubted that 'the great news (of the discovery of St Peter's tomb) corresponded with the truth',[31] and she believed that her discoveries with her associates M. Prandi and D. Mustilli filled in 'various disquieting gaps', including the most significant, that the name of the apostle himself was nowhere associated with the Aedicula.[32] This contrasted with the numerous invocations of St Peter and St Paul in graffiti found on the walls of the cult-centre on the Appian Way.[33]

The claim she made for herself in a short article (under 'Vatican') in the *Encyclopedia of the Early Church* may be quoted. 'But it fell to me alone to fill those gaps. Thus, I recognised the name Peter both on wall "g" (a wall running perpendicular to the Red Wall) and in a mausoleum in the necropolis (mausoleum of the Valerii). I completely deciphered the graffiti on wall "g" which were revealed as an outstanding example of mystical cryptography and a wonderful page of Christian spirituality (with among other things, numerous acclamations of the victory of Christ, Peter and Mary). I traced and identified the surviving relics of Peter, which through a set of strange but explicable happenings had escaped the excavators of 1940–1949 and demonstrated that they had been transferred from the earth tomb under the "trophaeum of Gaius" to the specially prepared resting-place (*loculus*) inside wall "g". I attained certainty in the identification of the relics in 1964.'[34] Pope Paul VI agreed with her, and announced the identification in 1968. Nearly thirty years later it may not be so easy to accept all Guarducci's findings. She certainly had luck and showed acute observation but already in 1955 Toynbee and Ward Perkins questioned the relevance of the inscription she had copied in the central niche in the north wall of the tomb of the Valerii, traced first in red lead and then partially retraced in charcoal.[35] Guarducci read 'Petrus roga Christus Iesus pro sanctis hominibus Chrestianis ad corpus tuum sepultis' (Peter, pray Christ Jesus for the holy Christian men buried near your body). Above was a rough drawing of a head and some indistinct black lines thought to be a head of Christ accompanied by a phoenix, the symbol of resurrection. These soon became illegible. Guarducci's interpretation was quickly challenged. At the least impossible it could have been a graffito scrawled by one of the Constantinian workmen, and hence have little bearing on the presence or not of St Peter's grave.

Doubts were also raised concerning Guarducci's interpretation of the welter of graffiti seen by her, inscribed in the plaster on the north side of wall 'g' above the *loculus* over a number of years. This wall had been built perpendicular to the Red Wall about AD 250, ostensibly to stabilize it after a fissure had appeared on the north side of the shrine. The new wall damaged this side of the shrine, damage which was covered up by facing the walls with marble while the open space in front of the shrine was now paved with mosaic. Wall 'g' became a centre of attraction. Pilgrims and visitors left a profusion of graffiti on its plastered surface mainly commemorating deceased relatives. Though some may be earlier (*c.* 290 onwards), most date from the period between the Peace of the Church, following Constantine's victory over Maxentius in 312, and the building of the basilica replacing the shrine *c.* 322, a time when the ☧ had become a recognized Christian symbol and Latin had finally replaced Greek as the language of Roman (and other Western) Christians. 'Nicasi vibas in ☧' or 'Gaudentius vibatis in ☧' are typical graffiti.[36] Of particular interst is the graffito '[In?] hoc vin[ce]' (with this conquer)[37] above a ☧ which echoes Eusebius' account of Constantine's vision in the late afternoon of the day before the decisive battle with Maxentius (i.e. 27 October 312): while the day was already fading he had seen a shining cross in the sky, more brilliant than the sun, accompanied by the words 'with this conquer' (*Life* i.28). This shows that by *c.* 320 the account of Constantine's experience recorded later by Eusebius was already current – another example of an archaeological find supporting information from a literary source. These readings are certain and perhaps one may add from the Red Wall, a faintly traced Πετ(ρος) εν(ι) for ενεστι = 'Peter (is) in (here)'?[38] But this somewhat arcane graffito is the only possible direct reference to the apostle among a multitude of graffiti and squiggles left by Christian visitors to the area of the shrine at a time when the cult of martyrs was growing in popularity. On the walls of the cult-centre on the Appian Way there were very numerous (over 200 recognizable)[39] invocations to Peter and Paul by name at this time. Given the confined space (less than 1 metre square) for writing it may be that some of the lines and squiggles had a cryptic reference to Peter and his keys,[40] but this would be hard to prove. Christians had long used abbreviations to denote the *nomina sacra* (names relating to the Godhead) inherited from the Jews,[41] and extended to include specifically Christian terminology. Secret language, however, was more in keeping with Qumran[42] or Gnosticism than orthodox practice, and after 312 there would be little need for it. The existence, between *c.* 290 and 320, of an organized system of cryptography in use among the Christians of Rome to hide the secrets of their faith from persecutors and uninitiated remains speculative.

Similarly the suggestion that 'Christ, Peter and Mary are therefore linked together'[43] on the basis of the appearance of the name Maria among those of the deceased encounters the difficulty that Maria was not an uncommon name among Western Christians; no less than 39 examples are listed by Diehl.[44] Their presence among the graffiti left by the dedicants gives no sure indication of a cult of the Virgin in third- and fourth-century Rome.

Guarducci believed that Peter was buried in a simple grave over which the *tropaion* was raised, and that subsequently his relics were transferred to a worthier resting-place in the form of a small marble cist (*loculus*) enclosed within wall 'g' below the graffiti. The transfer would have had to take place after *c.* 250 when wall 'g' was built, but that was the time when the Appian cult-centre was beginning to come into prominence. There is a problem too, of the bones themselves found reburied below the lowest niche in the Red Wall. Supposing Peter had met his fate in the circus nearby during the Neronian persecution of AD 64, what chance would Christians have had of securing his body for burial among those of other criminals destined for the Tiber or a common grave?[45] The contamination of human bones from the spot with those of domestic animals suggests that even though the site was used occasionally for burials, there was a long period, extending down to the middle of the second century, when it was not considered of special sanctity. Altogether, the suggestion that between 258 and 320 the apostle's bones were divided between three separate resting-places, i.e. below niche '1', in the reliquary in wall 'g', and at the Appian cult-centre, stretches credence.[46] Research has been made less easy by the rifling of the reliquary, perhaps by the Visigoths in 547–552,[47] and not least by the removal of bones from below niche '1' during the first period of excavation without proper record.

All in all Guarducci's exhaustive investigations still leave the earliest visible memorial to the two apostles as the 'Gaius trophy', the shrine in the Red Wall erected *c.* 160. This, however, raises an additional question, why so sacred a spot was not chosen for the site of the catacomb of the Popes, or even why, if the actual area was not available, the successive Popes were not buried nearby. There is also the long interval of nearly a century between *c.* 190 and *c.* 290 when the shrine seems to have attracted little attention. This was a critical time for the emergence of monarchical episcopacy and the Petrine tradition at Rome. The shrine was kept in good order, but throngs of visitors would soon have worn away the mosaic pavement laid *c.* 250 in front of it. There are no signs reported of patching or repairs. Then, *c.* 290 there is an upsurge of interest, which no doubt influenced Constantine's choice of the site for his basilica in honour of St Peter, just as the caves and grottoes in Palestine associated by legend with Jesus' birth, crucifixion, and ascension three centuries before, were chosen as the sites of commemorative churches. At Rome, the tomb itself was not buried beneath the altar of the church, but encased in marble, to stand above the floor on the architectural focus of the building in a similar position to the shrine in the church of the Holy Sepulchre.[48] We do not know why in the years immediately following Constantine's victory over Maxentius wall 'g' and its cavity became so attractive to pilgrims. Lactantius, our best authority for that period, is silent.

Let us, however, leave the situation as it appeared to Eusebius, another contemporary, writing some twenty years later *c.* 333, near the end of Constantine's reign. He wrote of Peter.[49] 'He is known throughout the world, even in the western countries, and his memory among the Romans is still more alive than the memory of all those who lived before him: so much so that he is honoured with a splendid tomb overlooking the city. To this tomb, countless crowds come from all parts of the Roman empire as to a great sanctuary and temple of God.' This was high praise from one whose veneration for Holy Places was never more than lukewarm.[50]

B. *Toura* presents altogether fewer difficulties, and those are connected mainly with questions whether all the manuscripts have survived for study. The site was some 10 km south of Cairo and the find was made, as already mentioned, early in August 1941 by one of the workmen who was clearing out a large cavern needed by the Eighth Army as an ammunition store. The cavern had once formed part of a quarry-area from which granite had been mined to be shaped into monuments in the time of the Pharaohs. The deposit of manuscripts had been placed against a wall of the cavern and covered with loose rubble as if hidden in a hurry. The workman immediately informed his foreman, who is said to have reported the find to the police who safeguarded it. However, it seems certain that some documents fell into the hands of dealers and traffickers whose unskilled attempts to divide their spoil caused considerable damage to the manuscripts.[51]

These latter consisted of codices containing the works of Origen and Didymus the Blind (*c.* 390) respectively. Since both theologians had been condemned at the Fifth General Council in 553, a reasonable suggestion would be that the deposit was hidden by a supporter who, however, never had the chance of retrieving it. Didymus' works included commentaries on the Books of Genesis, Job, and Zechariah. Origen's were contained in another codex: Books i and ii of *Contra Celsum* (corrupted to the extent that they could be students' notes), Books 5 and 6 of a 15-book *Commentary on Romans*, the opening section of an address on the Pasch,[52] a commentary on 1 Samuel 28 (the witch of Endor, the subect of a bitter rejoinder by Eustathius of Antioch, written post-311),[53] and, most interesting of all, the *Dialogue with Heracleides*, a hitherto unknown work which throws new light on the personality as well as the ideas of Origen. The passage from *On the Pasch* shows how Origen was in the habit of treating his audience like students. 'Let us start, brethren, with the etymology of the word Pasch',[54] he begins, as he might to a class. Heracleides was to be given Origen's full measure of condescension.[55]

The issue which brought Origen into an encounter with Bishop Heracleides was probably Monarchianism and the place may have been Bosra, the capital of the Roman province of Arabia. Monarchianism, as we know from Eusebius, was a burning issue at this time (*c.* 240) and nowhere more than in Arabia. The question for Christian theologians in the third century was how to understand the relations of God and Christ within the Godhead. In his *First Apology* written *c.* 155, the apologist Justin Martyr had emphasized the independent being (*hypostasis*) of the Son in relation to the Father. This had provoked a strong reaction among those who held that this belief was incompatible with monotheism. The critics, however, quickly separated into two opposing camps. Some claimed Jesus Christ was God without qualification, in which case if Christ suffered then so did God, suffering with Christ on the cross. The other party believed that Christ was a man like other men, but one in whom the Spirit dwelt to a unique degree. He was not God, but the greatest of all the prophets and adopted on his death into the Godhead. Neither system was satisfactory, but it would seem that the first, known in the East as Sabellianism after its Libyan exponent Sabellius (*c.* 220), was the form most threatening to the unity of the Church in Arabia. Origen loathed both forms of Monarchianism and had travelled to that province to controvert its upholders.[56] His dialogue with Heracleides that took place before not only clergy, but lay Christians also, may have formed part of his campaign and be placed *c.* 244–249.

It is clear from the *Dialogue* that Monarchianism was the enemy.[57] From the outset he has Heracleides wriggling. The bishop attempts to head off criticisms by bringing forward a creed (probably the creed of his Church) and reciting it. The creed accepted the Johannine Logos – 'I believe what the sacred Scriptures say: In the beginning was the Word ... ', followed by unexceptionable statements: 'we believe that Christ took flesh, that he was born, that he went up to heaven in the flesh in which he rose again, that he is sitting at the right hand of the Father, and thence he shall come to judge both the living, and the dead, being God and man.'[58] Origen was not satisfied. 'I charge you, Father Heracleides, "God is the almighty, the uncreated, the supreme God who made all things". Do you hold this doctrine?' Heracleides agreed, but Origen's aim was to force Heracleides to accept that understanding of the Godhead began with an acceptance of a clear distinction between God the Father and Christ ('Is the Son distinct from the Father?', he asks), even to the extent of believing in two Gods, though they formed a unity. Heracleides eventually acknowledged the existence of 'two Gods', though with the saving phrase, 'but the power is one'.

On the way Origen treats the bishop like an ignoramus. 'You do not appear to have answered my question. Explain what you mean; for perhaps I have failed to follow you. Is the Father God?'[59] No wonder Heracleides' colleagues took offence and Origen was forced into a long explanation. The debate moved on to the nature of the soul, whether or not it had blood, i.e. was in some sense bodily. Origen tried to grapple with the text 'Ye shall not eat the soul with the flesh' (Lev 17:11ff.; Deut 12:23), explaining that this was an aspect of a larger problem, that regarding the role of the 'inner man' made in the image of God. The audience became restive. Origen also had had enough. He turned on them. 'These questions are highly delicate. We need hearers who have an acute understanding. I therefore, charge those who listen to pay heed to themselves lest they should make me liable to the accusation of casting holy things to the dogs, shameless souls who think of nothing else but fornication and abuse.'[60] So it went on, two full pages of the English text, and that, said Origen, when he had regained some self-control, was only an introduction. 'To speak makes me embarrassed and not to speak makes me embarrassed'; but finally he attempts to find answers derived from scriptural texts for the relations between the outward appearance and inner soul of man. He had hardly finished when he is stung again, when one of his hearers, Bishop Demetrius, tells a colleague who had just come in: 'Brother Origen teaches that the soul is immortal' (i.e. resurrection was not bodily). Origen protests. He will not reply with reference to the Greeks (i.e. Platonists) but from 'meanings as found in the divine Scripture'.

In the end, he sums up what must have been a difficult experience with a ringing defence of the human will. Through its right use, 'let us take up eternal life. Let us take up that which depends on our decision. God does not give it us. He sets it before us ... It is in our power to stretch out our hand, to do good works and to lay hold on life and deposit in our soul.'[61] Free will was Christ's gift to all: nothing could be further from Augustine's ideas two centuries later, and define more clearly the different outlooks of Eastern and Western Christians towards free will and grace. This unscripted discussion, found by chance, shows Origen as he really was. There is, on the one hand, the subtle theologian sure of his ground, immensely learned, who knew practically the whole Bible by heart and could quote from any part at will. There is also the Platonist who may have disliked 'the Greeks' but could not dispense with an outright philosophical understanding of Scripture. On the other hand, there was the pedant and the bore, harassing those less competent than himself and trying his audience beyond limits of endurance; finally however, we see the idealist and missionary; the man of the Church who respected the Rule of Faith and upheld its unity, but also believed Christianity to be the highest form of wisdom, sought by toil and meditation, that enabled each individual to 'be saved in all things', and 'become one with the God of the universe and his only-begotten Son'.[62]

C. *Nag Hammadi*. The Toura ammunition store served its purpose. The victory of the Commonwealth forces at El Alamein (23 October to 5 November 1942) removed any Axis threat to Cairo. The inhabitants of the Nile valley could now live their lives in peace. Three hundred miles south of the Egyptian capital, where the Nile bends sharply towards the east, were a group of ancient sites associated with the early development of the monastic movement through Pachomius *c*. (285–346). His monastery at Chenoboskion (el Qasr) was on the right bank of the river, and three miles away was a cemetery contemporary with it. The site, however, was to take its name from the modern village of Nag Hammadi on the opposite bank. It was on the site of the cemetery, however, that late in 1945, some peasants were digging for *sebakh*, the rich loam deposited by the river floods, but sometimes marking ancient occupation, and used as fertilizer. One of the group, Muhammed Ali el Sannam, came upon a large storage pot lying exposed at the base of a boulder. Curious, he broke it only to find that instead of hoped for gold or treasure there appeared twelve leather-bound codices, on average 25 cm high and 15 cm broad. Ali and his brother decided to take them back to their village.[63] What happened next is confusing, but it seems that the el Sannam clan was involved in a blood feud with another, more powerful family in the village. Learning that the books were Christian and fearing prolonged harassment from the suspicious and hostile neighbours, they deposited their haul with the local Coptic priest. It needed, however, the latter's educated brother-in-law Raghib before the potential value of the codices was recognized. Raghib took one (codex III) to Cairo and showed it to a Coptic friend who took it to the Department of Antiquities. At length, on 4 October 1946 it was acquired by the Coptic Museum and Raghib received £250. Meantime unfortunate events in Ali's village had resulted in his wife burning much of one of the codices (XII) in her oven thinking it was the source of the family's continued ill luck. Others, however, escaped and were now bought up by local merchants at derisory prices. As early as March 1946 some were finding their way into the hands of antiquities dealers in Cairo.[64]

The ensuing saga was to extend over thirty years until 1977 when J. M. Robinson, Director of the Institute for Antiquity and Christianity at Claremont Graduate School in California, published in English the twelve codices and eight pages of a thirteenth that was found detached and tucked into the cover of codex VI. Almost simultaneously, French and German editions of the Coptic library of Nag Hammadi followed. Thus the entire surviving collection of 52 Gnostic or Gnostic-orientated writings, consisting of more than 1,000 large leaves, became available to scholars and general readers alike.

A generation had elapsed between discovery and full publication. Why?[65] First, the codices had very soon become dispersed among numerous antiquities dealers, and this, combined with the discovery of the more prestigious Dead Sea Scrolls in 1947, delayed immediate assessment of their true significance. Secondly, the rapidly changing complexion of Egyptian governments between 1947 and 1954 prevented the Coptic Museum acquiring the funds necessary to buy out the dealers. Thirdly, and perhaps most tragically, the young French scholar Jean Doresse, who realized the importance of the find as soon as he saw the first codex in September 1947, did not possess the academic 'clout' needed for pushing the discovery to the centre of attention and keeping it there. His transfer to Ethiopia for archaeological work there was a disaster for scholarship. Finally, it must be said, that reluctance or inability of national institutions and universities to co-operate, not least in Britain where there had been a leading interest in Coptic scholarship, prevented the gap left by Doresse's departure from being adequately filled. These factors, along with a desire by some scholars to monopolize what was available for study, allowed the delays to accumulate to preposterous proportions.

At first, however, few could have foreseen the trouble to come. Togo Mina, the Director of the Coptic Museum, contacted Doresse and his wife Marianne, whom he had known as students at the Ecole Normale. Doresse was lecturing in Paris on Coptic Gnostic texts and in September 1947 visited Cairo, sponsored by the Institut français d'Archéologie orientale au Caire. Finding himself prevented from visiting the site of Pachomius' monastery at Chenoboskion, owing to an outbreak of cholera in the area, he visited Togo Mina at the Coptic Museum. The latter opened a drawer in his desk and showed the astonished Doresse a book cover enclosing pages of papyrus covered with Coptic writing. It did not take Doresse long to see that he was gazing on hitherto unknown Coptic texts.[66]

Doresse's lectures had been starved of material. At that moment only the two codices included in the Codex Bruce and Codex Askew had been edited. (See above, p. 145.) Another four Coptic texts obtained by Dr Rheinhardt for Berlin in 1896 and handed to Carl Schmidt for publication had not been published before Schmidt died in 1938. Eventually, the Gnostic texts they contained, the *Gospel of Mary*, the *Apocryphon* (secret teaching) *of John*, the *Sophia* (Wisdom) *of Jesus Christ* and the *Acts of Peter*, were published by the Austrian scholar Walter Till, in 1955.[67] Up to that time scholars still had to rely for their study of Gnosticism almost exclusively on the works of their opponents, Irenaeus, Hippolytus, Tertullian, and in the late fourth century Epiphanius.

What Doresse saw would change this immediately. The packet contained five treatises, the *Apocryphon of John*, the *Gospel of the Egyptians*, the *Dialogue of the Saviour* (with his disciples, Mary and Mariamne), *Eugnostos the Blessed* and the *Sophia of Jesus Christ* (two versions of the same treatise). These added up to 134 pages of text, plus fragments of eighteen further pages.[68] It was a rare moment in the history of Christian archaeology.

In the next few months it seemed that progress towards full publication would be rapid. On 20 February 1948 Professor Henri-Charles Puech, Doresse's supervisor for his doctorate, announced jointly with Doresse at a regular meeting of the Académie des Inscriptions et Belles-Lettres the detailed discovery of Doresse's codex, emphasized its importance and indicated its possible value in substantiating a link between Gnosticism and Manichaeism.[69] Apart, however, from a brief statement in *Le Monde* of 23 Febuary, followed by the *Manchester*

Guardian, practically nothing was reported. Meantime, Doresse and Togo Mina had been active. In June they had published successive articles in *Vigiliae Christianae*,[70] Doresse's describing and analysing three of the tracts from codices in the Museum's possession. One, the *Wisdom of Jesus Christ*, included questions asked by the disciples to the heavenly Jesus of Gnosticism. 'How was man revealed?' 'how many aeons are there?' or 'how are things themselves produced?'[71] These amply bore out the questing curiosity of the Gnostics to which orthodoxy, represented by Irenaeus and Tertullian, was so strongly opposed.

About the same time Doresse received a packet through the post. It contained photographs of more texts. He was able to return to Cairo and there met Phokion Tano (d. 1972), a Cypriot-born proprietor of an antiquities gallery who was representing the interests of Marika Dattari, daughter of the numismatist. She had bought eight codices from him,[72] and sent photographs to Doresse. Now the codices themselves were produced. Doresse found himself confronted with up to 1,000 pages of papyrus of which 794 seemed to be undamaged. Included was a complete text of the *Gospel of Thomas*, fragments of which had been identified by Grenfell and Hunt at the beginning of the century. There was another Gnostic gospel, the *Gospel of Philip*, liturgical works such as *The Prayer of Thanksgiving*, mystic tracts like the *Discourse on the Eight and the Ninth*, didactic writings such as the *Teaching of Silvanus*, apocalypses such as the *Apocalypse of Peter*, hitherto lost texts such as *Asclepius*, of which only a Latin translation existed, and *Zostrianus*, possibly the Gnostic work criticized by the Neo-Platonist Plotinus in his lectures in Rome *c.* 230.[73] There were also Hermetic writings, indicating a link between the Gnostics and those Egyptians accepting the divine inspiration of the works of Hermes Trismegistus. It was a treasure chest. At the meeting of the Académie des Inscriptions et Belles-Lettres, on 17 June 1949 Doresse himself announced the discovery of nine codices containing 42 hitherto unknown Gnostic texts, emanating possibly from a school of Gnostic copyists in the period 250–350, using both Sahidic and a Thebaid(?) dialect of Coptic. The documents, Doresse had little need to add, were immensely important for the study of religion, philology and literature.[74]

Doresse, however was not destined to enjoy the same good fortune as Johannes Divjak, the young Austrian scholar whose discovery of 30 new letters and memoranda written by Augustine has galvanized Augustinian studies (see below, p. 362). Some enthusiasm was by now awakened. Doresse published another article outlining his new find in the *Vigiliae*[75] and a shorter account in the semi-popular American journal *Archaeology*.[76] Puech himself published a preliminary inventory of the texts in *Coptic Studies in Honor of*

Walter Ewing Crum[77] (1950) but the Coptic Museum lacked the resources to buy the Tano/Dattari codices, though in 1952 these were transferred to the safe keeping of the Museum. International co-operation proved inadequate. Crum's fellow-countrymen still remained on the sidelines.

Meantime, Togo Mina had died (October 1949) and Doresse's luck began to run out. A new but paradoxically less hopeful chapter had begun with Gilles Quispel's book *Gnosis als Weltreligion*, published at Zürich on the basis of lectures given at the C. G. Jung Institute.[78] The appearance of the Jung Institute on the scene and the division of the codices between it and the Coptic Museum was to prove a mixed blessing for the rapid and complete publication of the codices. The story has been told by James Robinson and the detail need not be recorded again here.[79] Suffice it to say that one of the codices had escaped possession by the Coptic Museum, and had been taken out of Egypt by Albert Eïd, a Belgian antiquities dealer who intended to sell it in the United States. He died, however, before he could effect a sale but after much negotiation and haggling, the codex, which comprised most of what became known as 'codex I', was bought in the name of the Jung Institute at Zürich in May 1952. It was designated the 'Jung codex' and displayed at a ceremony in Zürich on 15 November 1953.[80] At the time it contained 100 complete pages – a number of fragments of pages from the codex being in the Tano/Dattari collection – out of a total of about 138. There were four major treatises, the *Apocryphon of James* (a tract expounding 'secret knowledge of the Beyond' addressed to an unknown individual), a *Letter to Rheginos* (a treatise on resurrection), *The Gospel of Truth* (a devotional contemplation on the person and work of Christ), and a *Treatise on the Three Natures* (*Tripartite Tractate*; a long Gnostic account of the origin and history of the universe). This told how the Fall led to the creation of three different human types: the spiritual, the material and those, like the Hebrews, a mixture of both, and finally, how the Saviour would release humanity from death and restore all things.[81]

Quispel had been largely responsible for the purchase. He and Puech were prepared to work together on the codex publication, forming a committee with Till and Antoine Guillaumont, but Puech was anxious that France should retain a leading role in the publication of the whole collection of codices. On the other hand, in a letter written to Puech at the end of 1950, Quispel requested that Doresse should not be included in the publication team.[82] Puech agreed on 7 March 1951. No reason for this extraordinary demand and its acceptance was given. Uneasy though the relations with Quispel were,[83] the two senior scholars with their colleagues combined in the next step which was to publish the text of what proved to be the most important document of all, namely the *Gospel of Thomas*. This had been bound up in a codex (codex II) containing seven tracts, including another copy of *John* and the *Gospel according to Philip* and was housed at the Coptic Museum. In October 1956, members of Puech's committee were in Cairo, within a month of the Suez conflict that was to shut out further co-operation between Egypt and the French and British over the library for years. Togo Mina's successor, Pahor Labib, the Director of the Museum, handed over facsimiles of the *Gospel of Thomas* which he himself had already published.[84] In June 1957, Puech (inevitably!) announced to a meeting of the Académie des Inscriptions et Belles-Lettres the recovery of this text, claiming that he had identified it from fragments as long ago as 1952. His account of the 114 *logia* or sayings of Jesus contained in the gospel played down any connections with the canonical Gospels. He emphasized instead its 'esoteric' character and possible links with Manichaean works. He pointed to an important fact, however, that 'Thomas', whether in the form of the (Gnostic) *Acts of Thomas* or now the *Gospel of Thomas*, appeared to be connected closely with early Christianity in Edessa.[85]

Quispel's lecture in Oxford on 18 September 1957, however, marks the real beginnings of the study of this text. Quispel had been on good terms with the Oxford Faculty of Theology, and in 1955 had shared with Puech and a colleague, W. C. van Unnik, the publication of an analysis of the contents of the Jung codex, which F. L. Cross, Lady Margaret Professor of Divinity, edited. This was to remain for years a standard work on these texts.[86]

Quispel dismissed about half the 'Sayings' as Gnostic and syncretist, perhaps derived from 'The Gospel of the Egyptians' and not important for New Testament and early Christian studies. The other half were a different matter. Comparing some surviving texts of Tatian's *Diatessaron* with the logia (Sayings) in *Thomas*, Quispel was able to demonstrate that Tatian and *Thomas* must in every probability be borrowed from a common source. Similarities were too striking to be an accident. Thus in the Tuscan *Diatessaron* one reads 'He that shall speak a word against the Father it shall be forgiven him'. *Logion* 44 reads 'He that shall blaspheme against the Father it shall be forgiven him'. That the scribes and Pharisees had 'hidden the keys' of knowledge and not merely taken them away (Luke 11:52) could be paralleled in second-century writings such as Justin (*Dialogue with Trypho* 17.4) and Marcion (Tertullian, *Adv. Marcionem* iv.27).'Immense perspectives' were opening up, including the possibility that parts of *Thomas* could be an early Aramaic gospel, composed even before the fall of Jerusalem in 70 (the *Thomas* version of the parable of the vineyard, for instance, ends without vengeance being taken on the murderers of the king's son i.e by Jerusalem's capture)[87] The wildest dreams of those who two generations before had found the first evidence of the existence of *Thomas* at Oxyrhynchus seemed to be fulfilled. (See above, p. 148.)

The publication of the text of *Thomas* and the immediate interest it aroused redoubled demands for the publication of the remainder of the texts. In 1958 Doresse published his own account of the discovery and researches, suggesting that the originators belonged to a Sethian sect of Gnostics whose ideas were allied to those of Egyptian Hermetists (see also p. 281). With some prescience he designated the library 'The Library of Chenoboskion' (i.e. he thought it had a connection with Pachomius' monastery there). His chapter 'Quarante-quatre livres et inédites' betrays profound and justified disappointment.[88]

Meantime at Zürich a publication team had been formed under the leadership of Puech and Quispel and including Jan Zandee of Utrecht and R. McL. Wilson of St Andrews as associates. Exasperation, however, was rising among scholars who were not included. The Belgian scholar Gerard Garitte (soon, however, to be nominated as a member of the International Committee set up in October 1961) commented in *Le Muséon* of 1960 that after fifteen years only 47 out of more than 1,000 pages of manuscript had been published in their original language. The total consisted of 27 pages from the *Gospel of Truth* and 20 from the *Gospel of Thomas*. A mentality akin to that of the *Tour de France* prevailed.[89] Hans Jonas, the veteran Gnostic specialist, was even more scathing. The documents, he wrote in the 1962 issue of the *Journal of Religion*, had been beset by the curse of political roadblocks, litigation, scholarly jealousies that resulted from a craze for 'firstmanship'.[90] The situation was not quite as tragic, for in 1960 German translations of the *Gospel of Philip* and the *Hypostasis of the Archons* (i.e. 'the real being of the Rulers'), both from codex II, had been published in German by Leipoldt and Schenke[91] but it was bad enough. At length in 1961, stung into action by increasingly bad publicity, the Egyptian Ministry of Culture and National Guidance agreed with the General Director of UNESCO (René Maheu) to name a committee to publish and translate all the manuscripts. This at least had the merit of bringing on to the scene able younger scholars, including Martin Krause and Gerard Garitte. But delays continued. Photography was painfully slow, not least because the Egyptian photographers were engaged in recording threatened archaeological remains in Nubia, and not until August 1963 were 423 negatives of facsimiles, rather under half the total, handed to UNESCO. Another three years elapsed before the photography was completed.[92]

Work would probably have progressed at this snail's pace to the end of the century but for the energy of Martin Krause and James Robinson. Krause took advantage of the conference on the origins of Gnosticism held at Messina

TOP
Mortuary chapel at Theveste
(Tebessa)

MIDDLE
Martyr's tomb at
Mechta Zaoura

BOTTOM
Relics beneath the altar
at Mechta Azrou

Kherbet Bahrarous, lintel (as discovered by the author),
Noah's Ark pilaster and engraved fish,
from Oued Rzel, found by André Berthier

in April 1966 to read a paper and propose that the conference should request UNESCO for a statement on its plans for further publication of the texts.[93] The conference itself represented in some ways a step backwards. It was, as its organizer Ugo Bianchi pointed out, a 'Colloquium of historians of religion', and much of the discussion centred on the ideas of the *Religionsgeschichtliche Schule* applied to Gnosticism. There was much debate on how far Zoroastrianism had influenced the Gnostics – 'Gnosticism and the Indo-Iranian world' – and the pre-Christian origins of the movement. These were comparative methods of study, important in themselves but to become increasingly outdated by the evidence of what the Gnostics themselves believed – if only the Nag Hammadi documents could be published![94]

The year 1970 saw the beginning of the final turn of the tide. *The Gospel of Thomas* had shown the riches to be uncovered in the codices. The Congress of the International Association for the Study of Religions in Stockholm in August 1970 added urgency to the demand for their publication.[96] In December the International committee met and at last decided on a plan of action. The missing fragments of the original Eïd codex were reunited with those from the same codex held in the Coptic Museum. Publication of the codices began to follow in rapid succession. At Claremont, James Robinson saw his efforts rewarded. The team of young scholars, mainly Classicists who had extended their range of abilities to a mastery of Coptic, were setting to work studying and translating the entire range of 49 separate works. In 1975 a series of papers were read at the seventh International Conference on Patristic Studies at Oxford, setting the codices in the context of general Gnostic studies.[96] In 1977 *The Nag Hammadi Library* was given to the public: the publishers claimed, fairly, that 'for the first time in one volume one of the most dramatic archaeological finds of the century' had been published. Thirty-two years of procrastination and bickering had been brought to an end.

Was it all worthwhile? What contribution had the codices made to our understanding of the Gnostic movement? *Thomas* apart, the Nag Hammadi library has added enormously to our knowledge of Gnosticism. Texts now existed that enabled studies of the movement independent of the criticisms of the orthodox heresiologists. Further, they demonstrated the 'hydra-headed' quality of Egyptian Gnosticism. Apart from the 'straight' Gnostic treatises, such as the *Secret Teaching (Apocryphon) of John* or the *Paraphrase of Shem*, to choose two at random, there are works that show a width of scope extending beyond Christianity, such as the short extract (588B–589B) from Plato's *Republic*.[97] There were Hermetic writings, such as the *Discourse on the Eighth and Ninth*; works which were plainly Jewish, such as the *Apocalypse of Adam*;

works that were used by orthodox Christians, such as the *Sentences of Sextus*;[98] and Gnostic expositions of the baptismal and eucharistic liturgies.[99] In these the spiritual character of the rites are stressed. The first baptism is the forgiveness of sins. The true baptism was to enable the souls to become 'perfect spirits, while Eucharist witnessed to the completeness of the recipients' in every spiritual gift and every purity.[100] Far from being followers of Greek philosophy, there is an interesting passage in the *Treatise on the Three Natures* in which the author criticizes philosophers. 'They did not possess the possibility of knowing the cause of existing things because this was not communicated to them. Therefore they introduced other explanations.' Some attributed events to a Providence. Others denied the existence of Providence. There was confusion.[101] These strictures suggest that the critics of the Gnostics, such as Hippolytus, were off the mark when they attempted to trace Gnostic ideas back to pagan philosophies. In fact, the Gnostics are shown to have owed far more to Jewish speculations, especially about the creation narratives in Genesis, than to contemporary philosophy. Clearest of all, however, is the evidence the codices provide for the religious situation in Egypt *c.* 360. Some of the copyists seem to have included monks, one preserving his 'name in the flesh Gongessos (Concessus?)', and describing the text he was copying as 'God-written'.[102] One piece of cartonage carried the name 'Chenoboskion'.[103] It would appear that if the Meletians caused most trouble to Athanasius at the outset of his episcopate, in the last part it was the emergence of a strong Gnostic element among the Pachomian monks (see above, p. 202).

Far from being semi-pagan, self-centred élitists believing in absurdities. the codices show the Egyptian Gnostics to have been sure enough of their ground to belabour their orthodox opponents as 'dried up river beds',[104] to have emphasized the 'joy of believing',[105] and to have regarded themselves as missionaries. Christians were the only individuals whom people heeded![106] Origen was not far off the mark when he said that the (Gnostic) sect had arisen because 'several learned men (among the Greeks) had made a serious attempt to understand the doctrines of Christianity'.[107] The result was not a 'new world religion', but a first attempt to make Christianity the religion of the educated world.

D.   *The Dead Sea Scrolls.* At present nothing connected with the Dead Sea Scrolls can be dated later than AD 68/69, when Vespasian's forces took and destroyed the Covenanters' Essene[108] settlement at Kherbet Qumran. 'The greatest manuscript discovery of all times',[109] as it was called in the 1940s and 1950s, even exceeding the Nag Hammadi library, shared some features with the latter. Both were found by accident and in both discoveries a local Christian leader was among the first to realize their value. It was in March 1947 that an Arab shepherd, Mohammed ed Di'b, was looking for a goat that had wandered up among the rocky cliffs that rise above the marl terrace bordering the western shores of the Dead Sea, $7\frac{1}{2}$ miles south of the modern Jericho. It was getting hot and Mohammed sat down in the shade of a hollow in the rock. To amuse himself he threw a stone into a cleft in the cliff face in front of him. Instead of driving out his missing goat, he heard the clink of something breaking inside. He looked in, saw potsherds, retired in haste but returned next day with his cousin. Together they wormed their way into the narrow cavern, and saw, beside broken potsherds, six complete pots with their lids still on. Five were empty, but the sixth contained three rolls of leather parchment wrapped in linen.[110] One of these, the largest, was to be identified as the Isaiah Scroll.[111]

As at Nag Hammadi there followed a family discussion as to the scrolls' identity and value. Writing that was not Arabic could be seen, so they were not Koranic. Finally, the boys' uncle decided to take them into Bethlehem to a local Syrian antiquities dealer, Halil Iskandar Salim (Kando). He thought the writing was Syriac and took them to someone he believed might be interested, the Syrian metropolitan Mar Athanasius Yeshue Samuel, who resided in St Mark's convent in the Old City of Jerusalem. Meantime other Bedouin had been trying their luck in Mohammed's cave, and those nearby. They had found more scrolls and fragments. By the autumn of 1947 these were being hawked around to antiquities dealers and Jerusalem's learned institutions. Mar Samuel himself bought four scrolls which included the Isaiah Scroll and *Manual of Discipline* (IQS). At first, however, the scrolls were treated with scepticism, until on 25 November 1947 E. L. Sukenik, now Professor of Palestinian Archaeology at the Hebrew University of Jerusalem, recognized the ancient character of the script on fragments which the Bedouin had sold to a dealer. On the 29th he and an Armenian friend were at Bethlehem and there purchased three scrolls. These were *The Rule of War* (the War of the Children of Light against the Children of Darkness), a collection of *Psalms of Thanksgiving* and a second fragmentary scroll of Isaiah.[112] He was just in time, for the United Nations had voted to end the British Mandate and establish Israel. In the next six months, before the Mandate formally ended on 15 May 1948, Palestine gradually slipped into anarchy and further trips to Bethlehem became unsafe for Sukenik. He was however, able to enlist the interest of members of the American School of Oriental Studies, J. C. Trever and William Brownlee, who in turn persuaded Mar Athanasius to let the scrolls in his possession be photographed.

The first Arab–Israeli war (May to June 1948) left the Old City of Jerusalem as well as the Jordan valley in Jordanian hands. This meant that there was no direct Israeli participation in the investigations and excavations that now started in earnest. Between February and March 1949 the Jordanian Department of Antiquities under L. Lankester Harding co-operated with the Ecole Biblique, occasionally assisted by the American School of Oriental Research in Jerusalem to clear Cave 1 completely. In the next seven years ten more scroll-bearing caves were found. Cave 3 produced the Copper Scroll, a cylindrical scroll of copper which recorded a fantastic number of items of treasure allegedly hidden in identifiable places east of Jerusalem.[113] Cave 7 seems to have been a library on its own with exclusively Greek texts, including conceivably Christian texts.[114] The most prolific, however, was Cave 4, first discovered by Bedouin in 1952.[115] It contained fragments of hundreds of manuscripts (more than 380 identifed by 1959). Unfortunately these had not been stored in pots but laid on the ground. Time and damp had taken their toll. The manuscripts had matted and disintegrated into more than 15,000 fragments that required reassembling before identification was possible. At the time of writing (1994) the majority have yet to be deciphered.

Meantime, Lankester Harding's friend Roland de Vaux, now Director of the Ecole Biblique, was excavating the settlement of Kherbet Qumran. The remains of a complete self-supporting community were found, with its pottery, workshop, cisterns, kitchen, communal rooms, a cemetery and, above all, what appeared to be a scriptorium where scrolls could have been copied. In addition, the large amount of pottery found on the site corresponded with that found in the caves. A firm chronology was established during the five seasons of work, giving the main period of activity of the settlement as after *c.* 131 BC when the original buildings were destroyed by an earthquake and its capture by the Romans in AD 68/69. There was a short Roman-period occupation *c.* 69–75 and the site was a refuge during the Second Jewish Revolt (132–135) before it fell into oblivion.[116] These discoveries effectively ended controversies about the age and authenticity of the scrolls, now fixed as post-200 BC (the date of the earliest MS in Cave 4) to AD 68, and made the Essenes, whose settlements Pliny the Elder had located on the western shore of the Dead Sea, the most likely identity of the Covenanters.[117] One question that remains to be answered is whether scrolls such as the text of the psalms, found by Origen in a pot near Jericho, were deposited by the Covenanters or by some other organization, such as Jerusalem priests anticipating the siege of their city by Titus in AD 70.[118]

The leader of the community was a mysterious being known as the 'Teacher of Righteousness' (or 'Righteous Teacher'), who was opposed and persecuted by the 'Wicked Priest' and 'Man of Lies' referred to in the *Commentary on Habbakuk*.[119] The Teacher was himself a priest to whom God had given power in the final age to explain the hidden meaning of 'all the words of his servants the prophets'.[120] It is not possible to say exactly when these events took place, but the commentators relate the verses of the book of the prophet to events of their own day. Thus, in the *Commentary on Nahum* there is a reference to '[Deme]trius the king of Greece ... who sought to enter Jerusalem'. This is usually referred to Demetrius III and the event in 88 BC when he defeated the Hasmonaean ruler, Alexander Jannaeus (104–76 BC).[121] In one of the recently-deciphered (1989) fragments from Cave 4, there is a reference to Aemilius Scaurus, Pompey's general in Syria and Palestine at the time of Pompey's capture of Jerusalem in 63 BC.[122] The supposition must be that the events involving 'The Teacher of Righteousness' and the Wicked Priest took place sometime between 88 and 63 BC, and hence, of course, the Teacher could not be Jesus of Nazareth.

The Teacher, however, headed a community with strict rules of conduct elaborated in the *Manual of Discipline* (IQS3). 'Everyone who wishes to join the community must pledge himself to respect God and man; and to live according to the communal rule.'[123] Below the Teacher himself the community was ruled by three priests and twelve laymen elected by a general council,[124] at whose meetings 'everyone is to have an opportunity to render his opinion'.[125] There were rules about 'misrepresenting one's wealth'[128] (as Ananias did: Acts 5:2) 'and various indecorous acts' (e.g. raucous laughter) that could entail punishment.[127] Purity and blamelessness of conduct combined with scrupulous obedience to the Law were the ideals set out for each member.

Thus two generations before the birth of Christ there had been a revival of the prophetic tradition of Israel, fuelled by strong expectations of the cataclysmic end of the existing age reflected in the War Scroll and the stream of apocalyptic works that have been found in the caves.[128] This places the prophetic ministries of both John the Baptist and Jesus within a firm historical context.

After the crucifixion it seems clear that in many ways the Jerusalem Church not merely paralleled but continued this and other Qumran traditions. James the Lord's brother was known as The Righteous, and according to the (Jewish-Christian?) writer Hegesippus *c.* 170 was regarded as such even by his Saducean opponents.[129] In these years Jesus himself was thought of as a messianic prophet (Acts 3:32) and the Christian community was governed by three senior disciples, Peter, James and John, the 'pillars of the Church' (Gal. 2:9), similar to the three priests who governed the community at Qumran. The body of believers formed an assembly inspired by the Spirit awaiting the return of Christ and the coming of his kingdom, as did their Qumran counterparts with regard to the Righteous Teacher. This event was expected also in the same apocalyptic form as found at Qumran (but not, it would appear, 'in the desert'). The Essenes/Covenanters, as F. M. Cross pointed out, 'prove to be the bearers and in no small part the producers, of the apocalyptic tradition of Judaism', to which the Christians in the first century AD were the heir.[130] Even at the end of the century, at the time when the *Didachē* was compiled, the eucharistic meal was celebrated in anticipation of the messianic banquet.[131] For Christians and Covenanters alike it was reserved for those who were deservedly invited to the Festival or Banquet.[132] When one considers also the Light–Darkness,[133] Love–Hate symbolism, common in both the scroll literature and the Fourth Gospel, of 'knowledge' as a technical religious term and the use of the same calendar in both, one may conclude that many important aspects of the way of life and beliefs of the first generations of Christians continued those of the Essenes/Covenanters. The sect formed the bridge between the Old Israel and the New.

This was the situation when in 1959 de Vaux gave his Schweich Lectures to crowded audiences at the British Academy. Two years later he published with Milik and Benoît a comprehensive report of their excavations in caves in the Wadi Murabb'at on the Dead Sea some 11 miles south of Qumran.[134] These had been occupied sporadically from Chalcolithic times (*c.* 1500 BC) to the fourteenth century AD. But the most important discovery was a series of papyri written in Aramaic or Hebrew dating from the Second Jewish Revolt of 131–135. These show how complete was the authority exercised by Bar-Kochba over the area he controlled. The imperial lands had been seized and appropriated to the state of Israel, coinage was in circulation dating from 'the first year of the liberation of Israel' (131), dues were collected from tenant farmers, whose daily lives with weddings and land deals went on much as before.[135] While Justin Martyr, a native of Neapolis (Nablus) in Samaria, denounced the oppression of Christians by Bar Kochba,[136] an urgent, signed letter from the rebel leader to one of his commanders orders in strong terms that Galileans 'should not be unjustly treated' (probably in the distribution of supplies). Whether these Galileans were Christians or simply refugees from villages in Galilee retaken by the Romans is not known, but Bar-Kochba's evenhandedness towards them is evident.[137]

This fine publication of the Murabb'at document was followed the next year by another two-volume study in the *Discoveries in the Judaean Desert* series by de Vaux and Baillet devoted to discoveries in Qumran Caves 3–10, 'Les petites grottes de Qumran' (excluding Caves 4 and 11) and the Copper Scroll.[138] With this, the climax of the first period of scrolls discovery and research had been reached. An immense amount had been achieved. Publication, particularly by the American School of the *Manual of Discipline* and the *Commentary on Habakkuk*, had been prompt. There had been vigorous debates but with the result that many of the problems connected with the caves and their contents appeared to have been solved.[139] A period of consolidation was needed. The Jordanian Government had established an international team of scholars to work towards the publication of the discoveries. The team, drawn from the USA, France, Great Britain, Poland and Germany, represented the main Christian traditions.[140] A *Journal of Qumran Studies* provided a quarterly outlet for their results. Another ten years perhaps, and the world could have expected something approaching final assessments.

Unfortunately, it did not work out like that. The basic cause was probably the immense labour needed to assemble and decipher the thousands of fragments from Cave 4, some only a centimetre square and containing a single letter. With the daily routine of hard tedious study went perfectionism and a creeping institutional sloth. The scribes of Qumran may have become 'old friends' to the team but their attentions were destructive.[141] More ambitious members of the group moved on to senior university posts, leaving the work increasingly in the hands of resident members of the Ecole Biblique and its allies. Events also conspired to delay the work. In 1967 Israel smashed the Arab coalition in the Six-Day War. The Jordan valley and the Old City of Jerusalem fell to the victors, as did those scrolls that had not been acquired by American and European institutions. These included the great Temple Scroll, originally from Cave 11 and recovered from a dealer in Bethlehem (who received $105,000). Relations, however, between the Israeli Department of Antiquities and the Ecole Biblique were never better than correct and tended to deteriorate. When de Vaux died in 1971 shortly after his revision and updating of the Schweich Lectures, the Ecole lost a wise, experienced and ecumenically-minded scholar as its director, who commanded worldwide respect. One of the few major publications of the decade 1970–80 was J. T. Milik's edition of the Aramaic fragments of the *Book of Enoch* from Cave 4.[142] The scrolls were fading from public consciousness.

Underlying hostility on the part of the Israelis against the Ecole and Western scholars in general simmered – perhaps not unjustifiably. In 1986 an

Israeli official at the Antiquities Department was alleged to have told an American and British enquirer 'You will not see the scrolls in your lifetime'.[143] The gauntlet had been thrown down. The challenge to international scholarship could not be avoided. Next year a new chapter in scrolls research opened.

The great manuscript discoveries from Nag-Hammadi and Qumran had suffered from massive hindrances to research and publication, though for different reasons. Today, publication of the scrolls fragments is still unfinished nearly 50 years after their first discovery. It is evident, however, that their primary value is to Old Testament and inter-Testamentary scholarship, particularly in establishing the earliest known texts of the Hebrew Bible and the Septuagint. For early Christianity their significance lies mainly as illustrating the background of prophetic, apocalyptic and messianic expectations against which Jesus preached and healed. The Essenes emerge forcefully as an influence in these years. How far were John the Baptist[144] and the writer of the Fourth Gospel[145] influenced by them? Why did the Essene and sectarian centre of Damascus become a Christian centre so early? What if the probable identification of the fragment from Cave 7 (7Q5) as coming from Mark 6:53–54 (mentioning Lake Gennesaret) is authenticated?[146] The question could be followed by others, and the possibility opened up of Palestinian origins of both Mark's Gospel and the Fourth Gospel. The 'greatest manuscript find of all times' has not given up all its secrets. It also has its place in Christian archaeology.

NOTES

1. R. E. M. Wheeler, *Still Digging* (London, 1955), p. 152.
2. Own observation during visit to Ravenna in January 1945 after interrogating some German POWs at Rimini POW Camp.
3. Wheeler, op. cit., p. 154, and for ribald treatment of underclad statues at Leptis by members of the Highland Division, pp. 152–3.
4. Wheeler gives his 'Regulations for the safeguarding of antiquities' in Leptis Magna, Sabratha and Tripoli, dated 2 February 1943, op. cit., pp. 156–7.
5. The story is told by J. M. C. Toynbee and J. Ward Perkins in *The Shrine of St Peter and the Vatican Excavations* (London, Longmans, 1956), which I have followed (see pp. xi–xvii). See also Erik Sjöquist, 'The Shrine of St Peter; a review', *Antiquity* 31 (1957), pp. 15–18; and Toynbee, 'The shrine of St Peter and its setting', *JRS* 43 (1953), pp. 1–26.
6. Ibid., p. xvi.
7. Ibid., p. 12. The authors frequently compare the arrangement of the pagan cemetery with that of the cemetery of the Isola Sacra.
8. Ibid., p. 24.
9. Ibid., plate 4.
10. Ibid., p. 106.
11. Toynbee and Ward Perkins, pp. 79–80 and plate 18.

12. Ibid., plate 17 (Tomb V)
13. Ibid., plate 16.
14. Ibid., pp. 54–5; also ibid., p. 57 (mutilated epitaph of a Christian woman with formula 'deposita (in pace)' and palm branch and dove).
15. Described by Toynbee and Ward Perkins, op. cit., pp. 116–17 and plate 32.
16. The face of the figure resembles a youthful Christ, while the horses drawing his chariot have their gaze fixed firmly on him.
17. H. Lietzmann, *Petrus und Paulus in Rom. Liturgische und archaeologische Studien* (Bonn, 1915; 2nd edn, Berlin-Leipzig, W. de Gruyter, 1927). Lietzmann believed that Peter was buried in a pagan cemetery in use from the first half of the second century to the end of the third, and that Constantine's architect knew the position – a shrewd anticipation of the discoveries made by the excavators from 1940 onwards. See also Toynbee, *Shrine*. pp. 2–3.
18. Most convincingly put by Karl Heussi, *Die römische Petrus-tradition in kritischer Sicht* (Tübingen: Mohr, 1955), espec. pp. 54–7.
19. The setting of 1 Peter seems to be Asia Minor, for the churches addressed by the author include all provinces in Asia Minor except the south coast. The problem for the Christians appears to be general unpopularity, not a specific (Neronian) persecution.
20. *1 Clement* 5 (to the Church at Corinth).
21. For the huge bibliography occasioned by the report, see A. A. de Marco, *The Tomb of St Peter* (annotated bibliography with 870 entries: Leiden: Brill, 1964).
22. Toynbee and Ward Perkins, plate I, shows datable fragments of amphorae and a dish left on the side of the excavation of the Clivus. I saw pottery lying unrecorded in some of the pagan tombs I was able to visit, as well as more loose earth within the tombs than I would have liked to see in so important an excavation.
23. Dating, op. cit., p. 32. A drain under the floor of the tomb of which the Red Wall was one side, including tiles with stamps dated to the period 147–161. For the relation between the Red Wall and surrounding tombs and other features, see figs 10–13.
24. Described ibid., pp. 138–44.
25. Cited by Eusebius, *HE* ii.25, 6–7.
26. See J. B. Ward Perkins, 'The Shrine of St Peter and its twelve spiral columns', *JRS* 42 (1952) p. 21.
27. Op. cit., p. 146. These inhumations could be Jewish. There were numerous Jewish families in the Trastevere. Ralegh Radford's suggestion that one of the tombs was that of Pope Anencletus (d. *c.* 95) is not convincing. See *JRS* 47 (1957), p. 278.
28. Op. cit., pp. 154, 159–61.
29. Op. cit., p. 154: 'no detailed report had yet been issued about these bones' (i.e. by the end of 1955).
30. Pius XII, Radio Allocution of Christmas Eve 1950, *Acta Apostolicae Sedis* (Vatican City) 42 (1950), p. 132 and ibid., 43 (1951), pp. 51–2. See di Marco, op. cit., pp. 227–8.
31. M. Guarducci, art. 'Vatican', *EEC* (Eng. trans., 1994) II, 862.
32. Ibid.
33. Ibid. Her detailed study is contained in her *I graffiti sotto la Confessione di San Pietro in Vaticano* (3 vols; Vatican City, 1958): reviewed by P. M. Fraser, *JRS* 52 (1962) pp. 214–19.
34. Ibid. See Toynbee and Ward Perkins, op. cit., pp. 14–16: thorough discussion, ending with a verdict that Guarducci had not proved her case.
35. Ibid., p. 165
36. Guarducci, *The Tomb of St Peter*, Eng. trans J. McLellan (New York/London, 1960), pp. 123–4.
37. Discussed by Fraser, op. cit., p. 217.
38. Guarducci, *Tomb*, p. 132 (fig. 39). For a criticism of this view, see J. Carcopino, *Les Reliques de Saint Pierre à Rome* (Etudes d' Histoire chrétienne 2; Paris: Editions Albin Michel, 1965), pp. 32ff.
39. See. H. Last, *JRS* 44 (1954) p. 114, review of Carcopino.
40. Guarducci, *Tomb*, pp. 97–112.
41. For the early Christian use of abbreviations of *nomina sacra* see Colin H. Roberts, *Manuscript, Society and Belief in Early Christian Egypt* (Schweich Lectures 1977; OUP for British Academy, 1979), ch. 2.
42. See F. M. Cross, *The Ancient Library of Q'mran* (1956), p. 35.
43. Guarducci, op. cit., pp. 102–3 and 122.
44. *ILCV* III, p. 106. There was a *Maria filia Petri*, but from the Donatist stronghold of Lemellefensis in Mauretania Sitifensis: *ILCV* 4027 C.
45. See Last, art. cit., p. 115.

46. The problem of the bones is discussed by Guarducci and Venerando Correnti in *Le Reliquie di Pietro sotto la Confessione della Basilica Vaticana* (Vatican City, 1965), pp. 83ff, in the belief that they are St Peter's; excellent colour photograph of the graffiti on wall 'g', ibid., figs 4 and 5; and black and white in *Tomb*, plates iv–xiii. See, for a contrary view, Jerome Carcopino, op. cit. Rather pedantic in criticisms at times, but convincing that Guarducci's arguments are far from compelling. Last's review, *JRS* 44 (154), pp. 114–16, agrees with Carcopino. Also Toynbee, *Shrine*, pp. 13–14.

47. 'Ecclesiae et corpora martyrum exterminatae sunt a Gothis': *Liber Pontificalis* ed. Duchesne, I.291.

48. Ward Perkins, op. cit., p. 22.

49. Eusebius, *Theophania* iv.7: ed. E. Klostermann, *GCS*, *Eusebius* III (Leipzig, 1904).

50. See P. W. L. Walker, *Holy City, Holy Places?* (OUP, 1990), pp. 70ff.

51. The story of the find is told by O. Guérand, 'Note préliminaire sur les papyrus d'Origène découverts à Toura', *RHR* 131 (1946), pp. 85–108.

52. Ibid., p. 93.

53. For Eustathius's objections to Origen's exegesis, see R. V. Sellers, *Eustathius of Antioch* (Cambridge, 1928), pp. 75–81. His 'bitter spirit' against Origen is asserted by Socrates, *HE* vi.13.

54. Guérand, op. cit., p. 93.

55. *The Dialogue* is ed. and translated into French by J. Scherer in *SC* 67 (1960) and into English by H. Chadwick in *Alexandrian Christianity* (Library of Christian Classics II; London: SCM, 1954), pp. 437–55. See also B. Capelle, 'L'Entretien d'Origène avec Héraclide', *JEH* 2 (1951), pp. 143–57.

56. Eusebius, *HE* vi.33, 2. His dislike of both forms of monarchianism, see *Dialogue*, ed. Chadwick, p. 439.

57. Scherer, op. cit., p. 21.

58. Chadwick, p. 437: an early use of a creed to extablish its holder's orthodoxy.

59. Ibid., p. 438.

60. Ibid., p. 442.

61. Ibid., p. 454.

62. Ibid., p. 455.

63. See J. M. Robinson, *The Nag Hammadi Library in English* (New York: Harper and Row, 1977), pp. 21–5.

64. For this episode, ibid., p. 23; John Dart, *The Laughing Savior* (New York: Harper and Row, 1976), ch. 2.

65. Robinson tells the story of the delays in study and publication, perhaps with some bias, in 'The Jung Codex, the rise and fall of a monopoly', *Religious Studies Review* 3 (1977), pp. 17–30.

66. Jean Doresse, *Les Livres Secrets des Gnostiques d'Egypte* (Paris: Librairie Plon, 1958), p. 134.

67. W. Till, 'Die gnostischen Schriften der koptischen Papyrus, Berolinens 8502', *TU* 60 (1955).

68. This was codex III. The titles are translated in Robinson, *Nag Hammadi*, pp. 98ff. and 195–238.

69. *CRAI* (1948), Séance de 20 Février, pp. 87–95.

70. Togo Mina, 'Le Papyrus gnostique du musée copte', *VC* 2 (1948), pp. 129–36.

71. J. Doresse, 'Trois livres gnostiques inédites', ibid., pp. 137–60. Some extracts are given in translation.

72. Doresse, *Livres sécrets*, pp. 139–40; Dart, op. cit., pp. 13–17.

73. *Codex* viii.1: Robinson, *Library*, pp. 369–93, comprising 132 pages of the codex. Criticism by Plotinus: *Enneads* ii.9 (ed. A. H. Armstrong), as recorded by his biographer Porphyry (232–302), *Vita Plotini* 16. In the West, see Arnobius, *Contra Gentes* 1.52.

74. Doresse, 'Nouveaux documents gnostiques coptes découverts en Haute Egypte', *CRAI*, Séance du 17 juin (1949), pp. 176–180.

75. 'Nouveaux textes gnostiques coptes découverts en Haute-Egypte', *VC* 3 (1949), pp. 129–41.

76. 'A Gnostic Library from Upper Egypt', *Archaeology* 3 (1950), pp. 69–73.

77. H. C. Puech, 'Les nouveaux écrits gnostiques découverts en Haute-Egypt' in *Coptic Studies in Honor of W. E. Crum* (Boston and Paris: Byzantine Institute, 1950), pp. 91–154; 'Gnostische Evangelien und verwandte Dokumenten' in E. Hennecke and W. Schneemelcher (eds), *Neutestamentliche Apokryphen* (Tübingen, 1959), pp. 158–271.

78. Zürich: Origo Verlag (1951).

79. Robinson, 'The Jung Codex', pp. 19–22.

80. One of the terms of the purchase made in May 1952 was that it should not be made public for eighteen months! See W. C. van Unnik, *Newly Discovered Gnostic Writings*, Eng. trans. (Studies in Biblical Theology 30, London: SCM Press, 1960), p. 11, and a less dramatic account of events.

81. See van Unnik's summary, op. cit., esp. on the *Apocryphon of John*: pp. 69–79.

82. Robinson, 'The Jung Codex', p. 20. It would seem from the correspondence extracted by Robinson that, as he says, 'The first monopolistic dimension of the planning (to acquire the Jung Codex from the Eïd family) had to do with the exclusion of Doresse'. Doresse, on the other hand, behaved entirely honourably, informing Puech of each step he took to acquire the codex, while Puech was proposing to exclude him from the publication team.

83. Thus Puech appears also to have tried to exclude Quispel from the publication committee of material for whose availability he depended on Doresse (which included the text of the *Gospel of Thomas*) and excluded Doresse from the publication of the Jung codex. He wished, it appears, to take the lion's share of the credit for all publication and ensure that the honour was reserved to France: Robinson, op. cit., p. 23. An alternative account would seem to be desirable.

84. Pahor Labib (ed.), *Coptic Gnostic Papyri in the Coptic Museum of Old Cairo*, I (1956), plates 80–99.

85. H. C. Puech, 'Une collection des paroles de Jésus récemment retrouvée: L'Evangile selon Thomas', *CRAI* (1957), pp. 146–67.

86. *The Jung Codex*, ed. F. L. Cross (London: Mowbray, 1955).

87. Text reproduced in *VC* 11 (1957), pp. 187–207 under the title 'G. Quispel, The Gospel of Thomas and the New Testament'. See also R. McL. Wilson, *Studies in the Gospel of Thomas* (London: Mowbray, 1960).

88. *Les Livres sécrets*, ch. v.

89. G. Garitte, 'Bibliographie', *Le Muséon* 73 (1960), pp. 210–22, at pp. 211 and 214.

90. Hans Jonas, review of Doresse, Eng. trans. of *Les livres secrets*, *Journal of Religion* 42 (1962), pp. 262–73.

91. J. Leipoldt and H. M. Schenke, 'Koptisch-gnostische Schriften aus den Papyrus-Codices von Nag-Hammadi', *Theologische Forschungen* 12.4 (Hamburg 1960).

92. Robinson, 'The Jung Codex', p. 25. The final batch of 314 negatives and prints were delivered to UNESCO on 9 June 1966.

93. M. Krause, at the opening session of the conference (p. 66 of *Proceedings*). Cited from Robinson, op. cit., p. 25.

94. Ugo Bianchi, 'Perspectives de la recherche sur les origines du Gnosticisme' in *Selected Essays on Gnosticism, Dualism and Mysteriosophy* (Leiden: Brill, 1978), pp. 237–94; 'En effet, le Colloque de Messine à été un Colloque d'historiens des religions, dans un contexte régi par les intérêts typiques de cette science': p. 237.

95. Robinson, 'The Jung Codex', pp. 25–6.

96. M. Krause, (ed.) *Gnosis and Gnosticism* (Papers read at the Seventh International Conference on Patristic Studies, Oxford, 8–13 September 1975; Leiden: Brill, 1977).

97. Robinson, *Nag Hammadi Library*, pp. 290–2 (Codex vi.5).

98. Ibid., pp. 454–9 (Codex xii.1).

99. Ibid., pp. 435–43 (Codex xi.2); see E. Pagels, *The Gnostic Gospels* (London: Weidenfeld and Nicolson, 1979), p. 104 (baptism) and 'A Valentinian interpretation of baptism and the Eucharist and its critique of "orthodox" sacramental theology', *HTR* 65 (1972), pp. 153–69.

100. Codex xi.42, 1–43, 19; Robinson, pp. 441–2.

101. Translation quoted from F. L. Cross (ed.) *The Jung Codex*, p. 59. The spiritual group was 'light from light and spirit from spirit'.

102. Robinson, *Library*, p. 17.

103. Ibid., 16. relating to the cartonage in Codex I.

104. Pagels, *The Gnostic Gospels*, p. 106, quoting the *Apocalypse of Peter*.

105. The opening words of the *Gospel of Truth*: Robinson, p. 37.

106. *The Gospel of Philip*: Robinson, p. 138: 'If you say, "I am a Jew", no one will be moved, If you say, "I am Roman", no one will be disturbed. If you say, "I am Greek, a barbarian, a slave, a free man", no one will be troubled. [If] you [say] "I am a Christian" the [world] will tremble. Would that I [may receive] a name like that!' Gnostic Christians believed in their innate superiority over pagans (who had 'never lived in order that they might die') and Jews.

107. *Contra Celsum* 3.12.

108. Personally I believe that the Covenanters of the Dead Sea were Essenes, but accept the less exact definition preferred by some scholars.

109. W. F. Albright's instinctively correct judgement in a letter to John Trever: cited from F. M. Cross, *The Ancient Library of Q'mran* (London: Duckworth, 1956), p. 6.

110. I have taken the account from J. T. Milik, *Ten Years of Discovery in the Wilderness of Judaea*, Eng. trans. (SCM Press, 1959), pp. 11–12, and J. van der Ploeg, *The Excavations at Qumran*, Eng. trans. K. Smyth (London: Longmans, 1957), ch. i.

111. A very large document (known as IQ Is^a), 8 m long and 60 cm wide: Milik, p. 23.

112. See A. Dupont Sommer, *The Dead Sea Scrolls*, Eng. trans. E. M. Rowley (Oxford: Blackwell, 1952), pp. 10–11.

113. For the Copper Scroll, see P. Kyle McCarter Jr, 'The mystery of the Copper Scroll' in H. Shanks (ed.), *Understanding the Dead Sea Scrolls* (New York: Random House, 1993), ch. 18.

114. Thus C. P. Thiede, 'The origin and tradition of the gospel of Mark in the light of recent investigations', *Rendiconti, Istituto Lombardo, Accademia di Scienze e Lettere* (Milan, 1994), pp. 130–47, at pp. 139–40.

115. F. M. Cross, op. cit., p. 19: 'the main lode'.

116. Described by L. de Vaux, *Archaeology and the Dead Sea Scrolls: The Schweich Lectures 1959*, rev. edn in Eng. trans. (OUP, 1973), pp. 41–5.

117. Outlined by de Vaux, ibid., pp. 126–38, J. L. Teicher still held to the view that the Covenanters were Jewish-Christians: *Studia Patristica* 1.1 = *TU* 63 (1957), pp. 540–5, and *Antiquity* 37 (1963), p. 30.

118. Eusebius, *HE* vi.18 (above, p. 6); and see N. Golb, 'The Dead Sea Scrolls, a new perspective', *The American Scholar* (Spring 1989), pp. 177–207.

119. *Commentary on the Book of Habakkuk* (IQ P Hab), Eng. trans. Theodor H. Gaster, *The Scriptures of the Dead Sea* (London: Secker and Warburg, 1957), 1.5 and 2.1–2 and 7.8 ('wicked priest'). The term 'righteous' referred 'to the teacher who expounds the law aright' (1.1).

120. See also Cross, op. cit., pp. 95–119; *Habakkuk* 1.5: Gaster, p. 235.

121. *Comment on Nahum* ii.11: Gaster, p. 231.

122. R. Eisenman and M. Wise, *The Dead Sea Scrolls Uncovered* (Shaftesbury: Element Books, 1992), pp. 119–22 (4Q 323–324 A–B).

123. *Manual* i:1: Gaster, p. 49.

124. Ibid., viii.1: Gaster, p. 64.

125. Ibid., vi.8–13: Gaster, p. 59.

126. Ibid., vi.24: Gaster, p. 61.

127. Ibid., vii.14: Gaster, p. 63.

128. Cross, op. cit., p. 149, n.6, pp. 153ff.

129. Eusebius, *HE* ii.23; Josephus, *Antiquities* xx.9.1.

130. Cross, op. cit., p. 179.

131. *Didache* 9.2 and 10.6 and compare 1 Cor 12:26: 'For as often as you eat this bread and drink the cup, you proclaim the Lord's death until he comes'.

132. Parable of the banquet (Luke 14:15–24: none of those invited to the banquet will participate); for the Essenes the feast is for 'the men of the Name who are invited to the Festival': Cross, p. 179.

133. See Eisenman and Wise, op. cit., pp. 152 and 156; Michael 'the Prince of Light is opposed to Belial', Prince of Darkness and King of Evil, in the *Testament of Amram* (4Q 543, 545–548).

134. P. Benoît, J. T. Milik and R. de Vaux, 'Les Grottes de Murabb'at' in *Discoveries in the Judaean Desert of Jordan*, II (2 vols; OUP, 1961).

135. A land sale, p. 119; evidence for Bar Kochba's appropriation of imperial land, p. 123. Dues were to be paid to him.

136. Justin, 1 *Apol.* 31.

137. *Discoveries*, pp. 159–61.

138. M. Baillet and R. de Vaux, 'Les petites grottes de Qumran' in *Discoveries*, III (OUP, 1962), pp. 201–302 for the Copper Scroll; criticized by P. K. McCarter, op. cit. (note 113 above).

139. A good summary of progress and ideas to 1959 is given by D. Winton Thomas, *Antiquity* 33 (1959), pp. 189–94.

140. F. M. Cross, op. cit., p. 28. 'A catalogue of the Library', giving an excellent description of the early (productive and harmonious) work of the international team.

141. Ibid., p. 29.

142. J. T. Milik (ed.), *The Books of Enoch: Aramaic Fragments of Qumran Cave 4* (OUP, 1976).

143. The incident is recounted in Eisenman and Wise, op. cit., p. 3.

144. See O. Betz, 'Was John the Baptist an Essene?' in Hershel Shanks (ed.), *Understanding the Dead Sea Scrolls* (London; SPCK, 1992), ch. 16; J. A. T. Robinson, 'The baptism of John and the Qumran community', *HTR* 50 (1957), pp. 175–91.

145. See W. F. Albright, 'Discoveries in Palestine and the Gospel of St John' in W. D. Davies and D. Daube (eds), *The Background of the New Testament and its Eschatology: Studies in Honour of C. H. Dodd* (CUP, 1956), pp. 153–71; J. T. Vanderkam, 'The Dead Sea Scrolls and Christianity' in Shanks, op. cit., ch. 14.
146. C. P. Thiede, 'The origin and tradition of the Gospel of Mark in the light of recent investigations'. Thiede's views have not found universal acceptance. See Professor Graham Stanton's letter in *The Times* (29 December 1994) concerning the Magdalen Papyrus of Matthew's Gospel, but also attacking Thiede's claims on behalf of the Markan fragment from Cave 4. On the Magdalen Papyrus, see also D. C. Parker, 'Was Matthew written before 50 CE?', *The Expository Times* (October 1995), pp. 40–3.

FURTHER READING

W. F. Albright, 'Discoveries in Palestine and the Gospel of John' in W. D. Davies and D. Daube (eds), *The Background of the New Testament and its Eschatology* (CUP, 1956), pp. 153–71.

B. Capelle, 'L'entretien d'Origène avec Heraclide', *JEH* 2 (1951), pp. 143–57.

F. L. Cross, *The Jung Codex* (London: Mowbray, 1955).

F. M. Cross, *The Ancient Library of Qumran* (London: Duckworth 1956).

J. Doresse, *Les livres sécrets des Gnostiques d'Egypte* (Paris: Librairie Plon, 1956).

R. Eisenman and W. Wise, *The Dead Sea Scrolls Uncovered* (Shaftesbury: Element Books, 1992).

H. Gaster, *The Scriptures of the Dead Sea* (London: Secker and Warburg, 1957).

M. Guarducci, *The Tomb of St Peter: The New Discoveries in the Sacred Grottos of the Vatican*, Eng. trans. J. McLellan (New York/London, 1960).

M. Krause, *Gnostics and Gnosticism* (Papers read at the Seventh International Conference on Patristics Studies, Oxford 1975: Leiden: Brill, 1977).

J. T. Milik, *Ten Years of Discovery in the Wilderness of Judaea*, Eng. trans. (London: SCM Press, 1959).

E. Pagels, *The Gnostic Gospels* (London: Weidenfeld and Nicolson, 1979).

J. A. T. Robinson, 'The baptism of John and the Qumran community', *HTR* 50 (1957), pp. 175–91.

James M. Robinson, *The Nag Hammadi Library in English* (New York: Harper and Row, 1977).

James M. Robinson, 'The Jung Codex: the rise and fall of a monopoly', *Religious Studies Review* 3 (1977), pp. 17–30.

J. M. C. Toynbee and J. Ward Perkins, *The Shrine of St Peter and the Vatican Excavations* (London: Longmans, 1956).

R. de Vaux, *Archaeology and the Dead Sea Scrolls* (Schweich Lectures 1959), rev. and Eng. trans. (OUP, 1973).

12

Save Nubia ...
Save Carthage ...
Save everything

NUBIA

One of the explanations offered by Pahor Lalib for the slow work of the technicians detailed to photograph the Nag Hammadi codices was that they were away photographing Nubian monuments. These were destined to be engulfed by Lake Nasser to be formed from the rising waters that would be piling up behind the High Dam, whose construction was to begin in 1963 a few miles south of Aswan. 'Save (the Monuments of) Nubia' was an epoch-making event. Twenty-three countries from around the world co-operated, sending more than 50 separate teams of archaeologists to handle what could be recorded and salvaged within a five-years' grace, from 1960 to 1965. This effort of international co-operation would be repeated on a smaller scale at Carthage a decade later, and again in Iraq in the 1980s and in northern Sinai in the early 1990s. It marked the end of archaeology directed to purely national ends, as had prevailed during the previous century. The saga of Nag Hammadi had been a turning-point. From the close-knit cabal of scholars 'confident of the solidarity and commitment that unites us in this affair' (Puech to Quispel, 8 July 1955),[1] there came a call first 'for all who were adequately trained' to have the chance of studying and publishing the documents, and then a genuine, if American-led, co-operation between the Americans and European scholars that at last achieved a publication of the documents in English, French and German. A new spirit had been born which would now be tested.

In 1955 the Antiquities' Service in Khartoum awoke to the possibility that every trace of ancient civilization from Pharaonic times onwards, between Aswan and Wadi Halfa and beyond, was likely to be drowned under metres of water as the result of the High Dam.[2] The situation foreseen by Ugo Monneret de Villard in the early 1930s would become a reality. The cause was, quite simply, demography. Egypt at that time had little if any oil revenue, yet its population (in 1994 estimated at 58 million) was continuing to grow alarmingly. Cities and countryside alike were becoming densely overcrowded, but the Nile valley as it then was, was subject to the vagaries of the yearly flood, and could not sustain the increased pressure on its resources.

The Nile has no tributaries north of the Atbara river. As one flies down from Cairo south towards the Sudanese frontier one can see on one's left (east) a great number of dried-up wadis that once fed the Nile. Ten thousand years ago rainfall was abundant. Today if there are sometime destructive storms, it is usually minimal. On both sides of the river the banks slope just steeply enough to make irrigation difficult without sophisticated equipment beyond a fringe of about one and a half miles from the water. Thereafter the desert begins. The change from cultivation to sandy waste can be sudden, as I found taking evening walks in 1963 and 1964 from the Egypt Exploration Society's boat moored at Aniba, opposite Qasr Ibrim, westwards across the settlement into the desert beyond. In half an hour one had moved from the river through a small but flourishing community with its school, community centre and hospital, into the desert. Now the intention was to cover the whole area beneath a lake some 15 miles across and 200 ft deep in order to provide, as was hoped, additional cultivated land independent of the seasonal flow of the river, for the people living to the north. Egyptian Nubia and part of Sudan would be paying the price for this improvement to national well-being.

Nubia was fortunate in that a great amount of survey coupled with some excavation had been going on since the beginning of the century. In Sudan also, an exceptionally efficient Antiquities Service had been built up, not least by its last two British Commissioners for Archaeology, A. J. Arkell and P. L. Shinnie. Arkell made his mark in prehistory and written records; Shinnie combined a knowledge of Egyptology and early Christianity with flair and expert technique. The British Academy too, encouraged by the success of the Oxford University expeditions of the interwar years, decided to send out an expedition in the winter of 1951–52, led by O. G. S. Crawford, editor of *Antiquity*. Its purpose was to survey the forts and churches and other ancient sites on both banks of the Nile between its confluence with the Atbara and Abu Hamed, but also to include the fort at El Kab on the great bend of the Nile further west (i.e. much the Nubian kingdom of Makurrah).[3] In all the fifteen sites he recorded in detail Crawford found a fort, a church and other early-Christian remains, such as a cemetery dating from the tenth century onwards.

In two cases a church had been converted into a mosque, but elsewhere the Christian villages seem simply to have been abandoned and gradually become ruins.[4]

Meantime, Shinnie was embarking on two important pieces of work before the end of the Anglo-Egyptian condominium in 1956, and with it his appointment as Commissioner for Archaeology. Four miles south-east of Khartoum on the north bank of the Blue Nile were the ruins of the ancient town of Soba, the capital of the southern Nubian kingdom of Alwah. They covered an area of no less than a square mile, containing a great number of occupation-sites, mostly indicated by low mounds, but with only one obviously Christian building marked by upright granite columns still in place. Shinnie had two seasons, winter 1950–51 and 1951–52, on the site.[5] In contrast, however, to practically every other excavation outside the British Isles, he first made a cutting through one of the larger mounds in order to establish a sequence of pottery for dating purposes. This he considered essential before he excavated the church or any other of the mounds.[6] He also substituted the usual method of work on Egyptian sites, where one man armed with a mattock (*toria*) filled his colleague's basket whose contents the latter placed on his shoulder and dumped, with the pick, shovel and barrow normal on Romano-British sites. There was also continuous supervision of work carried out by a relatively small team of labourers.[7] The introduction of Wheeler-inspired Romano-British methods on to Nubian sites where stratification was all-important was a major innovation, though one which would not always be followed by the international teams in the next decade. Apart from providing the first classification of pottery and glass on a Nubian Christian site,[8] the excavations confirmed the impression gained by Crawford of a decline and abandonment of the site (in this case, probably as late as early years of the sixteenth century) rather than its destruction.[9] This result would be repeated in the northern kingdom's cathedral-fortress of Qasr Ibrim.

Shinnie, however, left Soba with many questions still unanswered, to concentrate with his colleague H. N. Chittick for the 1953 and 1954 seasons on the church and monastery at el Ghazali on the Wadi Abu dam not far from the town of Merowe.[10] The site had been known since Linant de Bellefonds had visited it in 1821 and Lepsius in 1849, the latter finding some twenty inscribed stones which he removed to Berlin.[11] It was a promising area, a monastic settlement occupied in the long period when Nubian Christianity was thriving. One could expect it to throw light on the life and organization of the Nubian Church. As a building, the Ghazali church was large by Nubian standards (28.1 m × 13.9 m). Its lower half had been well constructed with small, dressed

sandstone blocks, while the upper half was of mud-brick. The plan was basilican. Ghazali, in fact, could be taken as the Nubian type-church, with its main
nave and two side aisles divided by arcades, a pulpit half way down the north
side of the nave, the *haikal* (sanctuary) closed off by a wooden partition from
the nave, and beyond the *haikal*, a flight of steep, shallow steps leading to an
apse-shaped tribunal. Outside the church on the north side was a small construction containing either a baptismal font or an Epiphany tank. Except for
this latter, Ibrim also contained all these features. The church was at the centre
of a group of monastic buildings forming a self-contained settlement.[12]

Shinnie's excavation confirmed the importance of monasticism in Nubian
Christianity, and the continued use of Nubian, Greek and Coptic as Church
languages, as stated by Arab travellers. Inscriptions on epitaphs also followed
the Byzantine pattern. Enlarging on his experience at Soba, Shinnie concentrated on the pottery, great quantities of which were found on the site. His
detailed classification of types was to provide the most reliable basis for
dating sites, not entirely superseded by William Adams' more detailed results
derived from his work on the pottery kilns at Meinarti and Faras.[13]

Shinnie was succeeded briefly by the French archaeologist Professor Jean
Vercoutter before the Commission was 'Sudanized'. The new Commissioner,
Thabit Hassan Thabit, had been Chief Inspector of Antiquities and was
determined to do all possible to salvage for scholarship whatever could be
salvaged. He was assisted by the (posthumous) appearance of Monneret de
Villard's final volume of *La Nubie Medioévale*, in 1957, containing the plans and
photographs of the Milanese scholar's discoveries, a work of genius and
another indispensable guide.

Meantime UNESCO had not been idle. Plans had been prepared the
moment the High Dam project was proposed in 1955. Dr (later Professor)
W. Y. Adams of the University of Kentucky was invited to conduct a thorough
survey of threatened sites in northern Sudan.[14] An aerial survey was undertaken in the latter part of 1959, followed by intensive field work in the
following months. As a result, as nations volunteered their services, sites were
allocated. Adams lists 59 projects worked on between 1959 and 1969 by the
international teams. There was, as he says, a virtual 'gold rush' of archaeologists to the banks of the Nile. Following the formal launch of the international
campaign by UNESCO on 8 March 1960, the sites were allocated. In the
summer of 1960 the Polish Centre of Mediterranean Studies at Cairo directed
by Professor Kazimierz Michałowski received Faras and a four-mile (7 km)
surrounding area, the Scandinavians Serra West, Ghana Debeira West, a
Franco-Argentine team Aksha, and Spain Argin, all in the area between Faras

and Wadi Halfa. The Egypt Exploration Society would be working at Buhen, the impressive Pharaonic fort below Abu Simbel.[15]

At this stage, there was a bias towards saving the great Pharaonic monuments either side of the Egyptian–Sudanese border. Not surprisingly perhaps, for on the Egyptian side were the temples of Abu Simbel, and further north, of Amada and Kalabsha. A survey similar to that by Adams had been carried out by Dr Harry Smith of the British Museum for the area between Aswan and the 20-mile finger of Sudanese territory that jutted north-east along the Nile north of Wadi Halfa.[16] These monuments had been designated the prime targets for salvage, and the process of raising block by block the temples and statues of Abu Simbel by West German and Scandinavian companies began in the first months of 1964.[17] The temples of Amada, Wadi es Sebua and Kalabsha were among the 35 that had to be moved to higher ground.

Faras and Ibrim were, however, to become the stars in the first period of salvage, but these would have stood isolated without the success of the other international teams working on Nubian-Christian sites. As mentioned, excavations on Christian-date pottery kilns at Meinarti and Faras provided Adams with the means of supplementing and correcting Shinnie's classifications of Nubian pottery.[18] Djebel Adda, excavated by Nicolas Millet for the Americans, was a smaller but similar fort and administrative centre to Ibrim. Adolf Klasen's work on the church at Abdullah Nirqi, north of Abu Simbel, provided additional examples of the liturgical paintings, particularly of the military saints found at Faras. The Meroitic cemetery of Mas-Mas, dug by a Spanish team, supplemented Emery's finds in the cemetery south of Ibrim. All worked with a will, fighting against time. The coloured painting of Noah's ark on the wall of a room in the (monastic?) settlement of Debeira West, excavated by the University of Ghana under Shinnie's leadership, was a reminder of what would be happening before 1965 was out.[19]

At first the Nubians themselves, due for displacement north to the Kom Ombo area, were not too interested in the international effort to learn as much as possible about the civilization of their Christian ancestors. When Michałowski and his team arrived at Faras late in January 1961 only one village volunteered for work. The problem was daunting, as Faras lacked even the elementary facilities provided at Aniba for the British team at Ibrim. But Michałowski did not lack resource and courage. He was a scholar who had survived six years in a German POW camp (he had been attending a conference in Berlin only a week before Hitler's armies invaded Poland!). He had carried out excavations at Palmyra in the 1950s, but Faras was a challenge. Despite the initial setback a workforce of 90 *guftis* was soon recruited, mainly from Wadi

Halfa, and after an event, paradoxically for a then-Communist country, involving a strike by a third of the force for higher pay, work began in earnest.[20]

Michałowski had been interested in a sandy mound rising some 60 ft above the surrounding area. An Arab fort and a ruined Coptic church crowned its summit, but Griffith had begun to excavate there and had found late-Meroitic material; in places, tops of walls were showing through the surface. The problem was that this was likely to be a deep sand excavation with the accompanying danger of collapsing trench walls. To counter this, Michałowski laid out a main trench 20 m wide with sloping sides so that if the worst happened those working in the trench could escape. There was a preliminary scare caused by the recovery of sandstone blocks suggesting that the mound concealed only the ruins of a temple of Thutmosis III. Then the real nature of what lay below began to appear. The season ended with the discovery of two magnificent wall paintings, one of the archangel Michael, decorating the burial crypt of Bishop Johannes (d. 1005), and the other of the Virgin together with the names of three other bishops of Faras (Pachoras), Petros, Georgios and Jesu. The wonders of Faras had begun to emerge.[21]

Michałowski now packed four more 'seasons' into the next four years. The results were stupendous. The basilican-type cathedral that arose from the sands had been dedicated about AD 630 in honour of the Virgin. The walls had been covered with frescos, some as old as the eighth century, others, inferior in design and execution, were as recent as the twelfth, but the most brilliant were those of the Classical period of Nubian Christianity, the ninth and tenth centuries, matching the superb decorated pottery of that era.[22]

It was in these seasons that the achievement of Christian Nubia was revealed and the part played by the Monophysite religion inspiring its rulers and people. It was a religion centred first and foremost on the Virgin and the birth-narratives, including apocryphal accounts, such as the *First Gospel* or *Book (Protoevangelium) of James* that feature so fully the life of the Virgin's mother, Anna.[23] A ninth-century repair, blocking the original west entrance of the cathedral, had allowed the creation of a fresco showing the Virgin standing in the midst of the stars of the firmament, the Child in her arms and flanked by two angels, with the inscription 'The Holy Mary, Virgin Mother of Christ', and to the right 'Jesus Christ, the Saviour'.[24] Another impressive mural features the Virgin and the birth of Jesus with shepherds, and the three kings. The shepherds are given the names of Arnias and Lekotes.[25] Other paintings represented 'The Three Kings',[26] Peter, 'chief of the apostles',[27] and the saints particularly venerated in the Monophysite Church, 'Ignatius, archbishop of Antioch',[28] and John Chrysostom.[29] There were heroic episodes from Scripture, such as the great mural 10 ft long and 8 ft high depicting the three youths in the fiery furnace,[30] and in places of honour, the protectors of the kingdom, the archangel Michael[31] and the military saints.[32] Rulers, clergy and anchorites had not been omitted,[33] one of the most famous portraits being that of Bishop Marianos (*c*. AD 1020), resembling Henry VIII with his broad face and beard.[34] Differences of style were related to different periods. The 'violet' style, owing much to Coptic inspiration, exemplified by the magnificent St Anne painting of the eighth to ninth century,[35] succeeded by the 'white' style (also influenced by Coptic Christian art), the 'red-yellow' style, of the later Classic period, and finally by a cruder, more garish hieratic Ethiopian-type fresco of the final period, when the cathedral gradually became a prey to silt and sand.[36] The latter prevailed. The struggle was given up and the building abandoned sometime early in the thirteenth century.

Apart from discovery, post-war advances in conservation enabled the frescos, laid layer on layer, to be moved, cleaned and restored. Whereas Mileham and his colleagues could only marvel at the colours of the wall-paintings and lament that they would fade, in the 1960s they could be removed and conserved in museum laboratories.[37] To this extent the 'Save Nubia' campaign came at the right moment.

'The history and art of Nubia in the Christian period': this is what the paintings in the cathedral revealed. The succession of bishops listed on a wall fresco featuring royal and official personages[38] and precise dating of epitaphs of clergy combined to lessen the number of 'unanswered questions' in Nubian history, and raise others about the religious allegiance of the kingdoms (did the Melkites oust the Monophysites for a short time in the eleventh century?),[39] questions which could not have been asked without the 'wonder of Faras'.

What were the results of this sensational excavation? First, regarding the history of Christianity in Nubia, the story of the conversion of the Nubians could now be pushed back long – perhaps a century – before the arrival in 542 of the presbyter Julianus and his mission sent by Justinian's empress Theodora. The earliest building on the cathedral site was shown to be a mudbrick built church, rhomboid in shape, perhaps dating to the mid-fifth century.[40] At some stage the site was wanted for the royal palace, and the Christians may have been given one of the other early, mud-brick churches, 'the Great Church', or 'Rivergate Church' of the Oxford expeditions. Nubia was still pagan: witness the savage splendour of the royal tombs of Q'ustul and Ballana. Yet Christianity retained its adherents, particularly among the ordinary people of Faras. The turning-point may have been the victory of King Silko over his formidable heathen enemies the Blemmyes and their allies.[41] Did he, like Constantine, put his trust in the Christian God, and was rewarded? At least, his conversion *c.* 535 would place the Christian (Monophysite) mission of 542 in the context of events, and explain its rapid success.[42] The ground would have been prepared and Julianus and his companions assured of at least a hearing from the warlike king.

Thereafter for 900 years the Nubian kingdoms were Christian even though cut off from Byzantine Christendom by Muslim Egypt. A succession of bishops could be traced from Bishop Aetios, whose episcopate *c.* 620 preceded the destruction of the ruler's palace to make way for the cathedral. This replaced the Rivergate Church as the main centre of worship. In 707 it was rebuilt;[43] Monophysitism was confirmed as the religion of the now joint kingdom of Makurrah and Nobatia, and Faras became the seat of the eparch, subordinate to the king at Old Dongola.[44] At the same time, the Coptic monks, refugees from Muslim persecution in Egypt, established themselves in cells west of the city. Thereafter the names of Nubian monarchs and 24 bishops were preserved, ending with Tamar (d. 31 March(?) 1193), whose tombstone, copied by Count Vidua, was recovered from the Rivergate Church by Griffith.[45] The most prosperous age of Nubian Christianity and Nubian political influence is shown to be the tenth century, coinciding with the revival of Byzantine power. The decline was long. Sometime early in the thirteenth century the cathedral silts up with sand. One great effort is made to bring it back into service, and a massive North Monastery is erected[46] on the site of the Old Monastery. In vain! Nothing could turn back the desert. The memory of the sacred character of the spot was preserved by a small Coptic church on the summit of the *kôm* that had formed, until that in turn was replaced by a Turkish fort using the vantage-point it afforded.

The Church at Faras was well organized. The bishops had a staff, including an archpriest, priests and deacons, many of whose names were recorded.[47] The paintings show the detail of their vestments, the chasuble and stoles decorated or actually bejewelled, Byzantine in inspiration throughout but not greatly different from the vestments worn by Orthodox, Roman Catholic and Anglican clergy today.[48] The paintings, too, leave no doubt as to the close dependence of the king's and the eparch's authority on religious support. The queen mother, Martha, places herself under the protection of the Virgin.[49] God crowns the 'Christ-loving' (note the ecclesiastical title!) King Mercurius on the foundation stone of the cathedral.[50] In the tenth century, King Georgios II is represented as under the protection of the Virgin and Child.[51]

Within this theocratic system the Byzantine titles and forms of administration prevail as Griffith and de Monneret had shown. On the dedication inscription just mentioned the eparch is given the title of *Illustris*, the highest administrative rank in the Byzantine hierarchy.[52] Greek may even have been the official language of Makurrah, Mercurius' kingdom, as the inscription has Greek and Coptic versions. The bishopric of Pachoras (Faras) had the status of a Metropolitan possessed by senior bishoprics in the Byzantine empire. The outlines of Nubian ecclesiastical and civil administration and history set down by scholars of the previous generation had been filled in, at least partially just in time.

It might have been expected that Faras would be allocated to the British, work there having been carried out by successive British expeditions, and important Christian remains, such as the North Church and the Rivergate Church with its frescos, discovered by Oxford University expeditions. The distribution of sites in 1960 came at a time, however, when the Egypt Exploration Society and its Director, Walter Emery, were already committed to Buhen. This was one of the most southerly of Rameses II's forts and was endangered by the prospective flooding. Buhen therefore became the British no. 1 site, but in 1961 Emery was also interested himself in the cemeteries extending up a valley to the south of Ibrim and was also convinced (rightly) that there was a considerable Christian settlement on the edge of the Nile below the cathedral-fort. Ibrim itself had been allotted provisionally to the West Germans, but their reconnaissance party had apparently concentrated their inspection on the north half of the site, where the prevailing north wind had scarped the soil down almost to the bare rock. It was turned down. Emery then visited Ibrim, found carved blocks with cartouches of Thutmosis III, Rameses IV and Taharqa, and accepted the site as available to a second British team. As a first step he instructed his assistants Professor J. M. Plumley and Dr Richard Dale of Yale University to make a rapid survey of the buildings that lined the fortress walls, carry out a trial excavation within the church, and count the later (Bosnian) buildings whose ruins still had remained practically untouched since the capture of Ibrim from the Mamelukes in 1812.

Plumley and Dale were successful. The Bosnian houses were counted, 312 being identified. Then, on visiting the cathedral site, Plumley's eye caught a carved wooden border at ground level on the wall of an arcade near the Muslim *mihrab* that had been cut into the south wall to orientate worshippers toward Mecca. A skirting-board made no sense, and so Plumley and Dale dug down to find that some 5 ft (1.50 m) and at least three occupation levels separated the surface from the flagstones of the cathedral floor. Leaving the cathedral they walked down to the southern edge of the site. This was dominated by a large fortress-watch-tower, whose foundations seemed to rest on a solid stone balcony. Again small-scale excavations sufficed. The balcony was bounded at each end by solid stone railings which extended some distance north in the direction of the cathedral. The *podium* or, more probably, temple forecourt proved to be a second important site on Ibrim, which was now chosen for work by a British team.[53]

Dr Dale had to return to Yale and the present writer was invited to act as Professor Plumley's associate. The invitation for 1963–64 coincided with his turn for a sabbatical year and was accepted with alacrity. The expedition consisting of Plumley, self, with architects Ken Fraser and Andrew Mahaffy arrived at Aniba on 18 December. Conditions were rough. The Society's *dahibya* was put at our disposal, but it seemed as though it had been laid up since 1905 when it was the pride of Thos. Cook's Nile tourist fleet. Alas, no more! How those first days were survived is anyone's guess. Plumley's expertise as a cook was one reason, so too, as a mechanic, repairing an outboard motor, which made the writer's 'skill' sailing a *feluka* across the Nile to Ibrim unnecessary.

The excavation was almost as notable a success as that at Faras. The first task was to clear the mass of debris which littered the surface of the cathedral before testing Plumley's and Dale's theories. It was found that the mosque occupied the uppermost level. Arabic texts written on paper, including one magic text, were recovered. Below, there were unsuspected features, including the foundations of a large secular building that occupied the whole of the centre and west side of the church. Below this the original granite columns began to appear, all lying prone in an east–west (geographical) direction,[54] as if struck down simultaneously, perhaps by an earthquake. On this level there was burning, probably from the roof of the church. Below this in turn, on the west side, was a level of domestic occupation represented by a hard, beaten earth floor in which a large globular pot had been sunk.[55]

Gradually the remains of this fine stone-built building emerged, even more impressive than the cathedral at Faras, with a total length of 29.50 m by 20 m width. There were five aisles divided by stone arcades and within them a line of six granite columns on each side, resting on a firm flagstone floor. There was a tower at the south-west corner, and on the south (geographical) side the entrance had been built up on a great artificial mound erected over earlier X Group houses. Excavation had been carried on by the traditional methods, which in this instance had advantages. They enabled work to continue uninterrupted at a rhythm sustainable by the workforce of 46 *guftis*. Satisfaction was expressed by practically continuous songs, many of which seemed to centre on long-lost loves in 'Alexandriya'. Slack work was rewarded by the *reis* (foreman) with a sharp stroke with his cane on the offender's *gallabiya* (long, cloak-like outer garment). With Plumley, our Inspector, Ali-al-Goholy and the writer always on the scene, very little if anything was lost. As the writer found in 1972 it was quite possible to combine these methods with straight trenches and attention to levels.

The effectiveness of these traditional methods was shown by two events. First, on 23 December Ali-al-Goholy, produced a piece of parchment that had been used by a Bosnian occupant as a bottle-stopper was found undamaged by one of the workmen using his *toria*. It had been stretched and the equivalent of an invocation to 'Michael' could be read. We were put on the track of liturgical documents for which Ibrim would be famed. Then, working on the west side (geographical), the men came on a stairway leading to a crypt. Among the wind-blown silt that covered the steps was another document, this time papyrus containing two pages of an offertory prayer from a Eucharistic sequence.[56] In a short time the mattocks were scraping at the decorated archway that marked the entrance to the crypt. Work suddenly stopped. I came over and saw, within, a body hunched up against a wall which was blocking off this part of the crypt from a passage that ran behind the apse. The body was covered by a coating (some 0.50 m thick) of dust; that is, it had been deposited where it lay and not buried.[57] I called Plumley over. The body was taken out and laid on its back. Below a white shroud one could discern a brown habit of an ecclesiastic, and a bronze pectoral cross attached to his neck lying on his breast. Desiring 'the comfort station', I said to Plumley, 'He's an ecclesiastic. He's your man.' When I returned he was kneeling as though transfixed. Beside him lay two tightly-rolled paper scrolls. 'I thought he had too many bones, so I shook him', he said. The scrolls which had been placed beneath the body were put into polythene bags, copiously breathed upon so as to keep them damp. They survived. Unrolled to a total length of nearly 5 metres and 54 cm in width in the Department of Antiquities at Cairo, they revealed that they were Coptic and Arabic testimonial letters in favour of Bishop Timotheos from Gabriel IV, Pope of Alexandria, resident in Cairo (1370–1378). Timotheos was to be bishop of Ibrim and Pachoras and praised as a 'good Christ-loving man' who had risen through monastic ranks to become bishop. The date could not be earlier than 1372, the date of his consecration. At a stroke the survival of a fully-organized Nubian Church in communication with the Coptic Church in Egypt had been extended by a half-century.[58]

More followed. On the east (geographical) side and in front of the *haikal* the original floor of the church had been repaired with untidily laid flag-stones. Below these, separating them from the original stone floor, was a layer of wind-blown silt. It soon became clear that at sometime (one suspected during the brief Muslim occupation of the area by Shams-ed-Doula's forces in 1173–75), the cathedral library had been burnt and ransacked and fragments of liturgical and other sacred documents scattered. When the Christians regained possession these fragments had already been covered with wind-blown debris and were not recovered. At least 100 torn pieces, over-whelmingly in Greek and Nubian, were found.[59] They comprised parts of the *Acta* of the military saints Mercurius and George,[60] biblical fragments, includ-ing one fragment of beautifully illuminated manuscript, showing a bishop seated in brown habit holding a Bible and teaching.[61] There were Eucharistic prayers and, above all, hymns to the Virgin,[62] as well as the Monophysite ver-sion of the Trisagion ('Holy, holy, holy God ... who was crucified for us').[63] The discoveries at Qasr Ibrim were already complementing those from Faras.

From 11 January 1964 the main effort of the dig was concentrated on the podium. Believing that we only had this season to complete the work excava-tion had to move on at almost breakneck speed. The area produced storage jars but not many other signs of Bosnian occupation, the high watch-tower made of mud brick being the last ostensible evidence of occupation. The tower surviving to a height of about 7 m (22 ft) faced westwards across the Nile and was designed evidently to give early warning of the approach of ene-mies from that quarter. Below the tower were large rectangular chambers used for storing provisions. These had to be removed to expose houses of Christian date below. Lying across a sill, perhaps forming part of a stairway, was a palm beam used to support a roof or a second storey. Pulling it away I found it had fallen across a large pot lying aslant, though near to its original position. (See plate.) Its neck was encased in clay in which, however, there were marks of seals.[64] The neck had been broken and the contents could therefore be inspected without causing further damage. It was heavy and I suspected it had served as a grain store for the last inhabitants of the house. Plumley had doubts. He put his hand in and drew out a cylindrical leather scroll. To my astonishment, he unrolled it without further ado. Fortunately, it was supple; stitch marks at the edges suggested it had once formed part of a leather gar-ment made from gazelle skin. There was writing on the inside done with a hard reed pen in Nubian script but preceded by a ☧.[65] There were nine scrolls in all, legal documents, of the greatest historical importance. The latest, which had been inserted last, was dated 'from the era of the martyrs'[66] (*apo mart(yribus)* in Nubian) to the equivalent of AD 1464. A King Joel of Dotawo and a *papas* (metropolitan) of Phrim (Ibrim) called Markos were mentioned on the scroll as well as five other high officials.[67] (See plate.)

Once more, a single find had proved the survival of Christian Nubia for another century, to the second half of the fifteenth century. It was still a kingdom with its organized Church and administration. Since the pot had been sealed beneath the floors of the magazines that had replaced the dwelling, one must accept the probability that the Christian Nubian kingdom of Dotawo ('Lower Do') including Pachoras (Faras) and Djebel Adda survived until the beginning of the sixteenth century.[68] How it ended is still unclear. The podium site was covered by deep deposits of brown windblown sand but there was no destruction level. There was the same story in the cathedral. The final Christian level was succeeded by domestic occupation, and the fire that left its mark on the (geographical) west side divided two levels of this type of occupation. The Bosnian garrison that arrived towards the middle of the sixteenth century must have found an abandoned or practically abandoned site. Perhaps the diminutive, square Coptic church perched on a rock just above the 1963 level of the Nile, with its invocation of the Holy Trinity incised in Greek above the altar-space, represented the last flicker of Christianity at Ibrim. (See plate.)

The other documents in the pot were of the same type, but earlier. They were all Christian, beginning with an invocation of the Holy Trinity, referring to individual rulers and bishops of the previous two centuries. Compared to this find the discovery of four leaves of John Chrysostom's *Homily on the Four Living Beasts* in Coptic, beneath an upright stone outside the south (geographical) front of the cathedral, and of biblical manuscripts stored in pits cut in the flagstone surface of the podium, seemed merely consolation prizes.[69] When the dig ended on 27 February Ibrim had established itself as a site second only in importance to Faras, and unlike Faras, likely to survive the formation of Lake Nasser.

This was in fact the case. Though the east entrance with its watch-towers collapsed into the waters in 1965, work proved to be possible despite the dangers of seepage and capillary action. In 1966 another small mud-brick church was found on the east (geographical) side of the cathedral. It had served as a burial chapel for some of the bishops of Ibrim and was also found to be the repository of beautifully-written biblical MSS in Greek and Coptic,[70] and nearby the burial stele of Bishop Marianos of Pachoras (Faras) (d. 1036) was found on the site. Why the bishop had come to Ibrim to die there is not known but its presence indicates probably continuous contact between the two centres.[71]

In 1970 another church was discovered, in all likelihood the earliest, to the east of the cathedral, the 'South Church'. It had been converted out of a New Kingdom temple,[72] continued in use under the Ethiopian Pharaoh, Taharqa

(689–663 BC), and was probably the traditional religious centre at Ibrim. The blocks with cartouches of the kings were still in place, but one of the eastern rooms had been made into an apse by the insertion of a semicircular wall of masonry into what had previously been a rectangular chamber.

The date was certainly 'early', i.e. before the cathedral was built probably sometime in the seventh century. There was, however, a deposit of 0.45 m deep of occupational earth between the paved walkway associate with it and a similar walkway that ran alongside the Meroitic temple nearby. In thin layers of hardened mud around a plinth, possibly the base for a statue, were 150 bronze coins extending from AD 277 (Probus) into the fifth century (local imitations of small bronze of the house of Theodosius).[73] These may have been associate with libations, suggesting a period not much before AD 500 for the transformation of the area for Christian worship.

If that were so Ibrim may have witnessed a development similar to that of Faras. A small mud-brick church on the site of the future cathedral could have been superseded by a larger stone-built secular building on the site, and the Christian centre moved to the South Church.[74] Later, the secular building was replaced by the cathedral and the South Church became secondary. The cathedral itself was conceived on a monumental scale, being the only entirely stone-built church in Nubia.

The results from Faras and Ibrim were confirmed from other sites. At the smaller fort of Djebel Adda the American excavation produced a leather scroll also containing the names of King Joel and Bishop 'Merki'[75] (Markos?) And a date possibly as late as 1484. If this date is correct, Dotawo had survived as an organized state to the end of the fifteenth century. At Abdallah Nirqi, the Netherlands expedition found a series of magnificent frescos[76] including the military saints Theodore and Epimachos;[77] also John Chrysostom, a superb rendering of a priest in brown monastic habit, and another of the head and shoulders of a little figure emerging from a storage jar.[78] Most of these frescos, like those of Faras, were saved. At another site, Arminna West,[79] evidence suggested continuous occupation from Meroitic (*c.* first century BC) to late-Christian times, with the Classical period being the most prosperous. Other sites contributed their increase to knowledge of Christian Nubia. The call to 'Save Nubia' had been answered beyond expectation. In a very short time much had been salvaged. Equally important was the spirit of international co-operation, in particular between the British, Americans, Poles and Dutch, co-operation which would continue in the 'Save Carthage' expeditions a decade later.

The year 1965 saw the flooding of all the low-lying area north of Wadi Halfa. Ibrim alone survived for work to continue biennially until the time of writing (1994). South of Wadi Halfa flooding was less extensive and in April 1966 representatives of UNESCO met in Venice to decide what more could be done. A second phase of work was agreed, concentrating on the Batn el Hajar area between the Second and Third Cataracts. Its importance had been pointed out by Chittick in 1957.[80] The next five years drew a number of new teams, notably from Germany,[81] Geneva,[82] and the United States (University of Kentucky).[83] The Poles, under Stefan Jakobielski, Michałowski's student, began a new enterprise on the site of the capital of Makurrah, Old Dongola.[84] This site and Ibrim were destined to continue beyond 1972. The Batn el Hajar excavations at Kulb, Kulubnati, Sunnarti, Sai and Tangur, to mention a few of the more important sites, confirmed the main results of the Lower Nubian excavations. The watch-towers and forts facing west across the Nile showed clearly the quarter whence danger would come. Their existence strengthened the view that their kingdoms succumbed to continuous pressure from Sahara nomads, acting perhaps on behalf of Muslim tribes further west to force an unrestricted passage to the Red Sea and thence to Mecca.

Islam itself was, however, less of a danger. Dated Arabic inscriptions from a number of sites indicate that from the tenth century onwards there were groups of Muslims, probably traders, settled apparently peaceably in Nubian centres.[85] It would seem even as though the destructive raid on Ibrim by Shams ed Doula in 1173 was something of an aberration, a single punitive expedition against the presumptuous 'Lord of the Mountain' who thought himself secure in his eyrie. The threat of action, however, was never far away. At the very end of the 1972 season a trial excavation in a building next door to the cathedral, which in all probability was the governor's palace, produced an astonishing manuscript find. Documents stored in a stone (?) cist included an exchange of letters in 758 between the eparch at Ibrim and the emir at Aswan. The latter was insisting on the payment of tribute accepted by the Nubians in the *Baqt* (*pactum* or treaty) with the Egyptian Muslims in 652. The eparch's reply, written in Coptic, indicated a healthy respect for the emir who had threatened him with imprisonment for default.[86] Relations, however, remained on a diplomatic level. The real enemies to Nubian Christianity were the nomads, the same enemy that destroyed Christianity in North Africa and Anatolia.[87]

The emphasis of the work at Ibrim now tended to concentrate on the Bosnian remains or the pre-Christian, Meroitic, X-Group and Roman period. In 1976 a remarkable letter in barbarous Greek, written to the ruler of Ibrim, was mentioned. It complained of the depredations of Silko and invoked his assistance,[88] thus confirming Silko's own claims of success against the Blemmyes and others. Two years before, a lucky find by the writer in the last days of the 1974 dig resulted in the recovery of no fewer than 40 fragments of papyri including part of Book II of the *Iliad* and lists of expensive stores for the Roman garrison.[89] It indicated the Roman origin of the great south-west tower and also that the Roman occupation lasted much longer than the two years ascribed to Petronius' punitive expedition against the Ethiopians in 23 BC by Strabo.[90] Ibrim as Augustus' southern frontier, and an occupation lasting until the Year of the Four Emperors (AD 68–69) seems likely.[91] As a site, 'Ibrim never disappointed!'[92]

'Save Nubia' had more than justified itself. If only about one third of the sites in Lower Nubia had been saved great advances had been made in our knowledge of Nubia and its Christian civilization. Michałowski will always be associated with Faras and its treasures. Thanks to him and his colleagues many of the gaps in the record of Nubian political and administrative history had been filled. A new dimension had been created for the study of Christian art. The EES expedition to Ibrim had opened a new field for the study of Monophysite eucharistic liturgy, showing that while it was based on that of St Mark, it had retained some independent indigenous forms. The day-to-day life of the Christian Nubians was also revealed. Even elements in their diet in the latter stages of the long survival of the kingdom of Dotawo was shown through the excavation of the storage pits and magazines on the site. To William Adams goes the credit for building on the work of Shinnie to establish (perhaps with some over-elaboration) a firm classification of Nubian church architecture[93] and pottery types,[94] and also a new fundamental study of the role of Nubia as a link between Mediterranean and black Africa.

The four symposia on Nubian studies held between 1969 and 1978 in Germany, Poland, France and Britain ensured the continued interest in Nubian research.[95] Unlike the story of the scrolls and the Nag Hammadi documents, international co-operation has never failed, and publication has normally been rapid and scholarly. The example of Nubia was to be carried forward when a new challenge to the archaeology of Christian antiquity emerged, this time at Carthage.

CARTHAGE

Over-population had been a major factor prompting the building of the High Dam. It was to play a similar part in threatening the destruction of the archaeological heritage of Carthage. Urban sprawl between Tunis and Carthage and the accompanying roads were steadily encroaching on the ruins and, worse, the remains still to be discovered below ground. In 1970 a group of Tunisian and international scholars were brought together under UNESCO's auspices to try to identify what should be saved on scientific grounds from the tide of urbanization. Punic, Classical, early Christian and Byzantine remains, all were threatened. Their report was published next year.[96] By 1975 overseas teams from nine nations (to be joined by Canada in 1976 and later by Sweden) were working on sites allocated by the Tunisian government.[97] The appeal for 'Tunis–Carthage' had been justified.

The relatively small but potentially plum site from the early Christian standpoint was the Damous el Karita and its surroundings. Unfortunately the Bulgarians were hampered by technical problems relating to land-ownership on the site.[98] When the road to the north of the site was widened in the 1980s much of the important cemetery containing sarcophagi that lay in the way was extensively damaged. Elsewhere the teams fared better. The French under Serge Lancel concentrated on the Punic remains on Byrsa, citadel of Carthage, the British too worked successfully, mainly on the Carthaginian and Classical periods of occupation on the port installations and temple on Admiralty Island, and the Italians, Danes and West Germans also excavated largely Classical sites. The two important early-Christian discoveries were made by the French section of the Canadian mission under Paul Senay of the University of Trois Rivières,[99] and the Michigan University team from Ann Arbor under John Humphrey and John Pedley.

The object of the French-Canadian team was the 'Round Monument' located at the extreme north of an *insula* at the north end of the city, in the same *cardo* that contained the theatre and odeon. It enjoyed a magnificent view over the gulf of Tunis towards the sanctuary of Saturn on the summit of the Bou Kournein, and as far as the mountains of Zaghouan whose springs supplied Carthage with water. All these monuments had been excavated but in isolation and no attempt had been made to associate them in a general pattern of occupation of the area. Moreover, the Round Monument had been subjected to a sort of circular excavation which left it in the middle of a deep rubbish-covered pit whose sloping sides rendered accurate stratigraphy almost impossible.[100]

The site was particularly well known. It had been mentioned in 1833 by Charles Falbe, in 1861 by Norman Davis and in some detail by Audollent. In 1951, however, Alexandre Lézine had undertaken excavations that enabled him to draw up a plan (but not ascertain the date) of the monument and discover the existence of a Christian building immediately to the west.[101] Three years of careful, perhaps at times hesitant, work, however, enabled Professor Senay and his team to establish the likely identity of the building itself and set it in its context with its neighbours. In contrast to Lézine's excavation in the tradition of French architect-archaeologists, Senay concentrated on stratigraphy and chronology. The painstaking approach repaid. Though superficially the Round Monument resembled a hexagonal temple (Building 3) on the Admiralty Island, it became clear gradually that it was a Christian building connected with other Christian buildings immediately to the west.

Senay was able to demonstrate that the Round Building consisted of two concentric structures laid out apparently on a system of measurement associated with some of the major *martyria* of the eastern Roman Provinces.[102] 'In effect', Senay and colleague Marc Beauregard argued, 'the Round Monument shares with certain constructions in the Holy Land similarities of dimensions and proportions that cannot be due to chance alone but, rather, afford proof that they belong to the same architectural [school]; that which doubtless has its origins in the great Constantinian foundations in Palestine.'[103]

This was a big claim, but arguable in view of the authors' comparison of the Round Building with the rotundas in the church of the Nativity and Holy Sepulchre, both of which had almost exactly the same dimensions.[104] It was strengthened, moreover, by the discovery to the immediate west of the building not of a simple basilican-plan church but traces of a trifoliate *martyrium* of which the east and north apses survived. There were prospects of further Christian buildings lying to the west that could throw more light on the problem.[105]

The excavators dated the Round Building to the second half of the fourth century, with improvements in the reign of Theodosius I.[106] The Vandal occupation had witnessed its decay and temporary abandonment, a process reversed completely with the arrival of the Byzantines in 533. For three quarters of a century embellishments were lavished on the monument and surrounding Christian buildings. Floors were paved with mosaics, the last, the Mosaic of the Birds, dating probably to the early years of the seventh century,[107] therefore among the very latest mosaics to be found in the city. The seventh century, however, also saw neglect. Poorly-furnished burials of this period seem to be later than the final use of the building.[108] In whose honour was this building, reminiscent at least of the Constantinian monuments in Palestine and Rome, erected? The answer that springs to mind is that it was a cenotaph in honour of the martyr-bishop Cyprian (d. 258). This would identify the site with the hill 'near the governor's palace' near where the body of Cyprian was buried, according to the *Acts of Maximilian*, and with the Ager Sextii 'behind the proconsular residence' where Cyprian was executed.[109] In that case, why the long interval between the Peace of the Church and the second half of the fourth century before the monument was built? Moreover, this period coincides with the maximum power of the Donatists. If for them Cyprian was the vindicator of their tradition, would they choose to commemorate him with a building laid out on the same plan as those of Constantine who was their persecutor? True, they had contacts with the Holy Land but were these sufficient to prompt imitation of churches associated with the Holy Places (see above, p. 4)? Questions such as these can be asked but not answered. To Senay and his colleagues goes the credit of having made some sense of this, the most enigmatic Christian building so far found in Carthage.

Compared with this the University of Michigan (Ann Arbor)'s excavation of what proved to be a south annexe of a large Byzantine church was straight-forward. Difficulties were mainly administrative. As luck would have it the site lay at the northern edge of the American concession which ran north–south, bounded by the Avenue Habib Bourguiba to the west and the TGM railway line to the east, and included the newly-built supermarket. (Hence the basilica has been called the *Basilique du Supermarché*.) The basilica itself had been excavated by the Tunisian Institut d'Archéologie et d'Art, directed by Mme Liliane Ennabli in 1969–71. The mosaics that had covered the floor of the nave and side aisles had been moved for safe-keeing, leaving a somewhat forlorn appearance. It had been an imposing building 42 m long × 15 m wide with apses at each end and possibly a pulpit half way down a the nave on the north side, reminiscent of its counterparts elsewhere in the Byzantine word.[110] It must have played its part in the Byzantine restoration of Carthage (perhaps even on the archdeacon's church of Regio VI). It had replaced a smaller late fourth-century church (coin of Theodosius I in the masonry) whose axis lay slightly to the south, but whose destruction in the fifth century was indicated by a layer of rubble 1.20 m thick overlying it.[111] Fragments of masonry from the earlier church were re-used by the Byzantines.

The American concession ended 5 m short of the south wall of the Byzantine basilica, but for a considerable period the Tunisian authorities were unwilling to permit its extension northwards so as to examine the remains of the earlier church. Between 1976 and 1978 a baulk 5 m wide existed between the two sites, and a Byzantine baptistery which was situated within it remained in a sort of nomansland until it was agreed in 1978 that the American team could excavate there, which they did in 1979. Meantime in 1977 the writer had been able to confirm the destruction layer over the earlier church through observation of levels revealed by the gradual erosion of the north side of the baulk.

Despite these handicaps the annexe itself proved to be unexpectedly inform-ative about the final century of the Byzantine occupation. For the first time a

Graffiti found in the Roman catacombs, including a dove and the Good Shepherd.

Sealed pot containing Nubian manuscripts *in situ* at Qasr Ibrim

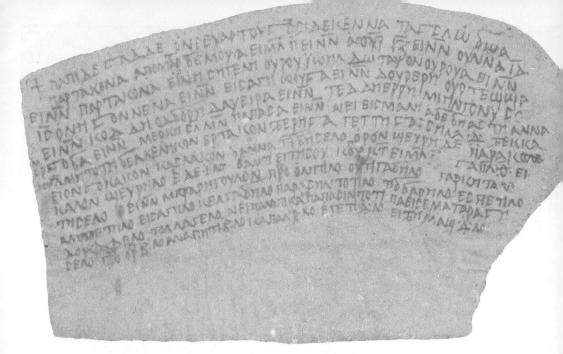

series of intact seventh-century levels were encountered. The latest mosaic floor had been covered by five phases of occupation, the last recognizably ecclesiastical phase ending *c.* 695, to be succeeded by four levels of domestic occupation. These ended with a possible Fatimid Arab occupation for a short time in the early eighth century.[112] The excavation among occupation levels to the south revealed no sudden break between a relatively prosperous Christian Carthage and the final Arab conquest in 698. Rather, a gradual, irreversible impoverishment set in, shown by an ever smaller area occupied that preceded final abandonment. The same picture of shoddy decline was reproduced on the Admiralty Isle and in the British sector around the southern portion of the walls of Theodosius II (built *c.* 425). Humble graves were found on previously occupied sites nearby.[113]

The international excavations revealed a good deal that had been missing in the history of Christian Carthage. Prosperity throughout the fourth century was succeeded by neglect and decay of Christian buildings under the Vandal kings, shown at both the Monument and Byzantine basilica sites as well as on Admiralty Island. The Byzantine restoration ushered in a period of brilliant and lavish reconstruction, in Carthage, as elsewhere in Justinian's empire. No fewer than four large Byzantine churches have been found in an area of half a square kilometre west of the port.[114] But it was not maintained. Some wealthy houses, such as the House of the Greek Charioteers to the west of the Byzantine basilica in the US sector, continued to be occupied in the seventh century.[115] In other parts there was growing poverty. Whether this was due to the decline of trade or to supplies not reaching the city in a quantity sufficient to sustain the city's population or some other cause, is not known. But the signs are that civic and ecclesiastical life alike declined through the seventh century. The view that both were suddenly extinguished by the arrival of the Arab invaders needs revision.

ELSEWHERE

Twelve years after the waters of Lake Nasser rose to cover some two-thirds of surviving Nubian monuments there was another call for international co-operation to salvage antiquities. In *Iraq* the Saddam dam across the Tigris north of Mosul would cause the flooding of the Hamrin Basin from April 1985 on, and the destruction of a large number of sites ranging from Palaeolithic through the periods of Babylonian history to Hellenistic and Islamic times. From 1978 to 1985 some 80 sites were explored by teams drawn from Great Britain, the United States, West Germany, Poland, France, Italy and Japan, among the most prominent, all co-operating with the Iraqi State Antiquities Organization.[116] The British School of Archaeology at Baghdad, founded in 1932 in memory of Gertrude Bell, took on a leading role. Very few early Christian remains, however, were found in the threatened area. Remains which might be identified as a monastery were found by the Japanese at Ain Shayi,[117] and further south near Eski Mosul (Old Mosul) a rather more finely-constructed church in use between the seventh and ninth centuries was excavated by a Franco-Iraqi team.[118] Christianity did not apparently achieve much success in this part of Persian Mesopotamia. It may have been confined largely to the main centres of population, while the people as a whole remained true to the traditional Zoroastrian cult so long as the Persian empire survived. Thereafter they passed direct to Islam.

Finally, we return to Egypt, this time to *Northern Sinai* and the area round Pelusium not far from the Sinai coast, part of the area handed back by Israel in 1982. As in Nubia the cause was a massive irrigation project. This time the aim was to irrigate western Sinai by cutting a huge canal running east from the Suez Canal into the desert lands which would eventually feed a series of irrigation water courses and so enable the desert to be cultivated. A number of ancient sites were threatened with flooding and in 1991 the Egyptian Antiquities Organisation appealed for international co-operation from already established missions to work with their Egyptian colleagues to survey and excavate these sites while there was time. The first in the field were the British led by Dr Steven Snape of Liverpool University and the French Institut archéologique du Caire. The British excavation centred on Pelusium itself (Tell el Farama) that lay just north of the course of the principal canal.[119] Pelusium had been a port and frontier town but the sea has retreated there, leaving a large *tell* (mound) some $2\frac{1}{2}$ miles from the coast. In the fifth century it was a Christian bishopric whose bishop, Isidore, wrote among his 2,000 extant letters a stinging attack on Cyril's conduct at the council of Ephesus in 431. 'Many of those who were assembled at Ephesus', he wrote, 'speak satirically of you as a man bent on pursuing his private animosities, not as one who seeks in correct belief the things of Jesus Christ.' Cyril was an apt disciple of his uncle, Theophilus, who 'openly expended his fury against the inspired and beloved John (Chrysostom)'.[120] Isidore had been monk and presbyter before becoming bishop.

In 1994, an industrial complex (probably connected with salt extraction) of the late-Roman period and pottery of the fourth to sixth centuries had been found but there were as yet no traces of Isidore's church. A cemetery containing bodies laid out with their heads facing east was found. The absence of grave-goods may have been due to robbing or to the Christian faith of the deceased.[121] During the 1992 season the British team was housed at the French expedition house at Babruza on the south side of the canal where the French were concentrating their work.[122] Indeed one of the features of the international salvage operations in Egypt, Iraq and Carthage was the complete co-operation between the nations and their teams. At Ibrim, Polish architects were members of the EES team, and the writer enjoyed the unstinted hospitality and encouragement of the Polish team on his way to Ibrim in November 1972. William Adams shared the leadership of the expedition with J. M. Plumley, in 1972 and 1974. There were British members of the Michigan team at Carthage. Many other examples of close international co-operation in the field could be quoted. The problem that faced everyone concerned was how best to salvage as much as possible of the threatened heritage of the past in face of the demands of the modern state. Their answer gives hope for the same immediate international response to similar challenges in the new millennium.

It may be necessary, for in 1994 a new threat was emerging in the form of a projected dam across the Euphrates which would threaten important Roman and early Christian sites at Samosata, Melitene and Zeugma.[123] A rescue dig under Dr David Kennedy of the University of Western Australia, with help from Glasgow University and the British Institute of Ankara, was at Zeugma in the winter 1993–94. Will it be in time?

NOTES

1. James M. Robinson, *Religious Studies Review* 3 (1977), 24 (see above, p. 284), p. 24.
2. The project was graphically described by J. M. Plumley, 'The Aswan Dam', *Antiquity* 34 (1960), p. 62.
3. O. G. S. Crawford, *Castles and Churches in the Middle Nile Region* (Sudan Antiquities Service, Occasional Papers 2; Khartoum, 1953).
4. Ibid., pp. 14 (Artul Mosque Church, Site 10) and 31 (el Koro Mosque-church, Site 31, fig. 10).
5. P. L. Shinnie, *Excavations at Soba* (Occasional Papers 3; Khartoum, 1955), 'Glass' (D. B. Harden). For the church, pp. 26–7.
6. Ibid., pp. 10 and 18.
7. Ibid., pp. 10 and 78–81.
8. Ibid., 'pottery', pp. 28–50; 'Glass', pp. 60–76.
9. Ibid., p. 76: end may have been due to 'slow decay rather than to violent overthrow' (by the Funj).
10. P. L. Shinnie and H. N. Chittick, *Ghazali – A Monastery in the Northern Sudan* (Occasional Papers 5; Khartoum, 1961). For the larger and more elaborate monastery at Basr el Wizz near Faras, see G. Scanlon, *JEA* 57 (1971), fig. I.
11. References given by Shinnie, *Soba*, pp. 8 and 17.
12. Ibid., p. 19.
13. W. Y. Adams, 'The Christian pottery kilns at Faras', *Kush* 9 (1961), pp. 20–43.
14. W. Y. Adams, *Nubia: Corridor to Africa* (London: Allen Lane, 1977), pp. 81ff. for his account of the massive conservation programme preceding the construction of the High Dam.
15. W. Y. Adams, 'The Archaeological Survey of Sudanese Nubia', *Kush* 9 (1961), pp. 7ff.

16. H. S. Smith, *Preliminary Reports of the Egypt Exploration Society's Nubian Survey* (London, 1961).
17. F. Hinkel, 'Report on the dismantling and removal of endangered monuments in Sudanese Nubia', *Kush* 12 (1964), pp. 111–18.
18. See W. Y. Adams, 'The evolution of Christian Nubian pottery' in E. Dinkler (ed.), *Kunst und Geschichte Nubiens in christlicher Zeit* (Recklinghausen: Bongers, 1970), pp. 111–23; 'The Christian potteries at Faras', *Kush* 11 (1963), pp. 30–45: 13 (1965), pp. 148–76 (Meinarti).
19. P. L. Shinnie, 'The University of Ghana excavations at Debeira West', *Kush* 11 (1963), pp. 257–63, plate LXVI b.
20. The story is told by Michałowski in *Faras: Die Kathedrale aus dem Wüstensand* (Cologne/Zürich/Einsiedeln, 1967), pp. 14–17.
21. Ibid., plates 3–4 (Archangel Michael and the Three Youths in the fiery furnace) and 72 (Madonna and Child in Bishop Johannes' funerary chapel).
22. Illustrated throughout *Faras* (Warsaw, 1974) and *Faras: Die Kathedrale*.
23. *The Book of James* ii–v; ed. M. R. James in *The Apocryphal New Testament* (OUP, 1924), pp. 39–41.
24. *Faras: Die Kathedrale*, plates 24 and 25, and pp. 106–7. The Virgin is represented in the 'violet' style of the tenth century, but the accompanying angels are some two centuries earlier in 'white style'.
25. Ibid., plates 63–69, pp. 143–7.
26. Plate 26, pp. 107-9.
27. Plate 30, p. 112, and plates 57–59: Bishop Petros protected by the apostle Peter, *c.* 975.
28. Plate 29, p. 111.
29. Plate 39, p. 119.
30. Plates 3–4 and 60–61, pp. 138–9. The youths are protected by Michael (see note 21 above). See also Adams, *Nubia*, p. 483.
31. Plates 62 and 71, p. 149 (eleventh century).
32. Thus Mercurius, plate 48, p. 128. See below, note 52.
33. Plates 31 (the anchorite Anamone), 37 (Bishop Kyros), 94 (a Nubian princess).
34. Plates 81–83, pp. 157–9. The comparison with Holbein's portrait of Henry VIII was not lost on Michałowski: p. 159.
35. Plate 27: St Anne guarding her secret, eighth–ninth century. The figures are classified in Michałowski's *Faras*, pp. 42ff.
36. Discussed by Michałowski, 'Open problems of Nubian art and culture in the light of dicoveries at Faras' in *Kunst und Geschichte*, pp. 11–20, at p. 15. The Ethiopian influence seems clear in *Faras: Die Kathedrale*, plates 89–95, especially in the cast of the eyes of the figures and stylized crown on the head of the young prince, plate 98. See also S. Jakobielski in *Nubia Christiana*, I (Warsaw, 1982), pp. 142–72.
37. Plate 15 shows Josef Gazy at work on a fresco before its removal.
38. See Stefan Jakobielski, *Faras*, III: *A history of the Bishopric of Faras* (Warsaw, 1972) pp. 206–11. (Conspectus of bishops and main events in Faras).
39. Asked by Michałowski, loc. cit., *Kunst und Geschichte*, p. 14: Jakobielski, *Faras*, III, ch. 9. But note Martin Krause, 'Zur Kirchen- und Theologiegeschichte Nubiens' in *Kunst und Geschichte*, pp. 71–86. The writer found a MS fragment, tenth to eleventh century in date, bearing the Monophysite version of the Trisagion ('Holy God, Holy Almighty, Holy Immortal, *who was crucified for us*'): *JbAC* 35 (1992), pp. 126–7.
40. See Michałowski, *Faras: Die Kathedrale*, p. 48 (plan).
41. On Silko, see above, p. 46, and Adams, *Nubia*, pp. 422–3, Michałowski dates his reign to *c.* 536: *Faras: Die Kathedrale*, p. 183.
42. A concise account of the stages of the conversion of the Nubians is given by Adams, pp. 438–45.
43. Transcription of the Greek and Coptic dedications, see Jakobielski, *Faras*, op. cit., ch. 2, at p. 38 (illustration).
44. Ibid., p. 41. Mercurios was 'king'; 'the great eparch' Marcos 'administered the kingdom'. Mercurius is called 'the new Constantine' in *Histroy of the Patriarchs* i, ch. xviii (*PO* 5), p. 140. The same title was accorded to the emperor Marcian by the bishops at the Council of Chalcedon in 451.
45. Jakobielski, *Faras*, op. cit., Annexe i, pp. 190–5. The text of the Tamar inscription is reproduced p. 205. (The actual place where the epitaph was found originally is not known: p. 167.) For Count Vidua see Chapter 4 above, pp. 46–7.

46. Ibid., pp. 167–8. The cathedral was renovated once during the thirteenth century when drifting sand had already accumulated to the level of the windows. The North Monastery was built about this time.

47. Ibid., pp. 190-201.

48. The Nubian bishop's garb is illustrated by Michałowski, *Faras* (1974), p. 46.

49. Michałowski, *Faras: Die Kathedrale*, plate 77.

50. Jakobielski, *Faras*, p. 41: text of inscription.

51. Michałowski, *Faras* (1974), pp. 47-9 and plate 34.

52. Jakobielski, *Faras*, p. 41, line 5 of inscription.

53. J. M. Plumley and R. Dale. 'Qasr Ibrim: Exploration Society Expedition 1963', unpublished; supplemented by information from J. M. Plumley to the writer.

54. The cathedral faced down river which flowed practically due north–south. The orientation was due also to its having been built on the foundations of a secular building (governor's palace?), a fact not known in 1963–64. Where I have used geographical rather than ecclesiastical orientation I have indicated this.

55. See Frend, 'The Qasr Ibrim Expedition (Dec. 1963–Feb. 1964)', *Acta* VII (Trier, 1965, published Rome, 1968), pp. 531–8 (= *Expedition*).

56. Publ. by Frend and I. A. Muirhead, 'The Greek manuscripts from the Cathedral of Q'asr Ibrim', *Le Muséon* 89 (1976), pp. 43–9.

57. Illustrated in *Illustrated London News* (11 July 1964).

58. Published by J. M. Plumley, 'The scrolls of Bishop Timotheos: two documents from mediaeval Nubia', *Texts from Excavations*, I (OUP, 1975). The documents consisted of 166 lines of Coptic and 58 lines of Arabic.

59. See Frend, 'Coptic, Greek and Nubian at Qasr Ibrim', *Byzantino–slavica* 33 (1972), pp. 224–9.

60. Publ. by Frend, 'Fragments of an Acta Martyrum from Qasr Ibrim' *JbAC* 29 (1986), pp. 66–70; 'Fragments of a version of the Acta S. Georgii from Qasr Ibrim',, *JbAC* 32 (1989), pp. 89–104; 'The cult of military saints in Christian Nubia' in *Theologia Crucis – Signum crucis* (Festschrift Dinkler; 1979), pp. 155–63.

61. Frend, *Expedition*, plate 5.

62. Frend, 'Some further liturgical fragments from Qasr Ibrim', *JbAC* 35 (1992), pp. 119–34 at pp. 119–26.

63. Ibid., pp. 126–7.

64. J. M. Plumley, 'Qasr Ibrim 1963–1964', *JEA* 50 (1964), pp. 3–5, plate II.2.

65. Frend, *Expedition*, plate 8.

66. I.e. from the beginning of the reign of Diocletian (AD 284).

67. Frend, *Expedition*, pp. 537–8. Plumley, in his lecture 'The Christian period at Qasr Ibrim; some notes on the MSS finds' (Warsaw, 1973), dates four other scrolls to the equivalent of 1281, 1287 and 1334. I owe this information to him.

68. W. Y. Adams, J. A. Alexander and R. Allen, 'Qasr Ibrim, 1980 and 1982', *JEA* 69 (1983), pp. 43–60, at p. 54 extends the Christian period at Ibrim to '*c.* 1550 AD'; Plumley, 'New evidence on Christian Nubia in the light of recent discoveries' in *Nubia Christiana*, I, p. 34.

69. Frend, *Expedition*, p. 538, plate 9.

70. The best, a Greek fragment of Mark in uncials and a Sahidic Coptic fragment of Isaiah: see Plumley and Adams, 'Qasr Ibrim 1972', *JEA* 60 (1974), p. 214.

71. See Plumley, *JEA* 52 (1966), p. 11: and Jakobielski, op, cit., pp. 146–7, suggesting that Marianos belonged to a succession of Melkite bishops in the first half of the eleventh century.

72. Plumley and Adams, op. cit., pp. 229–33. At Adisha also, a Pharaonic temple was turned into a church, see J. Vercoutter, *Kunst und Geschichte*, p. 155.

73. Plumley, 'Qasr Ibrim 1974', *JEA* 61 (1975), p. 16. The writer catalogued 165 coins (report forthcoming) though some of these came from other than the temple site.

74. See Mark Horton, 'First Christians at Qasr Ibrim', *Egyptian Archaeology* (1991), pp. 9–12. The presence of a large secular building below the cathedral was suggested by the non-regular plan of the east (ecclesiastical) end, and to the writer in 1964 by a solid stub of walling protruding low down half way along the south (ecclesiastical) wall.

75. Nicholas B. Millet, 'The Gebel Adda Expedition. Preliminary Report', *JARCE* 3 (1964), pp. 7–14. Six churches were discovered on the site, one of which had been converted into a mosque. Arabic documents dated from 1590 onwards.

76. P. van Moorsel, J. Jacquet and H. Schneider, *The Central Church of Abdallah Nirqi* (National Museum of Antiquities at Leiden; Brill, 1975), pp. 110–11 and plates 63 and 67, and p. 92; *Kunst und Geschichte*, plates 39–42).

77. Ibid., plate 83.

78. Moorsel, plates 78, 82 and 83.

79. Bruce G. Trigger, 'The cultural ecology of Christian Nubia' in *Kunst und Geschichte*, pp. 347–86, at p. 363: Adams, op. cit., pp. 357, 493–4.

80. H. N. Chittick, *Kush* 5 (1957), pp. 45ff, and plate 2.

81. For the German expeditions see, E. Dinkler *et al.*, 'Deutsche Nubien Unternehmung 1967', *Arch. Anzeiger* (1968), Heft 4, pp. 717–38; for 1968 ibid. (1971), Heft 1; for 1969, ibid. (1971), Heft 3, pp. 456–91; ibid., (1972), Heft 4, pp. 643–713; and *Kunst und Geschichte*, pp. 259–80.

82. Charles Maystre, 'Fouilles americano-suisses aux églises de Kageras, Ukuna Est et Songi Sud', in *Kunst und Geschichte*, pp. 181–208.

83. W. Y. Adams, 'The University of Kentucky Excavations at Kulubnarti 1969', ibid., pp. 141–54.

84. Stefan Jakobielski, 'Polish Excavations at Old Dongola', ibid., pp. 171–80.

85. See P. L. Shinnie, 'Debeira West', *Kush* 11 (1963), p. 262; Adams, *Corridor*. Also Shinnie, 'Trade in mediaeval Nubia', *Etudes Nubiennes* (1975), pp. 253–63.

86. Plumley and Adams, *JEA* 60 (1974), pp. 236–38 and plate CIII.3. I witnessed (the workman is holding my trowel!) the discovery, but unfortunately no stratigraphic record was kept to support the photographs which Plumley took.

87. See Frend, 'Nomads and Christianity in the Middle Ages', *JEH* 26 (1975), pp. 209–21 (see above, p. 30).

88. Adams, op. cit., p. 423.

89. Reported at the Fourteenth Congress of Papyrologists at Oxford in 1974: *Proceedings*, pp. 103–11; and fully analysed by M. E. Weinstein and E. G. Turner, 'Greek and Latin papyri from Qasr Ibrim', *JEA* 62 (1976), pp. 115–30.

90. Strabo, xvii. 53–4; cf. Dio Cassius, liv.5–6.

91. Frend, 'Augustus' frontier Qasr Ibrim', *BAR* (Internat. Ser.) 71 (1980), pp. 926–30; a similar result independently arrived at by Adams, 'Primis and the "Aethiopian Frontier"', *JARCE* 20 (1983), pp. 93–104.

92. Plumley's apt comment on the site in 1974.

93. Adams, 'Architectural evolution of the Nubian Church', *JARCE* 5 (1966), pp. 87–139; and P. M. Garthiewicz, 'An introduction to the history of Nubian Church architecture' in *Nubia Christiana* I (Warsaw, 1982), pp. 43–133.

94. Adams, 'The evolution of Christian Nubian pottery', in *Kunst und Geschichte*, pp. 111–28; 'Varia Ceramica', *Etudes nubiennes* (Chantilly Conference Proceedings, 2–6 July 1975; Inst. français d'Archéologie orientale du Caire 77: Cairo, 1978), pp. 1–23.

95. Four more have been held since 1978, including the retrospective 'Nubia Thirty Years Later', at Lille (11–17 September 1994).

96. Entitled 'Mise en valeur du patrimoine monumental de la région de Carthage en vue du développement économique'.

97. The teams in 1975 were Germany, Bulgaria, Denmark, France, Great Britain, Italy, Poland (resistivity survey; no digging), USA (two teams) and a combined Maghrebian team.

98. Partly from what I heard on the spot in 1976. Apparently, the owner of land immediately to the west of the basilica refused permission to excavate; but the large (9.15 m diameter) late Roman subterranean round tomb, converted into a baptistery(?) at one period, situated in the cemetery, beyond his boundary was re-examined and cleared by Professor S. Boyadjev and his team: see 'La Rotonde souterraine de Damous-el-Karita', *Atti* IX.2, pp. 117–31, No definite conclusions as to use after abandonment as a baptistery; earlier discussion: A. Lézine, *Architecture romaine d'Afrique* (Tunis, 1963), pp. 80–6. No attempt, however, was made to probe for remains below the floor-level of the basilica, or across the road to the north, to locate the wealthy cemetery there.

99. The English-speaking Canadians under Colin Wells and Edith Wightman worked on a sector of the Theodosian wall marking the northern boundary of the city. The British team had a party working on the corresponding sector on the south side.

100. Described by Senay, 'Fouille du Monument circulaire' in *Cahiers des études anciennes* 6: *Carthage* I (Les Presses de l'Université du Québec, 1976), pp. 23–4.

101. A. Lézine, *Fasti Archaeologici* VI (1953). Correctly estimated that the building was 'un édifice cultuel chrétienne' of late fourth-century date.

102. P. Senay and M. Beauregard, 'Parallèles palestiniens' in *Cahiers des Etudes anciennes* 13 *Carthage* V: (Université du Québec à Trois Rivières, 1981), p. 8 n. 4.
103. Ibid., p. 8.
104. Ibid., pp. 14–19. I am not sure whether other parallels cited, such as the Dome of the Rock in Jerusalem, add substantially to the authors' case.
105. *Cahiers* 12 (1980) (*Carthage* IV), plate II.
106. *Cahiers* 12 (Texte), p. 14.
107. Ibid., pp. 15 and 35.
108. *Cahiers* 6 (*Carthage* I), p. 33.
109. Charles-Picard's view expressed in *BAC* (1948), pp. 507–11; (1951–52), pp. 191–5, plate XVIII. See *Acta Maximiliani* 3: Musurillo, 249; *Acta Cypriani* 5: Musurillo, 175. Cyprian was buried in the existing cemetery of Macrobius Candidanus on the Via Mappalia.
110. See Noel Duval, 'Chronique', *Bulletin Monumental* 139 (1979), pp. 377–8; 140 (1982), pp. 227–9.
111. *Bulletin Monumental* (1982), p. 227 (col. A).
112. Simon Ellis, 'The ecclesiastical complex: stratigraphic report 1976' in J. Humphrey (ed.), *Excavations at Carthage 1976 Conducted by the University of Michigan*, III (Ann Arbor, 1977) ch. 3. The huge Antonine Baths were also abandoned in Vandal times and refurbished by the Byzantines.
113. See Henry Hurst, 'Excavations at Carthage, Fourth Interim Report', *AJ* 60 (1979), p. 44. Burials near Building 8 near the centre of the island.
114. See the writer, 'The Early Christian Church in Carthage', *Excavations at Carthage*, III, ch. 2, esp. pp. 21, 23–34.
115. The last phase of the house built in the late fourth century was probably 575–650: see J. Humphrey (ed.), *Excavations at Carthage 1975*, I, p. 17.
116. 'Excavations in Iraq, 1977–78', *Iraq* 41 (1979), pp. 159–81 (threatened sites).
117. 'Excavations in Iraq, 1985–86', *Iraq* 49 (1987), pp. 234–5.
118. 'Excavations in Iraq, 1982–83', *Iraq* 43 (1983), p. 217.
119. Steven Snape, 'Salvaging ancient Sinai', *Egyptian Archaeology* 3 (1993), pp. 21–2 (map); EES, Annual Report for 1994, pp. 11–12.
120. Isidore, *Ep.* 1.310. Cited from J. Stevenson, rev. W. H. C. Frend, *Creeds, Councils and Controversies* (SPCK, 1989), document 228, p. 319.
121. Snape, loc. cit., p. 22; 'Cisterns and cemeteries', ibid., 4 (1994), pp. 17–18.
122. Snape (1993), p. 22.
123. *The Times*, Report (9 March 1994).

FURTHER READING

W. Y. Adams, *Nubia*, chs 14–17.

W. Y. Adams, 'Architectural evolution of the Nubian church', *JARCE* 5 (1966), pp. 87–139.

W. Y. Adams with J. A. Alexander and R. Allen, 'Qasr Ibrim, 1980 and 1982', *JEA* 69 (1983), pp. 43–60.

E. Dinkler (ed.), *Kunst und Geschichte Nubiens in Christlicher Zeit* (Recklinghausen: Bongers, 1970; essays).

S. Jakobielski, 'A History of the Bishopric of Faras' in *Faras*, III (Warsaw, 1972).

K. Michałowski, *Faras: Die Kathedrale aus dem Wüstensand* (Cologne–Zürich–Einsiedeln, 1967).

J. M. Plumley, 'The scrolls of Bishop Timotheos: two documents from medieval Nubia' in *Texts from Excavations* (OUP, 1975).

J. M. Plumley, 'Qasr Ibrim 1963–64', *JEA* 50 (1964) and subsequent reports to 1980 in *JEA*.

P. L. Shinnie, *Excavations at Soba* (Occasional Papers no. 3; Khartoum, 1955).

P. L. Shinnie with H. N. Chittick, *Ghazali, a Monastery in the Northern Sudan* (Occasional Papers no. 5; Khartoum, 1961).

13

From war's end
to Trier, 1945–1965

The international salvage operations achieved much. They consolidated an international approach to archaeology, not least to Christian archaeology, as well as being immensely rewarding to the participating teams. A great many otherwise doomed sites were saved. A great deal was added to knowledge. In this chapter we return to more bread-and-butter themes. The twenty years that followed the end of the war witnessed both a consolidation in large scholarly volumes of previously garnered results, and also a gathering momentum of new discoveries. While these continued to be made in established archaeolo-gical areas on the southern shores of the Mediterranean, fresh fields were opening up elsewhere, in the state of Israel, Cyprus, western Europe and in one-time Roman territories along the Danube, including Austria and northern Yugoslavia (now Croatia). This was a broad band of territory where Christianity had made slowest progress, but even here the mission was becoming effective in the last decades of the fourth century. In that period the foundations were laid everywhere in the West, except in Roman Britain, for a Latin-dominated and Christian mediaeval Europe, that never lost sight of its continuity with the Roman provincial past.

Dramatic advances in knowledge were often the result of advances in archaeological techniques. In the field, the methods worked out by Mortimer Wheeler were now being applied almost universally, though 'déblayage excavation' died hard. The archaeologist also had to come to terms with a variety of techniques and skills borrowed from other fields of study. Air photography had become a precise science during the war.[1] Sites could now be pin-pointed and identified with an exactness impossible previously. Carbon dating from wood, charcoal and other organic material, and radiology, invaluable to the prehistorian, could also be used to date burnt-out Christian buildings and skeletal remains.[2] With ever greater precision demanded of excavators it became no longer possible to ignore pottery and apparently uninteresting small finds as had happened too often in the past.

A new generation of scholars was replacing the leaders and pioneers of the pre-war period. The war years had taken their toll; Dölger had left the scene in 1940 at the early age of 61. J. P. Kirsch followed him in February 1941 and Eugène Albertini the same year. Hans Lietzmann never recovered from the news of his son's death on the Russian front in July 1941 and succumbed to cancer at Locarno in June 1942. Neither Auguste Audollent nor Franz Cumont survived the war. Nor did the greatest of all self-taught practitioners. Henri Leclercq completed his *opus maximus*, the *Dictionnaire d'Archéologie chrétienne et de Liturgie*, in mid-1943. He handed in his reader's card to the British Museum and departed. His work was done. He died in March 1945 without revealing the secret of his encyclopaedic knowledge, powers of assimilation, and single-minded application to the task in hand.[3]

The *Dictionnaire* was not only the greatest in every respect of the compendia of existing knowledge concerning the early Church attempted at this time, but others, such as the *Dictionnaire d'histoire et géographie ecclésiastique*, floundered, not having a Leclercq to drive them forward, nor a H. I. Marrou to see that a final volume published in 1953, which included a report on the Vatican excavations, was kept right up to date. Van de Meer's and Mohrmann's *Atlas of the Early Christian World* (1958) aimed similarly at providing a thorough survey through maps and splendid illustrations of archaeological sites of the progress of the Church from apostolic times to *c.* AD 600 as known at the time. It remains an essential guide though it may be faulted for failing to take into account physical geography as a factor influencing both the missions and the divisions in the early Church.

The other great event in the 1950s was the appearance of the first volumes of the *Lexikon für Antike und Christentum* (first volume in 1950). Dölger's hopes had been fulfilled, for despite immense difficulties arising from the war, including the loss of manuscripts, publication had gone ahead.[4] Eight years later the Franz Josef Dölger Institut at Bonn University began publishing the annual *Jahrbuch für Antike und Christentum* with Theodor Klauser as editor, combining literary and archaeological discoveries in the field of early Christianity and Late Antiquity.

Large-scale reports on major sites explored before the war were also appearing. In 1947 Talbot Rice published the excavations on the Great Palace at Constantinople.[5] Jean Lassus brought out his *Sanctuaires chrétiens de Syrie,* describing the Christian remains he had worked on in Syria before the onset of hostilities. Doro Levi published the mosaics recovered by the Princeton expedition at Antioch (1948) and during the 1950s Final Reports on the excavations Dura Europos began to appear, including the church and the synagogue. In 1956 the seventh volume of the *Monumenta Asiae Minoris antiqua* was published, recording inscriptions found in Phrygia before the war. These included the appeal to Constantine by the citizens of Orkistus for a return to the status of *civitas* on the grounds that 'they were all Christians'(!).[6] For Christianity in southern Gaul, Fernand Benoît republished in 1954 Leblant's two catalogues of early-Christian sarcophagi from Arles (100 in number) and Marseilles (22). A steady stream of information about early Christianity based on archaeological evidence was becoming available to scholars and the public.

The process was furthered by the three International Congresses of Christian Archaeology held during this time, at Aix-en-Provence in 1954, Ravenna in 1962 and Trier, in 1965. They provided additional continuity with pre-war work as well as a platform for new discoveries to be discussed. At Ravenna in particular, those attending had the memorable privilege of seeing the sixth-century mosaics of San Vitale and San Apollinare Nuovo restored to their full glory,[7] as well as the new mosaics discovered during excavations in San Giovanni Evangelista, one of the few serious war casualties in the Byzantine city.[8]

At these gatherings church typology still held pride of place. The *martyria* replaced the basilica as the subject for debate. André Grabar had found hospitality and opportunity to work in the United States and in 1946 he had published his study of *martyria*.[9] In this he had associated the plan of the church buildings with the cult of martyrs and relics, and had stressed the influence of the attendant liturgy on the origins of Christian art.[10] He believed rightly that the liturgy had developed largely from simple ceremonies at the martyr's grave. The buildings in which the rites of remembrance were, however, held were modelled on existing pagan mausolea.[11] In the West, martyrs' relics would be buried beneath the altar of a church, but in the East they would be housed in a separate building centred on the tomb with a dome-roof. Byzantine churches would eventually follow this basic plan.

Grabar's theory held until examined in detail by John Ward Perkins in a lecture at the Trier Congress.[12] The pagan heritage, he argued, was not the only source of inspiration for the *martyrium*. If there was no specifically Christian architecture before the Peace of the Church (312),[13] there was also no counterpart to the trefoil (trifoliate) *martyrium* (such as at Theveste) nor for other Christian types, such as the cruciform shrine erected at Antioch in

381. In the fourth century Christianity was above all an innovative and even revolutionary religion, demonstrated in its art and architecture as well as its teaching and liturgy. Often, as Ambrose of Milan had stated, the shape of a building, in the form of a cross, reflected the witness of the martyr to the cross of Christ.[14] The case, however, was not closed, but a solution required greater flexibility than Grabar was perhaps prepared to accept.

A second typological dicussion also involved Grabar's *martyrium*, namely Dyggve's theory of some cemetery churches being 'roofless churches', the *basilica discoperta*. At the Rome Congress in 1938 Dyggve commented on the results of his excavations on the Marusinac site at Salona.[15] In comparing the structure, especially the size of the pillars, of the two churches there, he had concluded that the northern church, where he believed bishops of Salona had been buried, had been built round a rectangular courtyard that had been left open to the sky. He cited the example of the church of Abraham at Hebron which had been described by a sixth-century traveller as 'Basilica aedificata in quadriporticus in medio atrio discoperta'.[16]

This would have been a novel form of church architecture in Latin-speaking Christendom even for cemetery churches. It would have meant that this type of Christian architecture was indebted to the open courtyard of Semitic shrines, a possibility at Salona, though unlikely. While Grabar was prepared to assent,[17] other critics were practically unanimous in rejecting Dyggve's theory.[18] The argument was settled eventually in the simplest possible way. Excavations in 1993 and 1994 unearthed roofing materials in the area supposed to have been unroofed. Fragments of tiles lying where they fell were there for members of the Centenary Congress to see. The penalty for not taking trenches down to natural ground level can seldom have been better illustrated.

Meantime ever more new material was coming to light. In December 1964, Crawford, writing in *Antiquity*, claimed that 'the summer of 1964 has been full of exciting discoveries'.[19] He was not referring in particular to early Christianity, but he might as well have been. The three international congresses had shown how new discoveries were being made throughout the whole area once occupied by the Roman empire. The year 1961 had seen the first textbook designed to correlate literary with archaeological remains. Though Michael Gough gave too much space to the prevailing study of typology in Christian architecture and art, his *The Early Christians* was a pioneering work, a pointer to future writing of early-Church history, which integrated literary and archaeological studies.

Even at the risk of being episodic, the story of what was being found in these years should now be told. The British, as we have seen, were quick to safeguard the Classical and early-Christian monuments in Libya after the occupation of the territory in 1943. When Denys Haynes returned to the British Museum in 1946 and Ward Perkins became Director of the British School in Rome, the main responsibility for the Antiquities Departments in Tripolitania and Cyrenaica fell to Richard Goodchild (1918–68) who had returned to Tripolitania in 1946 as Antiquities Officer, after a year's post-war study in England. The choice could not have been better. Goodchild was a lifelong field archaeologist, trained in the skills needed for work in Roman Britain, and able to adapt these to the far more complicated sites in Libya. He was, moreover, able to work with others, with Ward Perkins in particular, in describing, discovering and excavating the Christian antiquities in the territory, and with the Italians in the task of rehabilitating and where feasible restoring major archaeological remains. From 1953 onwards he was training Libyans to take over the responsibility for their archaeological heritage. Goodchild was Controller of Antiquities in Cyrenaica 1954–66 (with an interval in 1960–61 when he was working in East Africa) but he died in February 1968 shortly after election to a Chair in London University. That so much was accomplished throughout Libya before the onset of the revolution in September 1969 was due largely to his energy, skill and tact.[20]

In the immediate aftermath of the war, there were two main tasks. The first was the restoration of the Classical, early-Christian and Byzantine monuments in the coastal towns already excavated. The second involved the use of information and resources built up during the Eighth Army's advance through the semi-desert areas of Tripolitania. This information was now used to promote archaeological research among the settlements that had developed on the Roman frontier in the third and later centuries.

The urban churches could now be dated more accurately than before the war. At Sabratha, where four were identified, the former great Severan judiciary basilica had been converted into a church,[21] probably not much later than 400, while a similar transformation had taken place at Leptis under Justinian.[22] The excavators were able also to establish how as part of Justinian's deliberate policy of urban restoration carved marble fittings were shipped already shaped, quarried from imperial quarries, and that the splendid mosaics were laid by craftsmen brought in from the East. It was as Ward Perkins and Goodchild claimed, 'part of a deliberate and carefully planned policy, designed to knit more closely the cultural ties between the provinces and the central authority'.[23]

Equally important was the exploration of the semi-desert areas south of the coastal cities by the same two scholars assisted by other British archaeologists, and in 1951 by an expedition from the British School at Rome. The

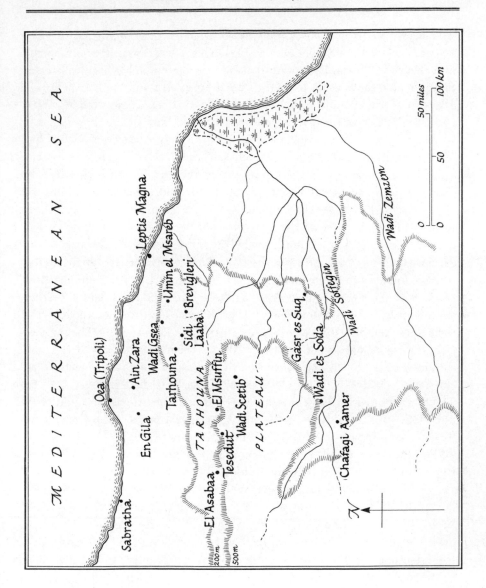

Principal Christian Sites in Tripolitania

sites investigated were villages and farm settlements, many of which were fortified and included Roman-period mausolea. This feature apart, the settlements
resembled their Numidian counterparts in the large number of olive presses
that provided the key to their agricultural prosperity, and the complete lack
of anything that could be called a civic public building. There were, however,
churches.[24] Most of these were basilican-type buildings with three aisles, a
single raised apse and probably a timber roof. There were, however, two differences from the Numidian village churches. These show no sign of a baptistery
attached whereas baptisteries were often present in the Tripolitanian
churches. Secondly, the altar generally stood a considerable distance from the
apse resulting in a larger chancel, and so far as their discoveries record there
were no reliquaries beneath the altar. None of the pre-Justinian churches had
pulpits (*ambon*) as was the norm in the Byzantine East.[25] At the same time,
carvings on the surface of the plinths and column bases were strikingly similar
to those found in the Numidian churches. In the church at Breviglieri shallow
carvings in relief featuring vines, ℞ symbols, birds and rams flanking either
side of a cross were to be found with rosettes incised in the same woodcarving
technique exemplified by carvings at Tigzirt and Khenchela.[26] The population, though using Latin on some inscriptions, seems to have been Berber and
Libyan-speaking.[27] The one inscription that betrays a religious allegiance is an
emphatic '[L]audes [D]omino Om[nipote]nti Deo et Christo Ei[us]' carved by
a certain Aemilianus on the lintel of a well-constructed Christian building of
uncertain use. 'Laudes Domino' and the suggestion of subordination in
'Christo Eius' indicates strongly-held Donatist views.[28]

This, however, stands alone among numerous inscriptions left behind by
this population of native farmer-soldiers. Decline rather than catastrophe
seems to have been the fate of their settlements. On one site investigated a
hovel, the home of a herdsman or peasant, occupied part of what had once
been a prosperous farmstead.[29] At another site, Gasr-es-Suq el-Oti in the
lower Sofegin valley south-east of Leptis Magna, a church had been converted
into a mosque,[30] witness to some continuity from Byzantine to Muslim times
before the site was abandoned.

Goodchild was interested in the Byzantine period, especially the latter
part. Taking up his post as Controller of Antiquities in Cyrenaica he soon
added to the two Christian churches already excavated by the Italians in
Cyrene. To these would be added by 1960 two more at Cyrene, two at
Apollonia and one at Teuchira (Tokra) on the coast.[31] In addition, a small
rural church at Theodorias (Gasr-el-Lebia), outside Apollonia yielded a building with magnificent mosaics,[32] a further indication of the prosperity enjoyed

in the countryside in the reign of Justinian. Goodchild concentrated on a palace at Apollonia, erected in the late-fifth or early-sixth century. It had been a fine, two-storey building with sets of rooms placed round a central court-yard leading to what was presumably the council chamber. On the exterior of one side had been an audience chamber and on the other, a chapel. This had contained a fine marble reliquary in the form of a sarcophagus having a central hole bored through the lid for pouring in libations. Who the saint was or the purpose of this elaborate reliquary is a matter for debate, but the possibility of taking and exchanging of oaths between the Byzantine authorities and marauding tribes such as the Louata seems plausible. 'Mutual pledge concerning the peace' in 543 between the two, violated by the Byzantines, fits this possibility.[33]

There had been squatter occupation in the early Arab period, and Goodchild became increasingly immersed in the problem of the transition from Byzantium to Islam in Egypt and Cyrenaica.[34] One of his later papers examined the attitude of some of the Copts and the Byzantines towards the Arab invaders and how one at least of the Coptic Byzantine leaders, Sanutius (Shnoudi/Shenouda?), supported the invaders.[35] There can be little doubt that had Goodchild lived more attention would have been paid in British universities to this topic and to the general problem of this momentous development throughout the whole southern shore of the Mediterranean, with its impact even today.

Another tantalizing scrap of information emerged from R. M. Harrison's excavation of the church at Ras al Hillal with the assistance of Libyan members of the Department of Antiquities.[36] The church itself was a three-naved basilica with an *ambon* (pulpit) projecting from the sanctuary into the nave. It had been built near the end of Justinian's reign and abandoned probably not long after the Arab conquest in 642. This, however, was not the end of the story. There was Arab occupation, and a graffito on wall plaster in Kufic characters gave a date of 722,[37] suggesting that in Cyrenaica, in contrast to Egypt itself, Christianity may not have survived more than a generation or so after the Arab conquest. Why, remains unsolved.

Revolution put a brake on the progress of archaeological exploration in Libya though valuable work has continued at Benghazi and other Cyrenaican sites. In *French North Africa* archaeology was even more severely damaged by the downfall of French predominance. By 1962 Tunisia, Algeria and Morocco were all independent states having parted with their former overlords amid varying degrees of acrimony. Morocco reverted to rule by its royal house in 1956. In Algeria where there was only the colonial rule of the Ottoman empire to look back to, there were seven and a half years of war and revolution ending with the breaking of all ties with France and the progressive expropriation of the European settler population. In December 1994 it was stated that 'less than a thousand non-essential French nationals remained in Algeria' (*Daily Telegraph*, 27 December 1994). In 1950 there had been about one million Europeans in what was regarded as part of France. In Tunisia matters appeared to be settled more amicably in 1956, but events in Algeria spilled across the Tunisian frontier. Tunisian opinion turned against France and there too most of the French settlers had to leave.

The full effects of the end of French rule in North Africa have still to be felt. How will relations between the countries north and south of the Mediterranean be stabilized? To this observer the die was cast in 1937 when the *Projêt Violette* was rejected by the successors to Léon Blum's Popular Front government. The *Projêt* had been swimming with the tide when it proposed the granting of French citizenship to a large group of middle-class Algerians, and wider powers to locally-elected councils. Had it been accepted and its privileges extended to the numerous group of former soldiers and their families, France might have forged a lasting Franco-Algerian society. At this stage most Algerians wanted assimilation with France. There were obvious benefits from French rule. The eradication of malaria from its last breeding grounds in the Constantine area was one,[38] the growing prosperity and Westernization of Algerian urban Muslims and Jews was another. Perceptions were unfortunately altered by France's defeat in June 1940. The change of sentiment was hastened by the Vichy government's anti-Semitic legislation in 1941 that deprived the Algerian Jews of their French citizenship, and threw them into the arms of the growing number of nationalists who now aimed at independence. The Allied presence in Algeria 1942–45 combined disruption of the economy with a scarcely concealed contempt for the Algerians ('Ayrabs' as the Americans called them). Revolutionary politics began to take over. On 8 May 1945 what had begun at Setif as a victory celebration turned into an anti-European riot in which 103 Europeans lost their lives. Reprisals were harsh and from that moment on opposition between Algerians, whether Jews or Muslims, and the settler population polarized.

Nonetheless, down to the end of 1953 it seemed as though the French might weather the storm. Effective control over Algeria was restored. With the exception of the high plains with their Donatist villages, archaeological work continued unabated. In December 1951 the *Gouvernement-Général* of Algeria (Direction de l'Intérieur et des Beaux-Arts) published a list of archaeological publications sponsored by his Direction since the end of the war. It makes impressive reading. Alongside military sites, such as Gilbert Charles-Picard's excavation of the Severan fortress on the Saharan borderlands at Dimmidi (Messad, south of the Chott el Hodna) and Colonel Jean Baradez' *Fossatum Africae* (aerial survey of the North African *limes*), were accounts of early-Christian excavations, such as Louis Leschi's re-examinations of Djemila and Tipasa, and Erwan Marec's work on the Christian quarter at Hippo. At the Fifth Congress of Christian Archaeology held at Aix (1954) Picard was able to announce a notable catalogue of new discoveries.[39]

The most important was at Hippo. By 1949 the authorities had bought up many of the smallholdings that covered most of the site of the Punic and Roman city, Erwan Marec, who had been working on the site as chance offered since the 1920s, directed the excavations. Behind the row of fine villas that had once dominated the ancient shoreline he came upon an entire Christian quarter.[40] This was dominated by a church 49 m long, and 20 m across. The apse (7 m in depth) was raised 0.55 m above the nave, enough to emphasize the status of the bishop and clergy, but not as in some of the Donatist churches, to exaggerate it.[41] The floor of this vast three-aisled building was covered with mosaic; on the right side was the baptistery, on the left, separated from the basilica by other rooms, was a trefoil building, similar to that found at Theveste (perhaps a martyr's chapel?)

By the time of the 1,600th anniversary celebrations of Augustine's birth (1954), it was evident that the Christian quarter occupied as much as 5,000 square metres (eventually 5,460) and containing 120 separate chambers. The most likely conclusion was that this huge complex was centred on Augustine's cathedral, the Basilica Pacis.[42] Not far away, across a street that surrounded the whole area, was another, perhaps older church with five naves and a square apse. This was possibly the Donatist church[43] whose festivities celebrating the episcopal martyr of Hippo, Leontius (d. 259), Augustine had once complained of having to hear.[44]

It was a vast excavation but also the last great *déblayage*. Plans were drawn up, mosaics over the whole complex photographed, but stratigraphy and detailed history were largely lacking. The presence of a Vandal grave dug into the surface of the forum remains a silent witness of the decline of Hippo under the Vandal kings, though the Basilica Pacis was still used for Teutonic burials.[45] Much later, poorly constructed tombs encroaching on some of the rooms within the Christian quarter raise the question of the date of its abandonment as such. Did this take place during the Berber interregnum (*c.* 660–700), or as part of a relatively short Muslim occupation of the site?[46]

More information on the latter was to come from the excavation of Tiddis. This was a prosperous Numidian native township (*castellum*) built along a rocky hillside some fifteen miles north-west of Constantine. André Berthier's excavation managed to continue through the crisis years following the all-out Algerian revolt in 1954, and important results were gained. Mithras as well as Saturn had apparently won the support of many of the inhabitants. The basilica which represented the ultimate victory of Christianity had been built directly opposite the cave that served as a Mithraeum.[47] Curiously, little trace of Byzantine renovation and fortification was found but, in contrast, considerable evidence for post-Byzantine occupation emerged. No fewer than 60 Abbasid glass tokens (weights or coins?) were found during the excavation, as well as a quantity of Arab-Berber pottery and fine glazed Muslim wares.[48] That occupation ended violently, probably sometime in the eleventh century, providing surprising evidence for continuity between Byzantine and Islamic North Africa, and adding weight to the theory that the Roman-Byzantine legacy of settled communities did not end before the invasion of the Hillalian nomads in the eleventh century.

Timgad, Tipasa and Tebessa also added to the religious history of North Africa, Timgad yielding a succession of three Donatist churches built on the site occupied by the cathedral of Bishop Optatus,[49] and Tipasa a new basilica near the eastern ramparts dedicated to the apostles Peter and Paul.[50] This, and tombs of martyrs found below the floor of and around the church of Bishop Alexander,[51] raises the question whether at Tipasa there had not been a change of allegiance from Donatism to Catholicism, perhaps during the Catholic ascendancy 348–361, similar to that of Thagaste.[52] Such a change might account for the ferocity of the pro-Donatist rebel Firmus' assault on the town in 373. Tebessa (Theveste), as always, provided some striking discoveries in the 1950s. A vast pagan cemetery was found beneath the existing basilica complex.[53] In the Christian *area* that succeeded this, there were burials 'ad sanctos', and one threatening 'If anyone violates this (tomb), God will violate him'.[54] Catholics as well as Donatists might use intemperate language, but these discoveries heightened the suspicion that at some time during its three centuries of Christian history Theveste had been a Donatist stronghold. (See below, chapter 14, p. 364.)

On 1 November 1954 the Algerians began a general uprising. Excavations in central Algeria at Timgad, Lambaesis and Diana (Zana) were curtailed or halted.[55] But elsewhere some work continued. At Tigzirt on the coast Serge Lancel reassessed in detail Gavault's excavation on the site in 1894–95. If his claim was justified that the church dated from the late fifth century and evidently succeeded three earlier more modest churches, then the carvings in the flat relief of the wood-carver, similar to those recorded by Gsell at Khenchela would date from the period of the Berber kingdoms. These art motifs would be anchored even more firmly to a Berber-Christian tradition.[56] Lancel was working in 1955. That year a new museum was due to open at Tipasa and restorations, in particular to the mosaics, foreshadowed at Djemila. The centenary celebrations of the *Revue Africaine* in 1956 also looked forward to the future with some optimism. Speaker after speaker referred to the lasting imprint of France on Algeria, though regretting that the policy of assimilation that had succeeded so well with the Jewish population had so far failed to secure similar results with the Arabs. Had it done so the present political claims, it was thought, would not be numbered among the country's problems.[57]

Alas, they were; the situation got worse not better. If the actual fighting ended in stalemate, all the political advantage lay with the Algerians who now outnumbered the settler population by nine to one. Negotiations for a settlement ended at Evian on 18 March 1962, with an agreement for a cease-fire and a referendum on the question of independence, to be held on 1 July. The vote was overwhelmingly in favour. On 3 July General de Gaulle accepted the result and declared Algeria an independent country. In a few years the great majority of the settler-population who had done so much to ensure the prosperity of the territory had returned to France.

Among those who left Algeria for Aix-en-Provence was one man who could have succeeded to the genius of Stéphane Gsell. Paul-Albert Février (1931–91) had hoped he might be able to build on Gsell's work, and had the situation been different would almost certainly have succeeded.[58] Like Goodchild he was a lifelong archaeologist, describing to the Sixth Congress of Christian Archaeology in 1962, at the age of 31, the revival of Christian archaeology in France that had taken place in the previous decade.[59] Essentially, however, he was an *africainiste* and he set out on his career as did most French *africainistes* as a student in the Ecole française de Rome. His article on 'Ostie et Porto à la fin d'Antiquité: topographie religieuse et vie sociale' (*Mélanges* 70 (1958), pp. 295–330) awoke him to the continuities between the Classical and early Christian world. In the second and third centuries AD Ostia had been one of the centres of Mithraic worship with a dozen or more Mithraea, but by the mid-fourth century the Church had replaced Mithras and one of the bath-buildings associated with the god had been converted into a church. How Christianity successfully took root in the city after a long period when its centre seems to have been confined to the cemeteries outside, where the cathedral was built, was impossible to say. Civic life, however, had moved from the patronage of the sun-god to Christianity within two generations.

Next year, still in Rome, Février showed his ability as a critic in re-examining some of the celebrated paintings in the catacomb of Priscilla.[60] He was able to argue that the famous mid-third-century scene centred on the *orante* with figures in the background, one of whom was holding a young woman holding an open scroll, represented some theme of instruction and of the intellectual life of the deceased, rather than an early example of a virgin receiving the veil, as Wilpert had claimed.[61]

Going on to North Africa, Février concentrated on Setif and its surroundings. Unlike many of his contemporaries his approach was that of an archaeologist rather than an architect. He was concerned with stratigraphy and precise dating.[62] Fortune favoured him, for in the north-west quarter of the town he found not only two funerary basilicas but accompanying mosaics precisely dated by the provincial era. In one of these basilicas these were dated 378–429 and in the other 383–429, with one epitaph dating to 471. It might look as though the Vandal invasion of 429 brought the life of these churches in Setif to a complete if temporary halt. Février, however, was able to use the decoration on these tombs dominated by simple geometric and vegetal designs with garlands and interlaces and a ☧ monogram flanked α/ω to date other similar funerary mosaics, including some found at Tabarka.[63] His later excavations established evidence for continuity between Byzantine and early Muslim Setif, and established that Setif continued to function as a town as late as the twelfth century.[64]

Continuities and transitions derived from archaeological evidence have not always been easy to establish. Deep layers of silt over city fora, as at Dougga and Timgad, suggest a lack of urban continuity through Vandal times however little the rural population was affected. Continuity between Byzantine and Muslim Algeria, despite Février's and Berthier's discoveries at Setif and Tiddis respectively, has been even more elusive and likely to remain so.

Février was able, however, to move research from concentration on religion and in particular on Donatism back to a more balanced study of Roman North Africa. Discoveries in central Algeria in the 1930s had made possible some correlation between material remains and literary evidence concerning the schism. In my study of the Donatist Church, published in 1952, I had asked the question 'Why Numidia?' What factors caused Optatus of Milevis and Augustine on the one hand, and archaeological evidence on the other, to indicate central Numidia and eastern Mauretania Sitifensis as the heartland of Donatism? This led to a study of possible non-theological, or economic and social causes of the movement, as well as its inspiration from the exclusive view of the Church and emphasis on confession and martyrdom represented by

Tertullian and Cyprian. The same emphasis, though with less experience of Numidian archaeology, was made by J. P. Brisson in 1955 in an independent study of the literary and published archaeological evidence.[65] Brisson was severely criticized by André Mandouze,[66] and in 1962 the Danish scholar Emin Tengström wrote what in retrospect would be among the first of the revisionist accounts of an important aspect of early Church history. Working from literary sources he claimed that the social and economic aspects of Donatism, as well as its reflection of Berber nationalism, had been much exaggerated, and the schism should be regarded first and foremost as a religious movement.[67]

Février agreed. In 1966 he wrote in the *Rivista di storia e letteratura religiosa* 'Toujours le Donatisme: à quand l'Afrique?' He did not accept everything Tengström had said, epecially concerning his reduction of the Circumcellions to seasonal workers on the Numidian olive plantations. Février considered, however, that too much had been made of the Donatists in the last few years, and too little to connect their movement with the history of North Africa in the fourth century. He pleaded for an interdisciplinary approach aimed at treating the religious and secular history of the provinces as an entity.[68]

His plea came too late. The sun had set on French influence and archaeology in Algeria. The last number of the *Revue Africaine* appeared in 1962. The *Recueil de Constantine* ceased regular publication the same year but managed one more issue for 1969–71. The *Bulletins* for Hippo and Oran ended in 1960–61 except for a few irregular numbers. Except when collaborating with Jürgen Christern at Tebassa in 1965, Février himself now worked from where he became Professeur d'Histoire romaine at the University of Aix-la-Provence. In 1989 he produced his *Approches du Maghreb romain: pouvoirs, différences et conflits*. A swathe was cut through the plethora of evidence, and after a panorama of French explorations of the antiquities of North Africa a coherent picture presented of how the inhabitants had lived under Roman rule. Without underestimating the power exercised by the Church in the fourth and early fifth centuries, as instanced by the imposing councils, effective works of charity, the cult of the martyrs and the vast episcopal areas and churches as at Tipasa, Djemila and Hippo,[69] religious controversy, including the Donatist schism, was cut down to size – half a chapter out of twelve on 'conflicts' – and some of its apologists (including the writer) severely if not always reasonably, criticized.[70] Though towns may have continued to flourish through the fifth century (doubtful, in view of literary and archaeological evidence for the practical abandonment of some, such as Timgad and Sabratha), Février was unable to describe convincingly the steady decline of standards in towns and countryside in the seventh century.[71] The Arab invasion accelerated the end of Latin North Africa, but this was well on the way to extinction before the invaders arrived at the gates of Sbeitla in 647. He had signalled, however, a new approach to the history of North Africa from the fourth to the eighth century waiting to be applied if and when circumstances make further work possible.

In *Tunisia* the situation was never so fraught. The nationalist Neo-Destours under Habib Bourguiba were less rigid in their views and in a weaker position than their Algerian counterparts. Not only had their supporters unwisely hailed the Axis forces when they recaptured Gafsa in January 1943, but in the existence of the Bey, Tunisians had an alternative and moderate rallying-point. Had General Mast, the Resident-General following the end of the North Africa campaign in May 1943, been more flexible and far-sighted, he might have initiated a settlement which would have divided powers between the Bey and the Neo-Destours while leaving real control in his hands. Unfortunately he was a 'disciplinarian' as he described himself, and any suggestion that Tunisia as a French protectorate might evolve towards 'dominion status' within a French 'commonwealth' was regarded with hostility. In March 1956 France was obliged to concede Tunisian independence, while two years later an air-raid on a frontier village suspected of harbouring Algerian insurgents disrupted relations. Archaeological work by French scholars suffered as a result.

The ten years 1945–55, before these events took place, had not been valueless. Noel Duval, like Paul-Albert Février, had been a member of the Ecole française de Rome. He both excavated new Christian sites and re-excavated successfully old ones, and introduced new methods of digging in which stratigraphy was applied properly and the association sought between the building being excavated with its surroundings. In 1951 he and Alexandre Lézine discovered the underground funerary 'chapel of Asterius'. This was an elaborate mausoleum built within a previously existing *souterrain* (man-made subterranean chamber). It had been built in the form of a small basilica and had served as the family tomb of the Asterii. A reliquary had been robbed, but fine mosaics featuring birds and fishes represented as swimming below a panel that showed two peacocks flanking a eucharistic chalice were almost intact. The most interesting feature was the date, secured from bronze coins found in the surface below the mosaic showing this had been laid down soon after the sixth Indiction during the reign of Maurice Tiberius (587/588).[72] This was the latest securely datable mosaic from Carthage and showed that even at this period the art of the mosaicist had not declined. It also provided further evidence for the existence of wealthy families who stuck to old-fashioned Latin burial formulae ('fidelis in pace') at the very end of the sixth century.[73] Another souterrain, this time on the hill Ste Monique, contained an epitaph of a certain Redemtus, an official of 'the Fifth Region', suggesting that ecclesiastical organization into *regiones* each presided over by an archdeacon was also surviving at this time.[74] Serious decline was delayed until the seventh century.

South-eastern Tunisia and the sites of Sbeitla and Ammaedara formed the focus of Duval's next work. At Sbeitla he recorded the existence of no fewer than eight churches, the earliest, mid-fourth century, on the site of a disused public building[75] and including one dedicated to Sts Trypho, Gervasius and Protasius, possibly an example of a connection between that town and Milan.[76] Some of the many Christian inscriptions threw light on the beliefs of Christians in the sixth century concerning Paradise. One epitaph recorded how the deceased 'had been called to the Lord's kingdom, where he had his eternal abode and everlasting peace'.[77]

In 1934 Ammaedara (Haidra) had produced an important Byzantine inscription relating to the Great Persecution. This listed 34 names of men and women, layfolk, who had suffered under 'the divine laws of the emperors Diocletian and Maximian', thus effectively answering scholars who questioned whether the Fourth Edict of persecution (spring 304) had ever been enforced in North Africa.[78] The site, and the basilicas discovered by Sadoux in 1897 and Gauckler and Gsell in 1900, were in a neglected state. Beyond the inscription honouring the martyrs the excavation by Dr Dolcemascolo, an Italian doctor at a mining site some eight miles away, had yielded few results and no report. Fighting in the area during February 1943 had also taken its toll. Duval found himself with the task of bringing some order into the site, restoring half-excavated basilicas, cataloguing the Christian inscriptions and preparing for a major excavation. This, however, was delayed until 1967 but as the first major excavation by a joint team of Tunisians and French under Duval's direction, it proved to be as important politically as it was for its important archaeological results.[79]

With the end of French rule many questions, especially concerning the final period of Byzantine Africa, remained unanswered. What could be made, for instance, of the tombs dug into the sanctuary of a large church at Bulla, and the small deposit of Ummayad coins (eighth century) recovered from one of them?[80] Unfortunately, the French had been slow to train North Africans in the archaeological skills needed to protect their heritage, including their immediate pre-Islamic past. The legacy of Lavigerie illustrated by the enormous cathedral on the Byrsa could not be renounced easily. The successful joint excavations, however, at Ammaedara in 1967 and the following years showed how new relations between French and Tunisians were possible. This opened the way for the excellent co-operation between the Tunisians and the international teams in the 'Save Carthage' campaign in the 1970s.

As one area for early-Christian research became more difficult another opened up. In *Israel* research into early-Christian antiquities was moving apace. While the Scrolls and Masada were the primary concerns of scholars in the new state, the influx of thousands of Jews, including a huge number of refugees in the years following 1948, required a great deal of new building. This often revealed hitherto unsuspected antiquities. Between 1948 and 1954 Avi Yonah was able to recover the remains of eleven churches and three monasteries. In Byzantine times every village could be reckoned to have its church. In the fifth century continuous influx of immigrants into the Holy Land and the inflow of capital had, as we have seen, turned Palestine into a largely Christian territory and its prosperity continued for another hundred years. More land was being taken into cultivation and the desert, especially in Negev, was being pushed back. One church, at Evron 10 km north of Acre, might have been typical of the steady progress of Christianity. It was a large basilican building (30 × 25 m) with a central nave and two side aisles built in 415. It was repaired in 442. In 492 it was enlarged, the porch being replaced by a narthex and the altar surrounded by a chancel screen. The floors were paved with mosaics some bearing a date and the names of its wealthy donors. Fourteen deacons with children were mentioned on one mosaic. Their names were Latin or Greek, Syriac being a small minority in nomenclature and language amid this prosperous, largely immigrant Christian community. [81]

Israel was to continue to be one of the main centres for new early-Christian discoveries. Israel's neighbour *Jordan* had taken a lion's share of exploring the caves of the Dead Sea and publishing the results. An excavation of a different type resulted in a valuable correction of an opinion held by H. C. Butler and his colleagues concerning earliest datable traces of Christianity in Jordan. Butler had believed that the church of Julianos at Umm el Jemal, east of Jerash, had been built in 344. (See above, p. 142.) A season's work in 1956 by G. U. S. Corbett showed that the dated dedication on which this was based referred not to the church but to 'the public cemetery of the people of Christ', where the dedicant hoped 'the better people would sing the praises of the deceased publicly'. Christians there certainly were in the town in 344, but the church itself, basilican in plan, was later. It was found to embody the more interesting feature of an earlier, monumental building, probably a temple, as well as a house. Useful as were preliminary surveys of sites through many of these expeditions of fifty years before, they could also be seriously misleading on important details, which then found their way into textbooks.[82]

Further north, in *Syria* and *Asia Minor*, the excavations revealing early civilizations of great historical importance overshadowed work on Christian sites. Ras Shamra, and Mari in Syria, Beyčesultan, Gordion, and Boghaz Köy in Asia Minor engaged the energies of French and British teams respectively. The Institut français d'archéologie à Beyrouth (Beirut), however, was responsible for one major piece of research affecting early Christianity. Georges Tchalenko's survey of village sites in northern Syria provided further evidence for the prosperity of these, but also for their progressive dependence in the sixth century on the monasteries. During this period most of these latter favoured the anti-Chalcedonian (Monophysite) cause. Thus, the Syrian Christians moved gradually from their support of Nestorius in the years preceding the council of Chalcedon in 451 to the opposite standpoint. The north Syrian monasteries provided a vital link in the chain that bound Christians from Armenia to Ethiopia in a single anti-Chalcedonian movement, a Church taking its lead from Alexandria whose territorial extent exceeded that of Rome and Constantinople put together.[83]

A large but orthodox monastery was the object of successive seasons' work by Michael Gough and the British Institute at Ankara (founded in 1950). Alahan (Koja Kalessi) in Isauria stood on a rock some 3,000 ft above sea level. The site had been visited by Ramsay in 1890 and worked on by the Turks, as already mentioned, at the turn of the century. Dating was not the main question, for there was an epitaph dated to February 462 of Tarasis, the guest-master, and the monastery church showed 'no sign of rebuilding'.[84] Nor was there any reason to suspect Alahan as being other than Chalcedonian in allegiance. Gough's interest was mainly in the plan of the complex and the architecture of the church. He found that the latter was basilican with a wooden roof, and indicated that in this part of Asia Minor the cupola did not precede the reign of Zeno (474–491).[85] Its introduction might reflect perhaps the slight but perceptible shift in official Byzantine religious attitudes towards the One-Nature (Monophysite) view of Christ.

Gough's excavation coincided with Calder's final contribution to the history of another Christian tradition, namely Montanism, through the discovery of an inscription in Phrygia proclaiming the deceased as a *Moïstēs* and *Koinonōs*. The latter term identified the dead man as a senior cleric in the Montanist hierarchy, though the title 'Moïstēs' remains obscure.[86] Finally, the last of the Pauline cities, Derbe, was identified by Michael Ballance as Kerti Hüyük in Lycaonia.[87]

In the Turkish capital, *Istanbul*, post-war work built on previous achievement. Thomas Whittemore died in 1950, but his Byzantine Institute of

America was firmly based, and his successor, Paul Underwood, extended the work of restoration in Sancta Sophia to the mediaeval frescos in the Kariye Djami.[88] Near the Byzantine Bucoleon harbour, the British, sponsored as previously by St Andrews University, took advantage of open land south of the peristyle belonging to the Grand Palace to uncover another suite of apartments of the period of Justinian and Theodora. More and more of the classic period of Constantinople was being recovered.[89]

The same period was occupying American scholars working in the Agora at *Athens*. In contrast to the major excavations of fifty years before, there was no *déblayage*. The Herulian invasion of 267 had wrought great damage, despite Dexippus' valiant defence of the city. The post-Herulian period could be demarcated sharply on the ground from the Classical period before. Homer Thompson was able to show that while the Agora never recovered its former glory, there were two centuries of developing Christian life that showed itself in the conversion of the temple of Hephaistos into a church in the fifth century and Christian incriptions found on the site. On the Acropolis the Parthenon and the Erechtheum were also both transformed into churches at the same period. Destruction came, as elsewhere in Greece and the Balkans, with the invasions of Avars and Slavs from *c.* 580 onwards, though some occupation lingered on for another century.[90]

One site in the *Balkans* showed how catastrophic these invasions could be. The Byzantine ruins known as Tsaritsin Grad (the fortress of the emperor) are situated between Nish and Skoplje. Work on the site had started in 1937 and was resumed by the Serbian Academy of Sciences in 1947. It is not a big site, but the original village had been Justinian's birthplace and he was determined to honour it. The result was a Christian town, with an episcopal quarter set on the Acropolis (possibly the site of the original village) and at least four other churches. There was a colonnaded main street and aqueduct bringing water from springs located some miles away. The interesting feature of the city is the shortness of its life, at most 75 years, *c.* 550–625. No coins later than Phocas (602–610) were found. The hovels erected by invading Slavs among the ruins and rough hand-made pottery found in these testify to the collapse of civilization that resulted from their invasion.[91] Salona, as we have seen, suffered a similar fate. The year 612 marks the last dated inscription there and in 641 Pope John IV had the relics of the Salonitan martyrs transferred to Rome. In the years between, life in the once populous capital of Dalmatia had become impossible.[92]

The Greek islands afforded refuges for many of those driven out of the towns on the mainland by the Slav invaders. These islands had been Christianized probably in the early fifth century, if not earlier, and in the post-war years numerous new churches were found in Cyprus particularly,[93] Lesbos,[94] Cos,[95] Delos[96] and Crete.[97] In the last-named a large church whose life, to judge from coin-evidence, may not have extended beyond the reign of Heraclius (610–641) was found accidentally, when a new nurses' wing was being added to the south end of Heraklion hospital about a mile from Knossos.[98] The site was interesting. The church, probably fifth century, was oriented 40° off the normal east–west orientation, and as at St Peter's the builders had given themselves what appeared to be an unnecesary amount of trouble. Though the ground to the immediate north was comparatively level they had chosen to build the west end of the church into a steep hill, while at the east end they had to bring in no less than 2.50 m depth of rubble from the nearby ruins of the Hellenistic and Roman city of Knossos in order to form a level platform on which to build. The reasons for their labours soon became clear. The ground on which the church stood was honeycombed with graves on the same alignment as the church. Some were substantial stone-lined tombs covered by heavy capstones, and despite their relative wealth they were usually without grave-goods of any kind. One of the graves had been given a special place of honour within the church, filling a space in the north-east corner of the nave. The top had been covered with a rich design using cubes of marble and porphyry. Over the place where the head would have lain was the bottom part of a small decorated Late Minoan bowl of black gypsum through which a hole had been bored to receive libations. At the foot of the skeleton was a large complete spindle vase. He was obviously held in high honour in the church, perhaps as a martyr.[99]

The dating of the cemetery beneath the church had to await the very last moment of the dig. A coin of Constantine II dating to *c.* 328 had been found first and we had concluded that the tombs were probably post-312. Suddenly the foreman, Manoli Markoiannakis, arrived in the middle of lunch before we left for the plane home. He had a gold earring in the palm of his hand. The skeletons had been left in place but the earring had fallen on to the ground from one. It was of a rare type that could be dated, however, to the first half of the third century.[100] Though no specifically Christian remains were found in the cemetery the suspicion remains that we had found a Christian *area*, perhaps even one connected with the bishopric of Knossos whose existence could be traced back to AD 170.[101] It had, moreover, been laid out within a pagan cemetery whose graves were found either side of the church.[102]

A great deal was being found, which as Dyggve's *History of Salonitan Christianity* (1951) showed could be integrated into a general history of early Christianity. In Salona, Dyggve had traced every aspect of the Church's rise and decline, from the first missionary-traders from the eastern Mediterranean and beyond, the martyrs of the Great Persecution, the triumph of the Church in the fourth century, evidence for the monastic movement, the prosperous and proud Christian city under Justinian, and its final slow, agonized decline and collapse before the Avar and Slav invasions. All this was demonstrable from excavation.

In the *West* outside North Africa, there was a different development, first a longer period when Christianity and paganism co-existed in apparent harmony, as demonstrated by the new Via Latina catacomb. Secondly, on the European mainland there was an ability to absorb the Germanic invaders into a Catholic Christian civilization without the destructive hiatus caused by new barbarian invasions in the seventh century which the Balkans and East suffered.

First, in *Rome*: the Vatican excavations and the claims that the tomb of St Peter had been found held the centre of the stage. Work on the catacombs, however, never ceased and often produced the unexpected. In 1955 building operations near the Via Latina revealed a small self-contained area in which some 400 individuals had been buried. Unlike the great catacombs this catacomb seems to have belonged to a comparatively wealthy group of families who could afford to be buried in individual family graves (*cubicula*) whose walls were richly decorated with frescos. The catacomb post-dated the Peace of the Church (312), was not dedicated to any martyr, and ceased to be used *c*. 360 before all the spaces in the *cubicula* had been filled. The paintings, however, provided the main interest. There were in total 115, a 'fourth-century picture gallery', as Iosi described them. Of these 41 were pictures from the Old Testament, including Adam and Eve being driven from Paradise, episodes from the life of Joseph and of Samson, of Phineas transfixing Zimri and Cozbi with his spear, of Jacob blessing Ephraim and Manasseh, which do not occur elsewhere in the catacombs. The New Testament was represented by thirteen scenes which included Christ delivering the Sermon on the Mount to the assembled people, the tomb of Lazarus in which Jesus escorted by a crowd of 80 figures is shown calling to the dead man still in his tomb, and a enigmatic painting of a soldier casting his lot into an urn hanging against the outer wall of a building – very curious, if casting lots for Christ's tunic at the crucifixion was in the artist's mind. Symbolism, or simply the free expression of the artist's genius, it is impossible to say.[103]

Among these biblical scenes were, however, others which by no stretch of imagination could be Christian. The death of Cleopatra(?), the goddesses Ceres and Abundantia, the return of Alcestis, the centrepiece of a magnificently decorated tomb, a whole cycle of the labours of Hercules, and finally, a vivid portrayal of a medical class with students standing round a prone patient. The only certainty is that pagan and Christian pictures were intermingled in catacomb art during the first half of the fourth century. Whether one is dealing with families of different religions or members of the same family some of whom were pagan, and how the Hercules paintings relate to similar representations on Roman sarcophagi, remains obscure.[104]

A second small family catacomb, on the Via Appia, also unrecorded on the *Itineraries* and not dedicated to a martyr, had a different message. It was only sporadically used, but while most of the burials date from the period 380–410, some extend back to the early third century, while one burial could be as early as 170. The epitaph of Glycera, a freedwoman of Aelius, prepares 'a pure place' ('loci puri') for herself and freedmen and women and their descendants, her husband being a freedman of (Marcus) Aurelius; and she marked the epitaph with a fish and an anchor.[105] The catacomb with its wide, well-cut stairway and gallery breathed, as the excavator claimed, 'an austere antiquity'.[106]

A third discovery related to a painting in the catacomb of Praetextatus, much examined since de Rossi's and Marchi's explorations in 1851. The story of Susanna and the elders was not an unusual theme, with Susanna representing the Church and the wicked elders representing Jews and Gentiles (cf Hippolytus, *In Danielem* 1.14.6). But on this *arcosolium* the *matrona* Celerina gave the story a contemporary twist. There was Susanna painted as a sheep flanked by the elders, 'seniores', shown as wolves, but on either side of this scene were large standing figures of saints, one plausibly identified by the letters LIB as Pope Liberius, the others possibly as the Roman martyrs Pope Xystus II and the deacon Laurentius executed in 258 during the Valerianic persecution. The theme thus was persecution, and it would not take a skilled interpreter to recognize Pope Liberius exiled by the emperor Constantius II as a victim, and the two wolves as his persecutors, the emperor and his puppet-bishop Felix.[107] Celerina herself would be identified with Susanna. The demonstration by the Roman *matronae* in favour of Liberius on Constantius' visit to Rome in 357 was perhaps enshrined for eternity in Celerina's grave.[108]

Over the *rest of Italy and Sicily* there was also continuous activity. In Sicily there was further exploration of the Syracusan catacombs, especially the Vigna Cassia.[109] In north Italy there were excavations in Aquileia, Verona and Concordia as well as Pula (Pola) and other sites in Istria. These excavations confirmed on the ground information provided by Zeno of Verona, Ambrose of Milan and Chromatius of Aquileia concerning Christian progress and controversies, especially in the period after 380. Excavations at Concordia[110] and

Verona as well as Milan were beginning to build up a pattern of large mediae-val churches in these cities being erected on the sites of early Christian churches, or cemeteries, the mediaeval city continuing the late Roman Christian centre.

Aquileia supported literary evidence in a different way. The sermons of Chromatius (bishop 387–*c*. 408) are full of denunciations of the Jews as though these outshone heretics and pagans in enmity to the Church.[111] In 1949 Bovini and Brusin published two mosaics from the site of the monastery of St Martin in the middle of Aquileia. One of the mosaics included the invo-cation 'D(omi)no Sab(aoth)' indicating (as it must) the existence of a synagogue next door to a Christian church.[112] Elsewhere in the city, on the site of the church of St Theodore, Brusin pared down the date of the building of the south *aula* to 313, associated with symbols in mosaic of the fish, Good Shepherd, Jonah, and the Eucharist. The area devoted to Christian use was doubled to 73 m × 31 m. after Bishop Theodore's death *c*. 320.[113] Some idea of the devotion that inspired some Christians who donated portions of these large mosaics can be illustrated from examples surviving in the cathedral church at Pula. There, Damianus and Laurentia provided 200 ft (*pedes*) of mosaic for the church on the site, and Donatianus gave the same amount 'in fulfilment of a vow'.[114] Christianity had become the living religion of the north Italian provinces on the eve of the barbarian invasions.

Finally, Ravenna, the choice for the Sixth International Congress in 1962, saw active work undertaken to prepare for the event. Bovini and his assistant Rafaella Farioli were able to clarify the sequence of the magnificent early-Christian buildings. It would appear that, as one might expect, Christianity first penetrated the area via the port and the first church was erected in the fourth century on the site of the basilica of San Apollinari in Classe, and is the earliest surviving record of that period. In the early sixth century Theodoric was determined to enforce parity between his Arian Goths and the Catholic Italian-Roman inhabitants who lived in the shadow of the visible reminders of the days when the court of Valentinian III and Galla Placidia was in Ravenna. He established a series of ecclesiastical and secular buildings, including the Palace of Theodoric, the Arian Baptistery and a cathedral designed to match point by point the existing Catholic buildings. Theodoric died in 526, and in 540 Ravenna was back in orthodox hands. San Vitale with its famous panels representing Theodora and her attendants, and Justinian, was among the results of the Reconquest.[115]

Christianity in Ravenna and Aquileia may be supposed reasonably to have provided the springboard for Christian advance north into the province of

Noricum (modern Carinthia). A fifth-century basilica was found by Rudolf Egger at Theurnia (St Peter in Holz) but the bishopric on this site as well as that at Maria Saal fell victim to the Slavs (Avars?).[116] More resistant was the Christian community at Ulrichberg, where the early-Christian church became the site of a mediaeval monastery.[117]

Further west in *Rhaetia* (covering modern Tyrol) Franz Miltner, returned from Ephesus, carried out a series of excavations within a fortified complex at Kirschbiechl above the Roman town of Agutum. The site had been a pagan sanctuary but seems to have been chosen by the bishop of Agutum as his epis-copal centre after that city became threatened by barbarians.[118] Two other sites, at Imst and Martinsbühl in relatively inaccessible areas, had churches and Christian communities in the years immediately before these events.[119] In these rural areas the Church's advance was sometimes resisted by the inhabi-tants. Literary sources tell the tale of the murder of missionaries by enraged pagans in 397.[120] The mission had been inspired by Ambrose of Milan and sent up the Adige valley where the members met their fate. In northern Gaul at this same time, Martin of Tours had to use strong-arm methods before he could subdue the pagan villagers.[121]

In the *Gallic Prefecture* itself, comprising Tingitana (area around Tangier), Spain, Gaul, the Rhineland and Britain, archaeological discoveries were rein-forcing literary evidence about the progress of Church in the period 370–420. In *Spain*, literary sources enable the rise of the Christian ascetic movement to be followed, represented by Priscillian of Avila and the wealthy family of Melania, and record in some detail the views of Priscillian himself.[122] Archaeology provided evidence for aristocratic house-churches, such as at Merida (discovered in 1917),[123] and for a growing number of urban Christian centres such as at Ampurias (Emporió) north of Tarragona, Alberea (province of Murcia, Espiel (Córdoba) and near Málaga.[124] Much, however, still remained undetected. Even so, sufficient Visigothic and Christian inscrip-tions were being found for Fr Vives to catalogue and comment on them.[125]

Southern France (Roman province of Narbonensis) benefited from the scaling-down of activity in North Africa. Paul-Albert Février among others trans-ferred from the insecurity of Algeria and provided a leadership and expertise that had been largely wanting. Important discoveries followed almost at once. At Cimiez near Nice, Christians had taken over derelict public baths *c.* 350 to build a church and baptistery[126] and there was a similar situation at Montferrand (Aude) where baths also provided space and building material for a funerary church.[127] Sulpicius Severus' establishment of two churches and a baptistery on his estate at Primulacum in *c.* 402 could not have been an isolated event.[128] In southern Gaul, as in north Italy, archaeology shows that the countryside as well as the towns was swinging over to Christianity from *c.* 380 onwards. Himerius of Tarragona's claim that 'myriads were seeking baptism'[129] seems to be borne out on the ground. A generation later, when the Visigoths arrived in 413, Priscillianism was the threat to orthodoxy in the province of Tarragona.[130] Paganism was a distant memory.

Février always insisted that any buildings associated with churches must be explored, and that the study of pottery found during excavations was indispensible.[131] His words were heeded in an area which had hitherto been practically monopolized by amateur 'diggers'. As an exception, Raymond Lantier's excavation of the Christian Visigothic cemetery at Estagel (Pyrénées Orientales) was thorough and scientific. He found nearly 200 graves which he dated to the mid-sixth century, and from this sample concluded that here there had been an admixture of Visigoth and Gallo-Roman types, with the Visigoths forming a ruling class and the Gallo-Romans their subjects.[132]

The most important discoveries of these years belonged to the same period but were connected with the Visigoths' conquerors, the Frankish rulers and nobility. The sites were carefully excavated, and the finds treated under laboratory conditions.[133] The abbey church of St Denis outside the old city walls of Paris had been erected over what was allegedly the tomb of a third-century martyr, Dionysius. He had been buried in an existing Roman cemetery. In the Merovingian period the church had retained its character as a mausoleum used for the burial of members of the Frankish royal house. Alterations to the crypt resulted in the discovery of a large limestone coffin containing the remains of a woman's body. She had been about 5 ft tall and had died at the age of approximately 45. A gold ring on her finger was inscribed 'Arnegundis Regine', identifying her as Queen Arnegunde, wife of the Frankish king Chlothar I (561–584). She had died about the year 570. No cost had been spared at her funeral. She had been laid on a bright red woollen blanket and wore a tunic, over which was an ankle-length gown of dark red silk, with broad cuffs embroidered in gold thread. There was an amazing assemblage of gold jewellery, brooches and trinkets. A bottle lay at her feet, reminiscent of the glass bottle that had been placed at the feet of the dignitary buried in the church at Knossos. The significance is not known, but nearly a century after the baptism of Clovis in 496 (or 499) pagan burial ritual and belief were far from extinct in the Frankish royal house.

This was even more evident in a second burial, a generation or so earlier (*c.* 530–540), found beneath the choir of Cologne cathedral.[134] Two burials were discovered, one of a young woman, the other of a boy about six years old.

The woman – she must have been a princess – was small, only 4 ft 7 in tall, and had died when she was about 30. No inscription gave her name, but she also was accompanied by jewellery that included gold earrings and a massive gold bracelet on her left forearm. Bottles, one perhaps containing wine, were laid at her feet. There were also four gold coins of Anastasius (491–518), Theodoric the Ostrogoth (493–526), and his successor Athalaric (526–534). The boy's grave was even more fascinating. He had been buried in a superbly-made wooden cot,[135] in what appeared to be full military regalia, including a helmet, a bow and three arrows, sword, two spears, battle axe, and also a wooden sceptre(?).[136] The pagan ritual in both burials is obvious, and so too the parallels with Sutton Hoo. The grave contained almost exactly the same equipment as in the ship-burial of the Anglian king. Yet this was in what had been the most Christianized part of the Rhineland. In Trier alone a double church datinq to 326 or a little later and over 800 Christian inscriptions had been found.[137] The two parts of the church were used in all probability for the commemoration of a martyr and episcopal burials, and for congregational worship, respectively. It is difficult to resist the conclusion that but for the leadership exercised by the Gallo-Roman nobility, such as Remigius of Reims, Pope Gregory I might have had to send his missionaries to the Franks as well as their Jutish allies in Kent in 597.

Why was it Kent only? Why was Britain a special case? While evidence for outright hostility to the new faith had to await discoveries in the 1980s (see below, p. 378), significantly more was being found that suggested that the Church in Britain differed from that of its neighbours in the West. The Church presented a strange picture of episcopal poverty alongside the obvious wealth of some individual communities and members. As we have seen, at the Council of Ariminum in 359, three British bishops were alone among an assemblage of more than 400 who accepted the emperor Constantius' offer of their travel expenses. The remainder refused to touch money offered by an heretical emperor. The British bishops, however, pleaded poverty, a plea that was generally accepted.[138] However, at Mildenhall (Suffolk) a discovery gave a totally different picture of some of the Christians in Britain at this period. It was first found in 1942 in a shallow trench by farmers ploughing slightly deeper (ten inches) than usual.[139] The 32 separate objects comprised the most important hoard of silver found in Britain south of the Wall. Its most famous piece was the superb round dish (60.5 cm in diameter and weighing 8,256 g) magnificently preserved and covered all over with figure-reliefs, centred on a mask of Oceanus. This figure was surrounded by two concentric zones, the inner showing Nereids, sea-centaurs and other marine beasts, the outer a

Bacchic revel. There was nothing Christian in the design nor on some other, smaller dishes featuring Pan and centaurs fighting wild beasts. But among these manifestations of vigorous paganism were spoons with a ☧ monogram, one bearing an inscription 'Pascentia vivas', and another 'Papitte (in) Do(mino?) vivas'[140] ('Pappita (or '-us') may you live in the Lord'). Comparison with the Corbridge *lanx* for style, date and content is obvious. The treasure seems to have belonged originally to Eutherios who held the office of *praepositus sacri cubiculi* (chief of the sacred bedchamber) under Julian in Gaul 355–361. His name is scratched on the back of two Bacchic platters. He returned to Rome and must have disposed of his silverware to a colleague. It was buried not long afterwards. There was wealth but also insecurity. This culminated in the concerted attack by the Saxons, the Picts, and Scots assisted by local dissidents in 367–368 and could be a possible cause for concealing the silver.[141] To bury such a treasure does not suggest peace and quiet in eastern Britain, where Christianity was relatively strong in the 360s.

A decade before, all seemed to be going well. The Church in Britain was united with that in the remainder of the West in its support of Athanasius.[142] Two discoveries in Roman villas show how it was gaining support among the wealthier native landowners. At Lullingstone (Kent) there was no indication when the excavation started that the villa would include a house-church in its basement. Built originally in the late first century, it was occupied to the end of the second century by a wealthy owner. For some reason the site was partially abandoned for about 50 years after *c.* 200, but reoccupied and remodelled in the latter part of the third century.[143] Mosaics were laid down, including one of Bellerophon slaying the Chimera, in the *triclinium* (dining room).[144] The reconstructed house, however, contained a basement at the north end which down to *c.* 355 was used probably for drying, airing and bleaching cloth over a flame. This use was then replaced by an entirely different and Christian use. The excavators found thousands of broken pieces of coloured wall-plaster. These were laboriously assembled in the British Museum and by the end of 1951 enough piecing together had taken place to identify two large ☧ symbols set in ornate wreaths. In addition, a row of six *orante* figures, one apparently giving a blessing, were found on plaster decorating a wall. They were richly dressed in long-sleeved half-leg tunics, divided by a blue or ochre horizontal sash with a vertical beaded band extending from one end of the garment to the other, the band and sash forming a cross. As each figure was standing between a pair of pillars below a tiled roof it would be difficult to deny their identity as clergy in a church, or perhaps even apostles.[145] The Christian rooms were entered by a separate entrance cut off from the rest of the house, suggesting perhaps use by

Christian villagers and workers on the estate. No mediaeval church, however, succeeded this house-church, which shared the fate of the villa, destroyed by fire probably early in the fifth century.[146]

The mosaic in the villa at Hinton St Mary in Dorset came to light on 12 September 1963, after traces had been found by the owner of a field digging post-holes for the foundations of a building.[147] Excavation revealed a large rectangular room (28 ft 4 in × 19 ft 6 in) divided into two unequal parts separated by a small passage. In the centre of the smaller room was a roundel showing Bellerophon slaying the Chimera, as at Lullingstone but in a more vivid and lifelike style. The mosaic floor of the larger room, however, was dominated by the head and shoulders of a youthful figure draped with a *tunica* (tunic) and *pallium* (woven cloak worn over the shoulder). Behind him was a ☧ and, on either side, pomegranates. The figure was obviously Christ, though without a nimbus and with the features borrowed perhaps from an imperial portrait (from coinage?) of Constans or Constantius. The pomegranates were recognized symbols of eternal life. As Jocelyn Toynbee pointed out, if the bust is Christ the remainder of the symbolism on the mosaics in both rooms falls into place. Bellerophon could have a Christian interpretation both in Britain and in Gaul, representing the triumph of good over evil.[148] In these cases Evil is banished from the house, and the symbol of Christ represents the reception of Good. The animals in the hunting scenes on the mosaic were noticeably different from those in pagan settings. The dogs chase the birds but do not catch and kill them. The great tree below the bust of Christ could be the tree of Life.[149] The four seasons, however, occupying the corners of the same mosaic are less easy to Christianize, but may have represented the continuity of God's creation through the seasons of the year, or simply have retained a similar pagan significance.[150]

The mosaic can properly be compared with that from another Dorset site, namely Frampton, where a ☧ had been figured on the mosaic dividing two large rooms of the same type as those at Hinton St. Mary.[151] Three and a half miles south of the latter was a villa at Fifehead Neville which produced a similar type of mosaic (now lost) and two rings bearing the ☧ monogram.[152] All these mosaics seem to be of the same date, *c.* 340, and came perhaps from the same workshop.[153] Clearly there was a strong Christian presence among these Dorset villa owners. They remain, however, anonymous, and unlike their counterparts in Gaul produced no known leadership in the Church.

Such leadership as penetrated Britain originated in Gaul. Martin of Tours was gathering disciples around him as he established his monastic settlement at Ligugé near Tours. One of those who may have joined him was a Briton,

Ninian. Ninian evidently came from the northern province of Britain. Bede's *Ecclesiastical History* (iii.4) relates what must have passed into legend by the time he wrote (731). He tells how Ninian, 'a most reverend and saintly man', preached the word succesfully among the Picts. He claims that 'he was properly instructed at Rome in the faith and mysteries of the truth', but, more relevantly, that he honoured Martin by naming his episcopal residence (*sedem*) after him, and built a stone church, 'which was unusual among the Britons', at a place called popularly 'The White House'.[154]

Archaeology has supported part of the legend. Excavations at Whithorn, inland from the coast of Galloway, by C. A. Ralegh Radford in the 1950s revealed a small late-Roman settlement,[155] and below the east end of Whithorn priory church were traces of a small building (oratory?) with plastered wall surrounded by a number of inhumations oriented east-west. This could have been Ninian's 'bishopric'. The possibility of a Christian settlement in the early fifth century was heightened by the discovery of an inscribed tombstone commemorating Latinus and his unnamed daughter, erected by a unnamed nephew or grandson (*nepos*) of Barrovadus. The inscription starts 'Te Dominum laudamus' (We praise thee, O Lord), suggesting that Barrovadus and his family had been Christian for three generations, i.e. to about the time of Ninian's recorded mission.[156]

Christianity may therefore have been continuous among the 'southern Picts' from the early fifth century onwards and thus provided a basis for the success of Columba's mission in the 560s. In England the final transition between paganism and Christianity did not take place, as we have seen, until the mid-seventh century. In 1952, just when Redwald seemed secure as the ruler honoured by the Sutton Hoo ship burial,[157] the numismatists who were challenged to disprove the date of 625 for the burial, obliged. Three eminent experts, Dr John Allan, sometime Keeper of Coins at the British Museum, M. Jean Lafaurie at the Cabinet des Médailles, and Philip Grierson of Gonville and Caius College, Cambridge, all agreed that from the point of view of the coins found with the burial, 625 was '*impossibly* early' (Lafaurie's emphasis) and the date must be around 650–660.[158] If so, who was the East Anglian king who still harboured pagan leanings? Fortunately perhaps, after an interval of eleven years, Lafaurie approached the problem again. Examining a hoard of 66 Merovingian gold coins found at Escharen in eastern North Brabant, he put the question: at what dates and in what regions most concerned did coins circulate together, and what types, whether minted in the Byzantine East, Italy, England or parts of the Merovingian dominions, were involved? This form of analysis, applied to Sutton Hoo, produced a date of 625! The problem of coins that previously seemed to have been minted later was still unanswered, but for the time being Redwald and 625 could be accepted as a working hypothesis.[159] In the British Museum, Rupert Bruce Mitford and his colleagues could at last contemplate resumption of work on the site in final preparation for writing a definitive report.[160]

There was more mystery about the origins and date of one further hoard recovered from St Ninian's Isle in the Shetland Islands. This was a hoard of 27 items of silverware and bone concealed beneath a slab marked with a cross near the chancel of a chapel dedicated, according to tradition, to St Ninian. It included a silver hanging bowl, seven silver bowls, twelve penannular brooches, a spoon, a single-pronged fork, a gilt sword-pommel and a porpoise bone. This last was probably a 'relic'. The hoard was buried probably about AD 800 in response to the danger of raids by Norsemen, but the mixture of Celtic and Pictish elements prevents any firm answer to the question what community or church the articles belonged. In many ways, these seem to continue the artistic traditions of some of the objects found at Sutton Hoo, and, though Christian, there is also the same curious mixture of paganism and Christianity; the helmet at Sutton Hoo and the sword-pommel at St Ninian's. With the hanging bowl, penannular brooches and silver bowls, one had the feeling of still being in the world of Late Antiquity prolonged into a period when much of the remainder of Europe was falling under the spell of the Carolingian empire.[161]

The immediate post-war years saw the same upsurge of interest in early Christian sites, as had followed the end of the Great War. While the aristocrats in the field continued to debate the typology of Christian art and architecture, the foot-sloggers, helped by vastly improved scientific aids and in many cases a resolve not to repeat the destructive errors of the past, pushed forward the pace of exploration. Except in Algeria and Morocco, successful revolutionary governments put little in the way of archaeological work – indeed, so far as 'Save Nubia' was concerned, the opposite was true. In Crete, despite tension between the British and Greek governments over Cyprus during 1956–62, archaeological work, including the writer's dig at Knossos, went on unhindered and indeed, encouraged by the Orthodox Church authorities. The output of new material remained just within bounds, the *Acta* of the three International Congresses of Christian Archaeology being confined to one volume plus plates. This situation, however, was not destined to continue. In the next quarter of a century an avalanche of new material descended. The growth of an 'academic industry' throughout the world opened a veritable Pandora's Box.

NOTES

1. See also the survey by O. G. S. Crawford, 'A century of air photography', *Antiquity* 28 (1954), pp. 206-11.
2. See W. F. Libby, *Radiocarbon Dating* (Chicago, 1952). P. R. Ritchie and J. Pugh, 'Ultra-violet radiation and excavation', *Antiquity* 37 (1963), pp. 259-63; W. F. Libby, 'The accuracy of radiocarbon dates', ibid., pp. 213-19; and for the consolidation of scientific techniques in archaeology, D. Brothwell and E. H. Higgs, *Science in Archaeology: A Comprehensive Survey of Progress and Research* (London, 1963).
3. See T. Klauser, *Henri Leclercq 1869–1945; vom Autodidakten zum Kompilator grossen Stils (JbAC* Ergänzungsband 5; 1977): unanswered questions, pp. 53-5; and above, p. 125.
4. Difficulties are outlined in the introduction to *RAC* I (1950).
5. For this and other collections listed in this paragraph, see Bibliography.
6. For Orkistus, *MAMA* VII, no. 305, lines 39-42. They objected to being a *vicus* under the jurisdiction of Nakolea, and after making out a case for promotion on economic grounds added 'Quibus omnibus quasi / cumulus accedit quod omnes sanctissimae reli / gionis habitare dicantur'. A final flourish! The petition was made in 331 when Constantine's pro-Christian credentials were well established.
7. See G. Bovini, *Eglises de Ravenne/The Churches of Ravenna* (Novara, 1960), pp. 86ff, for description and colour illus.
8. Recorded by M. Mazotti, *RAC* 32 (1956), pp. 204-18; Bovini, op. cit., pp. 40-1.
9. André Grabar, *Martyrium; recherches sur le Culte des reliques et l'art chrétien antique* (2 vols; Paris: Collège de France, 1946).
10. Ibid., II, p. 8: nearly all early Christian art was concerned in some way with the after life; figurative art on behalf of the dead preceded art for the benefit of the living.
11. Ibid., I, p. 54 (*martyrium* of Asterius at Salona). Grabar claimed (p. 14) that 'l'art chrétien à ses débuts n'invente guère de formes artistiques nouvelles'. It sought to adapt pagan forms to its needs.
12. J. Ward Perkins, 'Memoria, martyr's tomb and martyr's church', *Akten* VII (Vatican City/Berlin, 1967), pp. 3-27.
13. He did not mention the Christian Church buildings at Antioch *c.* 270 and Nicomedia *c.* 300.
14. Ambrose, dedication of the church of the Apostles in Milan in 382: 'Forma crucis templum est, templum victoria Christi sacra, triumphalis signat imago locum'; Ward Perkins, op. cit., p. 21, thus presenting an alternative to Grabar's theory, though Grabar has a long section (op. cit., I, p. 152ff.) on the subject of 'Martyria cruciformes', quoting Gregory of Nyssa, *Oratio* xviii.39 on the significance of this form of Christian building: p. 153 n.1.
15. E. Dyggve, 'Basilica Discoperta, un nouveau type d'edifice cultuel paléochrétien', *Atti* IV.1 (1940), pp. 415-32; for his imagined plan of Marusinac, Basilica II, p. 422, fig. 11; also art. in *Zeitschrift fur Kunstgeschichte* 39 (1940), pp. 103ff.
16. Quoting Placentinus, a contemporary of Procopius: *Atti* IV.1, p. 425.
17. Grabar, op. cit., I, pp. 121-5. He believed that the pagan *heröon* provided the model for the *basilica discoperta*: I, p. 135.
18. For instance, A. M. Schneider, 'Basilica discoperta', *Antiquity* 24 (1950), p. 131; and R. M. Milenovic, 'Zum Problem der Basilica Discoperta', *JÖAI* 41 (Beiblatt) (1954), pp. 129-58.
19. Crawford, *Antiquity* 38 (1964), Editorial, p. 245 (December 1964).
20. For a memoir on Goodchild's life and work see Joyce Reynolds (ed.) *Libyan Studies: Select Papers by R. G. Goodchild* (1976), pp. xiii–xvii.
21. J. B. Ward Perkins and R. G. Goodchild, 'The Christian antiquities in Tripolitania', *Archaeologia* 95 (1953), pp. 1-84, at pp. 7-22.
22. Ibid., pp. 22-4: six churches in all, four built by Justinian: Procopius, *De Aedif.* vi. 4. 4-5. Two of these latter had not been identified in 1952.
23. Ward Perkins and R. G. Goodchild, op. cit., p. 61.
24. R. G. Goodchild, 'Roman sites on the Tarhuna plateau of Tripolitania', *PBSR* 19 (1951), pp. 43-79; economic decline set in from the mid-sixth century: p. 65.
25. Ward Perkins and Goodchild, op. cit., p. 66.
26. Ibid., plates XVII and XVIII.

27. Goodchild, 'Tarhuna', p. 74: 'Latino-Libyan Inscriptions from Tripolitania', *AJ* 30 (1950), pp. 135–44.
28. Ward Perkins and Goodchild, op. cit., pp. 37–43 and Fig. 20 on p. 41.
29. David Oates, 'Ancient settlements in the Tripolitanian Gebel II', *PBSR* 22 (1954), pp. 91–117, at p. 113.
30. Ward Perkins and Goodchild, op. cit., pp. 54–6 and plate XXIV.
31. W. Widrig and R. G. Goodchild, 'The West Church at Apollonia in Cyrenaica', *PBSR* 28 (1960), pp. 70–90, and plates. XXVI–XXXIII.
32. See Ward Perkins, *Atti* VI, pp. 647–8 and figs 13–19, and *Atti* VIII, p. 228; also *Rivista* (1958), pp. 183 and 188–92. In general, see Joyce Reynolds, 'Christian inscriptions in Cyrenaica', *JTS* n.s. 11 (1960), pp. 284–94. One of the inscriptions (no. 8) mentions Hesychius the Libyarch, who was a high official and friend of Bishop Synesius (410).
33. R. G. Goodchild, 'A Byzantine palace at Apollonia', *Antiquity* 34 (1960), pp. 246–58.
34. Ibid., p. 254.
35. Goodchild, 'Byzantines, Berbers and Arabs in 7th century Libya', *Antiquity* 41 (1967), pp. 115–24.
36. R. M. Harrison, 'A sixth century church at Ras el Hillal in Cyrenaica', *PBSR* 32 (1964), pp. 1–20. Nine churches had been excavated in Cyrenaica by the end of 1960.
37. Ibid.
38. The work of Dr Robert Ambialet, among others, whom the writer was privileged to accompany on an inoculation tour through some villages near Constantine.
39. G. Charles-Picard, 'L'archéologie chrétienne en Afrique 1938–1953', *Atti* V (1957), pp. 47–59.
40. E. Marec, *Hippone la royale* (Algiers, 1950), pp. 53–67; J. Christern, *BZ* 55 (1962), pp. 188ff.
41. Augustine had a good description of the popular support enjoyed along with the exaggerated respect paid to a Donatist bishop: *Ep.* 23.3 (to Maximin of Sinitum).
42. E. Marec, 'Les dernières fouilles d'Hippo Regius, ville épiscopale de Saint Augustin', *Augustinus Magister* (Etudes augustiniennes; Paris, 1955), pp. 6–17 and Plan. Also J. Lassus, 'Les édifices du culte autour de la Basilique', *Atti* VI, pp. 581–610, esp. pp. 587ff. Opposition to Marec's interpretations: see H. I. Marrou, *Revue des études augustiniennes* 6.2 (1960), pp. 109ff. For Février's description see *Approches*, II, pp. 29–32.
43. Not accepted by J. Lassus, introduction to E. Marec, *Monuments chrétiens d'Hippone* (Algiers, 1958), pp. 6–7.
44. Augustine, *Ep.* 29,. Site described by Marec, 'Dernières fouilles', pp. 4–7; *Monuments*, Part III, 'L'Eglise à cinq nefs'.
45. Marec, 'Dernières fouilles', 13: burial of Ermengon, a Suevic noble; *Monuments*, pp. 62–5.
46. Marec, *Hippone*, p. 58.
47. A. Berthier, *Tiddis, antique Castellum Tidditanorum* (Algiers, 1951; 2nd edn, Algiers, 1972), p. 29.
48. Ibid., pp. 51–2 (pottery) and 50 (glass coins, contrasting with the lack of Vandal and Byzantine coins).
49. Charles-Picard, op. cit., p. 57; *BCTH* (1950), p. 40.
50. J. Baradez, *Tipasa* (Algiers, 1952), pp. 98–100.
51. Ibid., pp. 55–60; L. Leschi, report on *BCTH* (1941–42: Séance du 16 Nov. 1942), pp. 355–9.
52. Augustine, *Ep.* 93.5.17, for Thagaste's change of allegiance.
53. Charles-Picard, op. cit., p. 56 and *BCTH* (1950), p. 41 (pagan cemetery), report by M. Serée de Roch.
54. For the imprecation see L. Leschi, *BCTH* (1948–49), pp. 429ff.
55. As recorded in L. Balout and M. Leglay, 'L'archéologie algérienne en 1954', *RAfr* 98 (1955), pp. 223–4. Timgad had attracted 10,583 visitors during 1954.
56. Serge Lancel, 'L'architecture et décoration de la grande basilique de Tigzirt', *MEFR* 68 (1956), pp. 299–333.
57. N. Yacono, 'L'Algérie depuis 1830', *RAfr* 100 (1956; *Centenaire de la Société historique Algérienne 1856–1956*), p. 185. Yacono provides a bibliography of Algerian nationalism 1945–55 in n. 160, p. 189. For the opening addresses, see ibid., pp. 6–37.
58. The great influence of Gsell, even though he felt he himself was unable to continue his work, Février confesses in *Approches du Maghreb romain*, I, p. 14 (final para.), written in 1987.
59. 'L'archéologie chrétienne en France', *Atti* VI (Ravenna), pp. 57–93.

60. A. Février, 'Les peintures de la Catacombe de Priscille. Cubiculum de l'Orante', *MEFR* 71 (1959), pp. 301–19, especially pp. 306–7. To the writer, the young woman appears to be holding an open scroll (not a veil), while the standing figure at her shoulder appears to be female, aged about 40, rather than a youthful deacon. The other principal figure in the scene, a seated authoritative, rubicund personage, is more reminiscent of a philosopher (Pythagoras?) imparting knowledge than of St Peter.

61. J. Wilpert, *Die gottgeweihten Jungfrauen in den ersten Jahrhunderten der Kirche* (Fribourg, 1892), pp. 52–62, and *Pitture*, pp. 188–93, plates 79–82.

62. See Février's description of his aims and work in Introduction to *Approches*, I.

63. Février, 'Mosaiques funéraires chrétiennes datés d'Afrique du Nord', *Atti* VI, pp. 433–56.

64. Février, *Approches*, I, p. 7.

65. J. P. Brisson, *Autonomisme et christianisme dans l'Afrique romain* (Paris: Boccard, 1958).

66. A. Mandouze, 'Toujours le Donatisme', *Antiquité classique* 29 (1960), pp. 61–107.

67. E. Tengström, *Donatisten und Katholiken: soziale wirtschaftliche und politische Aspekte einer nord-afrikanischen Kirchenspaltung* (Göteborg, 1964). For a critical estimate of the influence of social and religious factors on religious controversies in Late Antiquity, see A. H. M. Jones, 'Were ancient heresies national or social movements in disguise?', *JTS* n.s. 10 (1959), pp. 280–98; B. Kriegbaum, *Kirche der Traditoren oder Kirche der Märtyrer* (Innsbruck, 1986).

68. P. A. Février, 'Toujours le Donatisme: à 'quand l'Afrique?', *RSLR* 2 (1966), pp. 228–40.

69. Février, *Approches*, II, pp. 27ff.: 'Bâtir pour le vrai Dieu'.

70. The tone of the author towards the writer may pehaps be characterized as 'désobligeant' (thus II, p. 174) on the mistaken ground that he had been a correspondent in the Spanish Civil War (ibid.) and had been influenced by adverse options gained there concerning Spanish clergy (p. 183). In fact as an Oxford undergraduate at the time, he shared the views of the overwhelming majority of his generation concerning the Spanish Civil War and, as a consequence, of the Roman Catholic Church.

71. His 'En guise de conclusion' does not add anything substantially new.

72. N. Duval and A. Lézine, 'La Chapelle funéraire dite d'Astérius à Cathage', *MEFR* 71 (1959), pp. 339–57; dating: p. 351.

73. Ibid., fig. 2.

74. Duval and Lézine, 'Nécropole chrétienne et Baptistère souterrain à Carthage', *CArch* 10–11 (1959–60), pp. 71–147, at pp. 95–9, esp. p. 97. For the name Redemtus, see *BTCH* (1946), p. 228.

75. N. Duval, *Les églises africaines à deux absides*, I: *Les basiliques de Sbeitla à deux sanctuaires opposés* (*BEFAR* 218; 1971).

76. This church (or monastery?) had been excavated soon after the war, and an epitaph of an official on the staff of the Praetorian Prefect in Africa found: one of many officials and aristocrats buried in the Sbeitla churches: *BCTH* (1949), pp. 631–2; 'Sbeitla', *DACL* XV.1, 978 (Pompeianus).

77. N. Duval, 'Nouvelles recherches d'archéologie et d'épigraphie chrétiennes à Sbeitla', *MEFR* 68 (1956), pp. 247–98, at p. 277, fig. 8.

78. See for discussion and literature, Y. Duval, *Loca Sanctorum Africae*, I (Collection de l'Ecole française de Rome 58: Rome, 1982), pp. 105–15. For the suggestion that the Fourth Edict was not enforced in North Africa see G. E. M. de Ste Croix, 'Aspects of the Great Persecution', *HTR* 47 (1954), pp. 86–96.

79. N. Duval, *Recherches archéologiques à Haidra*, II: *La Basilique I dite de Melleus* (Collection de l'Ecole française de Rome 18; Rome 1981); 'Inscriptions chrétiénnes d'Haidra', ibid. I (Rome, 1975).

80. Charles-Picard, op. cit., p. 46.

81. Avi Yonah, 'Christian archaeology in Israel 1948–1954', *Atti* V, pp. 117–24, esp. pp. 117–20.

82. G. U. S. Corbett, 'Excavations at Julianos Church at Umm el Jemal', *PBSR* 25 (1957), pp. 39–66.

83. G. Tchalenko, *Villages antiques de la Syrie du Nord* (Paris, 1953–58) and, shortly, 'La Syrie du Nord: étude économique' in *VIe Congrès International d'Etudes Byzantines* (1950), pp. 389–97. Other discoveries are summarized by C. Mondésert, *Syria* 37 (1960), pp. 116–30.

84. Michael Gough, *The Early Christians* (London, 1961), pp. 154–5. See above, p. 142.

85. Ibid., fig. 30. For Gough's further work on the sites in southern Turkey see 'Anazarbus', *AS* 2 (1952), pp. 85–150: 'Temple and church at Ayas (Cilicia).', ibid., 4 (1954), pp. 49–64. The church was built at the south-east end of the abandoned temple.

86. W. M. Calder, 'Early Christian epitaphs from Phrygia', *AS* 5 (1955), pp. 25–38, at p. 37. Calder also believed he had found the earliest dated Christian inscription; Paul son of Gaius standing and holding a round loaf marked with a cross, dated 179–180: pp. 33–5.

87. M. Ballance, 'The site of Derbe: a new inscription', *AS* 7 (1957), pp. 147–51. The return of the Austrians to Ephesus in 1954 under the direction of Franz Miltner completes the record of early Christian work in Asia Minor in this period: see *JÖAI* 43 (1956–58), Beiblatt, pp. 1–63, at pp. 56–8, for Christian graffiti on the walls of the shrine in a cave on the Bul Bül Dag.

88. See P. Lermerle's memoir on Thomas Whittemore, *Byzantion* 21 (1951), p. 21, and for Underwood's work, *AS* 4 (1954), p. 17.

89. D. Talbot Rice and G. U. S. Corbett, 'Archaeological summary of work', *AS* 3 (1953), p. 11: working on behalf of the Walker Trust. The buildings continued to be used until the period of the Latin conquest (1204).

90. Homer Thompson, 'The Athenian twilight 267–600', *JRS* 50 (1959), pp. 61–72: J. Creaghen and A. E. Raubitschek, 'Early Christian epitaphs from Athens', *Hesperia* 18 (1947), pp. 1–54, esp. pp. 37–50.

91. C. A. Ralegh Radford, 'Justiniana Prima (Tsaritsin Grad)', *Antiquity* 28 (1954), pp. 15–19.

92. E. Dyggve, *History of Salonitan Christianity*, pp. 14, n.1 and 125.

93. Basilica excavated by A. H. S. Megaw in the town site on Cape Drepanum (three aisles and three apses with an annexe to the north and an atrium to the west; mosaic pavement in nave). Recorded by J. M. Cook, 'Archaeology in Greece 1948–49', *JHS* 70 (1950), p. 15. Two other basilicas were reported by Megaw in same area: ibid., 74 (1954), p. 175. Coin hoards ending with Heraclius (641) indicate that there too Christian/Byzantine civilization suffered severely at the hands of raiders, this time Arabs, e.g. ibid., 73 (1953), p. 137 from Limassol; and Larnaka, ibid., 72 (1952), pp. 116–17. See also T. B. Mitford, 'New inscriptions from early Christian Cyprus', *Byzantion* 20 (1956), pp. 105–79.

94. *Atti* V, pp. 112–13.

95. Ibid.

96. Recorded by C. Delvoye, *Byzantion* 19 (1948), p. 369.

97. A. K. Orlandos, *Kritika Chronica* (1953), referring to work at Syia in western Crete; and on the peninsula at Panormus on the north coast, possibly succeeding a pagan shrine (own observation).

98. Recorded in detail by the writer and D. E. Johnston, 'The byzantine basilica church at Knossos', *ABSA* 57 (1962), pp. 186–238.

99. Ibid., pp. 194–5 and fig. 9.

100. Ibid., pp. 205 (Tomb I) and 230, plate 53c.

101. Eusebius, *HE* iv.23, 7–8: governed by Bishop Pinytus.

102. *ABSA* (1962), p. 203.

103. See A. Ferrua, 'Le pitture della Nova Catacomba di Via Latina' in *Monumenti di Antichità Cristiana*, 2nd series, VIII (Vatican City, 1960); reviewed by J. M. C. Toynbee, *JRS* 52 (1962), pp. 356–7: P. Testini, *Le Catacombe*, pp. 156, 298–301, and plates 184–195; see also M. Simon, 'Remarques sur la Catacombe de la Via Latina', *Mullus* (1964), pp. 327–35.

104. Simon, for instance, is unable to decide whether the representations of Hercules were pagan or Christianized or 'on the way that led to Christianization': op. cit., p. 335; see also his *Hercule et le Christianisme* (Strasbourg/Paris, 1955).

105. Ferrua, 'La Catacomba della Santa Croce', *Rivista* 29 (1953), pp. 7–45, at p. 19.

106. Ibid., p. 44.

107. Discussed by C. Dagens, 'Autour du Pape Libère: d'iconographie de Suzanne et des Martyrs romains sur l'arcosolium de Celerina', *MEFR* 78 (1966), pp. 327–81, esp. 341 and n. 1: Gerke's identification of Susanna with Celerina in 1934. Another important discovery, relating to the end of the Valerianic persecution, was made by R. Marichal, researching the graffiti in the San Sebastiano. He deciphered one text mentioning the consular dates of P. Cornelius Saecularis II and Iunius Donatus II = 260. This provided the first dated example of minuscule writing in the West, and also suggested a date by which Gallienus had called off the persecution of the Christians. See R. Marichal, 'Les dates des graffiti de Saint Sebastien', *CRAI* (1953), pp. 60–8.

108. Theodoret, *HE* ii.17: *GCS* 19, 137; Dagens, pp. 363–4.

109. C. A. Agnello, *Rivista* 31 (1955), pp. 1–50; 32 (1956), pp. 9–27 and see by the same author, *La Pittura paleocristiana della Sicilia* (Vatican, 1952).

110. For Concordia, see P. L. Zovatto, *Antichi Monumenti Cristiania di Iulia Concordia Sagittaria* (Vatican 1950), pp. 12ff.; and below, Chapter 14.

111. Chromace d'Aquilée, *Sermons* I and II, ed. J. Lemarié, *SC* 154 and 164 (Paris, 1969 and 1971), nos 9, 19.1, 27.1, 28.1 and 2: 'Jews, philosophers and heretics' denounced. Also Ambrose, *Ep.* 40.8 on a Jewish synagogue being burnt down, allegedly on the instigation of the local bishop: *PL* 16, 1103.

112. G. Brusin, 'Un grande edificio cultuale a Monastero di S. Martino Aquileia', *Aquileia nostra* 20 (1949), pp. 25–30. See also, for an alternative interpretation (the church used by Eastern immigrants), F. Forlati Tamaro, *Atti* VI, pp. 659–72; C. Jäggi, *JbAC* 33 (1990), pp. 82–3. Seeing the mosaics in 1962, it seemed impossible to think otherwise than that they were Jewish and not earlier than the mid-fourth century.

113. G. Brusin, 'Interpretazione dei mosaici cristiani nella zona della basilica di Aquileia', *Atti* V, pp. 433–55, see also L. Voelkl, *RQ* 50 (1955), pp. 102–4 for a suggestion that the Christian complex may have formed part of the emperor Maximian's palace (rather than Bishop Theodore's family residence) before conversion to Christian use.

114. Own observation during visit to the cathedral at the time of the Thirteenth Congress of Christian Archaeology (October 1994). Jerome scorned this sort of donation: *Ep.* 52: ed. Wright, p. 215.

115. Recorded by C. Delvoye, *Byzantion* 31 (1961), pp. 505–9.

116. Work on the site had gone on spasmodically since 1910. Published fully by Rudolf Egger, *Die römischen und frühchristlichen Altertümer Oberkärntens* (Klagenfurt, 1973), pp. 26ff.; for its destruction by Avars (not Slavs) see F. Miltner, *JÖAI* 41 (1954), p. 83.

117. For Ulrichberg see R. Noll, 'Altchristliche Funde in Oesterreich', *Atti* V, pp. 261–8.

118. Miltner, 'Grabungen auf der Kirchbichl von Lavant/Osttirol', *JÖAI* 41 (1954), Beiblatt, pp. 45–84; 43 (1956), pp. 84–124.

119. See A. Wotschinsky, 'Archaologische Zeugnisse in den ersten drei Jahrhunderten in Tirol', *Tiroler Heimatblatt* 1/3 (1965), pp. 23–6.

120. Vigilius, *Ep.* 1, to Simplicianus, bishop of Milan: *PL* 13, 550: see C. E. Chaffin, 'The martyrs of Val de Non', *TU* 107 (Berlin, 1970), pp. 263–9.

121. Sulpicius Severus, *Vita S. Martini* (*CSEL* 1), 13.9.

122. Thus Henry Chadwick, *Priscillian of Avila* (OUP, 1976); and for Melania, see *DCB* III, 888–889: she was Rome-based but of Spanish descent.

123. H. Leclercq, 'Mérida', *DACL* XI.1, 466–467, inscriptions 468–477.

124. H. Schlunk, 'Archaologische Funde und Forschungen in Spanien', *JDAI* 69 (1954), pp. 451–66.

125. J. Vives, *Inscripciones cristianas de la España romana y visigoda* (Barcelona, 1st edn 1942, 2nd edn 1969).

126. P. A. Février, 'L'archéologie en France', *Atti* VI, pp. 57–93 at p. 67; *CRAI* (1962), pp. 99–102; also F. Benoît, 'Le Baptistère de Cimiez', *Atti* VI, pp. 147–58; 'Les fouilles de Cimiez', *CRAI* (1962), pp. 207–19.

127. Noel Duval, 'L'architecture cultuelle', *Naissance des arts chrétiens*, pp. 186–219, at pp. 206–7 (plan).

128. Paulinus of Nola, *Ep.* 32.1.

129. Himerius, quoted by Pope Siricius: 'Innumerae, ut asseris, plebes, baptismi mysterium consequantur': *Ep.* i.2.3: *PL* 15, 1134.

130. Consentius, letter to Augustine: published as *Letter* II in the Divjak *Letters of Augustine*: *CSEL* 88 (Vienna, 1981).

131. Février, *Atti* VI, op. cit., p. 93. New inventories of Christian inscriptions were also needed.

132. R. Lantier, *CRAI* (1948), pp. 154–63.

133. See J. Werner, 'The Frankish royal tombs in the cathedrals of Cologne and Saint Denis', *Antiquity* 38 (1964), pp. 201–15, with ample bibliography.

134. Ibid., pp. 206–14.

135. Ibid., fig. 6.

136. Ibid., pp. 210–11, figs 8–10.

137. P. Gose, 'Frühchristliche Inschriften in Trier', in *Trierer Grabungen und Forschungen*, III (Berlin, 1958). Other discoveries were being made in the Rhineland at this time, for instance, another small late-Roman church below the church of St. Severin at Cologne: *Germania* 25 (1961), pp. 180ff.; and also at St Gereon's, where the church was found to stand on late-Roman foundations. See T. Kempf, 'Früchristliche, Funde und Forschungen in Deutschland', *Atti* V, pp. 60–72, at p. 64; J. G. Deckers, 'St Gereon in Köln: Ausgrabungen 1978/79', *JbAC* 25 (1992), pp. 102–31.

138. Sulpicius Severus, *Chron.* ii. 31.

139. See K. S. Painter, 'The Mildenhall Treasure: a reconsideration', *BMQ* 37.3–4 (1955), pp. 154–5, plates 71 and 72.

140. Painter, pp. 158–9. My reconstruction.

141. Suggested by the writer, 'Pagans, Christians and the Barbarian Conspiracy of AD 367', *Britannia* 23 (1992), pp. 121–31.

142. For example, Hilary of Poitiers, *De Synodis* i (written *c.* 358): *PL* 10, 479.

143. G. W. Meates, *The Lullingstone Roman Villa* (London, 1955), Ch. 10.

144. Ibid., plate 3.

145. Illustrated in plates xi–xiv in Meates, *The Lullingstone Roman Villa*, II (final report) (Maidstone: Kent Archaeological Society, 1987).

146. Meates, *Roman Villa*, pp. 165–6.

147. See J. M. C. Toynbee, 'A new Roman mosaic pavement found in Dorset', *JRS* 54 (1964), pp. 7–14.

148. See J. M. C. Toynbee, 'Mosaïques au Bellérophon', *Gallia* 13 (1955), pp. 91–7; M. Simon, 'Bellérophon chrétien' in *Mélanges Jérome Carcopino* (Paris: Hachette, 1966), pp. 889–904.

149. Toynbee, *JRS* 54, pp. 13–14. Note the contrast in the hunting scene to the savage hunting scene depicted on the late-third-century mosaic of the Villa Armerina in Sicily. (See H. I. Marrou, *Tempora Christiana*, facing p. 258)

150. Toynbee, op. cit., p. 14, but not convincing concerning a Christian interpretation. But see also H. Leclercq, 'Saisons', *DACL* XV.1, 580–581.

151. Discussed by Toynbee, op. cit.

152. Illustated in the *B.M. Guide to Early Christian and Byzantine Antiquities* (1921), p. 58.

153. D. J Smith, 'Three fourth century schools of mosaics in Roman Britian' in *La Mosaique gréco-romaine* (Paris: CNRS, 1965), pp. 95–116.

154. Bede, *HE* iii.4. See also Charles Thomas, *The Early Christian Archaeology of North Britain* (OUP, 1971), pp. 14–16.

155. C. A. Ralegh Radford, 'Excavations at Whithorn 1949', *TDGNHAS* 27 (1948–49), pp. 85–126.

156. Charles Thomas, *Christianity in Roman Britain*, pp. 283–4.

157. See Gordon Ward, 'The silver spoons from Sutton Hoo', *Antiquity* 26 (1952), pp. 9–14, at p. 11; Also *Atiquity*, ibid., Editorial, pp. 4–8.

158. P. Grierson, 'The dating of the Sutton Hoo coins', *Antiquity* 26, pp. 83–6. Grierson suggests *c.* 650 as the date of the burial. See also the same, *Antiquity* 44 (1970), pp. 14–18 on the purpose of the coins.

159. J. Lafaurie, quoted by Christopher Hawkes, 'Sutton Hoo: twenty-five years after', *Antiquity* 38 (1964), pp. 252–8.

160. See Bruce Mitford's brief report, 'Sutton Hoo excavations 1965–67', *Antiquity* 42 (1968), pp. 35–9; M. O. H. Carver, *The Age of Sutton Hoo* (London, 1992).

161. A. C. O'Dell and colleagues, 'St Ninian's Isle silver hoard', *Antiquity* 33 (1959), pp. 241–69; Kenneth Jackson, 'St Ninian's Isle Inscription', ibid., 34 (1960), pp. 38–43.

FURTHER READING

M. Avi-Yonah, 'Christian archaeology in Israel 1948–1954', *Atti* V, pp. 117–24.

J. Baradez, *Tipasa* (Algiers, 1952; 2nd edn 1957).

A. Berthier, *Tiddis, antique Castellum Tiddditanorum* (Algiers, 1951).

A. Berthier, *L'Algérie et son passé* (Paris: Editions Picard, 1951).

G. Bovini, *Eglises de Ravenne/The Churches of Ravenna* (Novara, 1960): fine illustrations.

J. P. Brisson, *Autonomisme et christianism dans l'Afrique romaine* (Paris: Boccard, 1958).

G. Brusin, *Aquileia e Gardo, Guida breve* (2nd edn; Padua, 1959).

N. Duval, *Les ruines de Sheitla* (Tunis, 1973).

N. Duval, *Recherches archéologiques – Haidra*, II: *La Basilique dite de Melleus* (Collection de l'Ecole française de Rome 18; 1981).

E. Dyggve, 'Basilica discoperta, un nouveau type d'édifice cultuel paléochrétien', *Atti* IV.1 (1940), pp. 419–32.

A. Ferrua, 'Le pitture della nuova catacomba di Via Latina' in *Monumenti di antichità cristiana* (Vatican City, 1960); rev. J. M. C. Toynbee, *JRS* 42 (1962), pp. 356–7.

P. A. Février, *Djemila* (Algiers, 1968): Arabic resumé.

P. A. Février, 'Mosaïques funéraires chrétiennes dans l'Afrique romain', *Atti* VI (1959), pp. 433–56.

W. H. C. Frend, *The Donatist Church: A Movement of Protest in Roman North Africa* (OUP, 1952; 3rd edn 1985).

W. H. C. Frend, 'The Byzantine basilican church at Knossos', *ABSA* 57 (1962), pp. 186–238.

R. G. Goodchild, 'Roman sites on the Tarhouna Plateau', *PBSR* 19 (1951), pp. 43–79.

R. G. Goochild, 'A Byzantine palace at Apollonia', *Antiquity* 34 (1960), pp. 246–58.

R. G. Goodchild, 'Byzantines, Berbers and Arabs in the 7th century', *Antiquity* 41 (1967), pp. 115–24.

R. G. Goodchild, *Libyan Studies*, ed. J. Reynolds (London, 1976).

M. Gough, *The Early Christians* (London: Thames and Hudson, 1961).

A. Grabar, *Martyrium: Recherches sur le culte des reliques et de l'art chrétien antique* (2 vols; Paris: Collège de France, 1946).

T. Klauser, *Henri Leclercq, 1869–1945, vom Autodidakten zum Kompilator grossen Stils* (*JbAC* Ergänzungsband 5; 1977).

S. Lancel, 'L'architecture et décoration de la grande basilique de Tigzirt', *MEFR* 68 (1956), pp. 299–333.

W. F. Libby, *Radiocarbon Dating* (Chicago, 1952).

A. Mandouze, 'Toujours le Donatisme', *Antiquité Classique* 29 (1960), pp. 61–107: review article; criticizing Brisson's work.

E. Marec, *Hippone le royale* (Algiers, 1950).

G. W. Meates, *Lullingstone Roman Villa* (London, 1955).

T. B. Mitford, 'New inscriptions from early Christian Cyprus', *Byzantion* 20 (1955), pp. 105–79.

A. C. O'Dell and colleagues, 'St Ninian's Isle silver hoard', *Antiquity* 33 (1959).

K. S. Painter, 'The Mildenhall Treasure, a reconsideration', *BMQ* 37 (1955), pp. 154–75.

A. M. Schneider, 'Basilica Discoperta', *Antiquity* 24 (1950), pp. 131–9.

V. Tchalenko, *Villages antiques de la Syria du nord* (3 vols; Paris, 1953–58).

E. Tengström, *Donatisten und Katholiken: soziale, wirtschaftliche und politische Aspekte einer nord-afrikanischen Kirchenspaltung* (Göteborg, 1964).

P. Testini; *Le Catacombe, antichi cimitieri cristiani in Roma* (Bologna, 1966).

Charles Thomas, *Early Christian Archaeology of North Britain* (OUP, 1971).

Homer Thompson, 'Athenian twilight 267–600', *JRS* 50 (1959), pp. 61–72.

J. M. C. Toynbee, 'A new Roman mosaic pavement found in Dorset', *JRS* 54 (1964), pp. 7–14.

J. Ward Perkins, 'Memoria, martyr's tomb and martyr's church', *Akten (Atti)* VII (Vatican–Berlin, 1967), pp. 3–27.

J. Ward Perkins with R. G. Goodchild, 'The Christian antiquities in Tripolitania', *Archaeologia* 95 (1953), pp. 1–84.

J. Werner, 'The Frankish royal tombs in the cathedrals of Cologne and St Denis', *Antiquity* 38 (1964), pp. 201–15.

14

Pandora's Box, 1965–1990

In the 1930s the Modern History school at Oxford ended its syllabus with the year 1914. Everything later was 'Current Affairs', too recent for an historian to assess adequately. Something similar may be said of Christian archaeology these last thirty years. Ever more discoveries and discussions of previous ones have resulted from rising standards of education and living world-wide that have produced an army of professionals and ever greater numbers of students interested in the Christian past. Pandora's Box had been blown apart by the sheer volume of research and discovery.

One instance may be quoted. At the Centenary Conference of Christian Archaeology held at Split and Porec in September 1994, Yoran Tsafrir of the Hebrew University at Jerusalem stated that no fewer than 1,000 early Byzantine sites had been found west of the Jordan. These included 150 synagogues, and he estimated that in Justinian's time the large and flourishing Palestinian population was two-thirds Christian and one-third Jewish. From Galilee to the Negev the country was prosperous, not least in the reign of Anastasius (491–518) whom excavations in Scythopolis in Galilee had shown to have been as great a builder as Justinian himself.[1]

This type of information could be repeated all over the Greco-Roman world, as for instance, in southern Asia Minor where over 100 Christian monuments had been recorded by 1990.[2] Istria also, whither the 1994 conference migrated from Split, which was previously only moderately well-known for its early Christian sites, emerges as a major Christian province. A map of sites drawn for the eleventh Congress in 1986 included no fewer than 19 churches at Pula and its surroundings, another 11 at Porec (Praesentum) and a further 33 scattered in various hardly-explored sites in the peninsula.[3] The Black Sea coast with Constanza (Tomi) as its centre had been revealed as another Christianized area, with its own record of martyrs, where archaeology has confirmed literary evidence.[4] Bulgaria,[5] Montenegro,[6] Albania,[7] the islands of the Adriatic coast of Croatia[8] have all produced early-Christian churches, as have Sardinia,[9] Corsica[10] and the Iberian peninsula.[11] Excavations have been carried out skilfully by a new generation of students.

Reports of these discoveries have occupied the six congresses of Christian archaeology held since Trier in 1965. Barcelona, Rome, Salonica, Lyons–Vienne–Grenoble–Geneva–Aosta, Bonn, and Split–Porec have been hosts to up to 500 delegates each. Their *Proceedings* have overflowed into volumes of print. Rome 1975 with two volumes totalling 1,284 pages was easily surpassed by the *Acta* of the Eleventh Congress. This mass of scholarship perambulated round five centres in three different countries in the late summer of 1986, and in 1989 produced a monster three-volume *Proceedings* of more than 3,000 pages. Added to these international gatherings have been national congresses, such as those of the Italian congresses of Christian archaeology, reviewing research and excavation on Italian soil.[12]

Important literary discoveries such as Johannes Divjak's identification of 31 new Augustinian letters and memoranda,[13] and new sermons by the same North African Father discovered at Mainz[14] have given fresh impetus to this generation of early Christian research. At Cologne the tiny Manichaean book researched and published by A. Henrichs and L. Koenen show how Mani himself describes his spiritual odyssey from membership of an Elkasaite baptist sect to the world mission of his own extreme Gnostic creed.[15] Archaeology and literary studies are now seen as inextricably linked, a process helped by growing interest by Classical faculties and Institutes in Continental countries in Late Antiquity. This relatively new lay participation in Catholic countries has contributed to the archaeology of the early Church as an essential connecting link between Classics and theology.

It will not be all plain sailing. 'Confessional' and even 'national' archaeology make little sense today, but thanks to the legacies of a not-so-recent past, suspicions between Classicists and theologians in the field of archaeology have persisted. Their continued existence was brought into the open by H. I . Marrou in an address at the opening of the Rome Congress in 1975.[16] Marrou was commemorating the fifty years of the existence of the Pontifical Institute of Christian Archaeology (see above, Chapter 9). He praised the progressive adoption of scientific techniques embodying, in particular, stratigraphy now taught to students of the Institute, but then spoke of the continued division (not least in Rome itself) between the disciplines of Classical and Christian archaeology. In some ways, he admitted, this was a legacy of the treatment of archaeology as an arm of (Catholic) apologetics, but in others, the fault lay with Classicists refusing to study beyond

Diocletian. The rest was 'Decadence' for which the Christians were largely responsible (shades of Gibbon!). Marrou appealed for co-operation between members of the two disciplines in the field of 'Late Antiquity' in studying its material remains.[17] The plea was timely. More still needs to be done, even in Britain, before ecclesiastical history and archaeology are accepted fully by Classicists and historians as kindred disciplines.

Marrou, as befitted a pupil of Franz Cumont, combined in himself Classical and patristic scholarship with the archaeology of the period 250–600. He refused to accept as 'decadent' or 'in decline' a period of human history that produced the great figures of Augustine, Ambrose, Jerome and Gregory Nazianzen.[18] His final article, written for the *Mélanges de l'Ecole française de Rome*, was a long study of the great hunting mosaics in the imperial villa of the Piazza Armerina. It breaks off in mid-sentence before he had reached a conclusion, after a vigorous criticism of a view attributed to Charles Seltman that the young woman-athletes represented 'the life lived among country people in central Sicily, where girls could still be gay, happy and natural', without the stultifying burden of Christian ethic and morality. Nonsense, he wrote, for the Christian empire was not to be identified with 'Anglo-Saxon puritanism'.[19]

Marrou was also an *Africaniste*, the natural consequence of being a scholar at the Ecole française de Rome in 1930–32.[20] His study in 1953 of what appears to be a seventh-century inscription from Hippo is remarkable.[21] The text, the funerary inscription of a certain Constantina, who died at the age of twelve, was atrociously written but concealed amidst an attempt at hexameters reminiscences of lines from Virgil's *Aeneid*. In this, among the latest Latin inscriptions from eastern Algeria, one can see how despite all efforts to grasp at a past heritage the Latin language was fading along with, it would seem, the Christian religion.[22] It was symbolic of the end of Latin North Africa.

In *Algeria* the first two decades of independence however witnessed further activity, particularly by non-French scholars. Denis Pringle was able to investigate anew the defences of Byzantine Africa,[23] and Elizabeth Fentress to work on the continuity between Byzantine and Islamic Setif.[24] But the most important event during these years was Jürgen Christern's detailed and immensely successful study of the Christian complex at Theveste (Tebessa). Theveste had been mentioned whenever Christian archaeology in North Africa has been discussed, but Christern's work was one of those rare instances where what must be regarded as a last chance was seized on, and a satisfactory solution to many outstanding problems arrived at. Christern spent three years on the site, 1965–67, with a colleague. Prompted by Février, who was able to take part in the work in 1965,[25] Christern started his study not with the basilica itself, but with the trefoil chapel attached to its south-west side (ecclesiastical south). The consequence was a drastic revision of Ballu's conclusions in the 1890s.[26] He found what could have been suspected, that the original Christian building was a small rectangular room, oriented north—south and had been erected within a pagan cemetery. It had housed a reliquary and a sarcophagus. It was covered with a mosaic floor and dated probably to the first half of the fourth century. Considerably later, in the second half of the century, it was enlarged, and a new mosaic laid down by the deacon Novellus, in the centre of which were recorded the names of seven martyrs. Surrounding this central panel were the names of deacons, lectors and women (wives?). This was the original *memoria*, in all probability erected over the supposed tomb of the martyr Crispina and her companions executed according to the date on the mosaic, 22 December (XI Kal. Jan.), presumably 304.[27]

What about the basilica? Here Christern was assisted by a single, significant find. In the foundations of the stairway connecting the chapel with the basilica a newly-minted gold solidus of Theodosius I, datable to 388,[28] had been found in 1954. A gold coin in mint condition could hardly be a stray find, and Christern concluded that it was intended as a foundation deposit. If this was so, then the basilica would date to 388 and subsequent years. His architect's eye told him that the whole majestic complex had been built at one and the same time, a mighty effort with the single object of erecting a building worthy of the martyr Crispina.[29] Why at that time? Here perhaps is an idea which Christern did not mention; it was the time of Timgad's eminence as a place of pilgrimage under the aegis of the Donatist bishop Optatus.[30] Did Theveste not wish to be outdone, and hence the tremendous activity? A speculation, but one that might fit the known facts. Thus the basilica was not a monastery but a vast pilgrimage centre, the impressive approaches seen from afar across the plain to the north, Once arrived, the pilgrim's sense of awe would be heightened as he made his way through the great basilica down the stairway to the trefoil sanctuary where the remains and reliquary of Crispina rested. The horse-troughs surrounding the courtyard were for pilgrims' horses;[31] other buildings served as hostelries, and in the writer's view, apartments on the north and west sides of the complex would be best explained less by monastic quarters,[32] than to house those belonging to a permanent staff needed to organize the continuous throngs of pilgrims. Though the problem of a possible earlier church beneath the foundations of the basilica remains, Christern's demonstration remains a convincing final word before the curtain fell on nearly all field work in Algeria.

Christern's opportunity was exceptional. The main contribution by French scholars to the archaeology of the Church in their former possessions in North Africa was to consolidate previous results largely from the Centre de Recherches sur l'Afrique mediterranée established at Aix-en-Provence. An enormous amount of material had been recovered in the previous three-quarters of a century. Much had been recorded, but apart from Leclercq's *Dictionnaire* reports were scattered about, often in now obsolete journals. It was greatly to the credit of the Duvals that they sought to tackle this problem before it was too late. In the 1970s Noel Duval had compiled a series of *Etudes* of Christian archaeology in North Africa with J. Cintas,[33] but realized that a full descriptive catalogue and bibliography of Algerian churches had become a necessity. An attempt to delegate this work to a research student was only partially successful and the main task fell to him. The two volumes of *Basiliques chrétiennes de l'Afrique du Nord* (I: *Algérie*),[34] record the discovery, description, date where possible, and most useful of all for the future, the last known state of preservation of each building. More specialized was Yvette Duval's study of the cult of martyrs in North Africa.[35] This was another vital work of cataloguing and preservation covering the whole of Roman North Africa. It was unfortunate, perhaps, that the author did not take enough account of the statement by Jerome in 393 that Donatus of Carthage had 'deceived nearly all Africa'[36] i.e. that throughout the fourth century Donatism was the majority religion there. To attempt to identify as many of the North African martyrs as possible with saints mentioned in orthodox martyrologies was doomed to failure. The *clan donatiste*, as the author termed them,[37] deserved better treatment and Bishop Marculus was surely more than a 'pretended (or even 'claimed') martyr'.[38] Indeed, an opportunity to study a non-orthodox liturgy in the West, based on the cult of martyrs in the fourth century, was lost.

In *Tunisia* similar valuable service has been done by Liliane Ennabli, French-born wife of M. Abdelmajib Ennabli, Inspector-General of Antiquities at Carthage. Here the problem was the salvage and cataloguing of what remained of the vast number of fragments of inscriptions found by Delattre during his excavation of the Damous el Karita, Basilica Majorum (Basilique de Mcidfa) and the Cyprian (Saint-Monique) basilicas.[39] Sketchy records only of this harvest of inscriptions had been kept. A considerable number of fragments had been stuck into the wall opposite the entrance of the White Fathers' museum on the Byrsa. Alas, many of these had fallen victim to the successive Axis and Allied occupations of Tunis (November 1942–May 1945) (see above, p. 215 n. 19). Only a little of what had been found was available for catalogue. Nonetheless 791 had survived from the several thousand which Delattre claimed to have found on the site of the Basilica Majorum,[40] but only 403 from the Sainte-Monique site.[41] The overwhelming number of these were simple epitaphs, expressions of piety such as 'Pascentea in pacem vixi(t) annis LX',[42] or 'Dynamius fidelis in pace'.[43] Only occasionally were the inscriptions a little more informative. Delattre's view that the Basilica Majorum was indeed dedicated to Perpetua and Felicitas may be upheld. The fragments, probably Byzantine in date, recording in monumental epigraphic style the names of the martyrs, would appear to leave no doubt.[44] Only a few provided information about the deceased, though there was a 'medicus synodi' recorded,[45] and in Sainte-Monique the presence of Germanic names (as was the case at Ammaedara) suggested some Vandal use of this church.[46] Generations of Christians, however, lived and died in Carthage without leaving more than their names behind them.

Cyrenaica, despite Libyan government attitudes toward foreigners, provided an opportunity for another French scholar to show how literary and accumulated archaeological evidence could be integrated so as to throw light on a crucial period of the province's history. The life and episcopate of Synesius of Cyrene (bishop 411–413) is excellently documented from his correspondence. Less well known are the material circumstances of the province during his lifetime.[47] Denis Roques had been a member of the Mission archéologique française at Apollonia and formed the ambitious plan of rewriting the history of Cyrenaica round the career of Synesius with the emphasis on 'change' rather than 'decline'.[48] Change there certainly was, not least from paganism to Christianity, and as in Numidia, the Christians seem to have triumphed in the final decades of the third century.[49] The last dated inscriptions recording priests of Apollo are 285–288,[50] a time when the Christian Cyrenaican congregations were already conscious enough of their strength to cross swords with their Metropolitan Bishop Dionysius of Alexandria (d. 264).[51] At this time pagan buildings such as the sanctuary of Demeter and the Odeon were already ruined and their sites occupied by 'rough houses belonging to the second half of the third century', as Goodchild described them.[52] Synesius himself had never been other than a Christian, though a Platonizing one. As elsewhere in North Africa he lived in a period where despite a relative prosperity of the countryside, there were immense social divisions, typified by the town houses of the wealthy with their mosaic floors and the dwellings of the poor. Synesius' concern for the latter and his struggle with the civic authorities in Ptolemais for justice on their behalf is fully recorded, but Roques was able to assemble more evidence for conditions in the countryside at this time.[53] His work was typical of an increasing integration of text and material remains into a single convincing story of changing provincial life in the late Roman empire.

Roques' interest was in the fifth rather than the seventh century. *Jordan* provided some hitherto unsuspected evidence of the world of John of Damascus (*c.* 654–754). Research leading to these discoveries was carried out largely by the Franciscans centred on Jerusalem in co-operation with the Jordan Service of Antiquities. While the Dominicans of the Ecole Biblique were becoming increasingly bogged down with the fragments of Cave 4 in the Dead Sea Scrolls the Franciscans were seizing the initiative as field archaeologists. Some of their work, particularly their attempts to prove the existence of a Jewish-Christian community through the second and third centuries in Palestine on the basis of finds in cemeteries round about Jerusalem, was open to justified criticism,[54] but the excavations by Fr Picirillo in Jordan were outstandingly successful. The results of Fr Picirillo's and his colleagues' excavations on the church of the Virgin at Madaba, and other churches at Ayoun Mousa, Quweismeh (near Amman) and Kherbet-es-Samra were as splendid a sequence of mosaics as to be found anywhere in the Greco-Roman world.[55] They show that in the second half of Justinian's reign, and in those of his successors, when prosperity in other parts of the Byzantine dominions was tending to decline, the three Palestine provinces which occupied present-day Jordan experienced an era of unexampled wealth. Churches, chapels, official buildings, such as baths, and private dwellings of this period were all paved with grandiose and elaborate mosaics. The finest was a great 5.15 × 7.35 m expanse covering the floor of the chapel of the presbyter John at Kherbet Mukhayet not far from Mount Nebo, and laid down in 562. Significantly, apart from two candles to be seen either side of a room within a pillared building that could pass for the front of a Greek temple, and the dedicatory inscription, the theme of mosaic is pastoral rather than religious. The four rows of figures that comprise the central field include a hunting scene with a huntsman attacking a bear; an allegorical figure representing Earth in the form of a woman crowned with fruits and grain, scenes of harvest and a shepherd standing with his sling defending a sheep from an attack by a wild boar. There are bunches of fruit and flowers and fish swimming in the open spaces.[56] The mosaic harmonizes exactly with those found in official buildings. In one, at Madaba, subsequently covered by the floor of the church of the Virgin, personifications of Christian Rome, Madaba and Gregoria (identity unknown) take their place beside Tychai (Fortunes). There is also Cupid (Eros) placed by Charis (Grace) in the path of a Countrywoman (Agroikēs), no doubt to tempt her, and in another scene Aphrodite is seated while Adonis punishes (mildly!) Eros.[57]

This Hellenized Christian society survived the Muslim conquest after 636. Bishops continued to be consecrated, churches rebuilt and renovated, monasteries to be populated through the seventh century and the first decades of the eighth century. There are examples of renovation and new mosaics being laid down in the reign of Omar II (717–720) at Quweismeh,[58] Ma'in[59] and at the church of St Stephen at Umm er-Rasas/Katron Mefaa.[60] It was also, however, a conservative society that still continued to use the Greco-Roman provincial (Pompeian) dating system on their mosaics three-quarters of a century after the Muslim conquest.[61]

One may ask why this civilization declined and virtually disappeared. A change of attitude by the Muslim rulers after Omar's death may have contributed. Yezid II (720–724) is known to history as an iconoclast, and in 723 he prohibited representations of living creatures in art throughout his dominions. His attitude was reinforced later in the century by that of the Iconoclast Byzantine emperors, but the churches seem to have weathered the storm. Rough plant-based patterns have been found replacing the heads of figures on some mosaics. At this time, however, churches become smaller, the language of the inscriptions weakens in syntax, grammar, and vocabulary. These are symptoms of decline, perhaps accentuated further by the earthquake of 746 that destroyed a major church at Jerash (see above, p. 201). But a major factor in the decline of the Christian population would seem to be the progressive worsening of material conditions. The upkeep of cisterns and systems of irrigation became increasingly uneconomical under the pressure of heavy, discriminatory taxation, brigandage, and the advance of nomadism and transhumance as ways of life. Christianity in Palestine and Jordan was the religion of a sedentary rural population, as it was on the high plains of Algeria. It seems that during the eighth century the Negev reverted once more to desert, and this may have happened elsewhere. The coincidence of the return to desert conditions and the decline of Christianity is too great to ignore.[62] Similar events may provide a clue to the religious history of all the territories that line the southern shores of the Mediterranean.

Jordan had provided evidence for the survival of an introspective but relatively prosperous Christianity through the first century of the Muslim conquest. In 1975 the Rome Congress examined material features of the *first expansive phases of Christianity*. What remains could without any doubt be attributed to the period before Constantine? Architecture, inscriptions, cemeteries, art – what had survived from that era? Not architecture; one scholar stated 'an early Christian architecture did not exist in the third century'.[63] It was a risky statement in view of Dura, or the 'bishop's house' referred to in the petition of the congregation of the Church of Antioch to the Emperor Aurelian (270–275) against Paul of Samosata;[64] or the large building opposite the imperial palace at Nicomedia destroyed as the first action by the authorities in the Great Persecution.[65] And were celebrations of the cult of the martyrs held only in the open air in cemeteries? The two small chambers within the 'Callistus catacomb' (San Callisto) suggest worship in buildings was not unusual in the third century and was becoming more elaborate by 300.[66] The discovery of actual third-century church buildings remains a possibility.

On the other hand, the tally of third-century inscriptions brought little new, Rome and Asia Minor providing an overwhelming proportion. Africa contributed few beyond the long-known Euelpius inscription from Caesarea, dated to 309 (or 315), in which the grave of the presbyter Victor is termed 'accubit-orium' and his congregation 'fratres', the latter terminology reminiscent of Tertullian and anticipating a Donatist outlook.[67] Elsewhere, Arles and Autun contributed most to a somewhat meagre harvest.

Not so of course the Roman *catacombs*, to which could be added the nuclei that eventually formed the catacombs of Vigna Cassia, Santa Maria e Gesù and Santa Lucia at Syracuse, possibly the earliest part of San Gennaro at Naples, and the area round the alleged tomb of St Felix at Cimitile. Research on these sites in the previous twenty years had become more exact in its methods. A number of the best-known cemeteries could now be proved to have originated in the first half of the third century. A landslip during work in the catacomb of Calepodius on the Via Aurelia west of the city revealed wholly unexpectedly the tomb of Pope Callistus (217–222) and, even more so, fragments of an inscription in the earth at the foot of the tomb, alluding to what had been regarded as a pious legend, namely his martyrdom by being thrown down a well. The discovery of the tomb proved that the catacomb must have been in existence by 222.[68] Probably almost as early was Area 1 of San Callisto, the 'catacomb of the Popes' which could have been the 'cemetery' whose supervision Pope Zephyrinus entrusted to his deacon (later Pope) Callistus *c.* 210.[69] The Lucina catacomb must also have been in use by the time Pope Cornelius was buried there,[70] while inscriptions dating to 266 and 270 respectively, the earliest dated memorials in the catacombs, confirmed the early date of the catacomb of Novatian.[71] At this period even the most prominent Christians, the Popes, were buried in simple graves whose decoration was confined to plaster and linear paintwork despite their fame and the numbers of pilgrims visiting them. Only in Damasus' time (366–384) did their tombs become monumental, a policy that fitted well with Damasus' reputation for ostentation and display.[72]

Styger therefore had been right in the 1930s in his conviction that there has been no Christian catacombs before the end of the second century. Previously it would seem, though from only one fairly sure example from the Isola Sacra, that Roman Christians were buried in ordinary, pagan cemeteries.[73] In the Roman provinces too, pagans and Christians appear to have been buried in the same cemeteries, such as the east necropolis at Tipasa in the fourth century. Two questions remained to be answered. First, how was it that the Chrsitians began to construct catacombs for the burial of their dead *c.* 200, and secondly what if any was the relation between the Christian and Jewish catacombs and their pictorial art, given that they appear to have begun at about the same time?

One answer to the first question was that by *c.* 200 the Christians in Rome began to hold land, as is clear from Hippolytus' reference to 'the cemetery' whose administration Zephyrinus entrusted to Callistus.[74] In this context it's not so surprising that the Christians were able to secure a lease (or sale) of a plot of land within the cemetery of the *Equites singulares* (Praetorian cavalry) that occupied a space in the imperial property known as *Ad Duos Lauros* three Roman miles along the Via Labicana south-east of the city. Jean Guyon's exhaustive study of the catacomb shows how this grew from an original nucleus into the vast necropolis of Peter and Marcellinus. By the end of the third century this already contained about 11,000 graves and whose galleries extended over 2 km.[75] Progress seems to have been particularly rapid from 260–300.[76] A similar development seems to have taken place in the Domitilla catacomb, where the first Christian graves appear to have been those of the Christian freedman family of the Ampliati in the early third century,[77] and the advance continued uninterrupted from that time.

At the time of the Rome Congress the writer believed that the figurative art of the catacombs derived largely from that of the Jewish artists at work in their own catacombs in Rome in the second and early third centuries, not least on the grounds that even at that time Jews and Christians were closely associated in the public mind as members of a single religious tradition (see Origen, *Contra Celsum* ii.2 and 4). The reverse, however, was now shown to have been a possibility.[78] In any event, the Christians of Rome in the third century were self-confident enough to develop their own art in order to demonstrate their trust in Jesus' message depicted through his authoritative teaching and acts of healing, and their hopes for the life beyond. These were uniquely their own.

At this stage the researches of Testini, Ferrua, Fasola and their colleagues had taken research regarding the catacombs, their origins and their art beyond the stylistic comparisons that previously had dominated these studies.[79] Evidence from coins, though seldom from pottery, had contributed towards a definitive dating of the third-century catacombs. The perennial debate on catacomb art had also moved away from the doctrinal and liturgical discussions of the previous generation to a more open and better informed debate, which enabled a large measure of originality to be claimed for the Christian artists of the day while still leaving some questions unanswered concerning the precise nature of their debt to their pagan contemporaries.

Ten years later discoveries of ever larger numbers of early Christian churches, not least in Italy, enabled more questions relating to the *impact of Christianity on society in Late Antiquity* to be asked and to some extent answered. The great peripatetic conference was held at a time when new early-Christian churches were being recorded from the Black Sea to the Channel coast and once more beyond the bounds of the empire as, for instance, the Sassanian church on the island of Kharg.[80]

The theme of the conference was 'The Christian city'. The exploration of areas near the cathedral in a number of Italian cities was revealing much about their early Christian history. The original Christian centre had indeed been outside the town walls in a cemetery where perhaps a martyr had been buried and a shrine erected in his memory. Even after Constantine's conversion and in the reigns of his sons, churches 'within the walls' were rare, a notable exception being that built by Fortunatus, bishop of Aquileia *c.* 345, which Athanasius witnessed.[81] The change takes place *c.* 380 onwards, when churches were being built in what had previously been the forum, and these developed into the cathedrals and episcopal centres.[82] The movement was accompanied by a decline in some of the traditional symbols of provincial urban life, baths, amphitheatres, and civil basilicas. Temples, however, do not seem to have been transformed into churches until the mid-fifth century, as already noted regarding the Parthenon and temples in Athens (above, p. 342). Across the Adriatic at Salona, the gladiators' rooms in the amphitheatre were transformed probably early in the fifth century into oratories in honour of martyrs killed there during the Great Persecution.[83] All this indicates a profound change of outlook taking place in the western provinces as a whole at this time. The forms of city administration, like Classical education, were surviving into the fifth century. Gradually, however, urban government was coming into the hands of the bishop. He was replacing the *defensor civitatis* as defender of the city and its people.[84] The relics of martyrs housed in the sanctuary of the cathedral became their final guarantee of safety from their enemies. How intensively Ambrose and Augustine, to name but two of the great bishops of the fourth and fifth centuries, had been obliged to busy themselves in secular business is well-known. Now this type of activity had become usual.

Geneva and Aosta were both stopping-places for the international caravan that was the Congress of 1986. Both illustrate the rise to dominance of the cathedral within the boundaries of a Roman urban community. Geneva (Genua) was a relatively small town, whose walls in the fourth centry enclosed no more than 5½ hectares. It had apparently become a *civitas* only during the Tetrarchy (293–305). Christian remains had been known since 1933, when, as recorded, Louis Blondel had carried out exploratory excavations in the area of the cathedral of St Pierre.[85] In 1979 Charles Bonnet, who had worked previously in Nubia as a member of the Franco-Swiss team, was entrusted with further excavations made possible through repairs to the fabric of the cathedral. The results were spectacular. A veritable maze of walls and floors on different levels were uncovered beneath the cathedral, which Bonnet was able to disentangle gradually and present a convincing account.

The earliest church buildings dated from the second half of the fourth century and were situated to the north of the present axis of the cathedral. They consisted of a large rectangular chamber that may have formed part of one of the aristocratic houses that occupied this part of the town.[86] An apse was soon added to the east end, but the baptistery that probably had existed at that time had been destroyed during repairs to the cathedral in the eighteenth century. About the year 400 the cathedral and the buildings that formed the *groupe épiscopal* (episcopal complex) began to take shape and new building continued during the fifth century. At the end of this period two basilicas had been built parallel to each other and two baptisteries, that placed between the two churches being the more important.[87] A bishop's palace equipped with an audience chamber, paved with mosaic and heated had been built adoining the south church. A peculiarity at both Geneva and Aosta was a corridor, built at Geneva along the south side of the north church. There was no access from it to the nave of the church, and Bonnet suggested the possibility of a *schola cantorum* (a practice area for choristers). The principal development, however, at Geneva in the sixth century and later centuries was the extension of the baptistery originally located between the two basilicas.[88] This provided the axis on which the mediaeval cathedral was to be built, while the progressive diminishing of the size of the baptismal basin indicated a change of liturgy involving the replacement of baptism by immersion by affusion, i.e. sprinkling water on to the head of the catechumen.[89]

Augusta Praetoria (Aosta) was a bigger and more important centre than Genua (Geneva). The original Christian basilica was built at the edge of the city's forum also in the second half of the fourth century. The earliest Christian graves in the cemeteries connected with the Roman town also were not earlier than this period.[90] While less complicated as a building, the basilica indicated that the Christians shared with their fellows at Geneva a strong sense of the importance of the baptismal liturgy. As at Geneva there were two separate baptisteries, perhaps, it is suggested, for men and women respectively. The basin in the larger was nearly 3 m in diameter. While it retained its octagonal shape, the flights of steps by which the neophyte descended into the waters were designed to form a Greek cross reminding him of the life and death of Christ with which he was associating himself. There was also a corridor extending along the north side of the basilica similar to that at Geneva, suggested by Bonnet as a *schola cantorum*.[91]

Whatever the function of these rooms may have been, both basilicas indicate a continuity of life through the Germanic-Arian occupation in the fifth century, and the dominance of the Church throughout that period. The episcopal complex occupied nearly one-third of the area enclosed within the city's walls at Geneva. It dominated. When a fire ravaged part of the cathedral there *c*. 500, the damage was swiftly repaired. Together with the cathedrals in the Italian towns and the episcopal complex within the walls at Salona, they represented stability and relative prosperity in an era of violent changes in the West. When in 476 the Rugian King Odoacar deposed Romulus Augustulus, the last West Roman emperor, many of the Italian cities would have seen their bishop's seat of authority rising on the one-time site of the forum. Confronted by this visible sign of the Church's power there was little that a barbarian ruler, even as long-living and prestigious as Theodoric the Ostrogoth (493–526), could do to secure equality of status for his Arian Goths.[92] Equality might exist by royal decree, but pre-eminence rested with the nominally subject people. Out of that predominance emerged not only the complete defeat of Arianism in Europe, but the first signs of an independent Italian nationhood.

The *sarcophagi* of the wealthier Christians buried within the precincts of many of the churches complete the picture of the gradual Christian conquest of the West. Ever since the recovery of the sarcophagus of Junius Bassus from below the floor of Old St Peter's in 1593, sarcophagi have been studied by historians of Christian art and belief. Leblant's catalogues of the Gallic sarcophagi in 1878 and 1886 had been classic works of scholarship but were confined to Gallic sites. In the post-war years enough new material was being discovered to enable systematic studies to be made of sarcophagi in Rome,[93] Salona,[94] as well as Gaul.[95]

In general, the sarcophagi of the Christian Roman nobility proclaim essentially the same message as the catacomb paintings, namely the confident hope of the deceased and his relatives concerning happiness beyond the grave through belief in Christ. Thus the raising of Lazarus, the Good Shepherd, the miracle of Cana and the miracles of healing, along with Old Testament themes, such as the Jonah cycle and Daniel, are all frequently represented. The sculptor was often able to portray more and different scenes than those painted in a mural on an *arcosolium*. One example may be quoted. The so-called 'Dogmatic Sarcophagus' in the Vatican Museum (dated 325–350) has two levels of figures.[96] The upper, incised to the left-hand side of a portrait of the deceased husband and wife, was a remarkable Creation scene, featuring first, the creation of Eve, not in the way described in Genesis 1:27 or 2:21–22, but 'by the hand of the Father through the Son and the Spirit' (Irenaeus, *Adv. Haer.* v.6.1) i.e. through an act of the Trinity; and adjoining this, Adam and Eve shown standing, representing mankind as the completed image of God, with the serpent curled round the tree of life. On the other side is the miracle of Cana and the raising of Lazarus. In the centre of the lower level Daniel stands among the lions, preceding to his left an Epiphany scene, the miracle of the healing of the blind man, while Daniel is offered a basket of loaves signed with a cross. To the right is the cycle of Peter's betrayal, remorse, and performance of the miracle of the spring.[97] In this praise for the dead couple, full of Christian teaching and symbolism, the pagan past is not forgotten, for winged Victories support the central roundel portraying the pair. These could hardly have been less than members of the senatorial aristocracy, and while the number of Christian sarcophagi so far identified (363) dating to the Constantinian era (312–363) shows that Christianity was making increasing advances among the aristocracy of the city of Rome, the latter never lost touch with their pagan past.[98] With biblical scenes expressing their hope of deliverance after death went Cupids, Genii, Tritons, Victories, and other traditional pagan or 'neutral' images. Like Classical education, the imagery of the pagan hope of bliss hereafter would not be abandoned when the new religion was adopted. It was merely integrated into the new set of beliefs.

Arles was the second major centre where a class of wealthy families buried their dead in elaborately decorated sarcophagi. Among these were senators whose wives had become Christians, such as Marcia Romana Celsa, wife of the consul Flavius Januarinus, *consul ordinarius* for the year 328, who died at the age of 38, and Hydria Tertulla, described as 'Clarissima'.[99] The sarcophagi found in the cemeteries of Trinquetaille and Alyscamps date from the first to the end of the fourth centuries. Conversion to Christianity might appear to have been prepared by the moral tone of some of the epitaphs in the third century, such as the words 'paci et quieti aeternae et memoriae aeternae, pax aeterna' ('to external peace and rest and to [their] eternal memory, eternal peace') emphasizing the eternity of peace and rest and the memory of the deceased, and in another instance stressing the virtues of Iulia Tyrannia, 'quae moribus pariter et disciplina ceteris feminis exempla fuit' ('her manner of life and moral discipline was an example to other women').[100] Such sentiments could easily find their place among Christians, and Christianity begins to make its presence felt *c.* 310.[101] But as in Rome the slow Christianization of members of the upper class is shown by the choice of pagan sequences on Christian sarcophagi, such as scenes from the chase or the countryside, as well as biblical scenes. The Arelate nobility seem to have been no different from the Roman. Some of their sarcophagi were manufactured in workshops in Arles, but many others were imported from Rome, as well as Attica or the quarries of Proconnesos, not far from the capital city.

The Arles manufactory ended by the beginning of the fifth century, but immediately new workshops started up in Narbonne and further west in Aquitaine quarrying marble from the Pyrenees. The style of these sarcophagi differs from the Arles groups. They are carved in flatter relief. They employ more plant motifs, fewer biblical scenes and the Christian symbol of the cross has more emphasis.[102] It was this tradition that survived into the Visigothic and Merovingian periods providing the link between the late-Roman province and mediaeval France.

In *Roman Britain* almost the opposite development seems to have been taking place. Excavations on sites near cathedrals have yielded only slight evidence of Christianity. At Exeter on the site of the church of St Mary Major six tombs were found aligned, of which two could be dated by carbon-14 testing to the fifth century.[103] At Lincoln the earliest phase of the church of St Paul-in-the-Bail appears to be early seventh century,[104] associated perhaps with Paulinus' missionary visit in 628–629, though still earlier buildings may await discovery. At Wells, however, the earliest building on the site of the Anglo-Saxon minister church was a Roman mausoleum. An extra skull found on one of the tombs of the Anglo-Saxon bishops had a sword-cut in the forehead; perhaps a martyr or simply a battle casualty.[105] Nor can one be certain of the Christianity of the Poundbury cemetery with its 1,400 graves outside Dorchester excavated by Christopher Sparey Green in 1977–82. There are as yet no certain archaeological evidences of continuity from a Roman to an Anglo-Saxon Christian centre, apart from Alban's shrine at Verulamium.[106]

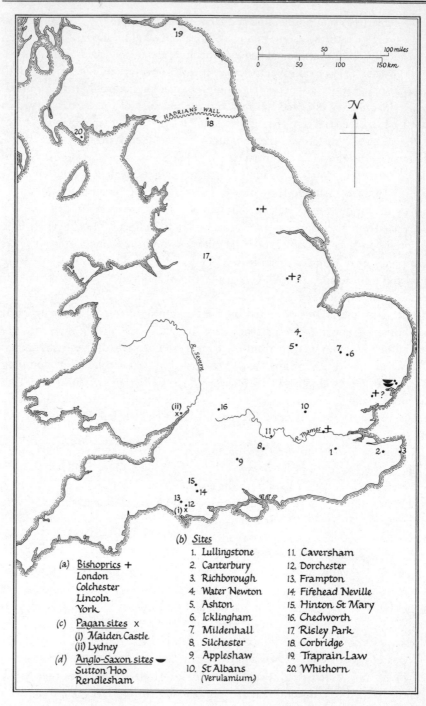

(b) Sites

1. Lullingstone
2. Canterbury
3. Richborough
4. Water Newton
5. Ashton
6. Icklingham
7. Mildenhall
8. Silchester
9. Appleshaw
10. St Albans
    (Verulamium)
11. Caversham
12. Dorchester
13. Frampton
14. Fifehead Neville
15. Hinton St Mary
16. Chedworth
17. Risley Park
18. Corbridge
19. Traprain Law
20. Whithorn

(a) Bishoprics +
London
Colchester
Lincoln
York

(c) Pagan sites x
(i) Maiden Castle
(ii) Lydney

(d) Anglo-Saxon sites ⏦
Sutton Hoo
Rendlesham

Roman Britain

There is, however, less speculation about the hoard of 29 pieces of church silver found by Mr A. J. Holmes, an amateur archaeologist, at Water Newton near Peterborough.[107] The treasure was found buried within the small (44 acres) Roman town of Durobrivae; unfortunately, the exact spot remains to date unknown. It had, however, been packed into a large dish on whose internal base had been inscribed $\alpha \text{☧} \omega$.[108] The dish (perhaps a large paten) was one of nine silver vessels in the treasure, which included a handled chalice, a strainer, a finely decorated silver jug, inscribed bowls and the base of a silver hanging lamp. The chalice was not only the earliest, early fourth century at the latest, but the finest piece of church silverware found in the West.[109] The jug and strainer have parallels with the Traprain Law hoard (see above, p. 208) but the silver bowls inscribed with the names of donors had not been found hitherto in the western provinces.

The hoard was entirely different from the Mildenhall treasure. That was the personal possession of a highly-placed individual, buried in haste, probably in a time of crisis. The Water Newton treasure was buried perhaps in similar circumstances but it was a major part of an altar-set with the addition of plaques, mostly reminiscent of pagan offerings, and must have belonged to a church.[110] There were also some curious features which did not come to light at once. The chalice was found separated from its two handles. The surviving base of the altar lamp had once been richly ornamented with roundels: they had disappeared. The interior of the dish or paten showed signs of burning. This could all be accidental; the handles could have been fixed badly, the roundels similarly, and a careless acolyte could have allowed the flame of a lamp to burn the dish. These are all possibilities. But suspicions remain. The treasure was unceremoniously buried. The handles could have been removed deliberately and so too, the roundels. They could have formed part of a distribution of loot, and the burning on the paten caused by the firing of a building whence they had been seized.[111]

By the middle of the fourth century Christians were forming a noticeable part of the community. A lead *defixio* (plaque) found during excavations in the bath-building at Bath includes the first occurrence of the term 'Christians' in Roman Britain. The text in fourth-century cursive runs 'Seu gen(tilis) seu C/h(r)istianus quaecunque utrum vir/utrum mulier ...' (Whether pagan or Christian, whether man or woman) and goes on to demand retribution on thieves (suspects named) who had stolen six silver coins (*argenteos*) from his purse.[112] The text may have been written by a Christian, but one who had no belief in forgiving his enemies. And enemies there apparently were. Evidence for this comes from the fate of large lead water tanks often marked with a ☧

used from baptism or perhaps other liturgical functions. One, from Walesby in Lincolnshire, depicts an actual baptism, a young woman, naked, standing between two severe-looking matrons 'thickly veiled and draped' who stand within two columns (of a church) flanked by three figures on each side dressed in tunic and cloaks.[113] But only one side of the tank survived. What happened to the rest may perhaps be guessed from a discovery made while constructing a roundabout and new road layout at Ashton, outside Oundle (Northamptonshire). At the bottom of a well a badly damaged lead font was found, its side smashed in, its base damaged, while fragments of another similar lay immediately below.[114] At Caversham on the Thames, near Reading, a similar find was made, but this time the font had been burnt as well as battered.[115] There could be no conceivable liturgical acts justifying such usage. Destruction in both cases was a sign of hostility. But by whom? The writer had suggested action by anti-Christian peasants at the time of the 'barbarian conspiracy' of 367–369.[116] This was the great invasion by combined forces of Saxons, Picts, Scots and Attecotti described vividly by Ammianus Marcellinus,[117] and he has suggested that a deposit of lead objects divided up as though for distribution as loot, found on a site three miles from Oundle, at North Lodge Farm, could also possibly be connected with these events.[118]

Archaeology can seldom answer the question 'why', but these separate finds of hoards and destroyed fonts seem to converge on a date in the 360s, and the known events of 367–369 may provide an answer, and explain in part at least why Christianity did not flourish in the reign of Valentinian I in Britain, as it did in the other Roman provinces of western Europe.

It is impossible to do full justice to the story of Christian archaeology in the period since the Trier Conference. International salvage work, chance discoveries, organized excavation and detailed research regarding the results have all played their part in exploding Pandora's Box. A feature had been the universal acceptance of up-to-date methods of excavation and the use of laboratory skills to obtain the most possible information from individual finds. Some hoary legends have been exposed. The 'Turin Shroud' had been shown beyond most peradventure to be of mediaeval date rather than the shroud in which Jesus was buried, leaving the imprint of his face on the cloth. The results of the three past decades have been wholly creditable, contrasting with the rush of discoveries before the First World War, when the aim of excavators was too often the embellishment of national museums and the finding of valuable small objects for private collections. Today the archaeology of the Christian Church had proved its worth. But what of tomorrow?

NOTES

1. To be published in *Acta* of the Conference. In his paper 'Palestine between Christianity and Islam (6th and 7th centuries)' Tsafrir showed how by the end of the fifth century Scythopolis was a purely Christian city. Its amphitheatre was disused and the space occupied by small dwellings. See also Yoran Tsafrir, 'Christian archaeology in Israel in recent years', *Atti* XI.2, pp. 1737–70: Moshe Fischer, 'A Byzantine settlement at Kh-Zikrin', ibid., pp. 1789–1807.

2. H. Hellenkamper, 'Early church architecture in southern Asia Minor' in *Churches Built in Ancient Times*, pp. 213–38, at p. 215.

3. Rajko Bratoz, 'Early Christian research in Slovenia and Istria', *Atti* XI.3, pp. 2345–88, map on p. 2364.

4. A. Radulescu and V. Lungu, 'Le Christianisme en Scythie Mineure', *Atti* XI.3, pp. 2561–2615. For Christianity *c.* 180 on the Black Sea coast, Eusebius, *HE* v.19.3 (Debeltum: see *Atlas of the Early Christian World*, p. 4).

5. Julia Valeva, *Atti* XI.2, pp. 1234–58 (fourth–fifth-century painted tombs); and Nelly Tchaneva-Detchevska, 'Les édifices cultuels sur le territoire Bulgare', ibid., pp. 2491–2509.

6. Ivanka Nicholojevic, *Atti* XI.3, pp. 2441–62.

7. G. Karaiskaj, 'Die albanische Stadt Sarda', ibid., pp. 2637–56.

8. For example, A. Sonje, 'La Chiesa paleocristiana ... sull' Isola Kok (Veglia)', *Atti* IX.2, pp. 507–24: N. Combi, 'Unpublished excavations in Jugoslavia', ibid., pp. 141–50.

9. P. Testini, 'Il complesso paleocristiano di Cornus (Regione Columbaris) in Sardegna', *Atti* VIII (1972), pp. 537–61.

10. G. Morachinic-Mazel, 'La fouille des basiliques paléochretiénnes de Corse. Nouvelles découvertes', ibid., pp. 361–6.

11. Articles in *Atti* VIII: Almeida and Matos (Portugal), pp. 239–43; Hanschild, (Marialba, León), pp. 327–32: the same (Centecelles, Tarragona) pp. 333–8; Palol and Sotomayor (Quesada, Jaén), pp. 375–82; Riu (hermits' caves in eastern Andalusia), pp. 431–44; San Martín Moro and Palol (Cartagena), pp. 447–58; and Verrié (Barcelona), pp. 605–10.

12. The Seventh Congresso Nazionale di Archeologia Cristiana (September 1993) reviewed the progress of Christian archaeology in Italy between 1983 and 1993 (held under the auspices of the Università degli Studi di Cassino; publication forthcoming).

13. Published in *CSEL* 88 (Vienna 1981). The collection includes one letter from Jerome to Aurelius of Carthage, then archdeacon (Letter 27). See *Les Lettres de Saint Augustin découvertes par Johannes Divjak* (Paris: Etudes Augustiniennes, 1983).

14. Ed. Jacques Dolbeau, 'Nouveaux sermons d'Augustin', *Recherches augustiniennes* (1992 and 1993).

15. A. Henrichs and L. Koenen, 'Ein griechischer Mani-Codex', *ZPE* 5.2 (1970), pp. 97–216; 19 (1975), pp. 1–85; 32 (1978) pp. 78–199.

16. Marrou, *Atti* IX.1, pp. 96–7: 'Il y a quelque chose d'excessif dans le cloisonnement qui a fait d'archéologie chrétienne un domaine séparé du reste de l'enquête sur l'ensemble des premiers siècles de notre ère' (p. 96). For similar views, see T. Klauser, 'Studien zur Entstehungsgeschichte der christlichen Kunst IV', *JbAC* 7 (1964), p. 74; also his earlier articles, ibid. (1958–63).

17. Marrou, op. cit., p. 97.

18. See Marrou, 'Culture, civilisation, decadence' and other similar essays in *Christiana Tempora* (Collection de l'Ecole française de Rome 35; Rome, 1978), ch. 1ff., and in his final work *Decadence romaine ou Antiquité tardive* (Paris, 1977).

19. H. I. Marrou, 'Sur deux mosaïques de la villa romaine de Piazza Armerina', ibid., pp. 253–95, at p. 295.

20. An example of Marrou's interest in North African archaeology was his brilliant description of the collection of early Christian, pagan and rural antiquities collected by the eccentric Gaston de Vulpillières mainly from around the oasis of el-Kantara: 'La collection Vulpillières à el-Kantara', *MEFR* 50 (1933), pp. 42–86.

21. 'Epitaphe chrétienne d'Hippone à réminiscences virgiliennes' in *Christiana Tempora*, pp. 124–44.

22. Perhaps the latest dated epitaph is of a Greco-Latin stone, also from Hippo, commemorating the infant Theodosius who died on 13 December 602: Marrou, ibid., p. 153.

23. D. Pringle, *The Defence of Byzantine Africa from Justinian to the Arab Conqeust* (*BAR* Internat. series 99; Oxford, 1981).

24. A. Mohamedi and E. Fentress, 'Fouilles de Sétif 1978–1982; la structure de la ville islamique', *BCTH* n.s. 19.3 (Paris, 1985), pp. 469–78.
25. P. A. Février, *Atti* XI, p. xc.
26. Above, pp. 127–8. Ballu believed the major part of the basilica complex to be Byzantine.
27. J. Christern, *Die frühchristliche Pilgerheiligtum von Tebessa* (Wiesbaden, 1976), pp. 106 and 293.
28. Ibid., p. 301.
29. Interestingly no inscription refers to Crispina by name. I myself suspected a fourth-century building in one phase, but earlier than 390. Many of the carefully cut building stones bore masons' marks of a similar type and hence probably of the same date. The basilica did not look Byzantine. Its relation to the equally finely built trefoil building 3 km away at Tébessa-Khalia remains unsolved.
30. See my *Donatist Church*, ch. 14, 'The rule of Optatus and Gildo 388–398'. But if Donatist, when and where did Augustine preach his sermon in honour of Crispina?
31. Christern, p. 303.
32. Ibid., p. 297.
33. Published in *MEFR* (1973) onwards.
34. Collection des Etudes Augustiniennes, Série Antiquité 130 (Paris, 1992). See Bibliography.
35. Y. Duval, *Loca Sanctorum Africae: Le culte des martyrs en Afrique du IVe au VIIe siècle* (2 vols; Collection de l'Ecole française de Rome 58; Rome, 1982); rev. by the writer, *JbAC* 27 (1984), pp. 243–6.
36. Jerome *De Viris Illustribus* 93: 'paene totam Africam decepit' and in particular (praecipue) Numidia.
37. Y. Duval, op. cit., p. 446.
38. Ibid., p. 705; 'le prétendu martyr'.
39. L. Ennabli, *Les inscriptions funéraires chrétiennes de Carthage*,
    1: *De la basilique dite de Sainte Monique à Carthage* (Collection de l'Ecole française de Rome 25: Rome, 1972) (= Collection).
    2: *La basilique de Mcidfa* (Collection 62: Rome, 1982).
40. Ennabli, op. cit., p. 337.
41. Ibid., p. 357. Delattre, she believes, may have exaggerated greatly the number of fragments of inscriptions he found.
42. Ste Monique, no. 15, p. 137.
43. Ibid., no. 26, p. 149.
44. Ibid., no. 1, p. 35 (gives bibliography).
45. Ibid., no. 292, pp. 28 and 222. Whether he was a physician attached to a synod when he died remains unknown.
46. Ibid., *Sainte-Monique*, p. 398: six names.
47. See Synesius, *Epistolae*: *PG* 66, 1322–1561; *Letters*, ed. and trans. A. Fitzgerald (New York and London: OUP, 1926).
48. D. Roques, *Synésios de Cyrène et la Cyrénaique du Bas-Empire* (Etudes d'Antiquités africaines; Paris: CNRS, 1987); rev. by the writer, *JbAC* 32 (1989), pp. 203–6.
49. Roques, op. cit., p. 322: disagreeing with Robin Lane Fox, *Pagans and Christians* (1986), pp. 585–95.
50. Roques, op. cit., p. 318.
51. Eusebius, *HE* vii.26.
52. R. G. Goodchild, 'A coin hoard from Balagrae (el Beida) and the earthquake of 365 AD', *Libyan Studies* (1976), pp. 229–38, at pp. 233–4.
53. Roques, op. cit., ch. 3, 'Les réalités religieuses'; also ch. 2.
54. Thus Joan E. Taylor, *Christians and the Holy Places: The Myth of Jewish-Christian Origins* (OUP, 1993), chs 1 and 2.
55. Beautifully illustrated in H.R.H. Princess Sumaya el-Hassan and Fr Michele Piccirillo (eds), *The Mosaics of Jordan* (Sothebys, 1993) (includes map with main sites).
56. Ibid., p. 33. The space within the columns of the aedicule commemorates the names of the donors of the mosaic.
57. Ibid., p. 26; M. Piccirillo, 'La Chiesa della Vergine a Madaba', *Liber Annuus Studii Biblici Franciscani* 34 (1984), pp. 373–402 and plates 68, 70, 72 and 77 (sixth century).
58. E. Puech, 'L'inscription Christo-Palestinienne du Monastère du el-Quweisne', *Liber Annuus* 34 (1984), pp. 341–6: (dated to 717/718).
59. See R. de Vaux, 'Une mosaique byzantine à Ma'in', *RB* (1938), pp. 227–58 (see above, p. 238); M. Piccirillo, 'Le antichità byzantine de Ma'in e dintorni', *Liber Annuus* 35 (1985), pp. 339–64.

60. Piccirillo, 'Ricercea in Giordania', *Liber Annuus* 32 (1982), p. 499: *Mosaics*, p. 36; A. Desremaux, *CRAI* (1983), p. 22, figs 6–7. For similar, seventh-century, churches in Lebanon, see N. Duval and J. P. Caillet, 'Khan Khalidé' in *Archéologie au Levant: Recueil R. Saidah* (Lyon, 1982), pp. 312–94.

61. Piccirillo, *Liber Annuus* (1984), p. 333 (referring to the church at Quweisne).

62. See N. Duval, 'L'architecture chrétienne en Jordanie' in *Churches Built in Ancient Times*, pp. 149–212, at pp. 206–8. See also Hugh Kennedy, 'From Polis to Madina; urban change in late Antique and early Islamic Syria', *Past and Present* 106 (1985), pp. 1–27.

63. B. M. Apollonj Ghetti, 'Problemi relativi alle origini dell'architettura paleocristiana', *Atti* IX.1, pp. 491–511 at p. 491: 'Un architettura paleocristiana del secolo III non esiste'.

64. Eusebius, *HE* vii.30.19–21.

65. Lactantius, *De Mortibus Persecutorum* 12.2–5.

66. See Krautheimer, pp. 34–7.

67. *CIL* VIII, 9586. See also A. Ferrua, 'L'epigraphia cristiana prima di Costantino', *Atti* IX.I, pp. 585–635, at p. 604; and *DACL* I, 813 (photo).

68. See A. Nestori, *Rivista* 47 (1971), pp. 169–278; and U. M. Fasola and P. Testini, 'I cimiteri cristiani', *Atti* IX.I, pp. 103–39, at p. 106.

69. Ibid., p. 107. (See above, p. 78.)

70. Ibid.

71. Ibid., p. 109.

72. Ammianus Marcellinus, xxvii. 3.14–15: Frend, *Rise of Christianity* (note 92 below), p. 627.

73. *Atti*, IX.1, pp. 105–6.

74. Hippolytus, *Philosophoumena* ix.12.14.

75. J. Guyon, *Le Cimitière aux deux Lauriers: recherches sur les catacombes romaines* (*BEFAR*; Rome, 1987); rev. F. Tolotti, *JbAC* 32 (1989), pp. 221–5; see pp. 96–102 on the historical context that favoured the creation of the catacomb.

76. Guyon, op. cit., p. 96.

77. P. Testini, 'Nuove osservazioni sul cubicolo di Ampliato in Domitilla', *Atti* IX.I, pp. 141–57.

78. Ibid., pp. 478–80. Finney's suggestion (ibid., pp. 391–405) of a Gnostic input, though interesting in view of the Hypogaeum of the Aurelii paintings, still needs further evidence. In general, however, see H. Brandenburg, 'Überlegungen zum Ursprung der frühchristlichen Bildkunst', ibid., pp. 331–60. He regarded Christian art in the third century as a part of late-Antique art, drawing on its forms and adapting its designs for its own needs: p. 360. Also Deichmann, *Christliche Archaeologie*, pp. 113–16. Catacomb painting was in his view 'not Christian nor Jewish but Roman': p. 116.

79. On some weaknesses in the stylistic approach, see Guyon, op. cit., pp. 94–6. For the debate in the first decade of the twentieth century, see above, pp. 161–2.

80. On Kharg, see J. Bowman, 'The Sassanian church in the Kharg Island' *Acta Iranica* 1.1. (1974); pp. 217–20.

81. Athanasius, *Apol. ad Constantium* 15. See also G. Brusin and P. L. Zovatto, *Monumenti paleo-cristiani di Aquileia* (1957).

82. P. Testini, G. Cantino Wataghin and E. L. Pani Ermini, 'La cattedrale in Italia', *Atti* XI.1, pp. 5–232, at p. 13.

83. E. Dyggve, *History of Salonitan Christianity*, p. 86.

84. See Noel Duval, 'Les evêques bâtisseurs', *Naissance des Arts chrétiens*, pp. 50–69; for the role of the bishop among his people, see Charles Pietri, 'Aux origines', ibid., p. 39.

85. Louis Blondel, 'Les premiers édifices chrétiens de Genève', *Geneva* 11 (1933), pp. 77–101; and see above, p. 245.

86. C. Bonnet, 'Les origines du groupe épiscopale de Genève', *CRAI* (1981), pp. 414–33: and 'Aoste et Genève: aménagements liturgiques', *Atti* IX.2, p. 1409.

87. Bonnet, 'Développement urbain et topographie chrétienne de Genève', *CRAI* (1985), pp. 323–38.

88. Bonnet, *CRAI* (1981), p. 419; 'Aoste et Genève', pp. 1424–5.

89. Bonnet, 'Aoste et Genève', p. 1413.

90. Renato Perinatti, 'Le necropoli di Augusta Pretoria', *Atti* IX.2, pp. 1215–26, at p. 1223.

91. Bonnet, 'Aoste et Genève', pp. 1419–23 with additional references.

92. *Excerpta Valesiana* (ed. Rolfe) xii.60. See W. H. C. Frend, *The Rise of Christianity* (Philadelphia/London, 1984), pp. 806–7.

93. Thus, Wolfgang Wischmeyer, 'Die Tafeldeckel der christlichen Sarkophage konstantinischer Zeit in Rom' *RQ* 40 Supplementheft (1982) with full bibliography to 1981.

94. See Nenad Cambi, *The Good Shepherd Sarcophagus and Its Group* (Salona, 1994; Serbo-Croat and English).

95. P. A. Février, 'Les sarcophages décorés du Midi' in *Naissance*, pp. 270–87; P. Périn, 'Les sarcophages mérovingiens', ibid., pp. 288–305.
96. F. W. Deichmann (ed.), *Repertorium der christlichen antiken Sarkophage*, I (Rome and Ostia–Wiesbaden, 1967), Tafel 14, Abb. 43, pp. 39–41; and see U. Schubert, 'Eine jüdiche Vorlage für die Darstellung der Erschaffung des Menschen in der sogennante Cotton-Genesis-Rezension?', *Atti* IX.1, pp. 433–49, at pp. 434–6.
97. See illustration in *EEC* II, fig. 147. Schubert (p. 436) points to the anticipation in Josephus, *Antiquities of the Jews* 1.1.2 for God sending Spirit (*pneuma*) and Soul (*psychē*) into Adam and Eve whom he had created.
98. The significance of these figures is discussed by Wischmeyer, op. cit., pp. 76–87; also Deichmann, *Entstehung*, ch. 8, 'Die Anfänge einer christlichen Kunst', pp. 141ff.: no purely Christian art before the Theodosian period, 380 onwards. In addition, G. M. A. Hanfmann, *The Seasons Sarcophagus in Dumbarton Oaks* (2 vols; Dumbarton Oaks Studies 2; 1951): application of this idiom to both pagan and Christian sarcophagi in third and fourth centuries.
99. Février, 'Sarcophages', illustration, p. 277.
100. Février, op. cit., p. 273.
101. Ibid., p. 275.
102. Ibid., p. 280–6.
103. K. S. Painter, 'Recent discoveries in Britain', *Atti* XI.3, pp. 2031–72, at pp. 2039–41.
104. Ibid., p. 2043. The possibility of Romano-British date has been discussed with me by M. J. Jones, the excavator of the site.
105. Ibid., p. 2037.
106. C. S. Green, 'The Early Christian cemetery at Poundbury', ibid., pp. 2073–5.
107. Published by K. S. Painter, *The Water Newton Early Christian Silver* (British Museum Publications, 1977).
108. Ibid., plate i.
109. Ibid., plate 6 (p. 30).
110. Ibid., plates 15–19 (pp. 38 and 39).
111. I have suggested this in a paper read to the Thirteenth Congress of Christian Archaeology at Split in September 1994.
112. Painter, *Atti* XI.3, pp. 2049–51; R. S. O. Tomlin in B. Cunliffe, *The Temple of Sulis Minerva at Bath*, II (Oxford, forthcoming), no. 98.
113. Painter, op. cit., p. 2056; Charles Thomas, *Christianity in Roman Britain to A.D. 500* (London, 1981), pp. 221–4 and fig. 41.
114. C. J. Guy, 'The lead tank from Ashton', *Durobrivae* 5 (1977), pp. 10–11.
115. Recorded in *Britannia* 20 (1989), pp. 333–4, and plate XXVI.
116. W. H. C. Frend, 'Pagans, Christians and the "Barbarian Conspiracy" of A.D. 367 in Roman Britain', *Britannia* 23 (1992), pp. 121–31.
117. Ammianus Marcellinus, *Res Gestae* xxvii.8.
118. Publ., with J. A. Hadman, in *Britannia* 25 (1994), pp. 224–6 and plate XVIA.

FURTHER READING

C. Bonnet, 'Les origines du groupe épiscopale de Genève', *CRAI* (1981), pp. 414–33; and *CRAI* (1985), pp. 323–38.

J. Christern, *Die frühchristliche Pilgerheiligtum von Tebessa* (Wiesbaden, 1976).

N. Duval, 'L'architecture chrétienne en Jordanie' in K. S. Painter (ed.), *Churches Built in Ancient Times* (London, 1994), pp. 149–217.

N. Duval and J. P. Caillet, *Archéologie au Levant* (Collection de la Maison de l'Orient Mediterranéen 12, Série archéologique 9; Lyon, 1982).

W. H. C. Frend, 'Pagans, Christians and the barbarian conspiracy of A.D. 367', *Britannia* 23 (1992), pp. 121–31.

Y. Hirschfeld, *The Judaean Monasteries in the Byzantine Period* (New Haven: Yale University Press, 1992).

Hugh Kennedy, 'From Polis to Madina; urban change in late antique and early Christian Syria', *Past and Present* 105 (1985), pp. 1–27.

H. I. Marrou, *Christiana Tempora* (Collection de l'Ecole française de Rome 35; Rome, 1978).

K. S. Painter, *The Water Newton Early Christian Silver* (British Museum Publications, 1977).

K. S. Painter, 'Recent discoveries in Britain', *Atti* XI.3, pp. 2031–72.

M. Piccirillo, *Mount Nebo* (Amman, 1989).

D. Roques, *Synésios de Cyrène et la Cyrenaique du Bas-empire* (Paris: CNRS, 1987).

Les sarcophages d'Aquitaine (Association pour l'Antiquité tardive 1; Brepols, 1993).

H. R. H. Sumaya el-Hassan and Fr Michele Piccirillo, *The Mosaics of Jordan* (London: Sothebys, 1993) (Piccirillo's individual excavations are referred to in the notes to this chapter).

Joan E. Taylor, *Christians and the Holy Places* (OUP, 1993),

Charles Thomas, *Christianity in Roman Britain to A.D. 500* (London, 1981).

(Attention is also drawn to the articles published in *Atti* IX and XI cited in the notes to this chapter.)

15

Whither Christian archaeology?

Here we must bring down the curtain for the time being. In this study we have followed the story of Christian archaeology from its curious beginning with the search for the True Cross by the empress Helena in Jerusalem in 326 to the avalanche of discoveries in our own day. The great scholars who have furthered these studies have passed in review, Bosio, de Rossi, Ramsay, Gertrude Bell, Gsell, Carl Schmidt, Crowfoot, Michałowski and Février, among many others. Whether strictly speaking ecclesiastical historians, as Bosio and de Rossi, or Classicists by training, all were interested in practical and field archaeology. They shared a realization that the successful study of Late Antiquity must be combined with an understanding of the causes of the spread of Christianity and of the origins of its liturgy and organization as demonstrated by material remains. Their achievements were placed on permanent record available to all by the stupendous work of Henri Leclercq in the *Dictionnaire d'Archéologie chrétienne et de liturgie* (1907–53) and F. J. Dölger's posthumous inspiration of the Franz Dölger Institut at Bonn (founded in 1955) and the *Reallexikon für Antike und Christentum*. These assure that their legacy will not be lost to future generations of scholars or be remembered only as a short episode in the cultural history of humanity.

Meantime, new discoveries continue apace. In Britain yet another late-Roman treasure was found by accident (a farmer searching for a lost hammer in a field with a metal detector!) at Hoxne in Suffolk in November 1992.[1] The wealth was amazing: 14,865 coins of which 569 were gold, 14,205 silver and 24 bronze, most dating from the reigns of Arcadius and Honorius (issues *c.* 394-405) but three of Constantine III (407–411), and an array of gold and silver vessels, spoons, ladles and an ivory box (?). The hoard shows once again the character of Romano-British Christianity, immensely wealthy adherents at the top, but with little evidence of support among the population as a whole,[2] and perhaps a language divide between a minority of Latin-speakers and the majority who spoke a language akin to Welsh. At the other extreme of the *oik-oumenē* new discoveries at Aksum by David Phillipson's excavations in 1993, 1994 and continuing, are unravelling the mysteries surrounding the great 'false door' obelisks and associated tombs and the transition from paganism to Christianity in Nubia.[3]

Two examples from many. And meantime the new finds, particularly of documents, have been accelerating the integration of literary and archaeological discoveries relating to the early Church. The ten successive studies by Carsten Colpe on the significance for Jewish, pagan, and Christian studies arising from the Nag Hammadi library have show how this discovery is influencing our perceptions of religious life and thought in the Roman empire in the third and fourth centuries.[4] The work of A. D. Nock has been continued through the spade of the excavator. *Jahrbuch für Antike und Christentum* and the Institut des études méditerranées at Aix-en-Provence are ensuring that that impetus will not readily be lost.

Apart from the intrinsic value of the discoveries, the churches, catacombs, manuscripts, frescos, and the multitude of small objects which tell us about the life of the early Christians, the historical significance of Christian archaeology falls under two main headings. First, the discoveries have helped to throw light on the major transitions in the history of the early Church, from paganism to Christianity in the late-third century, from Late Antiquity to Byzantinism in the second half of the fifth century, and from Byzantium to Islam during the seventh century. Secondly, major finds have enabled the non-orthodox traditions to speak for themselves. Church history is no longer a history of 'orthodoxy and heresy'. A whole new world of divergent beliefs and teaching has been opened up. We now know a great deal more than we did about Montanism, Donatism, Manichaeism and Monophysitism. Something of the fullness of the Christian heritage has been revealed and the vivid kaleidoscopic character of the lives and beliefs of its different adherents.

The third century was decisive for the victory of the Church. That seems evident, and also that the Church was able to take advantage of the long breathing-space of toleration that characterized the period. A congregational church and baptistery at Dura Europos was not entirely unexpected in the reign of Alexander Severus (222–235) in which it was said that Christians 'were allowed'.[5] The real change came with Gallienus' rescript in 260 to the

Egyptian bishops allowing them to resume possession of their cemeteries.[6] From that moment on we find the first dated Christian inscriptions and these begin to multiply. Some Roman catacombs grow into vast necropoleis in this period. There are dated Christian inscription from Philippi and the Tembris valley and the first material evidence for Christianity in the Rhineland.[7] In contrast, important territorial deities such as Saturn in North Africa and Apollo in Cyrenaica appear to lose popularity. There are few dedications to them after the end of the third century. The Great Persecution of 303–312 was foredoomed to failure.

We need, however, to be careful. The Church might be advancing but in some parts of Asia Minor its importance in the community was overshadowed by that of the local Jews. At Sardis, for instance, there had been a Christian bishop since the mid-second century, and Melito was as articulate and passionate an adherent as one could want. But the Christians could boast nothing approaching the huge synagogue sited in one of the best areas of the city that the Jews possessed in the third century, nor the open support of local councillors and other prominent citizens.[8] At Aphrodisias, the capital of Caria, a large inscription discovered inscribed on a square marble pillar contains the names of 55 Jews, including three proselytes and 52 God-fearers. It dates to the early third century and the object was to commemorate the erection of the building for a charitable purpose. A number of the God-fearers state that they were traders and some were city councillors. The Jews in these two cities were a powerful force, well integrated into their communities.[9] It would take another century before the same could be said for the Christians.

In the fifth century, however, the Church in the West, with the exception of Roman Britain, was strong enough to resist any threat from the Arian or pagan Germanic invaders. An inscription such as that of Bishop Rusticus, dedicating the cathedral of Narbonne in 445 that he had rebuilt after a fire and on whose behalf he received nearly 3,000 gold solidi from contributions, speaks for itself.[10] Cathedrals (the bishop's seat) came to dominate the towns, regardless of whether the ruler was a Visigoth or Burgundian Arian or a Catholic Frank. But victory over the Germanic barbarians was combined with a steady estrangement from Eastern Christendom. Here the study of church architecture in the two halves of the empire is revealing. In the West the basilican plan continues to prevail, but in the East the cupola, or domed church, becomes progressively the rule. Behind these differences in architecture lay differences of Christological doctrine and concepts concerning martyrs and martyrdom. The Council of Chalcedon could paper over the cracks, but it could not conceal the real divergences between Eastern and Western theologies. Justinian's attempted *reconquista* won few friends in the West.

The third period of transition was that from Byzantine Christianity to Islam. What happened in the provinces newly conquered by the Arabs from the 630s onwards is obscure. One Arab writer indicates that when faced with the prospect of higher taxation as the price of defeat some populations immediately embraced Islam. This may have happened in parts of North Africa following the defeat of the Kahena by the Muslim armies *c.* 703.[11] Here we have tried to gather up as much of the extant archaeological material as possible. Occasionally town life continued, as in Setif, but in the majority of instances where anything can be known there was a steep decline in living standards. Hovels succeed the relatively prosperous farmsteads of the olive-centred economies that characterized many parts of the Mediterranean in the seventh century. Cultivation is replaced by desert, the farmer by the semi-nomad. In Syria, Jordan, Palestine and Egypt Christianity declines to a minority status. Elsewhere from Cyrenaica to Morocco, it seems to succumb almost completely not much later than 700. How and why this happened remains a crucial challenge for future research.

Information about the non-orthodox traditions have come in a variety of ways. Ramsay's, Calder's and now Mitchell's researches in Phrygia revealed the existence of farmers on a great imperial estate occupying much of the Tembris valley, who proclaimed their Christianity sometimes in militant terms before the Peace of the Church in 312, held beliefs corresponding to what was known about the Phrygian Montanists from literary sources. Similar methods extending over two generations of scholars reveal the extent of the Donatist movement in southern Numidia in the fourth century. Sensational manuscript finds have contributed fundamental new knowledge about Gnosticism and Manichaeism. The discovery of the splendours of the Nubian Monophysite civilization in the Nile valley has been due to the work of the international teams engaged in the UNESCO 'Save Nubia' project. The results, however obtained, have been a widening of horizons in the history of the early Church. Henceforth *Antike* and *Christentum* can never be divorced and the successful study of early Christianity must embrace every aspect of its different traditions.

It's an inviting prospect but one that cannot be assured even in the medium term. The main threat comes from the population explosion of the present century and the ever-expanding and destructive infrastructure needed to sustain it.

The opposition of settler-population and road-builder ransacking convenient ruins for stone that confronted Commandant Tripier at Orléansville in

1845 was the first example of a situation that has become familiar. Where population is rising as in Tunisia and Algeria, ancient sites will be robbed.

More international salvage operations and a greater awareness of the permanent threat to humanity's cultural and religious heritage may slow the process, but unless world population stabilizes it cannot halt it.

Another danger lies in what may be termed the 'academic industry'. Today the numbers of aspiring doctorate candidates in the humanities threaten to outrun the sum of worthwhile topics available for research. If the number of early Christian sites declines, Christian archaeology may well suffer the fate of New Testament studies and become starved of new material. As a symptom of this we are already witnessing the appearance of revisionist theories regarding Montanism from scholars operating far from Asia Minor. The process is likely to continue. Reworking a static data base is the way to fossilization and irrelevance.[12]

Meantime chances of working in some of the promising areas of the Mediterranean are being lost. In Britain research into Christian antiquity overseas suffers from the same problems that Ramsay pointed to with regard to his excavations at Bin Bir Kilisse. There, £300 was needed to pay an architect to plan the churches and £5,000 to finance a full-scale excavation. Neither sum was forthcoming. So in the last decade in Tunisia, though intergovernmental relations have been excellent, no resources have been pledged from the United Kingdom for work on early-Christian or Byzantine and Berber sites before these are swallowed up by urban sprawl or intensive agriculture. While hundreds of millions of pounds have been raised through appeals put out by senior universities, the relatively small sum needed to fund a yearly Fellowship at the British School at Rome for work on these topics has not been voted. Too often, short-sighted 'committee arguments' appear to have carried the day.

It is sad to end this study on a pessimistic note, but the dangers to the environment and historical heritage are obvious and pressing. 'Save Nubia' came too late, 'Save Carthage' was probably just in time. 'Save the Euphrates valley monuments' still hangs on the balance. In this survey I have attempted to describe what has been done and point out what still remains. In four centuries Christian archaeology has moved from apologetic to scientific study. May the progress toward an interdisciplinary approach to its problems continue. It is for the next generation to reach an answer to the question, 'And what of tomorrow?'

NOTES

1. Reported by Catherine Johns and Roger Bland, 'The Hoxne Late Roman Treasure', *Britannia* 25 (1994), pp. 165–73; 85 more coins (four gold and 81 silver) were found during ploughing in September 1993, and have been added to the total.
2. Bede records, for instance, that in 429 the Romano-British army opposed the barbarian invaders successfully after 'the greatest multitude' of it had been baptized by Bishop Germanus of Auxerre, i.e. they were pagans: *EH* i. 20.
3. David Phillipson, 'The significance and symbolism of Aksumite stelae', *Cambridge Archaeological Journal* 4 (1994), pp. 189–210.
4. Carsten Colpe, series of articles published in *JbAC* (1972–82).
5. Lampridius, *Vita Alexander Severi* 22.4: 'Christianos esse passus est'.
6. Eusebius, *HE* vii. 13.
7. Carsten Thiede, *Heritage of the First Christians* (Eng. trans.; London, 1992), p. 52 (Albana sarcophagus).
8. See A. R. Seager and A. T. Kraabel, 'The synagogue and the Jewish community' in G. M. A. Hanfmann, *Sardis From Prehistoric to Roman Times* (1983), pp. 168–90.
9. J. Reynolds and T. Tannenbaum, *Jews and Godfearers at Aphrodisias* (Cambridge, 1987).
10. See *DACL* XII.2, 828 and 846–850.
11. See the account given of the conversion of the Fezzan oasis Berbers to Islam by Ibn Abd al-Hakam: *Conquête de l'Afrique du Nord et de l'Espagne*, ed. A. Gateau (Algiers, 1942), p. 59.
12. See Barry Cunliffe, 'The public face of the past', p. 194 of offprint.

The Roman Empire

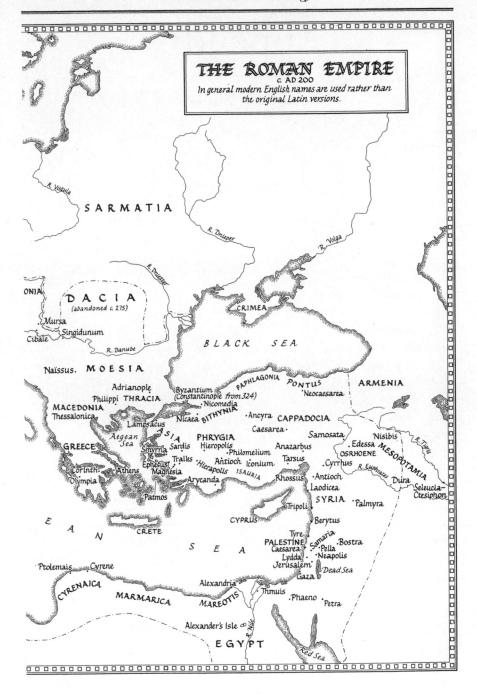

THE ROMAN EMPIRE
c. AD 200
*In general modern English names are used rather than
the original Latin versions.*

Appendix

The International Congresses of Christian Archaeology

1894 Split–Salona
1900 Rome
1932 Ravenna
1938 Rome
1954 Aix-en-Provence
1962 Ravenna
1965 Trier
1969 Barcelona
1975 Rome
1980 Thessalonica (Salonica)
1986 Lyons–Grenoble–Geneva–Aosta
1991 Bonn
1994 Centenary Congress, Split–Porec

Select Bibliography

Detailed information about discoveries relating to the early Church may be found in *Mélanges de l'Ecole de Rome* (North Africa), *Bulletin de Correspondence hellénique* (French projects in Asia Minor and on the Greek mainland), the *Jahreshefte der Öesterreichischen archaeologischen Instituts* (Austrian excavations at Ephesus), *Journal of Egyptian Archaeology* (work of the Egypt Exploration Society at Qasr Ibrim and other Nubian and Egyptian sites), and the annual reports of excavations in the eastern Mediterranean published in the *Journal of Hellenic Studies* and in *Byzantion*. There are also the periodic progress reports on new excavations and discoveries in the Proceedings (*Atti*) of successive International Congresses of Christian Archaeology (1894–1994).

I have reserved this selection for major scholarly reference works and useful smaller studies not represented in 'Further Reading' in individual chapters.

INSCRIPTIONS

S. L. Agnelli, *Silloge di inscrizione paleocristiane della Sicilia* (Rome, 1953).

W. Boppert, *Die frühchristlichen Inschriften des Mittel-rheingebietes* (Römisch-Germanisch Zentralmuseum zu Mainz; Mainz: Philipp von Zabern, 1971).

W. M. Calder and colleagues, *Monumenta Asiae Minoris Antiqua* (Manchester University Press, 1931–88).

E. Diehl, *Inscriptiones Latinae Christianae Veteres* (3 vols; 2nd edn, Berlin: Weidmann, 1961).

Liliane Ennabli, *Les Inscriptions funéraires chrétiennes de Carthage*, I: *La basilique dite de Sainte-Monique*; II: *La basilique de Mcidfa* (Institut national d'archéologie et d'arts de Tunis/Ecole française de Rome, 1975, 1982).

A. Ferrua, *Epigrammata Damasi* (Vatican City, 1942).

A. Ferrua, 'Le antichi inscrizioni cristiane della Spagna', *RAC* 20 (1943).

S. Gsell, *Inscriptions latines de l'Algérie*, I: *Inscriptions de la Proconsulaire* (Paris: Champion, 1922), II: *Inscriptions de la Confédération Cirtéenne*, ed. H. G. Pflaum (1952).

Inscriptiones Christianae Urbis Romae, ed. A. Silvagni and successors (1922–).

G. Vantini, *Oriental Sources of Nubian History*, ed. E. Dinkler and K. Michalowski (Warsaw: PWN/Editions scientifiques de Pologne, 1966).

Since 1990 the annual *Bulletin d'Information et de liaison* of the Association Internationale d'Etudes patristiques has contained sections on current archaeological and epigraphical studies (published by Brepols).

MAJOR COMPENDIA

F. Cabrol and H. Leclercq (eds), *Dictionnaire d'Archéologie chrétienne et de Liturgie* (15 vols; Paris: Letouzey, 1907–53).

A. Baudrillart (ed.), *Dictionnaire d'Histoire et de Géographie ecclésiastique* (Paris: Letouzey, 1912–).

E. Everett Ferguson and associates (eds), *Encyclopaedia of Early Christianity* (New York/London: Garland Publishing Inc., 1990).

Angelo de Berardino (ed.), Institutum Patristicum Augustinianum, *Encyclopedia of the Early Church*, Eng. trans. Adrian Walford (2 vols; Cambridge: James Clarke, 1992).

E. Kirschbaum (ed.), *Lexikon für christlichen Ikonographie* (Rome/Freiburg/ Basel/Vienna: Herder, 1968–).

T. Klauser and colleagues (eds), *Reallexikon für Antike und Christentum* (Stuggart: Hiersemann, 1950–).

G. Krause and G. Müller, *Theologische Realenzyklopädie* (Berlin/New York, 1977–).

MAPS AND ATLASES

H. Chadwick and G. R. Evans, *Atlas of the Christian Church* (London, 1987).

S. Gsell, *Atlas archéologique de l'Algérie* (Algiers: Jourdan, 1911).

F. van der Meer and Christine Mohrmann, *Atlas of the Early Christian World* (London and Edinburgh: Nelson, 1958).

See also the maps, plans and many illustrations at the end of *Encyclopedia of the Early Church*, II (Cambridge: James Clarke, 1992).

BIBLIOGRAPHIES AND TOOLS FOR STUDY

Bibliografia dell'Antichità cristiana = *RAC* 37.1–2 (1961).

G. Bovini, *Principale Bibliografia su Ravenna romana paleocristiana e paleobizantina* (Faenza: Università degli Studi di Bologna, 1962).

Y. Duval, *Loca Sanctorum Africae: Le Culte des Martyrs en Afrique du IVe au VIIIe siècle* (2 vols; Ecole française de Rome, 1982).

I. Gui, N. Duval and J.-P. Caillet, *Basiliques chrétiennes d'Afrique du Nord*, I: *Inventaire de l'Algérie*, i: *Texte*, ii: *Illustrations* (Institut d'Etudes augustiniennes, 1992).

R. Krautheimer *et al.*, *Corpus Basilicarum Christianarum Romae* (Vatican City, 1937–)

C. Lepelley, *Les Cités romaines de l'Afrique au Bas-Empire* (2 vols; Paris: Etudes augustiniennes, 1979, 1981).

Liber Pontificalis, ed. L. Duchesne (Paris, 1886–92).

A. Mandouze, *Prosopographie chrétienne du Bas-Empire*, I: *Afrique (303–533)* (Paris, 1982).

P. Testini, *Archeologia cristiana* (Bari, 1980).

A. van Tongerloo, S. N. C. Lieu and J. van Oost, *Corpus Fontium Manichaeorum* (Brepols, 1995–).

Various authors, *Naissance des arts chrétiens: Atlas des monuments paléochrétiens de la France* (Paris: Imprimerie Nationale, 1991).

There are useful bibliographies (up to 1990) at the end of each entry in the *Encyclopedia of the Early Church*; and accounts of many individual sites in *Atti* XI.2 and 3.

SELECT BIBLIOGRAPHY

F. M. Abel with L. H. Vincent, *Jérusalem, recherches de topographie, d'archéologie et d'histoire* (2 vols; Paris, 1926).

W. V. Adams, Archaeological survey of Sudanese Nubia', *Kush* 11 (1961), pp. 7ff.

W. V. Adams, 'The evolution of Christian Nubian pottery' in E. Dinkler (ed.), *Kunst und Geschichte Nubiens in christlicher Zeit* (Recklinghausen: Bongers, 1970), pp. 111–23.

G. Agnello, *La Pittura paleocristiana della Sicilia* (Collezione Amici delle Catacombe 17; Vatican, 1952).

E. Albertini, 'Actes de vente du Ve siècle trouvés dans la région de Tébessa (Algérie)', *JS* (January 1930), pp. 23–30.

E. Albertini, 'Stéphane Gsell' (a memoir), *RAfr* 73 (1932), pp. 20–53.

E. Amélineau, 'Codex Brucianus. Notice sur le papyrus gnostique Bruce', *Notices et extraits des monuments Coptes de la Bibliothèque nationale* 29, part i.

E. Amélineau, 'Le Christianisme chez les anciens Coptes', *RHR* 14 (1886).

F. Anfray, A. Caquot and P. Nautin, 'Une nouvelle inscription grecque d'Ezana, roi d'Axoum', *JS* (October 1970), pp. 260–73.

B. Bagatti, *Excavations in Nazareth* (Jerusalem, 1967; Eng. trans. by E. Hoade of *Gli Scavi di Nazeret*).

A comprehensive list of Bagatti's publications is given by Joan E. Taylor, *Christians and the Holy Places* (OUP, 1993), pp. 346–8.

M. Baillet and R. de Vaux, *Les petites grottes de Q'umran* (*Discoveries in the Judaean Desert*, III; OUP, 1962).

J. Baradez, *Tipasa ville antique de la Maurétanie* (Algiers, 1951).

I. Barnea, *Christian Art in Romania*, I (Bucharest, 1979).

X. Barral i Altet, 'Mensae et repas funéraires dans les nécropoles d'époque chrétienne de la périnsule ibérique', *Atti* IX.2, pp. 49–70.

A. Baruffa, *Giovanni Battista de Rossi* (Vatican, 1994).

G. L. Bell, *Churches and Monasteries of the Tur Abdin* (1913).

H. I. Bell and T. C. Skeat, *Fragments of an Unknown Gospel* (British Museum, 1935).

F. Benoît, J. T. Milik and R. de Vaux, *Discoveries in the Judaean Desert of Jordan* II (OUP, 1961).

C. Bonnet, 'L'Eglise Saint-Laurent d'Aoste', *Atti* IX.2, pp. 105–17.

C. Bonnet, 'L'aménagement du site archéologique de la cathédrale Saint-Pierre de Genève' in *Das Denkmal und die Zeit* (Festschrift Alfred Schmid: Lucerne, 1990), pp. 251–8.

A. Bosio, *Roma Sotteranea*, ed. P. G. Severani (4 vols; Rome, 1632).

G. Bovini, Il *cosidetto Mausoleo di Galla Placidia in Ravenna* (Vatican, 1950).

G. Bovini, *I sarcophagi cristiani, determinazione della loro cronologia mediante l'analisi dei ritratti* (Vatican, 1949).

A. Boyadjev, 'La rotonde souterraine de Damous-el-Karita à Carthage', *Atti* IX.2, pp. 117–31.

British Museum, *Guide to Early Christian Antiquities*.

T. L. Bruce Mitford, *The Sutton Hoo Ship Burials* (British Museum, 1975–83).

Marquis du Buisson, *Les peintures de la Synagogue de Dura Europos 246–256 après J. C.* (Rome, 1939).

J. L. Burckhardt, *Travels in Nubia* (London, 1819; reprint 1968).

A. J. Butler, *Coptic Churches in Egypt* (London, 1884).

J. Carcopino, *Aspects mystiques de la Rome païenne* (Paris; Artisan du Livre, 1942).

J. Carcopino, *Les reliques de Saint Pierre, à Rome* (Paris: Albin Michael, 1965).

M. O. Carver, *The Age of Sutton Hoo: The Seventh Century in North-western Europe* (London, 1992).

H. Chadwick, *Alexandrian Christianity* (Library of Christian Classics 2; London, 1954), pp. 430–55 for Origen's *Dialogue with Heracleides*.

Marcel Christofle, *Rapport sur les fouilles et consolidations effectuées 1933–1936 par le Service des Monuments Historiques de l'Algérie* (Algiers, 1937).

P. Collart, 'Inscriptions de Philippes', *BCH* 56 (1932), pp. 192–231.

J. Comfry and M. Fayel, 'Inscriptions de Philippes', *BCH* 60 (1936), 37–58.

P. Courcelle, 'Une seconde campagne des fouilles à Ksar el Kelb', *MEFR* 53 (1936), pp. 166–97.

C. Courtois, *Les Vandales et L'Afrique* (Algiers: Gouvernement-Général de l'Algérie, 1955).

Rosemary Cramp, 'Monkwearmouth and Jarrow in their European context' in K. S. Painter (ed.), *Churches Built in Ancient Times* (1994), pp. 279–95.

J. Dart, *The Laughing Savior* (New York: Harper and Row, 1976).

Ernst Dassmann (ed.), *Das Reallexikon für Antike und Christentum und das F. J. Dölger-Institut in Bonn* (Stuttgart, 1994).

F. Decret and Mhamed Fantar, *L'Afrique du Nord dans l'Antiquité* (Paris: Payot, 1981).

R. Dévreese, 'L'Eglise de l'Afrique durant l'occupation byzantine', *MEFR* 57 (1940), pp. 141–66.

C. Diehl, *L'Afrique byzantine* (Paris: Leroux, 1896).

E. Dinkler (ed.), *Kunst und Geschichte Nubiens in christlicher Zeit* (Recklinghausen: Bongers, 1970).

E. Dinkler, 'Deutsche Nubienunternehmungen' in successive numbers of *AA* (1967–72).

J. Doresse, 'Nouveaux textes gnostiques coptes découverts en Haute-Egypte', *VChr* 3 (1949), pp. 129–41.

A. Dupont Sommer, *The Dead Sea Scrolls*, Eng. trans. E. M. Rowley (Oxford: Blackwell, 1952).

N. Duval, 'Les édifices de culte des origines à l'époque constantinienne', *Atti* IX.1, pp. 513–29.

N. Duval, *Les basiliques à deux sanctuaires opposés* (*Recherches archéologiques à Sbeitla*, I; Paris, 1971; and II: Paris, 1973).

N. Duval, 'L'architecture chrétienne et des pratiques liturgiques en Jordanie en rapport avec le Palestine: recherches nouvelles' in K. S. Painter (ed.), *Churches Built in Ancient Times*, pp. 149–212.

N. Duval, 'Plastique chrétienne de Tunisie et d'Algérie', *BCTH* n.s. 8 (1972); *Bulletin archéologique* (Paris, 1975), pp. 53–165.

R. Egger with F. Bulić, *Die Altchristliche Friedhof Manastirine* (2 vols; Salona, 1917).

Simon Ellis, 'The ecclesiastical complex: stratigraphical report 1976' in J. Humphrey (ed.), *University of Michigan Excavations at Carthage 1976*, III (1977), ch. 3.

W. B. Emery and L. P. Kirwan, *The Royal Tombs of Ballana and Q'ustul* (2 vols; London, 1932).

S. Eyice, 'Le baptistère de Sainte Sophie à Istanbul,' *Atti* IX.2, pp. 199–257.

U. M. Fasola, 'Le recenti scoperte nelle Catacombe sotto Villa Savoia. Il coemeterium Iordanorum ad S. Alexandrum', *Atti* VIII, pp. 273–98.

P. A. Février, *Approches au Maghreb romain* (2 vols; Aix-en-Provence: Edisud, 1987–89).

P. A. Février, with N. Duval, 'Les monuments chrétiens de la Gaule Transalpine', *Atti* VIII, pp. 107–26.

P. Corby Finney, *The Invisible God: The Earliest Christians on Art* (New York: OUP, 1994).

Alison Frantz, 'From paganism to Christianity in the temples of Athens', *DOP* 19 (1985).

W. H. C. Frend, 'The Memoria Apostolorum in Roman North Africa', *JRS* 30 (1940), pp. 27–49.

W. H. C. Frend, 'The Qasr Ibrim expedition of 1963–64', *Atti* (*Akten*) VII (Rome, 1968), pp. 531–8.

W. H. C. Frend, 'The cult of military saints in mediaeval Nubia' in Carl Andresen (ed.), *Theologia Crucis–Signum Crucis* (Festschrift E. Dinkler: Tübingen: Mohr, 1979), pp. 155–64.

W. H. C. Frend, *The Rise of Christianity* (Philadelphia: Fortress Press/London: Darton, Longman and Todd, 1984).

W. H. C. Frend, 'Early Christian Nubia: progress and prospects of research' in *Proceedings of the PMR Conference* VI (Villanova, PA, 1985), pp. 51–74.

W. H. C. Frend, *Archaeology and History in the Study of Early Christianity* (essays; London: Variorum Press, 1988).

P. Gauckler, *Eglises chrétiennes de la Tunisie 1894–190X* (Paris, 1907).

E. F. Gautier, *Le Passé de l'Afrique du Nord* (Paris: Payot, 1937).

A. von Gerkan, 'Petrus in Vaticano et in Catacumbas', *JbAC* 5 (1962), pp. 23–42.

H. Grégoire, 'Un voyage dans le Pont et en Cappadocie', *BCH* 33 (1909), pp. 3–170.

H. Grégoire, 'Sainte-Salse', *Byzantion* 12 (1937), pp. 217–24.

S. Gsell, 'Chronique d'archéologie africaine', *MEFR* 20 (1895)–29 (1904).

S. Gsell, 'Satafis (Périgotville) et Thamalla (Tocqueville)', *MEFR* 15 (1895), pp. 33–70.

S. Gsell, 'Les fouilles de Bénian', *CRAI* (1899), pp. 277ff.

S. Gsell, *Khamissa, Mdaourouch, Announa* (2 fascicules; Paris, 1914–18).

S. Gsell, 'Le Christianisme en Oranie', *Bulletin de 50e année de la Société de géographie et d'archéologie d'Oran* (Oran, 1928).

M. Guarducci, *I graffiti sotto la Confessione di San Pietro in Vaticano* (3 vols; Vatican City, 1958); rev. P. M. Fraser, *JRS* 52 (1962), pp. 214–19.

M. Guarducci, 'Vatican', *EEC* II, 862.

M. Guarducci with V. Correnti, *Le reliquie de Pietro sotto la Confessione della Basilica Vaticana* (Vatican City, 1965).

Commandant E. Guénin, 'Inventaire archéologique du Cercle de Tébessa', *Nouvelles archives des Missions scientifiques* 17 (1908), pp. 36ff.

O. Guérand, 'Note préliminaire sur le papyrus d'Origène découvert à Toura', *RHR* 131 (1946), pp. 85–108.

M. Gutschow, 'Das Museum des Praetextatus', *Pontificia Accademia Romana, Memorie* 4 (1938), pp. 46ff.

S. Guyer, 'Edifices à coupole de l'Orient', *Atti* IV.2, pp. 3ff.

G. M. A. Hanfmann, *The Seasons Sarcophagus in Dumbarton Oaks* (Dumbarton Oaks Studies 2; 2 vols, 1951).

D. B. Harden (ed.), *Dark Age Britain: Studies Presented to E. T. Leeds* (London: Methuen, 1955).

A. Harnack, 'Die älteste Kircheninschrift', *SBAW* (October 1915).

R. M. Harrison and N. Firath, 'Excavations at Sarachane in Istanbul (First Prelim. Report)', *DOP* 19 (1965).

W. Harvey, *Structural Survey of the Church of the Nativity at Bethlehem* (1935).

H. Hellenkemper, 'Early church architecture in southern Asia Minor' in K. S. Painter (ed.), *Churches Built in Ancient Times*, pp. 213–38.

E. Hennecke and W. Schneemelcher, *Neutestamentliche Apokryphen* (Tübingen: Mohr, 1959).

K. Heussi, *Die römische Petrus-tradition in historischer Sicht* (Tübingen: Mohr, 1955)

History of the Patriarchs: PO 5.

J. Humphrey (ed.) *Excavations at Carthage Conducted by the University of Michigan* (American Schools of Oriental Research, 1976–).

E. Iosi, *Il cimitero di Callisto* (Collezione di Amici delle Catacombe 2; Rome, 1933).

H. Jaubert, 'Anciens évêchés et ruines chrétiennes de la Numidie et la Sitifienne', *RC* 46 (1912), pp. 1–218.

M. J. Jones, 'St. Paul-in-the-Bail, Lincoln, Britain in Europe' in K. S. Painter (ed.), *Churches Built in Ancient Times*, pp. 325–48.

J. van der Kamm, *The Dead Sea Scrolls To-day* (Eerdmans/SPCK, 1994).

J. P. S. Kent and K. S. Painter, *The Wealth of the Roman World* (British Museum, 1987).

L. P. Kirwan, 'The Oxford University excavation in Nubia', *JEA* 21 (1935), pp. 191–8.

E. Kitzinger, *Byzantine Art in the Making* (Cambridge, MA, 1977).

T. Klauser, 'Studien zur Entstehungsgeschichte der christlichen Kunst', *JbAC* (1958), pp. 20–51; and nine essays in subsequent numbers in *JbAC*.

T. Klauser, *Gesammelte Arbeiten*, ed. E. Dassmann (*JbAC* Ergänzungsband 3; Münster, 1974).

T. Klauser, *Henri Leclercq, vom Autodidakten zum Kompilator grossen Stils* (*JbAC* Ergänzungsband 5: Münster, 1977).

J. R. Knipfing, 'The *libelli* of the Decian Persecution', *HTR* 16 (1923), pp. 363ff.

J. Kollwitz, 'Christusbild', *RAC* 3 (1957), pp 1–20.

J. Kollwitz, 'Die Malerei der konstantinischer Zeit', *Atti* VII.1 (1968), pp. 29–158.

M. Krause, 'Zur Kirchen- und Theologiegeschichte Nubiens' in E. Dinkler (ed.), *Kunst und Geschichte Nubiens*, pp. 71–86.

M. Krause, *Gnosis and Gnosticism* (Papers read at the Seventh International Conference on Patristic Studies, Oxford 1975; Leiden: Brill, 1977).

R. Krautheimer, *Early Christian and Byzantine Arcitecture* (Pelican History of Art, 1975).

Serge Lancel, 'Africa' in *Augustinus-Lexikon* I (Stuttgart, 1986).

Serge Lancel, *Actes de la Conférence de Carthage en 411* (*SC* 194, 195, 224: Paris, 1972–75).

P. G. Lapeyre, 'La basilique chrétienne de Tunisie', *Atti* IV.1, pp. 169–244.

G. La Piana, 'The Roman Church at the end of the second century', *HTR* 18 (1925), pp. 201–77.

J. Lassus, 'Les mosaïques d'Antioche', *CRAI* (1936), pp. 33–42.

J. Lassus, 'L'Eglise cruciforme d'Antioch Kouassie' in R. Stillwell (ed.), *Antioch on the Orontes*, II, pp. 5–44.

J. Lassus, 'Questions sur l'architecture de l'Afrique du Nord', *Atti* VIII, pp. 107–26.

Cardinal Charles Lavigerie, *De l'utilité d'une mission permanente à Carthage* (Algiers, 1881).

Bentley Layton, *The Gnostic Treatise on the Resurrection from Nag Hammadi* (Harvard University, 1979).

E. Leblant, 'Les premiers chrétiens et les dieux', *MEFR* 12 (1892), pp. 1–16.

E. T. Leeds, *Celtic Ornament* (OUP, 1933).

M. Leglay, *Saturne africain: histoire* (Paris, 1966).

L. Leschi, 'Basilique et cimitière donatistes de Numidie', *RAfr* 78 (1936), pp. 27–42.

L. Leschi with F. Logeart, 'Les épitaphes funéraires chrétiennes de Djebel Nif en Nisr', *RAfr* 83 (1940), pp. 5–36.

Abbé A. L. Leynaud, 'Les fouilles des Catacombes de Sousse', *CRAI* (1905), pp. 504–17.

A. Lézine, *Architecture romaine d'Afrique* (Tunis, 1963).

H. Lietzmann, *Petrus und Paulus in Rom: liturgische und archaeologische Studien* (2nd edn, Berlin/Leipzig: de Gruyter, 1927).

E. Littmann with D. Krenker and T. von Lüpke, *Die Deutsche Aksumexpedition* (1913).

A. Loisy, *Les mystères païens et le mystère chrétien* (Paris: Nourry, 1912).

Cyril Mango, *The Date of the Narthex Mosaics of the Church of the Domition at Nicaea* (*DOP* 13; 1959).

Cyril Mango, *Materials for the Study of the Mosaics of St Sophia at Istanbul* (Dumbarton Oaks Studies 8; 1962).

A. Merlin, 'Forum et églises de Suffetula', *Bulletin des Antiquaires de France* (1912).

J. Mesnage, *Afrique chrétienne, évêchés et ruines antiques* (Paris: Leroux, 1912).

K. Michałowski, 'Open problems of Nubian art and archaeology' in E. Dinkler (ed.), *Kunst und Geschichte Nubiens*, pp. 11–28.

Togo Mina, 'Le papyrus gnostique du Musée Copte', *VC* 2 (1948), pp. 129–36.

P. Monceaux, *Histoire littéraire de l'Afrique chrétienne* (7 vols; Paris: Leroux, 1901–23).

U. Monneret de Villard, *La Nubie medioévale*, I and II (Cairo, 1935), III and IV (Cairo, 1957).

U. Monneret de Villard, *Storia della Nubia cristiana* (*OCA*: Rome, 1938).

A. Orlandos, 'Délos chrétienne', *BCH* 60 (1936), pp. 68–100.

E. Pagels, 'A Valentinian interpretation of baptism and the eucharist', *HTR* (1972), pp. 153–69.

K. S. Painter (ed.) *Churches Built in Ancient Times: Recent Studies in Early Christian Archaeology* (Society of Antiquaries of London, 1994).

K. S. Painter, 'Villas and early Christianity in Roman Britain', *Atti* VIII, pp. 149–65.

P. de Palol, 'Los monumentos de Hispaña en la arqueología paleocristiana', *Atti* VIII, pp. 167–85.

P. Pergola, 'La région dite du Bon Pasteur dans la cimitière de Domitilla sur l'Ardeatina', *RA* 51 (1973), pp. 65–96.

P. Pergola, 'La région dite des Flavii Aurelii dans la catacombe de Domitille', *MEFR* (A) 95 (1983), pp. 183–268.

Flinders Petrie, *Seventy Years in Archaeology* (London, 1938).

C. Pietri, *Roma christiana, Recherches sur l'Eglise de Rome, son organisation, sa politique, son idéologie de Militiade à Sixte III, 311–440* (*BEFAR* 224; Rome, 1976).

J. M. Plumley, *The Christian Period at Qasr Ibrim: Some Notes on the MSS Finds* (Warsaw, 1973).

A. Poulle, 'Nouvelles inscriptions de Timgad, de Lambèse et d'Announa', *RC* 22 (1882), pp. 331–48.

Andrew Poulter, 'Churches in space; the early Byzantine city of Nicopolis' in K. S. Painter (ed.), *Churches Built in Ancient Times*, pp. 249–68.

H. C. Puech, 'Nouveau écrits gnostiques découverts en Haute Egypt' in *Coptic Studies in Honour of W. E. Crum* (Boston, 1950).

H. C. Puech, 'Une collection des Paroles de Jésus récemment retrouvée: L'Evangile selon Thomas', *CRAI* (1957), pp. 146–67.

J. Quasten, 'Der gute Hirt in der frühchristlichen Totenliturgie', *Studi e Testi* 121 (1946), pp. 373–406.

G. Quispel, 'The Gospel of Thomas and the New Testament', *VC* 2 (1957), pp. 189–207.

W. M. Ramsay, *The Letters to the Seven Churches in Asia* (London, 1906).

A. Ravoisié, *Exploration scientifique de l'Algérie pendant les années 1840–1842* (2 folio vols; Paris, 1846).

L. Reekmans, *La Tombe du Pape Corneille et sa région cemétériale* (Vatican City, 1964).

G. A. Reisner, *Archaeological Survey of Nubia* (report for 1907–1908) (Cairo, 1910).

I. A. Richmond, *Archaeology and the Afterlife in Pagan and Christian Imagery* (Oxford, 1950).

I. A. Rodwell, 'The archaeology of the Early Church in the Channel Isles' in K. S. Painter (ed.), *Churches Built in Ancient Times*, pp. 294–310.

J. B. de Rossi, *Roma Sotteranea* (3 vols; Rome, 1861–77).

M. Ryan, 'Early Christian metalwork: new evidence from Ireland' in K. S. Painter (ed.), *Churches Built in Ancient Times*, pp. 313–24.

Paul Salama, 'Recherches sur la sculpture géométrique traditionelle', *El Djezair* 16 (Algiers, 1977).

M. Schaffler, 'Ein Kirchengrabung in Steiermark 1973', *Atti* IX.1, pp. 485–95.

C. Schmidt, 'Gnostische Schriften in koptischer Sprache aus den Codex Brucianus', *TU* 8.2 (Leipzig, 1891).

C. Schmidt, 'Ein vorirenäisches gnostisches Original-Werk in koptischer Sprache', *SBAW* (1896), pp. 839–47.

A. M. Schiender, 'Mensae oleorum oder Totenspeistische', *RQ* 35 (1927), pp. 287–301.

H. H. R. Seeliger, 'Christliche Archaeologie oder Spätantike Kunstgeschichte', *RAC* 61 (1985), pp. 167–87.

Pierre Senay, 'Fouille du Monument circulaire', *Cahiers des études anciennes* 6 (*Carthage*, I; Université de Québec, à Trois Rivières, 1976). (*Carthage*, II–V = *Cahiers* 10–13 (1977–81).)

W. Seston, 'Sur les derniers temps du Christianisme en Afrique', *MEFR* 56 (1936), pp. 101–24.

Herschel Shanks (ed.), *Understanding the Dead Sea Scrolls* (London: SPCK, 1992).

P. L. Shinnie, 'The University of Ghana Excavation at Debeira West,' *Kush* 11 (1963), pp. 257–69.

P. L. Shinnie, 'Trade in mediaeval Nubia', *Etudes nubiennes* (1975), pp. 257–63.

Marcel Simon, *Hercule et le Christianisme* (Strasbourg/Paris, 1955).

H. S. Smith, *Preliminary Report of the Egypt Exploration Society Nubian Survey* (London, 1961).

M. Smith, *Jesus the Magician* (San Francisco, 1978).

Steven Snape, 'Salvaging ancient Sinai', *Egyptian Archaeology* 3 (1993), pp. 21–2.

R. Stillwell, *Antioch on the Orontes* (Princeton, 1938).

J. Strzygowski, 'Die christliche Denkmaler Aegyptens', *RQ* 13 (1898), pp. 1–41.

Paul Styger, *Il monumento apostolico a San Sebastiano sulla Via Appia* (Rome, 1925).

Paul Styger, 'Heidnische und christliche Katakomben' in *Pisciculi* (Festschrift Dölger; Münster, 1939), pp. 266–75.

L. von Sybel, *Christliche Antike* (2 parts; Marburg 1906, 1909).

P. Testini, *Archeologia cristiana* (Rome, 1958).

P. Testini, '*Basilica paleocristiana a Tharros*', Atti IX, p. 525.

P. Testini, *La Catacombe e gli antichi cimiteri cristiani in Roma* (Bologna, 1966).

P. Testini, 'Il complesso paleocristiano di Cornus (regione Columbaris) in Sardegna', *Atti* VIII, pp. 537–61.

C. P. Thiede, *Heritage of the First Christians* (A Lion Book: Oxford, 1992).

W. Till, 'Die gnostischen Schriften der koptischen Papyrus Berlinensis 8502', *TU* 60 (Berlin, 1955).

Franklin K. B. Toker, 'An early Christian Church beneath the cathedral of Florence', *Atti* IX.2, pp. 545–54.

G. Tomasevic, 'Une mosaïque du Ve siècle de Heraklea Lynkestis', *Atti* VIII, pp. 567–81.

J. M. C. Toynbee, *Death and Burial in the Roman World* (London, 1971).

Bruce Trigger, *History and Settlement in Lower Nubia* (Yale University Publications in Anthropology 69: 1965).

E. P. Urbach, 'The rabbinical laws of idolatry in the second and third centuries in the light of archaeological and historical evidence', *Israel Exploration Journal* 9 (1959), pp. 149–65.

W. C. van Unnik, *Newly Discovered Gnostic Writings* (London: SCM Press, 1960).

R. de Vaux, 'Une mosaïque byzantine à Ma'in', *RB* 47 (1938), pp. 276–86.

E. Vincent, 'Fouilles exécutées à Ain el Kebira, Satafis', *RC* 16 (1876–77), pp. 303–26.

L. H. Vincent, 'Le Père Lagrange' *RB*, (1938), pp. 321–54.

L. H. Vincent with F. M. Abel, *Bethléhem, le sanctuaire de la Nativité* (Paris, 1914) (see also under W. Harvey).

C. Melchior de Vogüé, *Syrie centrale, architecture civile et religieuse du Ier au VIIIe siècles* (Paris, 1865–67).

D. Watts, *Christians and Pagans in Roman Britain* (London and New York, 1991).

M. E. Weinstein and E.G. Turner, 'Greek and Latin papyri from Qasr Ibrim', *JEA* 62 (1976), pp. 115–30.

C. Wessely, *Les plus anciens monuments du Christianisme* (*PO* IV.2; Paris, 1907).

R. E. M. Wheeler, *Still Digging* (London, 1955).

T. Whittemore, *The Mosaics of St Sophia at Istanbul* (4 vols; Paris/Oxford, 1933–53).

Edith M. Wightman, *Gallia Belgica* (London: Batsford, 1985).

J. Wilpert, *Le Pitture delle Catacombe romane* (2 vols; Rome, 1903).

J. Wilpert, *La Fede della chiesa nascente secondo i monumenti dell'arte funeraria antica* (Rome, 1938).

C. G. Zammit, 'The Tal Bistra catacombs', *Bulletin of the Museum, Valletta* (Malta, 1935), pp. 165–87.

P. L. Zovatto, *Antichi Monumenti cristiani di Iulia Concordia Sagittaria* (Vatican City, 1950).

Index